| TO THE STUDENT

This text was created to provide you with a high-quality educational resource. As a publisher specializing in college texts for business and economics, our goal is to provide you with learning materials that will serve you well in your college studies and throughout your career.

The educational process involves learning, retention, and the application of concepts and principles. You can accelerate your learning efforts by utilizing the supplements accompanying this text.

The **Study Guide,** prepared by the author, provides for each chapter a statement of purpose, suggestions on how to study, a study outline, and a series of questions for self evaluation plus answers to those questions.

The **Working Papers** include all forms needed for solving homework assignments. The forms contain captions and information that you would otherwise have to copy from the text.

The **Manual Practice Set,** *The Jenelle Corporation,* covers the complete information processing cycle. It can be used anytime after Chapter 5 and concluded anytime after Chapter 11. A computerized version of the practice set is also available.

A **Computerized Practice Set,** *It's Your Corporation* by Don Saftner, is a three-month general ledger software program that includes a practice set. This practice set take the reader through the accounting process. Each month the practice set introduces new concepts and procedures, and integrates them with concepts previously presented.

These learning aids are designed to improve your performance in the course by highlighting key points in the text and providing you with assistance in mastering basic concepts.

Check your local bookstore, and ask the manager to place an order for you today.

We at Irwin sincerely hope that this text package will assist you in reaching your goals both now and in the future.

FUNDAMENTALS OF
FINANCIAL ACCOUNTING

FUNDAMENTALS OF FINANCIAL ACCOUNTING

Daniel G. Short
Glenn A. Welsch
both of
The College of Business Administration
The University of Texas at Austin

Sixth Edition
IRWIN
Homewood, IL 60430
Boston, MA 02116

© RICHARD D. IRWIN, INC., 1974, 1977, 1981, 1984, 1987, and 1990

Sponsoring editor: *Ron M. Regis*
Developmental editor: *Cheryl D. Wilson*
Project editor: *Suzanne Ivester*
Production manager: *Irene H. Sotiroff*
Designer: *Michael Warrell*
Artist: *Penny Nickels and Alice Thiede and Rolin Graphics*
Compositor: *Better Graphics, Inc.*
Typeface: *10/12 Palatino*
Printer: *R. R. Donnelley & Sons Company*

Library of Congress Cataloging-in-Publication Data

Short, Daniel G.
    Fundamentals of financial accounting/Daniel G. Short, Glenn A.
Welsch.—6th ed.
        p.   cm.
    Welsch's name appears first on the earlier edition.
    Includes index.
    1. Accounting.   I. Welsch, Glenn A.   II. Title.
HF5635.W458   1990
657—dc20   89–15360
                                                           CIP

Printed in the United States of America
1 2 3 4 5 6 7 8 9 0 DO 6 5 4 3 2 1 0 9

PREFACE

The preparation of the sixth edition of *Fundamentals of Financial Accounting* represents a dramatic departure from the preparation of previous editions. A group of experienced accounting educators was assembled to provide detailed and comprehensive reviews of the manuscript. A team of developmental and copy editors then worked with the authors to synthesize the reviewers' suggestions and incorporate them into the text. As a result, the sixth edition continues the Short and Welsch tradition, but it also reflects substantial revisions suggested by reviewers (both current adopters and nonadopters). In no cases were changes made for the sake of change. We believe that each change represents a significant improvement.

Reorganized Coverage to Increase Flexibility

Key revisions to the sixth edition include:

- Expanded discussion of the FASB rule-making process.
- Introduction of simplified statement of cash flow in Chapter 1.
- Sections on financial statement analysis in many chapters to illustrate how accounting alternatives affect decision making.
- More focused discussion of transaction analysis in Chapter 2.
- Rearranged organizational structure in Chapter 4 to provide better explanation of the accounting cycle.
- Aging of accounts method integrated into Chapter 6.
- Expanded discussion of closing entries for sales revenue and bad debt expense.
- Simplified discussion of bank reconciliation.
- New supplement in Chapter 2 to illustrate preparation of a simple statement of cash flows.
- More thorough discussion of chart of accounts.
- Expanded explanation of partial year depreciation.
- Simplified discussion of federal income taxation with focus on corporations.
- New supplement on ethics in accounting.
- Greater emphasis on computers with computerized practice set and homework problems.
- Discussion of inflation accounting reduced to a chapter supplement to reflect *FASB Statement 82.*
- Deferred-tax section rewritten to reflect *FASB Statement 96.*
- Consolidations chapter expanded to reflect requirements contained in *FASB Statement 94.*
- Chapter 15 completely rewritten to incorporate *FASB Statement 95.*
- Effective-interest amortization integrated into the bond chapter.
- Introduction to capital leases included in the liabilities chapter.

- Comparison of ordinary annuities and annuities due presented in a chapter supplement.
- Complete rewrite of the discussion on LCM (*FASB Statement 12*).
- Major rewrite of the consolidations chapter for improved clarity.
- Sixteen new illustrations of financial reporting from current annual reports.
- A large number of revisions to exercise and problem material.
- A new case based on an actual annual report in each chapter.

In addition to major changes, there have been literally hundreds of minor revisions to improve the text's clarity and comprehensiveness. Many reviewers have commented that the sixth edition is unusually easy to read and understand. We have achieved that objective through careful writing and selection of illustrations. The book discusses a number of advanced topics ignored in many other fundamentals textbooks. Clarity has not been attained at the expense of ignoring or "sliding over" difficult topics.

Acknowledgments

The authors express special gratitude to the following faculty members who have made major contributions to the sixth edition:

Wagih G. Dafshy
College of William and Mary

Dinah Gottschalk
James Madison University

David Marcinko
State University of New York, Albany

Joseph R. Razek
University of New Orleans

George Violette
University of Southern Maine

Kenneth P. Sinclair
Lehigh University

Donald E. MacGilvra
Shoreline Community College

Kenneth Simmonds
California State University, Los Angeles

Leland Mansuetti
Sierra College

Philip H. Empey
Purdue University, Calumet

M. J. Hubbert
Cornell University

Kenneth M. Hiltebeitel
Villanova University

Charles J. Davis
California State University, Sacramento

Robert W. Koehler
Penn State University

Harry Dickinson
Virginia Commonwealth University

Leon Hanouille
Syracuse University

Finally, we express our thanks to numerous users of the prior editions for their valuable suggestions.

Our thanks to the American Institute of Certified Public Accountants, American Accounting Association, Financial Accounting Standards Board, and the authors identified by citations for permission to quote from their publications. To J.C. Penney, Company, Inc. our special thanks for permission to use its annual report.

Daniel G. Short
Glenn A. Welsch

CONTENTS IN BRIEF

CONTENTS

CHAPTER NINE

Operation Assets—Property, Plant, and Equipment; Natural Resources; and Intangibles   414

CHAPTER TEN

Measuring and Reporting Liabilities   472

A NOTE TO INSTRUCTORS

Discussions with a large number of accounting educators have convinced us that there is no single "best" way to teach accounting. We selected topics for this text and organized them in a sound and logical way, but we have given you the flexibility to easily include or exclude topics and to rearrange the organization. Adopters have told us that this text permits them to custom-design their courses based on their preferences and the needs of their students.

Most chapters are divided into two parts, an arrangement that permits the instructor to give balanced reading assignments. Also, it provides additional flexibility in selecting topic coverage. With this arrangement each instructor can easily emphasize or eliminate selected topics.

There are supplements at the end of many chapters that discuss either procedural or advanced topics. While it is unlikely that any instructor would assign all of the supplements, should the objectives of the course require it, there is sufficient additional material available.

A brief statement of objectives is given at the start of each exercise, problem, and case. These statements are designed to assist the student, but they can also help the instructor to select appropriate assignment material.

The book places an important emphasis on understanding accounting terminology. Each chapter has at least one exercise on terminology that can be assigned to assess student comprehension.

There is an unusually large number of homework assignments. Instructors are able to vary assignments from semester to semester. In addition, each chapter contains assignments at different levels of difficulty. Exercises tend to be applications of a single concept discussed in the chapter; problems are more difficult and may require an understanding of several concepts; cases typically require analysis and judgment. All end-of-chapter material is keyed either to a chapter part or supplement.

Each chapter gives a case based on the J.C. Penney Company, Inc. financial statements included in the appendix at the end of the book. These cases provide an excellent overview of current accounting practice.

Supplements

The support package for *Fundamentals of Financial Accounting* offers several teaching aids to assist the instructor.

Solutions Manual

This comprehensive manual includes answers (with detailed computations) to all questions, exercises, problems, and cases. It was independently reviewed for accuracy by Don MacGilvra of Shoreline Community College.

New Lotus Template

To give students hands-on experience in using computers to solve accounting problems, a LOTUS template is available. It features 27 problems from the text (identified by a computer symbol). This aid is **free** to adopters.

Examination Materials

This extensive bank of examination questions was prepared by Harry Dickinson of Virginia Commonwealth University. The material is organized by chapter and coded by topic, type of question (multiple-choice, short problem, etc.), and level of difficulty.

CompuTest

An improved test-generation program, CompuTest allows editing of questions, provides up to 99 different versions of each test, and permits question selection based on type of question or level of difficulty.

TeleTest

By telephoning Richard D. Irwin, Inc. and specifying the questions to be drawn from the test bank, you can obtain laser-printed tests custom designed for your course.

New   ## Instructor's Lecture Guide

Prepared by Ken Simmonds of California State University—Los Angeles, the guide includes chapter overviews, teaching objectives, and lecture outlines. It also contains teaching transparencies for use during lectures or in the development of suggested assignments.

Manual Practice Set

Revised for the sixth edition by Leon Hanouille of Syracuse University, the manual practice set—The Jenelle Group, Inc.—is a complete, integrated problem covering the entire information-processing cycle. It can be introduced after Chapter 5 and concluded any time after Chapter 11. The section on the statement of cash flows can be completed after Chapter 15.

New   ## Computerized Practice Set

New to the sixth edition is a computerized version of the practice set, The Jenelle Group, Inc.

Solution Transparencies

These transparencies feature the solutions to **all** exercises, problems, and cases, as well as selected teaching transparencies.

Fundamentals of Financial Accounting, sixth edition, is an introduction to the communication of relevant financial information to investors, creditors, analysts, and other individuals. This book is designed to meet the needs of students who plan to major in accounting as well as those who do not. If you understand the material in *Fundamentals of Financial Accounting*, it will be much easier for you to be successful in subsequent business courses. Nonaccounting majors will benefit from their study of this book because they must understand the language of business as well as the uses and limitation of accounting infor mation. Senior business executives often tell us that they need a better understanding of accounting. Careful study of this text will prepare you for the future.

This book is able to meet the needs of both accounting and nonaccounting majors because of its emphasis on concepts. The text gives a sound introduction to accounting practice. And with a continuing emphasis on concepts, it clarifies the "why" of each practice. Our discussion of this conceptual framework ties together topics that might otherwise seem unrelated. Also, you will be able to generalize your knowledge and, for example, see similarities between accounting for inventory and property, plant, and equipment. Your understanding of these concepts will (1) aid in your study of accounting, (2) permit you to adapt to changes in accounting practice, and (3) help you to appreciate the uses and limitation of accounting information.

Special Features for Students

There is a complete package of study aids available to help you. Each study aid was reviewed by the authors of the text to ensure consistency in terminology, approach, and quality. These aids are:

1. A Study Guide that includes chapter outlines, additional illustrations, and sample exam questions with detailed solutions.
2. Working Papers that include all forms needed for solving homework assignments. The forms contain captions and information that you would otherwise have to copy from the text.
3. A Practice Set that covers the complete information processing cycle. It can be used anytime after Chapter 5 and concluded anytime after Chapter 11. A computerized version of the Practice Set is also available.
4. A LOTUS template for IBM compatible computers is available to provide experience in using the computer to solve accounting problems. The problems in the text that are featured on the template are identified with a computer symbol.
5. A list of Check Figures for exercises, problems, and cases.

Each chapter begins with a special introduction that gives you a complete overview of the topics to be covered. The introduction includes a brief statement of purpose and explains how the chapter relates to prior discussions. The introduction also includes broad learning objectives to provide a "road map" for your study of the chapter. Each introduction provides a financial reporting perspective that relates the topics in the chapter to actual financial statements.

Accounting has its own technical language and jargon. The book will help you learn these new words by providing both a comprehensive index and, at the end of each chapter, a list of "important terms used in this chapter." This list includes the key words, the definition of the word, and the page reference that tells you where the word was first introduced.

A unique format is used in many of the exhibits. To facilitate your study, these exhibits give the illustrative data, analysis, and accounting entries and reporting on a single page.

Each exercise, problem, and case begins with a brief statement of the purpose of the assignment. You will get much more out of homework assignments when you understand your role more clearly.

An actual set of financial statements is included at the end of the text to help you learn how various accounting issued are handled by a typical company.

The discussions in each chapter have been carefully integrated with other chapters. When we refer to a topic from a prior chapter, a reference is provided to help you locate and review the prior discussion.

FUNDAMENTALS OF FINANCIAL ACCOUNTING

ONE

PERSPECTIVES—ACCOUNTING OBJECTIVES AND COMMUNICATION

PURPOSE

In our environment, people need information to make rational economic decisions. Most consumers use product and price information prior to purchasing a specific item. Investors and creditors need financial information before they provide funds to a business entity. A primary source of financial information is the periodic financial statements provided by a business entity. The primary purpose of this chapter is to define accounting, review the environment in which accounting is done, and describe how accounting serves our society.

The financial reporting perspective on the opposite page is from the PepsiCo financial statement. It illustrates that financial statements provide information concerning business activities that are part of our daily lives.

LEARNING OBJECTIVES

1. Write and explain the objectives of accounting.
2. Explain how accounting reports help decision makers.
3. Tell how the business environment influences accounting.
4. Give an overview of the financial statements used to communicate information.
5. Expand your accounting vocabulary by learning the "Important Terms Defined in This Chapter."
6. Apply the knowledge learned from this chapter by completing the homework assigned by your instructor.

ORGANIZATION

Part A—objectives and environment of accounting
1. Accounting defined.
2. Use of accounting information by decision makers.
3. Historical accounting perspectives.
4. Groups involved in accounting innovation.

Part B—communication of accounting information
1. Communication concepts and approaches.
2. Overview of external financial statements.

PART A—OBJECTIVES AND ENVIRONMENT OF ACCOUNTING

Accounting Defined

Accounting can be defined as the collection and processing (analysis, measurement, and recording) of financial data about an organization and the reporting of that information to decision makers. An accounting system processes data concerning the (a) flows of resources into and out of an organization, (b) resources controlled (i.e., assets) by the organization, and (c) claims against those resources (i.e., debts). The flow of accounting information is summarized in Exhibit 1–1. Notice that the end products of an accounting system are **financial statements** that are prepared for decision makers.

Economics has a special relationship with accounting. Economics is the study of how people and society choose to employ scarce productive resources that could have alternative uses to produce various commodities and distribute them for consumption, now or in the future, among various persons and groups in society. Like economics, accounting has a conceptual foundation that provides guidelines for the collection, measurement, and communication of financial information about an organization. In general, accounting reports how an entity has allocated its scarce resources. Thus, accounting collects, measures, interprets, and reports financial information on the same activities that are the focus of economics. Economics explains economic relationships on a conceptual level, whereas accounting reports the economic relationships primarily on a practical level. However, accounting measurements are as consistent with economic concepts as is possible. Accounting must cope with the complex and practical problems of measuring in monetary terms the economic effects of **exchange transactions** (i.e., resource inflows and outflows). These effects relate to the resources held and the claims against the resources of an entity. Throughout this textbook, the theoretical and practical issues that arise in the measurement process are discussed from the accounting viewpoint.

Accounting Operates in a Complex Environment

The environment in which accounting operates is affected by such forces as the type of (a) government (e.g., democracy versus communism), (b) economic system (e.g., free enterprise versus socialism), (c) industry (e.g., technological versus agrarian), (d) organizations within that society (e.g., labor unions), and (e) regulatory controls (i.e., private sector versus governmental). Accounting is influenced significantly by the educational level and economic development of the society.

Fundamental to a dynamic and successful society is the ability of each organization to measure and report its accomplishments; to undergo critical self-analysis; and, through sound decisions, to strengthen itself and grow. Essentially, society, and the various organizations that comprise it, thrive in direct proportion to the efficiency with which scarce resources of human talent, mate-

Exhibit 1-1 Flow of economic information in an accounting system

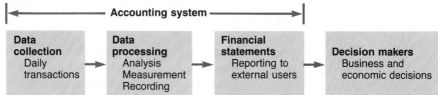

* Financial statements are prepared primarily for investors and creditors and those that advise investors and creditors. Financial statements are prepared under the assumption of reasonably sophisticated and diligent users (FASB, *Statement of Financial Accounting Concepts No. 1*, "Objectives of Financial Reporting by Business Enterprises" [Stamford, Conn., November 1978]).

rials, services, and capital are allocated. To achieve their goals, organizations need information about how resources are obtained and used. Accounting information is designed to meet this need.

Accounting is a system that is continuously changing to meet the evolving needs of society. The environmental characteristics of a society are diverse and complex; therefore, accounting is always facing new challenges. For example, during a period of significant inflation, special accounting concepts and procedures are able to report "real" effects separately from purely inflationary effects.

Throughout this textbook, you will study how accounting responds to the unique environment of the United States. In the next few paragraphs, we will discuss two environmental characteristics—types of business entities and measurement in dollars. These characteristics have pervasive effects on accounting concepts and procedures.

Types of Business Entities

This textbook emphasizes **accounting for profit-making business entities.** There are three main types of business entities—sole proprietorship, partnership, and corporation. Their primary characteristics are given in the paragraphs that follow.

A **sole proprietorship** is an unincorporated business owned by one person. This type of business entity is usually small in size and is common in the services, retailing, and farming industries. Often, the owner is the manager. Legally, the business and the owner are not separate entities. However, accounting views the business as a separate entity that must be accounted for separately from its owner.

A **partnership** is an unincorporated business that is owned by two or more persons known as partners. Some partnerships are large in size (e.g., international public accounting firms). The agreements between the owners are specified in a partnership contract. This contract deals with such matters as division of income each reporting period and distribution of resources of the business upon termination of its operations. A partnership is not legally separate from its owners. Legally, each partner in a general partnership is responsible for the debts of the business (i.e., each general partner has **unlimited liability**). However, accounting views the partnership as a separate business entity to be accounted for separately from its several owners.

A **corporation** is a business that is incorporated under the laws of a particular state. The owners are called stockholders or shareholders. Ownership is represented by shares of capital stock that usually can be bought and sold freely. When an approved application for incorporation is filed by the organizers, the state issues a charter. This charter gives the corporation the right to operate as a separate legal entity, separate and apart from its owners. The stockholders enjoy **limited liability.** Stockholders are liable for the debts of the corporation only to the extent of their investments. The corporate charter specifies the types and amounts of capital stock that can be issued. Most states require a minimum of two or three stockholders and a minimum amount of resources to be contributed at the time of organization. The stockholders elect a governing board of directors, which in turn employs managers and exercises general supervision of the corporation.[1] Accounting also views the corporation as a separate business entity that must be accounted for separately from its owners.

In terms of economic importance, the corporation is the dominant form of business organization in the United States. This dominance is caused by the many advantages of the corporate form: *(a)* limited liability for the stockholders, *(b)* continuity of life, *(c)* ease in transferring ownership (stock), and *(d)* opportunities to raise large amounts of money by selling shares to a large number of people. The primary disadvantages of a corporation are that *(a)* they tend to be impersonal and *(b)* their income is subject to double taxation (corporate income is taxed when earned and then again when it is distributed to stockholders as dividends). In this textbook, we emphasize the corporate form of business. Nevertheless, the accounting concepts and procedures that we discuss also apply to the other types of businesses.

Measurement in Dollars

In a barter system, it is difficult to determine the value of goods and services that are exchanged. In a monetary system, the unit of exchange (dollars in our case) is the common denominator used to measure value. Thus, the monetary unit provides a means for expressing the available resources and the resource flows of an entity.

Accounting uses the monetary system of each country within which it operates. One of the critical problems in accounting is the conversion of financial amounts from one monetary system (e.g., British pounds) to another monetary system (e.g., U.S. dollars) in measuring resources and resource flows for multinational activities.

---

[1] We do not discuss a number of specialized types of entities such as joint ventures, mutual funds, cooperatives, investment trusts, and syndicates. Consideration of these entities is appropriate for advanced accounting courses.

Measurement Fundamentals

To measure something, we need a precise definition of what is to be measured. If we want to measure the population of California, we must decide if our definition of a California resident includes such people as military personnel, college students, and hotel guests. Similarly, in accounting, it is necessary to have a precise definition of what is to be measured.

In the measurement of the resources of a business, accounting requires a precise definition of the specific entity for which financial data are to be collected. When the entity is defined, it is called an **accounting entity.** Accounting focuses on business transactions that affect the entity and ignores transactions that affect only related entities (e.g., the owners of the company). This focus is called the **separate-entity assumption.**[2] The separate-entity assumption requires that for accounting purposes, the particular entity being accounted for be distinguished carefully from all similar and related entities and persons. An entity is viewed as owning the resources (i.e., assets) used by it and as owing the claims (i.e., debts) against those resources. For measurement purposes, the assets, debts, and activities of the entity are kept separate from those of the owners and other entities. The separate-entity assumption is used for all types of business entities (i.e., sole proprietorships, partnerships, and corporations).

Use of Accounting Information by Decision Makers

In making decisions, a decision maker is concerned about the future because a decision cannot change the past. However, an effective decision maker should not neglect to consider past events and outcomes. An understanding of what has happened in the past can aid in making decisions because history may shed considerable light on what the future is likely to hold. One of the fundamental inputs to decision making is dependable and relevant historical data. A large portion of the historical data that are relevant to business decisions is accounting information. This information includes costs (i.e., resources expended), revenues (i.e., resources earned), assets (i.e., things owned), liabilities (i.e., amounts owed), and owners' equity (i.e., total assets less total liabilities of the entity). Accounting information must be understandable and relevant if it is to be used by decision makers. This is a primary reason why measurements in accounting must adhere to acceptable standards and concepts.

Financial statements serve decision makers in three related ways:

1. Accounting provides information that is helpful in making decisions. Most important decisions are based, in part, on complex financial considerations. Accounting provides an important information base and a particular analytical orientation that help the decision maker assess

---

[2] A list of the fundamental assumptions and principles underlying accounting is summarized in Exhibit 4–5.

the future financial implications and potential outcomes of various alternatives that are considered.

2. Accounting reports the economic effects of past decisions on the entity. Once a decision is made and implementation starts, economic effects on the entity occur. These economic effects often are critical to the success of the endeavor. The evolving effects of past decisions must be measured and reported so that the decision maker can be informed of developing problems, and of successes, over time. Accounting provides a continuing feedback of the economic effects of decisions already made, the results of which are communicated by means of periodic financial statements.

3. Accounting keeps track of a wide range of items to meet the stewardship (or safeguarding) responsibilities that must be assumed by all organizations. These include how much cash is available for use; · how much customers owe the company; what debts are owed by the organization; what items are owned by the company, such as machinery and office equipment; and inventory levels on hand.

Accounting Information in Decision Making for a Typical Business

Many business activities occur over a period of time. During this time, resources are used with the expectation that there will be desirable results in the future. Decision makers need information about the continuing amounts of resources committed, resources used, resources on hand, and outputs (goods and services). The accounting process is designed to provide a continuing flow of such information to all interested parties. A typical flow of accounting information in an entity is diagrammed in Exhibit 1–2. The financial statements constitute the primary source of relevant information on a continuing basis. This information is important feedback concerning the outcome of particular decisions.

Now we will examine information flows in a typical business.

The manager of a company usually will develop a **business plan** for operating the business. As the business operates, resources flow in from the sale of goods and services and flow out for expenses. On a continuing basis, the manager needs information about sources and amounts of funds, revenues (products and services sold), expenses, the amounts invested in equipment and inventory, the cash situation, the amount spent for research and development, and the amount of money used in the sales efforts.

The manager needs such information for two reasons. First, accounting information will help the manager make sound decisions that can improve the effectiveness and efficiency of the business. Second, accounting information reports what the score was during the immediate past periods. This scorekeeping is important to the evaluation and control of performance. Exhibit 1–2 shows that financial evaluations are important information inputs to the decision-making process.

Exhibit 1-2 Accounting information flows in a decision and implementation cycle

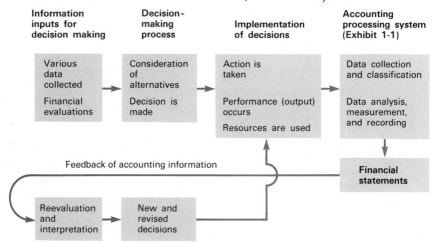

Stockholders (owners) of the business also have information needs. Owners must continuously select from among three alternatives: (1) retain their ownership interest, (2) expand or contract it, or (3) dispose of it completely. Stockholders are also interested in management decisions that will expand the business and make it more profitable. Therefore, stockholders need financial information about the trend of sales, the level of expenses, the amount of earnings, the amount invested by the entity in various assets (such as inventory and machinery), the debts of the business, and cash flow. Stockholders need to know how the management is allocating the scarce resources provided by the owners and the creditors. The primary objective of periodic financial statements is to provide, on a continuing basis, information bearing on the three alternatives listed. The accounting information provided should be an important part of the decision-making process of the owners in ways similar to those depicted in Exhibit 1-2.

Historical Accounting Perspectives

Accounting is as old as the exchange processes (whether barter or monetary) that gradually developed with civilization. The earliest written records, including the Scriptures, contain references to what now is called accounting.

Accounting evolved in response to the economic needs of society. Prior to the 15th century, accounting had no well-defined pattern except that it developed in answer to governing and trading needs of the era. The first known treatment of the subject of accounting was written in 1494, two years after the discovery of America. An Italian monk and mathematician, Fr. Luca Paciolo, described an approach developed by Italian merchants to account for their activities as owner-managers of business ventures. Paciolo laid the foundations of the accounting model that is used to this day. As economic activity progressed from the feudal system to agriculture and then to the Industrial Revolution, accounting continued to adapt to the needs of society. As business units became more complex and broader in scope, accounting evolved in response to the increased planning and control responsibilities of management.

In the 17th and 18th centuries, the Industrial Revolution in England provided the impetus for developing new approaches in accounting that focused on the accumulation of data about the cost of manufacturing each product. In the latter half of the 19th century, English accountants appeared on the American scene to assist in accounting for British interests in U.S. companies. By 1900, the lead in accounting developments, provided earlier by the English, began to shift to Americans. Since the turn of this century, spearheaded by the accounting profession in the United States, accounting has experienced dynamic growth.

The Accounting Profession Today

Since 1900, accounting has attained the stature of such professions as law, medicine, engineering, and architecture. As with all recognized professions, accounting is subject to professional licensing, observes a code of ethics, requires a high level of professional competence, is dedicated to service to the public, requires a high level of academic study, and rests on a "common body of knowledge." An accountant may be licensed as a **Certified Public Accountant,** or **CPA.** This designation is granted only on completion of requirements specified by each state. Although the CPA requirements vary among states, they include a college degree with a specified number of accounting courses, good character, one to five years of professional experience, and successful completion of a three-day examination. The CPA examination, scheduled in each state simultaneously on a semiannual basis, is prepared by the American Institute of Certified Public Accountants. This examination covers accounting theory, auditing, business law, and accounting practice.

Accountants (including CPAs) commonly are engaged in professional practice or are employed by businesses, government entities, nonprofit organizations, and so on. Accountants employed in these activities often take and pass a professional examination to become a **Certified Management Accountant,** or **CMA.** The CMA examination is administered by the Institute of Management Accountants which was created by the National Association of Accountants.

Practice of Public Accounting

A CPA can offer professional services to the public for a fee, as does the lawyer and physician. In this role, the accountant is known as an **independent CPA** because certain responsibilities extend to the general public rather than being limited to the specific business that pays for the services. Independent CPAs, although paid by their clients, are not employees of their clients. This independence from the client is a unique characteristic of the accounting profession. Independence has important implications for accountants. In case of malpractice, physicians are subject to potential lawsuits only from the patient involved (and the family). In contrast, in case of malpractice in the audit function, the independent CPA is subject to potential liability that may extend to all parties (whether known to the CPA or not) who have suffered loss because of reliance on financial statements "approved" by the CPA.

While an individual may practice public accounting, usually two or more individuals organize an accounting firm in the form of a partnership (in some states, incorporation is permitted). Accounting firms vary in size from a one-person office to regional firms and the Big Eight firms, which have hundreds of offices located worldwide. Accounting firms usually render three types of services: auditing, management advisory services, and tax services.

Auditing

The most important service performed by the CPA in public practice is the **audit or attest function.** The purpose of an audit is to lend credibility to the financial reports; that is, to assure that they are relevant, accurate, and not biased. An audit involves an examination of the financial reports (prepared by the management of the entity) to assure that they conform with **generally accepted accounting principles (GAAP).** We will discuss GAAP later. In performing an audit, the independent CPA examines the underlying transactions, including the collection, classification, and assembly of the financial data incorporated in the financial reports. To appreciate the magnitude of these responsibilities, the number of transactions involved in a major enterprise such as General Motors involves billions of dollars each year. However, the CPA does not examine each of these transactions; rather, professional approaches are used to ascertain beyond reasonable doubt that transactions were measured and reported properly.

There are many intentional and unintentional opportunities to prepare misleading financial reports. The audit function performed by an independent CPA is the best protection available to the public. Many investors have learned the pitfalls of making investments in enterprises that do not have their financial reports examined by an independent CPA.

Management Advisory Services

Many independent CPA firms offer consulting services. These services usually are accounting based and encompass such activities as the design and installation of accounting, data processing, profit-planning and control (i.e., budget) systems; financial advice; forecasting; inventory controls; cost-effectiveness studies; and operational analyses. This facet of public practice is growing rapidly.

Tax Services

CPAs in public practice usually provide income tax services to their clients. These services include both tax planning as a part of the decision-making

Exhibit 1–3 Typical organization of the financial function

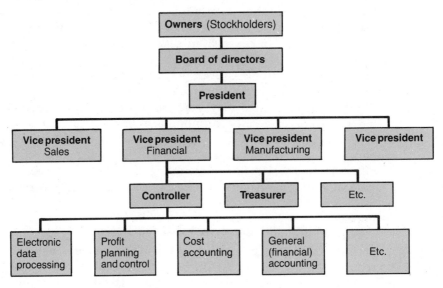

process and determination of the income tax liability (reported on the annual income tax return). Because of the increasing complexity of state and federal tax laws, a high level of competence is required that can be provided by CPAs specializing in taxation. The CPA's involvement in tax planning often is quite significant. Most major business decisions have significant tax impacts; in fact, tax-planning considerations often govern certain business decisions.

Employment by Organizations

Many accountants, including CPAs and CMAs, are employed by profit-making and nonprofit organizations. An organization, depending on its size and complexity, may employ from a few to hundreds of accountants. In a business enterprise, the chief financial officer (usually a vice president or controller) is a member of the management team. This responsibility usually entails a wide range of management, financial, and accounting duties. Exhibit 1–3 shows a typical organizational arrangement of the financial function in a business.

In a business entity, accountants typically are engaged in a wide variety of activities, such as general management, general accounting, cost accounting, profit planning and control (i.e., budgeting), internal auditing, and electronic data processing. A primary function of the accountants in organizations is to provide data that are useful for internal managerial decision making and for controlling operations. Also, the functions of external reporting, tax planning, control of assets, and a host of related responsibilities normally are performed by accountants in industry.

Employment in the Public Sector

The vast and complex operations of governmental units, from the local to the international level, create a need for accountants. Accountants employed in the public sector perform functions similar to those performed by their counterparts in private organizations. Also, the General Accounting Office (GAO) and the regulatory agencies, such as the Securities and Exchange Commission (SEC), Interstate Commerce Commission (ICC), Federal Power Commission (FPC), and Federal Communications Commission (FCC), use the services of accountants in carrying out their regulatory duties.

Groups Involved in Accounting Innovation

In the United States, five groups lead in the development of financial accounting concepts and practice. A general knowledge of their roles is important to your understanding of accounting. The groups are the American Institute of Certified Public Accountants (AICPA), Financial Accounting Standards Board (FASB), Securities and Exchange Commission (SEC), American Accounting Association (AAA), and Financial Executives Institute (FEI). The past and present roles of each group are briefly reviewed below.

American Institute of Certified Public Accountants (AICPA)

The AICPA was organized a few years before the turn of the century by a group of accountants engaged in public and industrial accounting. Membership currently is limited to CPAs. The AICPA publishes the *Journal of Accountancy* which contains articles of interest to the practicing CPA. During the period from 1939 to 1959, the AICPA's **Committee on Accounting Procedure** issued a number of *Accounting Research Bulletins (ARBs)* that enunciated certain recommended financial accounting principles and procedures. These recommendations were followed by much of the accounting profession. Realizing the need for a more concentrated effort to develop accounting standards and more adherence to prescribed accounting guidelines, in 1959 the AICPA organized the **Accounting Principles Board (APB)** to replace the former committee. The APB issued 31 numbered *Opinions* during its existence from 1959 through mid-1973. The *Opinions* dealt with many of the difficult issues of financial accounting; therefore, many of them were controversial. Throughout this textbook, you will notice a few references to the *ARBs* and numerous references to APB *Opinions* because some of them are still recognized by the accounting profession.

As a result of increasing criticism of the APB in the early 1970s, the AICPA created a special committee to review the process that was used to establish accounting principles and procedures. The committee completed its study and recommended the creation of a new independent body, the Financial Accounting Standards Board (FASB).

Financial Accounting Standards Board (FASB)

The FASB began operating June 1, 1973. It was organized to be independent and has seven full-time members who are appointed by an independent board of trustees. The sole function of the FASB is the **establishment and improvement of accounting concepts and standards.** Through the FASB, the accounting profession intends to keep the standards-setting function in the private sector rather than to have the standards imposed by laws and governmental agencies. The FASB issues **FASB Statements** which are formal rules that establish new accounting standards.

The FASB has adopted the following process for establishing new accounting standards:

1. A problem is identified and placed on the FASB agenda. A task force is assigned to deal with the problem.
2. A Discussion Memorandum is issued. This document is neutral in content and discusses the various accounting alternatives that are available.
3. A public hearing is held. Accountants, lawyers, financial analysts, business executives, and the general public may express their opinions before the members of the FASB.
4. An Exposure Draft is issued. This draft is the proposed standard that the FASB intends to issue.
5. Another public hearing is held. Once again, anyone who is interested in the proposed rule is given the opportunity to testify before the board. The FASB may issue a revised exposure draft after this public hearing.
6. A standard is issued.

The standards-setting process may take a month or two in the case of a minor rule, or over a year in the case of a controversial rule. The final decisions concerning new standards are made by the FASB, but there is considerable input from the public. In fact, some accountants believe that the FASB is essentially a political process where the Board attempts to find solutions that are acceptable to its constituents. This characterization has a negative connotation to some people and is not completely valid. Nevertheless, it is important to recognize that rules in accounting are established by groups of people and are not like basic rules of science.

Securities and Exchange Commission (SEC)

The SEC is a government regulatory agency that operates under authority granted by the Securities Acts of 1933 and 1934. These acts were enacted in response to the manipulations, irrational speculation, and lack of credible financial information that existed when the stock market crashed in 1929–30. The acts gave the SEC authority to **prescribe accounting guidelines for the financial reports required to be submitted by corporations that sell their securities in interstate commerce** (i.e., registered companies, which are primarily those listed on the stock exchanges). This list includes most of the large, and some medium-size, corporations. The SEC requires these corporations to submit periodic financial reports, which are maintained in the files of the Commission as a matter of public record. Also, a **prospectus,** which is a preliminary statement presented to prospective buyers or investors, is required before the sale of securities. As a matter of policy, the SEC usually has followed the accounting concepts, standards, and procedures established by the accounting profession. The SEC issues *Financial Reporting Releases (FRR)*, which prescribe the guidelines to be followed by registered companies in preparing the financial reports submitted in conformance with the Securities Acts. Throughout its existence, the SEC has had a significant impact on accounting. Its staff has worked closely with the accounting profession on the evolution and improvement of accounting standards.

American Accounting Association (AAA)

The AAA was organized during the World War I period by a group of college accounting professors. The Association sponsors and encourages the improvement of accounting teaching and research and publishes *The Accounting Review*, which contains the results of academic research. Its committees issue reports that exert a pervasive influence on the development of accounting theory and standards.

Financial Executives Institute (FEI)

The membership in the FEI is primarily CPAs and CMAs employed in industry. They are financial vice presidents, controllers, and other accounting executives. This group provides important and responsible inputs to the FASB.

Summary of Part A

Economic success in a competitive business economy means earning reasonable profits and providing funds (cash) to meet broad reinvestment needs. Adequate reinvestment in businesses means more jobs, better wages, continuing technological advances, expansion of efficient productive capacity, adequate dividends for investors, and more tax revenue to the government (to support socially desirable programs and other governmental activities). The decisions that lead to this success are often based, in part, on information communicated in accounting reports.

PART B—COMMUNICATION OF ACCOUNTING INFORMATION

This part of the chapter presents an overview of the end product of the accounting process—the **periodic financial statements** of a business. These statements are the primary way to communicate financial information about an entity. Chapter 2 continues this overview of the basic financial statements.

The remaining chapters discuss how the financial statements are developed. Those chapters focus on the economic analyses, measurements, and recording of transactions that precede the preparation of financial statements.

Communication Concepts and Approaches

Communication is a flow of information from one party to one or more other parties. **Effective communication** means that the recipient understands what the sender intends to convey. Communication involves problems in understanding the words, symbols, and sounds used by the parties involved. Accounting uses words and symbols to communicate financial information that is relevant to decision makers.

The terminology of accounting was developed to communicate financial information effectively. As is common with other professions, the terminology of accounting is technical because precision is essential. Accounting has developed in direct response to the needs of its environment. Therefore, accounting is continuously evolving new concepts, terminology, procedures, and means of communication. In the chapters to follow, you will learn the basic terminology of accounting. Your understanding of accounting terminology will permit you to effectively communicate with others concerning important business topics. Accounting terminology is referred to as the "language of business."

Overview of External Financial Statements

Financial statements often are classified as (1) internal (i.e., management accounting) statements and (2) external (i.e., financial accounting) statements. **Internal accounting statements** are not given to parties outside the entity. They are used exclusively by the managers of the entity; therefore, they are prepared to meet specific internal policies and guidelines established by those managers.

External financial statements are given to parties outside the entity (which include stockholders and creditors). External parties are unable to specify guidelines for preparation of the statements.

To ensure that external parties can rely on the information reported in financial statements, the entity is required to conform to **generally accepted accounting principles (GAAP)** that are developed by the accounting profession. GAAP will be discussed in the remaining chapters.

This textbook discusses the **preparation and interpretation** of external financial reports only. The next several pages present an overview of the external financial statements required by GAAP.

A general understanding of financial statements at the outset helps you to understand the accounting process when it is discussed in later chapters. The three required financial statements for a profit-making entity for **external reporting** to owners, potential investors, creditors, and other decision makers are:

1. **Income statement.**
2. **Balance sheet** (also called the statement of financial position).
3. **Statement of cash flows (SCF).**

These three required statements summarize the financial activities of the business entity for each specific period of time. They can be prepared at any time (such as end of the year, quarter, or month) and can apply to any time span (such as 10 years, 1 year, 1 quarter, or 1 month). The heading of each statement has a specific statement of the **time dimension** of the report. The time covered by the report (e.g., one year) is called an **accounting period.** First, we will illustrate these statements for a simple business case. Chapter 2 discusses them in a more complex case.

The Income Statement

The income statement reports the **profit performance** of a business entity. The term **profit** is used widely in our language, but accountants prefer to use the technical term **net income.** The **model** for the income statement is:

$$\text{REVENUES} - \text{EXPENSES} = \text{NET INCOME}$$

An income statement reports the revenues and expenses for a specified period. Revenues cause inflows of resources into a business, and expenses cause outflows of resources. Income statements report revenues, expenses, and net income for a specific period of time, which is called the **time-period assumption** (e.g., "For the Year Ended December 31, 19A").

Illustration. The income statement of Business Support, Inc., is presented in Exhibit 1–4. Business Support is a company that provides professional secretarial services for a fee. Business Support was organized by three individuals as a **corporation.** Each owner (called a stockholder) received 1,000 shares of capital stock as proof of ownership. The **heading** of the income statement specifically identifies the name of the entity, the title of the report, and the **time period** over which the net income was earned (one year). Notice that the income statement has three major captions: **revenues, expenses,** and **net income.** The details given under each caption meet the needs of decision makers interested in Business Support. This latter point is significant because the composition and the details of a financial statement vary, depending on the characteristics of the business entity and the needs of the decision makers.

Exhibit 1–4   Income statement (simplified)

<table>
<tr><td colspan="2"> BUSINESS SUPPORT, INC.
Income Statement
For the Year Ended December 31, 19A </td><td>←Name of entity
←Title of report
←Time period</td><td>} HEADING</td></tr>
</table>

Revenues:		
Stenographic revenue	$30,000	
Printing revenue	20,000	
Mailing revenue	13,000	
Total revenues		$63,000
Expenses:		
Salary expense	30,750	
Payroll tax expense	1,100	
Rent expense for office space	2,400	
Rental payments for copiers	6,600	
Utilities expense	400	
Advertising expense	960	
Supplies expense	90	
Interest expense	100	
Depreciation expense on office equipment	600	
Total expenses (excluding income tax)		43,000
Pretax income		20,000
Income tax expense ($20,000 × 17%)		3,400
Net income		$16,600
Earnings per share (EPS) ($16,600 ÷ 3,000 shares)		$5.53

Next, we will discuss the four primary elements on an income statement—revenues, expenses, net income, and earnings per share (EPS).

Revenues

Revenues are earned from the sale of goods or services rendered by the entity to others for which the entity will receive (or has received) cash or something else of value. When a business sells goods or renders services, it may receive cash immediately. If goods or services are sold on credit, the business receives an **account receivable,** which is collected in cash later. In either case, the business recognizes revenue for the period as the sum of sales of goods and services for cash and on credit. Revenue is measured in dollars as the bargained **cash-equivalent** price agreed on by the two parties to the transaction.[3] Various terms are used in financial statements to describe revenue, such as sales revenue,

---

[3] Revenue sometimes is called income, such as rent income, interest income, and royalty income, but this practice causes confusion. Ideally, **income should be used to refer only to the difference between revenues and expenses.**

service revenue, rental revenue, and interest revenue. Revenues are discussed in more detail in Chapter 4.

Expenses

Expenses represent the dollar amount of resources used up by the entity during a period of time to earn revenues. Expenses may require the immediate payment of cash and/or some other resource such as an inventory item. The expense may be on credit so that cash or some other resource is paid after the expense is incurred, such as paying the employees at the end of the month for services provided during the month. For accounting purposes, the **period in which an expense is incurred is the period in which goods are used or services are received.**[4] The expense may be incurred in one accounting period, and the payment made in another accounting period.

An expense may represent the cost of **using** equipment or buildings that were purchased in one accounting period for use in several accounting periods. Through use, each one is worn out over an extended period of time known as **useful life.** As such items are used in operating the business, a portion of their cost becomes an expense. This kind of expense is called **depreciation expense.** For example, on January 1, 19A, Business Support purchased office equipment for its own use at a cash cost of $6,000. It was estimated that the office equipment would have a useful life of 10 years. Therefore, the depreciation expense each year for using the equipment is measured as $6,000 ÷ 10 years = $600. The income statement for 19A (Exhibit 1–4) reports this amount as an expense.[5]

Business Support also reported **interest expense** for one year on the $1,000, 10% note payable (i.e., $1,000 × 10% = $100) because this debt was outstanding for all of 19A.

As a corporation, Business Support has a 17% income tax rate on income. Therefore, Business Support incurred **income tax expense** of $3,400 (i.e., $20,000 × 17% = $3,400).

Net Income

Net income (often called profit by nonaccountants) is the excess of total revenues over total expenses. If the total expenses exceed the total revenues, a **net loss** is reported. When revenues and expenses are equal for the period, the business has operated at **break even.**

Notice that Business Support reported (*a*) pretax income; (*b*) income tax expense; and (*c*) net income, which is an **aftertax** amount.[6]

---

[4] Incurred, as used in this context, means that the amount involved should be accounted for (i.e., recorded in the accounting system) during the specific period.

[5] Accounting for depreciation is discussed in Chapter 9.

[6] Corporations, except those that qualify under Subchapter S of the Internal Revenue Code, are required to pay federal income taxes. The income tax rates are determined by Congress and are changed periodically. Sole proprietorships and partnerships, as business entities, and Subchapter S corporations are not subject to income taxes. In each of these cases, the owner, or owners, must report the income of the entity on their own individual income tax returns. For illustrative purposes, an average tax rate is used herein to ease the arithmetic.

Earnings per Share (EPS)

The amount of earnings per share (EPS) is reported on the income statement of corporations. EPS is computed by dividing net income by the number of shares of **common** stock outstanding. Because Business Support had 3,000 shares of common stock outstanding (i.e., 1,000 shares were owned by each of the three stockholders) and a net income of $16,600, EPS was computed as $16,600 ÷ 3,000 shares = $5.53 per share for the year. EPS is given extensive attention by security analysts and investors.

The Balance Sheet

The purpose of the balance sheet is to report the financial position of a business at a particular point in time. Financial position is the amount of resources (i.e., assets) and the liabilities (i.e., debts) of a business. Therefore, the balance sheet is frequently called the statement of financial position. The **accounting model** for the balance sheet is:[7]

$$\text{ASSETS} = \text{LIABILITIES} + \text{OWNERS' EQUITY}$$

Assets represent resources owned by the entity, liabilities are the debts (obligations) of the entity, and owners' equity represents the interests of the owners.

Illustration.   The balance sheet of Business Support, Inc., is presented in Exhibit 1–5. Notice that the **heading** specifically identifies the name of the entity, the title of the report, and the specific date of the statement. Note that the specific point in time—in this case, December 31, 19A—is stated clearly on the balance sheet. This contrasts with the dating on the income statement, which indicates a period of time (such as one year). After the statement heading, the **assets** are listed on the left and the **liabilities** and **owners' equity** (called stockholders' equity for a corporation) on the right. Notice that the two sides "balance" in conformity with the accounting model given above. In the following chapters, you will learn that the accounting model for the balance sheet is the basic building block for the entire accounting process.

Next, we will discuss the three elements reported on a balance sheet—assets, liabilities, and owners' equity.

Assets

Assets are the resources owned by the entity. Assets may be tangible (physical in character) such as land, buildings, and machinery; or they may be intangible (characterized by legal claims or rights) such as amounts due from customers (legal claims called accounts receivable) and patents (protected rights).

---

[7] The accounting model is an algebraic equation that can be rearranged. For example, it frequently is expressed as Assets − Liabilities = Owners' Equity.

Exhibit 1–5   Balance sheet (simplified)

BUSINESS SUPPORT, INC.
Balance Sheet
At December 31, 19A

Assets			Liabilities		
Cash		$13,600	Accounts payable	$ 900	
Accounts receivable		13,000	Income taxes payable	500	
Land		20,000	Note payable (10%)	1,000	
Office equipment	$6,000		Total liabilities		$ 2,400
Less: Accumulated			**Stockholders' Equity**		
depreciation	600	5,400*	Contributed capital:		
			Capital stock (par $10;		
			3,000 shares)	$30,000	
			Contributed capital in excess		
			of par value	3,000	
			Retained earnings	16,600	
			Total stockholders'		
			equity		49,600
			Total liabilities and		
Total assets		$52,000	stockholders' equity		$52,000

* This is the **undepreciated** cost; it is usually called the book value of the asset.

Notice in the balance sheet given in Exhibit 1–5 that each **asset** listed has an assigned dollar amount. An asset should be measured on the basis of the total cost incurred to acquire it. For example, the balance sheet for Business Support reports "Land, $20,000"; this is the amount of resources paid for the land when it was acquired. Even if the market value of the land changes, the balance sheet will report the land at its **original acquisition cost.** Balance sheets do not purport to show the **current market value** of the assets listed. Some unsophisticated users of financial statements do not understand this limitation and can easily misinterpret the financial position of a business.

Accountants do not change the measurement of each asset to reflect the new market values because the acquisition cost is factually objective (i.e., not an estimate), whereas the current market value of the assets owned by the entity would have to be estimated at the end of each year. The estimate would be subjective because the assets are not sold each year-end. Such subjectivity could reduce the reliability of the financial statements.

Notice that the balance sheet in Exhibit 1–5 reports "Office equipment, $6,000," which was its **acquisition cost.** Accumulated depreciation of $600 is subtracted from the original cost. This $600 is the same as the amount of depreciation expense on the income statement (Exhibit 1–4). This amount is deducted because it represents the portion of the original cost that is "worn out or used up" to earn the revenues. Since this is a cumulative amount, at the end of the next year (19B) the deduction for accumulated depreciation will be $1,200 (i.e., $600 × 2 years).

Liabilities

Liabilities are the debts or obligations of the entity. They arise primarily because of the purchase of goods or services from others on credit and through cash borrowings to finance the business.

If a business does not pay its creditors, the law may give the creditors the right to force the sale of assets sufficient to meet their claims.

Business entities often borrow money by entering into a formal contract. In this case, a liability called **notes payable** is created. A note payable specifies a definite maturity or payment date and the rate of interest charged by the lender. Many businesses purchase goods and services on credit that do not involve formal notes. This transaction creates a liability known as **accounts payable.** Another type of liability arises because income taxes often are paid, at least in part, several months after the balance sheet date. Therefore, a liability to the government, **income taxes payable,** must be reported until the taxes are fully paid. Notice in Exhibit 1–5 that Business Support listed three liabilities and the amount of each.

Owners' Equity

The accounting model (Assets = Liabilities + Owners' Equity) shows that owners' equity is equal to total assets minus total liabilities of the business. Because creditors' claims legally come first, owners' equity represents a **residual interest** in the assets. Owners' equity sometimes is called net worth. However, the preferable designations are *(a)* "owner's equity" for a sole proprietorship, *(b)* "partners' equity" for a partnership, and *(c)* "stockholders' equity" for a corporation. Owners' equity in a business comes from two sources: (1) **contributed capital,** which is the investment of cash and other assets in the business by the owners; and (2) **retained earnings,** which is the amount of accumulated earnings kept in the business.[8]

In Exhibit 1–5, the stockholders' equity section reports the following:

1. **Contributed capital.**   The three stockholders invested a total of $33,000 in the business. Each stockholder received 1,000 shares of capital stock having a par value of $10 per share (par value is discussed in Chapter 12). They invested an average price of $11 per share, or $1 per share above par value. The 3,000 shares issued are reported at their par value (3,000 × $10) as "Capital stock," and the remainder (3,000 shares × $1 = $3,000) is reported as "Contributed capital in excess of par value."

---

[8] The term **retained earnings** usually is used by businesses organized as corporations. In contrast, sole proprietorships and partnerships usually do not use this term because it is included in the owners' capital account(s). These distinctions are discussed later.

2. **Retained earnings.** The accumulated amount of earnings less all losses and dividends paid to the stockholders since formation of the corporation is reported as "Retained earnings." During the first year, Business Support earned $16,600, as shown on the income statement (Exhibit 1–4). This amount is reported as retained earnings on the balance sheet for Business Support at this date because no dividends were declared or paid to the stockholders during the first year (since organization).

3. **Total stockholders' equity.** The sum of the owners' investment is the original capital ($33,000) plus the retained earnings ($16,600), which equals $49,600. This amount may be verified in terms of the accounting model: Assets ($52,000) − Liabilities ($2,400) = Stockholders' Equity ($49,600).

A cash dividend is the payment by a corporation of an equal amount to each share of capital stock outstanding. For example, if a cash dividend of $6,000 had been declared and paid by Business Support to the three stockholders during the year, the balance sheet would have reflected cash of $7,600 (i.e., $13,600 − $6,000) and retained earnings of $10,600 (i.e., $16,600 − $6,000).

Statement of Cash Flows (SCF)

Each financial statement has a primary purpose. The balance sheet shows the resources that are owned and owed to others by a business at a point in time. The income statement reports the revenues that were earned during an accounting period and the expenses that were incurred to earn the revenue. As discussed earlier in this chapter, revenue is not always equal to cash collected from customers because some sales may be on credit. Also, expenses reported on the income statement may not be equal to the cash paid out during the period because expenses may be incurred in one period and payment made in another. As a result, net income (revenues minus expenses) is usually not the amount of cash earned during the period. In fact, many successful companies may earn large amounts of income and, nevertheless, go out of business because they do not have sufficient cash to meet their obligations. Because the income statement does not provide any information concerning cash flows, accountants prepare the **statement of cash flows (SCF)** which reports cash flows from various activities.

There are three primary categories of cash flows in a typical business:

1. **Cash flows from operating activities.** These cash flows are directly related to earning income (i.e., normal business activity). Examples of this type of cash flows include cash collected from customers and cash paid to employees.

2. **Cash flows from investing activities.** This category includes cash flows that are related to the acquisition or sale of productive assets used by the company. Examples include the purchase of a new factory and the sale of a used delivery truck.

Exhibit 1–6   Statement of cash flows (SCF) (simplified)

BUSINESS SUPPORT, INC.
Statement of Cash Flows
For the Year Ended December 31, 19A

Cash flows from operating activities:
Cash collected from customers $50,000
Cash paid for expenses . . . . (44,400)
    Net cash inflow from operating activities . . . . $ 5,600

Cash flows from investing activities:
Cash paid to purchase equipment . . . . (6,000)
Cash paid to purchase land . . . . (20,000)
    Net cash outflow from investing activities . . . .   (26,000)

Cash flows from financing activities:
Cash received from owners' investment 33,000
Cash received from loan   1,000
    Net cash inflow from financing activities   34,000

Net increase in cash during the year $13,600

---

3. **Cash flows from financing activities.**   These cash flows are directly related to the financing of the enterprise itself. Examples of these cash flows include cash received from owners for their initial investment in the business and cash used to repay a loan from a bank.

Many analysts believe that the SCF is the most important financial statement because it is useful for predicting the future cash flows that may be available from an investment in a particular business.

Illustration.   The SCF for Business Support, Inc., is shown in Exhibit 1–6. Notice that the period of time covered (i.e., for the year ended December 31, 19A) is usually the same as the income statement.

The SCF is developed by analyzing the balance sheet and the income statement. For example, the income statement for Business Support (Exhibit 1–4) reported revenue of $63,000, but $13,000 of the revenue was on credit (notice the "Accounts receivable" in Exhibit 1–5). Therefore, the amount of cash collected from customers was $50,000, which is reported in Exhibit 1–6.

A detailed discussion of the SCF is deferred to Chapter 15 because its preparation requires a more complete knowledge of accounting. At this point, you only need to understand the type of information reported on the SCF and how it differs from the income statement.

Exhibit 1-7 Format of financial statements—demonstration case

---

ABC SERVICE CORPORATION
Income Statement

Date _____

		Computations
Revenues:		
Service revenue	$ ____	_____
Expenses:		
Various expenses . . . . . $ ____		_____
Interest expense . . . . . . ____		_____
Depreciation expense . . . ____		_____
Total expenses	____	
Pretax income	____	
Income tax expense	____	_____
Net income	$ ____	
Earnings per share	$ ____	_____

ABC SERVICE CORPORATION
Balance Sheet

Date _____

Assets:		
Cash	$ ____	_____
Accounts receivable	____	_____
Service trucks . . . . . . $ ____		_____
Less: Accumulated		
depreciation . . . . . ____	____	_____
Total assets	$ ____	
Liabilities:		
Note payable (15%) . . . . $ ____		_____
Income taxes payable . . . ____		_____
Total liabilities	$ ____	
Stockholders' equity:		
Capital stock (par $ ____;		
_____ shares)	____	_____
Contributed capital in		
excess of par value . . .	____	_____
Retained earnings	____	_____
Total stockholders'		
equity	____	
Total liabilities and		
stockholders' equity . . .	$ ____	

Exhibit 1–8 Suggested solution—demonstration case

ABC SERVICE CORPORATION
Income Statement

Date ___For the Year Ended December 31, 19A___

		Computations
Revenues:		
Service revenue	$100,500	*Given*
Expenses:		
Various expenses $54,000		*Given (minus interest)*
Interest expense 1,500		*$10,000 × 15%*
Depreciation expense . . . 5,000		*$20,000 ÷ 4 years*
Total expenses	$ 60,500	
Pretax income	40,000	
Income tax expense	8,000	*$40,000 × 20%*
Net income	$ 32,000	
Earnings per share	$ 10.67	*$32,000 ÷ 3,000 shares*

ABC SERVICE CORPORATION
Balance Sheet

Date ___At December 31, 19A___

Assets:			*$36,000 + $10,000 + $94,500*
Cash		$58,000	*− $55,500 − $7,000 − $20,000*
Accounts receivable		6,000	*$100,500 − $94,500*
Service trucks $20,000			*Given, cost of trucks*
Less: Accumulated			
depreciation 5,000		15,000	*$20,000 ÷ 4 years = $5,000*
Total assets		$79,000	
Liabilities:			
Note payable (15%) $10,000			*Given, bank loan*
Income taxes payable . . . 1,000			*Given, amount unpaid*
Total liabilities		$11,000	
Stockholders' equity:			
Capital stock (par $ _10_;			
_3,000_ shares) 30,000			*3,000 × $10*
Contributed capital in			
excess of par value . . . 6,000			*3,000 × ($12 − $10)*
Retained earnings 32,000			*From income statement**
Total stockholders'			
equity		68,000	
Total liabilities and			
stockholders' equity . . .		$79,000	

* Beginning RE ($-0-) + Net income ($32,000) − Dividends ($-0-) = Ending RE ($32,000).

Financial Statement Analysis

Some students mistakenly believe that accounting is unimportant and uninteresting. They probably hold this belief because they can only see financial statements as the end of a process. While it is true that financial statements represent the end of the accounting process, they also represent the beginning of the decision-making process. Accountants are information specialists who provide important input for managers, bankers, investors, and financial analysts. Accountants must have a clear understanding of many areas of business in order to provide relevant information for decision makers. Similarly, decision makers must have a clear understanding of accounting in order to properly use information to make optimal decisions. A swim coach would never try to evaluate a swimmer's time in the 100 freestyle without first asking if the time was for a race in meters or in yards. Likewise, a decision maker should never attempt to use accounting information without first understanding the procedures, concepts, and assumptions that were used to develop the information.

Even at this early stage of your study of accounting, we can provide some examples of how an analyst might review Business Support, Inc.

1. The company is in a strong cash position. Its cash on hand is more than five times larger than its liabilities ($13,600 ÷ $2,400).
2. The company earned net income in its first year of operation, which is often unusual. The income represents a 50% return on the owners' initial investment ($16,000 ÷ $33,000). A return that is this large is very unusual.
3. The cash flow from operations is significantly less than the net income that was earned. This is typical for a new, growing company because it often does not collect all of its sales revenue in cash.

These observations are intended to illustrate that even in the highly simplified case of Business Support, it is possible to gain important insight into the operations of a company by using accounting data. Later in this textbook, you will see how various accounting assumptions can affect decisions made by users of financial statements.

DEMONSTRATION CASE

At the end of most chapters, one or more demonstration cases are presented. These cases provide an overview of the primary issues discussed in the chapter. Each demonstration case is followed by a recommended solution. The case should be read carefully; then you should prepare your own solution before you study the recommended solution. This self-evaluation is highly recommended.

The introductory case presented below will start you thinking in monetary terms of some of the resource inflows and outflows of a business. (Note: The case will test your comprehension of Part B of the chapter and also your analytical skills.)

ABC Service Corporation was organized by Able, Baker, and Cain on January 1, 19A. On that date, each investor bought 1,000 shares of capital stock (par value $10 per share) at $12 cash per share. On the same day, the corporation borrowed $10,000 from a local bank and signed a three-year, 15%, note payable. The interest is payable each December 31. On January 1, 19A, the corporation purchased two service trucks for $20,000 cash. Operations started immediately.

At the end of 19A, the corporation had completed the following additional business transactions (summarized):

a. Performed services and billed customers for $100,500, of which $94,500 was collected in cash by year-end.

b. Paid $55,500 cash for expenses (including the annual interest on the note payable).

c. Paid $7,000 cash to the Internal Revenue Service (IRS) for income taxes. At the end of the year, ABC still owed the IRS $1,000 (the average income tax rate was 20%).

d. Depreciated the cost of the two service trucks on the basis of a four-year useful life (disregard any residual value at the end of the four-year life).

Required:
Complete the two 19A financial statements shown in Exhibit 1–7 by entering the correct amounts. The suggested solution is given in Exhibit 1–8.

SUMMARY OF CHAPTER

Accounting interacts with almost all aspects of the environment: social, economic, and political. Any organization in our society, whether local, national, or international, can be an **accounting entity.** The essence of accounting is the measurement and reporting of financial information for an accounting entity. **Measurement** and **reporting** of the financial effects of transactions on accounting entities are relevant to interested decision makers. Your decision-making potential is enhanced if you understand the financial impacts of alternative solutions to particular problems.

Part B of the chapter explained and illustrated the basic features of the three required external financial reports—the income statement, the balance sheet, and the statement of cash flows (SCF).

The income statement is a statement of operations that reports revenues, expenses, and net income for a stated period of time. Earnings per share (EPS), which gives the relationship between net income and the number of shares of common stock outstanding, was illustrated.

The balance sheet is a statement of **financial position** that reports dollar amounts for the assets, liabilities, and owners' equity at a specific point in time.

The financial statements for a small company were illustrated. In the next chapters, you will move one step forward by learning more about the accounting model and the analysis of business transactions.

The accounting model for the balance sheet, **Assets = Liabilities + Owners' Equity,** is the **foundation for the entire accounting process.**

The statement of cash flows reports inflows and outflows of cash for a specific period of time.

IMPORTANT TERMS DEFINED IN THIS CHAPTER

AAA American Accounting Association. *p. 15*

Accounting Entity A business or other organization; separate and distinct from its owners. *p. 7*

AICPA American Institute of Certified Public Accountants. *p. 13*

Assets Items owned; have value. *p. 20*

Auditing Attest function; reliability; auditor's opinion. *p. 11*

Balance Sheet Position statement; Assets = Liabilities + Owners' Equity. *p. 20*

Contributed Capital Total amount invested by stockholders. *p. 22*

Corporation A separate legal entity; shares of stock represent ownership. *p. 6*

CMA Certified Management Accountant. *p. 10*

CPA Certified Public Accountant. *p. 10*

Depreciation Allocation of the cost of operational assets; based on use. *p. 19*

Dividend (Cash) A cash payment from a corporation to its stockholders based on the number of shares held. *p. 23*

EPS Earnings per share; common stock. *p. 20*

Expenses Outflow of resources; for goods and services used. *p. 18*

FASB Financial Accounting Standards Board. *p. 14*

FEI Financial Executives Institute. *p. 15*

GAAP Generally accepted accounting principles. *p. 16*

Income Statement Required report; operations; net income; EPS. *p. 17*

Liabilities Obligations; debts; promises to pay. *p. 22*

Management Advisory Services Service rendered by CPA firms; consulting; complements audit and tax services (MAS). *p. 11*

Net Income Revenues − Expenses = Net Income. *p. 17*

Owners' Equity Assets − Liabilities = Owners' Equity. *p. 22*

Partnership Nonstock; two or more owners. *p. 5*

Retained Earnings Accumulated earnings; reduced by dividends. *p. 23*

Revenues Inflow of resources; from sale of goods and services. *p. 18*

SCF Statement of cash flows. *p. 23*

SEC Securities and Exchange Commission; government. *p. 14*

Separate-Entity Assumption An entity must be accounted for separately and apart from its owners. *p. 7*

Sole Proprietorship Nonstock; one owner. *p. 5*

Stockholders' Equity Assets − Liabilities = Stockholders' Equity. *p. 23*

QUESTIONS

Part A: Questions 1–7

1. Define accounting.
2. Explain the use of the monetary unit in accounting.
3. Briefly distinguish among a sole proprietorship, partnership, and corporation.
4. What is an accounting entity? Why is a business treated as a separate entity for accounting purposes?
5. Briefly explain the three ways that financial statements serve statement users.
6. List and briefly explain the three primary services provided by CPAs in public practice.
7. Briefly explain the role of the:
    a. FASB.
    b. SEC.
    c. AAA.

Part B: Questions 8–23

8. Financial statements are the end products of the accounting process. Explain.
9. Define communication.
10. The accounting process generates financial reports for both "internal" and "external" users. Identify some of the groups of users.
11. Complete the following:

Name of statement	A more descriptive name
a. Income statement	*a.* _____
b. Balance sheet	*b.* _____
c. Statement of cash flows (SCF)	*c.* _____

12. What information should be included in the heading of each of the three required financial statements?
13. Explain why the income statement and the SCF are dated "For the Year Ended December 31, 19X," whereas the balance sheet is dated "At December 31, 19X."
14. Define revenue.
15. Define expense.

16. Briefly define the following: net income, net loss, and break even.

17. What are the purposes of *(a)* the income statement, *(b)* the balance sheet, and *(c)* the SCF?

18. Explain the accounting model for the income statement. What are the three major items reported on the income statement?

19. Explain the accounting model for the balance sheet. Define the three major components reported on the balance sheet.

20. Explain the accounting model for the SCF. Explain the three major components reported on the statement.

21. Why is owners' equity referred to frequently as a residual interest?

22. What are the two primary sources of owners' equity in a business?

23. What are the appropriate titles for owners' equity for *(a)* sole proprietorship, *(b)* partnership, and *(c)* corporation?

EXERCISES

(Note: The booklet of working papers that accompanies this textbook provides forms with the problem data already entered.)

Part A: Exercises 1–1 to 1–2

E1–1   (Identifying Important Accounting Organizations)
Below is a list of important abbreviations used in Part A of the chapter. These abbreviations also are used widely in business. For each abbreviation give the full designation. The first one is an example.

Abbreviations	Full designations
(1) CPA	Certified Public Accountant
(2) APB	_____
(3) GAO	_____
(4) AAA	_____
(5) CMA	_____
(6) AICPA	_____
(7) SEC	_____
(8) FASB	_____
(9) ICC	_____
(10) FEI	_____

E1–2   (Match Definitions with Terms or Abbreviations)
Match each definition with its related term or abbreviation by entering the appropriate letter in the space provided.

Terms or abbreviations	Definitions
_____ (1) SEC	A. The collection, analysis, measurement, recording, and reporting information about an entity to decision makers.
_____ (2) Auditing	
_____ (3) Sole proprietorship	
_____ (4) Corporation	B. Measurement of information about an entity in the monetary unit—dollars.
_____ (5) Accounting	
_____ (6) Separate entity	C. An unincorporated business owned by two or more persons.
_____ (7) Auditor's report	
_____ (8) CMA	D. An entity defined for accounting purposes, separate from its owners.
_____ (9) Partnership	
_____ (10) AICPA	E. An incorporated entity that issues shares of stock as evidence of ownership.
_____ (11) FASB	
_____ (12) CPA	F. Certified Management Accountant.
_____ (13) Unit of measure	G. Attest function by an independent CPA.
_____ (14) FEI	H. Certified Public Accountant.
_____ (15) American Accounting Association	I. An unincorporated business owned by one person.

J. Independent CPA's statement that indicates whether the financial statements are appropriate and not misleading.

K. Securities and Exchange Commission.

L. Financial Accounting Standards Board.

M. American Accounting Association.

N. Financial Executives Institute.

O. American Institute of Certified Public Accountants.

P. American Institute of Certified Public Accountants.

Part B: Exercises 1–3 to 1–11

E1–3   (Using the Income Statement and Balance Sheet Models)

Review the chapter explanations of the income statement and the balance sheet models. Apply these models in each independent case below to compute the two missing amounts for each case. Assume it is the end of 19A, the first full year of operations for the company.

Independent Cases	Total Revenues	Total Assets	Total Expenses	Total Liabilities	Net Income (Loss)	Stockholders' Equity
A	$95,000	$150,000	$88,000	$85,000	$	$
B		112,000	61,000		10,000	60,000
C	80,000	92,000	86,000	26,000		
D	50,000			40,000	9,000	77,000
E			81,000	73,000	(6,000)	92,000

E1-4   **(Analyzing an Income Statement)**

Merry Corporation was organized by three individuals on January 1, 19A, to provide electronic repair services. At the end of 19A, the following income statement was prepared:

MERRY CORPORATION
Income Statement
For the Year Ended December 31, 19A

Revenues:		
Service revenue (cash)	$168,000	
Service revenue (credit)	12,000	
Total revenues		$180,000
Expenses:		
Salaries expense	71,000	
Rent expense	18,000	
Utilities expense	10,000	
Advertising expense	11,000	
Supplies expense	18,000	
Interest expense	7,000	
Depreciation expense	5,000	
Total expenses		140,000
Pretax income		40,000
Income tax expense		12,000
Net income		$ 28,000
EPS		$2.80

Required:

a. What was the average monthly revenue amount?

b. What was the monthly rent amount?

c. Explain why supplies is reported as an expense.

d. Explain why interest is reported as an expense.

e. Explain what is meant by "Depreciation expense, $5,000."

f. What was the average income tax rate for Merry Corporation?

g. How many shares of capital stock were outstanding?

h. Can you determine how much cash the company had on December 31, 19A? Explain.

E1-5   **(Preparing a Simple Income Statement)**

Assume you are the owner of "The Drop-In Shop," which specializes in items that interest college students. At the end of January 19A, you find that (for January only):

a. Sales, per the cash register tapes, totaled $100,000, plus one sale on credit (a special situation) of $1,000.

b. With the help of a friend (who majored in accounting), you determined that all of the goods sold during January had cost you $30,000 when they were purchased.

c. During the month, according to the checkbook, you paid $35,000 for salaries, utilities, supplies, advertising, and other expenses; however, you have not yet paid the $600 monthly rent for January on the store and fixtures.

On the basis of the data given, what was the amount of income for January (disregard income taxes)? Show computations. (Hint: A convenient form to use would have the following major side captions: revenue from sales, expenses, and the difference—net income.)

E1-6   (Analysis of Cash Inflow from Operations)

Lawn Care Company, a service organization, prepared the following special report for the month of January 19A:

Service Revenue, Expenses, and Income

Service revenue:

Cash services (per cash register tape)	$95,000	
Credit services (per charge bills; not yet collected by end of January)	30,000	$125,000

Expenses:

Salaries and wages expense (paid by check)	50,000	
Salary for January not yet paid	2,000	
Supplies used (taken from stock, purchased for cash during December) . . .	1,000	
Estimated cost of wear and tear on used delivery truck for the month (depreciation)	500	
Other expenses (paid by check)	21,500	75,000
Pretax income		50,000
Income tax expense (not yet paid)		10,000
Income for January		$ 40,000

Required:

a. The owner (who knows little about the financial part of the business) asked you to compute the "amount that cash increased in January 19A from the operations of the company." You decided to prepare a detailed report for the owner with the following major side captions: cash inflows (collections), cash outflows (payments), and the difference—net increase (or decrease) in cash.

b. What was the average income tax rate?

c. See if you can reconcile the "difference—net increase (or decrease) in cash" you computed in (a) with the income for January 19A.

E1-7   (Preparing a Simple Income Statement and Balance Sheet)

Sandy Corporation was organized by five individuals on January 1, 19A. At the end of January 19A, the following monthly financial data are available:

Total revenues	$110,000
Total expenses (excluding income taxes)	80,000
Cash balance, January 31, 19A	18,000
Receivables from customers (all considered collectible)	12,000
Merchandise inventory (by inventory count at cost)	35,000
Payables to suppliers for merchandise purchased from them (will be paid during February 19A)	9,000
Capital stock (par $10; 2,600 shares)	26,000

No dividends were declared or paid during 19A.

Assume a 30% tax rate on the income of this corporation; the income taxes will be paid during the first quarter of 19B.

Required:
Complete the following two statements:

SANDY CORPORATION
Income Statement
For the Month of January 19A

Total revenues . . . . $ _____	
Less: Total expenses (excluding income tax) . . . . _____	
Pretax income . . . . _____	
Less: Income tax expense . . . . _____	
Net income . . . . $ _____	

SANDY CORPORATION
Balance Sheet
At January 31, 19A

Assets:
Cash . . . . $ _____
Receivables from customers . . . . _____
Merchandise inventory . . . . _____
Total assets . . . . $ _____

Liabilities:
Payables to suppliers . . . . $ _____
Income taxes payable . . . . _____
Total liabilities . . . . _____

Stockholders' equity:
Capital stock . . . . $ _____
Retained earnings . . . . _____
Total liabilities and stockholders' equity . . . . $ _____

E1–8 **(Completing a Simple Balance Sheet)**

Best Seller Bookstore was organized as a corporation by Terry Lloyd and James Stewart; each contributed $40,000 cash to start the business. Each received 3,000 shares of common stock, par $10 per share. The store completed its first year of operations on December 31, 19A. On that date, the following financial items for the year were determined: December 31, 19A, cash on hand and in the bank, $41,100; December 31, 19A, amounts due from customers from sales of books, $19,000; store and office equipment, purchased January 1, 19A, for $50,000 (estimated useful life, five years; depreciate an equal amount each year); December 31, 19A, amounts owed to publishers for books purchased, $7,000; and a note payable, 10%, one year, dated July 1, 19A, to a local bank for $2,000. No dividends were declared or paid to the stockholders during the year.

Required:

a. Complete the balance sheet at the end of 19A shown below.

b. What was the amount of net income for the year?

c. Show how the $100 liability for interest payable was computed. Why is it shown as a liability on this date?

	Assets				Liabilities		
Cash	. . . .	$ ____		Accounts payable	. . . .	$ ____	
Accounts receivable	. . . .	____		Note payable (10%)	. . . .	____	
Store and office equipment	. . . $ ____			Interest payable	. . . .	100	
Less: Accumulated				Total liabilities	. . . .	$ ____	
depreciation to date	. . . . .	____	____				

Stockholders' Equity

Common stock	. . . .	____
Contributed capital in excess		
of par	. . . .	____
Retained earnings	. . . .	11,000
Total stockholders' equity	. . .	____

Total assets	. . . .	$ ____	Total liabilities and stockholders' equity	. . . . . .	$ ____

E1-9 (Preparing a Simple Statement of Cash Flows)

FUJI Manufacturing Corporation is preparing the annual financial statements for the stockholders. A SCF must be prepared. The following data on cash flows were developed for the entire year ended December 31, 19D: cash inflow from operating revenues, $250,000; cash expended for operating expenses, $190,000; sale of unissued FUJI stock for cash, $20,000; cash dividends declared and paid to stockholders during the year, $15,000; and payments on long-term notes payable, $50,000. During the year, a tract of land was sold for $10,000 cash (which was the same price that FUJI had paid for the land in 19C), and $33,000 cash was expended for two new machines. The machines were used in the factory.

Required:
Prepare a SCF for 19D. Follow the format illustrated in the chapter.

E1-10 (Completing a Simple Income Statement)

Quality Reality, Incorporated has been operating for five years and is owned by three investors. J. Doe owns 60% of the total outstanding stock of 9,000 shares and is the managing executive in charge. On December 31, 19C, the following financial items for the entire year were determined: commissions earned and collected in cash, $140,000, plus $14,000 uncollected; rental service fees earned and collected, $16,000; salaries expense paid, $56,700; commissions expense paid, $40,000; payroll taxes paid, $3,000; rent paid, $2,200 (not including December rent yet to be paid); utilities expense paid, $900; promotion and advertising paid, $6,000; and miscellaneous expenses paid, $400. There were no other unpaid expenses at December 31. Quality Realty rents its office space but owns the furniture therein. The furniture cost $6,000 when acquired and has an estimated life of 10 years (depreciate an equal amount each year). The average income tax rate for this corporation is 30%. Also during the year, the company paid the owners "out of profit" cash dividends amounting to $10,000. Complete the following income statement:

Revenues:		
Commissions earned	$ _____	
Rental service fees	_____	
Total revenues		$ _____
Expenses:		
Salaries expense	_____	
Commission expense	_____	
Payroll tax expense	_____	
Rent expense	_____	
Utilities expense	_____	
Promotion and advertising expense	_____	
Miscellaneous expenses	_____	
Depreciation expense	_____	
Total expenses (excluding income taxes)		_____
Pretax income		_____
Income tax expense		_____
Net income		$ 42,000
Earnings per share (EPS)		$ _____

E1–11 **(Applying the Balance Sheet Model)**

On June 1, 19F, Remington Corporation prepared a balance sheet just prior to going out of business. The balance sheet totals showed the following:

Assets (no cash)	$100,000
Liabilities	70,000
Stockholders' equity	30,000

Shortly thereafter, all of the assets were sold for cash.

Required:

a. How would the balance sheet appear immediately after the sale of the assets for cash for each of the following cases? Use the format given below.

	Cash received for the assets	Balances immediately after sale		
		Assets	− Liabilities	= Stockholders' Equity
Case A	$110,000	$ _____	$ _____	$ _____
Case B	100,000	_____	_____	_____
Case C	90,000	_____	_____	_____

b. How should the cash be distributed in each separate case? (Hint: Creditors have a priority claim over owners upon dissolution.) Use the format given below.

	To creditors	To stockholders	Total
Case A	$_____	$_____	$_____
Case B	_____	_____	_____
Case C	_____	_____	_____

PROBLEMS

(Note: The booklet of forms that accompanies this textbook provides forms with the problem data already entered.)

Part A: Problems 1–1 to 1–3

P1–1   (Analyzing Transactions)
Below are listed five transactions completed by Baxter Company during the year 19A:

a. Sold services for cash, $40,000.
b. Purchased a microcomputer for use in performing the accounting function of the company: cost, $6,000; paid cash.
c. Paid salaries, $20,000 cash.
d. Borrowed $15,000 cash on a 12% interest-bearing note.
e. The owner of Baxter Company purchased a special pickup for his personal use: cost, $16,000; paid cash from his personal funds.

Required:
Complete the tabulation given below. Indicate the effects (in dollars) of each of the above transactions on the balance sheet, income statement, and SCF of Baxter Company. Consider only the effects on the date the transactions were completed. Provide explanatory comments to support your response for each transaction. Use "+" for increase and "−" for decrease on the income statement and balance sheet.

	Transaction				
Financial Statements	*(a)*	*(b)*	*(c)*	*(d)*	*(e)*
Income statement: Revenues Expenses	$	$	$	$	$
Balance sheet: Assets Liabilities Owners' equity					
SCF: Cash inflow Cash outflow					
Explanations:					

P1-2 (Analysis of Data to Support a Loan Application)

On January 1, 19A, three individuals organized Box Company. Each individual invested $7,500 cash in the business. On December 31, 19A, they prepared a list of resources (assets) owned and a list of the debts (liabilities) to support a company loan request of $50,000 submitted to a local bank. None of the three investors had studied accounting. The two lists prepared were as follows:

Company resources:

Cash	$ 10,000
Service supplies inventory (on hand)	5,000
Service trucks (four practically new)	64,000
Personal residences of organizers (three houses)	190,000
Service equipment used in the business (practically new)	24,000
Bills due from customers (for services already completed)	13,000
Total	$306,000

Obligations of the company:

Unpaid wages to employees	$ 18,000
Unpaid taxes	6,000
Owed to suppliers	8,000
Owed on service trucks and equipment (to a finance company)	40,000
Loan from organizer	15,000
Total	$ 87,000

Required:

a. If you were advising the local bank about the two lists, what issues would you raise? Explain the basis for each question and include any recommendations that you have (consider the separate-entity assumption).

b. In view of your response to *(a)*, what do you think the amount of **net resources** (i.e., assets minus liabilities) of the company would be? Show your computations.

P1–3   (Comparison of Income with Cash Flow)

Rush Service Company was organized on January 1, 19A. At the end of the first quarter (three months) of operations, the owner prepared a summary of its operations as shown in the first column of the following tabulation:

	Computation of—	
Summary of Transactions	Income	Cash
1. Services performed for customers, $66,000, of which one sixth remained uncollected at the end of the quarter.	$ +66,000	$ +55,000
2. Cash borrowed from the local bank, $20,000 (one-year note).	_____	_____
3. Purchased a small service truck for use in the business: cost, $8,000; paid 20% down, balance on credit.	_____	_____
4. Expenses, $42,000, of which one fifth remained unpaid at the end of the quarter.	_____	_____
5. Purchased service supplies for use in the business, $2,000, of which one fourth remained unpaid (on credit) at the end of the quarter. Also, one fifth of these supplies were unused (still on hand) at the end of the quarter.	_____	_____
6. Wages earned by employees, $18,000, of which one sixth remained unpaid at the end of the quarter.	_____	_____
7. Purchased land for future use for $20,000 cash.	_____	_____
Based only on the above transactions, compute the following for the quarter: 　　Income (or loss) 　　Cash inflow (or outflow)	$ _____	$ _____

Required:

a. For each of the seven transactions given in the tabulation above, enter what you consider the correct amounts. Enter a zero when appropriate. The first transaction is illustrated.

b. For each transaction, explain the basis for your dollar responses.

Part B: Problems 1–4 to 1–8

P1–4   (Completing a Simple Balance Sheet)

Light Corporation was organized by Kelly Ditmore and Cynthia Baldwin; they had previously operated the company as a partnership. Each owner has 10,000 shares of capital stock of Light Corporation. At the end of the accounting year, 19H, the company bookkeeper prepared the following incomplete balance sheet.

LIGHT CORPORATION
Balance Sheet

(1)	Assets:		
(2)	Cash		$28,000
(3)	Accounts receivable		15,000
(4)	Equipment* . . . . $ ____		
(5)	Less: Accumulated depreciation	10,000	40,000
(6)	Total _____		$83,000
(7)	_____		
(8)	Accounts payable	8,000	
(9)	Income taxes payable	1,000	
(10)	Note payable, short term (15%)†	4,000	
(11)	_____		____
(12)	_____		
(13)	Capital stock (par $____)	20,000	
(14)	Contributed capital in excess of par	10,000	
(15)	Retained earnings	40,000	
(16)	_____		70,000
(17)	Total liabilities and stockholders' equity		$_____

* Equipment has a 10-year estimated life; equal amounts expensed each year.
† Note dated July 1, 19H, time to maturity, 12 months.

Required (the lines are numbered above for problem reference purposes):

1. Define the term **assets** as used on the balance sheet.
2. What would be the company's checking account balance in the bank assuming the company has $500 petty cash on hand on December 31, 19H?
3. Explain why "Accounts receivable" represents an asset.
4. Compute the amount that the equipment cost when it was acquired by Light Corporation.
5. Explain "Accumulated depreciation." What does the $10,000 indicate?
6. Enter the correct caption.
7. Enter the correct caption.
8. Explain why "Accounts payable" is a liability.
9. Explain what this liability represents.
10. What amount of interest expense applies to the year 19H? Note that the amount computed will be shown on the income statement as "Interest expense."
11. Enter the appropriate caption and amount.
12. Enter the appropriate caption.
13. Enter the amount of the par value per share of capital stock.
14. What was the total issue price per share of capital stock?
15. Explain what the $40,000 amount means.
16. Enter appropriate caption.
17. Enter correct amount.
18. Do you have any suggestions about the heading of the statement?

P1-5   (Redraft an Incorrect Income Statement)

Donald Realty Company was organized early in 19A as a corporation by four investors, each of whom invested $6,000 cash. The company has been moderately successful, even though internal financial controls are inadequate. Although financial reports have been prepared each year (primarily in response to income tax requirements), sound accounting procedures have not been followed. Therefore, the financial performance of the company is known only vaguely by the four stockholders. Recently, one of the stockholders, with the agreement of the others, sold his shares to a local accountant. The new stockholder was amazed when handed the report below. This report was prepared by an employee for the last meeting of the board of directors. The accountant could tell immediately that the reported profit was wrong. She quickly observed that no interest expense was shown on a $10,000, 12%, note payable that had been outstanding throughout the year. Also, no recognition had been given to depreciation expense of office equipment that was purchased on January 1, 19D, at a cost of $12,000 with an estimated six-year useful life.

DONALD REALTY
Profit Statement
December 31, 19D

Commissions earned (all collected)	$155,400
Property management revenue (exclusive of $2,000 not collected)	9,000
Total	164,400
Salaries paid	35,000
Commissions paid	36,000
Payroll taxes paid	3,200
Office supplies expense	150
Rent paid	3,000
Utilities paid	600
Advertising (excluding the December bill for advertising of $6,000 not yet paid)	26,000
Miscellaneous expenses	450
Total	104,400
Profit for the year (pretax)	$ 60,000

EPS: $60,000 ÷ 15,000 shares = $4.

Required:
You were asked to redraft the income statement, including corrections. Assume an average income tax rate of 30%.

P1-6   (Prepare a Simple Income Statement and Balance Sheet)

Assume you are president of Solar Company. At the end of the first year (December 31, 19A) of operations, the following financial data are available for the company:

Cash	$ 20,000
Receivables from customers (all considered collectible)	10,000
Inventory of merchandise (based on physical count and priced at cost)	80,000
Equipment owned, at cost	45,000
Depreciation expense (equipment)	2,500
Note payable, one year, 12% annual interest, owed to the bank (dated July 1, 19A) . . .	30,000
Interest on the note through December 31, 19A (due to be paid to the bank on	
June 30, 19B; $30,000 × 12% × 6/12)	1,800
Salary payable for 19A (on December 31, 19A, this was owed to an employee	
who was away because of an emergency; will return around January 10, 19B,	
at which time the payment will be made)	1,000
Total sales revenue	120,000

Expenses paid, including the cost of the merchandise sold (excluding income taxes
at a 30% rate; the taxes will be paid during the first quarter of 19B) $75,000
Capital stock, 7,000 shares outstanding 80,000
No dividends were declared or paid during 19A.

Required (show computations):

a. Prepare a summarized income statement for the year 19A.

b. Prepare a balance sheet at December 31, 19A.

P1–7 (Analyze a Student's Business and Prepare a Simple Income Statement)

During the summer between her junior and senior years, Jenni Brown needed to earn
sufficient money for the coming academic year. Unable to obtain a job with a reasonable
salary, she decided to try the lawn-care business for three months. After a survey of the
market potential, Jenni bought a used pickup truck on June 1 for $1,200. On each door
she painted "Jenni's Lawn Service, Phone 471-4487." Also, she spent $600 for mowers,
trimmers, and tools. To acquire these items she borrowed $2,000 cash on a note at 10%
interest per annum, payable at the end of the three months (ending August 31).

At the end of the summer, Jenni realized that she had "done a lot of work, and her
bank account looked good." This fact prompted her to become concerned about how
much profit the business had earned.

A review of the check stubs showed the following: Deposits in the bank of collections
from customers totaled $11,400. The following checks were written: gas, oil, and lubrica-
tion, $830; pickup repairs, $175; repair of mowers, $80; miscellaneous supplies used,
$100; helpers, $4,400; payroll taxes, $175; payment for assistance in preparing payroll tax
forms, $25; insurance, $150; telephone, $90; and $2,050 to pay off the note including
interest (on August 31). A notebook kept in the pickup, plus some unpaid bills, reflected
that customers still owed her $600 for lawn services rendered and that she owed $100 for
gas and oil (credit card charges). She estimated that the "wear and tear" for use of the
truck and the other equipment for three months amounted to $400.

Required:

a. Prepare a quarterly income statement for Jenni's Lawn Service for the months
June, July, and August 19A. Use the following main captions: revenues from services, expenses, and net income. Because this is a sole proprietorship, the
company will not be subject to income tax.

b. Do you see a need for one or more additional financial reports for this company
for 19A and thereafter? Explain.

P1–8 (Analyze a Student's Business and Prepare a Simple Income Statement)

Upon graduation from high school, Jack Kane immediately accepted a job as a plumber's
helper for a large local plumbing company. After three years of hard work, Jack received a
plumber's license and decided to start his own business. He had saved $10,000 which he
invested in the business. First, he transferred this amount from his savings account to a
business bank account for "Kane Plumbing Company, Incorporated." His lawyer had
advised him to start as a corporation. He then purchased a used panel truck for $8,000
cash and secondhand tools for $1,400; rented space in a small building; inserted an ad in
the local paper; and opened the doors on October 1, 19A. Immediately, Jack was very
busy; and after one month, he employed a helper. Although Jack knew practically
nothing about the financial side of the business, he realized that a number of reports were
required and that costs and collections had to be controlled carefully. At the end of the

year, prompted in part by concern about his income tax situation (previously he only had to report salary), Jack recognized the need for financial statements. His wife, Jane, "developed some financial statements for the business." On December 31, 19A, with the help of a friend, she gathered the following data for the three months just ended: Deposits in the bank account of collections for plumbing services totaled $30,000. The following checks were written: plumber's helper, $7,550; payroll taxes paid, $150; supplies purchased and used on jobs, $9,000; oil, gas, and maintenance on truck, $1,100; insurance, $650; rent, $500; utilities and telephone, $650; and miscellaneous expenses, $400 (including advertising). Also, there were uncollected bills to customers for plumbing services amounting to $2,000. The rent for December amounting to $100 had not been paid. The average income tax rate is 20%. The "wear and tear on the truck and tools due to use during the three months" was estimated by Jack to be $900.

Required:

a. Prepare a quarterly income statement for Kane Plumbing for the three months October–December 19A. Use the following main captions: revenue from services, expenses, pretax income, and net income.

b. Do you think that Jack may have a need for one or more additional financial reports for 19A and thereafter? Explain.

CASES

Part A: Cases 1–1 to 1–2

C1–1   (Analysis of the Assets and Liabilities of a Business)

David Jones owns and operates the Jones Sporting Goods Company (a sole proprietorship). An employee prepares a financial report for the business at each year-end. This report lists all of the resources (assets) owned by Jones (including such personal items as the home owned and occupied by Jones). It also lists all of the debts of the business (but not the "personal" debts of Jones).

Required:

a. From the accounting point of view, in what ways do you disagree with what is being included in and excluded from the report of business assets and liabilities?

b. Upon questioning, Jones responded, "Don't worry about it, we use it only to support a loan from the bank." How would you respond to this comment?

C1–2   (Decision about a Proposed Audit)

You are one of three partners who own and operate the Tasty Refreshments Company. The company has been operating for seven years. One of the other partners has always prepared the company's annual financial statements. Recently you proposed that "the statements should be audited each year because it would benefit the partners and preclude possible disagreements about the division of profits." The partner that prepares the statements proposed that his "Uncle Ray, who has a lot of financial experience, can do the job and at little cost." Your other partner remained silent.

Required:

a. What position would you take on the proposal? Justify your response.

b. What would you strongly recommend? Give the basis for your recommendation.

Part B: Cases 1–3 to 1–4

C1–3 (Identifying Deficiencies in an Income Statement and Balance Sheet)

Young Corporation was organized on January 1, 19A. At the end of 19A, the company had not yet employed an accountant. However, an employee who was "good with numbers" prepared the following statements at that date:

YOUNG CORPORATION
December 31, 19A

Income from sales of merchandise	$180,000
Total amount paid for goods sold during 19A	(95,000)
Selling costs	(30,000)
Depreciation (on service vehicles used)	(15,000)
Income from services rendered	50,000
Salaries and wages paid	(60,000)
Income taxes (at tax rate of 30% on pretax income)	(9,000)
Profit for the year 19A	$ 21,000

YOUNG CORPORATION
December 31, 19A

Resources:		
Cash		$ 28,000
Merchandise inventory (held for resale)		44,000
Service vehicles		45,000
Retained earnings (profit earned in 19A)		21,000
Grand total		$138,000
Debts:		
Payables to suppliers		$ 15,000
Note owed to bank		20,000
Due from customers		12,000
Total		47,000
Supplies on hand (to be used in rendering services)	$12,000	
Accumulated depreciation (on service vehicles)	15,000	
Capital stock, 10,000 shares	70,000	
Total		97,000
Grand total		$144,000

Required:

a. List all of the deficiencies in the above statements that you can identify. Give a brief explanation on each one.

b. Prepare a proper income statement (correct net income is $21,000) and balance sheet (correct balance sheet total is $126,000).

C1-4   **(Introduction to an Actual Set of Financial Statements)**

JCPenney   Refer to the financial statement of J.C. Penney Company, Inc. given in the appendix immediately preceding the index.

1. What is the amount of net income for the current year?
2. How much revenue was earned in the current year?
3. How much cash does the company have at the end of the current year?
4. What is the amount of retained earnings at the end of the current year?
5. Who is the auditor for J.C. Penney?

TWO

THE ACCOUNTING MODEL AND TRANSACTION ANALYSIS

PURPOSE

Chapter 1 emphasized the importance of the communication of accounting information to certain decision makers. It also presented an overview of external financial statements. The purpose of Chapter 2 is to begin our discussions of how the accounting function collects data about business transactions and how those data are processed to provide the periodic financial statements. To accomplish this purpose, this chapter discusses the accounting model, transaction analysis, and how the results of transaction analysis are recorded in an accounting system.

The balance sheet on the opposite page is complex, but it illustrates the accounting model that is discussed in this chapter. Notice that Assets = Liabilities + Shareholders' Equity.

LEARNING OBJECTIVES

1. Explain what constitutes a business transaction.
2. Analyze some simple business transactions in terms of the accounting model: Assets = Liabilities + Owners' Equity, and Debits = Credits.
3. Record the results of transaction analysis in two basic ways: (a) journal entries and (b) T-accounts.
4. Use the T-account balances to prepare a simple income statement and balance sheet.
5. Expand your accounting vocabulary by learning the "Important Terms Defined in This Chapter."
6. Apply the knowledge learned from this chapter by completing the homework assigned by your instructor.

ORGANIZATION

1. The accounting model.
2. Nature of business transactions.
3. Debits = Credits.
4. Transaction analysis.
5. Journal entries and T-accounts.

The Limited, Inc.

Consolidated Balance Sheets

[thousands]	January 30, 1988	January 31, 1987
Assets		
Current Assets		
Cash and Equivalents	$ 47,953	$ 3,256
Accounts Receivable	95,060	72,878
Inventories	353,693	361,489
Other	47,906	31,608
Total Current Assets	544,612	469,231
Property and Equipment	889,155	734,727
Investment in Finance Subsidiary	77,487	105,503
Other Assets	76,669	67,628
Total Assets	$1,587,923	$1,377,089
Liabilities and Shareholders' Equity		
Current Liabilities		
Accounts Payable	$ 149,974	$ 169,112
Accrued Expenses	131,602	131,829
Income Taxes	48,740	33,963
Total Current Liabilities	330,316	334,904
Long-Term Debt	343,000	70,420
Deferred Income Taxes	174,209	169,414
Other Long-Term Liabilities	11,227	20,809
Shareholders' Equity		
Common Stock	94,837	94,398
Paid-in Capital	205,328	199,424
Retained Earnings	677,232	487,720
Unrealized Loss on Marketable Equity Securities	(8,219)	—
	969,178	781,542
Less Treasury Stock, at Cost	(240,007)	—
Total Shareholders' Equity	729,171	781,542
Total Liabilities and Shareholders' Equity	$1,587,923	$1,377,089

The Accounting Model

Chapter 1 presented the accounting model:

$$\text{Assets (A)} = \text{Liabilities (L)} + \text{Owners' Equity (OE)}$$

The accounting model can also be thought of in the following terms:

$$\begin{array}{rl}
\text{Resources} = & \text{Sources} \\
\text{(A)} = & \text{(L + OE)}
\end{array}$$

The assets of a business are its resources which must be supplied by someone. The liabilities and owners' equity represent the sources of the assets.

The accounting model is an algebraic model, and it expresses common sense. As an algebraic model, it can be rearranged in various ways, such as Assets − Liabilities = Owners' Equity. It also expresses a basic truism: "What I own less what I owe equals my equity in the business." For example, if on December 31 you own assets of $100,000 and owe debts of $30,000, your equity in the business is $70,000.

Let's carry our personal example one step further to see how you stand at the end of the next month. To do this, you must use the accounting model and **record each and every transaction** that you complete. The amounts for assets, liabilities, and owners' equity will change as follows:

Transactions	Assets	=	Liabilities	+	Owners' Equity
Your beginning financial situation	$100,000		$30,000		$70,000
a. Received $3,000 salary	+3,000		–0–		+3,000
Revised situation	103,000		30,000		73,000
b. Paid monthly bills, $2,000	−2,000		–0–		−2,000
Revised situation	101,000		30,000		71,000
c. Paid a debt, $10,000 (no interest now)	−10,000		−10,000		–0–
Revised situation	91,000		20,000		71,000
d. Paid cash for IBM stock as an investment, $5,000	−5,000				
	+5,000				
Your ending financial situation	$ 91,000		$20,000		$71,000

Notice two important points in the above schedule: (1) each transaction had a **dual** effect in the model (i.e., at least two items in the model changed); and (2) after each transaction is recorded, the model is in balance (i.e., A = L + OE).

The **separate-entity assumption** (Chapter 1) requires that a business be accounted for as an entity separate and apart from its owners. From the previous personal illustration, we saw that (*a*) revenues **increase** owners' equity, (*b*) expenses **decrease** owners' equity, and (*c*) dividends (i.e., withdrawals) paid by the corporation **decrease** owners' equity in the company. Therefore, for a business, we can elaborate on the accounting model as follows:

Assets = Liabilities + Owners' Equity

Decreased by:	Increased by:
• Owner withdrawals	• Owner investments
• Expenses	• Revenues

Each transaction has a dual economic effect which is recorded in terms of this expanded accounting model. An example of the dual economic effect of a transaction can be seen when you borrow money from a bank. One effect is an increase in your assets (cash) and the other effect is an increase in your liabilities. Transactions are recorded in terms of this model regardless of whether the accounting system is handwritten, mechanized, or computerized. Let's examine the model based on transactions that affect Bass Cleaners, Inc.

The Accounting Model Illustrated

When Bob Bass and three others organized Bass Cleaners, Inc., on January 1, 19A, each of the four organizers invested $5,000 cash, and each received 200 shares of capital stock. The company immediately started operations. Each transaction completed by the business must be recorded in the company's accounting system in terms of the accounting model:

Assets = Liabilities + Stockholders' Equity

Notice that for a corporation, owners' equity is usually called stockholders' equity.

Exhibit 2–1 lists a series of transactions completed during the year 19A. The exhibit shows how each transaction is recorded in terms of the accounting model for Bass Cleaners. Study it carefully and notice that (1) each transaction is recorded separately; (2) in recording each transaction, the equality of the accounting model is maintained (that is, assets will always equal liabilities plus owners' equity); and (3) the dual effect, as discussed in the preceding section, is recorded for each transaction.

Each transaction is **analyzed,** then entered in terms of the accounting model. The last line of Exhibit 2–1 shows the financial position of the business at December 31, 19A (end of year 1):

Assets, $38,700 = Liabilities, $6,500 + Stockholders' Equity, $32,200

Exhibit 2–1 Transaction analysis illustrated

BASS CLEANERS, INC.
Transaction Analysis—19A

Dual effect of each transaction on the entity

Transactions	Assets	=	Liabilities	+	Stockholders' Equity
a. Bass Cleaners received $20,000 cash invested by owners; 800 shares ($25 par value) of stock issued to the four owners	Cash + $20,000				Capital stock (par $25; 800 shares) + $20,000
b. Borrowed $5,000 cash on 12% note payable	Cash + 5,000		Note payable + $5,000		
c. Purchased delivery truck for cash at cost of $8,000	Cash − 8,000 Delivery truck + 8,000				
d. Cleaning revenue collected in cash, $40,000	Cash + 40,000				Cleaning revenue + 40,000
e. Cleaning revenue earned in 19A, but the bill is not collected, $4,000	Accounts receivable + 4,000				Cleaning revenue + 4,000
f. Operating expenses paid in cash, $25,800	Cash − 25,800				Operating expenses − 25,800

52

g. Operating expenses incurred in 19A but not paid, $2,000 . . . . Accounts payable + 2,000   Operating expenses — 2,000

h. Paid 12% interest on the $5,000 note payable, (h) above, with cash ($5,000 × 12% = $600) . . . . Cash — 600   Interest expense — 600

i. Depreciation expense for one year on truck ($8,000 ÷ 5 years = $1,600) . . . . Truck — 1,600   Operating expenses, depreciation — 1,600

j. Cash dividend of $1,800 declared and paid to stockholders* . . . . Cash — 1,800   Retained earnings (or dividends paid) — 1,800

k. Collected $1,000 cash on accounts receivable in (e) . . . . Cash + 1,000
Accounts receivable — 1,000

l. Paid $500 cash on accounts payable in (g) . . . . Cash — 500   Accounts payable — 500

Totals (end of accounting period) . . Total assets $38,700 = Total liabilities $6,500 + Total stockholders' equity $32,200

* A cash dividend is not an expense; it is a withdrawal of resources from the business and is paid to the owners.

53

The method used in Exibit 2–1 to record each transaction would be inefficient for a business that had numerous transactions. This data collection process can be facilitated in an accounting system by establishing a separate record for each item included in the financial statements. These separate records are called **accounts.**

The Account

To facilitate the preparation of financial statements, most accounting systems have separate accounts, individually labeled, for each **asset** (such as cash, inventory, accounts receivable, equipment, and land); for each **liability** (such as accounts payable, note payable, and taxes payable); and for each item of **owners' equity**[1] (such as capital stock, sales revenue, service revenue, and various kinds of expenses). The **Cash account** for Bass Cleaners is shown in Exhibit 2–2. This account format is called a T-account.

Accounts (*a*) facilitate preparation of the financial statements and (*b*) attain accuracy in the accounting system in the following ways:

a. **Keeping track of amounts.** Each account is designed so that all **increases** are entered on one side (e.g., on the left side of the Cash account in Exhibit 2–2) and all **decreases** are entered on the other side (e.g., on the right side of the Cash account in Exhibit 2–2). You can see the increased efficiency by comparing the list of plus and minus amounts on the cash lines of Exhibit 2–1 with the arrangement in Exhibit 2–2. Also, imagine thousands or millions of such increases and decreases during the year in a typical business. The Cash account shown in Exhibit 2–2 reflects a left side total of $66,000 and a right side total of $36,700. The difference, $29,300, is the ending cash balance (which is reported on the balance sheet). The account system is very flexible; for example, instead of being set up in the "T-account" format shown in Exhibit 2–2, it can be set up in other formats (which will be discussed in Chapter 3). The account system can be used with either (or a combination of) handwritten, mechanical, or computerized approaches.[2]

---

[1] Owners' equity usually is designated to indicate the kind of ownership arrangement used as follows:

Corporation	Stockholders' equity
Partnership	Partners' capital
Sole proprietorship	Owners' capital

[2] Handwritten or manually maintained accounts in the formats shown here are used in small businesses. Highly mechanized and computerized systems retain the concept of the account but not this format. T-accounts are useful primarily for instructional purposes.

Exhibit 2-2 Account (T-account format) illustrated

Cash*			
Left or Debit Side		**Right or Credit Side**	Acct. No. 101
(Increases)		(Decreases)	
Investment by owners	20,000	To purchase truck	8,000
Loan from bank	5,000	Operating expenses	25,800
Cleaning revenue	40,000	Interest expense	600
Collections on accounts		Dividends declared and paid	1,800
receivable	1,000	Payment on accounts payable	500
	66,000		36,700

* The data shown in this account were taken from Exhibit 2–1.

b. **Providing a systematic method of checking for accuracy during the recording process.** It is useful to think of an account as having two sides. The **left side** is always called the **debit** side, and the **right side** is always called the **credit side.** These designations were used in Exhibit 2–2.

In addition to the accounting model (A = L + OE), another algebraic **balancing feature** can be created by simply **reversing** the position in the account of the increases and decreases on the **opposite sides** of the accounting model in the manner shown below.

Assets		=	Liabilities		+	Owners' Equity	
Debit	Credit		Debit	Credit		Debit	Credit
+	–		–	+		–	+

Notice that **debit** always refers to the left side of an account and **credit** always refers to the right side of an account. Thus, debit and credit positions do not change; only the plus and minus signs change positions. The addition of this algebraic concept results in a second balancing feature, that is, for every transaction **debits always should equal credits.** Thus, the system used for recording increases and decreases in the accounts may be tabulated as follows:

	Increases	Decreases
Assets	Debit	Credit
Liabilities	Credit	Debit
Owners' equity	Credit	Debit

Refer back to Exhibit 2–1, transaction (*a*). Accountants record this transaction with a debit (increase) to Cash for $20,000 and a credit (increase) to Capital Stock for $20,000. Notice the two equalities that minimize the possibility of recording errors: (1) the accounting model, which is in balance; and (2) debits equal credits. For practice, express transactions (*b*) and (*c*) in debit-credit terms before you look at the correct answer in the footnote.[3]

Many students have trouble with accounting because they forget that the only meaning for "debit" is the left side of an account and the only meaning for "credit" is the right side of an account. Perhaps someone once told you that you were a "credit" to your school or your family. As a result, you may think that there is a "goodness" attached to credits and perhaps a "badness" attached to debits. Such is not the case. Just remember that debit means left and credit means right. It should also be easy to remember when a debit increases an account and when it decreases an account. A debit (left) increases asset accounts because assets are on the left side of the accounting model (A = L + OE). A credit (right) increases liability and owners' equity accounts because they are on the right side of the accounting model.

Debits and Credits for Revenues and Expenses

Some students are confused about the proper terms to reflect changes in revenue and expense accounts. Remember that owners' equity is increased by credits and decreased by debits. Revenues increase owners' equity; therefore, **revenues are recorded as credits.**

Expenses decrease owners' equity; therefore, **expenses are recorded as debits.** In other words, the debit-credit relationship for owners' equity accounts is applied to revenues and expenses.[4]

In summary, the balance features of the accounting model are:

1. **Assets = Liabilities + Owners' Equity.**
2. **Debits = Credits.**

Notice that each transaction has a dual effect (i.e., a debit and a credit). Because of this dual effect, the accounting model is often called a **double-entry** system.

Journals and Ledgers

Transactions are initially recorded in a journal, which is a chronological listing of transactions. After analyzing the business documents that describe a transaction, the accountant prepares a journal entry in the following format:

---

[3] Transaction (*b*) is a debit to Cash for $5,000 and a credit to Note Payable for $5,000. Transaction (*c*) is a debit to Delivery Truck for $8,000 and a credit to Cash for $8,000. Notice that both equalities are maintained as each transaction is recorded. If debits did not equal credits, an error was made.

[4] The words **debit** and **credit** are used as both verbs and nouns.

```
Account name (debit) . . . . . . . . . . . . . . . . . . . . . . . . . . . . . . . . xxx
    Account name (credit) . . . . . . . . . . . . . . . . . . . . . . . . . . . . .        xxx
```

After the journal entries have been recorded, the accountant posts (transfers) the dollar amounts to each account that was affected by the transaction. As a group, the accounts are called a ledger. In a manual accounting system, the ledger is often a notebook with a separate page for each account. In a computerized system, each account is stored on a disk.

Chart of Accounts

Each company must establish a chart of accounts to facilitate recording transactions. A chart of accounts is the listing of all the account names contained in the ledger (e.g., Cash, Land, Sales Revenue, Wages Payable, etc.).

Every company will have a different chart of accounts, depending on the nature of their business activities. For example, a small lawn-care service may have a revenue account called Mowing Revenue, but it is unlikely that General Motors would have need for such an account.

Because each company has a different chart of accounts, you should not try to memorize a typical chart of accounts. When you prepare journal entries for homework problems, either you will be given the account names or you should select appropriate descriptive names. Once a name is selected for an account, the exact name must be used in all journal entries that affect the account.

Basic categories of accounts are discussed in Chapter 3.

Nature of Business Transactions

Accounting focuses on certain events that have an economic impact on the entity. Those events are recorded as a part of the accounting process and are called **transactions.** A broad definition of transactions includes (1) exchanges of assets and liabilities between the business and one or more other parties; and (2) certain events that are not between the business and other parties but have a direct and measurable effect on the accounting entity. Examples of the first category of transactions include the purchase of a machine, the sale of merchandise, the borrowing of cash, and the investment in the business by the owners. Examples of the second category of transactions include (1) **economic events,** such as a drop in the replacement cost of an item held in inventory, and (2) **time adjustments,** such as depreciation of an operational asset and the "using up" of prepaid insurance. Throughout this textbook, the word **transaction** will be used in the broad sense to include both types of events.

Most transactions create some type of **business (or source) document.** In the case of a sale on credit, a charge ticket is prepared; and in the case of a purchase of goods for resale, an invoice is received. In other transactions, such as a cash sale, the only document may be the cash register tape. It is important to capture the data on each transaction as it occurs. Once this is done, the accounting system records, analyzes, and summarizes the economic impact of each transaction on the entity.

Most transactions with external parties involve an exchange where the business entity both gives up something and receives something in return. In the case of a sale of merchandise for cash, the entity gives up the goods sold and receives cash in return. In the case of a credit sale of merchandise, the resource received at the time of sale is an account receivable (an asset). When the account receivable is collected, another transaction occurs. In this case, the resource given up is the account receivable, and the resource received is cash. In the purchase of an asset, the entity acquires the noncash asset and gives up cash, or in the case of a credit purchase, the entity incurs a liability. Another transaction occurs later when the debt is paid. At that time, the entity gives up cash and receives satisfaction of the debt.

Transaction Analysis

Transaction analysis is the process of studying a transaction to determine its dual effect on the entity in terms of the accounting model. Transaction analysis starts when a business document is available that indicates a completed transaction. Based on transaction analysis, the effects of the transaction are recorded in the accounting system.

Accounting principles require the use of **accrual basis accounting.** This means that assets, liabilities, owners' equity, revenues, and expenses should be recognized (i.e., recorded) when the transaction that caused them was completed. The related cash collected or paid at a later date is recorded as a separate transaction. For example, a credit sale made on the last day of year 1 must be recorded in year 1, and the cash collection must be recorded in year 2. In contrast, **cash basis accounting** (which is not appropriate) would record the sale only in year 2 when the cash is collected. Accrual accounting requires that revenues and expenses be measured and reported in the accounting period in which the transactions occur rather than when the related cash is received or paid.

Recall that for each transaction recorded, **two separate balances** must be maintained: (1) Assets = Liabilities + Owners' Equity, and (2) Debits = Credits.

Transaction Analysis and Recording

Bass Cleaners, Inc., will be used again to demonstrate transaction analysis and the basic recording process. We analyze each transaction (given in Exhibit 2–1) and trace the manner in which the dual effect is recorded in the accounting model by using T-accounts (rather than using the simple plus and minus signs shown in Exhibit 2–1). The transactions (repeated for convenience) are identified with letters for ready reference.

For each transaction, Exhibit 2–3 gives its (*a*) nature, (*b*) transaction analysis, (*c*) journal entry, and (*d*) T-account effect. The **journal entry** is an accounting

Exhibit 2–3   Transaction analysis, journal entries, and T-accounts illustrated, Bass Cleaners, Inc.

BASS CLEANERS, INC.

a. **Received $20,000 cash invested by the four owners and in turn issued 800 shares of capital stock (par value $25 per share).**

Transaction analysis—This transaction increased the company's cash by $20,000, which is recorded in the **Cash** account as a debit (increase); liabilities were unaffected; and owners' equity was increased by $20,000, which is recorded in the **Capital Stock** account as a credit (increase). The journal entry (recording) in the accounting system may be summarized conveniently in what often is called a **journal entry**. This format lists the **debit** first—account name and amount—then lists the credit—account name and amount (which is indented for clarity).

Journal Entry

		Debit	Credit
(*a*) Cash (asset)		20,000	
Capital stock (owners' equity)			20,000

The two T-accounts would appear as follows:

Cash (asset)			Capital Stock (owners' equity)		
Debit	Credit		Debit	Credit	
(*a*) 20,000				(*a*) 20,000	

Dual check for accuracy—The entry meets both tests: Assets (+$20,000) = Liabilities (-0-) + Owners' Equity (+$20,000), and Debits ($20,000) = Credits ($20,000).

b. **Borrowed $5,000 cash from the bank on a 12% interest-bearing note payable.**

Transaction analysis—This transaction increased cash by $5,000, which is recorded in the **Cash** account as a debit (increase); liabilites were increased by $5,000, which is recorded in the **Note Payable** account as a credit (increase); and owners' equity was not changed. The journal entry may be summarized as follows:

(*b*) Cash (asset)		5,000	
Note payable (liability)			5,000

The accounts affected would appear as follows (new items are boxed):

Cash (asset)			Note Payable (liability)		
Debit	Credit		Debit	Credit	
(*a*) 20,000				(*b*) 5,000	
(*b*) 5,000					

Dual check for accuracy—The entry meets both tests: Assets (+$5,000) = Liabilities (+$5,000) + Owners' Equity (-0-), and Debits ($5,000) = Credits ($5,000).

Exhibit 2–3 *(continued)*

c. **Purchased a delivery truck for cash at a cost of $8,000.**

Transaction analysis—This transaction increased the asset, **Delivery Truck,** by $8,000, which is recorded in that asset account as a debit (increase); and the cash was decreased by $8,000, which is recorded in the asset account **Cash** as a credit (decrease). Liabilities and owners' equity were not affected. The journal entry may be summarized as follows:

(*c*) Delivery truck (asset)   8,000
      Cash (asset)   8,000

The two accounts affected would appear as follows:

	Delivery Truck (asset)				**Cash (asset)**	
	Debit	Credit			Debit	Credit
(*c*)	8,000		(*a*)	20,000	(*c*)	8,000
			(*b*)	5,000		

Dual check for accuracy—The entry meets both tests: Assets (delivery truck, +$8,000, and cash, −$8,000) = Liabilities (–0–) + Owners' Equity (–0–), and Debits ($8,000) = Credits ($8,000).

d. **Cleaning revenue earned and collected in cash, $40,000.**

Transaction analysis—This transaction increased cash by $40,000, which is recorded in the asset account **Cash** as a debit (increase); liabilities were not affected; and owners' equity was increased by $40,000 as a result of earning revenue. Owners' equity is credited (increased) for $40,000. A separate owners' equity account, **Cleaning Revenue,** is used to keep track of this particular revenue. The journal entry may be summarized as follows:

(*d*) Cash (asset)   40,000
      Cleaning revenue (owners' equity)   40,000

The two accounts affected would appear as follows:

	Cash (asset)			**Cleaning Revenue (owners' equity)**	
	Debit	Credit		Debit	Credit
(*a*)	20,000	(*c*) 8,000			(*d*) 40,000
(*b*)	5,000				
(*d*)	40,000				

Dual check for accuracy—The entry meets both tests: Assets (+$40,000) = Liabilities (–0–) + Owners' Equity (+$40,000), and Debits ($40,000) = Credits ($40,000).

Exhibit 2–3 *(continued)*

e. **Cleaning revenue earned, but the cash was not yet collected, $4,000.**

Transaction analysis—This transaction increased the company's asset, **Accounts Receivable,** by $4,000, which is recorded as a debit (increase) to that account; liabilities were not affected; and owners' equity was increased by $4,000. Owners' equity is credited (increased) by $4,000 using a separate account, **Cleaning Revenue,** which is used to keep track of this particular revenue. The journal entry may be summarized as follows:

    (e) Accounts receivable (asset)   4,000
           Cleaning revenue (owners' equity)   4,000

The effect on the two accounts would appear as follows:

Accounts Receivable (asset)			Cleaning Revenue (owners' equity)		
Debit		Credit	Debit		Credit
(e)	4,000			(d)	40,000
				(e)	4,000

Dual check for accuracy—The entry meets both tests: Assets (+$4,000) = Liabilities (–0–) + Owners' Equity (+$4,000), and Debits ($4,000) = Credits ($4,000).

f. **Expenses incurred and paid in cash, $25,800.**

Transaction analysis—This transaction decreased cash by $25,800, which is recorded in the **Cash** account as a credit (decrease); liabilities were not affected; and owners' equity was decreased by $25,800 as a result of paying expenses. Owners' equity is decreased by debiting a separate account **Operating Expenses,** which is used to keep track of this particular type of expense. The journal entry may be summarized as follows:

    (f) Operating expenses (owners' equity) 25,800
         Cash (asset)   25,800

The effect on the two accounts would appear as follows:

Operating Expenses (owners' equity)			Cash (asset)			
Debit		Credit	Debit			Credit
(f)	25,800		(a)	20,000	(c)	8,000
			(b)	5,000	(f)	25,800
			(d)	40,000		

Dual check for accuracy—The entry meets both tests.

Exhibit 2-3 *(continued)*

g. **Expenses incurred, but the cash not yet paid, $2,000.**

Transaction analysis—This transaction did not affect the company's assets; liabilities were increased by $2,000, which is recorded as a credit (increase) to **Accounts Payable;** and owners' equity was decreased $2,000 by debiting a separate account, **Operating Expenses,** which is used to keep track of this particular type of expense. The journal entry summarized is:

(*g*) Operating expenses (owners' equity)   2,000
          Accounts payable (liability)   2,000

The two accounts affected would appear as follows:

Operating Expenses (owners' equity)		**Accounts Payable (liability)**	
Debit	Credit	Debit	Credit
(*f*) 25,800		(*g*)	2,000
(*g*) 2,000			

Dual check for accuracy—The entry meets both tests.

h. **Paid cash interest incurred on note payable in (*b*) ($5,000 × 12% = $600).**

Transaction analysis—This transaction decreased cash by $600, which is recorded as a credit (decrease) in the **Cash** account; the principal amount of the related liability ($5,000) was not changed; however, owners' equity was decreased by the amount of the interest ($600) because the payment of interest (but not the principal of the note) represents an expense. Owners' equity is decreased by debiting a separate account, **Interest Expense,** which is used to keep track of this particular type of expense. The journal entry summarized is:

(*h*) Interest expense (owners' equity)   600
          Cash (asset)   600

The two accounts affected would appear as follows:

Interest Expense (owners' equity)		**Cash (asset)**			
Debit	Credit	Debit		Credit	
(*h*) 600		(*a*)	20,000	(*c*)	8,000
		(*b*)	5,000	(*f*)	25,800
		(*d*)	40,000	(*h*)	600

Dual check for accuracy—The entry meets both tests.

Exhibit 2–3 *(continued)*

i. **Depreciation expense on the truck for one year ($8,000 ÷ 5 years = $1,600).**

Transaction analysis—This transaction is caused by the **internal** use (wear and tear) of an asset owned for operating purposes (rather than for resale). This use is measured in dollars and recorded as depreciation expense. Owners' equity was decreased by this expense, which is recorded as a debit to a separate account for this type of expense, **Operating Expenses** (alternatively, a separate expense account, called Depreciation Expense, could have been used). Assets (i.e., the delivery truck) were decreased because a part of the cost of the asset was "used up" in operations. Instead of directly crediting (decreasing) the asset account, Delivery Truck, a related **contra account**, **Accumulated Depreciation, Delivery Truck,** is credited so that the total amount of depreciation can be kept separate from the cost of the asset. This procedure will be explained and illustrated in detail in Chapter 9. The journal entry summarized is:

> (*i*) Operating expenses (owners' equity) 1,600
> Accumulated depreciation, delivery truck
> (contra account) 1,600

The two accounts affected would appear as follows:

Operating Expenses (owners' equity)		**Accumulated Depreciation, Delivery Truck (contra account)**	
Debit	Credit	Debit	Credit
(*f*) 25,800			(*i*) 1,600
(*g*) 2,000			
(*i*) 1,600			

Dual check for accuracy—The entry meets both tests: Assets (−$1,600) = Liabilities (−0−) + Owners' Equity (−$1,600), and Debits ($1,600) = Credits ($1,600).

j. **Declared and paid cash dividends to stockholders, $1,800.**

Transaction analysis—This transaction decreased the company's cash by $1,800, which is recorded in the **Cash** account as a credit (decrease); liabilities were unaffected; owners' equity was decreased by $1,800 as a result of the resources (cash) paid out of the business to the stockholders. Owners' equity is debited (decreased) by using a separate account, **Retained Earnings,** which is used to keep track of this kind of decrease in owners' equity (and certain increases explained later). Dividends declared and paid decrease owners' equity but do not represent an expense (which also decreases owners' equity), rather dividends represent a cash distribution of "earnings" to the owners. The journal entry summarized is:

> (*j*) Retained earnings (or dividends paid) 1,800
> Cash (asset) 1,800

Exhibit 2–3 *(continued)*

The two accounts would appear as follows:

Retained Earnings (owners' equity)				Cash (asset)			
Debit		Credit		Debit		Credit	
(j)	1,800			(a)	20,000	(c)	8,000
				(b)	5,000	(f)	25,800
				(d)	40,000	(h)	600
						(j)	1,800

Dual check for accuracy—The entry meets both tests.

k. Collected $1,000 cash on accounts receivable in (e).

Transaction analysis—This transaction increased the asset cash by $1,000, which is recorded as a debit (increase) in the **Cash** account; another asset, **Accounts Receivable,** was decreased, which is recorded as a credit (decrease) of $1,000. Liabilities and owners' equity were not affected because there was a change in two assets with no change in total assets. The journal entry summarized is:

(k) Cash (asset) 1,000
      Accounts receivable (asset) 1,000

The two accounts would appear as follows:

Cash (asset)				Accounts Receivable (asset)			
Debit		Credit		Debit		Credit	
(a)	20,000	(c)	8,000	(e)	4,000	(k)	1,000
(b)	5,000	(f)	25,800				
(d)	40,000	(h)	600				
(k)	1,000	(j)	1,800				

Dual check for accuracy—The entry meets both tests.

l. Paid $500 cash on accounts payable in (g).

Transaction analysis—This transaction decreased cash by $500, which is recorded as a credit (decrease) in the **Cash** account; the $500 decrease in liabilities is recorded as a debit (decrease) to the **Accounts Payable** account. Owners' equity was not affected because there was no revenue or expense involved in this transaction. The journal entry summarized is:

(l) Accounts payable (liability) 500
      Cash (asset) 500

Exhibit 2–3 *(concluded)*

The two accounts would appear as follows:

	Accounts Payable (liability)			Cash (asset)	
	Debit	Credit		Debit	Credit
(*l*)	500	(*g*) 2,000	(*a*)	20,000 (*c*)	8,000
			(*b*)	5,000 (*f*)	25,800
			(*d*)	40,000 (*h*)	600
			(*k*)	1,000 (*j*)	1,800
				(*l*)	500

Dual check for accuracy—The entry meets both tests.

method of expressing the results of transaction analysis in a Debits = Credits format. Notice that for each transaction: (*a*) the debits are written first, (*b*) the credits are written below all of the debits, and (*c*) the credits are indented (both words and amounts).

You should study Exhibit 2–3 carefully (including the explanations of transaction analysis). Careful study of Exhibit 2–3 is essential to understand (*a*) the accounting model, (*b*) transaction analysis, (*c*) recording the dual effects of each transaction, and (*d*) the dual-balancing system. Notice that the amounts for each additional entry illustrated are shown in boxes to facilitate your study of this exhibit.

In summary, Exhibit 2–3 presented the following features of an accounting system:

1. **Collecting information about each completed transaction** that is necessary for accounting purposes.
2. **Analyzing each transaction** to determine how it affected the accounting model—Assets = Liabilities + Owners' Equity.
3. **Recording the effects of transactions is accomplished in the "journal entry format"** commonly used in accounting as follows:

Account name (debit) xxx
    Account name (credit) xxx

4. **Showing the effects in T-accounts** which provide for increases and decreases in each account as follows:

Assets		=	Liabilities		+	Owners' Equity	
(Debit)	(Credit)		(Debit)	(Credit)		(Debit)	(Credit)
+	−		−	+		−	+

Exhibit 2–4 Income statement and balance sheet illustrated

BASS CLEANERS, INC.
Income Statement
For the Year Ended December 31, 19A

Cleaning revenue ($40,000 + $4,000)		$44,000
Operating expenses ($25,800 + $2,000 + $1,600)	$29,400	
Interest expense	600	30,000
Net income		$14,000

Note: To simplify the illustration, income taxes are disregarded.

BASS CLEANERS, INC.
Balance Sheet
At December 31, 19A

Assets

Cash ($20,000 + $5,000 − $8,000 + $40,000 −		
$25,800 − $600 − $1,800 + $1,000 − $500)		$29,300
Accounts receivable ($4,000 − $1,000)		3,000
Delivery truck	$ 8,000	
Less: Accumulated depreciation	1,600	6,400
Total assets		$38,700

Liabilities

Note payable (12%)	5,000	
Accounts payable ($2,000 − $500)	1,500	
Total liabilities		$ 6,500

Stockholders' Equity

Contributed capital:		
Capital stock (par $25; 800 shares)	20,000	
Retained earnings (beginning retained earnings, $–0–, plus net income,		
$14,000, minus dividends declared and paid, $1,800)	12,200	
Total stockholders' equity		32,200
Total liabilities and stockholders' equity		$38,700

---

5. **Preparing periodic financial statements** from the data accumulated in the accounts (discussed in Chapter 3). The income statement and balance sheet for Bass Cleaners are shown in Exhibit 2–4.

Some Misconceptions

Some people confuse bookkeeping with accounting. In effect, they confuse a part of accounting with the whole. Bookkeeping involves the routine, clerical part of accounting and requires only minimal knowledge of accounting. A bookkeeper may record the repetitive and uncomplicated transactions in most businesses and may maintain the simple records of a small business. In contrast, the accountant is a highly trained professional, competent in the design of information systems, analysis of complex transactions, interpretation of financial data, financial reporting, auditing, taxation, and management consulting.

Another prevalent misconception is that all transactions are subject to precise and objective measurement and that the accounting results reported in the financial statements are exactly what happened that period. In reality, accounting numbers are influenced by estimates, as will be illustrated in subsequent chapters. Some people believe that financial statements report the market value of the entity (including its assets), but they do not. To understand and interpret financial statements, the user must be aware of their limitations as well as their usefulness. One should understand what the financial statements do and do not try to accomplish.

Finally, financial statements are often thought to be inflexible because of their quantitative nature. As you study accounting, you will learn that it requires considerable **professional judgment** on the part of the accountant to capture the economic essense of complex transactions. Accounting is stimulating intellectually; it is not a cut-and-dried subject. It calls on your intelligence, analytical ability, creativity, and judgment. Accounting is a communication process involving an audience (users) with a wide diversity of knowledge, interest, and capabilities; therefore, it will call on your ability as a communicator. The language of accounting uses concisely written phrases and symbols to convey information about the resource flows measured for specific organizations.

To understand financial statements, you must have a certain level of knowledge of the concepts and the measurement procedures used in the accounting process. You should learn what accounting "is really like" and appreciate the reasons for using certain procedures. This level of knowledge cannot be gained by reading a list of the concepts and a list of the misconceptions. Neither can a generalized discussion of the subject matter suffice. A certain amount of involvement, primarily problem solving (similar to the requirement in mathematics courses), is essential in the study of accounting focused on the needs of the user. Therefore, we provide problems aimed at the desirable knowledge level for the user (as well as the preparer) of financial statements.

DEMONSTRATION CASE

On January 1, 19A, an ambitious college student started the ABC Service Company. Completed transactions (summarized) through December 31, 19A, for ABC Service Company (a sole proprietorship) were:

a. Invested $5,000 cash in the business.
b. Purchased service supplies, $600; paid cash. These supplies were placed in a storeroom to be used as needed.
c. Revenues earned, $32,000, collected in cash, except for $2,000 on credit.
d. Operating expenses incurred, $17,000; paid cash except for $1,000 on credit.

e. Used $500 of the service supplies from the storeroom for operating purposes.

f. Owner withdrew $3,000 cash from the business.

g. At year-end purchased a tract of land for a future building site. Paid cash, $5,000.

Requirement 1:

Set up T-accounts for Cash, Accounts Receivable (for services on credit), Service Supplies (for supplies on hand in the storeroom), Land, Accounts Payable (for operating expenses on credit), Owner's Equity, Service Revenues, and Operating Expenses. Next, analyze each transaction, prepare journal entries, and then enter the effects on the accounting model in the appropriate T-accounts. Identify each amount with its letter given above.

Requirement 2:

Use the **amounts in the T-accounts** developed in Requirement 1 to prepare an income statement (Exhibit 1–4) and a balance sheet (Exhibit 1–5) for ABC Service Company. The solutions to these two requirements are shown in Exhibit 2–5.

Preparation of the 19A **income statement** involved selection of the **account balances** for all revenues and expenses. The **income statement model** is applied: Revenues − Expenses = Net Income.

The 19A **balance sheet** required use of the **account balances** for **all** assets and liabilities. The **balance sheet model** is applied: Assets = Liabilities + Owners' Equity. Notice that owner's equity includes the net income amount ($14,500) reported on the income statement because it increased owner's equity.

Exhibit 2–5 Transaction analysis, journal entries, T-accounts, and financial statements— a demonstration case

---

Requirement 1—transaction analysis and journal entries:

a. Increase Cash, $5,000; increase Owner's Equity account, $5,000.

Journal entry:

Cash	5,000	
Owner's equity		5,000

b. Increase asset, Service Supplies, $600; decrease Cash, $600 (supplies are not an expense until used).

Journal entry:

Service supplies	600	
Cash		600

c. Increase assets, Cash, $30,000, and Accounts Receivable, $2,000; increase Service Revenue (an owner's equity account), $32,000.

Journal entry:

Cash	30,000	
Accounts receivable	2,000	
Service revenue		32,000

Exhibit 2–5 *(continued)*

Requirement 1 (continued):

d. Decrease asset, Cash, $16,000; increase liability, Accounts Payable, $1,000; increase Operating Expenses, $17,000 (which decreases owner's equity).

Journal entry:

Operating expenses	17,000	
Cash		16,000
Accounts payable		1,000

e. Decrease asset, Service Supplies, $500; increase Operating Expenses, $500 (which decreases owner's equity).

Journal entry:

Operating expenses	500	
Service supplies		500

f. Decrease asset, Cash, $3,000; decrease Owner's Equity account, $3,000.

Journal entry:

Owner's equity	3,000	
Cash		3,000

g. Increase asset, Land, $5,000; decrease asset, Cash, $5,000.

Journal entry:

Land	5,000	
Cash		5,000

T-accounts:

Cash

(a)	5,000	*(b)*	600
(c)	30,000	*(d)*	16,000
		(f)	3,000
		(g)	5,000

Accounts Receivable

(c)	2,000

Service Supplies

(b)	600	*(e)*	500

Land

(g)	5,000

Accounts Payable

		(d)	1,000

Owner's Equity

(f)	3,000	*(a)*	5,000

Service Revenue

		(c)	32,000

Operating Expenses

(d)	17,000	
(e)	500	

Exhibit 2–5 *(concluded)*

Requirement 2—periodic financial statements:

ABC SERVICE COMPANY
Income Statement
For the Year Ended December 31, 19A

Revenues:
    Service revenue $32,000
Expenses:
    Operating expenses 17,500
Net income $14,500

ABC SERVICE COMPANY
Balance Sheet
At December 31, 19A

Assets		Liabilities	
Cash	$10,400	Accounts payable	$ 1,000
Accounts receivable	2,000	Total liabilities	1,000
Service supplies	100		
Land	5,000		
		Owner's Equity	
		Owner's equity	$ 2,000
		Net income (Req. 2)	14,500
		Total owner's equity	16,500
		Total liabilities and owner's	
Total assets	$17,500	equity	$17,500

SUMMARY OF CHAPTER

This chapter discussed the **accounting model** and illustrated its application in the accounting system for a business. For accounting purposes, transactions were defined as *(a)* exchanges of assets and liabilities between the business and other individuals and organizations; and *(b)* certain events that exert a direct effect on the entity (such as a fire loss) and events caused by the passage of time (such as depreciation of a building).

Application of the accounting model—Assets = Liabilities + Owners' Equity—was illustrated for a small business. The application involved: *(a)* transaction analysis, *(b)* journal entries, and *(c)* the accounts (T-account format).

An extended illustration, Exhibit 2–3 was presented. Each transaction causes at least two different accounts to be affected in terms of the accounting model— Assets = Liabilities + Owners' Equity. The model often is referred to as a **double-entry** system because each transaction has a dual effect.

The accounting model and the mechanics of the debit-credit concept in T-account format can be summarized as follows, where + means increase and − means decrease:

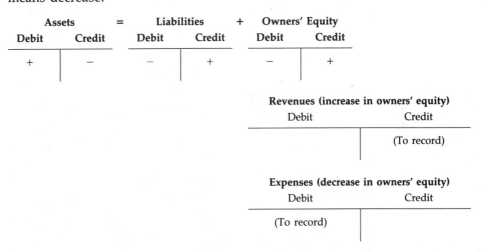

Assets		=	Liabilities		+	Owners' Equity	
Debit	**Credit**		**Debit**	**Credit**		**Debit**	**Credit**
+	−		−	+		−	+

Revenues (increase in owners' equity)

Debit	Credit
	(To record)

Expenses (decrease in owners' equity)

Debit	Credit
(To record)	

An increase in **revenues** (a credit) represents an **increase** in owners' equity. When a revenue is earned, the assets of the business are increased (or liabilities may be decreased); and because of the dual effect, owners' equity is increased by the same amount. In contrast, when an **expense** is incurred, the assets are decreased (or liabilities may be increased); and because of the dual effect, owners' equity is decreased by the same amount.

CHAPTER SUPPLEMENT 2A

Statement of Cash Flows (SCF)

The balance sheet and the income statement are both prepared directly from the balances contained in the various accounts, as illustrated in the demonstration case at the end of this chapter. Preparation of the statement of cash flows (SCF) requires an analysis of changes in the accounts. In this supplement, we will continue the demonstration case and will prepare the statement of cash flows.

Basically, the SCF summarizes increases and decreases in the Cash account and classifies the cash flows as being associated with operating, investing, or financing activities. In simple cases, it is possible to prepare the SCF by analyzing the Cash account. The Cash account for ABC Service Company (from the demonstration case in Exhibit 2–5) is summarized below. We have added some explanatory captions to identify the transaction that caused the cash inflow or outflow.

Cash (from Exhibit 2–5)

(a)	Owners' contribution	5,000	(b)	Bought supplies	600
(c)	Collected from customers	30,000	(d)	Paid operating expenses	16,000
			(f)	Paid to owner	3,000
			(g)	Paid for land	5,000

The SCF for ABC Service Company is shown in Exhibit 2–6.

Notice in Exhibit 2–6 that the SCF reports three types of cash flows: operating, investing, and financing activities. Operating activities are associated with earn-

Exhibit 2–6 Simplified statement of cash flows (SCF)

ABC SERVICE COMPANY
Statement of Cash Flows
For the Year Ended December 31, 19A

Cash flows from operating activities:		
Cash collected from customers	$30,000	
Cash paid for supplies and expenses	(16,000)	
Net cash inflow from operating activities		$13,400
Cash flows from investing activities:		
Bought land		(5,000)
Cash flows from financing activities:		
Cash contributed by owner	5,000	
Cash paid to owner	(3,000)	
Net cash inflow from financing activities		2,000
Net increase in cash during the year		$10,400

ing income; investing activities involve the acquisition of productive assets (other than inventory); and financing activities involve financing the company itself (e.g., borrowing money from creditors). The bottom line on the SCF is the net increase or decrease in cash during the year. ABC Service Company started with no cash at the beginning of 19A and had $10,400 at the end of the year (an increase of $10,400). The bottom line of the SCF also reports an increase of $10,400.

Preparation of the SCF from the Cash account of ABC Service Company demonstrates that it is possible to use just the Cash account to prepare the statement. Also, this simple example provides some insight into the information contained in the SCF. Unfortunately, for most companies this simple approach is impossible to use because thousands of transactions are recorded in the Cash account. In Chapter 15, we will discuss procedures that are used to prepare the SCF for more complex cases.

IMPORTANT TERMS DEFINED IN THIS CHAPTER

Account A standardized format used to accumulate data about each financial statement item. It provides for recording increases and decreases in these items caused by transactions. *p. 54*

Accrual Basis Accounting All financial statement items—assets, liabilities, revenues, expenses, etc.—are recognized (recorded) when the related transaction occurs. In contrast, cash basis accounting is not appropriate because it recognizes **only** cash transactions. *p. 58*

Business (Source) Document A document that evidences (supports) a business transaction. *p. 57*

Cash Basis Accounting See accrual basis accounting. *p. 58*

Debits and Credits Debit is the name for the left side of a T-account. Debits represent increases in assets and decreases in liabilities and owners' equity. Credit is the name for the right side of a T-account. Credits represent decreases in assets and increases in liabilities and owners' equity. *p. 55*

Journal Entry An accounting method of expressing the results of transaction analysis in a Debits = Credits format. *p. 56*

Periodic Financial Statements The financial statements that must be prepared each reporting period for external parties—balance sheet, income statement, and statement of cash flows. *p. 66*

Transaction An exchange between a business and one or more external parties and certain other events, such as a fire loss. *p. 57*

Transaction Analysis The process of studying a completed transaction to determine its economic effect on a business in terms of the accounting model: Assets = Liabilities + Owners' Equity. *p. 58*

QUESTIONS

1. Give the accounting model and define each category.

2. Assume your personal financial condition is assets, $30,000; and debts, $20,000. You pay a $10,000 debt plus 12% interest for the year. Show how your personal financial condition will change in terms of the accounting model.

3. Define a business transaction in the broad sense and give an example of the two different kinds of transactions.

4. Explain why owners' equity is increased by revenues and decreased by expenses.

5. Demonstrate the dual effect on the accounting model of (*a*) a cash sale of services for $1,000 and (*b*) a cash payment of $300 for office rent for the business.

6. Explain what the separate-entity assumption means in accounting.

7. What are the owners of a business organized as a corporation called? What is the basis for this name?

8. Explain why a business document is important in accounting for a business entity.

9. At December 31, 19A (end of year 1), the accounting model for YOUR Company showed the following: owners' equity, $70,000; and liabilities, $20,000.
   a. Show how YOUR Company stands in terms of the accounting model.
   b. Show the summarized balance sheet.

10. For accounting purposes, what is an account? Explain why accounts are used in an accounting system.

11. Explain what debit and credit mean.

12. Explain why revenues are recorded as credits and expenses as debits.

13. What is meant by the "two equalities" in accounting?

14. Complete the following matrix by entering either debit or credit in each cell:

Items	Increases	Decreases
Assets		
Liabilities		
Owners' equity		
Revenues		
Expenses		

15. Complete the following matrix by entering either increases or decreases in each cell:

Items	Debit	Credit
Assets		
Liabilities		
Owners' equity		
Revenues		
Expenses		

16. Briefly explain what is meant by transaction analysis.
17. Define accrual accounting. Contrast it with cash basis accounting.
18. What is a T-account? What is its purpose?
19. What is a journal entry?
20. Assume you and a friend started a new business called Y and M Corporation. Each of you invested $10,000. Give the effect of this transaction on the company in terms of:
    a. The accounting model.
    b. A journal entry.
    c. How it is shown in the T-accounts.
21. Complete the following tabulation:

Transactions	Assets	Liabilities	Owners' Equity
a. Investment of cash by organizers, $15,000			
b. Borrowed cash, $4,000			
c. Performed legal services for cash, $8,000			
d. Paid expenses, $6,000 cash			
e. Purchased equipment, $9,000 cash			
Ending balances			

22. XR Company paid a $10,000, 12%, one-year note on the due date. Show how this transaction would affect the accounting model.

EXERCISES

E2–1   (Match Definitions with Terms)

Match each definition with its related term by entering the appropriate letter in the space provided.

Terms	Definitions
_____ (1) Separate-entity assumption	A. = Liabilities + Owners' Equity.
	B. Reports assets, liabilities, and owners' equity.
_____ (2) Business document	C. Accounts for a business separate from its owners.
_____ (3) Credits	
_____ (4) Assets	D. Increase assets; decrease liabilities and owners' equity.
_____ (5) Transaction	
_____ (6) Income statement	E. An exchange between an entity and other parties.
_____ (7) T-account	
_____ (8) Balance sheet	F. Evidence of a completed transaction.
_____ (9) Debits	G. Decrease assets; increase liabilities and owners' equity.
	H. Reports revenues, expenses, and net income.
	I. A standardized format used to accumulate data about each item reported on financial statements.

E2–2   (Accounting Model—Personal)

You have just finished college and have been working for Dynex Business for one month. At the start of the month, your financial situation was shown in the following schedule. You are to complete the schedule by "recording" your transactions summarized in the first column and indicating your ending financial position on the last line.

Transactions	Assets	Liabilities	Owners' Equity
a. Beginning (personal items, including your rather used auto).	$4,000	$800	$3,200
b. Borrowed $1,000 to get through the first month.			
c. Paid rent on apartment, $500.			
d. Paid utility deposits, $200.			
e. Personal expenses: food, cleaning, etc., $700.			
f. Auto payment, $400 (including $300 interest).			
g. Trip to visit a special person, $500.			
h. Received a gift from your family, $150 cash.			
i. You gave your date a special present, $50.			
j. You received your first paycheck (net of deductions), $1,800.			
k. Your ending financial position.			

E2–3   (Use of T-accounts; Summarize the Results)

Vista Company has been operating one year (19A). At the start of 19B, its T-accounts were:

Assets:

Cash	Accounts Receivable	Land
4,000	1,000	3,000

Liabilities:

Accounts Payable	Note Payable	Income Taxes Payable
500	400	100

Owners' Equity:

Owners' Equity	Revenues	Expenses
7,000		

Required:

1. Enter the following 19B transactions in the T-accounts:
   a. Paid the income tax.
   b. Collected the accounts receivable.
   c. Paid the accounts payable.
   d. Revenue earned, $30,000; including 15% on credit.*
   e. Expenses incurred, $18,000; including $2,000 on credit.*

   * Hint: each of these transactions will affect three accounts.

2. Respond to the following by using data from the T-accounts:

   a. On January 1, 19B, amounts for the following were:
      Assets, $_____ = Liabilities, $_____ + Owners' Equity, $_____.
   b. Net income for 19B was $_____.
   c. On December 31, 19B, amounts for the following were:
      Assets, $_____ = Liabilities, $_____ + Owners' Equity, $_____.

3. Complete the following schedule at December 31, 19B:

Accounts	Assets	Liabilities	Owners' Equity
Cash Accounts receivable Land Accounts payable Note payable Income taxes payable Owners' equity	$	$	$
Total assets	$		
Total liabilities		$	
Total owners' equity			$

E2–4   (Match Definitions with Terms)

Match each definition with its related term by entering the appropriate letter in the space provided.

<table>
<tr><td colspan="2" align="center">Terms</td><td align="center">Definitions</td></tr>
<tr><td>_____</td><td>(1) Journal entry</td><td>A. Accounting model.</td></tr>
<tr><td>_____</td><td>(2) Note payable</td><td>B. The three required periodic financial state-</td></tr>
<tr><td>_____</td><td>(3) Assets = Liabilities</td><td>ments.</td></tr>
<tr><td></td><td>   + Owners' Equity</td><td>C. The two equalities in accounting that aid in</td></tr>
<tr><td>_____</td><td>(4) Expenses</td><td>providing accuracy.</td></tr>
<tr><td>_____</td><td>(5) Accounts payable</td><td>D. An accounting method of expressing the re-</td></tr>
<tr><td>_____</td><td>(6) A = L + OE, and</td><td>sults of transaction analysis.</td></tr>
<tr><td></td><td>   Debits = Credits</td><td>E. The account that is credited when money is</td></tr>
<tr><td>_____</td><td>(7) Balance sheet, in-</td><td>borrowed from a bank.</td></tr>
<tr><td></td><td>   come statement,</td><td>F. The account that is credited when a sale is</td></tr>
<tr><td></td><td>   statement of cash</td><td>made.</td></tr>
<tr><td></td><td>   flows</td><td>G. The account that is debited when an expense</td></tr>
<tr><td>_____</td><td>(8) Revenues</td><td>is incurred.</td></tr>
<tr><td>_____</td><td>(9) Accounts receivable</td><td>H. The account that is debited when a credit</td></tr>
<tr><td>_____</td><td>(10) Double-entry system</td><td>sale is made.</td></tr>
<tr><td></td><td></td><td>I. The account that is credited when an ex-</td></tr>
<tr><td></td><td></td><td>pense is incurred on credit.</td></tr>
<tr><td></td><td></td><td>J. Application of the accounting model—Assets</td></tr>
<tr><td></td><td></td><td>= Liabilities + Owners' Equity.</td></tr>
</table>

E2–5   (Preparing Simple Journal Entries)

Express the results of your transaction analysis for each of the following six transactions. Use only the journal entry format.

a. Example: Three investors organized XT Corporation, and each one invested $20,000 cash.

Cash ($20,000 × 3)	60,000	
Stockholders' equity		60,000

b. Borrowed $5,000 cash and signed a 10% note.

c. Earned revenues, $40,000, of which $4,000 was on credit.

d. Incurred expenses, $25,000, of which $3,000 was on credit.

e. Paid a debt, accounts payable, $1,000.

f. Collected an amount due, accounts receivable, $2,000.

g. Paid cash interest on note payable, $500.

E2–6   (Balance Sheet, Income Statement, and Cash Flow Relationships)

Gorden Corporation has been operating for one year, 19A. At the end of 19A, the financial statements have been prepared. Below are a series of independent cases based on the 19A financial statements. For each independent case and the financial relationship it relates to, you are to supply the missing item and its amount.

Cases	Data	Missing Item	Missing Amount
Example	Assets, $70,000; owners' equity, $20,000	Liabilities	$50,000
A	Revenues, $100,000; expenses, $60,000		
B	Liabilities, $30,000; owners' equity, $52,000		
C	Cash inflows, $80,000; increase in cash, $30,000		
D	Liabilities, $40,000; assets, $100,000		
E	Net income, $35,000; expenses, $60,000		
F	Net income, $20,000; revenues, $95,000		
G	Expenses, $80,000; revenues, $80,000		
H	Revenues, $80,000; expenses, $95,000		
I	Increase in cash, $20,000; cash outflows, $80,000		
J	Cash outflows, $60,000; cash inflows, $45,000		

E2–7 **(Transaction Analysis; Nonquantitative)**

For each transaction given below indicate the effect on assets, liabilities, and owners' equity by entering a plus for increase and a minus for decrease.

Transactions	Effect on Assets	Effect on Liabilities	Effect on Owners' Equity
a. Issued stock to organizers for cash (example).	+		+
b. Borrowed cash from local bank.			
c. Purchased equipment on credit.			
d. Earned revenue, collected cash.			
e. Incurred expenses, on credit.			
f. Earned revenue, on credit.			
g. Paid cash for (e).			
h. Incurred expenses, paid cash.			
i. Earned revenue, collected three-fourths cash, balance on credit.			
j. Theft of $100 cash.			
k. Declared and paid cash dividends.			
l. Collected cash for (f).			
m. Depreciated equipment for the period.			
n. Incurred expenses, paid four-fifths cash, balance on credit.			
o. Paid income tax expense for the period.			

E2–8   **(Understanding Transactions; Effects on Balance Sheet and Income Statement)**
During its first week of operations, January 1–7, Tiny Retail Company completed eight transactions, the dollar effects of which are indicated in the following schedule:

| Accounts | Dollar Effect of Each of the Eight Transactions | | | | | | | | Ending Balance |
	1	2	3	4	5	6	7	8	
Cash	$10,000	$15,000	$(4,000)	$80,000	$(9,000)	$(50,000)	$(11,000)	$7,000	$38,000
Accounts receivable				10,000				(7,000)	3,000
Store fixtures					9,000				9,000
Land		12,000							12,000
Accounts payable						20,000	(11,000)		9,000
Note payable (10%)		15,000	8,000						23,000
Capital stock	10,000								10,000
Revenues				90,000					90,000
Expenses						70,000			70,000

Required:

1. Write a brief explanation of each transaction. Explain any assumptions that you make.

2. Complete the following tabulation after the eight transactions:

Balance sheet:
Total assets . . . . $ _____
Total liabilities . . . . $ _____
Total owners' equity . . . . $ _____

Income statement:
Total revenues . . . . $ _____
Total expenses . . . . $ _____
Net income . . . . $ _____

E2-9 **(Applying the Accounting Model)**

Jack Service Company, Inc., was organized by five investors. The following transactions were completed:

a. The investors paid in $50,000 cash to start the business. Each one was issued 1,000 shares of capital stock, par value $10 per share.

b. Equipment for use in the business was purchased at a cost of $10,000, one quarter was paid in cash, and the balance is due in six months.

c. Service fees were earned amounting to $54,000, of which $10,000 was on credit.

d. Operating expenses incurred amounted to $33,000, of which $3,000 was on credit.

e. Cash was collected for $4,000 of the service fees performed on credit in (c) above.

f. Paid cash, $1,000, on the operating expenses that were on credit in (d) above.

g. Investor A borrowed $15,000 from a local bank and signed a one-year, 12% note for that amount.

Required:

Set up a schedule similar to the following and enter thereon each of the above transactions that should be recorded by Jack. Transaction (a) is used as an example.

Transactions	Assets	= Liabilities + Owners' Equity
a. Investment of cash in the business	Cash + $50,000	Capital stock + $50,000

After the last transaction (on the last line of the schedule), total each dollar column to prove the correctness of your situation.

E2-10 **(Application of Debits and Credits; Nonquantitative)**

The 12 transactions given below were completed by Duster Service Company during the year 19X:

1. The organizers paid in cash and in turn received 10,000 shares of capital stock.

2. Duster borrowed cash from the local bank.

3. Duster purchased a delivery truck, paid three-fourths cash, and the balance is due in six months.

4. Revenues earned, collected cash in full.

5. Expenses incurred, paid cash in full.

6. Revenues earned, on credit (cash will be collected later).

7. Expenses incurred, on credit (cash will be paid later).

8. Declared and paid a cash dividend to stockholders.

9. Collected half of the amount on credit in 6.

10. Paid all of the credit amount in 7.

11. A spare tire was stolen from the delivery truck (not insured).

12. At the end of 19X, the delivery truck is depreciated by a dollar amount (an expense).

Required:

For each transaction given above enter in the tabulation given below, a D for debit and a C for credit to reflect the increases and decreases of the assets, liabilities, and owners' equity (separate accounts are given for owners' equity). Transaction 1 is used as an example.

	Twelve Transactions											
Accounting Model	1	2	3	4	5	6	7	8	9	10	11	12
a. Assets	D											
b. Liabilities												
Owners' equity: *c.* Investments by owners	C											
d. Revenues												
e. Withdrawals (dividends)												
f. Expenses												

(Note: In some cases there may be both a D and C in the same box.)

E2–11   (Using T-accounts; Summarizing the Results)

American Company, Inc., was organized and issued 10,000 shares of its capital stock for $30,000 cash. The following transactions occurred during the current accounting period:

a. Received the cash from the organizers, $30,000.

b. Service fees earned amounted to $35,000, of which $25,000 was collected in cash.

c. Operating expenses incurred amounted to $23,000, of which $17,000 was paid in cash.

d. Bought two machines for operating purposes at the start of the year at a cost of $9,000 each; paid cash.

e. One of the machines was destroyed by fire one week after purchase; it was uninsured. The event to be considered is the fire. (Hint: Set up a Fire Loss Expense account.)

f. The other machine has an estimated useful life to American of 10 years (and no residual value). The event to be considered is the depreciation of the equipment because it was used for one year in rendering services.

g. Stockholder Able bought a vacant lot (land) for $25,000 cash.

Required:

1. Set up appropriate T-accounts and record in them the dual effects on the accounting model of each of the above transactions that should be recorded by American. Key the amounts to the letters starting with (a). Number the following required accounts consecutively starting with 101 for cash: Cash, Accounts Receivable, Machines, Accumulated Depreciation, Accounts Payable, Service Fees Earned, Operating Expenses, Fire Loss Expense, Depreciation Expense, and Capital Stock.

2. Use the data in the completed T-accounts (Requirement 1) to complete the following:

> Debits = Credits:
> Total debits . . . . $ _____
> Total credits . . . . $ _____
>
> Income statement:
> Total revenues . . . . $ _____
> Total expenses . . . . $ _____
> Net income . . . . $ _____
>
> Balance sheet:
> Total assets . . . . $ _____
> Total liabilities . . . . $ _____
> Total owners' equity . . . . $ _____

PROBLEMS

P2–1 (Transaction Analysis, Recording, and Reporting)

Ivy Company was organized on January 1, 19A, by four friends. Each organizer invested $8,000 in the company, and, in turn, each was issued 8,000 shares of capital stock. To date they are the only stockholders.

During the first quarter (January–March 19A), the company completed the following six transactions:

1. Collected a total of $32,000 from the organizers and, in turn, issued the shares of capital stock.
2. Purchased equipment for use in the business; paid $8,000 cash in full.
3. Purchased land for use in the business; paid $4,000 cash and gave a $6,000, one-year, 10% interest-bearing note for the balance; total cost, $10,000.
4. Earned service revenues of $40,000, of which $36,000 was collected in cash; the balance was on credit. (Hint: Two asset accounts are increased.)
5. Incurred $30,000 operating expenses, of which $25,000 was paid in cash; the balance was on credit. (Hint: Three different accounts will be affected.)
6. In addition, one stockholder reported to the company that 500 shares of his Ivy stock had been sold and transferred to another stockholder for a cash consideration of $8,000.

Required:

a. Was Ivy Company organized as a sole proprietorship, a partnership, or a corporation? Explain the basis for your answer.
b. What was the issue price per share of the capital stock?
c. During the first quarter, the records of the company were inadequate. You were asked to prepare the summary of transactions given above. To develop a quick assessment of their economic effects on Ivy Company, you have decided to complete the tabulation that follows and to use plus (+) for increases and minus (−) for decreases for each account. The first transaction is used as an example.

	Six Transactions—Effects						Ending Amounts (total)
Accounts	1	2	3	4	5	6	
Cash	$ + 32,000	$	$	$	$	$	$
Accounts receivable							
Land							
Equipment							
Accounts payable							
Note payable							
Capital stock	+ 32,000						
Service revenue							
Operating expenses							

d. Did you include the transaction between the two stockholders in the above tabulation? Why?

e. Based only on the completed tabulation above, provide the following amounts (show computations):
   (1) Income for the quarter.
   (2) Total assets at the end of the quarter.
   (3) Total liabilities at the end of the quarter.
   (4) Total owners' equity at the end of the quarter.
   (5) Cash balance at the end of the quarter.
   (6) Net amount of cash inflow from operations, that is, from revenues and expenses combined.
   (7) How much interest must be paid on the note at its maturity date?

P2–2   (Identifying Accounts for Assets, Liabilities, and Owners' Equity; Also, Usual Balance—Debit versus Credit)
Listed below are the accounts of the Rapid Rental Corporation:

a. Cash.
b. Accounts receivable.
c. Capital stock (issued to stockholders).
d. Bonds payable.
e. Rent revenue.
f. Insurance premium paid in advance of use.
g. Interest revenue.
h. Investments, long term.
i. Interest expense.
j. Machinery and equipment.
k. Patents.
l. Income tax expense.
m. Property taxes payable.
n. Loss on sale of machinery.
o. Land, plant site (in use).
p. Accounts payable.
q. Supplies inventory (held for use as needed).
r. Note payable, short term.
s. Retained earnings.
t. Investments, short term.
u. Certificates of deposit (CDs) held.
v. Operating expenses.
w. Income taxes payable.
x. Gain on sale of equipment.
y. Land held for future plant site.
z. Revenue from investments.
aa. Wages payable.
bb. Accumulated depreciation.
cc. Merchandise inventory (held for resale).

Complete a tabulation similar to the following (enter two check marks for each account listed above). Account *a* is used as an example.

| | | | Owner's equity (including revenues and expenses) | Usual balance | |
Account	Asset	Liability		Debit	Credit
a.	✓			✓	

Etc.

P2–3 **(Transaction Analysis; Recording; Financial Statements)**

Garden City Service Company has been operating for three years. At the end of 19C, the accounting records reflected assets of $320,000 and liabilities of $120,000. During the year 19D, the following summarized transactions were completed:

a. Revenues of $160,000, of which $10,000 was on credit.

b. Issued an additional 1,000 shares of capital stock, par $10 per share, for $10,000 cash.

c. Purchased equipment that cost $25,000; paid $10,000 cash, and the balance is due next year.

d. Expenses incurred were $85,000, of which $15,000 was on credit.

e. Collected $8,000 of the credit amount in *(a)*.

f. Declared and paid cash dividends to stockholders of $12,000.

g. Paid $10,000 of the credit amount in *(d)*.

h. Borrowed $20,000 cash on a 12% interest-bearing note from a local bank (on December 31, 19D); payable June 30, 19E.

i. Cash amounting to $400 was stolen (not covered by insurance).

j. Depreciation on equipment was $600 for 19D (because of use).

Required:

1. Enter each of the above transactions in the following schedule. The first transaction is used as an example.

| | Assets | | Liabilities | | Owners' Equity | |
Transactions	Debit	Credit	Debit	Credit	Debit	Credit
Balances, January 1, 19D	$320,000			$120,000		$200,000
a. Revenues	150,000					160,000
	10,000					
b.						
Etc.						

2. Respond to the following:
   a. Why were two debits entered in the above schedule for transaction (a)?
   b. Complete the following at the end of 19D:

   Income statement:
       Revenues . . . . $ _____
       Expenses . . . . $ _____
       Net income . . . . $ _____

   Balance sheet:
       Assets . . . . $ _____
       Liabilities . . . . $ _____
       Owners' equity . . . . $ _____

   c. Explain why the dividend declared and paid is not an expense.

P2–4 **(Transaction Analysis; Recording)**

Listed below is a series of accounts for Arbor Corporation, which has been operating for three years. These accounts are listed and **numbered** for identification. Below the accounts is a series of transactions. For each transaction indicate the account(s) that should be debited and credited by entering the appropriate account number(s) to the right of each transaction. The first transaction is used as an example.

Account No.	Account titles	Account No.	Account titles
1	Cash	10	Wages payable
2	Accounts receivable	11	Income taxes payable
3	Supplies inventory (on hand, pending use)	12	Capital stock (par $10)
4	Prepaid expense	13	Retained earnings
5	Equipment (used in the business)	14	Service revenue
6	Accumulated depreciation, equipment	15	Operating expenses
7	Patents	16	Income tax expense
8	Accounts payable	17	Interest expense
9	Note payable	18	None of the above (explain)

Transactions	Debit	Credit
a. Example—Purchased equipment for use in the business; paid one-third cash and gave a note payable for the balance.	5	1, 9
b. Investment of cash in the business; capital stock was issued (at par).	____	____
c. Paid cash for salaries and wages.	____	____
d. Collected cash for services performed this period.	____	____
e. Collected cash for services performed last period.	____	____
f. Performed services this period on credit.	____	____
g. Paid operating expenses incurred this period.	____	____
h. Paid cash for operating expenses incurred last period.	____	____
i. Incurred operating expenses this period, to be paid next period.	____	____
j. Purchased supplies for inventory (to be used later); paid cash.	____	____
k. Used some of the supplies from inventory for operations.	____	____
l. Purchased a patent; paid cash.	____	____
m. Made a payment on the equipment note (a) above; the payment was part principal and part interest expense.	____	____
n. Collected cash on accounts receivable for services previously performed.	____	____
o. Paid cash on accounts payable for expenses previously incurred.	____	____
p. Paid three fourths of the income tax expense for the year; the balance to be paid next period.	____	____
q. On last day of current period, paid in cash for an insurance policy covering the next two years.	____	____

P2-5 **(Transaction Analysis; Recording in the Accounts)**

Listed below is a series of accounts (with identification numbers) for Quality Service Corporation.

Account No.	Account titles	Account No.	Account titles
1	Cash	20	Capital stock (par $10)
2	Accounts receivable	21	Contributed capital in excess of par
3	Service supplies inventory	25	Service revenue
4	Trucks and equipment	26	Operating expenses
5	Accumulated depreciation	27	Depreciation expense
10	Accounts payable	28	Interest expense
11	Note payable	29	Income tax expense
12	Income taxes payable	30	None of the above (explain)

During 19X, the company completed the selected transactions given in the tabulation that follows.

Required:

To the right indicate the accounts (by identification number) that should be debited and credited and the respective amounts. The first transaction is used as an example.

Transactions	Debit Acct. No.	Debit Amount	Credit Acct. No.	Credit Amount
a. Example: Purchased panel truck for use in the business for $18,000; paid $10,000 cash and signed a 12% interest-bearing note for the balance, $8,000.	4	18,000	1 11	10,000 8,000
b. Service revenue earned, $150,000, of which $40,000 was on credit.				
c. Operating expenses incurred, $100,000, of which $20,000 was on credit.				
d. Purchased service supplies, $1,500; paid cash (placed in supplies inventory for use as needed).				
e. Collected $8,000 of the credit amount in (b).				
f. Paid $15,000 of the credit amount in (c).				
g. Used $400 of the service supplies (taken from inventory) for service operations.				
h. Depreciation on the truck for the year, $3,000.				
i. Paid six months' interest on the note in (a).				
j. Income tax expense for the year, $4,000; paid three-fourths cash; balance payable by April 1 of next year.				

CASES

C2–1   (Inspection of a Balance Sheet to Evaluate Its Reliability)

J. Doe asked a local bank for a $50,000 loan to expand his small company. The bank asked Doe to submit a financial statement of the business to supplement the loan application. Doe prepared the balance sheet shown below.

Balance Sheet
June 30, 19F

Assets:

Cash and CDs	$ 9,000
Inventory	30,000
Equipment	46,000
Residence (monthly payments, $2,800)	300,000
Remaining assets	20,000
Total assets	$405,000

Liabilities:

Short-term debt to suppliers	$ 62,000
Long-term debt on equipment	38,000
Total debt	100,000
Owners' equity, J. Doe	305,000
Total liabilities and owners' equity	$405,000

Required:

The balance sheet has several flaws; however, there is at least one major deficiency. Identify it and explain its significance.

C2–2   (Analyzing and Restating an Income Statement that Has Major Deficiencies; a Challenging Case)

Robert Smith started and operated a small service company during 19A. At the end of the year, he prepared the following statement based on information stored in a large filing cabinet:

SMITH COMPANY
Profit for 19A

Service fees income collected during 19A		$80,000
Cash dividends received		12,000
Total		92,000
Expense for operations paid during 19A	$58,000	
Cash stolen	300	
Supplies purchased for use on service jobs (cash paid) . . .	1,700	
Total		60,000
Profit		$32,000

A summary of completed transactions was:

a. Service fees earned during 19A, $95,000.

b. The cash dividends received were on some Dow Jones common stock purchased by Robert Smith six years earlier.

c. Expenses incurred during 19A, $64,000.
d. Supplies on hand (unused) at the end of 19A, $500.

Required:

1. Did Smith prepare the above statement on a cash basis or an accrual basis? Explain how you can tell. Which basis should be used? Explain why.
2. Revise the above statement to make it consistent with proper accounting and reporting. Explain (using footnotes) the reason for each change that you make.

C2–3 (Challenging Analytical Case Related to Application of the Accounting Model)

Tower Company was organized during January 19A by three individuals. On January 20, 19A, the company issued 5,000 shares to each of its organizers. Below is a schedule of the **cumulative** account balances immediately after each of the first 10 transactions.

Accounts	1	2	3	4	5	6	7	8	9	10
Cash	$75,000	$70,000	$87,000	$77,000	$66,000	$66,000	$70,000	$58,000	$55,000	$54,000
Accounts receivable			18,000	18,000	18,000	21,000	21,000	21,000	21,000	21,000
Office fixtures		20,000	20,000	20,000	20,000	20,000	20,000	20,000	20,000	20,000
Land				14,000	14,000	14,000	14,000	14,000	14,000	14,000
Accounts payable					2,000	2,000	2,000	7,000	4,000	4,000
Note payable		15,000	15,000	19,000	19,000	19,000	19,000	19,000	19,000	19,000
Capital stock*	75,000	75,000	75,000	75,000	75,000	75,000	79,000	79,000	79,000	79,000
Revenues			35,000	35,000	35,000	38,000	38,000	38,000	38,000	38,000
Expenses					13,000	13,000	13,000	30,000	30,000	31,000

Ten Transactions—Cumulative Balances

* Owners' equity.

Required:

1. Analyze the changes in the above schedule for each transaction; then explain the transaction. Transactions 1 and 2 are used as examples:
   a. Cash increased $75,000, and capital stock (owners' equity) increased $75,000. Therefore, transaction 1 was an issuance of the capital stock of the corporation for $75,000 cash.
   b. Cash decreased $5,000, office fixtures (an asset) increased $20,000, and note payable (a liability) increased $15,000. Therefore, transaction 2 was a purchase of office fixtures that cost $20,000. Payment was made as follows: cash, $5,000; note payable, $15,000.

2. Based only on the above schedule (disregarding your response to Requirement 1) respond to the following after transaction 10:

    a. Income statement:
        Revenues . . . . $ _____
        Expenses . . . . _____
        Net income . . . . $ _____

    b. Balance sheet:
        Total assets . . . . $ _____
        Total liabilities . . . . _____
        Total owners' equity . . . . _____

C2–4 **(Overview of an Actual Set of Financial Statements)**

JCPenney Refer to the financial statements of J.C. Penney Company, Inc. given in the appendix immediately preceding the index.

1. Assume that all of the company's sales were on credit during the current year. What journal entry would be prepared to record sales revenue?
2. If J.C. Penney repaid in cash all of its short-term debt at the end of the current year, what journal entry would be prepared?
3. Is J.C. Penney a corporation, a partnership, or a proprietorship?
4. Use the company's balance sheet to determine the amounts in the accounting model (A = L + OE).
5. The company shows inventory of $2,201 million on its balance sheet. Does this amount represent the expected selling price of the inventory?

THREE

THE ACCOUNTING INFORMATION PROCESSING CYCLE

PURPOSE

Chapter 2 emphasized the fundamental accounting model and transaction analysis. It also discussed the use of journal entries and T-accounts to record the results of transaction analysis for each business transaction. The purpose of Chapter 3 is to discuss the **accounting information cycle,** which processes financial data from the transaction to the end result—the periodic income statement, balance sheet, and statement of cash flows. This chapter will expand your knowledge of journal entries, accounts, and financial statements.

Even fairly simple financial statements (like the income statement on the opposite page) contain technical words that are explained in this chapter.

LEARNING OBJECTIVES

1. Identify and explain the characteristics of an accounting system.
2. List and explain the six sequential phases of the accounting system.
3. Apply the six phases of the accounting information processing cycle using simple situations.
4. Prepare simple financial statements—income statement, balance sheet, and SCF.
5. Expand your accounting vocabulary by learning the "Important Terms Defined in This Chapter."
6. Apply the knowledge learned from this chapter by completing the homework assigned by your instructor.

ORGANIZATION

1. Accounting information processing cycle—six sequential phases.
2. Classifications on the:
   a. Income statement.
   b. Balance sheet.
   c. Statement of cash flows (SCF).

Kellogg's

Consolidated Earnings and Retained Earnings

Year ended December 31,

(millions)	1987	1986	1985
Net sales	$3,793.0	$3,340.7	$2,930.1
Interest revenue	14.1	11.7	7.2
Other revenue (deductions), net	(8.4)	(31.0)	(2.8)
	3,798.7	3,321.4	2,934.5
Cost of goods sold	1,939.3	1,744.6	1,605.0
Selling and administrative expense	1,162.5	948.7	766.6
Interest expense	31.2	41.5	35.4
	3,133.0	2,734.8	2,407.1
Earnings before income taxes	665.7	586.6	527.4
Income taxes	269.8	267.7	246.3
Net earnings—$3.20, $2.58, and $2.28 a share	395.9	318.9	281.1
Retained earnings, beginning of year	1,481.5	1,288.5	1,118.4
Dividends paid — $1.29, $1.02, and $.90 a share	(159.5)	(125.9)	(111.0)
Retained earnings, end of year	$1,717.9	$1,481.5	$1,288.5

Accounting Information Processing Cycle

An accounting system, regardless of the size of a business, is designed to collect, process, and report financial information about the entity. **Financial reports** are prepared at the end of each **reporting period,** often called the **accounting period.** For external reporting, the accounting period is one year in length, and it may, or may not, be the calendar year (January 1 to December 31). During each accounting period, the accounting system systematically collects and processes economic data about all of the transactions completed by the entity. This collecting and processing activity is called the **accounting information processing cycle.** It is called a cycle because it is repeated each accounting period for the new economic data. This processing cycle involves a series of sequential phases (steps), starting with collecting information concerning transactions and continuing through the accounting period to the preparation of the required financial statements—income statement, balance sheet, and statement of cash flows. The phases are outlined in Exhibit 3–1.

The first six phases of a typical accounting information processing cycle are discussed in the following paragraphs. Each phase is discussed in order and illustrated by using Bass Cleaners, Inc. (Exhibit 2–3). At the end of this chapter, a comprehensive demonstration case, with its solution, is given to tie all of these six phases together.

Phase 1—Collect Original Data

The first phase in the accounting information processing cycle is the collection of data about each transaction affecting the entity. Data are collected continuously throughout the accounting period as transactions occur. Each transaction that involves **external** parties usually generates one or more source documents that provide essential information about that transaction. Examples are sales invoices, cash register tapes, purchase invoices, and signed receipts. Documentation must be generated **internally** for certain transactions that are not between entities, such as depreciation and the using up of office supplies already on hand.[1] The original source documents are not generated by the accounting function but through the various **operating** functions of a business. The quality of the **outputs** of an information processing system is determined primarily by the quality of the inputs of original data based on transactions. Therefore, a carefully designed and controlled data collection system is an essential part of an accounting information processing system.

To illustrate the collection of original data, return to Bass Cleaners, Inc. (Exhibit 2–3). The first transaction was the issuance of 800 shares of capital stock for $20,000 cash. The documents to support this transaction would be a copy of

---

[1] Recall from Chapter 2 that transactions include (a) events that involve an exchange between two or more separate entities (or persons) and (b) events that are not between entities but nevertheless have a particular economic impact on the entity being accounted for.

Exhibit 3-1 Phases of the accounting information processing cycle

---

ACTIVITIES DURING THE ACCOUNTING PERIOD

Phases

1   **Collect original data** about each transaction as it occurs.

2   **Analyze each transaction** in terms of (a) Assets = Liabilities + Owners' Equity, and (b) Debits = Credits.

3   **Record transactions in journal.**

4   **Post (transfer) data from journal to ledger.**

ACTIVITIES AT THE END OF THE ACCOUNTING PERIOD

5   **Prepare a trial balance** from the ledger.

6   **Prepare financial statements.**

7-11   Other phases at end of the accounting period—discussed in Chapter 5.

---

the cash receipt given to each stockholder and an internal memorandum that identifies the number of shares issued to the organizers.

Phase 2—Analyze Each Transaction

This phase in the accounting information processing cycle was illustrated in Exhibit 2-3. Recall from Chapter 2 that each transaction must be analyzed to determine **economic effects** on the entity in terms of the accounting model, Assets = Liabilities + Owners' Equity, and the equality, Debits = Credits. When this analysis is completed, the economic effects are formally entered into the accounting system in the Debits = Credits format.

Transaction analysis requires an understanding of the nature of business transactions, the operations of the business, and a sound knowledge of the concepts and procedures of accounting.

To illustrate, analysis of the first transaction of Bass Cleaners (Exhibit 2-3)—the issuance of 800 shares of capital stock to the organizers for $20,000 cash—would be:

$$\text{ASSETS} = \text{LIABILITIES} + \text{STOCKHOLDERS' EQUITY}$$

Cash debit, $20,000 = No effect + Capital stock credit, $20,000

Phase 3—Record Transactions in Journal

After transaction analysis, the economic effects of each transaction are formally entered into the accounting system in a record known as the **journal.** The journal is a simple form used to record each transaction using the Debits = Credits format.

In a simple situation, each transaction could be recorded directly in the separate accounts for each asset, liability, and owners' equity. However, in more complex situations, each transaction should be recorded in one place in **chronological order** (i.e., in order of date of occurrence). The accounting record designed for this purpose is the journal. Typically, the effects of transaction analysis are recorded first in the journal and later transferred to the appropriate accounts (refer to the various journal entries and T-accounts used for Bass Cleaners in Exhibit 2–3).

The journal contains a chronological listing of each entry for all of the transactions. For example, the first transaction by Bass Cleaners (Exhibit 2–3) would appear in the journal in the following format:

JOURNAL

	Debit	Credit
(Date) Cash	20,000	
Capital stock (par $25; 800 shares)		20,000
To record investment of cash by owners.		

Notice that the **debit always is listed first** and the **credit is listed last and indented** to avoid incorrect identification.

The journal entry is a physical linking of the dual effects of each transaction. This contrasts with the T-accounts, where the debits and credits associated with each transaction are separated physically between two or more accounts. For example, the economic effects of the above entry for Bass Cleaners appear in separate accounts as follows:

Cash		Capital Stock	
(Date) 20,000			(Date) 20,000

The **journal** is the place of initial (or first) entry of the economic effects of each transaction. Therefore, it is called the **book of original entry.** The journal serves three useful purposes:

1. It provides for the initial and chronological listing of each transaction immediately after its transaction analysis is completed.
2. It provides a single place to record the economic effects of each transaction without further subclassifications of the data.
3. It facilitates later **tracing:** checking for possible errors; and reconstruction of each transaction, its analysis, and its recording.

Knowledge of the approximate date of a transaction often is used in tracing activities. The journal is the only place in the accounting system where the economic effects of each transaction are linked physically and recorded chronologically.

The first three transactions for Bass Cleaners have been entered in a typical journal shown in Exhibit 3–2. Recording transactions in the journal in this manner is called **journalizing,** and the entries made are called **journal entries.**

Exhibit 3–2 Journal illustrated

	Journal			Page ___1___	
Date	Account Titles and Explanation	Folio	Debit	Credit
Jan. 1	Cash	101	20,000	
	Capital stock	301		20,000
	Investment of cash by owners			
Jan. 3	Cash	101	5,000	
	Note payable	202		5,000
	Borrowed cash on 12% note			
Jan. 6	Delivery truck	111	8,000	
	Cash	101		8,000
	Purchased delivery			
	truck for use in			
	the business			

To summarize the discussion about journal entries: (1) each transaction is first recorded in the journal as a separate entry; (2) each entry in the journal is dated, and entries are recorded in chronological order; (3) for each transaction, the debits (accounts and amounts) are entered first, the credits follow and are indented; and (4) for each transaction, the economic effects on the accounting model and the debits and credits are linked in one entry. These features provide an "audit or tracing trail" that facilitates subsequent examination of past transactions and assists in locating errors. Also, the journal is designed to simplify subsequent accounting (as will be shown later).

Phase 4—Post (Transfer) Data from Journal to Ledger

A separate account is set up for each asset, liability, and owners' equity. An accounting system typically contains a large number of such accounts. Collectively, these individual accounts are contained in a record known as the **ledger.** The ledger may be organized in many ways. Handwritten accounting systems

Exhibit 3–3 Ledger illustrated (T-accounts)

BASS CLEANERS, INC.
LEDGER at December 31, 19A

ASSETS	=	LIABILITIES	+	OWNERS' EQUITY

ASSETS = **LIABILITIES** + **OWNERS' EQUITY**

Cash 101   **Accounts Payable** 201   **Capital Stock** 301

(a)	20,000	(c)	8,000
(b)	5,000	(f)	25,800
(d)	40,000	(h)	600
(k)	1,000	(j)	1,800
		(l)	500

(Net debit balance, $29,300)

Accounts Payable:
| (l) | 500 | (g) | 2,000 |

(Net credit balance, $1,500)

Capital Stock:
| | (a) | 20,000 |

Retained Earnings* 310
| (j) | 1,800 |

Accounts Receivable 102   **Note Payable** 205   **Cleaning Revenue** 312

| (e) | 4,000 | (k) | 1,000 |

(Net debit balance, $3,000)

Note Payable:
| | (b) | 5,000 |

Cleaning Revenue:
| | (d) | 40,000 |
| | (e) | 4,000 |

(Net credit balance, $44,000)

Delivery Truck 120   **Operating Expenses 320**

| (c) | 8,000 |

Operating Expenses:
(f)	25,800
(g)	2,000
(i)	1,600

(Net debit balance, $29,400)

Accumulated Depreciation, Delivery Truck† 121   **Interest Expense** 325

| | (i) | 1,600 |

Interest Expense:
| (h) | 600 |

| Totals | $38,700 | = | $6,500 | + | $32,200 |

Note: The accounting model, Assets = Liabilities + Owners' Equity, given at the top of this exhibit and the totals at the bottom are shown for your convenience in studying; they would not appear in an actual ledger.

* Retained Earnings is an owners' equity account that reports accumulated earnings minus dividends paid to date. Dividends paid reduce cash and owners' equity (Chapter 12). Dividends paid is a distribution to owners—not an expense because it does not contribute to earning revenue.

† The delivery truck is depreciated over a five-year period because that is its estimated useful life to Bass Cleaners. Depreciation refers to the "wearing out" of the truck due to use. The truck is assumed to wear out at a steady rate each year throughout its life; therefore, the annual depreciation is $8,000 ÷ 5 years = $1,600. This amount is recorded in an account called Accumulated Depreciation, Delivery Truck; it is a negative, or contra, account to the Delivery Truck account. The $1,600 also is an expense for the year. For further explanation of depreciation, see Chapter 9.

may use a loose-leaf ledger—one page for each account. In a machine accounting system, a separate machine card is kept for each account. With a computerized accounting system, the ledger is kept on electronic storage devices, but there are still individual accounts under each system. Each account is identified by a descriptive **name** and an **assigned number** (e.g., Cash, 101; Accounts Payable, 201; and Capital Stock, 301).

Exhibit 3–3 shows the ledger for Bass Cleaners in T-account format. The ledger contains information that initially was recorded in the journal and then transferred to the appropriate accounts in the ledger. The transfer of information from the journal to the ledger is called **posting.** This transfer from the chronological arrangement in the journal to the account format in the ledger is important because the ledger reflects the data classified as assets, liabilities, owners' equity, revenues, and expenses. This reclassification of the data facilitates the subsequent preparation of financial statements.

Usually a business will record the transactions in the journal each day and **post** to the ledger less frequently, say, every few days. Of course, the timing of these activities varies with the data processing system used and the complexity of the entity.

The T-account format shown in Exhibit 3–3 is useful for instructional purposes. However, the typical account used is the columnar format shown in Exhibit 3–4. It retains the debit-credit concept, but it is arranged to provide columns for date, explanation, folio (F), and a running balance.

Exhibit 3–4 Ledger account in columnar format illustrated

Account Title _____ Cash _____   Account Number ___ 101 ___

Date	Explanation	Folio	Debit	Credit	Balance
Jan. 1	Investments	1	20,000		20,000
3	Borrowing	3	5,000		25,000
6	Truck purchased	3		8,000	17,000
7	Cleaning revenue	4	40,000		57,000
8	Operating expenses	4		25,800	31,200
10	Interest expense	5		600	30,600
15	Payments to owners	7		1,800	28,800
16	Collections on receivables	8	1,000		29,800
17	Payments on accounts payable	8		500	29,300

To post to the ledger, the debits and credits shown in the journal entries are transferred directly as debits and credits to the appropriate accounts in the ledger. Both the journal and the ledger have a **Folio** column for **cross-reference** between these two records. In the journal, the numbers in the Folio column indicate the account **to which** the dollar amounts were posted. In the ledger account, the numbers in the Folio column indicate the journal page **from which** the dollar amounts were posted. Folio numbers are used in the posting phase to (*a*) indicate that posting has been done and (*b*) provide an "audit trail."

The economic data concerning transactions end up in the ledger; therefore, it has been called the **book of final entry.**

At the end of the accounting period, the first four phases of the accounting information processing cycle will have been completed—data collection, analysis, journal entries, and posting to the ledger.[2] Phase 5 starts the end-of-period phases.

Phase 5—Prepare a Trial Balance

At the end of the accounting period, a **trial balance** is prepared directly from the ledger. A trial balance is a listing, in ledger account order, of the individual **accounts** and their respective **net ending** debit and credit balances. The ending balance shown for each individual account is the difference between the total of its debits and the total of its credits. Exhibit 3–5 shows the trial balance of Bass Cleaners at December 31, 19A. It was prepared directly from the ledger accounts given in Exhibit 3–3.

A trial balance has two purposes:

1. It provides a check on the equality of the debits and credits as shown in the ledger accounts at the end of the period.
2. It provides financial data in a convenient form to help in preparing the financial statements.

Phase 6—Prepare Financial Statements

Phase 6 is the preparation of the three required financial statements—income statement, balance sheet, and statement of cash flows. The trial balance (developed in Phase 5) provides basic data that are needed to prepare the financial statements at the end of the accounting period. The 19A income statement and balance sheet for Bass Cleaners are shown in Exhibit 3–6. Notice that the amounts on these statements were taken directly from the trial balance, except for retained earnings. Retained earnings is computed as: Beginning balance,

---

[2] Chapter 5 expands the accounting information cycle to include some additional activities to develop the financial statements in complex situations.

Exhibit 3–5 Trial balance illustrated

BASS CLEANERS, INC.
Trial Balance
December 31, 19A

Account No.	Account titles	Net balance Debit	Credit
101	Cash	$29,300	
102	Accounts receivable	3,000	
120	Delivery truck	8,000	
121	Accumulated depreciation, delivery truck		$ 1,600
201	Accounts payable		1,500
205	Note payable (12%)		5,000
301	Capital stock (par $25; 800 shares)		20,000
310	Retained earnings (explained later)	1,800	
312	Cleaning revenue		44,000
320	Operating expenses	29,400	
325	Interest expense	600	
	Totals	$72,100	$72,100

$-0- (this is year 1 for Bass Cleaners) + Net income (from the income statement), $14,000 − Dividends paid to stockholders, $1,800 = Ending balance, $12,200.[3]

The first six phases of the accounting information processing cycle are summarized in Exhibit 3–7. Before we present a comprehensive case that involves all six phases of the cycle, we will discuss the major classifications of the three required financial statements. An understanding of these classifications will facilitate the preparation of the statements (Phase 6 of the cycle).

Classifications of Elements Reported on the Financial Statements

To make financial statements more useful, **classifications** of information are included on the financial statements. There are a variety of acceptable classifications used in practice. You should not be confused when you notice different formats used by different companies.

Acceptable classifications for each of the three required financial statements are outlined on the next few pages. Following each classification, some of the

---

[3] Notice how much easier it is to prepare these statements from a trial balance than when the accounts are used directly (as was done in Chapter 2). Retained earnings, an element of stockholders' equity, will be discussed in detail later.

Exhibit 3–6 Income statement and balance sheet, Bass Cleaners, Inc.

BASS CLEANERS, INC.
Income Statement
For the Year Ended December 31, 19A

Cleaning revenue		$44,000
Expenses:		
Operating expenses	$29,400	
Interest expense	600	
Total expenses		30,000
Net income		$14,000

Earnings per share (EPS), $14,000 ÷ 800 shares = $17.50

BASS CLEANERS, INC.
Balance Sheet
At December 31, 19A

Assets

Cash		$29,300
Accounts receivable		3,000
Delivery truck	$ 8,000	
Less: Accumulated depreciation	1,600	6,400
Total assets		$38,700

Liabilities

Accounts payable		$ 1,500
Note payable (12%)		5,000
Total liabilities		6,500

Stockholders' Equity

Contributed capital:		
Capital stock (par $25; 800 shares)	20,000	
Retained earnings ($14,000 − $1,800)	12,200	
Total stockholders' equity		32,200
Total liabilities and stockholders' equity		$38,700

major distinctions are briefly discussed. Future chapters will discuss these classifications in more detail.

Classifications on the Income Statement

An income statement is classified as follows:

A. **Revenues** (often classified by type, such as sales, service, and interest revenue)

B. **Expenses**
    Cost of goods sold (an expense)

Exhibit 3–7 Sequential phases of an accounting information processing cycle summarized*

Activity	Flow of Data

Activity

(1) Collect raw data

(capture the economic data about each **transaction**)

(2) Analyze each transaction

(determine economic effects of each transaction on the entity)

(3) Journalize

(record the economic effects of each transaction on the accounting model in chronological order)

(4) Post to the ledger

(accumulate each asset, liability, and owners' equity in separate accounts)

(5) Develop a trial balance

(list of account balances to facilitate preparation of financial reports)

(6) Prepare financial statements

(to help decision makers make better decisions)

Flow of Data

Original source documents

| Invoices | Vouchers | Bills | Etc. |

Transaction Analysis
(effect on the enterprise in terms of accounting model A = L + OE)

Journal

Ledger

CASH   101

Trial balance

| Trial balance | | |
| Account | Debit | Credit |

Financial statements

| Income statement | Balance sheet | Statement of cash flows | Special reports |

Operating expenses:
 Selling expense
 General and administrative expense
 Interest expense
 Income tax expense
C. **Income before extraordinary items (A − B)**

D. Extraordinary items (unusual and nonrecurring)
  Gains and losses

E. Net income (C − D)

F. Earnings per share (EPS)

The major classifications of revenues and expenses were discussed in Chapter 1.

Cost of goods sold is an expense incurred when merchandise is sold. The merchandise was purchased by the company before it was sold to its customers. The amount paid to the supplier for the items sold is called cost of goods sold. Assume merchandise purchased for resale cost $40,000. If three fourths of it was sold for $50,000, the effect can be shown on an income statement as:

```
Sales revenue . . . . . . . . . . . . . . . . . . $50,000
    Less: Cost of goods sold ($40,000 × 3/4) . .   30,000
Operating expenses:
    Etc.
```

The merchandise that remains ($40,000 − $30,000) is listed on the balance sheet as an asset called "Inventory." Sales revenue minus cost of goods sold is called **gross margin.**

Operating expenses are the usual expenses that are incurred in operating a business during an accounting period. Often they are classified between selling expense and general and administrative expense. Selling expense includes all amounts incurred during the period in performing sales activities (such as salaries of salespeople). General and administrative expense includes the overall business expenses (such as the salary of the president).

Interest expense is incurred as the result of borrowing money. Interest expense on debt is sometimes combined ("netted out") with interest revenue so that only a single amount is reported.

Extraordinary (EO) items are gains and losses that are both *(a)* unusual in nature and *(b)* infrequent in occurrence. These items must be separately reported on the income statement. Since they seldom occur, separate reporting informs decision makers that they are not likely to recur.

Income tax expense is incurred by a corporation but not by a sole proprietorship or partnership.[4] Income taxes are payable each year (partially in advance on quarterly estimates). A corporation must report income tax expense on its income statement separately for operations and extraordinary items. Assume XT Corporation computed **pretax** amounts as follows: income from operations, $80,000; and an extraordinary gain, $10,000. If the income tax rate is 30%, the income statement would show the following:

---

[4] The earnings of a sole proprietorship and a partnership must be reported on the **personal** income tax returns of the owners. Under specified conditions, a closely held corporation can avoid corporate income tax as a Subchapter S corporation.

Pretax income from operations		$80,000
Less: Income tax ($80,000 × 30%)		24,000
Income before extraordinary items		56,000
Extraordinary gain	$10,000	
Less: Income tax ($10,000 × 30%)	3,000	7,000
Net income		$63,000

Notice that income tax expense is allocated separately to income from operations and the extraordinary gain.

Earnings per share (EPS) relates only to the common stock of a corporation. It is computed by dividing income by the average number of common shares outstanding during the reporting period. If an extraordinary gain or loss is reported, these earnings per share amounts must be reported. Assume ART Corporation reported the following **aftertax** amounts on its income statement:

Income before extraordinary items . . .	$100,000
Less: Extraordinary loss	20,000
Net income	$ 80,000

If 40,000 shares of common stock are outstanding, EPS would be reported as follows:

Income before extraordinary items . . .	($100,000 ÷ 40,000 shares) =	$ 2.50
Less: Extraordinary loss	($20,000 ÷ 40,000 shares) =	(0.50)
Net income	($80,000 ÷ 40,000 shares) =	$ 2.00

Classifications on the Balance Sheet

Typically a balance sheet is classified as follows:

A. **Assets (by order of liquidity):**[5]
   (1) Current assets (short term)
   (2) Long-term investments
   (3) Operational assets (property, plant, and equipment)
   (4) Intangible assets
   (5) Deferred charges
   (6) Other (miscellaneous) assets
       Total assets

B. **Liabilities (by order of time to maturity):**
   (1) Current liabilities (short term)
   (2) Long-term liabilities
       Total liabilities

---

[5] Liquidity refers to the average period of time required to convert a noncash asset to cash.

C. **Owners' equity (by source):**
    (1) Contributed capital (by owners)
    (2) Retained earnings (accumulated earnings minus accumulated dividends declared)

Current assets include cash and other assets that are expected to be converted into cash or used within one year from the balance sheet date or during the normal operating cycle of the business, whichever is longer. The **normal operating cycle** for a merchandising company is shown in Exhibit 3–8.

Typical current assets are cash, short-term investments, accounts receivable, inventory, and prepaid expenses (i.e., expenses paid in advance of use).

Long-term investments include assets that are not used in operating the businesss. Examples include investments in real estate and stocks and bonds of other companies. This classification may include cash set aside in special funds (such as savings accounts) for use for a specified long-term purpose.

Operational assets are often called property, plant, and equipment or fixed assets. This group includes tangible assets that were acquired for use in **operating the business** rather than for resale as inventory items or held as investments. The assets included are buildings; land on which the buildings reside; and equipment, tools, furniture, and fixtures used in operating the business. Operational assets, with the exception of land, are depreciated as they are used. Their initial cost is apportioned to expense over their estimated useful lives. This apportionment of cost is called **depreciation.** Land is not depreciated because it does not wear out like machinery, buildings, and equipment. The amount of depreciation computed for **each period** is reported on the income statement as depreciation **expense.** The **accumulated** amount of depreciation expense for all past periods is **deducted** from the initial cost of the asset to derive the **book or carrying value** reported on the balance sheet. To illustrate, Bass Cleaners purchased a delivery truck for $8,000. It had an estimated useful life of five years. Depreciation expense is computed as $8,000 ÷ 5 years = $1,600 per year. The balance sheets developed during the five-year period would report the following:

	19A	19B	19C	19D	19E
Delivery truck	$8,000	$8,000	$8,000	$8,000	$8,000
Less: Accumulated depreciation . . .	1,600	3,200	4,800	6,400	8,000
Book or carrying value	$6,400	$4,800	$3,200	$1,600	$ –0–

Intangible assets have no **physical existence** and have a long life. Their value is derived from the **legal rights and privileges** that accompany ownership. Examples are patents, trademarks, copyrights, franchises, and goodwill. Intangible assets usually are not acquired for resale but rather are directly related to the operations of the business.

Deferred charges are prepayments for goods and services that are expected to help generate revenue in the future. They are often included in the classification of "Other assets." Prepaid expenses and deferred charges are similar. The term **prepaid expense** is used typically for items classified as current assets; **deferred charges** is used for items classified as noncurrent assets.

Exhibit 3–8 Typical operating cycle of a business

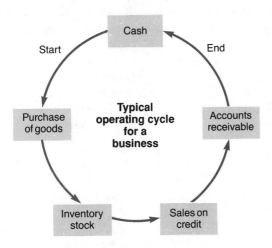

Current liabilities are short-term debts at the balance sheet date that are expected to be paid out of the current assets listed on the same balance sheet. Short-term liabilities are expected to be paid during the coming year or the normal operating cycle of the business, whichever is longer. Current liabilities include accounts payable, short-term notes payable, wages payable, income taxes payable, and other expenses incurred (used) but not yet paid.

The difference between total current assets and total current liabilities is called **working capital.** It is a widely used measure of a company's ability to pay its short-term obligations.

The relationship between current assets and current liabilities is sometimes expressed as a ratio called the current ratio:

$$\text{Current ratio} = \text{Current assets} \div \text{Current liabilities}$$

The current ratio is one of the key numbers that are studied by financial analysts. As you will see in Chapter 16, a low current ratio is often an early warning of financial difficulty including bankruptcy. Classification of the current ratio as high or low depends on a number of factors including analytical judgment.

Long-term liabilities are the other debts of a company that are not classified as current liabilities. Long-term liabilities have maturities that extend beyond one year (or one operating cycle, if longer than a year) from the balance sheet date. Examples include long-term bank loans, bond liabilities, and mortgages.

Owners' equity (called stockholders' equity for a corporation) represents the residual claim of the owners (i.e., A − L = OE). This claim results from the initial contributions of the stockholders (contributed capital) plus retained earnings, which is the accumulated earnings of the company less the accumulated dividends declared. Retained earnings represents the amount of earnings that have been left in the company for growth. Typically long-time successful companies have grown more from retained earnings than from additional contributions by investors for capital stock.

Capital stock usually has a par value, which is a legal amount per share. Par value has no relationship to the **market price** of the shares. When a corporation issues capital stock above the par value, the excess must be recorded in a separate account. Assume a corporation issued 6,000 shares of its capital stock, par $10 per share, for $80,000 cash. The required journal entry is:

```
Cash . . . . . . . . . . . . . . . . . . . . . . . . . . . . . . . . . . . . . . . . 80,000
     Capital stock (par $10; 6,000 shares)  . . . . . . . . . . . . . . . . . . .        60,000
     Contributed capital in excess of par ($80,000 − $60,000)  . . . . . . . .        20,000
```

Capital stock is discussed in Chapter 12.

Classifications of the Statement of Cash Flows (SCF)

The SCF is classified as follows:

1. **Cash flows from operating activities.**   This section reports cash flows associated with earning income.
2. **Cash flows from investing activities.**   Cash flows in this section are associated with buying and selling productive assets (other than inventory).
3. **Cash flows from financing activities.**   These cash flows are related to financing the business.

Each of these classifications was introduced in Chapter 1 and will be discussed in detail in Chapter 15.

DEMONSTRATION CASE

Accounting Information Processing Cycle

This case illustrates the **accounting information processing cycle** from the capture of the raw economic data during the accounting period to the financial statements prepared at the end of the accounting year. You should study each step in the solution carefully because it reviews the discussion in Chapters 1, 2, and 3.

On January 3, 19A, M. Hall and P. Garza organized a corporation, La Paloma Apartments, to build and operate apartment complexes. At the start, each one invested $40,000 cash and in turn received 3,000 shares of $10 par value capital stock. On that date, the following entry was recorded in the journal:

Exhibit 3–9 Trial balance and transactions for demonstration case

---

LA PALOMA APARTMENTS
Ledger Balances
July 1, 19C (start of year 2 of rental operations)

Account No.	Account titles	Debit	Credit
101	Cash	$ 18,000	
103	Accounts receivable (or rent receivable)		
105	Supplies inventory	2,000	
112	Prepaid insurance		
121	Land (apartment site)	30,000	
122	La Paloma apartment building	200,000	
123	Accumulated depreciation, apartment building		$ 10,000
125	Furniture and fixtures	60,000	
126	Accumulated depreciation, furniture and fixtures		12,000
131	Land for future apartment site		
201	Accounts payable		6,000
202	Property taxes payable		
203	Income taxes payable		
204	Mortgage payable (10%; apartment building)		180,000
205	Note payable, long term (12%)		
301	Capital stock (par $10; 6,000 shares)		60,000
302	Contributed capital in excess of par		20,000
303	Retained earnings (accumulated earnings to June 30, 19C)		22,000
401	Rent revenue		
521	Utilities and telephone expense		
522	Apartment maintenance expense		
523	Salary and wage expense		
524	Insurance expense		
525	Property tax expense		
526	Depreciation expense		
527	Miscellaneous expenses		
531	Interest expense		
532	Income tax expense		
	Totals	$310,000	$310,000

(Assets, $288,000 = Liabilities, $186,000 + Stockholders' Equity, $102,000)

January 3, 19A:

Cash	80,000	
Capital stock (par $10; 6,000 shares)		60,000
Contributed capital in excess of par ($80,000 − $60,000)		20,000

Then land was acquired for $30,000 cash, and a construction contract was signed with a builder. The first apartments were rented on July 1, 19B. The owners

Exhibit 3–9 *(concluded)*

Transactions, July 1, 19C, through June 30, 19D:

Date	Description

a. On November 1, 19C, paid $3,000 cash for a two-year casualty insurance policy covering the building, its contents, and liability coverage.

b. Rental revenue earned: collected in cash, $105,500; and uncollected by June 30, 19D, $2,000.

c. Paid accounts payable (amount owed from the prior year for expenses), $6,000.

d. Bought a tract of land, at $35,000, as a planned site for another apartment complex to be built in "about three years." Cash of $5,000 was paid, and a long-term note payable (12% interest per annum, interest payable each six months) was signed for the balance of $30,000.

e. Operating expenses incurred and paid in cash were:

Utilities and telephone expense	$23,360
Apartment maintenance expense	1,200
Salary and wage expense	6,000

f. At the end of the accounting year (June 30, 19D), the following bills for expenses incurred had not been recorded or paid: June telephone bill, $40; and miscellaneous expense, $100.

g. Paid interest for six months on the long-term note at 12% per annum. (Refer to item [*d*].) (Hint: Interest = Principal × Rate × Time.)

h. An inventory count at the end of the accounting period, June 30, 19D, showed remaining supplies on hand amounting to $400. Supplies used are considered a miscellaneous expense.

i. By the end of the accounting period, June 30, 19D, one third (8 months out of 24 months) of the prepaid insurance premium of $3,000 paid in transaction (*a*) had expired because of passage of time.

j. Depreciation expense for the year was based on an estimated useful life of 20 years for the apartment and 5 years for the furniture and fixtures (assume no residual or salvage value).

k. The property taxes for the year ending June 30, 19D, in the amount of $2,700 have not been recorded or paid.

l. Cash payment at year-end on the mortgage on the apartment was:

On principal	$20,000
Interest ($180,000 × 10%)	18,000
Total paid	$38,000

m. Income tax expense for the year ending June 30, 19D, was $5,940 (i.e., a 20% average rate). This obligation will be paid in the next period.

---

decided to use an **accounting year** of July 1 through June 30 for business purposes (instead of a period that agrees with the calendar year).

It is now July 1, 19C, the beginning of the second year of rental operations; therefore, certain **accounts in the ledger** have balances carried over from the prior accounting year ended June 30, 19C. A complete list of the accounts in the ledger that will be needed for this case, their folio numbers, and the balances carried over from the previous year is given in Exhibit 3–9. **Typical transactions** (summarized) for the 12-month accounting year—July 1, 19C, through June 30, 19D—are also given in Exhibit 3–9. Instead of using dates, we will use the letter notation to the left of each transaction.

Required:

Complete the accounting information processing cycle by doing each of the following:

1. **Analyze,** then **journalize** (i.e., enter in the journal), each transaction listed above for the accounting period July 1, 19C, through June 30, 19D. Number the journal pages consecutively starting with 1.

	Cash		101
Balance	18,000		

2. **Set up a ledger** with T-accounts that has all of the accounts listed on the trial balance given in Exhibit 3–9; include the account numbers as given. Enter the July 1, 19C, balances in each account in this manner:

3. **Post all entries** from the journal to the ledger; use the Folio columns for account numbers.

4. **Prepare a trial balance** at June 30, 19D.

5. **Prepare an income statement** for the reporting year ending June 30, 19D. Use the following classifications:

> Revenues
> Operating expenses:
>   Total operating expenses
> Income from apartment operations
> Interest expense
> Pretax income
>   Income tax expense
> Net income
> EPS

6. **Prepare a balance sheet** at June 30, 19D. Use the following classifications:

> **Assets**
> Current assets
> Operational assets
> Other assets
>
> **Liabilities**
> Current liabilities
> Long-term liabilities
>
> **Stockholders' Equity**
> Contributed capital
> Retained earnings

Suggested Solution:

Requirement 1:

JOURNAL   **Page 1**

Date	Account Titles and Explanation	Folio	Debit	Credit
a.	Prepaid insurance	112	3,000	
	Cash	101		3,000
	Paid insurance premium for two years in advance.			
	(Explanatory note: An asset account, Prepaid Insurance, is debited because a future service, insurance coverage, is being paid for in advance.)			
b.	Cash	101	105,500	
	Accounts receivable (or rent receivable)	103	2,000	
	Rent revenue	401		107,500
	To record rent revenues earned for the year, of which $2,000 has not yet been collected.			
c.	Accounts payable	201	6,000	
	Cash	101		6,000
	Paid a debt carried over from previous year.			
d.	Land for future apartment site	131	35,000	
	Cash	101		5,000
	Note payable, long term (12%)	205		30,000
	Bought land as a site for future apartment complex. (This is a second tract of land acquired; the present apartment building was built on the first tract.)			
e.	Utilities and telephone expense	521	23,360	
	Apartment maintenance expense	522	1,200	
	Salary and wage expense	523	6,000	
	Cash	101		30,560
	Paid current expenses.			
f.	Utilities and telephone expense	521	40	
	Miscellaneous expenses	527	100	
	Accounts payable	201		140
	Expenses incurred, not yet paid.			
g.	Interest expense	531	1,800	
	Cash	101		1,800
	Paid six months' interest on a long-term note ($30,000 × 12% × 6/12 = $1,800).			

Requirement 1 (concluded):

JOURNAL Page 2

Date	Account Titles and Explanation	Folio	Debit	Credit
h.	Miscellaneous expenses	527	1,600	
	Supplies inventory	105		1,600
	To record as expense supplies used from inventory during the year.			
	(Explanatory note: Supplies are bought in advance of use. Therefore, at that time they are recorded as an asset, Supplies Inventory. As the supplies are used from inventory, the asset thus used becomes an expense. Refer to Supplies Inventory account [$2,000 − $400 = $1,600].)			
i.	Insurance expense	524	1,000	
	Prepaid insurance	112		1,000
	To record as an expense the cost of the insurance that expired ($3,000 × 8/24 = $1,000).			
j.	Depreciation expense	526	22,000	
	Accumulated depreciation, apartment building	123		10,000
	Accumulated depreciation, furniture and fixtures	126		12,000
	Depreciation expense for one year.			
	Computation: Apartment: $200,000 ÷ 20 years = $10,000. Furniture and fixtures: $60,000 ÷ 5 years = $12,000.			
k.	Property tax expense	525	2,700	
	Property taxes payable	202		2,700
	Property taxes for the current year, not yet paid.			
l.	Mortgage payable	204	20,000	
	Interest expense	531	18,000	
	Cash	101		38,000
	Payments on principal of mortgage payable plus interest expense ($180,000 × 10%).			
m.	Income tax expense	532	5,940	
	Income taxes payable	203		5,940
	Income tax for the year; payable later.			

Requirements 2 and 3—Ledger:

LEDGER

Cash					101
Date	F	Amount	Date	F	Amount
Balance		18,000	(a)	1	3,000
(b)	1	105,500	(c)	1	6,000
			(d)	1	5,000
			(e)	1	30,560
			(g)	1	1,800
			(l)	2	38,000

(Net debit balance, $39,140)

Accounts Receivable			103
(b)	1	2,000	

Supplies Inventory			105
Balance	2,000	(h)	2	1,600

Prepaid Insurance			112
(a)	1	3,000	(i)	2	1,000

Land (Apartment Site)		121
Balance	30,000	

La Paloma Apartment Building		122
Balance	200,000	

Accumulated Depreciation, Apartment Building			123
		Balance	10,000
		(j)	2	10,000

Furniture and Fixtures					125
Date	F	Amount	Date	F	Amount
Balance		60,000			

Accumulated Depreciation, Furniture and Fixtures			126
		Balance	12,000
		(j)	2	12,000

Land for Future Apartment Site			131
(d)	1	35,000	

Accounts Payable			201
(c)	1	6,000	Balance		6,000
			(f)	1	140

Property Taxes Payable			202
		(k)	2	2,700

Income Taxes Payable			203
		(m)	2	5,940

Mortgage Payable (10%; apartment building)			204
(l)	2	20,000	Balance	180,000

Requirements 2 and 3 (continued):

Note Payable, Long Term (12%) 205							
Date	F	Amount	Date	F	Amount		
			(d)	1	30,000		

Insurance Expense				524	
Date	F	Amount	Date	F	Amount
(i)	2	1,000			

Capital Stock		301
Balance		60,000

Property Tax Expense		525
(k)	2	2,700

Contributed Capital in Excess of Par		302
Balance		20,000

Depreciation Expense		526
(j)	2	22,000

Retained Earnings		303
Balance		22,000

Miscellaneous Expenses		527
(f)	1	100
(h)	2	1,600

Rent Revenue		401
(b)	1	107,500

Interest Expense		531
(g)	1	1,800
(l)	2	18,000

Utilities and Telephone Expense		521
(e)	1	23,360
(f)	1	40

Income Tax Expense		532
(m)	2	5,940

Apartment Maintenance Expense		522
(e)	1	1,200

Salary and Wage Expense		523
(e)	1	6,000

Requirement 4:

LA PALOMA APARTMENTS
Trial Balance
June 30, 19D

Account No.	Account titles	Debit	Credit
		Balance	
101	Cash	$ 39,140	
103	Accounts receivable (or Rent receivable)	2,000	
105	Supplies inventory	400	
112	Prepaid insurance (16 months)	2,000	
121	Land (apartment site)	30,000	
122	La Paloma apartment building	200,000	
123	Accumulated depreciation, apartment building		$ 20,000
125	Furniture and fixtures	60,000	
126	Accumulated depreciation, furniture and fixtures		24,000
131	Land for future apartment site	35,000	
201	Accounts payable		140
202	Property taxes payable		2,700
203	Income taxes payable		5,940
204	Mortgage payable (10%; apartment building)		160,000
205	Note payable, long term (12%)		30,000
301	Capital stock (par $10; 6,000 shares)		60,000
302	Contributed capital in excess of par		20,000
303	Retained earnings (accumulated earnings to June 30, 19C)		22,000
401	Rent revenue		107,500
521	Utilities and telephone expense	23,400	
522	Apartment maintenance expense	1,200	
523	Salary and wage expense	6,000	
524	Insurance expense	1,000	
525	Property tax expense	2,700	
526	Depreciation expense	22,000	
527	Miscellaneous expenses	1,700	
531	Interest expense	19,800	
532	Income tax expense	5,940	
	Totals	$452,280	$452,280

Requirement 5:

LA PALOMA APARTMENTS
Income Statement
For the Year Ended June 30, 19D

Revenues:
 Rent revenue $107,500*

Operating expenses:
 Utilities and telephone expense $23,400
 Apartment maintenance expense 1,200
 Salary and wage expense 6,000
 Insurance expense 1,000
 Property tax expense 2,700
 Depreciation expense 22,000
 Miscellaneous expenses   1,700

    Total operating expenses   58,000

Income from apartment operations   49,500
 Interest expense   19,800

Pretax income   29,700
 Income tax expense   5,940

Net income . . . . $ 23,760

EPS ($23,760 ÷ 6,000 shares) $3.96

* Notes:
 a. These amounts were taken directly from Requirement 4, the trial balance.
 b. No products are sold by this business; therefore, gross margin cannot be reported.

Requirement 6:

LA PALOMA APARTMENTS
Balance Sheet
At June 30, 19D

Assets

Current assets:

Cash	$ 39,140*	
Accounts receivable	2,000	
Supplies inventory	400	
Prepaid insurance	2,000	
Total current assets		$ 43,540

Operational assets:

Land (apartment site)		30,000	
La Paloma apartment building	$200,000		
Less: Accumulated depreciation, building	20,000	180,000	
Furniture and fixtures	60,000		
Less: Accumulated depreciation, furniture and fixtures . . .	24,000	36,000	
Total operational assets			246,000

Other assets:

Land for future apartment site†		35,000
Total assets		$324,540

Liabilities

Current liabilities:

Accounts payable	$ 140	
Property taxes payable	2,700	
Income taxes payable	5,940	
Total current liabilities		$ 8,780

Long-term liabilities:

Mortgage payable	160,000	
Note payable, long term (12%)	30,000	
Total long-term liabilities		190,000
Total liabilities		198,780

Stockholders' Equity

Contributed capital:

Capital stock (par $10; 6,000 shares)	$60,000	
Contributed capital in excess of par	20,000	
Total contributed capital		80,000
Retained earnings (beginning balance, $22,000 +		
net income, $23,760)		45,760
Total stockholders' equity		125,760
Total liabilities and stockholders' equity		$324,540

* These amounts were taken directly from Requirement 4, the trial balance.
† Classified as "other" rather than "operational" because this land is not being used currently for operating purposes.

SUMMARY OF CHAPTER

An accounting system is designed to collect, process, and report financial information about an entity. During each period, an **accounting information processing cycle** starts with data collection and ends with the periodic financial statements. The phases of this sequential cycle were summarized in Exhibit 3–7.

The accounting model—Assets = Liabilities + Owners' Equity—gives the basic framework for transaction analysis and recording the dual effect of each transaction. The accounting model has two balancing features that must be met for each transaction: (1) assets must equal liabilities plus owners' equity and (2) debits must equal credits. After transaction analysis, the dual effects of each transaction are recorded first in the journal and then are posted to the ledger. The journal provides a chronological record of the transactions, and the ledger reflects a **separate account** for each kind of asset, liability, and owners' equity. Normally, asset accounts will have debit balances; liability accounts will have credit balances. Owners' equity accounts normally will show credit balances for the Capital Stock and Retained Earnings accounts; expenses will show debit balances; and revenues will show credit balances. The accounting information processing cycle accumulates the financial data needed to develop the periodic financial statements: the income statement, balance sheet, and statement of cash flows.

The chapter also gave an outline of the classifications on the required financial statements—income statement, balance sheet, and statement of cash flows.

IMPORTANT TERMS DEFINED IN THIS CHAPTER

Accounting Information Processing Cycle Sequential accounting phases used to process data from initial transaction to financial statements. *p. 94*

Accounting (or Reporting) Period Time period; usually one year; the period covered by the financial statements. *p. 94*

Accounting System Designed to collect, process, and report financial information about an entity. *p. 94*

Cost of Goods Sold An expense that represents the cost of purchasing goods and merchandise that were sold during the accounting period. *p. 104*

Current Assets Assets that are expected to be converted to cash within one year or the operating cycle if longer. *p. 106*

Current Liabilities Liabilities that will be paid by using current assets within one year or the operating cycle if longer. *p. 107*

Current Ratio The ratio of current assets divided by current liabilities. *p. 107*

Extraordinary Gain or Loss A gain or loss that is unusual and infrequent; separately reported on the income statement. *p. 104*

Gross Margin Sales revenue minus cost of goods sold. *p. 104*

Journal Entry   An original entry made in the journal in terms of: A = L + OE, and Debits = Credits. *p. 96*

Journalizing   Recording transactions in the journal; original entry; chronological order. *p. 96*

Ledger   Contains all of the individual accounts for assets, liabilities, and owners' equity. *p. 97*

Normal Operating Cycle of a Business   Used to define current assets and current liabilities; the time from cash to purchase of inventories; to sale on credit, and back to cash. *p. 106*

Operational Assets   Assets used to operate a business; not for resale; often called property, plant, and equipment. *p. 106*

Posting   Transferring data from the journal to the ledger. *p. 99*

Reporting Period   Same as accounting period (see above). *p. 94*

Trial Balance   A list of all of the accounts in the ledger and their balances. *p. 100*

Working Capital   Difference between total current assets and total current liabilities. *p. 107*

QUESTIONS

1. What is the function of an accounting system?
2. Explain the accounting information processing cycle.
3. How does a company collect the data needed for accounting purposes?
4. What is meant by transaction analysis?
5. Explain the meaning of "to debit" and "to credit."
6. Define the following terms: *(a)* accounting period and *(b)* reporting period.
7. What is the *(a)* book of original entry and *(b)* book of final entry?
8. Define the journal. What is its purpose?
9. Define the ledger. What is its purpose?
10. Explain the difference between journalizing and posting.
11. What is the purpose of the folio notations in the journal and in the ledger accounts?
12. What is a trial balance? What is its purpose?
13. What is an audit trail?
14. What is the primary purpose of the classifications of the information presented on financial statements?
15. What are the six major classifications on the income statement?
16. Define extraordinary items. Why should they be reported separately on the income statement?
17. List the six classifications of assets reported on a balance sheet.
18. Briefly define *(a)* current assets, *(b)* current liabilities, and *(c)* working capital.

19. What is a prepaid expense?
20. For operational assets, as reported on the balance sheet, explain *(a)* cost, *(b)* accumulated depreciation, *(c)* book value, and *(d)* carrying value.
21. What are the classifications of liabilities on a balance sheet?
22. Briefly explain the major classifications of owners' equity for a corporation.
23. What are the three major classifications on a statement of cash flows?

EXERCISES

E3–1 **(Match Definitions with Phases of the Accounting Information Processing Cycle)**
Match each definition with its related phrase by entering the appropriate letter in the space provided.

Phases (sequential order)	Definitions
_____ Data collection	A. Income statement, balance sheet, SCF.
_____ Transaction analysis	B. Transfer of amount for each account affected by the transaction; results in a reclassification of the data.
_____ Journalizing	C. A listing of each account and its debit or credit ending balance; checks Debits = Credits.
_____ Posting	D. Source documents that underlie each transaction.
_____ Trial balance	E. A chronological record is prepared that reflects the economic effects of each transaction.
_____ Financial statements	F. A careful study of each transaction and determination of its economic effects on the entity.

E3–2 **(Overview of the Accounting Information Processing Cycle)**
On January 1, 19A, Joe Hotstrike started the Hotstrike Electric Company (a single-owner business). During 19A, the company completed the following summarized transactions:

a. Cash invested by the owner, $20,000.
b. Service revenues earned, $80,000 (all cash).
c. Operating expenses incurred, $30,000 (all cash).
d. Cash withdrawn from the business by the owner, $4,000 per month for 12 months.

Required:
You are to process these four transactions through the accounting information processing cycle by phases as given below.

Phase 1—Collect information—already done above.

Phase 2—Analysis. Write your analysis of each transaction in terms of Assets = Liabilities + Owner's Equity, and Debits = Credits.

Phase 3—Journalize each transaction.

Phase 4—Post the journal entries to the ledger. Use only the following T-accounts: Cash, Owner's Equity, Hotstrike, Service Revenues, and Operating Expenses.

Phase 5—Prepare a trial balance.

Phase 6—Prepare the following financial statements:
  a. Income statement.
  b. Balance sheet.

E3–3 **(Write Journal Entries from T-accounts)**

The following T-accounts for Oakland Service Company, Inc., show five different transactions (entries). Prepare a journal entry for each transaction and write a complete description of each one. (Hint: Notice that some transactions have two debits or two credits.)

Cash					Accounts Payable				Capital Stock (Par $10)		
(a)	70,000	(c)	9,000	(e)	1,500	(c)	2,000		(a)		70,000
(b)	20,000	(e)	1,500								
(d)	2,000	(f)	5,000								

Accounts Receivable				Note Payable				Service Revenue		
(b)	4,000	(d)	2,000			(f)	15,000		(b)	24,000

Equipment			Operating Expenses		
(f)	20,000		(c)	11,000	

E3–4 **(Journalize and Compute Account Balances)**

On January 1, 19A, Wilson and Young organized the Metro Company, Inc. The completed transactions from January 1, 19A, through February 3, 19A, can be summarized as follows:

Jan. 1 Cash invested by the organizers was: Wilson, $30,000 (for 3,000 shares); and Young, $20,000 (for 2,000 shares).

  3 Paid monthly rent, $1,800.

  15 Purchased equipment for use in the business that cost $26,000; paid $2,000 down and signed a 10% note payable for the balance. Monthly payments made up of part principal and part interest are to be paid on the note.

  30 Paid cash for operating expenses amounting to $20,000; in addition, operating expenses of $4,000 were incurred on credit.

  30 Service fees earned amounted to $50,000, of which $40,000 was collected and the balance was on credit.

Feb. 1 Collected $6,000 on account for services performed in January and originally recorded as an account receivable and service revenue.

  2 Paid $3,000 on the operating expenses incurred in January and originally recorded as an account payable and operating expenses.

  3 Paid the first installment of $750 on the equipment note, including $200 interest expense.

Required:
1. Analyze and journalize each of the above transactions.
2. Based on your journal entries only, compute the following:
   a. Cash balance at February 3, 19A.
   b. Pretax income for the period January 1, 19A, through February 3, 19A.

E3–5 (Match Definitions with Terms)

Below are terms related to the income statement. Match each definition with its related term by entering the appropriate letter in the space provided.

Terms	Definitions
_____ Cost of goods sold	A. Sales revenue minus cost of goods sold.
_____ Interest expense	B. Items that are both unusual and infrequent.
_____ Extraordinary (EO) items	C. Sales of services for cash or on credit.
_____ Service revenue	D. Revenues + Gains − Expenses − Losses (including extraordinary [EO] items).
_____ Income tax expense on operations	E. Amount of resources used to purchase the goods that were sold during the reporting period.
_____ Income before EO items	F. Income tax on revenues minus operating expenses.
_____ Net income	G. Time cost of money (borrowing).
_____ Gross margin on sales	H. Income divided by shares outstanding.
_____ EPS	I. Income before EO items and the related income tax.
_____ Operating expenses	J. Total expenses directly related to operations.
_____ Pretax income from operations	K. Income before all income tax and before EO items.

E3–6 (Complete a Partial Income Statement with Income Tax and an Extraordinary Loss)

Orban Corporation (common stock, 10,000 shares outstanding) is preparing the income statement for the year ended December 31, 19D. The pretax operating income was $100,000, and there was a $30,000 pretax loss on earthquake damages to one of the plants (properly classified as an EO item). Total tax expense is $21,000 on the basis of a 30% tax rate on operations and on the earthquake loss.

Required:

1. Complete the following income statement:

    (Already completed to here)
    Pretax operating income
        Less: Income tax
    Income before EO items:
        EO loss
            Less: Income tax
    Net income
    Earnings per share

2. Why is the income tax of $21,000 separated into two parts?

E3–7   (Ordering the Classifications on a Typical Balance Sheet)

Following is a list of classifications on the balance sheet. Number them in the order in which they normally appear on a balance sheet.

No.	Titles
———	Current liabilities
———	Liabilities
———	Owners' equity
———	Long-term liabilities
———	Long-term investments
———	Intangible assets
———	Operational assets (property, plant, and equipment)
———	Current assets
———	Retained earnings
———	Contributed capital
———	Assets
———	Other assets
———	Deferred charges

E3–8 **(Match Definitions with Terms)**

Below are terms related to the balance sheet. Match each definition with its related term by entering the appropriate letter in the space provided.

Terms	Definitions
_____ Retained earnings	A. A miscellaneous category of assets.
_____ Current liabilities	B. Current assets minus current liabilities.
_____ Liquidity	C. Total assets minus total liabilities.
_____ Contra asset account	D. Nearness of assets to cash (in time).
_____ Accumulated depreciation	E. Assets expected to be collected in cash within one year or operating cycle, if longer.
_____ Intangible assets	
_____ Other assets	F. Same as carrying value; cost less accumulated depreciation to date.
_____ Shares outstanding	
_____ Normal operating cycle	G. Accumulated earnings minus accumulated dividends.
_____ Book value	H. Asset offset account (subtracted from asset).
_____ Working capital	I. Balance of the Capital Stock account divided by the par value per share.
_____ Liabilities	
_____ Operational assets	J. Assets that do not have physical substance.
_____ Owners' equity	K. Items owned by the business that have future economic values.
_____ Current assets	
_____ Assets	L. Liabilities expected to be paid out of current assets within the next year or operating cycle, if longer.
_____ Long-term liabilities	
	M. The average cash-to-cash time involved in the operations of the business.
	N. Sum of the annual depreciation expense on an asset from its acquisition to the current date.
	O. All liabilities not classified as current liabilities.
	P. Property, plant, and equipment.
	Q. Obligations to give up (pay) economic benefits in the future.

E3–9 **(Classification of Investments in Common Stock on the Investor's Balance Sheet)**

Brown Corporation is preparing its annual financial statements at December 31, 19B. The company has two investments in shares of other corporations:

a. Common stock of X Corporation: 1,000 shares purchased for $80,000 during 19A. X Corporation is a supplier of parts to Brown Corporation; therefore, the latter "intends to hold the stock indefinitely." The shares acquired represented 2% of the shares outstanding. X stock was selling at $95 at the end of 19B.

b. Common stock of Y Corporation: purchased 500 shares at a cost of $60 per share on August 15, 19B. Brown made this investment to "temporarily use some idle cash that probably will be needed next year." Y stock was selling at $80 at the end of 19B.

Required:

Illustrate and explain the basis for the classification and amount that should be reported for each investment on the 19B balance sheet of Brown Corporation.

E3–10   (Prepare a Simple Statement of Cash Flows)

At the end of the annual reporting period, December 31, 19B, the records of Xtra Company showed the following:

a. Cash account: beginning balance, $36,000; ending balance, $17,000.

b. From the income statement:
  - (1) Cash revenues $180,000
  - (2) Cash expenses   135,000

c. From the balance sheet:
  - (1) Additional capital stock sold: common stock, par $10; sold 2,000 shares at $15 per share.
  - (2) Borrowed cash on a long-term note, $25,000.
  - (3) Purchased equipment for use in the business: paid cash, $75,000.
  - (4) Paid a long-term note, $20,000.
  - (5) Declared and paid a cash dividend, $14,000.
  - (6) Purchased land for employee parking lot, $10,000.

Required:

1. Prepare the 19B statement of cash flows for Xtra Company.
2. Prove your answer.

PROBLEMS

P3–1   (Journalize, Post, and Compute Account Balances)

Art Air Conditioning Service Company, Incorporated, has been operating for three years. In the past, few records were kept; however, Art now realizes the need for a complete accounting system. The following selected transactions were completed during January 19E:

Jan. 1   Purchased three new service trucks at $12,000 each; paid $12,000 down and signed a one-year, 12% interest-bearing note for the balance. Twelve monthly payments, each including principal and interest, are to be made on the note.

31   Service revenue earned in January amounted to $85,000, which included $10,000 on credit (due in 90 days).

31   Operating expenses incurred in January amounted to $60,000, which included $4,000 on credit (payable in 60 days).

31   Dividends declared and paid of $8,000 in cash to the stockholders.

31   Paid $2,132 on the truck note, which included $240 interest.

31   Collected $4,400 on the services extended on credit in January.

Required:

1. Analyze and journalize each of the above transactions. Number the first journal page, 51; etc.

2. Post the journal entries to the following T-accounts. Use folio numbers.

Account No.	Account titles	Balance, January 1, 19E
101	Cash	$40,000 (debit)
102	Accounts receivable	20,000 (debit)
103	Trucks	None
104	Accounts payable	9,000 (credit)
105	Note payable	None
106	Retained earnings	80,000 (credit)
107	Service revenue	None
108	Operating expenses	None
109	Interest expense	None

Remaining accounts—not needed.

3. Compute the following amounts based on the above data only:
    a. Cash balance at the end of January 19E.
    b. Pretax income for the month of January 19E.

P3–2   (Complete Phase 2, Transaction Analysis, and Phase 3, Journalize)
Barton, Incorporated, was organized by four persons during January 19A. Each investor paid $12,500 cash, and each received 750 shares of $15 par value stock. During 19A, the transactions listed below occurred (Phase 1). The letters at the left of each item will serve as the date notation.

a. Received the $50,000 investment of cash by the organizers and issued the shares.
b. Purchased office equipment that cost $6,000; paid cash.
c. Paid $400 cash for a two-year insurance policy on the office equipment for 19A and 19B (debit the asset account, Prepaid Insurance, because the premium is paid in advance on this date).
d. Purchased a delivery truck at a cost of $12,000; paid $7,000 down and signed a $5,000, 90-day, 12% interest-bearing note payable for the balance.
e. Purchased office supplies for cash to be used in the stenographic and mailing operations, $2,000. The supplies are for future use (therefore, debit the asset account, Office Supplies Inventory—an asset account because they have not yet been used).
f. Revenues earned during the year were:

	Cash	On credit
Stenographic fees . . .	$55,000	$14,000
Mailing fees	8,000	2,000

g. Operating expenses incurred during the year were (excluding transactions [h] through [i]):

Cash	$26,000
On credit	14,000

h. Paid the $5,000 note on the panel truck. Cash paid out was for the $5,000 principal plus the interest for three months.
i. Purchased land for a future building site at a cost of $20,000; paid cash.

j. Depreciation on the truck for 19A was computed on the basis of a three-year useful life; on the office equipment, a useful life of five years was assumed (compute full-year depreciation on each and assume no residual value).

k. By December 31, 19A, insurance for one year had expired. Prepaid Insurance should be decreased and an expense recorded because half of the insurance was "used" during 19A.

l. An inventory of the office supplies reflected $300 on hand at December 31, 19A. Supplies Inventory should be reduced and an expense recognized because some, but not all, of the supplies were used in 19A.

m. Income tax expense, based on a 20% rate, was $5,190 (to be paid in 19B).

Required:

1. Analyze and journalize each of the above transactions. Write a brief explanation after each journal entry.
2. What was the balance in the Cash account at the end of 19A?

P3–3   (Complete an Income Statement with Income Tax, Extraordinary Gain, and EPS)
Spectra Company, Inc., was organized on January 1, 19A. On that date, 10,000 shares of common stock were issued to three owners for $150,000 cash.

At the end of the first year, December 31, 19A, the company records showed the following:

a. Merchandise sold: for cash, $200,000; on credit, $20,000.

b. Interest on debt; paid in cash, $2,000.

c. Salaries and wages paid in cash, $53,000.

d. Other operating expenses, $5,000, incurred (used) but not yet paid.

e. Cost of the merchandise sold, $100,000.

f. Services sold (all for cash), $10,000.

g. Extraordinary (EO) gain, $10,000 (subject to income tax).

h. Average corporate income tax rate on all items, 25%.

Required:

a. Complete the following income statement for the year, 19A:

Revenues

Expenses:
    Cost of goods sold
    Operating expenses
    Interest expense
Pretax income from operations
    Income tax expense
Income before EO item
    EO gain
        Less: Income tax
Net income
EPS

b. What was the total amount of income tax for 19A?

c. Explain why the cash paid by the organizers is not considered to be revenue.

P3–4   **(Prepare a Balance Sheet and Analyze Some of Its Parts)**

Master Jewelers is developing the annual financial statements for 19C. The following amounts were correct at December 31, 19C: cash, $41,200; accounts receivable, $55,200; merchandise inventory, $110,000; prepaid insurance, $600; investment in stock of Z corporation (long term), $31,000; store equipment, $50,000; used store equipment held for disposal, $9,000; accumulated depreciation, store equipment, $10,000; accounts payable, $50,000; long-term note payable, $40,000; income taxes payable, $7,000; retained earnings, $80,000; and common stock, 100,000 shares outstanding, par $1 per share (originally sold and issued at $1.10 per share).

Required:
1. Based on the above data, prepare a 19C balance sheet. Use the following major captions (list the individual items under these captions):

   Assets: Current assets, Long-term investments and funds, Operational assets, and Other assets.

   Liabilities: Current liabilities, and Long-term liabilities.

   Stockholders' equity: Contributed capital, and Retained earnings.

2. What is the book or carrying value of the:
   a. Inventory?
   b. Accounts receivable?
   c. Store equipment?
   d. Note payable (long term)?
   Explain what these values mean.
3. What is the amount of working capital?

P3–5   **(Prepare the Stockholders' Equity Section of a Balance Sheet)**

At the end of the 19A annual reporting period, the balance sheet of Balcones Corporation showed the following:

BALCONES CORPORATION
Balance Sheet
At December 31, 19A

Stockholders' Equity

Contributed capital:	
Common stock (par $10; 6,000 shares) . . .	$ 60,000
Contributed capital in excess of par	10,000
Total contributed capital	70,000
Retained earnings:	
Ending balance	40,000
Total stockholders' equity	$110,000

During 19B, the following selected transactions (summarized) were completed:

a. Sold and issued 1,000 shares of the common stock at $16 cash per share (at year-end).

b. Net income, $30,000.

c. Declared and paid a cash dividend on the beginning shares outstanding of $4 per share.

Required:

1. Prepare the stockholders' equity section of the balance sheet at December 31, 19B.

2. Give the journal entry to record the sale and issuance of the 1,000 shares of common stock.

P3–6 **(Complete Phase 6, Income Statement and Balance Sheet, from a Trial Balance)**
Mission Real Estate Company (organized as a corporation on April 1, 19A) has completed Phase 1 (data collection), Phase 2 (analyses), Phase 3 (journal entries), and Phase 4 (posting) for the second year, ended March 31, 19C. Mission also has completed a correct trial balance (Phase 5) as follows:

MISSION REAL ESTATE COMPANY
Trial Balance
At March 31, 19C

Account titles	Debit	Credit
Cash	$ 41,000	
Accounts receivable	53,800	
Office supplies inventory	200	
Automobiles (company cars)	26,000	
Accumulated depreciation, automobiles		$ 12,000
Office equipment	2,000	
Accumulated depreciation, office equipment		1,000
Accounts payable		12,150
Income taxes payable		
Salaries and commissions payable		1,000
Note payable, long term		20,000
Capital stock (par $1; 30,000 shares)		30,000
Contributed capital in excess of par		5,000
Retained earnings (on April 1, 19B)		7,350
Dividends declared and paid during the current year	10,000	
Sales commissions earned		90,000
Management fees earned		8,000
Operating expenses (detail omitted to conserve your time)	46,000	
Depreciation expense (on autos and including $333 on office equipment)	6,000	
Interest expense	1,500	
Income tax expense (not yet computed)		
Totals	$186,500	$186,500

Required:

1. Complete the financial statements, as follows:

   a. Income statement for the reporting year ended March 31, 19C. Include income tax expense, assuming a 30% tax rate. Use the following major captions: Revenues, Expenses, Pretax income, Income tax, Net income, and EPS (list each item under these captions).

   b. Balance sheet at the end of the reporting year, March 31, 19C. Include (1) income taxes for the current year in income taxes payable, and (2) dividends in retained earnings. Use the captions that follow (list each item under these captions).

Assets
Current assets
Operational assets

Liabilities
Current liabilities
Long-term liabilities

Stockholders' Equity
Contributed capital
Retained earnings

2. Give the journal entry to record income taxes for the year (not yet paid).

P3–7 **(Reporting Building, Land, and Depreciation Expense)**
Hudson Company is preparing the balance sheet at December 31, 19X. The following assets are to be reported:

1. Building, purchased 15 years ago (counting 19X): original cost, $330,000; estimated useful life, 25 years from date of purchase; and no residual value.
2. Land, purchased 15 years ago (counting 19X): original cost, $50,000.

Required:

a. Show how the two assets should be reported on the balance sheet. What is the total book value of these operational assets?

b. What amount of depreciation expense should be reported on the 19X income statement? Show computations.

P3–8 **(Prepare a Simple Statement of Cash Flows)**
Anderson Corporation is preparing its annual financial statements at December 31, 19A, its first year of operations. The following cash flow data have been determined to be correct for 19A:

a. Sales and service revenues, $300,000, including $15,000 on credit and not yet collected.

b. Expenses, $256,000, including $6,000 noncash items.

c. Borrowed cash, $20,000, on a three-year note payable (10% interest payable each year-end). The note was dated December 31, 19A.

d. Purchased a new delivery truck for $14,000 cash.

e. Issued stock for $15,000 cash.

f. Purchased a tract of land for a future building site that cost $24,000; paid cash.

g. Cash account: balance, January 1, 19A, $36,000; and balance, December 31, 19A, $68,000.

Required:

1. Prepare the 19A statement of cash flows for Anderson Corporation.

2. Prove your answer.

P3–9 **(Completion of the First Six Phases of the Accounting Information Processing Cycle)**
Spring Company, Inc., was started on January 1, 19A. During the first year ended December 31, 19A (end of the accounting period), the following summarized entries were completed:

Date	Transactions
a.	Issued 20,000 shares of its common stock (par $1 per share) for $80,000 cash.
b.	Purchased equipment for use in operations that cost $40,000 cash. Estimated life, 10 years.
c.	Borrowed $50,000 cash on a long-term note payable (10% interest).
d.	Revenues earned, $98,000, of which $8,000 was on credit (not yet collected at year-end).
e.	Expenses incurred (including interest on the note payable), $60,000, of which $5,000 was on credit (not yet paid at year-end).
f.	Paid cash dividend, $10,000. (Hint: Debit Retained Earnings.)
g.	Recorded depreciation expense. Assume no income tax.

Required:

Process the above transactions through the accounting information processing cycle by phases as follows:

Phase 1—Collect information about each transaction; already done above.

Phase 2—Analysis; write your analysis of each transaction in terms of: Assets = Liabilities + Stockholders' Equity, and Debits = Credits.

Phase 3—Journalize each transaction. Start your journal with page 1. Use the date letters for identification of transactions.

Phase 4—Post the journal entries to the ledger accounts (as you complete each journal entry or after the last journal entry). Set up the following ledger accounts and account numbers: Cash, 101; Accounts Receivable, 102; Equipment, 105; Accumulated Depreciation, 106; Accounts Payable, 201; Note Payable, Long Term, 205; Common Stock, 301; Contributed Capital in Excess of Par, 302; Retained Earnings, 303; Revenues, 310; and Expenses, 315.

Phase 5—Prepare a trial balance.

Phase 6—Prepare the following 19A financial statements:

    a. Income statement.

    b. Balance sheet.

P3–10 **(Comprehensive Problem: Completion of the First Six Phases of the Accounting Information Processing Cycle)**

Home Realty is a corporation that conducts a real estate and rental management business. The transactions listed below, representative of those during the first year (19A), were selected from the actual transactions.

Assume that these transactions comprise all of the transactions for 19A. All of the accounts needed in the ledger are given below (Phase 1). Use the letters given at the left as the date notation.

a. Received $60,000 cash invested by three stockholders and issued 4,500 shares of stock (par value is $10 per share).

b. On January 1, 19A, purchased office equipment that cost $6,000; paid one-third cash and charged the balance (one third due in 6 months, and the remaining third is due in 12 months). Credit Accounts Payable for the amount not paid in cash.

c. Purchased land for future office site: cost, $20,000; paid cash.

d. Paid office rent in cash, 12 months at $200 per month (debit Rent Expense).

e. Sold nine properties and collected sales commissions of $56,000.

f. Paid salaries and commissions expense to salespersons amounting to $52,000 and miscellaneous expenses amounting to $1,000.

g. Collected rental management fees, $30,000.

h. Paid utilities, $1,400.

i. Paid auto rental fees (auto rented for use in business), $3,600.

j. Paid for advertising, $7,500.

k. The estimated life of the office equipment was 10 years; assume use for the full year in 19A and no residual value.

l. Additional commissions earned during 19A on sale of real estate amounted to $64,000, of which $14,000 was uncollected at year-end.

m. Paid the installment of $2,000 on the office equipment (see [b] above). Assume no interest.

n. 19A income tax expense of $24,000 will be paid in 19B.

Required:

1. Set up T-accounts as follows (no beginning balances because this is the first year):

Account No.	Account titles	Account No.	Account titles
101	Cash	402	Rental management revenue
102	Accounts receivable	501	Rent expense
103	Office equipment	502	Salary and commission expense
104	Accumulated depreciation, office equipment	503	Miscellaneous expenses
105	Land for future office site	504	Utilities expense
201	Accounts payable	505	Auto rental expense
203	Income taxes payable	506	Advertising expense
301	Capital stock (par $10)	507	Depreciation expense
302	Contributed capital in excess of par	508	Income tax expense
401	Realty commission revenue		

2. Complete Phase 2 (analyze) and Phase 3 (journalize) each of the above transactions. Use the journal format shown in Exhibit 3–2. Use the letters for dates. Number the journal pages starting with 1. Write a brief explanation of each entry.

3. Complete Phase 4—Post each transaction from the journal to the ledger. Use folio cross-references when posting. You may post each entry as it is made, or wait until all of the journal entries are made.

4. Complete Phase 5—Prepare a trial balance.

5. Complete Phase 6—Prepare the following 19A financial statements:

   a. Income statement—major captions:
      Revenues, Expenses, Pretax income, Income tax expense, Net income, and EPS (enter individual items under each).

   b. Balance sheet—major captions:
      Assets: Current assets, Operational assets, and Other assets.
      Liabilities: Current liabilities.
      Stockholders' equity: Contributed capital, and Retained earnings.
      (Enter individual items under each.)

P3–11   **(A Challenging Analysis of the Amounts on an Income Statement)**

Below is a partially completed income statement of McDonald Corporation for the year ended December 31, 19B.

Items	Other Data		Amounts
Net sales revenue			$200,000
Cost of goods sold			
Gross margin on sales	Gross margin as percent of sales, 65%		
Expenses: Selling expense			
General and admin- istrative expense		$23,000	
Interest expense		2,000	
Total expenses			
Pretax income			
Income tax on operations			
Income before EO* items:			
EO gain		10,000	
Income tax effect			
Net EO gain			
Net income			
EPS (on common stock): Income before EO gain			1.00
EO gain			
Net income			

* EO = Extraordinary.

Required:

Based on the data given above, and assuming (1) a 20% income tax rate on all items and (2) 20,000 common shares outstanding, complete the above income statement. Show all computations.

CASES

C3-1   (Analysis of Financial Statements)

The amounts listed below were selected from the annual financial statements for Small Corporation at December 31, 19C (end of the third year of operations):

From the 19C income statement:

Sales revenue	$ 300,000
Cost of goods sold	(180,000)
All other expenses (including income tax)	(90,000)
Net income	$ 30,000

From the December 31, 19C, balance sheet:

Current assets	$ 100,000
All other assets	265,000
Total assets	$ 365,000
Current liabilities	$ 60,000
Long-term liabilities	79,000
Capital stock (par $10)	150,000
Contributed capital in excess of par	15,000
Retained earnings	61,000
Total liabilities and stockholders' equity	$ 365,000

Required:

Analyze the data on the 19C financial statements of Small by answering the questions that follow. Show computations.

a. What was the gross margin on sales?

b. What was the amount of EPS?

c. What was the amount of working capital?

d. If the income tax rate were 25%, what was the amount of pretax income?

e. What was the average sales price per share of the capital stock?

f. Assuming no dividends were declared or paid during 19C, what was the beginning balance (January 1, 19C) of retained earnings?

C3-2   (Identification and Correction of Several Accounting Errors)

The bookkeeper of Careless Company prepared the following trial balance at December 31, 19B:

Account titles	Debit	Credit
Notes receivable	$ 4,000	
Supplies inventory		$ 200
Accounts payable	800	
Land	16,000	
Capital stock		20,000
Cash	7,045	
Interest revenue	200	
Note payable		5,000
Operating expenses	19,000	
Interest expense		800
Other assets	9,583	
Service revenue		30,583
Totals	$56,583	$56,583

An independent CPA (auditor) casually inspected the trial balance and saw that it had several errors. Draft a correct trial balance and explain any errors that you discover. All of the amounts are correct except "Other assets."

C3–3   (A Complex Situation that Requires Technical Analysis of an Income Statement; Challenging)

Simon Lavoie, a local attorney, decided to sell his practice and retire. He has had discussions with an attorney from another state who wants to relocate. The discussions are at the complex stage of agreeing on a price. Among the important factors have been the financial statements on Lavoie's practice. Lavoie's secretary, under his direction, maintained the records. Each year they developed a "Statement of Profits" on a cash basis from the incomplete records maintained, and no balance sheet was prepared. Upon request, Lavoie provided the other attorney with the following statements for 1990 prepared by his secretary:

S. LAVOIE
Statement of Profits
1990

Legal fees collected		$92,000
Expenses paid:		
Rent for office space	$10,400	
Utilities expense	360	
Telephone expense	2,900	
Office salaries expense	19,000	
Office supplies expense	900	
Miscellaneous expenses	1,600	
Total expenses		35,160
Profit for the year		$56,840

Upon agreement of the parties, you have been asked to "examine the financial figures for 1990." The other attorney said: "I question the figures because, among other things, they appear to be on a 100% cash basis." Your investigations revealed the following additional data at December 31, 1990:

a. Of the $92,000 legal fees collected in 1990, $28,000 was for services performed prior to 1990.

b. At the end of 1990, legal fees of $7,000 for services performed during the year were uncollected.

c. Office equipment owned and used by Lavoie cost $3,000 and had an estimated remaining useful life of 10 years.

d. An inventory of office supplies at December 31, 1990, reflected $200 worth of items purchased during the year that were still on hand. Also, the records for 1989 indicate that the supplies on hand at the end of that year were about $125.

e. At the end of 1990 a secretary, whose salary is $12,000 per year, had not been paid for December because of a long trip that extended to January 15, 1991.

f. The phone bill for December 1990, amounting to $1,500, was not paid until January 11, 1991.

g. The office rent paid of $10,400 was for 13 months (it included the rent for January 1991).

Required:

a. On the basis of the above information, prepare a correct income statement for 1990. Show your computations for any amounts changed from those in the statement prepared by Lavoie's secretary. (Suggested solution format with four column headings: Items; Cash Basis per Lavoie Statement, $; Explanation of Changes; and Corrected Basis, $.)

b. Write a comment to support your schedule prepared in *(a)*. The purpose should be to explain the reasons for your changes and to suggest some other important items that should be considered in the pricing decision.

C3–4 **(Information Processing Based on an Actual Company)**

JCPenney · Refer to the financial statements of J.C. Penney Company, Inc. given in the appendix immediately preceding the index.

1. Give examples of business documents that are analyzed by the company's accountants to record sales transactions.

2. How should the company record the payment of $1,000 on account by one of its credit customers?

3. How should the company record the purchase of $12,000 of inventory on credit from one of its suppliers?

4. Does the collection of an account receivable by J.C. Penney affect its total assets?

5. The company does not report depreciation expense on the Statement of Income. Why?

FOUR

ADJUSTING ENTRIES AND THE CONCEPTUAL FRAMEWORK OF ACCOUNTING

PURPOSE

This chapter continues the discussion of the accounting information cycle. Certain transactions affect more than one accounting period. At the end of each accounting period, a group of entries called adjusting entries are made to allocate the effects of these transactions to the proper accounting periods.

Accounting procedures (such as adjusting entries) rest on a theoretical foundation called the conceptual framework of accounting. Part B of this chapter introduces this framework which explains the "why" of accounting.

The example on the opposite page illustrates the full-disclosure principle which requires reporting of relevant accounting and non-accounting information.

LEARNING OBJECTIVES

1. Explain the revenue and matching principles.
2. Prepare adjusting entries.
3. Identify and explain the essential characteristics of accounting information.
4. Give an overview of the conceptual framework of accounting.
5. Use the conceptual framework as a qualitative supplement while studying the other chapters.
6. Expand your accounting vocabulary by learning the "Important Terms Defined in This Chapter."
7. Apply the knowledge learned from this chapter by completing the homework assigned by your instructor.

ORGANIZATION

Part A—adjusting entries
1. Accrual basis accounting.
2. Types of adjusting entries.
3. Adjusting entries illustrated.

Part B—conceptual framework of accounting
1. Essential characteristics of accounting information.
2. Fundamental concepts of accounting: assumptions, principles, constraints, elements of financial statements, and detailed practices and procedures.

The Year in Numbers

The following is a presentation of selected financial and operational statistics for fiscal 1988 compared with fiscal 1987, which included results of Western Air Lines, Inc. ("Western") as a wholly-owned subsidiary after December 18, 1986. On April 1, 1987, Western was merged into Delta. Dollar amounts are expressed in thousands, except per share figures.

	1988	1987	Per Cent Change
Operating Revenues	$ 6,915,377	$ 5,318,172	+30%
Operating Expenses	6,418,293	4,913,647	+31
Operating Income	497,084	404,525	+23
Net Income	306,826	263,729	+16
Net Income Per Share	6.30	5.90	+ 7
Dividends Paid	58,456	44,397	+32
Dividends Paid Per Share	1.20	1.00	+20
Stockholders' Equity Per Share	44.99	39.84	+13
Average Number of Common Shares Outstanding	48,706,851	44,712,993	+ 9
Debt-to-Equity Position	25%/75%	35%/65%	—
Revenue Passengers Enplaned	58,564,507	48,172,626	+22
Revenue Passenger Miles (000)	49,009,094	38,415,117	+28
Available Seat Miles (000)	85,833,959	69,013,669	+24
Passenger Mile Yield	13.15¢	12.81¢	+ 3
Passenger Load Factor	57.10%	55.66%	+ 3
Breakeven Passenger Load Factor	52.69%	51.09%	+ 3
Cargo Ton Miles (000)	652,833	480,969	+36
Cargo Yield Per Ton Mile	53.58¢	58.27¢	− 8
Total Fuel Gallons Consumed (000)	1,753,538	1,435,801	+22
Average Fuel Price Per Gallon	56.09¢	46.80¢	+20
Revenue Passenger Miles Per Fuel Gallon	27.9	26.8	+ 4
Available Seat Miles Per Fuel Gallon	49.0	48.1	+ 2
Average Seats Per Aircraft Mile	169.0	169.2	—
Cost Per Available Seat Mile	7.48¢	7.12¢	+ 5
Average Passenger Trip Length in Miles	837	797	+ 5
Average Aircraft Flight Length in Miles	640	617	+ 4
Average Aircraft Utilization (Hours Per Day)	8.62	8.37	+ 3

PART A—ADJUSTING ENTRIES

In the previous chapter, we discussed the first phases of the accounting information processing cycle. This chapter introduces a special type of journal entry that is made at the end of the accounting period. These entries are called **adjusting entries.** Before we discuss how adjusting entries are made, we will see why these entries are necessary.

Accrual Basis Accounting

Accrual basis accounting is required under generally accepted accounting principles (GAAP). Accrual basis accounting means that all **completed transactions** are recorded when they occur, regardless of when any related cash receipts or payments occur. In contrast, **cash basis accounting** means that transactions are recorded only when the related cash is received or paid. Cash basis accounting is not in conformity with GAAP.

Accrual basis accounting requires application of the revenue and matching principles.

The **revenue principle** specifies that revenues are **earned** (i.e., recognized) in the period when the revenue transaction occurs, rather than when the cash is collected. Therefore, the total amount of revenues reported on the income statement should include sales and service revenue collected in cash and those on credit. Similarly, when revenue is collected in advance, revenue should be reported on the income statement for the period in which it is earned, rather than in the period that the cash is received. Assume rent revenue of $1,200 is collected on December 1, 19A, for 12 months' future occupancy ending November 30, 19B. If the accounting year ends on December 31, rent revenue **earned** in 19A would be $100 and, in 19B, $1,100. These amounts would be reported on the 19A and 19B income statements.

To apply the **revenue principle,** the general guideline is that revenue is considered earned when the **earning process** is substantially completed. In the case of the sale of merchandise, the earning process is substantially completed when the ownership of the merchandise passes from the seller to the buyer. In the case of the sale of services, the earning process is substantially completed as the services are performed (rather than when the services finally are completed in all respects).

Expenses are reported on the income statement for the period when the goods or services are **used or consumed.** In some cases, the expense-incurring services and merchandise are obtained on credit whereby the cash is paid in a later period; and in other cases, the cash is paid in advance of use of the merchandise or services. In each of these cases, the date of the cash flow is not used to determine the period in which the expense should be reported on the income statement. The general guideline for expenses is that they should be matched with the revenues they produce. This is called the **matching principle.** For example, the cost of a TV set that is sold in 19A should be matched with the revenue by reporting both on the 19A income statement. If the TV set had not sold until 19B, the cost of the set would be matched with revenue by reporting both on the 19B income statement.

To apply the matching principle, it is necessary to consider the **purposes** for which the expenses were incurred. If the expenses are associated with a specific revenue, as is the usual case, the expenses should be identified with the period in which that revenue was earned. Resources used in one period to earn revenues in other periods should be assigned to those other periods. Some expenses, such as general company overhead and institutional advertising, do not have a direct relationship to the revenues of a specific accounting period. Therefore, such expenses are recognized on the income statement of the period in which they were incurred.

Accrual Basis Accounting and the Time-Period Assumption

The life span of most businesses is indefinite. However, decision makers need **current** information about the business. Therefore, the life span of a business is divided into a series of short time periods, such as one year, for many financial reporting purposes. This division of the activities of a business into a series of equal time periods is known as the **time-period assumption.**

The accounting period usually is 12 consecutive months. Many companies use a year that corresponds to the natural cycle of their business, such as July 1 through June 30, rather than to the calendar year.

In addition to the annual financial statements, many businesses prepare and publish quarterly financial reports for external distribution. These statements are called **interim reports.** In addition to external reports, monthly financial statements often are prepared exclusively for **internal management** purposes. These internal reports may be prepared several times each year.

Dividing the life span of a business into short time periods, such as a year, for measurement purposes often causes complex accounting problems because **some transactions start in one accounting period and are concluded in a subsequent period.** For example:

a. A machine that is purchased in year 19A will be depreciated over its estimated useful life of 10 years.

b. Rent is collected in one year for six months in advance, and two of the occupancy periods (months) extend into the next year.

c. An insurance premium on property is paid in advance for two years of future coverage.

When a transaction overlaps two or more accounting periods, the effects of the transaction must be separated between the periods. Measurement of revenues and expenses is complicated because both revenue and expense transactions may start in one period and extend over one or more future periods. At the end of each accounting period, journal entries often must be made to reflect transactions whose effects extend beyond the year in which the initial transaction occurred. These entries are called **adjusting entries.**

Adjusting Entries

Adjusting entries are made to change certain account balances at the end of the accounting period. For example, assume a company purchased a machine for use in the business on January 1, 19A. The machine cost $50,000 and had an estimated useful life of five years (no residual value). On January 1, 19A, an asset account—Machinery—was debited (increased) for $50,000. By December 31, 19A (end of the first accounting period), the machine had depreciated to $40,000. Therefore, due to an internal economic event (use of the machine), an **adjusting entry** must be made to (a) decrease the book value of the asset by $10,000 and (b) record depreciation expense of $10,000.

Adjusting entries have four basic characteristics as follows:

1. An **income statement** account balance (revenue or expense) is changed.
2. A **balance sheet** account balance (asset or liability) is changed.
3. They usually are recorded at the end of the accounting period.
4. They never directly affect the Cash account.

The four different types of adjusting entries are as follows:

Revenues (revenue principle applied):

1. **Revenue collected in advance but not yet earned.**   Revenue collected in advance of being **earned** must be deferred to the future period or periods in which it will be earned. In this case, cash collection precedes revenue recognition.

    Example: On December 1, 19A, Alpha Company collected $1,000 cash for December 19A and January 19B rent (i.e., $500 per month). On the transaction date, the company debited Cash and credited Rent Revenue for $1,000.

    Analysis on December 31, 19A: Rent revenue was earned in 19A for only one month, December; the other monthly rent will be earned in 19B; however, cash was collected in 19A for both months. Therefore, on December 31, 19A, an **adjusting entry** for $500 must be made to (a) decrease (debit) Rent Revenue and (b) increase (credit) Rent Revenue Collected in Advance. The $500 credit balance in this account must be reported on the 19A balance sheet as a **liability** because the company owes the renter occupancy for one month (January 19B).

2. **Revenue earned but not yet recorded or collected.**   Revenue not collected or recorded but earned in the current accounting period should be recorded as **earned** in the current period, even though the related cash will be collected in a subsequent period. In this case, cash collection lags revenue recognition.

    Example: On December 31, 19A, Alpha Company finished two phases of a service job for a customer; the third phase will be done in January

19B. The total contract price was $1,200 (i.e., $400 per phase) cash, payable on completion of all phases.

Analysis on December 31, 19A: Service revenue of $800 (i.e., $1,200 × 2/3) was earned in 19A, although not yet recorded or collected. Therefore, an **adjusting entry** for $800 must be made on December 31, 19A. This entry will (*a*) increase (debit) Accounts Receivable and (*b*) increase (credit) Service Revenue because revenue for the first two phases has been earned in 19A. A receivable must be recorded because the collection of cash will be made in 19B.

Expenses (matching principle applied):

3. **Expense paid in advance but not yet incurred.** Expense paid in advance of use of the services or goods must be deferred to the future period, or periods, in which such services or goods will be used. In this case, cash payment precedes expense recognition.

Example: On January 1, 19A, Alpha Company paid a two-year premium of $800 for property insurance; the coverage is for 19A and 19B (i.e., $400 per year). The company recorded this transaction on January 1, 19A, as a debit (increase) of $800 to Prepaid Insurance (an asset) and a decrease (credit) to Cash.

Analysis on December 31, 19A: On this date, half of the benefit of the insurance coverage has been used (i.e., $800 ÷ 2 = $400); the other half remains prepaid. Therefore, on December 31, 19A, an **adjusting entry** for $400 must be made to (*a*) increase (debit) Insurance Expense and (*b*) decrease (credit) Prepaid Insurance. This entry records the $400 expense for 19A and leaves $400 in the asset account, Prepaid Insurance. Prepaid insurance is an asset because Alpha Company has an obligation from the insurance company to provide insurance coverage for 19B (the premium already has been paid).

4. **Expense incurred but not yet recorded or paid.** Expense incurred (the services or goods have been used) in the current accounting period but not yet recorded or paid should be recorded as expense in the current period. In this case, cash payment occurs after expense recognition.

Example: On December 31, 19A, Alpha Company employees have earned $1,000 in wages that will be paid in cash on the next payroll date, January 6, 19B.

Analysis on December 31, 19A: The company has incurred wage expense in 19A of $1,000 (the employees were helping to earn 19A revenues). Because the employees have not been paid, the company has a $1,000 liability on December 31, 19A. Therefore, an **adjusting entry** for $1,000 must be made on December 31, 19A. This entry will (*a*) debit (increase) Wage Expense and (*b*) credit (increase) Wages Payable. This liability will be reported on the 19A balance sheet and will be paid on the next payroll date, January 6, 19B.

In summary, adjusting entries usually are made at the end of each accounting period, after the regular entries are completed. At this time, the accountant must make a careful check of the records and supporting documents to determine whether there are any cases such as those listed above that need **adjusting entries.** In most cases, adjusting entries will be required. If any required adjusting entries are not made, revenue and expenses for the period may be measured incorrectly. The result would be an incorrect measurement of amounts on both the income statement and the balance sheet for both the current and subsequent period or periods.

Terminology—Accrued and Deferred

Accountants often use two technical terms in respect to adjusting entries and in a more general sense. **Accrued,** in the case of expenses, means not yet paid; in the case of revenues, not yet collected. **Deferred,** in the case of revenues, means collected in advance; in the case of expenses, paid in advance. To summarize:

Terms	Definitions	Examples
1. Accrued expense.	An expense incurred but not yet paid.	Wages earned by employees but not yet paid.
2. Accrued revenue.	A revenue earned but not yet collected.	Services performed in advance of collection.
3. Deferred (or unearned) revenue.	A revenue not yet earned but collected in advance.	Rent collected in advance of occupancy.
4. Deferred (or prepaid) expense.	An expense not yet incurred but paid in advance.	Insurance premium paid in advance.

Adjusting Entries Illustrated (a Case Study)

This section of the chapter continues the discussion of adjusting entries. It provides detailed illustrations and explanations of numerous adjusting entries. Our emphasis will be on the **analysis** of specific examples to determine the appropriate adjusting entry and the related entries that are made in subsequent periods. Throughout the examples we will refer to High-Rise Apartments, Inc. (organized as a corporation on January 1, 19A), and will assume that the current annual accounting period ends December 31, 19B. Adjusting entries are entered in the journal and posted to the ledger accounts. All adjusting entries are recorded and dated at the end of the accounting period.

Revenue Collected in Advance (Deferred Revenue)

Businesses may collect cash and record it in advance of earning the related revenue. The amount collected in advance is called **unearned or deferred revenue.** Unearned revenue must be apportioned to the period in which the services are performed or the sale is completed in conformity with the **revenue principle.**

When a business has unearned revenue, an **adjusting entry** usually is required. This entry will recognize (1) the correct amount of revenue **earned** during the current period and (2) the remaining obligation in the future to provide the related goods or services.

Example: On December 11, 19B, two tenants paid rent for one month from December 11, 19B, through January 10, 19C, in the amount of $1,500. The sequence of entries recorded by High-Rise is:

December 11, 19B—date of the transaction:

```
Cash . . . . . . . . . . . . . . . . . . . . . . . . . . . . . . . . . . . . . . . . 1,500
    Rent revenue . . . . . . . . . . . . . . . . . . . . . . . . . . . . . .        1,500
  To record one month's rent for the period December 11, 19B,
  through January 10, 19C.
```

December 31, 19B—end of the accounting period:

Analysis: The $1,500 cash collected included rent revenue for December 19B of $1,500 × 20/30 = $1,000, and rent revenue collected in advance for January 19C of $1,500 × 10/30 = $500. Therefore, an **adjusting entry** is required on December 31, 19B, to (*a*) reduce the balance in Rent Revenue by $500 and (*b*) record the obligation to furnish occupancy in 19C for one third of a month which was paid in advance of that year. This $500 is a current liability that will be paid in January 19C by providing occupancy rights.

   a. December 31, 19B (end of the accounting period) **adjusting entry:**[1]

```
Rent revenue . . . . . . . . . . . . . . . . . . . . . . . . . . . . . . .    500
    Rent revenue collected in advance . . . . . . . . . . . . . . . . .            500
  To adjust the accounts for revenue collected in advance as of the
  end of the current period.
```

    The $1,000 (i.e., $1,500 − $500) rent revenue is reported on the 19B income statement. The rent revenue collected in advance of $500 is reported on the 19B balance sheet as a current liability.

---

[1] The entry at collection date, December 11, 19B, could have been recorded so that it would preclude the need for an adjusting entry later:

```
Cash . . . . . . . . . . . . . . . . . . . . . . . . . . . . . . . . . . . . . . . . 1,500
    Rent revenue . . . . . . . . . . . . . . . . . . . . . . . . . . . . . .        1,000
    Rent revenue collected in advance . . . . . . . . . . . . . . . . . .            500
```

Also, it could be accounted for as follows with the same end result:

December 11, 19B:

```
Cash . . . . . . . . . . . . . . . . . . . . . . . . . . . . . . . . . . . . . . . . 1,500
    Rent revenue collected in advance . . . . . . . . . . . . . . . . . .          1,500
```

December 31, 19B—adjusting entry:

```
Rent revenue collected in advance . . . . . . . . . . . . . . . . . . . . 1,000
    Rent revenue . . . . . . . . . . . . . . . . . . . . . . . . . . . . . .        1,000
```

December 31, 19C (end of next accounting period)—adjusting entry:

Rent revenue collected in advance   500
Rent revenue   500
To transfer the rent revenue from the liability account to the
19C revenue account because it now has been earned.

Revenue Earned Prior to Collection (Accrued Revenue)

At the end of the current accounting period, analysis may reveal that some revenue has been **earned** but has **not yet been recorded or collected.** Earned but uncollected revenue is called accrued revenue.

The revenue principle states that if revenue was earned in the current accounting period, it must be recorded and reported in that period. This is accomplished by making an **adjusting entry** to recognize (*a*) a receivable for the amount earned but not yet collected and (*b*) the amount of revenue earned.

Example: On December 31, 19B, the manager of High-Rise Apartments analyzed the rental records and found that one tenant had not paid the December rent amounting to $600. The sequence of entries recorded by High-Rise is:

b. December 31, 19B (end of the accounting period)—adjusting entry:

Rent revenue receivable   600
Rent revenue   600
To record rent revenue earned in 19B but not collected by
year-end.

January 19C—date of collection:

Cash   600
Rent revenue receivable   600
To record collection of receivable for 19B rent revenue.

The adjusting entry at the end of 19B has two measurement purposes: (1) to record rent revenue earned in 19B of $600 and (2) to record a receivable (an asset) for occupancy provided in 19B for which $600 cash will be collected in January 19C. Rent revenue receivable is reported on the December 31, 19B, balance sheet as a current asset.

Expenses Paid in Advance (Deferred or Prepaid Expense)

A company may pay cash in one accounting period for services that will be used in future accounting periods to help earn revenues during those future periods. Such transactions create an asset because of the future benefits. The asset usually is called a **prepaid expense** (or a deferred expense). As the related revenues are earned, period by period, the prepaid expense amount must be apportioned to the appropriate periods in conformity with the **matching principle.**

For example, if the related revenues are earned over three accounting periods, the prepaid expense must be apportioned to each of those three periods in order to measure net income for each period.

Example: On January 1, 19B, High-Rise paid cash of $2,400 in advance for a two-year insurance policy on the apartment building. The entries by High-Rise for this prepaid expense are:

January 1, 19B—date of the transaction:

> Prepaid insurance (an asset account) 2,400
>   Cash   2,400
>   To record prepayment of a two-year premium on building.

December 31, 19B—end of the accounting period:

Analysis: The $2,400 cash paid on January 1, 19B, was for insurance coverage for two full years; therefore, insurance expense for each of the two years will be $1,200. At the end of 19B, an adjusting entry must be made to (*a*) reduce prepaid insurance by $1,200 and (*b*) record insurance expense of $1,200 for 19B.

> *c.* December 31, 19B (end of the accounting period)—adjusting entry:

> Insurance expense 1,200
>   Prepaid insurance   1,200
>   To record 19B insurance expense for 12 months ($2,400 ×
>   12/24 = $1,200).

The adjusting entry has two measurement purposes: (1) it apportions insurance expense to the current period for **matching** purposes and (2) it adjusts (reduces) the Prepaid Insurance account to the correct asset amount ($1,200) for the unexpired insurance remaining at the end of 19B. That is, at the end of 19B, the company was entitled to one more year of insurance protection (with a cost of $1,200), which is a current asset.

December 31, 19C (end of next accounting period)—adjusting entry:

> Insurance expense 1,200
>   Prepaid insurance   1,200
>   To record 19C insurance expense.

This entry apportions insurance expense to 19C and reduces the prepaid insurance balance to zero because the policy term ends on December 31, 19C.

Other Expenses Paid in Advance

A company may pay cash (or incur a liability) in one accounting period to acquire an asset that will be used to generate revenue in future accounting periods. The cost of the asset must be apportioned to the various accounting periods in conformity with the matching principle.

Example: On January 1, 19A, a contractor finished an apartment building for High-Rise. The contract price of $360,000 was paid in cash. The building has an **estimated useful life** of 30 years and an estimated $60,000 **residual value** at the end of the 30 years. This transaction involved the acquisition of an asset (building) that may affect the financial statements for the next 30 years (including 19A). The entries by High-Rise are discussed below.

January 1, 19A—date of acquisition of the building:

Apartment building 360,000
    Cash   360,000
    To record full payment for construction cost of the building.

d. December 31, 19B (end of the accounting period)—adjusting entry:

Depreciation expense 10,000
    Accumulated depreciation, building   10,000
    To record straight-line depreciation expense for one year
    ($360,000 − $60,000) ÷ 30 years = $10,000.

The adjusting entry for depreciation expense will be repeated at the end of each year over the 30-year life of the building. The estimated amount expected to be recovered when the asset is sold or disposed of is known as the **residual value** (sometimes called scrap or salvage value). For computing depreciation, the cost of the asset must be **reduced** by the residual value. The difference ($360,000 − $60,000 = $300,000) is the net amount of cost to be depreciated over the estimated useful life. Thus, the annual depreciation expense on the apartment building is ($360,000 − $60,000) ÷ 30 years = $10,000.[2] The residual value of $60,000 is deducted because it is the amount of cost that is expected to be recovered at the end of the useful life (of the building) to the company.

The adjusting entry has two measurement purposes: (1) it allocates a part of the cost of the building to expense for the current period for **matching** purposes and (2) it adjusts (reduces) the amount of the asset to its undepreciated cost. The credit to Accumulated Depreciation, Building could have been made directly to the building account with the same effect. However, it is desirable, for reporting purposes, to keep the balance of the asset account Apartment Building at original cost. This is accomplished by an asset **contra,** or **offset,** account titled Accumulated Depreciation, Building. The difference between the acquisition cost and accumulated depreciation is called **book** or **carrying value.** The book or carrying value does not represent the current **market** value of the asset because accounting for depreciation is a cost allocation process rather than a market valuation process.

Supplies Inventory

Some types of assets are acquired during an accounting period, but the cost of those assets that are "used up" during the period is not determined until the end of the accounting period. When the cost is determined, an adjusting entry must be made.

Example: High-Rise purchases maintenance supplies not for resale but for use as needed. They are kept in a small storeroom from which supplies are withdrawn as needed. On January 1, 19B, the inventory of maintenance supplies was $100; these were **unused** supplies on hand carried over from the previous year.

---

[2] This example assumes straight-line depreciation, that is, an equal amount of depreciation expense is apportioned to each period. Other methods of depreciation are discussed in Chapter 9.

On March 18, 19B, additional supplies were purchased for $500 and placed in the storeroom. No accounting entry is made when the supplies are withdrawn for use. To determine the amount of supplies **used** during the period, an inventory of the supplies remaining is taken at the end of the period. At December 31, 19B, the inventory of the supplies in the storeroom showed $200. The entries by High-Rise are:

March 18, 19B—date of purchase of supplies:

Inventory of maintenance supplies (an asset)	500	
Cash		500

To record purchase of maintenance supplies for addition to inventory.

Note: This entry increases the inventory account balance from $100 to $600.

e.   December 31, 19B (end of the accounting period)—adjusting entry:

Maintenance expense	400	
Inventory of maintenance supplies		400

To record the amount of supplies used from inventory:
Beginning inventory, $100 + Purchases, $500 − Ending inventory, $200 = Supplies used, $400.

Analysis: Before the adjusting entry is made, the balance in the Inventory of Maintenance Supplies account is $600 (i.e., beginning inventory, $100, plus the purchase, $500); however, the actual inventory count at this date showed $200, which means that usage of supplies was $400 (i.e., $100 + $500 − $200 = $400). The above adjusting entry is required to (*a*) reduce the inventory account by $400 (so that the asset, inventory, will be shown as $200 per the inventory count) and (*b*) to record an expense for the amount of supplies used, $400. Therefore, the 19B income statement will report supplies expense of $400. The 19B balance sheet will report a current asset––inventory of maintenance supplies—of $200.

Expenses Incurred Prior to Payment (Accrued Expenses)

Most expenses are incurred and paid for during a single accounting period; however, at the end of the period, there usually are some expenses that have been **incurred** but are **not yet paid for or recorded.** Such unpaid expenses are called **accrued expenses.** These expenses must be recorded in the current period because they must be **matched** with the revenues of the current period in conformity with the matching principle. Also, the liability for those unpaid expenses must be recorded and reported on the balance sheet of the current period. These effects are recorded by using an adjusting entry.

Example—Salary Expense: On December 31, 19B, the manager of High-Rise was on vacation and would return January 10, 19C. Therefore, the manager's December salary of $900 was not paid or recorded by December 31, 19B. The sequence of entries by High-Rise for the accrued salary expense (disregard payroll taxes at this time) is:

f. December 31, 19B (end of the accounting period)—adjusting entry:

```
Salary expense .................................    900
     Salaries payable (or accrued salaries payable) ...........          900
     To record salary expense and the liability for December salary
     not yet paid.
```

January 10, 19C—date of payment of the December 19B salary:

```
Salaries payable .................................    900
     Cash .................................                   900
     To record payment of a December 19B salary.
```

The adjusting entry had two measurement purposes: (1) to record an expense incurred in 19B for matching with revenues and (2) to record the liability for the salary owed at the end of 19B for balance sheet purposes. The entry in 19C recorded the payment of the liability.

Example—Interest Expense: On November 1, 19B, High-Rise borrowed $30,000 cash from a local bank on a 90-day note with an annual interest rate of 12%. The principal plus interest is due in three months. The entries by High-Rise are:

November 1, 19B—date of transaction:

```
Cash .................................  30,000
     Note payable, short term ...........................          30,000
     To record a loan from a bank.
```

Analysis: At December 31, 19B, the end of the accounting period, two months have passed since the note was signed. Therefore, interest expense for two months has accrued on the note because interest legally accrues with the passage of time. At year-end, there is a **liability** for interest for the two months. This expense and the related liability have not yet been recorded. Therefore, an **adjusting entry** is necessary to (*a*) debit interest expense for $600 (i.e., $30,000 \times 12\% \times 2/12 = \$600$) and (*b*) credit interest payable for the same amount. The adjusting and payment entries are:

g. December 31, 19B (end of the accounting period)—adjusting entry:

```
Interest expense .................................    600
     Interest payable (or accrued interest payable) .........          600
     To record accrued interest expense for two months on note
     payable ($30,000 × 12% × 2/12 = $600).
```

January 31, 19C—maturity date; payment of the principal of the note and interest:

```
Note payable, short term ...........................  30,000
Interest payable (per adjusting entry) .....................     600
Interest expense (19C—$30,000 × 12% × 1/12) ...............     300
     Cash .................................                  30,900
     To record payment of principal plus interest on note payable
     at maturity date.
```

Recording Adjusting Entries

The preceding examples showed the application of the revenue and matching principles at the end of the accounting period by using adjusting entries. In cases when certain economic effects have not been recorded, appropriate adjusting entries are necessary to ensure that both the income statement and balance sheet will be correct. Adjusting entries are made to allocate revenue and expense among the current and one or more future periods so that expenses are properly matched with revenues each accounting period.

Adjusting entries relate to transactions that start in one period and, in effect, continue into one or more subsequent periods. Therefore, an analysis to determine whether an adjusting entry is needed, and if so, how it should be made, must be based on the sequence of related events covering the periods affected. The demonstration case at the end of this chapter illustrates how adjusting entries are influenced by particular situations.

Adjusting entries are entered first in the journal (dated the last day of the accounting period) immediately after all of the regular transactions are recorded. Then the adjusting entries are posted from the journal to the ledger accounts. Recording in the journal and posting to the ledger are necessary because adjusting entries reflect economic events, and their effects must be processed through the accounting information system and into the financial statements in the same manner as the regular transactions. These procedures are illustrated in the next chapter within the context of a complete information processing cycle.

In some instances, it is difficult to draw a clear line between regular and adjusting entries. Adjusting entries (*a*) usually must be made at the **end** of the accounting period and (*b*) **update** certain income statement and balance sheet accounts. The important point is that adjusting entries (as well as many other entries) are necessary to appropriately measure periodic revenues and to match expenses with those revenues that were earned during the period.

The demonstration case at the end of this chapter is designed to give you additional experience with adjusting entries.

PART B—CONCEPTUAL FRAMEWORK OF ACCOUNTING

Importance of the Conceptual Framework

Our discussion of the accounting information processing cycle has emphasized accounting procedures. Now that you have a basic understanding of **how** an accounting system works, we want to change our focus and discuss **why** it works the way it does. All of our accounting procedures have theoretical support (i.e., a reason for doing things a particular way). The Financial Accounting Standards Board (FASB) has issued a series of publications that explain the **conceptual framework of accounting.** These publications are called *Statements of Financial Accounting Concepts,* and the discussions in this chapter are based on these statements.

An understanding of accounting concepts will be helpful as you study. It is much easier to learn and remember how to do something if you know why it must be done a certain way. Our objective in this chapter is to provide an overview of the conceptual framework of accounting. We will refer back to the conceptual framework many times in future chapters. Try to develop a general understanding of the concepts. You will learn more about the concepts as you study the rest of the textbook.

Essential Characteristics of Accounting Information

The conceptual framework of accounting starts with definitions of the **essential characteristics** that accounting information must possess. These essential characteristics are outlined in Exhibit 4–1. First, the **users** of accounting information are identified as **decision makers.** These decision makers are defined as average, prudent investors, creditors, and experts who provide financial advice. They are expected to have a reasonable understanding of accounting concepts and procedures (which may be one of the reasons you are studying accounting).

The primary objective of accounting is to provide information that helps users to make better decisions. To satisfy this objective, accounting information must have the primary **qualitative characteristics** of relevance and reliability. **Relevance** means that information must be capable of influencing decisions. **Reliability** means that information must be accurate, unbiased, and verifiable.

Also, accounting information must have a secondary qualitative characteristic called **comparability.** This means that users should be able to compare the current information of a business entity with current information about other

Exhibit 4–1   Essential characteristics of accounting information

ACCOUNTING INFORMATION	
With reference to:	**Essential characteristics**
1. Users	Decision makers who need financial information.
2. Objective	Decision usefulness—helps users make better decisions.
3. Primary qualities	• Relevance—to decisions. • Reliability—correct information.
4. Secondary quality	Comparability—with prior periods and other entities.
5. Threshold for recognition	Immaterial amounts—not large enough to influence important decisions.
6. Cost-benefit constraint	Cost of developing and reporting should be less than the value of the benefit to decision makers.

businesses and with information from prior time periods. Comparability is a secondary characteristic because it is not as important as relevance and reliability.

The two remaining characteristics given in Exhibit 4–1 focus on the cost of preparing accounting information. The **threshold for recognition** (often called materiality) means that accounting for a specific item (i.e., transaction) need not conform precisely to specified accounting guidelines if the amount of the item is not large enough to affect important decisions. Second, the **cost-benefit constraint** recognizes that it is costly to produce and report accounting information. Under this constraint, accounting should not use more resources to develop and report information than its value to decision makers—to do so would clearly be uneconomic. Measurement for the threshold for recognition and the cost-benefit relationship is very subjective. For example, accountants for a large company might not be concerned about a $100 error in measuring the cost of a $10,000,000 tract of land. They might be most concerned about a $100 error in the Cash account because it could be an indication of employee theft.

Fundamental Concepts of Accounting

Exhibit 4–2 gives an overview of the **fundamental concepts of accounting** that are based on the characteristics shown in Exhibit 4–1. Each of the five categories (assumptions, principles, constraints, elements of financial statements, and detailed practices and procedures) is discussed below.

Assumptions of Accounting

The four assumptions are primarily based on the business environment in which accounting operates. They reflect the scope of accounting and the expectations that set certain limits on the way accounting information is reported.

Separate-Entity Assumption
Each business must be accounted for as an individual organization, separate and apart from its owners, all other persons, and other entities. The personal transactions of the owners are not considered as transactions of the business. A business entity may be a sole proprietorship, partnership, or corporation; but in all cases, it will be accounted for as a separate entity.

Continuity Assumption
For accounting purposes, a business is assumed to have an indefinite life. This assumption is sometimes called the going-concern assumption because accounting assumes that a business will continue to follow its objectives indefinitely. This assumption means that assets can be reported on the balance sheet in terms of their cost instead of the value they would bring if the company were liquidated.

Exhibit 4–2   Fundamental concepts of accounting

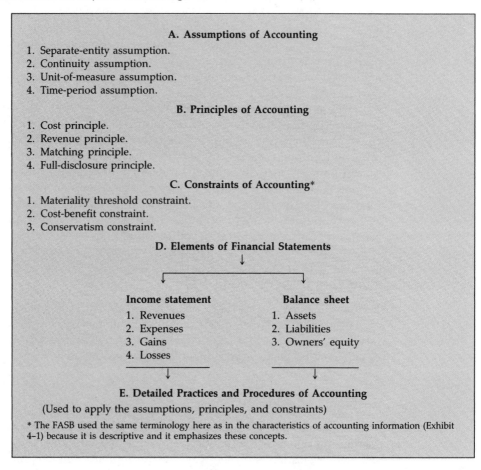

A. Assumptions of Accounting
1. Separate-entity assumption.
2. Continuity assumption.
3. Unit-of-measure assumption.
4. Time-period assumption.

B. Principles of Accounting
1. Cost principle.
2. Revenue principle.
3. Matching principle.
4. Full-disclosure principle.

C. Constraints of Accounting*
1. Materiality threshold constraint.
2. Cost-benefit constraint.
3. Conservatism constraint.

D. Elements of Financial Statements
↓

Income statement
1. Revenues
2. Expenses
3. Gains
4. Losses
↓

Balance sheet
1. Assets
2. Liabilities
3. Owners' equity
↓

E. Detailed Practices and Procedures of Accounting
(Used to apply the assumptions, principles, and constraints)

* The FASB used the same terminology here as in the characteristics of accounting information (Exhibit 4–1) because it is descriptive and it emphasizes these concepts.

Unit-of-Measure Assumption
Each entity will account for, and report, its financial results primarily in terms of the national monetary unit. Therefore, the financial statements of companies in the United States must use the dollar. This assumption implies that the monetary unit is a stable measuring unit, without a changing value. In recent years, this assumption has been questioned as the result of inflation.

Time-Period Assumption
The time-period assumption recognizes that decision makers require **periodic information** about the financial condition of a business. The **accounting period** does not have to conform to the calendar year, and most businesses issue quarterly financial statements (covering a three-month period) in addition to the annual statements.

Principles of Accounting

The four principles of accounting are important because they provide the conceptual guidelines for the measurement, recording, and reporting phases of the accounting information processing cycle. They can be characterized as "how to apply" concepts.

Cost Principle

The cost principle states that the **cash-equivalent** cost should be used for recognizing (i.e., recording) all financial statement elements (assets, liabilities, owners' equity, revenue, expenses, gains, and losses). Under the cost principle, cost is **measured** as the cash paid plus the current dollar value of all noncash considerations.

Revenue Principle

The revenue principle specifies when revenue should be **recognized** (i.e., recorded) and how it should be measured. Revenue should be recognized when the company has earned the revenue and there is an inflow of net assets (or a settlement of a liability) from the sale of goods or services. Revenue is **measured** as the cash received plus the current dollar value of all noncash considerations received (i.e., in accordance with the cost principle).

Matching Principle

Resources that are used to earn revenues are called **expenses.** The matching principle holds that when the period's revenues are properly recognized in conformity with the revenue principle, all of the expenses incurred in earning those revenues must be recorded with the revenues of that period. If the revenue from selling a television set is recognized in 19X, the purchase cost of the set must be recognized as an expense in 19X only.

Full-Disclosure Principle

The periodic financial statements of a business must clearly report all of the relevant information about the economic affairs of a business. This principle requires (*a*) complete financial statements and (*b*) notes to the financial statements to elaborate on the "numbers."

Constraints of Accounting

The constraints of accounting are practical guidelines to reduce the **volume** and **cost** of reporting accounting information without reducing its value to decision makers. The constraints are materiality, cost-benefit, and conservatism.

Materiality Threshold Constraint

Although items and amounts that are of low significance must be accounted for, they do not have to be separately reported if they would not influence reasonable decisions. Accountants usually designate such items and amounts as immaterial.

Cost-Benefit Constraint

The benefits of accounting information to decision makers should be higher than the cost of providing that information. This concept is economically sound; however, measurement of benefits is difficult.

Conservatism Constraint

Special care should be taken to avoid (*a*) overstating assets and revenues and (*b*) understating liabilities and expenses. This constraint produces conservative income statement and balance sheet amounts.

Elements of Financial Statements

The **elements** of financial statements are the broad classifications of information that are reported on the required financial statements. These elements were discussed briefly in Chapters 2 and 3. Exhibit 4–3 gives the formal definitions of all of the elements for the income statement and the balance sheet.

Practices and Procedures of Accounting

The "practices and procedures of accounting" were listed last in Exhibit 4–2 because they primarily involve implementation of the fundamental concepts. Practices and procedures are practical and detailed guidelines. They have been

Exhibit 4–3 Elements of financial statements defined*

Income statement:

1. **Revenues.**   Inflows of net assets or settlements of liabilities from sale of goods and services that constitute the entity's **ongoing or major operations.**
2. **Expenses.**   Outflows or using up of assets or incurrence of liabilities for delivery of goods or services and other activities that constitute the entity's **ongoing or major operations.**
3. **Gains.**   Increases in net assets from **peripheral or incidental transactions** and all other activities except those from revenues or investments by owners.
4. **Losses.**   Decreases in net assets from **peripheral or incidental transactions** and other events except those from expenses or distributions to owners.

Balance sheet:

1. **Assets.**   Probable future economic benefits owned by the entity as a result of past transactions.
2. **Liabilities.**   Probable future sacrifices of economic benefits as a result of past transactions; involves transfer of assets or services.
3. **Owners' equity.**   Residual interest of the owners after all debts are paid (i.e., Assets − Liabilities = Owners' Equity).

* Adapted from: FASB, *Statement of Financial Accounting Concepts No. 6*, "Elements of Financial Statements" (Stamford, Conn., December 1985).

developed to attain a reasonable degree of uniformity in applying the fundamental concepts. The practices and procedures of accounting are discussed in all of the chapters of this textbook. A major portion of the illustrations given in Chapter 3 involved accounting practices and procedures—journal, ledger, trial balance, classifications on the financial statements, depreciation, and so on.

Relationships among the Financial Statements

Exhibit 4–4 gives the basic relationships among the three required financial statements. The exhibit shows that the beginning balance sheet was changed to the ending balance sheet by the items reported on the income statement and

Exhibit 4–4   Relationships among the three required financial statements

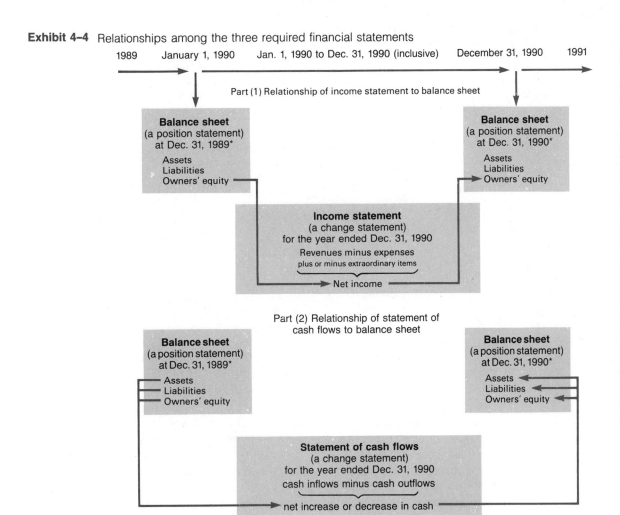

Exhibit 4–5 Summary of the conceptual framework of accounting (based on FASB *Statements of Financial Accounting Concepts Nos. 1, 2, 3,* and *5*)

Fundamentals	Brief explanations	Examples
USERS of financial statements (persons to whom they are directed—the audience)	Primarily decision makers who are "average prudent investors" and are willing to study the information with diligence.	Investors, creditors, including those who advise or represent investors and creditors.
OBJECTIVES of financial statements (decision usefulness)	To provide economic information about a business that is useful in projecting the future cash flows of that business.	The operations of a business are summarized in net income, which is the primary long-term source of cash generated by a business.
QUALITATIVE characteristics of financial statements (necessary to make the reported information useful to decision makers)	Characteristics that make financial statements useful: 1. **Relevance**—affects decisions; timely presentation; has predictive and feedback value. 2. **Reliability (believable)**—unbiased, accurate, and verifiable. 3. **Comparability**—comparable with other periods and entities.	1. The financial statements are available soon after their data have been audited and present complete information. 2. Audited financial statements. 3. Use straight-line depreciation from period to period.
IMPLEMENTATION ASSUMPTIONS of financial statements (imposed by the business environment)	1. **Separate-entity assumption**—each business is accounted for separately from its owners and other entities. 2. **Continuity (going-concern) assumption**—assumes the entity will not liquidate but will continue to pursue its objectives. 3. **Unit-of-measure assumption**—accounting measurements will be in the monetary unit. 4. **Time-period assumption**—accounting reports are for short time periods.	1. XYZ Company is a separate entity; its owners and creditors are other entities. 2. Accounting for XYZ Company will assume it will carry on its normal operations. 3. Assets, liabilities, owners' equity, revenues, expenses, etc., are measured in dollars in the United States. 4. Financial statements of XYZ Company are prepared each year.

statement of cash flows. You can see changes in the financial position of a business by comparing its balance sheets at the beginning and the end of the year.

The income statement and statement of cash flows are often referred to as **change** statements because they help users understand what caused the changes in balance sheet amounts. Exhibit 4–4 shows that the **income statement** explains one change in a balance sheet item—owners' equity (i.e., retained earnings). The income statement gives detailed information that "explains" net income. The **statement of cash flows** explains all of the changes on the balance sheet in terms of cash inflows and cash outflows.

The three financial statements are linked in important ways. This linking is called **articulation;** that is, an amount in one statement (e.g., net income on the

Exhibit 4–5 *(continued)*

Fundamentals	Brief explanations	Examples
IMPLEMENTATION PRINCIPLES of accounting	1. **Cost principle**—Cost (cash equivalent cost given up) is the appropriate basis for initial recording of assets, liabilities, owners' equity, revenues, expenses, gains, and losses.	1. XYZ Company purchased a machine; record the cash equivalent given up, $10,000, as the cost of the machine.
	2. **Revenue principle**—The cash equivalent amount received for the sale of goods or services is recognized as earned revenue when ownership transfers or as the services are rendered.	2. Sale of merchandise for $2,000, half cash and half on credit—record sales revenue of $2,000 on date of sale.
	3. **Matching principle**—Revenues are recognized in conformity with the revenue principle; then all expenses incurred in earning that revenue must be identified and recorded in the period in which those revenues are recognized.	3. Sales of merchandise during the period of $100,000 are recorded as earned; the cost of those goods, $60,000, is recorded as expense of that period.
	4. **Full-disclosure principle**—The financial statements of an entity should disclose (present) all of the relevant economic information about that entity.	4. Report inventory on the balance sheet and explain in a note the inventory accounting policies.
CONSTRAINTS OF ACCOUNTING (based on practical reasons)	1. **Materiality**—Amounts of relatively small significance must be recorded; however, they need not be accorded strict theoretical treatment (for cost-benefit reasons).	1. Purchase of a pencil sharpener for $4.98 (an asset) may be recorded as expense when purchased.
	2. **Cost-benefit**—The value of a financial item reported should be higher for the decision makers than the cost of reporting it.	2. An expense report costs $3,000; its potential cost saving is $1,000.
	3. **Conservatism**—Exercise care not to overstate assets and revenues and not to understate liabilities and expenses.	3. A loss and a gain are probable, but not for sure. Report the loss but not the gain.

income statement) is carried to another statement (e.g., retained earnings on the balance sheet). Decision makers can better interpret the financial statements when they clearly understand these relationships.

In summary, the conceptual framework of accounting explains why certain accounting procedures exist. As you study subsequent chapters, it will be useful to refer back to the discussions in this chapter. To make it easier to do so, we have summarized the conceptual framework in Exhibit 4–5. You should study it carefully and refer back to it often.

Exhibit 4–5 *(concluded)*

Fundamentals	Brief explanations	Examples
ELEMENTS of financial statements (basic items reported on the financial statements)	Income statement:	
	1. **Revenues**—inflows of net assets, or settlements of liabilities from sale of goods and services that constitute the entity's ongoing or major operations.	1. Sale of merchandise for cash or on credit.
	2. **Expenses**—outflows or using up of assets, or incurrence of liabilities for delivery of goods or services, and other activities that constitute the entity's ongoing or major operations.	2. Wages earned by employees paid in cash or owed.
	3. **Gains**—increases in net assets from peripheral or incidental transactions, and all other activities except those from revenues or investments by owners.	3. Sale of a tract of land for a price more than its cost when acquired.
	4. **Losses**—decreases in net assets from peripheral or incidental transactions and other events except those from expenses or distributions to owners.	4. Sale of a tract of land for a price less than its cost when acquired.
	Balance sheet:	
	5. **Assets**—probable future economic benefits owned by the entity as a result of past transactions.	5. Land, buildings, equipment, patent.
	6. **Liabilities**—probable future sacrifices of economic benefits as a result of past transactions; involves transfer of assets or services.	6. Note owed to the bank, taxes owed but not yet paid, unpaid wages.
	7. **Owners' equity**—residual interest of owners after all debts are paid (i.e., Assets − Liabilities = Owners' Equity).	7. Capital stock outstanding plus retained earnings.
DETAILED accounting practices and procedures (detailed measurement and recording guidelines)	1. Those related to asset and income measurement.	1. Straight-line versus accelerated depreciation.
	2. Those related to reporting accounting information.	2. Separate reporting of extraordinary items (net of income tax); terminology.
	3. Other accounting procedures.	3. Control and subsidiary ledgers, special journals, bank reconciliations, worksheets.

DEMONSTRATION CASE

(Try to resolve the requirements before proceeding to the suggested solution that follows.)

New Service Corporation is owned by three stockholders and has been in operation for one year, 19A. Cash flow and expenses are critical control problems. Minimal recordkeeping has been performed to save money. One secretary performs both the secretarial and recordkeeping functions. Because of a loan application made by the corporation, the bank has requested an income statement and balance sheet. The secretary prepared the following (summarized for case purposes):

NEW SERVICE CORPORATION
Profit Statement
Annual—December 31, 19A

Revenues:	
Service	$ 78,500
Expenses:	
Salaries and wages	(43,200)
Utilities	(1,800)
Miscellaneous	(4,000)
Net profit	$ 29,500

NEW SERVICE CORPORATION
Balance Sheet
December 31, 19A

Assets

Cash	$ 4,000
Accounts receivable	35,500
Supplies on hand	8,000
Equipment	40,000
Other assets	16,000
Total assets	$103,500

Liabilities

Accounts payable	$ 9,000
Income taxes payable	
Note payable, one year, 12%	10,000

Net Worth

Capital stock, par $10	50,000
Premium	5,000
Retained profits	29,500
Total liabilities and net worth	$103,500

After reading the two statements, the bank requested that an independent CPA examine them. The CPA found that the secretary used some obsolete captions and terminology and did not include the effects of the following data (i.e., the adjusting entries):

a. Supplies inventory on hand at December 31, $3,000.
b. Depreciation for 19A. The equipment was acquired during January 19A; estimated useful life, 10 years, and no residual value.
c. The note payable was dated August 1, 19A. The principal plus interest are payable at the end of one year.
d. Rent expense of $3,600 was included in miscellaneous expense.
e. Income taxes; assume an average tax rate of 17%.

Required:

1. Recast the above statements to incorporate the additional data, appropriate captions, preferred terminology, and improved format. Show computations.
2. Prepare the adjusting entries (in journal form) for the additional data at December 31, 19A.
3. Comment on any part of this situation that the bank loan officer should note if it appears to be unusual.

Suggested Solution

Requirement 1:

NEW SERVICE CORPORATION
Income Statement
For the Year Ended December 31, 19A

	Amounts reported	Effects of adjusting entries*	Corrected amounts
Revenues:			
Service revenue	$78,500		$78,500
Expenses:			
Salaries and wages expense	43,200		43,200
Utilities expense	1,800		1,800
Supplies expense		(a) + 5,000	5,000
Depreciation expense		(b) + 4,000	4,000
Interest expense		(c) + 500	500
Rent expense		(d) + 3,600	3,600
Miscellaneous expenses	4,000	(d) − 3,600	400
Total expenses	49,000		58,500
Pretax income	$29,500		20,000
Income tax expense ($20,000 × 17%)		(e) + 3,400	3,400
Net income			$16,600
EPS ($16,600 ÷ 5,000 shares)			$3.32

NEW SERVICE CORPORATION
Balance Sheet
At December 31, 19A

Assets

Cash	$ 4,000		$ 4,000
Accounts receivable	35,500		35,500
Supplies inventory	8,000	*(a)* − 5,000	3,000
Equipment	40,000		40,000
Accumulated depreciation		*(b)* − 4,000	(4,000)
Other assets	16,000		16,000
Total assets	$103,500		$94,500

Liabilities

Accounts payable	$ 9,000		$ 9,000
Income taxes payable		*(e)* + 3,400	3,400
Interest payable		*(c)* + 500	500
Note payable, short term (12%)	10,000		10,000
Total liabilities	19,000		22,900

Stockholders' Equity

Capital stock (par $10; 5,000 shares)	50,000		50,000
Contributed capital in excess of par	5,000		5,000
Retained earnings	29,500	− 29,500 + 16,600	16,600
Total liabilities and stockholders' equity	$103,500		$94,500

Note: Observe changes in captions, terminology, and format.
* The letters identify the adjustments shown under Requirement 2.

Requirement 2:
Adjusting entries at December 31, 19A:

a.	Supplies expense 5,000	
	Supplies inventory	5,000

To reduce supplies inventory to the amount on hand December
31, 19A, $3,000, and to record supplies expense, $8,000 − $3,000 =
$5,000.

b.	Depreciation expense 4,000	
	Accumulated depreciation	4,000

Depreciation for one year, $40,000 ÷ 10 years = $4,000.

c.	Interest expense 500	
	Interest payable	500

To record interest expense and the interest accrued (a liability)
from August 1 to December 31, 19A ($10,000 × 12% ×
5/12 = $500).

d.	Rent expense 3,600	
	Miscellaneous expenses	3,600

To record rent expense in the proper account.

e.	Income tax expense 3,400	
	Income taxes payable	3,400

To record income tax expense and the liability for unpaid
tax as computed on the income statement.

Requirement 3:

The loan officer should note particularly the following:

a. The overstatement of net income by 78% [i.e., ($29,500 − $16,600) ÷ $16,600] and total assets by 10% [i.e., ($103,500 − $94,500) ÷ $94,500]. This suggests either (1) an attempt to mislead or (2) a need for better accounting.

b. The high amount in accounts receivable compared to cash and total assets. This fact suggests inadequate evaluation of credit and/or inefficiency in collections.

c. The small amount of cash compared with accounts payable (a current liability).

d. Inclusion of rent expense in miscellaneous expenses.

e. Inappropriate captions, terminology, and format shown in the financial statements.

SUMMARY OF THE CHAPTER

To measure net income, the **revenue principle** states that revenues earned during the period from the sale of goods or services must be identified, measured, and reported for that period. The **matching principle** states that the expenses incurred in earning those revenues must be identified, measured, and matched with the revenues earned in the period to determine periodic net income. To implement the revenue and matching principles, certain transactions and events whose economic effects extend from the current period to one or more future accounting periods must be analyzed at the end of the accounting period. This analysis is the basis for allocating their effects to the current and future periods. The allocation of some revenues and expenses to two or more accounting periods requires the use of **adjusting entries.** Adjusting entries follow the same concepts and procedures as entries for the usual transactions except that they are made at the end of the accounting period.

Part B of the chapter discussed the conceptual framework of accounting which explains the "why" of accounting. The conceptual framework is summarized in Exhibit 4–5.

IMPORTANT TERMS DEFINED IN THIS CHAPTER

Accural Basis Accounting Record completed transactions when they occur, regardless of when the related cash is received or paid. *p. 140*

Accrue (Accrued) An expense incurred but no yet paid; a revenue earned but not yet collected. *p. 144*

Adjusting Entries   End-of-period entries required by the revenue and matching principles to attain a cutoff between periods. *p. 142*

Cash Basis Accounting   Record only cash basis transactions; not in conformity with GAAP. *p. 140*

Conceptual Framework of Accounting   See Exhibit 4–5. *p. 151*

Conservatism Constraint   Do not overstate assets and revenues; do not understate liabilities and expenses. *p. 156*

Contra Account   An account, related to a primary account, that is an offset (or reduction) to the primary account. *p. 148*

Cost-Benefit Constraint   Accounting information should have a higher use value than the cost of reporting it. *p. 156*

Cost Principle   All assets, liabilities, and owners' equity items are recorded initially at cost. *p. 155*

Defer (Deferred)   An expense paid in advance of use; a revenue collected in advance of being earned. *p. 144*

Depreciation   Expense of using (wearing out) a building, machinery, fixtures, etc., each period of useful life. *p. 148*

Elements of Financial Statements   Major classifications on the financial statements. *p. 156*

Expenses Incurred but Not Recorded   Expenses actually incurred but not yet paid or recorded. *p. 143*

Expenses Paid in Advance   Cash paid for goods or services before those goods or services are used; prepaid expenses. *p. 143*

FASB, *Statements of Financial Accounting Concepts*   Give the conceptual framework of accounting; summarized in Exhibit 4–5. *p. 151*

Full-Disclosure Principle   Financial statements must report all relevant information about the economic affairs of a business. *p. 155*

Interest Expense   Time value of money; the cost of borrowing money *p. 150*

Interim Reports   Financial reports for periods of less than one year; quarterly or monthly reports. *p. 141*

Matching Principle   All costs incurred to earn the revenues of the period must be identified and then matched with revenue by recording as expense. *p. 140*

Materiality Constraint   Items of low significance need not be separately reported. *p. 155*

Residual Value   Value (estimated) of an operational asset at the end of its useful life to the business (scrap or salvage value). *p. 148*

Revenue Collected in Advance   Revenue collected in cash before that revenue is earned; precollected revenue. *p. 142*

Revenue Earned but Not Yet Collected or Recorded   Revenue not yet collected, or recorded, but already earned; accrued revenue. *p. 142*

Revenue Principle Recognize revenue in the period earned rather when the cash is received; earning process completed. *p. 140*

Separate-Entity Assumption A business is accounted for separate and apart from its owners and all others. *p. 153*

Supplies Inventory Supplies purchased and still on hand; unused supplies at the end of period. *p. 148*

Time-Period Assumption Division of the operating activities of a business into a series of equal time periods (usually one year) for accounting purposes. *p.154*

Unit-of-Measure Assumption Financial statements measured in terms of the monetary unit—U.S. dollars. *p. 154*

QUESTIONS

Part A: Questions 1–7

1. Briefly explain why the time-period assumption and the accrual basis of accounting require a precise cutoff at the end of each accounting period.
2. Briefly explain adjusting entries. List the four types of adjusting entries.
3. AB Company collected $600 rent for the period December 15, 19A, to January 15, 19B. The $600 was credited to Rent Revenue Collected in Advance on December 15, 19A. Give the adjusting entry required on December 31, 19A (end of the accounting period).
4. On December 31, 19B, Company T recorded the following adjusting entry:

   Rent revenue receivable 500
       Rent revenue   500

   Explain the situation that caused this entry and give the subsequent related entry.
5. On July 1, 19A, M Company paid a two-year insurance premium of $400 and debited Prepaid Insurance for that amount. Assuming the accounting period ends in December, give the adjusting entries that should be made at the end of 19A, 19B, and 19C.
6. Explain estimated residual value. Why is it important in measuring depreciation expense?
7. Explain why adjusting entries are entered in the journal on the last day of the accounting period and then are posted to the ledger.

Part B: Questions 8–18

8. Briefly explain why a conceptual framework of accounting is important.
9. Explain the purpose of defining the six essential characteristics of accounting information.
10. Briefly explain the cost-benefit characteristic of accounting information.
11. An essential characteristic of accounting information that is considered to be a secondary characteristic involves what two comparisons?

12. What are the two primary characteristics of accounting information? Briefly explain each.

13. List the five categories that comprise the fundamental concepts of accounting. Briefly explain each.

14. List and briefly explain the three accounting constraints.

15. List the four elements reported on the income statement. Explain the primary difference between revenues and gains and expenses and losses.

16. Explain why the balance sheet is dated differently than the income statement and the statement of cash flows.

17. Explain the basic difference between accrual basis accounting and cash basis accounting.

18. What basis of accounting is required by GAAP on the (*a*) income statement, (*b*) balance sheet, and (*c*) statement of cash flows?

EXERCISES

Part A: Exercises 4–1 to 4–11

E4–1 (Match Definitions with Terms)

Below are terms related to adjusting entries. Match each definition with its related term by entering the appropriate letter in the space provided. There will be two answers for each term.

Terms	Definitions
_____ _____ (1) Accrued expense	A. A revenue not yet earned; collected in advance.
_____ _____ (2) Deferred expense	B. Office supplies on hand; will be used next accounting period.
_____ _____ (3) Accrued revenue	C. Interest revenue collected; not yet earned.
_____ _____ (4) Deferred revenue	D. Rent not yet collected; already earned.
	E. An expense incurred; not yet paid or recorded.
	F. A revenue earned; not yet collected.
	G. An expense not yet incurred; paid in advance.
	H. Property taxes incurred; not yet paid.

E4–2 (Two Simple Adjusting Entries)

Jones Company has completed its first year of operations on December 31, 19A. All of the 19A entries have been recorded, except for the following:

a. At year-end, employees have earned wages of $6,000. These wages will be paid on the next payroll date, January 6, 19B.

b. At year-end, interest revenue of $5,000 has been earned by the company. The cash will be collected March 31, 19B.

Required:

1. What is the annual reporting period for this company under the time-period assumption?

2. Give the required adjusting entry for transactions (*a*) and (*b*) above. Give appropriate dates and write a brief explanation of each entry.

E4–3   **(Matching Transactions with Terms)**

Match each transaction with its related term by entering the appropriate letter in the space provided.

Terms	Transactions
_____ (1) Deferred revenue	A. At the end of the year, wages payable of $2,500 had not been recorded or paid.
_____ (2) Accrued revenue	
_____ (3) Deferred expense	B. Supplies for office use were purchased during the year for $600, and $100 of the office supplies remained on hand (unused) at year-end.
_____ (4) Accrued expense	
	C. Interest of $300 on a note receivable was earned at year-end, although collection of the interest is not due until the following year.
	D. At the end of the year, service revenue of $1,000 was collected in cash but was not yet earned.

E4–4   **(Effects of Three Adjusting Entries on the Income Statement and Balance Sheet)**

California Company started operations on January 1, 19A. It is now December 31, 19A (end of the annual accounting period). The part-time bookkeeper needs your help to analyze the following three transactions:

a. On January 1, 19A, the company purchased a special machine for a cash cost of $15,000 (debited to the machine account). The machine has an estimated useful life of 10 years and no residual value.

b. During 19A, the company purchased office supplies that cost $1,200. At the end of 19A, office supplies of $400 remained on hand.

c. On July 1, 19A, the company paid cash of $300 for two years' premium on an insurance policy on the machine.

Required:

Complete the following schedule of the amounts that should be reported for 19A:

Selected Balance Sheet Amounts at December 31, 19A:	Amount to be reported
Assets:	
Machine	$ _____
Accumulated depreciation	_____
Carrying value	_____
Office supplies inventory	_____
Prepaid insurance	_____
Selected Income Statement Amounts for the Year Ended December 31, 19A:	
Depreciation expense	$ _____
Office supplies expense	_____
Insurance expense	_____

E4–5 **(Journalize Seven Typical Adjusting Entries)**

Grant Department Store is completing the accounting process for the year just ended, December 31, 19B. The transactions during 19B have been journalized and posted. The following data with respect to adjusting entries are available:

a. Office supplies inventory at January 1, 19B, was $120. Office supplies purchased and debited to Office Supplies Inventory during the year amounted to $500. The year-end inventory showed $180 of supplies on hand.

b. Wages earned during December 19B, unpaid and unrecorded at December 31, 19B, amounted to $1,400. The last payroll was December 28; the next payroll will be January 6, 19C.

c. Three fourths of the basement of the store is rented for $800 per month to another merchant, J. B. Smith. Smith sells compatible, but not competitive, merchandise. On November 1, 19B, the store collected six months' rent in advance from Smith for $4,800, which was credited in full to Rent Revenue when collected.

d. The remaining basement space is rented to Spears Specialty for $360 per month, payable monthly. On December 31, 19B, the rent for November and December 19B was not collected or recorded. Collection is expected January 10, 19C.

e. Delivery equipment that cost $21,000 was being used by the store. Estimates for the equipment were (1) useful life four years and (2) residual value at the end of four years' use, $1,000. Assume depreciation for a full year for 19B. The asset will be depreciated evenly over its useful life.

f. On July 1, 19B, a two-year insurance premium amounting to $2,000 was paid in cash and debited in full to Prepaid Insurance.

g. Grant operates an alteration shop to meet its own needs. Also, the shop does alterations for J. B. Smith. At the end of December 31, 19B, J. B. Smith had not paid for alterations completed amounting to $450. This amount has not been recorded as Alteration Shop Revenue. Collection is expected during January 19C.

Required:

Give the adjusting entry for each situation that should be recorded in the journal of Grant Department Store at December 31, 19B.

E4–6 **(Adjusting Entries for Interest on Two Notes Receivable)**

On April 1, 19B, Davis Corporation received a $4,000, 10% note from a customer in settlement of a $4,000 open account receivable. According to the terms, the principal of the note, plus interest, is payable at the end of 12 months. The annual accounting period for Davis ends on December 31, 19B.

Required:

a. Give the journal entry for Davis for receipt of the note on April 1, 19B.

b. Give the adjusting entry required on December 31, 19B.

c. Give the journal entry on date of collection, March 31, 19C, for the principal and interest.

On August 1, 19B, to meet a cash shortage, Davis Corporation obtained a $20,000, 12% loan from a local bank. The principal of the note plus interest expense is payable at the end of 12 months.

Required:

  d. Give the journal entry for Davis on the date of the loan, August 1, 19B.

  e. Give the adjusting entry required on December 31, 19B.

  f. Give the journal entry on date of payment, July 31, 19C.

E4–7   (Adjusting Entries for Prepaid Insurance—Two Cases)

Warde Company is making adjusting entries for the year ended December 31, 19B. In developing information for the adjusting entries, the accountant learned that on September 1, 19B, a two-year insurance premium of $3,600 was paid.

Required:

  a. What amount should be reported on the 19B income statement for insurance expense?

  b. What amount should be reported on the December 31, 19B, balance sheet for prepaid insurance?

  c. Give the adjusting entry at December 31, 19B, under each of two cases:

    Case 1—Assume that when the premium was paid on September 1, 19B, the bookkeeper debited the full amount to Prepaid Insurance.

    Case 2—Assume that when the premium was paid on September 1, 19B, the bookkeeper debited the full amount to Insurance Expense.

    (Hint: In Case 2 be sure that after the adjusting entry, you end with the same amount in the Prepaid Insurance account as in Case 1.)

E4–8   (Adjusting Entry for Supplies Inventory)

Long Company uses a large amount of shipping supplies that are purchased in large volume, stored, and used as needed. At December 31, 19B, the following data relating to shipping supplies were obtained from the records and supporting documents:

Shipping supplies on hand, January 1, 19B	$ 4,000
Purchases of shipping supplies during 19B	13,000
Shipping supplies on hand, per inventory December 31, 19B	2,000

Required:

  a. What amount should be reported on the 19B income statement for shipping supplies expense?

  b. What amount should be reported on the December 31, 19B, balance sheet for shipping supplies inventory?

  c. Give the adjusting entry at December 31, 19B, assuming the purchases of shipping supplies were debited in full to Shipping Supplies Inventory ($13,000).

  d. What adjusting entry would you make assuming the bookkeeper debited Shipping Supplies Expense for the $13,000? (Hint: In solving [c] and [d], be sure that each solution ends up with the same amount remaining in the Shipping Supplies Inventory account.)

E4–9   (Correct Income Statement and Balance Sheet Amounts for the Effects of Three Adjusting Entries)

On December 31, 19B, Dell Company prepared an income statement and balance sheet and failed to take into account three adjusting entries. The income statement, prepared on this incorrect basis, reflected a pretax income of $20,000. The balance sheet reflected total assets, $80,000; total liabilities, $30,000; and owners' equity, $50,000. Dell is not a corporation; therefore, it does not pay income tax. The data for the three adjusting entries were:

a. Depreciation was not recorded for the year on equipment that cost $55,000; estimated useful life, 10 years, and residual value, $5,000.

b. Wages amounting to $8,000 for the last three days of December 19B not paid and not recorded (the next payroll will be on January 10, 19C).

c. Rent revenue of $3,000 was collected on December 1, 19B, for office space for the period December 1, 19B, to February 28, 19C. The $3,000 was credited in full to Rent Revenue when collected.

Required:
Complete the following tabulation to correct the financial statement amounts shown (indicate deductions with parentheses):

Items	Net income	Total assets	Total liabilities	Owners' equity
Balances reported	$20,000	$80,000	$30,000	$50,000
Effects of depreciation				
Effects of wages				
Effects of rent revenue				
Correct balances				

E4–10   **(Prepare Correct Income Statement to Include Effects of Seven Adjusting Entries; Give Adjusting Entries)**
Lyons, Inc., completed its first year of operations on December 31, 19A. Because this is the end of the annual accounting period, the company bookkeeper prepared the following tentative income statement:

Income Statement, 19A

Rental revenue		$102,000
Expenses:		
Salaries and wages expense	$26,400	
Maintenance expense	10,000	
Rent expense (on location)	8,000	
Utilities expense	3,000	
Gas and oil expense	2,000	
Miscellaneous expenses (items not listed above)	400	
Total expenses		49,800
Income		$ 52,200

An independent CPA reviewed the income statement and developed additional data as follows:

1. Wages for the last three days of December amounting to $600 were not recorded or paid (disregard payroll taxes).

2. The telephone bill for December 19A amounting to $200 has not been recorded or paid.

3. Depreciation on rental autos, amounting to $20,000 for 19A, was not recorded.

4. Interest on a $20,000, one-year, 12% note payable dated November 1, 19A, was not recorded. The 12% interest is payable on the maturity date of the note.
5. Rental revenue includes $2,000 rental revenue for the month of January 19B.
6. Maintenance expense includes $1,000, which is the cost of maintenance supplies still on hand (per inventory) at December 31, 19A. These supplies will be used in 19B.
7. The income tax rate is 30%. Payment of income tax will be made in 19B.

Required:

a. Prepare a correct income statement for 19A, assuming 7,000 shares of stock are outstanding. Show computations.
b. Give the adjusting entry at December 31, 19A, for each of the additional data items. If none is required, explain why.

E4–11   (Prepare Three Adjusting Entries and Recast the Income Statement and Balance Sheet)
On December 31, 19C, the bookkeeper for Seattle Company prepared the income statement and balance sheet summarized below but neglected to consider three of the adjusting entries.

	As prepared	Effects of adjusting entries	Corrected amounts
Income statement:			
Revenues	$95,000		
Expenses	(83,000)		
Income tax expense			
Net income	$12,000		
Balance sheet:			
Assets			
Cash	$18,000		
Accounts receivable	26,000		
Rent receivable			
Equipment*	40,000		
Accumulated depreciation	(8,000)		
	$76,000		
Liabilities			
Accounts payable	$10,000		
Income taxes payable			
Owners' Equity			
Capital stock	50,000		
Retained earnings	16,000		
	$76,000		

* Acquired January 1, 19A, 10-year life, no residual value; straight-line depreciation.

Data on the three adjusting entries:

1. Depreciation on the equipment was not recorded for 19C.

2. Rent revenue earned of $1,000 for December 19C was neither collected nor recorded.

3. Income tax for 19C was not paid or recorded. The average rate was 20%.

Required:

a. Complete the two columns to the right in the above tabulation to show the correct amounts on the income statement and balance sheet.

b. Prepare the three adjusting entries (in journal form) that were omitted. Use the account titles given above.

Part B: Exercises 4–12 to 4–14

E4–12   (Match the Essential Characteristics of Accounting Information with Conceptual Designations)
Match the essential characteristics of accounting information with the related designation by entering the appropriate letter in the space provided.

Designations	Essential characteristics
_____ (1) Users	A. Comparability with prior periods and other entities.
_____ (2) Cost-benefit constraint	B. Decision usefulness—helps users make better decisions.
_____ (3) Secondary quality	C. Decision makers who need financial information.
_____ (4) Purpose	D. Relevance to decisions and reliability.
_____ (5) Threshold for recognition	E. Immaterial amounts—not large enough to influence important decisions.
_____ (6) Primary qualities	F. Cost of developing and reporting is less than the use value to decision makers.

E4–13   (Match Financial Statements with the Elements of Financial Statements)
Match the financial statements with the elements of financial statements by entering the appropriate letter in the space provided.

Elements of financial statements	Financial statements
_____ (1) Liabilities	A. Income statement.
_____ (2) Cash from operating activities	B. Balance sheet.
_____ (3) Losses	C. None of the above.
_____ (4) Assets	
_____ (5) Revenues	
_____ (6) Cash from financing activities	
_____ (7) Gains	
_____ (8) Owners' equity	
_____ (9) Expenses	
_____ (10) Assets owned by proprietor	

E4–14   (Match Definitions with Terms)

Match each definition with its related term by entering the appropriate letter in the space provided.

Terms	**Definitions**
_____ (1) Primary users of financial statements	A. To prepare the income tax return of the business.
_____ (2) Broad objective of financial reporting	B. Separate entity, going concern, time periods, and unit of measure.
_____ (3) Qualitative characteristics of financial statements	C. Guidelines to apply the assumptions and principles.
_____ (4) Implementation assumptions	D. To provide financial information that is useful in making decisions.
_____ (5) Elements of financial statements	E. Relevance and reliability.
_____ (6) Implementation principles	F. Investors, creditors, and those who advise and represent them (decision makers).
_____ (7) Exceptions to implementation principles	G. Materiality, cost-benefit, conservatism.
_____ (8) Detailed accounting practices and procedures	H. Assets, liabilities, owners' equity, revenues, expenses, gains and losses.
_____ (9) None of the above	I. Revenue, cost, matching, full disclosure.

PROBLEMS

Part A: Problems 4–1 to 4–10

P4–1   (Prepare Four Simple Adjusting Entries)

The annual accounting year used by Zane Company ends on December 31. It is December 31, 19X, and all of the 19X entries have been made except the following adjusting entries:

a. On September 1, 19X, Zane collected six months' rent of $2,400 on some storage space. At that date, Zane debited Cash and credited Rent Revenue for $2,400.

b. The company earned service revenue of $1,000 on a special job that was completed December 29, 19X. Collection will be made during January 19Y, and no entry has been recorded.

c. On November 1, 19X, Zane paid a one-year premium for property insurance, $1,800. Cash was credited and Insurance Expense was debited for this amount.

d. At December 31, 19X, wages earned by employees not yet paid, $400. The employees will be paid on the next payroll date, January 15, 19Y.

Required:

Give the adjusting entry required for each transaction. Provide a brief explanation for each entry.

P4–2   (Prepare Four Types of Adjusting Entries)
Hydro Company started operations on September 1, 19A. It is now August 31, 19C, end of its second year of operations. All entries for the annual accounting period have been journalized and posted to the ledger accounts. The following end-of-year entries are to be recorded:

a. Service revenue collected in advance, $1,500. On August 15, 19C, the company debited Cash and credited Service Revenue for this amount. The services will be performed during September 19C.

b. Revenue earned but not yet collected or recorded, $5,000. The company completed a large service job, which passed inspection on August 31, 19C. Collection is expected on September 6, 19C.

c. Expense paid in advance, $3,000. The company purchased service supplies on August 1, 19C, at which time Supplies Expense was debited and Cash credited for this amount. At August 31, 19C, one third of these supplies were on hand (will be used later on other jobs).

d. Expense incurred but not yet paid or recorded. The company used the consulting services of an engineer during the last two weeks of August 19C. The services have been performed, and the company expects to pay the $500 billing on September 15, 19C.

Required:

1. What is the accounting (i.e., reporting) year for this company? What accounting assumption supports your answer?

2. Prepare the required adjusting entry for each situation, including a brief explanation of each entry.

3. Explain the effect on net income if these entries are not made on August 31, 19C (disregard income tax).

P4–3   (Give Six Adjusting Entries and Related Balance Sheet Classifications)
Martha Company is preparing the adjusting entries for the year ended December 31, 19B. On that date, the bookkeeper for the company assembled the following data:

1. On December 31, 19B, salaries earned by employees but not yet paid or recorded, $6,000.

2. Depreciation must be recognized on a service truck that cost $10,000 on July 1, 19B (estimated useful life is five years with no residual value).

3. Cash of $1,000 was collected on December 28, 19B, for services to be rendered during 19C (Service Revenue was credited).

4. On December 27, 19B, the company received a tax bill of $200 from the city for 19B property taxes (on service equipment) that is payable (and will be paid) during January 19C.

5. On July 1, 19B, the company paid $840 cash for a two-year insurance policy on the service truck (2 above).

6. On October 1, 19B, the company borrowed $10,000 from a local bank and signed a 10% note for that amount. The principal and interest are payable on maturity date, September 30, 19C.

Required:

a. The bookkeeper has asked you to assist in preparing the adjusting entries at December 31, 19B. For each situation above, give the adjusting entry and a brief explanation. If none is required, explain why.

b. Based on your entries given in Requirement *(a),* complete the following schedule to reflect the amounts and balance sheet classifications:

Item No.	Accounts	19B amount	Balance sheet classification (one check on each line)		
			Assets	Liabilities	Owners' equity
1	Salaries payable . . . . $ _____		_____	_____	_____
2	Accumulated depreciation	_____	_____	_____	_____
3	Revenue collected in advance	_____	_____	_____	_____
4	Property taxes payable	_____	_____	_____	_____
5	Prepaid insurance	_____	_____	_____	_____
6	Interest payable	_____	_____	_____	_____

P4–4   (Prepare Seven Adjusting Entries and Recompute Income to Include Their Effects) Dover Company is at the end of its accounting year December 31, 19B. The company is not a corporation; therefore, it does not pay income tax. The following data that must be considered were developed from the company's records and related documents:

1. On July 1, 19B, a three-year insurance premium on equipment was paid amounting to $900 that was debited in full to Insurance Expense on that date.

2. During 19B, office supplies amounting to $1,000 were purchased for cash and debited in full to Supplies Inventory. At the end of 19A, the inventory count of supplies remaining on hand (unused) showed $200. The inventory of supplies on hand (unused) at December 31, 19B, showed $300.

3. On December 31, 19B, B&R Garage completed repairs on one of the company's trucks at a cost of $650; the amount is not yet recorded and, by agreement, will be paid during January 19C.

4. In December 19B, a tax bill, on trucks owned during 19B, amounting to $1,400 was received from the city. The taxes, which have not been recorded, are due and will be paid on February 15, 19C.

5. On December 31, 19B, the company completed a hauling contract for an out-of-state company. The bill was for $7,500 payable within 30 days. No cash has been collected, and no journal entry has been made for this transaction.

6. On July 1, 19B, the company purchased a new hauling van at a cash cost of $21,600. The estimated useful life of the van was 10 years, with an estimated residual value of $1,600. No depreciation has been recorded for 19B (compute depreciation for six months in 19B).

7. On October 1, 19B, the company borrowed $6,000 from the local bank on a one-year, 12% note payable. The principal plus interest is payable at the end of 12 months.

Required:

a. Give the adjusting entry required on December 31, 19B, related to each of the above transactions. Give a brief explanation with each entry.

b. Assume the company had prepared a tentative income statement for 19B that did not include the effect of any of the above items and that the tentative net income computed was $20,000. Considering the above items, compute the corrected net income for 19B. Show computations.

P4-5   **(Compute Income Statement Amounts for Three Items and Identify Any Adjusting Entries)**

The following information was provided by the records of Sea View Apartments (a corporation) at the end of the annual fiscal period, December 31, 19B:

Revenue:

a. Rent revenue collected in cash during 19B for occupancy in 19B (credited to
   Rent Revenue) $497,000

b. Rent revenue earned for occupancy in December 19B; will not be collected until
   19C 12,000

c. In December 19B, collected rent revenue in advance for January 19C (credited to
   Rent Revenue) 16,000

Salary expense:

d. Cash payment made in January 19B for salaries incurred (earned) in
   December 19A 3,000

e. Salaries incurred and paid during 19B (debited to Salary Expense) 58,000

f. Salaries earned by employees during December 19B; will not be paid until January
   19C 2,000

g. Cash advance to employees in December 19B for salaries that will be earned in
   January 19C (debited to Receivable from Employees) 2,500

Supplies used:

h. Maintenance supplies inventory on January 1, 19B (balance on hand) 2,000

i. Maintenance supplies purchased for cash during 19B (debited to Maintenance
   Supplies Inventory when purchased) 8,000

j. Maintenance supplies inventory on December 31, 19B 1,500

Required:

1. In conformity with the revenue and matching principles, what amounts should be reported on Sea View's 19B income statement for:

   a. Rent revenue . . . . $ _____
   b. Salary expense . . . .   _____
   c. Maintenance supplies expense . .   _____

   Show computations.

2. Check the items that would need an adjusting entry at the end of 19B:

   a. _____; b. _____; c. _____; d. _____; e. _____; f. _____; g. _____; h. _____;
   i. _____; j. _____.

P4–6   **(Determine the Effect of Five Adjusting Entries on the Income Statement)**
Delta Company has completed its annual financial statements for the year ended December 31, 19C. The income statement (summarized) reflected the following:

Revenues:
Service revenue $95,600
Rental revenue (office space)   2,400
Total revenues 98,000

Expenses:
Salaries and wages expense 44,000
Service supplies used   2,600
Depreciation expense   2,000
Maintenance of equipment   2,000
Rent expense (service building)   8,400
Oil and gas for equipment   1,800
Insurance expense   200
Utilities expense   800
Other expenses   6,200
Total expenses 68,000
Net income $30,000

The company is a partnership; therefore, it does not pay income taxes. An audit of the records and financial statements by a CPA revealed that the following items were not considered:

1. Service revenue of $700 earned but not collected on December 31, 19C, was not included in the $95,600 on the income statement.

2. The $2,600 of service supplies used included $600 of service supplies still on hand in the supplies storeroom on December 31, 19C.

3. Rent revenue of $100 that was collected in advance and not yet earned by December 31, 19C, was included in the $2,400 on the income statement.

4. Property tax for 19C of $400 was billed during December 19C, but will be due and paid during January 19D (not included in the above amounts on the income statement).

5. A two-year insurance premium of $400 was paid on July 1, 19B; no premiums were paid in 19C.

Required:

a. Recast the above income statement to include, exclude, or omit each of the items identified by the CPA. Use a format similar to the following:

Items	Amounts as reported	Corrections	Amounts that should be reported

b. The owner of the company asked you to explain the following:
(1) The insurance premium was paid in 19B; therefore, why was insurance expense reported in 19C?
(2) Although the company paid no cash for depreciation expense, $2,000 was included in 19C as expense. Why was this so?

P4–7 **(Determine the Effects of Six Entries on the Income Statement and Balance Sheet)**
It is December 31, 19B, end of the annual accounting period for Texan Company. Below are listed six independent transactions (summarized) that affected the company during 19B. The transactions are to be analyzed as to their effects on the balance sheet and income statement for 19B.

  a. On January 1, 19A, the company purchased a machine that cost $24,000 cash (estimated useful life six years and no residual value).
   (1) Show how the machine should be reported on the 19B balance sheet.
   (2) Show how the 19B income statement should report the effects of the machine usage.

  b. On September 1, 19B, the company signed a $9,000, one-year, 10% note payable. The principal plus interest is payable on maturity date.
   (1) Show how the liability should be reported on the 19B balance sheet.
   (2) Show how the effects of the note should be reported on the 19B income statement.

  c. During 19B, service revenues of $90,000 were collected, of which $10,000 was collected in advance.
   (1) Show how the $10,000 should be reported on the 19B balance sheet.
   (2) Show how the 19B income statement should report the effects of the transaction.

  d. In 19B, expenses paid in cash amounted to $60,000, of which $5,000 was paid for expenses yet to be incurred (prepaid).
   (1) Show how the 19B balance sheet should report the $5,000.
   (2) Show how the income statement should report this situation.

  e. In 19B, $85,000 cash revenues were collected; and in addition, revenues of $5,000 were on credit.
   (1) Show how the $5,000 should be reported on the 19B balance sheet.
   (2) Show how the 19B income statement should report the revenues.

  f. In 19B, expenses amounting to $56,000 were paid in cash; and in addition, expenses of $5,000 were on credit.
   (1) Show how the $5,000 should be reported on the 19B balance sheet.
   (2) Show how the expenses should be reported on the 19B income statement.

P4–8 **(Analytical—Compare Two Sets of Account Balances to Determine What Adjusting Entries Were Made)**
Nynex Company is completing the information processing cycle at the end of its fiscal year, December 31, 19B. Below is listed the correct balance at December 31, 19B, for each account (*a*) before the adjusting entries for 19B and (*b*) after the adjusting entries for 19B.

	Account balance, December 31, 19B			
	Before adjusting entries		After adjusting entries	
Items	**Debit**	**Credit**	**Debit**	**Credit**
a. Cash	$ 8,000		$ 8,000	
b. Service revenue receivable			400	
c. Prepaid insurance	300		200	
d. Operational assets	120,200		120,200	
e. Accumulated depreciation, equipment		$ 21,500		$ 25,000
f. Income taxes payable				5,500
g. Capital stock		70,000		70,000
h. Retained earnings, January 1, 19B		14,000		14,000
i. Service revenue		60,000		60,400
j. Salary expense	37,000		37,000	
k. Depreciation expense			3,500	
l. Insurance expense			100	
m. Income tax expense			5,500	
	$165,500	$165,500	$174,900	$174,900

Required:

a. Compare the amounts in the columns before and after the adjusting entries to reconstruct the four adjusting entries that were made in 19B. Provide an explanation of each.

b. Compute the amount of income assuming (1) it is based on the amounts before adjusting entries and (2) it is based on the amounts after adjusting entries. Which income amount is correct? Explain why.

P4–9 **(Compute Effects of Adjusting Entries on the Balance Sheet and Income Statement; Two Consecutive Years)**
On January 1, 19A, four persons organized Atlantic Company. The company has been operating for two years, 19A and 19B. Given below are data relating to six selected transactions that affect both years. The annual accounting period ends December 31.

a. On January 1, 19A, the company purchased a computer for use in the business at a cash cost of $15,000. The computer has an estimated useful life of five years and no residual value. It will be depreciated on a straight-line basis.

b. On July 1, 19A, the company borrowed $10,000 cash from City Bank and signed a one-year, 12% interest-bearing note. The interest and principal are payable on August 31, 19B.

c. The company owns its office building. On October 1, 19A, the company leased some of its office space to A. B. Smith for $6,000 per year. Smith paid this amount in full on October 1, 19A, and expects to use the space for one year only. The company increased (debited) Cash for $6,000 and increased (credited) Rent Revenue for $6,000 on October 1, 19A.

d. Office supplies were purchased for use in the business. Cash was decreased (credited), and Office Supplies Inventory was increased (debited). The unused supplies at each year-end are determined by inventory count. The amounts were:

Year	Purchased	Inventory
19A	$700	$200
19B	500	300

e. Wages are paid by the company at the end of each two weeks. The last payroll date in December usually is four days before December 31. Therefore, at each year-end, unpaid wages exist that are paid in cash on the first payroll date in the next year. The wages paid in cash and the wages incurred but not yet paid or recorded at each year-end were:

Year	Wages paid in cash during the year	Wages unpaid and unrecorded Dec. 31
19A	$30,000	$4,000
19B	36,000	3,000

f. On July 1, 19A, the company paid a two-year insurance premium (on the computer) of $240. At that date, the company increased (debited) an asset account—Prepaid Insurance—and decreased (credited) Cash, $240.

Required:

Complete the following schedule for 19A and 19B by entering the amounts that should be reported on the financial statements of Atlantic Company. Show computations.

	19A	19B
Balance sheet:		
Assets		
Computer	$ _____	$ _____
Less: Accumulated depreciation	_____	_____
Carrying value	_____	_____
Office supplies inventory	_____	_____
Prepaid insurance	_____	_____
Liabilities		
Note payable, City Bank	_____	_____
Interest payable	_____	_____
Rent revenue collected in advance	_____	_____
Wages payable	_____	_____
Income statement:		
Rent revenue	$ _____	$ _____
Depreciation expense	_____	_____
Interest expense	_____	_____
Office supplies expense	_____	_____
Wage expense	_____	_____
Insurance expense	_____	_____

P4–10   **(Comprehensive Problem; Prepare Six Adjusting Entries and Recast the Income Statement and Balance Sheet)**

Denver Corporation has been in operation since January 1, 19A. It is now December 31, 19A, the end of the annual accounting period. The company has not done well financially during the first year, although revenue has been fairly good. The three stockholders manage the company, but they have not given much attention to recordkeeping. In view of a serious cash shortage, they asked a local bank for a $10,000 loan. The bank requested a complete set of financial statements. The 19A annual financial statements given below were prepared by a clerk and then were given to the bank.

DENVER CORPORATION
December 31, 19A

Income Statement

Transportation revenue	$90,000
Expenses:	
Salaries expense	20,000
Maintenance expense	15,000
Other expenses	25,000
Total expenses	60,000
Net income	$30,000

Balance Sheet

Assets

Cash	$ 1,000
Receivables	4,000
Inventory of maintenance supplies	5,000
Equipment	30,000
Remaining assets	37,000
Total assets	$77,000

Liabilities

Accounts payable	$ 7,000

Capital

Capital stock	40,000
Retained earnings	30,000
Total liabilities and capital	$77,000

After briefly reviewing the statements and "looking into the situation," the bank requested that the statements be redone (with some expert help) to "incorporate depreciation, accruals, inventory counts, income taxes, and so on." As a result of a review of the records and supporting documents, the following additional information was developed:

1. The inventory of maintenance supplies of $5,000 shown on the balance sheet has not been adjusted for supplies used during 19A. An inventory count of the maintenance supplies on hand (unused) on December 31, 19A, showed $1,500. Supplies used are debited to Maintenance Expense.

2. The insurance premium paid in 19A was for years 19A and 19B; therefore, the prepaid insurance at December 31, 19A, amounted to $1,000. The total insurance premium was debited in full to Other Expenses when paid in 19A.

3. The equipment cost $30,000 when purchased January 1, 19A. It had an estimated useful life of five years (no residual value). No depreciation has been recorded for 19A.

4. Unpaid (and unrecorded) salaries at December 31, 19A, amounted to $1,500.

5. At December 31, 19A, hauling revenue collected in advance amounted to $5,000. This amount was credited in full to Transportation Revenue when the cash was collected earlier during 19A.

6. Assume an income tax rate of 30%.

Required:

a. Give the six adjusting entries (in journal form) required by the above additional information for December 31, 19A.

b. Recast the above statements after taking into account the adjusting entries. You do not need to use classifications on the statements. Suggested form for the solution:

| | | Changes | | |
| Items | Amounts reported | Plus | Minus | Correct amounts |
(List here each item from the two statements)

c. Omission of the adjusting entries caused:
   (1) Net income to be incorrect by: $_____, __ overstated, or __ understated.
   (2) Total assets on the balance sheet to be incorrect by: $_____, __ overstated, or __ understated.
   Write a brief, nontechnical report to the bank explaining the causes of these differences.

Part B: Problems 4–11 to 4–16

P4–11   (Match Definitions with Fundamental Concepts)
Match each definition with its related fundamental concept by entering the appropriate letter in the space provided.

Fundamental concepts

_____ (1) Separate-entity assumption
_____ (2) Continuity assumption
_____ (3) Unit-of-measure assumption
_____ (4) Time-period assumption
_____ (5) Cost principle
_____ (6) Revenue principle
_____ (7) Matching principle
_____ (8) Full-disclosure principle
_____ (9) Materiality threshold
_____ (10) Cost-benefit constraint
_____ (11) Conservatism constraint

Elements of financial statements

_____ (12) Income statement
_____ (13) Balance sheet
_____ (14) Practices and procedures of accounting

Definitions

A. Used to apply the assumptions, principles, and constraints.
B. The reporting period usually is one year.
C. Expenses are matched with revenues period by period.
D. Items of low significance do not need to be reported separately.
E. Account for the business separate from owners.
F. Report in terms of the monetary unit.
G. Inflow of net assets from the sale of goods and services that is measurable in dollars.
H. All relevant information about the financial activities must be reported.
I. The entity is a going concern.
J. Financial statement elements are initially recorded at cash equivalent cost.
K. Reports revenues, expenses, gains, and losses.
L. Value of user benefits must exceed cost of providing the item of financial information.
M. Reports Assets = Liabilities + Owners' Equity.
N. Do not overstate assets and revenues and do not understate liabilities and expenses.

P4–12   (Match Definitions with Elements of Financial Statements)
Match each definition with its related element by entering the appropriate letter in the space provided.

Elements

Income statement:

_____ (1) Revenues
_____ (2) Expenses
_____ (3) Gains
_____ (4) Losses

Definitions

A. Cash received during the accounting period.
B. Probable future sacrifices of economic resources.
C. Increase in net assets from peripheral transactions.
D. Outflow of assets for delivery of goods or services.

Elements	Definitions

Balance sheet:

_____ (5) Assets
_____ (6) Liabilities
_____ (7) Owners' equity

E. Residual interest of owners.
F. Inflow of net assets from major ongoing operations.
G. Cash paid out during the period.
H. Probable future economic benefits; owned by the entity.
I. Decrease in net assets from incidental transactions.

P4–13 **(Match Transactions with Concepts)**

Below are listed the concepts of accounting. Match each transaction with its related concept by entering the appropriate letter in the space provided. Use one letter for each blank.

Concepts	Transactions

_____ (1) Users of financial statements
_____ (2) Objective of financial statements

Qualitative characteristics:

_____ (3) Relevance
_____ (4) Reliability

Implementation assumptions:

_____ (5) Separate entity
_____ (6) Continuity
_____ (7) Unit of measure
_____ (8) Time period

Elements of financial statements:

_____ (9) Revenues
_____ (10) Expenses
_____ (11) Gains
_____ (12) Losses
_____ (13) Assets
_____ (14) Liabilities
_____ (15) Owners' equity

Implementation principles:

_____ (16) Cost
_____ (17) Revenue
_____ (18) Matching
_____ (19) Full disclosure

A. Recorded a $1,000 sale of merchandise on credit.
B. Counted (inventoried) the unsold items at the end of the period and valued them in dollars.
C. Acquired a vehicle for use in operating the business.
D. Reported the amount of depreciation expense because it likely will affect important decisions of statement users.
E. Identified as the investors, creditors, and others interested in the business.
F. Used special accounting approaches because of the uniqueness of the industry.
G. Sold and issued bonds payable of $1 million.
H. Paid a contractor for an addition to the building with $10,000 cash and $20,000 market value of the stock of the company ($30,000 was deemed to be the cash equivalent price).
I. Engaged an outside independent CPA to audit the financial statements.
J. Sold merchandise and services for cash and on credit during the year then determined the cost of those goods sold and the cost of rendering those services.
K. Established an accounting policy that sales revenue shall be recognized only when ownership to the goods sold passes to the customer.
L. To design and prepare the financial statements to assist the users in making decisions.
M. Established a policy not to include in the financial statements the personal financial affairs of the owners of the business.

Concepts	Transactions
Constraints of accounting:	

_____ (20) Materiality threshold

_____ (21) Cost-benefit constraint

_____ (22) Conservatism constraint

N. Sold an asset at a loss that was a peripheral or incidental transaction.

O. The user value of a special financial report exceeds the cost of preparing it.

P. Valued an asset, such as inventory, at less than its purchase cost because the replacement cost is less.

Q. Dated the income statement "For the Year Ended December 31, 19B."

R. Used services from outsiders—paid cash for some and the remainder on credit.

S. Acquired an asset (a pencil sharpener that will have a useful life of five years) and recorded as an expense when purchased for $1.99.

T. Disclosed in the financial statements all relevant financial information about the business; necessitated the use of notes to the financial statements.

U. Sold an asset at a gain that was a peripheral or incidental transaction.

V. Assets, $500,000 − Liabilities, $300,000 = Owners' Equity, $200,000.

W. The accounting and reporting assumes a "going concern."

P4–14 (Convert from Cash to Accrual Basis)

At the end of 19A, the accounting records of Brown Company showed the following data:

	For the year		
	19A	**19B**	**19C**
Service revenue:			
Cash	$40,000	$60,000	
On credit	15,000	11,000	
19C revenue collected in advance of 19C (not included in the $60,000)		3,000	
Additional cash collections for:			
19A service revenue	6,000	5,000	
19B service revenue		7,000	$3,000
Expenses:			
Paid in cash	25,000	30,000	
On credit	5,000	7,000	
19C expenses paid in advance of 19C (not included in the $30,000)		4,000	
Additional cash payments for:			
19A expenses	3,000	2,000	
19B expenses		3,000	3,000

Required:
Complete the following tabulation (show computations):

		For the year	
		19A	**19B**
a.	Service revenue that would be reported:		
	Accrual basis . . . . $ _____		$ _____
	Cash basis . . . . $ _____		$ _____
b.	Expenses that would be reported:		
	Accrual basis . . . . $ _____		$ _____
	Cash basis . . . . $ _____		$ _____

P4–15   **(Restate Income Statement from Cash Basis to Accrual Basis)**

Barton Company (not a corporation) prepared the income statement given below including the two footnotes:

BARTON COMPANY
Income Statement, Cash Basis
For the Year Ended December 31, 19B

Sales revenue (does not include $20,000 sales on credit because collection will be in 19C)	$120,000
Expenses (does not include $10,000 expenses on credit because payment will be made in 19C)	75,200
Profit	$ 44,800

Additional Data:

a. Depreciation on operational assets (a company truck) for the year amounted to $15,000. Not included in expenses above.

b. On January 1, 19B, paid a two-year insurance premium on the truck amounting to $400. This amount is included in the expenses above.

Required:

a. Recast the above income statement on the accrual basis in conformity with GAAP. Show computations and explain each change.

b. Explain why the cash basis does not measure income as well as the accrual basis.

P4–16   **(Challenging; Convert Income Statement and Balance Sheet from Cash to Accrual Basis)**

At the end of 19A, George Corporation prepared the following annual income statement and balance sheet:

GEORGE CORPORATION
Income Statement
For the Year Ended December 31, 19A

Revenues	$280,000
Expenses	248,000
Income before taxes	32,000
Income taxes (average rate, 30%)	9,600
Net income	$ 22,400

GEORGE CORPORATION
Balance Sheet
At December 31, 19A

Assets			Liabilities	
Cash		$ 18,000	Accounts payable	$ 8,000
Accounts receivable		22,000	Income taxes payable (this is the	
Inventory (by count)		76,800	one half unpaid)	4,800
Fixtures	$25,000		Note payable (12%; due June 20,	
Less: Accumulated			19B)	20,000
depreciation	7,000	18,000	Total liabilities	32,800
Total assets		$134,800		

Stockholders' Equity

Common stock (par $10;		
5,000 shares)	$50,000	
Contributed capital in excess		
of par	10,000	
Retained earnings	42,000	
Total stockholders' equity		102,000
Total liabilities and stockholders'		
equity		$134,800

An independent audit of the above statements and underlying records showed the following:

1. Depreciation expense included in total expense was $2,000 for 19A; it should have been $2,500.

2. A tentative order was received from a customer on December 31, 19A, for goods having a sales price of $10,000 and was included in sales revenue and accounts receivable. The goods were on hand (and included in the ending inventory). It is quite likely that a sale may not materialize; the customer will decide by January 20, 19B. This tentative order should not have been recognized as a sale in 19A.

Required:
Other than these two items, the amounts on the financial statements were correct. Recast the two statements to take into account the depreciation error and the incorrect recognition of the tentative order. Show computations and assume an average income tax rate of 30%.

CASES

Part A: Case 4–1

C4–1   (A Question of Full Disclosure)
Forbes Magazine (December 8, 1980, p. 57) reported the following: "One firm sold shares for a new coal mining company. The prospectus stated that the firm had acquired 15,000 acres of land with proven coal deposits. What the 'entrepreneurs' who raked in some $20 million didn't mention in the prospectus was that they had only leased surface rights to the land. So the only way they could possibly get any coal out of it was if the black stuff came popping out of its own volition."

Explanation:

A prospectus is defined in *Webster's Ninth New Collegiate Dictionary* as "A preliminary printed statement that describes an enterprise (as a business or publication) and that is distributed to prospective buyers, investors, or participants."

The company sold all of the shares in one state; therefore, it was not under the jurisdiction of the SEC (see Chapter 1 discussion of the Securities and Exchange Commission).

Required:

If the firm were to prepare a financial report for external decision makers should they disclose the facts cited above? Give the basis for your decision.

Part B: Cases 4–2 to 4–4

C4–2   **(Analysis of Four Transactions of a Real Estate Company that Involve Adjusting Entries)**

Fast Company, a closely held corporation, invests in commercial rental properties. Fast's annual accounting period ends on December 31. At the end of each year, numerous adjusting entries must be made because many transactions completed during current and prior years have economic effects on the financial statements of the current and future years. This case is concerned with four transactions that have been selected for your analysis. Assume the current year is 19D.

Transaction A:

On July 1, 19A, the company purchased office equipment for use in the business that cost $12,000. The company estimates that the equipment will have a useful life of 10 years and no residual value.

a. Over how many accounting periods will this transaction affect the financial statements of Fast? Explain.
b. Assuming straight-line depreciation, how much depreciation expense should be reported on the 19A and 19B income statements?
c. How should the office equipment be reported on the 19C balance sheet?
d. Would an adjusting entry be made by Fast at the end of each year during the life of the equipment? Prove your answer.

Transaction B:

On September 1, 19D, Fast collected $18,000 rent on some office space. This amount represented the monthly rent in advance for the six-month period, September 1, 19D, through February 28, 19E. Rent Revenue was increased (credited), and Cash was debited for $18,000.

a. Over how many accounting periods will this transaction affect the financial statements of Fast? Explain.
b. How much rent revenue on this office space should Fast report on the 19D income statement? Explain.
c. Did this transaction create a liability for Fast as of the end of 19D? Explain. If yes, how much?
d. Should an adjusting entry be made by Fast on December 31, 19D? Explain why. If your answer is yes, give the adjusting entry.

Transaction C:

On December 31, 19D, Fast owed employees unpaid and unrecorded wages of $5,000 because the payroll was paid on December 27, and between this day and year-end, employees worked three more days in December 19D. The next payroll date is January 5, 19E.

a. Over how many accounting periods would this transaction affect the financial statements of Fast? Explain.
b. How would this $5,000 affect the 19D income statement and balance sheet of Fast?
c. Should an adjusting entry be made by Fast on December 31, 19D? Explain why. If your answer is yes, give the adjusting entry.

Transaction D:

On January 1, 19D, Fast agreed to supervise the planning and subdivision of a large tract of land for a customer—J. Ray. This service job, to be performed by Fast, involved four separate phases. By December 31, 19D, three phases had been completed to the satisfaction of Ray. The remaining phase will be done during 19E. The total price for the four phases (agreed on in advance by both parties) was $40,000. Each phase involves about the same amount of services. On December 31, 19D, no cash had been collected by Fast for the services already performed.

a. Should Fast record any service revenue on this job for 19D? Explain why. If yes, how much?
b. If your answer to (a) is yes, should Fast make an adjusting entry on December 31, 19D? If yes, give the entry. Explain.
c. What entry will be made by Fast when the last phase is completed, assuming the full contract price is collected on completion date, February 15, 19E?

C4–3 (Analysis of How Alternative Ways of Recording a Transaction Affect Adjusting Entries)

General situation: On December 1, 19A, Voss collected $4,000 cash for office space rented to an outsider. The rent collected was for the period December 1, 19A, through March 31, 19B. The annual accounting period ends on December 31.

Required:

a. How much of the $4,000 should Voss report as revenue on the 19A annual income statement? How much of it should be reported as revenue on the 19B income statement?
b. What is the amount of rent revenue collected in advance as of December 31, 19A? How should Voss report this amount on the 19A financial statements?
c. On December 1, 19A, Voss could have recorded the $4,000 collection in one of three different ways as follows:

Approach A:

Cash	4,000	
Rent revenue		4,000

Approach B:

Cash	4,000	
Rent revenue collected in advance		4,000

Approach C:

Cash 4,000
    Rent revenue   1,000
    Rent revenue collected in advance   3,000

For each approach, give the appropriate adjusting entry (in journal form) at December 31, 19A. If no adjusting entry is required, explain why.

d. Do you believe one of the approaches shown above is better than the other two? Which one? Explain.

C4–4   **(Analysis of Notes to an Actual Financial Statement)**

JCPenney   The full disclosure principle requires reporting all relevant economic information concerning a business. The following questions are based on the notes to the financial statements. Refer to the financial statements of J.C. Penney Company, Inc. given in the appendix immediately preceding the index.

1. When does the company's fiscal year end?
2. Does the company generate more sales from stores or catalog operations?
3. What is the approximate sales per square foot in J.C. Penney metropolitan market stores?
4. What is the dollar amount of Land included in the Properties account reported on the balance sheet?
5. What was the amount of dividends payable at the end of the current year?
6. What was the amount of sales revenue for the first three months of 1988?

FIVE

INFORMATION PROCESSING IN AN ACCOUNTING SYSTEM

PURPOSE

Chapter 3 introduced the accounting information processing cycle, and Chapter 4 discussed an important phase of the cycle—adjusting entries. The purpose of Chapter 5 is to expand and complete the cycle. The expansion in this chapter involves additional phases that are performed at the end of the accounting period. Accounting worksheets, adjusting entries, closing entries, and financial statements are emphasized. A clear understanding of this chapter will help you learn more applications of the (a) conceptual framework of accounting and (b) accounting information processing cycle.

The complete accounting cycle is illustrated on the opposite page.

LEARNING OBJECTIVES

1. Define and explain the complete accounting information processing cycle.
2. Apply the four phases of the cycle that are performed during the accounting period.
3. Apply each of the seven phases of the cycle that are performed at the end of the accounting period.
4. Expand your accounting vocabulary by learning the "Important Terms Defined in This Chapter."
5. Apply the knowledge learned from this chapter by completing the homework assigned by your instructor.

ORGANIZATION

1. Phases of the accounting information processing cycle during the accounting period.
2. Phases of the accounting information processing cycle at the end of the accounting period.
3. Data processing approaches in an accounting system—manual, mechanical, computerized.
4. Interim financial statements.

FINANCIAL REPORTING PERSPECTIVES

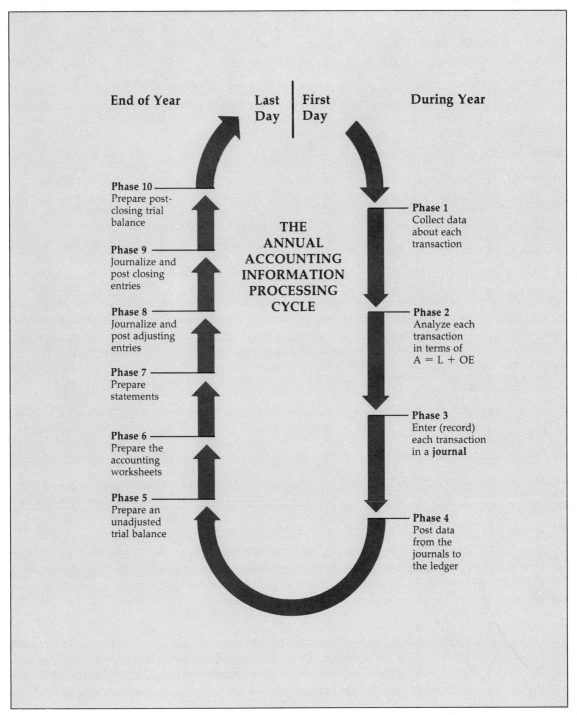

End of Year   Last Day | First Day   During Year

THE ANNUAL ACCOUNTING INFORMATION PROCESSING CYCLE

Phase 10
Prepare post-closing trial balance

Phase 9
Journalize and post closing entries

Phase 8
Journalize and post adjusting entries

Phase 7
Prepare statements

Phase 6
Prepare the accounting worksheets

Phase 5
Prepare an unadjusted trial balance

Phase 1
Collect data about each transaction

Phase 2
Analyze each transaction in terms of $A = L + OE$

Phase 3
Enter (record) each transaction in a **journal**

Phase 4
Post data from the journals to the ledger

Expanding the Accounting Information Processing Cycle

This section expands, but does not change, the **accounting information processing cycle** introduced in Chapter 3. The expansion has additional phases related to the end-of-period activities. Exhibit 5–1 shows the additional phases.

Phases Completed during the Accounting Period

The phases completed during the accounting period were discussed in Chapter 3. For study convenience, these phases are summarized below.

Phase 1—Collect Original Data

This phase is a continuing activity that collects **source documents** (such as sales invoices) from all of the transactions as they occur. The collection process involves all operations of the entity and a large number of employees (including nonaccountants). Source documents provide data to be analyzed and recorded in the accounting system. The source documents must be collected in a timely manner and must provide **complete and accurate data** about each transaction.

Phase 2—Analyze Each Transaction

This phase is an analysis of source documents to identify and measure the economic impact of each transaction on the entity in terms of the accounting model: Assets = Liabilities + Owners' Equity, and Debits = Credits. It requires determination of the specific accounts that should be increased or decreased to properly reflect the economic consequences of each transaction.

Phase 3—Record Transactions in Journal (Journalizing)

This phase involves recording by date the analysis of each transaction in the **journal** in the Debits = Credits format. The economic impacts of each transaction on the entity are recorded first in the journal in chronological order.

Phase 4—Post (Transfer) Data from Journal to Ledger

This phase involves transferring the data in the journal to the **ledger.** The ledger has separate accounts—one for each kind of asset, liability, and owners' equity. Posting to the ledger reorders the data from the chronological order in the journal to the classifications in the accounting model—Assets = Liabilities + Owners' Equity. The ledger provides appropriately classified economic data that will be used to **complete the remaining phases** of the accounting information processing cycle (including preparation of the periodic financial statements).

Phases of the Accounting Information Processing Cycle Completed at the End of the Accounting Period

The phases of the accounting information cycle discussed in Chapter 3 are expanded in this chapter. These additional phases facilitate the end-of-period accounting activities and minimize accounting errors. The specific procedures associated with the remaining phases are discussed in detail in this section.

Exhibit 5-1 Phases of the accounting information processing cycle expanded

Phases Completed During the Accounting Period

1. **Collect original data** about each transaction of the entity; supported with business documents.
2. **Analyze each transaction** (when completed) to determine the economic effects on the entity in terms of the accounting model.
3. **Record transactions in journal.** The entries are recorded in chronological order. This phase is called journalizing.
4. **Post (transfer) data from journal to ledger.**

Phases Completed Only at the End of the Accounting Period

5. **Prepare an unadjusted trial balance** from the ledger.
*6. **Prepare an accounting worksheet:**
   a. Collection of data for adjusting entries and analysis of the data in the context of the accounting model. Enter the adjusting entries on the worksheet.
   b. Separation of the adjusted data among the income statement, balance sheet, and statement of retained earnings. Prepare statement of cash flows (SCF) worksheet (discussed in Chapter 15).
7. **Prepare financial statements from the worksheet:**
   a. Income statement.
   b. Balance sheet.
   c. Statement of cash flows (SCF; discussed in Chapter 15).
*8. **Journalize and post adjusting entries** (at the end of the period):
   a. Recorded in the journal.
   b. Posted to the ledger.
*9. **Closing entries for the income statement accounts:**
   a. Recorded in the journal.
   b. Posted to the ledger.
*10. **Prepare a post-closing trial balance.**

Phase Completed Only at the Start of the Next Accounting Period

11. Optional **reversing entries** (Chapter Supplement 5A).

* Phases added in this chapter to expand the cycle.

Phase 5—Prepare an Unadjusted Trial Balance

At the end of the accounting period, after all current transactions have been recorded in the journal and then posted to the ledger, a listing of all **ledger accounts** and their balances is prepared. This listing is called the **unadjusted trial balance.** This trial balance can be used to check the two accounting equalities—Assets = Liabilities + Owners' Equity, and Debits = Credits.

This trial balance is called **unadjusted** because it does not include the effects of the **adjusting** entries (discussed in Chapter 4). The expanded phases—6 through 10—show how the adjusting entries are included in the (*a*) financial statements and (*b*) the accounting records.

Phase 6—Prepare an Accounting Worksheet

At the end of the accounting period, an **accounting worksheet** may be prepared. The worksheet is prepared before the adjusting and closing entries are recorded. The **completed worksheet provides all of the data needed to complete the remaining end-of-period phases** by bringing together in one place, in an orderly way, the (1) unadjusted trial balance, (2) adjusting entries, (3) income statement, (4) statement of retained earnings, (5) balance sheet, and (6) the closing entries (explained later).[1]

Illustration: The simplified case used in Chapter 4 for High-Rise Apartments, Inc., will be used to illustrate preparation of a worksheet at the end of the accounting period. To make the illustration easier, two exhibits are given:

Exhibit 5–2—Worksheet format with the unadjusted trial balance and adjusting entries.

Exhibit 5–3—Worksheet completed; shows the **income statement, statement of retained earnings, and balance sheet.**

The sequential steps used to develop the worksheet are:

Step 1—Set up the worksheet format by entering the appropriate column headings. This step is shown in Exhibit 5–2. The left column shows the account titles (taken directly from the ledger). There are six separate pairs of debit-credit money columns. Notice that the last six debit-credit columns show the data for the financial statements.

Step 2—Enter the **unadjusted** trial balance as of the end of the accounting period directly from the ledger into the first pair of debit-credit columns. When all of the current entries for the period, **excluding** the adjusting entries, have been recorded in the journal and posted to the ledger, the amounts for the **unadjusted** trial balance are the balances of the respective ledger accounts. Before going to the next step, the equality of the debits and credits in the unadjusted trial balance should be tested by totaling each column (totals $491,460). When a worksheet is used, there is no need to develop a **separate** unadjusted trial balance (Phase 5) because it can be developed on the worksheet.

Step 3—The second pair of debit-credit columns, headed "Adjusting Entries," is completed by developing and then entering the adjusting entries directly on the worksheet. The adjusting entries for High-Rise Apartments shown in Exhibit 5–2 were discussed in detail in Chapter 4. To facilitate examination (for potential errors), the adjusting entries usually are coded on the worksheet as illustrated in Exhibit 5–2. Some of the adjusting entries

---

[1] This entire section on the worksheet can be omitted without affecting the remaining chapters because it is only a facilitating procedure.

Exhibit 5–2 Worksheet format with unadjusted trial balance and adjusting entries (already entered)

HIGH-RISE APARTMENTS, INC.
Worksheet for the Year Ended December 31, 19B

Account Titles	Unadjusted Trial Balance		Adjusting Entries		Adjusted Trial Balance		Income Statement		Retained Earnings		Balance Sheet	
	Debit	Credit	Debit	Credit	Debit	Credit	Debit	Credit	Debit	Credit	Debit	Credit
Cash	12,297											
Prepaid insurance	2,400			(c) 1,200								
Inventory of maintenance supplies	600			(e) 400								
Land	25,000											
Apartment building	360,000											
Accumulated depreciation, building		10,000		(d) 10,000								
Note payable, long term		30,000										
Rent collected in advance				(a) 500								
Mortgage payable, long term		238,037										
Capital stock (par $10; 5,000 shares)*		50,000										
Contributed capital in excess of par		5,000										
Retained earnings, Jan. 1, 19B		29,960										
Dividends declared and paid	12,000											
Rent revenue		128,463	(a) 500	(b) 600								
Advertising expense	500											
Maintenance expense	3,000		(e) 400									
Salary expense	17,400		(f) 900									
Interest expense	19,563		(g) 600									
Utilities expense	34,500											
Miscellaneous expenses	4,200											
Insurance expense			(c) 1,200									
Depreciation expense			(d) 10,000									
Salaries payable				(f) 900								
Interest payable				(g) 600								
Rent revenue receivable			(b) 600									
	491,460	491,460	14,200	14,200								

* Average issue price per share: ($50,000 + $5,000) ÷ 5,000 shares = $11. This topic is discussed in Chapter 12.

Exhibit 5–3 Accounting worksheet completed

HIGH-RISE APARTMENTS, INC.
Worksheet for the Year Ended December 31, 19B

Account Titles	Unadjusted Trial Balance Debit	Unadjusted Trial Balance Credit	Adjusting Entries* Debit	Adjusting Entries* Credit	Adjusted Trial Balance Debit	Adjusted Trial Balance Credit	Income Statement Debit	Income Statement Credit	Retained Earnings Debit	Retained Earnings Credit	Balance Sheet Debit	Balance Sheet Credit
Cash	12,297				12,297						12,297	
Prepaid insurance	2,400			(c) 1,200	1,200						1,200	
Inventory of maintenance supplies	600			(e) 400	200						200	
Land	25,000				25,000						25,000	
Apartment building	360,000				360,000						360,000	
Accumulated depreciation, building		10,000		(d) 10,000		20,000						20,000
Note payable, long term		30,000				30,000						30,000
Rent collected in advance				(a) 500		500						500
Mortgage payable, long term		238,037				238,037						238,037
Capital stock (par $10; 5,000 shares)		50,000				50,000						50,000
Contributed capital in excess of par		5,000				5,000						5,000
Retained earnings, Jan. 1, 19B		29,960				29,960				29,960		
Dividends declared and paid	12,000				12,000				12,000			
Rent revenue		128,463	(a) 500	(b) 600		128,563		128,563				
Advertising expense	500				500		500					
Maintenance expense	3,000		(e) 400		3,400		3,400					

	Trial Balance Dr	Trial Balance Cr	Adjustments Dr	Adjustments Cr	Adjusted Trial Balance Dr	Adjusted Trial Balance Cr	Income Statement Dr	Income Statement Cr	Balance Sheet Dr	Balance Sheet Cr
Salary expense	17,400		(f) 900		18,300		18,300			
Interest expense	19,563		(g) 600		20,163		20,163			
Utilities expense	34,500				34,500		34,500			
Miscellaneous expenses	4,200				4,200		4,200			
Insurance expense			(c) 1,200		1,200		1,200			
Depreciation expense			(d) 10,000		10,000		10,000			
Salaries payable				(f) 900		900				900
Interest payable				(g) 600		600				600
Rent revenue receivable			(b) 600		600				600	
	491,460	491,460	14,200	14,200	503,560	503,560	92,263	128,563		
Income tax expense†			(h) 7,260		7,260		7,260			
Income taxes payable				(h) 7,260		7,260				7,260
Net income‡							29,040			29,040
							128,563	128,563		
									12,000	
									47,000	59,000
									59,000	59,000
Retained earnings, Dec. 31, 19B§									399,297	399,297

* Explanation of adjusting entries is provided in Exhibit 5–4.
† Revenues, $128,563 − Pretax expenses, $92,263 = $36,300; $36,300 × Tax rate, 20% = $7,260.
‡ Pretax income, $36,300 − Income tax, $7,260 = $29,040.
§ $59,000 − $12,000 = $47,000.

may need one or more account titles in addition to those of the original trial balance listing (see last four account titles in Exhibit 5–2). After the adjusting entries are completed on the worksheet, the equality of debits and credits for those entries is checked (totals $14,200).

The remaining steps to complete the worksheet are shown by the shaded area in Exhibit 5–3; these steps are:

Step 4—The pair of debit-credit columns headed "Adjusted Trial Balance" is completed. Although not essential, this pair of columns helps to assure accuracy. The adjusted trial balance is the line-by-line combined amounts of the unadjusted trial balance, plus or minus the amounts entered as adjusting entries in the second pair of columns. For example, the Rent Revenue account shows a $128,463 credit balance under Unadjusted Trial Balance. To this amount is **added the credit** amount, $600, **minus the debit amount,** $500, for combined amount of $128,563, which is entered as a **credit** under Adjusted Trial Balance. For those accounts that were not affected by the adjusting entries, the unadjusted trial balance amount is carried directly across to the Adjusted Trial Balance column. After each line has been completed, the equality of the debits and credits under Adjusted Trial Balance is checked (total, $503,560).

Step 5—The amount on each line, under Adjusted Trial Balance, is **extended horizontally** across the worksheet and entered under the financial statement heading (income statement, retained earnings,[2] or balance sheet) on which it must be reported. Debit amounts are carried across as debits, and credit amounts are carried across as credits.

You can see that (1) each amount extended across was entered under only one of the six remaining columns, and (2) debits remain debits and credits remain credits in the extending process.

Step 6—At this point, the two Income Statement columns are summed (subtotals). The difference between these two subtotals is the **pretax income (or loss).** Income tax expense then is computed by multiplying this difference by the tax rate. In Exhibit 5–3, the computation was (Revenues, $128,563 − Pretax expenses, $92,263) × Tax rate, 20% = $7,260. The **adjusting entry** for income tax then was entered at the bottom of the worksheet. Income tax expense and income taxes payable now can be extended horizontally to the Income Statement and Balance Sheet columns. Net income is entered as a **balancing debit** amount in the Income Statement column and as a credit in the Retained Earnings column.

Step 7—The two Retained Earnings columns are summed. The difference is the ending balance of retained earnings. This balance amount is entered as

---

[2] The statement of retained earnings is discussed below under Phase 7.

a balancing debit amount under Retained Earnings and also as a balancing credit amount under Balance Sheet (i.e., an increase to owners' equity). At this point, the two Balance Sheet columns should sum to equal amounts. The continuous checking of the equality of debits and credits in each pair of debit-credit columns helps to assure the correctness of the worksheet. However, the balancing feature alone does not assure that the worksheet has no errors. For example, if an expense amount (a debit) were extended to either the Retained Earnings debit column or to the Balance Sheet debit column, the worksheet would balance in all respects; however, at least two money columns would have one or more errors. Therefore, special care must be used in selecting the appropriate debit-credit columns during the horizontal extension process.[3]

The completed worksheet, Exhibit 5–3, provides the data needed to complete the remaining phases of the accounting information processing cycle as follows (summarized from Exhibit 5–1):

Phases	Phase descriptions	Source on worksheet
7	Prepare income statement	Income Statement columns
	Prepare balance sheet	Balance Sheet columns
	Prepare statement of retained earnings	Retained Earnings columns
8	Record adjusting entries in journal and post to ledger	Adjusting Entries columns
9	Record closing entries in journal and post to ledger	Income Statement and Retained Earnings columns
10	Post-closing trial balance	Prepare from ledger and check with Balance Sheet columns

Phase 7—Prepare Financial Statements from the Worksheet

The completed worksheet provides the accounts and amounts needed to prepare the income statement, balance sheet, and statement of retained earnings. The statement of retained earnings, although not a required statement, usually is prepared by corporations. The **retained earnings statement** ties together the income statement and the stockholders' equity section of the balance sheet.

The financial statements for High-Rise Apartments, prepared directly from the worksheet, Exhibit 5–3, are shown below. Notice that all of the figures were provided by the last three pairs of columns headed "Income Statement," "Retained Earnings," and "Balance Sheet."

---

[3] The number of paired columns on a worksheet can be reduced by omitting both, or either, the Adjusted Trial Balance columns and the Retained Earnings columns.

HIGH-RISE APARTMENTS, INC.
Income Statement
For the Year Ended December 31, 19B

Revenues:		
Rent revenue		$128,563
Operating expenses:		
Advertising expense	$ 500	
Maintenance expense	3,400	
Salary expense	18,300	
Interest expense	20,163	
Utilities expense	34,500	
Miscellaneous expenses	4,200	
Insurance expense	1,200	
Depreciation expense	10,000	
Total operating expenses		92,263
Pretax income		36,300
Income tax expense ($36,300 × 20%)		7,260
Net income		$ 29,040
EPS ($29,040 ÷ 5,000 shares)		$5.81

HIGH-RISE APARTMENTS, INC.
Statement of Retained Earnings
For the Year Ended December 31, 19B

Retained earnings balance, January 1, 19B	$29,960
Add net income of 19B	29,040
Total	59,000
Less dividends declared and paid in 19B	12,000
Retained earnings balance, December 31, 19B	$47,000

HIGH-RISE APARTMENTS, INC.
Balance Sheet
At December 31, 19B

Assets

Current assets:			
Cash		$ 12,297	
Rent revenue receivable		600	
Inventory, maintenance supplies		200	
Prepaid insurance		1,200	
Total current assets			$ 14,297
Operational assets:			
Land		25,000	
Apartment building	$360,000		
Less: Accumulated depreciation	20,000	340,000	365,000
Total assets			$379,297

HIGH-RISE APARTMENTS, INC.
Balance Sheet
At December 31, 19B

Liabilities

Current liabilities:		
Salaries payable	$ 900	
Interest payable	600	
Income taxes payable	7,260	
Rent collected in advance	500	
Total current liabilities		$ 9,260
Long-term liabilities:		
Note payable	30,000	
Mortgage payable	238,037	
Total long-term liabilities		268,037
Total liabilities		277,297

Stockholders' Equity

Contributed capital:		
Capital stock (par $10; 5,000 shares)	50,000	
Contributed capital in excess of par	5,000	
Total contributed capital	55,000	
Retained earnings (see statement of retained earnings)	47,000	
Total stockholders' equity		102,000
Total liabilities and stockholders' equity		$379,297

Phase 8—Journalize and Post Adjusting Entries

This phase is needed to enter the adjusting entries into the accounts. Immediately after finishing the worksheet, the financial statements are prepared. By using a worksheet, preparation of the financial statements is not delayed by the remaining phases of the accounting cycle. After the financial statements have been prepared, the **adjusting entries shown on the completed worksheet are entered in the journal and then posted to the ledger.** These entries are "dated" as of the last day of the accounting period. This task is a clerical one because the entries merely are copied from the worksheet into the journal. The adjusting entries for High-Rise Apartments, with a **folio notation** to show that posting is completed, are shown in Exhibit 5–4. Each adjusting entry was explained in Chapter 4, Part A. The ledger, with the adjusting entries posted (in color for identification), is shown in Exhibit 5–6. You should trace the posting from the journal to the ledger.

Phase 9—Closing Entries for the Income Statement Accounts

The revenue, gain, expense, and loss accounts are **income statement accounts.** The remaining accounts are **balance sheet accounts.** The revenue, gain, expense, and loss accounts are often called **temporary** (or nominal) accounts because they are used to accumulate data for the **current accounting period only.** At the end of each period, their balances are transferred, or **closed,** to the Retained Earnings account. This periodic closing (or clearing out) of the balances

Exhibit 5–4 Adjusting entries recorded in the journal

	HIGH-RISE APARTMENTS, INC.			
	JOURNAL			Page <u>6</u>
Date 19B	Account Titles and Explanation	Folio	Debit	Credit
Dec. 31	*a.* Rent revenue	340	500	
	Rent collected in advance	204		500
	To adjust the accounts for revenue collected in advance.			
31	*b.* Rent revenue receivable	102	600	
	Rent revenue	340		600
	To adjust for rent revenue earned in 19B but not yet collected.			
31	*c.* Insurance expense	356	1,200	
	Prepaid insurance	103		1,200
	To adjust for insurance expired during 19B.			
31	*d.* Depreciation expense	360	10,000	
	Accumulated depreciation, building	113		10,000
	To adjust for depreciation expense for 19B.			
31	*e.* Maintenance expense	351	400	
	Inventory of maintenance supplies	104		400
	To adjust for supplies used from inventory during 19B.			
31	*f.* Salary expense	352	900	
	Salaries payable	206		900
	To adjust for salaries earned but not yet recorded or paid.			
31	*g.* Interest expense	353	600	
	Interest payable	209		600
	To adjust for accrued interest expense for two months on note payable ($30,000 \times 12\% \times 2/12 = \$600$).			
31	*h.* An adjusting entry for income tax expense is computed on the worksheet when the pretax income is computed thereon. The entry is:			
	Income tax expense	370	7,260	
	Income taxes payable	208		7,260

of the income statement accounts into Retained Earnings is done by using closing entries. The closing entries have two purposes: (1) to transfer net income (or loss) to retained earnings and (2) to establish a **zero balance** in each of the temporary accounts to start the next accounting period. In this way, the **income statement accounts** again are ready for their **temporary** collection function for the next period.

In contrast, the **balance sheet accounts** (assets, liabilities, and owners' equity) are not closed periodically; therefore, they are often called **permanent** (or real) accounts. To illustrate, the ending cash balance of one accounting period must be the beginning cash balance of the next accounting period. The only time a permanent account has a zero balance is when the item represented (such as machinery) is no longer owned (or is fully depreciated). The balance at the end of the period in each balance sheet account is carried forward in the ledger as the **beginning** balance for the next period.

The **closing entries** made at the end of the accounting period to transfer the balances of all of the income statement accounts is only a clerical phase. To close an account means to transfer its balance to another designated account by means of an entry. For example, an account that has a credit balance (such as a revenue account) is closed by **debiting** that account for an amount equal to its balance and crediting the account to which the balance is transferred. In the closing process, a credit balance is always transferred to another account as a credit, and a debit balance is always transferred to another account as a debit. Closing entries are **dated** the last day of the accounting period, entered in the journal in the usual Debits = Credits format, and immediately posted to the ledger.

A special summary account, called Income Summary, sometimes is used in the closing process. All of the income statement accounts—revenues, gains, expenses, and losses—are closed to Income Summary. The difference between the total credits and the total debits is net income or net loss, which is then closed to the Retained Earnings account. The following summarized data for High-Rise Apartments (from Exhibit 5–3) are used to illustrate the Income Summary account: total revenues, $128,563; total expenses, $99,523; and net income, $29,040. The three closing entries, as they would be shown in the ledger accounts, are:

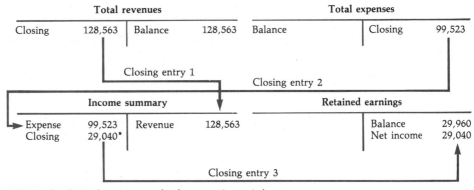

Total revenues				Total expenses		
Closing	128,563	Balance	128,563	Balance	Closing	99,523

Closing entry 1

Closing entry 2

Income summary				Retained earnings		
Expense	99,523	Revenue	128,563		Balance	29,960
Closing	29,040*				Net income	29,040

Closing entry 3

* Notice that this is the net income for the accounting period.

Exhibit 5–5   Closing entries recorded in the journal (source of data is Exhibit 5–3)

	HIGH-RISE APARTMENTS, INC.			
	JOURNAL			Page <u>7</u>
Date 19B	Account Titles and Explanation	Folio	Debit	Credit
Dec. 31	Rent revenue	340	128,563	
	Income summary	330		128,563
	To transfer revenues into Income Summary.			
31	Income summary ($92,263 + $7,260)	330	99,523	
	Advertising expense	350		500
	Maintenance expense	351		3,400
	Salary expense	352		18,300
	Interest expense	353		20,163
	Utilities expense	354		34,500
	Miscellaneous expenses	355		4,200
	Insurance expense	356		1,200
	Depreciation expense	360		10,000
	Income tax expense	370		7,260
	To transfer expense amounts into Income Summary.			
31	Income summary	330	29,040	
	Retained earnings	305		29,040
	To transfer Net Income into Retained Earnings.			
31	Retained earnings	305	12,000	
	Dividends declared and paid	306		12,000
	To transfer Dividends Declared and Paid into Retained Earnings.			

The detailed closing entries are shown in Exhibits 5–5 and 5–6. The data used in the detailed closing entries can be taken directly from the worksheet Exhibit 5–3.

The last journal entry shown on Exhibit 5–5 closed Dividends Declared and Paid (which is a temporary account) to Retained Earnings (not to Income Summary). High-Rise Apartments declared and paid a $12,000 cash dividend to its stockholders. Dividends Declared and Paid was debited, and Cash was credited for this amount. Dividends are payments to the stockholders out of earnings. A dividend reduces retained earnings. Therefore, the dividend account is closed to Retained Earnings.[4] Notice that the **ending** balance in the ledger account for

---

[4] When the dividend was declared and paid, the debit could have been made directly to Retained Earnings. In this case, the closing entry would not be made.

Exhibit 5-6 Ledger accounts illustrated with adjusting and closing entries

HIGH-RISE APARTMENTS, INC.
LEDGER—19B

Cash	101		Income Taxes Payable	208		Maintenance Expense	351
12,297			(h)	7,260		3,000	(7) 3,400
					(e)	400	

Rent Revenue Receivable	102		Interest Payable	209		Salary Expense	352
(b) 600			(g)	600		17,400	(7) 18,300
					(f)	900	

Prepaid Insurance	103		Mortgage Payable	251		Interest Expense	353
2,400	(c) 1,200			238,037		19,563	(7) 20,163
					(g)	600	

Inventory of Maintenance Supplies	104		Capital Stock	301		Utilities Expense	354
600	(e) 400			50,000		34,500	(7) 34,500

Land	110		Contributed Capital in Excess of Par	302		Miscellaneous Expenses	355
25,000				5,000		4,200	(7) 4,200

Retained Earnings is: $29,960 + $29,040 − $12,000 = $47,000. Net income and dividends paid are included in the statement of retained earnings (Exhibit 5–3).

After the closing process is completed, all of the temporary (i.e., the income statement) accounts have a zero balance. These accounts then are ready for reuse during the next accounting period for accumulating the revenues and expenses of the new period. When T-accounts are used, as in Exhibit 5–6, a zero balance is indicated by a double ruling on each side of the account. Notice that

(concluded)

Apartment Building 111		Retained Earnings 305		Insurance Expense 356	
360,000		(7) 12,000	29,960	(c) 1,200	(7) 1,200
			(7) 29,040		

Accumulated Depreciation, Building 113		Dividends Declared and Paid 306		Depreciation Expense 360	
	10,000	12,000	(7) 12,000	(d) 10,000	(7) 10,000
	(d) 10,000				

Note Payable, Long Term 201		Income Summary 330		Income Tax Expense 370	
	30,000	(7) 99,523	(7) 128,563	(h) 7,260	(7) 7,260
		(7) 29,040			

Rent Collected in Advance 204		Rent Revenue 340		
(a)	500	(a) 500	128,463	
		(7) 128,563	(b) 600	

Salaries Payable 206		Advertising Expense 350	
(f)	900	500	(7) 500

For illustrative purposes:
- Unadjusted balances are in black.
- Adjusting entries are in color.
- Closing entries are enclosed in boxes.

the closing process also updates the balance of Retained Earnings (a permanent account).

The permanent (i.e., balance sheet) accounts have an **ending** balance, which is carried forward as the beginning balance for the next period. The balance carried forward in a T-account can be shown as follows:[5]

---

[5] Exhibit 3–4 shows the columnar format for ledger accounts that is always used. The T-account format is used only for instructional convenience.

Retained Earnings			305
Dividends (19B)	12,000	Jan. 1, 19B, balance	29,960
Balance carried forward to 19C	47,000	Net income (19B)	29,040
	59,000		59,000
		Jan. 1, 19C, balance	47,000

Phase 10—Prepare a Post-Closing Trial Balance

A post-closing trial balance is a verification of the account balances after all closing entries have been posted. In computerized accounting systems, this verification can be done automatically. In other systems, it may be done with a printing calculator or an adding machine. All of the income statement accounts have been closed to Retained Earnings; therefore, the post-closing trial balance will show balances **only** for the permanent accounts classified as assets, liabilities, and owners' equity. These balances should be the same as those shown in the last two columns of the worksheet (Exhibit 5–3). The ending balances shown in the ledger accounts after the closing process will be the beginning balances for the next period.

Phase 11—Reversing Entries

Some accountants add an **optional phase** to the accounting information processing cycle called **reversing entries.** This phase is dated as of the first day of the next accounting period. It is used for the sole purpose of **facilitating** certain subsequent entries in the accounts. Reversing entries are related specifically to certain adjusting entries that already have been journalized and posted to the accounts. When appropriate, such adjusting entries are reversed on the first day of the next period (i.e., the debits and credits simply are reversed by the reversing entry). Reversing entries involve bookkeeping skills rather than accounting concepts and principles. Supplement 5A at the end of this chapter discusses reversing entries.

Data Processing Approaches in an Accounting System

Data processing in an accounting system refers to the flow of data through the information processing cycle. Although data processing can be time consuming and costly, a well-designed processing system provides an efficient flow of data from the daily transactions to the financial statements at the end of the accounting period. The processing of accounting data may be done in any combination of three approaches: manual data processing, mechanical data processing, and computerized data processing.

Manual Data Processing

With this approach, the accounting work is done by hand (i.e., manually). The manual approach is used in small entities. In large and medium-size businesses, certain parts of the information process are often done manually. The manual approach also is used in accounting textbooks to illustrate data processing because you can see what is being done. You cannot see what is going on inside a computer.

Mechanical Data Processing

Mechanical data processing is used to record repetitive transactions that occur in large numbers. Mechanical processing of accounting data uses accounting machines that vary in type and application. These mechanical devices range from cash registers to posting machines. Although mechanical data processing is used today, it is being rapidly replaced by computerized data processing.

Computerized Data Processing

When computerized data processing is used, the use of manual and mechanical activities in an accounting system is minimal. Because of the large capability to store data and the speed with which such data can be manipulated and recalled, computerized data processing is widely used in accounting. Computerized data processing needs **hardware** (the computer and equipment related to it) and **software** (the programs that are instructions to the computer). Computerized data processing is applied widely to such accounting problems as payrolls, billings for goods and services, accounts receivable, accounts payable, inventories, and to the preparation of detailed financial statements. Because of the rapid development of microcomputers and software "packages" for them, it is techically and economically feasible for even the smallest businesses (and individuals) to have a computerized accounting system.

Interim Financial Statements

Financial statements for a reporting period of less than one year are called **interim financial statements.** Such statements usually are prepared quarterly. **Monthly** financial statements almost always are for internal management uses only.

When interim financial statements are prepared, the company usually does not go through the phases of interim adjusting and closing entries. The formal phases of journalizing and posting adjusting entries typically are performed only at the end of the annual accounting period. Instead, the company prepares a worksheet to facilitate preparation of the interim financial statements. Therefore, the worksheet has another useful purpose when interim financial statements are prepared. At the end of each interim period, an unadjusted trial balance is taken from the ledger accounts and entered directly on a worksheet. The worksheet then is completed by entering the interim adjusting entries on it and extending the adjusted amounts to the Retained Earnings, Income Statement, and Balance Sheet columns. The interim statements are prepared on the basis of the worksheet. In such cases, the remaining phases of the accounting information processing cycle (adjusting entries recorded, closing entries recorded, and post-closing trial balance) are not completed at the end of each interim period.

SUMMARY OF THE CHAPTER

This chapter discussed the complete accounting information processing cycle. The cycle captures economic data on transactions as they occur, records their economic effects on the entity, and communicates these effects by means of the periodic financial statements. The accounting information system must be designed to measure net income, financial position, and cash flow accurately and effectively. Such an information system also must be designed to fit the specific characteristics of the entity.

The worksheet, the closing entries, and the post-closing trial balance phases are clerical data processing procedures and do not involve any new accounting principles. The 11 phases discussed in this chapter constitute the accounting information processing cycle that is repeated each accounting period.

Many adaptations of the procedures used to implement the cycle are observed in actual situations because entities have different characteristics such as size, type of industry, complexity, accounting expertise, and sophistication of the management.

The information processing activities in a particular entity can be effective in terms of the outputs (the financial statements), but unfortunately, the opposite may be true. The effectiveness of the system depends on the competence of those performing the data processing tasks and the importance attached by the management and owners to the measurement of operating results and financial position. In this context, the information processing system of an entity is significant to all parties interested in the entity because the financial statements are important in decision making.

CHAPTER SUPPLEMENT 5A (Reversing Entries Illustrated)

After preparing the post-closing trial balance, an **optional facilitating phase** may be added as Phase 11 (see Exhibit 5–1). This optional phase involves reversing entries. **Reversing entries are dated at the beginning of the next period and relate only to certain adjusting entries made at the end of the prior period.** Certain adjusting entries may be reversed on the first day of the next period solely to facilitate recording subsequent related transactions. Reversing entries are optional and involve only bookkeeping skills rather than accounting principles or concepts. The reversing entry phase is used in most companies, whether the system is manual, mechanical, or computerized.[6]

---

[6] Knowledge of reversing entries is important primarily to students who plan to study advanced accounting. This knowledge is not needed for study of the remaining chapters in this book.

Exhibit 5–7 Purpose of reversing entries illustrated with wages

DAY COMPANY

Situation: The payroll was paid on December 28, 19B; the next payroll will be on January 13, 19C. At December 31, 19B, wages of $3,000 were earned for the last three days of the year that had not been paid or recorded.

With reversing entry	Without reversing entry

a. **The preceding adjusting entry:**

December 31, 19B, adjusting entry to record the $3,000 accrued (unpaid) wages:

With reversing entry	Without reversing entry
Wage expense 3,000	Wage expense 3,000
Wages payable	Wages payable
(a liability) 3,000	(a liability) 3,000

b. **The closing entry:** The revenue and expense accounts are closed to Income Summary after the adjusting entries are completed and posted to the ledger.

December 31, 19B, closing entry:

With reversing entry	Without reversing entry
Income summary 3,000	Income summary 3,000
Wage expense 3,000	Wage expense 3,000

Reversing entries are given this name because they reverse, at the start of the next accounting period, the effects of certain adjusting entries made at the end of the previous period. Reversing entries are always the opposite of the related adjusting entry. It is efficient to "reverse" only certain adjusting entries; the other adjusting entries should not be reversed.

To illustrate reversing entries, assume that Day Company is in the process of completing the information processing cycle at the end of its accounting period, December 31, 19B. Exhibit 5–7 presents a situation that shows (1) an adjusting entry on December 31, 19B; (2) the reversing entry that could be made on January 1, 19C; and (3) the subsequent entry on January 13, 19C, that was facilitated or simplified. To demonstrate the facilitating effect of a reversing entry, we also have presented entries in the exhibit reflecting the same situation assuming no reversing entry. You should study carefully the two sets of entries and the explanatory comments in Exhibit 5–7. The reversing entry is shown in color for emphasis.

Exhibit 5–8 presents another illustration of the effects of reversing entries. It is presented to emphasize the facilitating feature of reversing entries as shown in both the journal and ledger. The reversing entry is shown in color to facilitate your study.

Certain adjusting entries can be reversed to facilitate or simplify subsequent related entries, but other adjusting entries should **not** be reversed. There is no

Exhibit 5–7 *(concluded)*

> *c.* **The reversing entry:** The information processing cycle in 19B is complete. All closing entries have been posted, and the post-closing trial balance has been verified. At this point in time, January 1, 19C, the accountant should decide whether it is desirable to reverse any of the 19B adjusting entries (i.e., any reversing entries) to simplify the **subsequent related entries.** Question: Would a reversing entry on January 1, 19C, simplify the entry to be made on January 13, 19C, when the wages are paid?
>
> January 1, 19C, reversing entry:
>
> | | | | |
> |---|---|---|---|
> | Wages payable (a liability) . . . . | 3,000 | | No reversing entry assumed. |
> | Wage expense . . . . | | 3,000 | |
>
> *d.* **The subsequent entry that was facilitated:** The payroll of $25,000 was completed and paid on January 13, 19C. This subsequent payment entry is to be recorded. Question: Did the reversing entry facilitate or simplify this entry?
>
> January 13, 19C, payroll entry:*
>
> | | | | | |
> |---|---|---|---|---|
> | Wage expense . . . . . . | 25,000 | | Wages payable . . . . . . | 3,000 |
> | Cash . . . . | | 25,000 | Wage expense . . . . | 22,000 |
> | | | | Cash . . . . | 25,000 |
>
> * **Explanation:** Observe that when the reversing entry was used, this last entry required only one debit, contrasted with two debits when no reversing entry was made. This difference was because the reversing entry served to (1) clear out the liability account, Wages Payable; and (2) set up a temporary **credit** in the Wage Expense account. After the last entry, to record the payment of the payroll, both accounts affected— Wage Expense and Wages Payable—are identical in balance under both approaches. If the reversing entry is not made, the company must go to the trouble of identifying how much of the $25,000 paid on January 13, 19C, was expense and how much of it was to pay the liability set up in the adjusting entry at the end of the prior period ([*a*] above).

inflexible rule that will help you decide which adjusting entries should be reversed. You must analyze each case and make a rational choice. In general, short-term accruals and deferrals are candidates for reversal.

The adjusting entry to record depreciation and other entries of this type should never be reversed. In these cases, the adjusting entry is not followed by a subsequent "collection or payment" entry; therefore, it would be not only pointless to reverse the adjusting entry for depreciation but would introduce an error into the accounts because the accumulated depreciation account would reflect a zero balance for the first period. Thus, many adjusting entries are not candidates for reversal. Those that are candidates are easily identified if one considers the nature of the subsequent related transaction (i.e., whether there is a subsequent collection or payment).

Perhaps the most compelling reason for reversing entries is to increase the likelihood that the effects of certain adjusting entries will not be overlooked when recording the next related transaction in the following period.

Exhibit 5–8 Reversing entries illustrated, journal and ledger (with interest revenue)

Situation: On September 1, 19A, Company X loaned $1,200 on a one-year, 10% interest-bearing note receivable. On August 31, 19B, the company will collect the $1,200 principal plus $120 interest revenue. The annual accounting period ends December 31.

JOURNAL

a. September 1, 19A—To record the loan:

Note receivable   1,200
   Cash   1,200

b. December 31, 19A (end of the accounting period)—Adjusting entry for four months' interest revenue earned but not collected ($1,200 × 10% × 4/12 = $40):

Interest receivable   40
   Interest revenue   40

c. December 31, 19A—To close interest revenue:

Interest revenue   40
   Income summary   40

d. January 1, 19B—To reverse adjusting entry of December 31, 19A:

Interest revenue   40
   Interest receivable   40

Observe that after this entry, the Interest Receivable account reflects a zero balance and Interest Revenue reflects a **debit** balance of $40 (four months' interest).

e. August 31, 19B—Subsequent entry; to record collection of note plus interest for one year:*

Cash   1,320
   Note receivable   1,200
   Interest revenue   120

LEDGER

Cash

	x,xxx	(a) 9/1/19A	1,200
(e) 8/31/19B	1,320		

Note Receivable

(a) 9/1/19A	1,200	(e) 8/31/19B	1,200

Interest Receivable

(b) 12/31/19A	40	(d) 1/1/19B	40

Interest Revenue

(c) 12/31/19A	40	(b) 12/31/19A	40
(d) 1/1/19B	40	(e) 8/31/19B	120

Income Summary

		(c) 12/31/19A	40

Note: To demonstrate the facilitating feature, assume the reversing entry (d) was not made. The August 31, 19B, entry would be more complex, viz:

Cash 1,320
  Note receivable   1,200
  Interest receivable   40
  Interest revenue   80

* Observe that after this entry, the Note Receivable account has a zero balance and the Interest Revenue an $80 balance which represents eight months' interest revenue earned in 19B.

IMPORTANT TERMS DEFINED IN THIS CHAPTER

Accounting Information Processing Cycle   Accounting phases (steps) from the time a transaction is completed to the financial statements. *p. 194*

Closing entries End-of-period entries to close all revenue and expense accounts to Retained Earnings (through Income Summary). *p. 203*

Computer Hardware Computer and other equipment used with it. *p. 210*

Computerized Data Processing Accounting process performed (in whole or in part) using computers. *p. 210*

Computer Software Computer programs and instructions for using an electronic computer. *p. 210*

Manual Data Processing Accounting process performed (in whole or in part) in handwriting; manually. *p. 209*

Mechanical Data Processing Accounting process performed (in whole or in part) using machines. *p. 210*

Permanent (Real) Accounts Permanent (or real) accounts are the balance sheet accounts; no closing entries. *p. 205*

Post-Closing Trial Balance Trial balance prepared after all of the closing entries have been posted. *p. 209*

Reversing Entries Recorded at beginning of next accounting period; backs out certain adjusting entries; facilitates subsequent entries. *p. 209*

Statement of Retained Earnings Reports increases and decreases in retained earnings; ties together the income statement and balance sheet. *p. 201*

Temporary (Nominal) Accounts Income statement accounts; closed at the end of the accounting period. *p. 203*

Unadjusted Trial Balance A trial balance that does not include the effects of the adjusting entries. *p. 195*

Worksheet A "spreadsheet" designed to minimize errors and to provide data for the financial statements. *p. 196*

QUESTIONS

1. Distinguish among manual, mechanical, and computerized data processing. How does each relate to accounting information processing?
2. Identify, in sequence, the 11 phases of the accounting information processing cycle.
3. Contrast transaction analysis with journalizing.
4. Compare journalizing with posting.
5. How does posting reflect a change in the classification of the data?
6. Contrast an unadjusted trial balance with an adjusted trial balance. What is the purpose of each?
7. What is the basic purpose of the worksheet?
8. Why are adjusting entries entered on the accounting worksheet?
9. Why are adjusting entries recorded in the journal and posted to the ledger even though they are entered on the worksheet?

10. What is the purpose of closing entries? Why are they recorded in the journal and posted to the ledger?

11. Distinguish among (*a*) permanent, (*b*) temporary, (*c*) real, and (*d*) nominal accounts.

12. Why are the income statement accounts closed but the balance sheet accounts are not?

13. What is a post-closing trial balance? Is it a useful part of the accounting information processing cycle? Explain.

14. What are reversing entries? When are reversing entries useful? Give one example of (*a*) an adjusting entry that should be reversed and (*b*) another one that should not be reversed (based on Chapter Supplement 5A)?

EXERCISES

E5–1 **(Match Definitions with the 11 Phases of the Accounting Information Processing Cycle)**
Match each definition with its related phase by entering the appropriate letter in the space provided.

Phases

_____ (1) Data collection
_____ (2) Transaction analysis
_____ (3) Journalizing
_____ (4) Posting
_____ (5) Unadjusted trial balance
_____ (6) Worksheet
_____ (7) Financial statements
_____ (8) Adjusting entries recorded
_____ (9) Closing entries recorded
_____ (10) Post-closing trial balance
_____ (11) Reversing entries

Definitions

A. Reduces income statement accounts to zero.
B. Converts chronological data to A = L + OE basis.
C. Collection of source documents.
D. Backs out certain adjusting entries.
E. Income statement, balance sheet, and SCF.
F. Recording the results of transaction analysis.
G. Checks equalities after the adjusting entries.
H. Determines effects of transactions on A = L + OE.
I. Records transactions and events at the end of the accounting period that are not yet recognized properly.
J. Checks equalities before the adjusting entries.
K. Facilitates, in an orderly way, completion of the remaining phases of the cycle.

E5–2 **(Match Definitions with Terms)**

Match each definition with its related term by entering the appropriate letter in the space provided.

Terms	Definitions
_____ (1) Interim financial statements	A. A "spreadsheet" used to facilitate completion of the financial statements.
_____ (2) Permanent accounts	B. Computer instructions and programs.
_____ (3) Closing entries	C. Reconciles the income statement with the balance sheet at the end of each accounting period.
_____ (4) Computer hardware	
_____ (5) Statement of retained earnings	D. Recorded only on the first day of each accounting period to facilitate subsequent entries.
_____ (6) Temporary accounts	
_____ (7) Accounting worksheet	E. A computer and dot matrix printer.
_____ (8) Adjusting entries	F. All of the income statement accounts.
_____ (9) Computer software	G. Cause all temporary accounts to have a zero balance.
_____ (10) Folio notation	
_____ (11) Reversing entries	H. Recorded to recognize items only at the end of the accounting period.
_____ (12) Adjusted trial balance	I. All of the balance sheet accounts.
	J. Prepared after adjusting entries and before closing entries to check equalities.
_____ (13) Income Summary account	
_____ (14) Nominal accounts	K. Used to indicate that posting has been done.
_____ (15) Real accounts	L. Financial statements that cover less than one year.
	M. A special clearing account used only during the closing process.

E5–3 **(Prepare a Simple Income Statement and Balance Sheet, Including Four Adjusting Entries, without a Worksheet)**

Haskins Company prepared the unadjusted trial balance given below at the end of the accounting year, December 31, 19B. To simplify the case, the amounts given are in thousands of dollars.

Account titles	Debit	Credit
Cash	$ 40	
Accounts receivable	27	
Prepaid insurance	4	
Machinery (10-year life; no residual value)	50	
Accumulated depreciation		$ 4
Accounts payable		6
Wages payable		
Income taxes payable		
Capital stock (no par; 3,000 shares)		62
Retained earnings		10
Dividends declared and paid during 19B	3	
Revenues (not detailed)		67
Expenses (not detailed)	25	
Totals	$149	$149

Other data not yet recorded at December 31, 19B:

1. Insurance expired during 19B, $3.
2. Depreciation expense for 19B, $4.
3. Wages payable, $5.
4. Income tax rate, 30%.

Required:

(Note: A worksheet may be used but is not required.)

a. Complete the income statement and balance sheet given below for 19B.
b. Give the adjusting entries for 19B.
c. Give the closing entries for 19B.

Income Statement
For the Year Ended December 31, 19B

Revenues (not detailed)	$ _____
Expenses (not detailed)	_____
Pretax income	_____
Income tax expense	_____
Net income	$ _____
EPS	$ _____

Balance Sheet
December 31, 19B

Assets		**Liabilities**	
Cash . . . . $ _____		Accounts payable . . . . . . $ _____	
Accounts receivable . . . . _____		Wages payable . . . . _____	
Prepaid insurance . . . . . _____		Income taxes payable . . . _____	
Machinery . . . . _____		**Stockholders' Equity**	
Accumulated			
depreciation . . . . _____		Capital stock . . . . _____	
		Retained earnings . . . . . _____	
Total . . . . $ _____		Total . . . . $ _____	

E5–4   (Determine How to Extend an Unadjusted Trial Balance to Complete a Worksheet; Uses Answer Codes)

The worksheet at December 31, 19B, for Wright Corporation has been completed through the adjusted trial balance. You are ready to extend each amount to the several columns to the right. The columns that will be used are listed below with code letters:

Code	Columns
A	Income Statement, debit
B	Income Statement, credit
C	Retained Earnings, debit
D	Retained Earnings, credit
E	Balance Sheet, debit
F	Balance Sheet, credit

Below are listed representative accounts to be extended on the worksheet. For each account, you are to give the code letter that indicates the proper worksheet column to the right of "Adjusted Trial Balance" to which the amount in each account should be extended. Assume normal debit and credit balances.

Account titles	Code
(1) Cash (example)	E
(2) Inventory of office supplies	
(3) Interest payable	
(4) Capital stock	
(5) Commission revenue earned	
(6) Rent revenue collected in advance	
(7) Salary expense	
(8) Prepaid insurance	
(9) Retained earnings, beginning balance (a credit)	
(10) Building	
(11) Mortgage payable	
(12) Income taxes payable	
(13) Sales commissions receivable	
(14) Accumulated depreciation on building	
(15) Contributed capital in excess of par	
(16) Dividends declared and paid	
(17) Income tax expense	
(18) Investment in bonds	
(19) Net income amount (indicate both the debit and credit on the worksheet)	
(20) Net loss amount (indicate both the debit and credit on the worksheet)	
(21) Retained earnings, positive ending balance amount (indicate both the debit and credit on the worksheet)	

E5–5   **(Completing a Worksheet Starting with an Unadjusted Trial Balance)**

Monroe Company is completing the annual accounting information processing cycle at December 31, 19B. The worksheet, as shown below, has been started (to simplify, amounts given are in thousands of dollars).

Account No.	Account titles	Unadjusted trial balance Debit	Unadjusted trial balance Credit
101	Cash	$ 25	$
102	Accounts receivable	38	
103	Inventory	22	
104	Prepaid insurance	3	
110	Equipment (10-year life, no residual value)	70	
111	Accumulated depreciation, equipment		7
119	Accounts payable		11
120	Wages payable		
121	Income taxes payable		
122	Revenue collected in advance		
123	Note payable, long term (10% each December 31)		20
130	Capital stock (par $10)		60
131	Contributed capital in excess of par		10
140	Retained earnings		15
141	Dividends declared and paid	8	
145	Revenues		104
146	Expenses	61	
147	Income tax expense		
	Totals	$227	$227

Data not yet recorded for 19B:

a. Insurance expense, $1.

b. Depreciation expense, $7.

c. Wages earned by employees; not yet paid, $2.

d. Revenue collected by Monroe; not yet earned, $3.

e. Income tax rate, 30%.

(Note: No accrued interest is recorded because interest is paid on each December 31.)

Required:

Complete the worksheet in every respect (you may use account numbers instead of account titles). Set up additional column headings for Adjusting Entries, Adjusted Trial Balance, Income Statement, Retained Earnings, and Balance Sheet. Record all revenues and expenses (except income tax) in the two accounts given (145 and 146).

E5–6   (Completing a Worksheet Starting with an Unadjusted Trial Balance)

Scott Corporation, a small company, is completing the annual accounting information processing cycle at December 31, 19B. The worksheet, prior to the adjusting entries, has been started as shown below.

Account Titles	Unadjusted Trial Balance	
	Debit	Credit
Cash	$ 24,000	
Accounts receivable	14,000	
Equipment	30,000	
Accumulated depreciation		$ 9,000
Other assets	64,000	
Accounts payable		11,000
Note payable, long term		10,000
Capital stock (par $10)		40,000
Contributed capital in excess of par		11,000
Retained earnings		14,000
Revenues		90,000
Expenses	53,000	
	$185,000	$185,000
Income tax expense		
Income taxes payable		
Net income		

Data not yet recorded for 19B:

a. Depreciation expense, $3,000.

b. Income tax rate, 25%.

Required:

Complete the worksheet in all respects. Set up additional column headings for Adjusting Entries, Adjusted Trial Balance, Income Statement, Retained Earnings, and Balance Sheet.

E5–7   **(Identifying Adjusting Entries by Comparing Unadjusted and Adjusted Trial Balances)**

Badger Company is in the process of completing the information processing cycle at the end of the accounting year, December 31, 19B. The worksheet and financial statements have been prepared. The next step is to journalize the adjusting entries. The two trial balances given below were taken directly from the completed worksheet.

| Account Titles | December 31, 19B | | | |
| | Unadjusted Trial Balance | | Adjusted Trial Balance | |
	Debit	Credit	Debit	Credit
a. Cash	$ 9,300		$ 9,300	
b. Accounts receivable			800	
c. Prepaid insurance	1,000		150	
d. Equipment	120,000		120,000	
e. Accumulated depreciation		$ 21,300		$ 26,300
f. Income taxes payable				3,300
g. Capital stock (par $10)		50,000		50,000
h. Retained earnings, January 1, 19B		16,000		16,000
i. Service revenue		61,000		61,800
j. Salary expense	18,000		18,000	
k. Depreciation expense			5,000	
l. Insurance expense			850	
m. Income tax expense			3,300	
	$148,300	$148,300	$157,400	$157,400

Required:

By examining the amounts in each trial balance, reconstruct the four adjusting entries that were made between the unadjusted trial balance and the adjusted trial balance. Give an explanation of each adjusting entry.

E5–8   **(Journalizing Adjusting and Closing Entries Based on a Completed Worksheet)**

The accountant for Rand Corporation has just completed the following worksheet for the year ended December 31, 19D (note the shortcuts used by the accountant to reduce the number of vertical columns on the worksheet—credits in parens, and no column for adjusted trial balance):

Account Titles	Unadjusted Trial Balance (credits)	Adjusting Entries Debit	Adjusting Entries Credit	Income Statement (credits)	Balance Sheet (credits)
a. Cash	15,000				15,000
b. Prepaid insurance	300		100		200
c. Accounts receivable	20,000				20,000
d. Machinery	80,000				80,000
e. Accumulated depreciation	(24,000)		8,000		(32,000)
f. Other assets	13,700				13,700
g. Accounts payable	(7,000)				(7,000)
h. Rent collected in advance			200		(200)
i. Interest payable			450		(450)
j. Income taxes payable			3,375		(3,375)
k. Note payable, long term	(10,000)				(10,000)
l. Capital stock (par $10)	(50,000)				(50,000)
m. Retained earnings	(18,000)				(18,000)
n. Revenues	(80,000)	200		(79,800)	
o. Expenses (not detailed)	60,000	100		60,100	
p. Depreciation expense		8,000		8,000	
q. Interest expense		450		450	
r. Income tax expense		3,375		3,375	
s. Net income				7,875	(7,875)
Totals	–0–	12,125	12,125	–0–	–0–

Required:

a. Prepare the adjusting entries in journal form required on December 31, 19D. Write a brief explanation with each entry.

b. Prepare the closing entries at December 31, 19D.

E5–9 (Recording Adjusting Entries in Journal Format)

For each of the 10 independent situations, give the journal entry by entering the appropriate code(s) and amounts.

Codes	Accounts	Codes	Accounts
A	Cash	K	Interest revenue
B	Office supplies inventory	L	Wage expense
C	Revenue receivable	M	Depreciation expense
D	Office equipment	N	Interest expense
E	Accumulated depreciation	O	Supplies expense
F	Note payable	P	Capital stock
G	Wages payable	Q	Retained earnings
H	Interest payable	R	Dividends declared and paid
I	Rent revenue collected in advance	S	Income summary
J	Service revenue	X	None of the above

	Debit		Credit	
Independent Situations	Code	Amount	Code	Amount
a. Accrued wages, unrecorded and unpaid at year-end, $400 (example).	L	400	G	400
b. Service revenue collected and recorded as revenue, but not yet earned, $700.				
c. Dividends declared and paid during year and debited to Dividends account, $900. Give entry at year-end.				
d. Depreciation expense for year not yet recorded, $650.				
e. Balance at year-end in Service Revenue account, $59,000. Give the closing entry at year-end.				
f. Service revenue earned but not yet collected at year-end, $300.				
g. Balance at year-end in Interest Revenue account, $360. Give the closing entry at year-end.				
h. Office Supplies Inventory account at year-end, $550; inventory of supplies on hand at year-end, $100.				
i. At year-end interest on note payable not yet recorded or paid, $180.				
j. Balance at year-end in Income Summary account after all revenue and expense accounts have been closed, $9,900 (credit).				

E5-10 **(Based on the Chapter Supplement 5A; Determining When to Use a Reversing Entry)**

England Company has completed the accounting information processing cycle for the year ended December 31, 19A. Reversing entries are under consideration (for January 1, 19B) for two different adjusting entries (of December 31,19A). For case purposes, the relevant data are given in T-accounts:

Prepaid Insurance

1/1/19A Balance	600	*(a)* 12/31/19A Adj. entry	400

Insurance Expense

(a) 12/31/19A Adj. entry	400	*(c)* 12/31/19A Closing entry	400

Accrued Wages Payable

		(b) 12/31/19A Adj. entry	1,000

Wage Expense

Paid during 19A	18,000	(d) 12/31/19A Closing entry	19,000
(b) 12/31/19A Adj. entry	1,000		

Income Summary

12/31/19A Closing entries		12/31/19A	
(c)	400	Closed to Retained Earnings	19,400
(d)	19,000		

Required:

Would a reversing entry on January 1, 19B, facilitate the next related entry for (a) Prepaid Insurance and (b) Accrued Wages Payable? Explain why.

PROBLEMS

P5-1   **(Prepare an Income Statement and Balance Sheet from an Unadjusted Trial Balance and Include the Effects of Five Adjusting Entries)**

American Company, Inc., a small service company, keeps its records without the help of an accountant. After much effort, an outside accountant prepared the following unadjusted trial balance as of the end of the annual accounting period, December 31, 19C:

Account titles	Debit	Credit
Cash	$ 40,000	
Accounts receivable	31,000	
Service supplies inventory	700	
Prepaid insurance	800	
Service trucks (5-year life; no residual value)	20,000	
Accumulated depreciation, service trucks		$ 8,000
Other assets	10,400	
Accounts payable		2,000
Wages payable		
Income taxes payable		
Note payable (3 years; 10% each December 31)		10,000
Capital stock (par $3)		30,000
Contributed capital in excess of par		3,000
Retained earnings		6,500
Dividends declared and paid	2,000	
Service revenue		85,000
Remaining expenses (not detailed)*	39,600	
Income tax expense		
Totals	$144,500	$144,500

* Excludes income tax expense.

Data not yet recorded at December 31, 19C:

1. The supplies inventory count on December 31, 19C, reflected $200 remaining on hand; to be used in 19D.

2. Insurance expired during 19C, $400.

3. Depreciation expense for 19C, $4,000.

4. Wages earned by employees not yet paid on December 31, 19C, $500.

5. Income tax rate, 30%.

Required:

Note: A worksheet may be used but is not required.

a. Complete the financial statements given below (show computations) for 19C to include the effects of the five transactions listed above.

b. Give the 19C adjusting entries. (Hint: Journalize the above five data items.)

c. Give the 19C closing entries. (Hint: Use the income statement column.)

Income Statement
For the Year Ended December 31, 19C

Service revenue		$ _____
Remaining expenses (not detailed) . . . . . $ _____		
Supplies expense . . . . _____		
Insurance expense . . . . _____		
Depreciation expense . . . . _____		
Remaining wage expense . . . . _____		
Total expenses		_____
Pretax income		_____
Income tax expense		_____
Net income		$ _____
EPS		$ _____

Balance Sheet
At December 31, 19C

Assets	Liabilities
Cash . . . . $ _____	Accounts payable . . . . . . $ _____
Accounts receivable . . . . _____	Wages payable . . . . _____
Service supplies inventory _____	Income taxes payable . . . _____
Prepaid insurance . . . . . _____	Note payable, long term . . _____
Service trucks . . . . _____	Total liabilities . . . . . . _____
Accumulated depreciation . _____	**Stockholders' Equity**
Other assets	Capital stock (par $1) . . . _____
(not detailed) . . . . _____	Contributed capital in
	excess of par . . . . _____
	Retained earnings . . . . . _____
	Total stockholders'
	equity . . . . _____
	Total liabilities and
Total assets . . . . $ _____	stockholders' equity . . . $ _____

P5–2 **(Use the Ledger Balances to Explain the Adjusting Entries Recorded and to Give
the Closing Entries; Three Analytical Questions)**
The ledger accounts of Sterling Company at the end of the second year of operations,
December 31, 19B (prior to the closing entries), were as shown below. The 19B adjusting
entries are identified by letters, and account numbers are given to the right of the account
name.

Cash   101
Bal. 20,000

Note Payable (10%) 201
Jan. 1, 19B
10,000

Capital Stock (Par $2)   301
Bal. 50,000

Inventory, Maintenance Supplies 102
Bal. 500	(a) 400

Wages Payable   202
(e) 600

Contributed Capital in Excess of Par   302
Bal 6,000

Service Equipment   103
Jan. 1, 19A 90,000

Interest Payable   203
(b) 1,000

Retained Earnings   303
Bal. 9,000

Accumulated Depreciation, Service Equipment   104
Bal. 18,000
(d) 18,000

Revenue Collected in Advance   204
(c) 7,000

Service Revenue   304
(c) 7,000	Bal. 220,000

Remaining Assets   105
Bal. 42,500

Income Taxes Payable 205
(f) 8,250

Expenses   305
Bal. 160,000
(a) 400
(b) 1,000
(d) 18,000
(e) 600
(f) 8,250

Required:

a. Develop three 19B trial balances of Sterling Company using the following format:

Account No.	Unadjusted Trial Balance		Adjusted Trial Balance		Post-Closing Trial Balance	
	Debit	Credit	Debit	Credit	Debit	Credit
101						

b. Write an explanation of each adjusting entry for 19B.

c. Give the closing journal entries (do not use Income Summary).

d. What was the apparent useful life of the service equipment? What assumptions must you make to answer this question?

e. What was the average income tax rate for 19B?

f. What was the average issue (sale) price per share of the capital stock?

P5-3 (Complete a Worksheet Starting with the Adjusted Trial Balance; Compute the Amounts for the Adjusting Entries; and Give the Closing Entries)

Oval Corporation has partially completed the following worksheet for the year ended December 31, 19E:

Account Titles	Unadjusted Trial Balance Debit	Unadjusted Trial Balance Credit	Adjusting Entries Debit	Adjusting Entries Credit
Cash	11,000			
Accounts receivable	26,000			
Supplies inventory	1,200			(a) 500
Interest receivable			(b) 200	
Long-term note receivable (10%; dated September 1, 19E)	6,000			
Equipment (10-year life)	80,000			
Accumulated depreciation		35,000		(c) 8,000
Accounts payable		11,000		
Note payable, short-term (12%; dated June 1, 19E)		8,000		
Interest payable				(d) 560
Income taxes payable				(e) 3,620
Capital stock (par $1)		33,000		
Contributed capital in excess of par		2,000		
Retained earnings		8,000		
Service revenue		68,000		
Interest revenue				(b) 200
Expenses (not detailed)	40,800		(a) 500	
Depreciation expense			(c) 8,000	
Interest expense			(d) 560	
Income tax expense			(e) 3,620	
Totals	165,000	165,000	12,880	12,880

Required:

1. Use additional columns for Adjusted Trial Balance, Income Statement, Retained Earnings, and Balance Sheet; and complete the worksheet.

2. Show how the following amounts were computed in the adjusting entries:
   a. $500.
   b. $200.
   c. $8,000.
   d. $560.

3. Give the closing entries.

4. Why are the adjusting and closing entries journalized and posted?

P5-4 (Start with a Partially Completed Worksheet and Complete Phases 6-9 in Order)

Virginia Corporation is completing the accounting information processing cycle for the year ended December 31, 19C. The unadjusted trial balance, taken from the ledger, was as follows:

Account No.	Account titles	Unadjusted trial balance	
		Debit	Credit
101	Cash	$ 43,550	
103	Accounts receivable	17,000	
105	Prepaid insurance	450	
107	Interest receivable		
120	Long-term note receivable (12%)	6,000	
150	Equipment (10-year life)	100,000	
151	Accumulated depreciation, equipment		$ 20,000
170	Other assets	30,000	
201	Accounts payable		14,000
203	Wages payable		
205	Interest payable		
210	Note payable, long-term (15%)		10,000
300	Capital stock (par $10)		80,000
301	Contributed capital in excess of par		12,000
310	Retained earnings		34,000
311	Dividends declared and paid during 19C	8,000	
320	Service revenue		150,000
322	Interest revenue		
350	Expenses (not detailed)*	115,000	
351	Depreciation expense		
360	Interest expense		
370	Income tax expense		
207	Income taxes payable		
	Totals	$320,000	$320,000

* Includes wage expense and insurance expense.

Additional data for adjusting entries:

a. Expired insurance during 19C was $150.

b. Interest on the long-term note receivable (dated September 1, 19C) is collected annually each August 31.

c. The equipment was acquired on January 1, 19A (assume no estimated residual value).

d. At December 31, 19C, wages earned but not yet paid or recorded amounted to $3,000.

e. Interest on the long-term note payable (dated May 1, 19C) is paid annually each April 30.

f. Assume a 20% average income tax rate.

Required:

a. Phase 6—Complete a worksheet for the year ended December 31, 19C. Key the adjusting entries with letters.

b. Phase 7—Prepare an income statement (use two captions: Revenues and Expenses), a statement of retained earnings, and a balance sheet; use three captions only (Assets, Liabilities, and Stockholders' Equity).

c. Phase 8—Write an explanation of each adjusting entry reflected on the worksheet.

d. Phase 9—Give the closing entries in journal form. Explain why they must be journalized and posted to the ledger.

P5-5 **(Comprehensive Problem to Cover Chapters 2 through 5, Starting with an Unadjusted Trial Balance and Ending with the Closing Entries)**
W&P Moving and Storage Service, Inc., has been in operation for several years. Revenues have increased gradually from both the moving and storage services. The annual financial statements prepared in the past have not conformed to GAAP. The newly employed president decided that a balance sheet, income statement, and statement of retained earnings would be prepared in conformity with GAAP. The first step was to employ a full-time bookkeeper and engage a local CPA firm. It is now December 31, 19C, the end of the current accounting year. The bookkeeper has developed a trial balance from the ledger. A member of the staff of the CPA firm will advise and assist the bookkeeper in completing the accounting information processing cycle for the first time. The unadjusted trial balance at December 31, 19C, is shown below.

Unadjusted Trial Balance
December 31, 19C

Debits		Credits	
Cash	$ 25,880	Accumulated depreciation	$ 18,000
Accounts receivable	2,030	Accounts payable	6,000
Office supplies inventory	150	Wages payable	
Prepaid insurance	600	Interest payable	
Land for future building site	6,000	Revenue collected advance	
Equipment	68,000	Income taxes payable	
Remaining assets (not detailed)	27,000	Note payable (12%)	30,000
Salary expense	74,000	Capital stock (par $1;	
Advertising expense	1,000	20,000 shares)	20,000
Utilities expense	1,270	Retained earnings,	
Maintenance expense	6,500	January 1, 19C	21,600
Miscellaneous expenses	570	Hauling revenue	106,400
Insurance expense		Storage revenue	14,000
Wage expense			
Depreciation expense			
Interest expense			
Income tax expense			
Dividends declared and paid	3,000		
	$216,000		$216,000

Examination of the records and related documents provided the following additional information that should be considered for adjusting entries:

a. A physical count of office supplies inventory at December 31, 19C, reflected $40 on hand. Office supplies used are a miscellaneous expense. Office supplies purchased during 19C were debited to this inventory account.

b. On July 1, 19C, a two-year insurance premium was paid amounting to $600; it was debited to Prepaid Insurance.

c. The equipment cost $68,000 when acquired. Annual depreciation expense is $6,000.

d. Unpaid and unrecorded wages earned by employees at December 31, 19C, amounted to $1,200.

e. The $30,000 note payable was signed on October 1, 19C, for a 12% bank loan; principal and interest are due at the end of 12 months from that date.

f. Storage revenue collected and recorded as earned before December 31, 19C, included $400 collected in advance from one customer for storage time to be used in 19D. (Hint: Reduce storage revenue.)

g. Gasoline, oil, and fuel purchased for the vehicles and used during the last two weeks of December 19C amounting to $300 have not been paid for or recorded (this is considered maintenance expense).

h. The average income tax rate is 20%, which produces income tax expense of $5,600.

Required:

a. Phase 6—Enter the unadjusted trial balance on a worksheet; then, based on the above data, enter the adjusting entries. Complete the worksheet.

b. Phase 7—Using the worksheet, prepare an income statement (use two captions: Revenues and Expenses), statement of retained earnings, and balance sheet.

c. Phase 8—Using the worksheet, prepare the 19C adjusting entries in journal form.

d. Phase 9—Using the worksheet, prepare 19C closing entries in journal form.

P5–6   **(Alternate Comprehensive Problem to Cover Chapters 2 through 5, Starting with an Unadjusted Trial Balance and Ending with the Closing Entries)**
Charter Air Service, Incorporated, was organized to operate a charter service in a city of approximately 350,000 population. The 10 organizers were issued 7,500 shares of $10 par value stock for a total of $75,000 cash. To obtain facilities to operate the charter services, the company rents from the city hangar and office space at the city airport for a flat monthly rental. The business has prospered because of the excellent service and the high level of maintenance on the planes. It is now December 31, 19D, end of the annual accounting period, and the accounting information processing cycle is in the final phases. Representative accounts and unadjusted amounts selected from the ledger at December 31, 19D, are as follows:

Unadjusted Trial Balance
December 31, 19D

Debits		Credits	
Cash	$ 24,600	Accumulated depreciation,	
Prepaid insurance	6,000	aircraft	$ 60,000
Maintenance parts inventory	18,000	Note payable (12%)	100,000
Aircraft	260,000	Capital stock (par $10)	75,000
Salary expense	90,000	Retained earnings,	
Maintenance expense	24,000	January 1, 19D	20,600
Fuel expense	63,000	Charter revenue	262,400
Advertising expense	2,000		
Utilities expense	1,400		
Rent expense	14,000		
Dividends declared and paid	15,000		
	$518,000		$518,000

For the 19D adjusting entries, the following additional data were developed from the records and supporting documents:

a. On January 1, 19D, the company paid a three-year insurance premium amounting to $6,000.

b. The aircraft, when purchased on January 1, 19A, cost $260,000; and the estimated useful life to the company is approximately 10 years. The equipment has an estimated residual value of $60,000. Annual depreciation expense is $20,000 (can you verify this amount?).

c. On July 1, 19D, the company borrowed $100,000 from the bank on a five-year, 12% loan. Interest is payable annually starting on June 30,19E.

d. Charter revenue, on occasion, is collected in advance. On December 31, 19D, collections in advance amounted to $1,000; when collected, this amount was recorded as Charter Revenue.

e. Rent amounting to $14,000 on hangar and office space was paid during the year and recorded as Rent Expense. This included rent paid in advance amounting to $2,000 for January and February 19E. The total amount was recorded as Rent Expense in 19D.

f. The inventory of maintenance parts at December 31, 19D, showed $7,000. All parts purchased are debited to Maintenance Parts Inventory when purchased.

g. For case purposes, assume an average income tax rate of 20%, which results in income tax expense of $6,000.

Required:

a. Enter the above accounts and unadjusted balances from the ledger on a worksheet. (The following accounts should be added at the bottom of the worksheet because they will be needed for the adjusting entries: Insurance Expense, Depreciation Expense, Interest Expense, Interest Payable, Revenue Collected in Advance, Prepaid Rent Expense, Income Tax Expense, and Income Taxes Payable.)

b. Based on the additional data given above, enter the 19D adjusting entries on the worksheet.

c. Phase 6—Complete the worksheet.

d. Phase 7—Based on the worksheet, prepare the 19D income statement (use two captions, Revenues and Expenses), statement of retained earnings, and the balance sheet.

e. Phase 8—Journalize the 19D adjusting entries.

f. Phase 9—Journalize the 19D closing entries.

P5–7 **(Mini-Practice Set Starting with Transactions and Continuing through a Complete Accounting Information Cycle; Simplified by Using Only 10 Basic Entries Plus 5 Adjusting Entries)**
Little Service Company (a corporation) began operations on January 1, 19A. The annual reporting period ends December 31. The trial balance on January 1, 19B, was as follows (rounded to even thousands to simplify):

Account No.	Account titles	Debit	Credit
01	Cash	$ 2	$
02	Accounts receivable	6	
03	Service supplies inventory	15	
04	Land		
05	Equipment	80	
06	Accumulated depreciation, equipment		8
07	Remaining assets (not detailed to simplify)	5	
11	Accounts payable		7
12	Note payable		
13	Wages payable		
14	Interest payable		
15	Income taxes payable		
21	Capital stock (par $1)		83
31	Retained earnings		10
35	Service revenue		
40	Depreciation expense		
41	Income tax expense		
42	Interest expense		
43	Remaining expenses (not detailed to simplify)		
50	Income summary		
	Totals	$108	$108

Transactions during 19B, summarized in thousands of dollars (the letters indicate dates):

a. Borrowed $12 cash on a 10% note payable, dated March 1, 19B.

b. Purchased land for future building site, paid cash, $12.

c. Revenues for 19B, $140, including $20 on credit.

d. Sold 2,000 shares of capital stock for $1 cash per share.

e. Remaining expenses for 19B, $80, including $6 on credit.

f. Collected accounts receivable, $14.

g. Purchased "remaining" assets, $10 cash.

h. Accounts payable paid, $9.

i. Purchased service supplies for future use, $10 (debit to Account No. 3).

j. Signed a $15 service contract to start February 1, 19C.

k. Declared and paid cash dividend, $15. (The accountant decided to debit Account No. 31 rather than a special account.)

Data for adjusting entries:

1. Service supplies inventory counted on December 31, 19B, $10 (debit Remaining Expenses).

2. Equipment, useful life 10 years (no residual or scrap value).

3. Accrued interest on note payable (to be computed).

4. Wages earned since the December 24 payroll; not yet paid, $16.

5. Income tax rate, 20%; payable in 19C.

Required:
Phases 1, 2, and 3—Analyze and journalize each of the 11 transactions. Give a description below each entry. Start with journal page 1 and provide a column for "Folio."

Phase 4—Set up the 20 ledger accounts. Use the following format (enter the beginning balances):

Account Title	Cash			Account Number	01
Date	Explanation	Folio	Debit	Credit	Balance
19B	Beginning balance	√			2
a	Borrowed cash	1	12		14

Note: Cash requires 10 lines; the remainder, 4 lines each.

Post the journal; use the Folio columns.

Phase 5—Set up an accounting worksheet like Exhibit 5–2 and enter the unadjusted trial balance at December 31, 19B.

Phase 6—Complete the worksheet.

Phase 7—Prepare the 19B income statement and balance sheet. To save time use only major captions.

Phase 8—Journalize and post the adjusting entries.

Phase 9—Journalize and post the closing entries.

Phase 10—Prepare a post-closing trial balance. (Use account numbers rather than titles to save time.)

Phase 11—Identify the two reversing entries that could be made.

P5–8   **(Based on Chapter Supplement 5A; Selecting Adjusting Entries that Often Are Reversed)**

Alvin Corporation has completed all information processing including the annual financial statements at December 31, 19D. The adjusting entries recorded at that date were as follows:

a.	Insurance expense	150	
	Prepaid insurance		150
b.	Interest receivable	200	
	Interest revenue		200
c.	Supplies expense	80	
	Supplies inventory		80
d.	Depreciation expense	2,000	
	Accumulated depreciation		2,000
e.	Wage expense	500	
	Wages payable		500
f.	Interest expense	300	
	Interest payable		300
g.	Income tax expense	4,000	
	Income taxes payable		4,000

Required:

For each of the above adjusting entries indicate whether it usually would be reversed. Give the reversing entry in each instance (if none, so state) and explain the basis for your response.

CASES

C5–1   **(Analyze Some Simple Errors to Determine the Effects of Each on Income, Assets, and Liabilities)**

Lax Company (not a corporation) was careless about its financial records during its first year of operations, 19A. It is December 31, 19A, end of the annual accounting period. An outside CPA examined the records and discovered numerous errors. All of those errors are described below. Assume each error is independent of the others. Analyze each error and indicate its effect on 19A and 19B income, assets, and liabilities **if not corrected.** Do not assume any other errors. Use these codes to indicate the effect of each dollar amount: O = overstated, U = understated, and N = no effect. Write an explanation of your analysis of each transaction to support your response. The first error is used as an example.

| | Effect on | | | | | |
| | Net Income | | Assets | | Liabilities | |
Independent Errors	19A	19B	19A	19B	19A	19B
a. Depreciation expense for 19A, not recorded in 19A, $950.	O $950	N	O $950	O $950	N	N
b. Wages earned by employees during 19A, not recorded or paid in 19A, but will be paid in 19B, $200.						
c. Revenue earned during 19A but not collected or recorded until 19B, $400.						
d. Amount paid in 19A and recorded as expense in 19A, but not an expense until 19B, $500.						
e. Revenue collected in 19A and recorded as revenue in 19A, but not earned until 19B, $600.						
f. Sale of services and cash collected in 19A. Recorded as a debit to Cash and as a credit to Accounts Receivable, $800.						
g. On December 31, 19A, bought land on credit for $9,000, not recorded until payment was made on February 1, 19B.						

Explanation of analysis of errors if not corrected:

a. Failure to record depreciation in 19A caused depreciation expense to be too low; therefore, income was overstated by $950. Also, accumulated depreciation is too low by $950, which causes assets to be overstated by $950 until the error is corrected.

C5-2 (Analytical—Prepare Adjusting and Closing Entries by Analyzing Unadjusted and Adjusted Trial Balances; Then Answer 10 Analytical Questions)

Delta Company was organized on January 1, 19A. At the end of the first year of operations, December 31, 19A, the bookkeeper prepared the following two trial balances (amounts in thousands of dollars):

Account No.	Account titles	Unadjusted trial balance Debit	Unadjusted trial balance Credit	Adjusted trial balance Debit	Adjusted trial balance Credit
11	Cash	$ 30	$	$ 30	$
12	Accounts receivable	25		25	
13	Prepaid insurance	3		2	
14	Rent receivable			1	
15	Operational assets	48		48	
16	Accumulated depreciation, operational assets . . .				6
17	Other assets	4		4	
18	Accounts payable		11		11
19	Wages payable				2
20	Income taxes payable				2
21	Rent revenue collected in advance				3
22	Note payable (10%; dated January 1, 19A)		30		30
23	Capital stock (par $1)		50		50
24	Retained earnings				
25	Dividends declared and paid	2		2	
26	Revenues (total)		92		90
27	Expenses (total including interest)	71		80	
28	Income tax expense			2	
	Totals	$183	$183	$194	$194

Required:

a. Based on inspection of the two trial balances, give the 19A adjusting entries developed by the bookkeeper (provide brief explanations).
b. Based on the above data, give the 19A closing entries with brief explanations.
c. Answer the following questions (show computations):
   (1) How many shares of stock were outstanding at year-end?
   (2) What was the estimated useful life of the operational assets assuming no residual value?
   (3) What was the amount of interest expense that was included in the total expenses?
   (4) What was the balance of Retained Earnings on December 31, 19A?
   (5) What was the average income tax rate?
   (6) How would the two accounts (a) Rent Receivable and (b) Rent Revenue Collected in Advance be reported on the balance sheet?

(7) Explain why cash increased by $30,000 during the year even though net income was very low comparatively.

(8) What was the amount of EPS for 19A?

(9) What was the average selling price of the shares?

(10) When was the insurance premium paid and over what period of time did the coverage extend?

C5-3 **(Adjusting and Closing Entries for an Actual Company)**

JCPenney   Refer to the financial statements of J.C. Penney Company, Inc. given in the appendix immediately preceding the index.

1. For fiscal year 1988, what dates should the company use for the (a) adjusting entries, (b) closing entries, and (c) reversing entries?

2. Give the closing entry for sales revenue at the end of the current year.

3. What company accounts would not appear on a post-closing trial balance?

4. What company accounts would appear on a post-closing trial balance?

5. Give the closing entry for Prepaid Expenses at the end of the current year.

6. It is possible to determine whether the company uses reversing entries?

SIX

ACCOUNTING FOR SALES REVENUE AND COST OF GOODS SOLD

PURPOSE

The previous five chapters discussed the various phases of the information processing cycle and the conceptual framework of accounting. In this chapter, you will apply that knowledge by examining typical business transactions that involve the purchase and sale of merchandise. Net income reported on the income statement is a measure of the operating success of a business. As a result, proper recording of sales revenue and the related cost of goods sold is important to both managers and users of financial statements.

The income statement on the opposite page illustrates how cost of sales (also called cost of goods sold) is emphasized by many companies. Also shown is a note explaining why cost of sales has changed.

LEARNING OBJECTIVES

1. Apply the revenue principle and record sales revenue.
2. Account for credit sales and sales discounts.
3. Use the allowance method to record bad debts.
4. Apply the matching principle to record cost of goods sold.
5. Identify and explain two inventory systems.
6. Describe the cost of goods sold model.
7. Make closing entries with each of the inventory systems.
8. Expand your accounting vocabulary by learning the "Important Terms Defined in This Chapter."
9. Apply the knowledge learned from this chapter by completing the homework assigned by your instructor.

ORGANIZATION

Part A—accounting for sales revenue
1. Recording sales revenue.
2. Measuring bad debt expense.
3. Sales returns and allowances.

Part B—accounting for cost of goods sold
1. Nature of cost of goods sold.
2. Inventory systems.
3. Taking a physical inventory.

Colgate-Palmolive Company

Consolidated Statement of Income

Thousands of Dollars Except Per Share Amounts

	1987	1986	1985
Net sales	$5,647,460	$4,984,576	$4,523,678
Cost of sales	3,169,323	2,892,322	2,680,693
Gross profit	**2,478,137**	2,092,254	1,842,985
Operating expenses and other items:			
Marketing and selling	1,539,783	1,302,262	1,144,623
General and administrative	554,466	457,705	421,604
Provision for restructured operations	211,000	—	—
Interest expense	89,014	76,235	53,908
Interest income	(26,173)	(30,381)	(43,291)
Earnings from equity investments	(12,770)	(10,577)	(9,314)
Total operating expenses and other items	**2,355,320**	1,795,244	1,567,530
Income from continuing operations before income taxes	**112,817**	297,010	275,455
Provision for income taxes	68,795	119,545	107,654
Income from continuing operations	54,022	177,465	167,801

Financial Review

Results of Operations

Gross Profit Margin

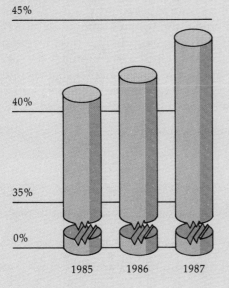

45%

40%

35%

0%

1985   1986   1987

Cost of Sales

The Company continues to benefit from cost reduction programs currently in place. Gross profit on sales improved in all business segments in 1987 to 44% on a worldwide basis, as compared to 42% in 1986 and 41% in 1985. These higher margins are the result of more efficient manufacturing facilities, a more favorable product/business mix and lower prices for certain raw materials.

PART A—ACCOUNTING FOR SALES REVENUE

Applying the Revenue Principle

Determination of the amount of revenue that should be recorded and the appropriate accounting period in which to record it sometimes presents complex problems. Sales may be for cash or on credit and may involve the trade in of a noncash asset. Sales activities often begin in one accounting period and end in another. Problems associated with accounting for sales revenue are easier to resolve if you know the revenue principle (Exhibit 4–5). The amount of revenue recorded is based on the **market value** of the considerations received, or the market value of the item sold, whichever is more clearly determinable. Also, sales revenue should be recognized in the accounting period when ownership of the goods passes from the seller to the buyer. Problems in implementing the revenue principle will be discussed in this chapter.

Observe the income statement for Campus Corner in Exhibit 6–1. Cost of goods sold[1] (an expense) is set out separately from the remaining expenses. Notice that the income statement shows gross margin on sales, which is the difference between net sales revenue and cost of goods sold.[2] In this chapter, we will discuss several transactions that affect the Campus Corner income statement.

Recognizing Sales Revenue

In most cases, the seller records sales revenue when ownership of goods passes from the seller to the buyer. Under the revenue principle, the sales price (net of any discounts) is the measure of the amount of revenue that should be recorded. If the sale is for cash, the amount of revenue to be recorded is the amount of cash that was received. If the sale is on credit, the revenue is the **cash equivalent** of the assets to be received excluding any financing charges (i.e., interest). If the sale involves the trade in of a noncash asset (such as the trade in of an old car for a new car), the amount of revenue is the cash equivalent of the goods received or given up, whichever is the more clearly determinable. Campus Corner would recognize a sale in 19F (i.e., when ownership passed) as follows:

a. Cash sales for the day per the cash register tapes:

Jan. 2	Cash	2,000	
	Sales revenue		2,000

---

[1] Similar titles sometimes used are "cost of sales" and "cost of products sold." Regardless of title, it is an **expense.**

[2] In this chapter, to simplify the illustrations, we ordinarily shall not show the detailed operating expenses. In the single-step format for the income statement, revenues would be reported as above under a major caption "Revenues." However, all expenses, including cost of goods sold, would be reported under a major caption "Expenses." Therefore, in the single-step format, gross margin on sales is not reported.

Exhibit 6–1 Income statement

CAMPUS CORNER
Income Statement (multiple-step format)
For the Year Ended December 31, 19F

		Amount
Gross sales revenue		$108,333
Less: Sales returns and allowances		8,333
Net sales revenue		100,000
Cost of goods sold		60,000
Gross margin on sales		40,000
Operating expenses:		
Selling expense (detailed)	$15,000	
Administrative expense (detailed)	10,000	25,000
Pretax income		15,000
Income tax expense		3,000
Net income		$ 12,000
EPS ($12,000 ÷ 10,000 shares)		$1.20

b. Credit sales for the day per all charge tickets:

```
Jan. 2   Accounts receivable . . . . . . . . . . . . . . . . . . . . . . . .  1,000
              Sales revenue . . . . . . . . . . . . . . . . . . . . . . . .       1,000
```

Alternatively, a **separate sales revenue** account could be kept in the ledger for the sales of each department. The two journal entries above would be as follows:

```
Jan. 2   Cash . . . . . . . . . . . . . . . . . . . . . . . . . . . . . . .  2,000
         Accounts receivable . . . . . . . . . . . . . . . . . . . . . . .  1,000
              Sales, Department 1 . . . . . . . . . . . . . . . . . . . . .       1,000
              Sales, Department 2 . . . . . . . . . . . . . . . . . . . . .       1,500
              Sales, Department 3 . . . . . . . . . . . . . . . . . . . . .        500
```

The managers of Campus Corner would be able to use information concerning sales revenue for each department for a variety of purposes. For example, an increase in the sales volume of Department 2 may indicate a need to assign additional salespeople to work in that department.

Credit Sales and Sales Discounts

A large portion of the sales made by many businesses is on credit. When merchandise is sold on credit, the terms of payment should be definite so there will be no misunderstanding as to the amounts and due dates. Credit terms usually are printed on each credit document. Often, credit terms are abbreviated using symbols such as, "n/10, EOM," which means the net amount (i.e., the sales amount less any sales returns) is due not later than 10 days after the end of the month (EOM) in which the sale was made. In other cases, **sales discounts** (often called cash discounts) are granted to the purchaser to encourage early payment. For example, the credit terms may be "2/10, n/30," which means that if cash payment is made within 10 days from the date of sale, the customer may deduct 2% from the invoice price; however, if not paid within the 10-day discount period, the full sales price (less any returns) is due in 30 days from date of sale.

Usually customers will pay within the discount period because the savings are substantial. For example, with terms 2/10, n/30, 2% is saved by paying 20 days early, which is approximately 37% annual interest. Credit customers conceivably may borrow cash from a bank to take advantage of cash discounts. Normally, the bank's interest rate is less than the high interest rate associated with failing to take cash discounts. Because the cash discount on sales almost always will be taken, many businesses record the amount of sales revenue based on the amount of cash that probably will be received rather than for the gross sales amount. A sale by Campus Corner of $1,000 with terms 2/10, n/30 is recorded as follows:

a. January 18—date of sale on credit:

Accounts receivable	980	
Sales revenue		980
Terms: 2/10, n/30 ($1,000 × 0.98 = $980).		

b. January 27—date of collection if payment is made **within** the discount period (the usual case):

Cash	980	
Accounts receivable		980

c. January 31—date of collection if payment is made **after** the discount period (the unusual case):

Cash	1,000	
Sales discount revenue*		20
Accounts receivable		980

* Interest revenue sometimes is used because conceptually it is in the nature of interest revenue earned.

The method for recording sales revenue illustrated above is called the **net method.** As an alternative, some companies use the **gross method of recording sales revenue.** Under the gross method, sales revenue is recorded without deducting the amount of the cash discount. The following journal entries would be made for a $1,000 sale if the gross method were used instead of the net method:

a. January 18—date of sale on credit:

Accounts receivable	1,000	
Sales revenue		1,000

b. January 27—date of collection if payment is made **within** the discount period (the usual case):

```
Cash  . . . . . . . . . . . . . . . . . . . . . . . . . . . . . . . . . . . . . .  980
Sales discounts  . . . . . . . . . . . . . . . . . . . . . . . . . . . .   20
    Accounts receivable  . . . . . . . . . . . . . . . . . . . . . . . . .          1,000
    Terms 2/10, n/30 ($1,000 × 0.98 = $980).
```

c. January 31—date of collection if payment is made **after** the discount period (the unusual case):

```
Cash  . . . . . . . . . . . . . . . . . . . . . . . . . . . . . . . . . . . 1,000
    Accounts receivable  . . . . . . . . . . . . . . . . . . . . . . . . .          1,000
```

The Sales Discounts account (used with the gross method) may be reported as (a) a contra revenue account or (b) an addition to selling expense. The gross method overstates both accounts receivable and sales revenue. The net method is theoretically preferable, but most companies choose the method that they believe involves the least clerical effort.

Cash discounts are not the same as **trade discounts.** A cash discount is a price concession given to encourage early payment of an account. A trade discount is sometimes used by vendors for quoting sales prices; the amount **after** the trade discount is the sales price. For example, an item may be quoted at $10 per unit subject to a 20% trade discount on orders of 100 units or more; thus, the price for the large order would be $8 per unit.

The use of cash discounts appears to be declining. In some jurisdictions, they are not legal in certain situations because the effect is to charge the cash customers more than the credit customers who pay within the discount period. Also, the discount not taken by credit customers is a hidden financing charge that may be governed by legislation dealing with credit practices.

Extending credit usually involves an increase in the amount of bookkeeping required because detailed records must be kept for each credit customer. Some businesses have their credit sales handled by a credit card company (such as Mastercard or Visa), which charges a fee for this service. The fee paid to the credit card company is recorded as a collection expense (and not a sales discount). Chapter Supplement 6A discusses some aspects of the detailed records kept for credit customers.

Measuring Bad Debt Expense

Despite careful credit investigations, a few credit customers will not pay their bills. If an account receivable is uncollectible, the business has incurred a **bad debt expense.** Businesses that extend credit know that there will be a certain amount of bad debt losses on credit sales. In fact, an extremely low rate of bad debt losses is probably not good because it may indicate too tight a credit policy. If the credit policy is too restrictive, many good credit customers may be turned away causing a loss of sales volume. Bad debt losses can be thought of as a necessary expense associated with generating credit sales.

In conformity with the matching principle, bad debt expense must be matched with the sales revenue that caused those losses. This requirement is difficult to implement because it may be one or more years after the sales were made before the business will know that the customers will be unable to pay.

To satisfy the matching principle, the **bad debt allowance method** is used to measure bad debt expense. The allowance method recognizes that bad debt expenses must be recorded in the year in which the sales that caused those losses were made rather than in the year that the customer is unable to pay. There is no way of knowing in advance which individual customers will not pay. Therefore, the allowance method is based on **estimates** of the probable amount of bad debt losses from uncollectible accounts. The estimate is made in each accounting period based on either (1) the total credit sales for the period or (2) an aging of accounts receivable.

Percent of Credit Sales. A company that has been operating for some years has sufficient experience to project probable future bad debt losses. New companies often rely on the experience of similar companies that have been operating for a number of years. Assume an analysis by Campus Corner indicated on average bad debt loss of 0.9% of total credit sales as follows:

Year	Bad debt losses	Credit sales
19A	$ 440	$ 54,000
19B	480	57,000
19C	620	53,000
19D	500	66,000
19E	660	70,000
	$2,700	$300,000

Aggregate: $2,700 ÷ $300,000 = 0.9%
average loss rate for the five-year period
19A–E.

Usually a company will adjust the historical average loss rate to reflect future expectations. Campus Corner expects a small increase in uncollectible amounts from 19F sales; therefore, it increased the expected loss rate to 1.0%.

Assuming net credit sales in 19F of $40,000, Campus Corner would record bad debt expense of $40,000 × 1% = $400 in 19F. The following **adjusting entry** would be made at the end of the accounting period, December 31, 19F:

Bad debt expense 400
    Allowance for doubtful accounts (or bad debts) 400
  To adjust for the estimated bad debt loss based on credit sales with an
average expected loss rate of 1% ($40,000 × 1% = $400).

Bad debt expense of $400 would be reported on the 19F income statement. It would be matched with the related sales revenue for 19F, the year in which the credit was granted. The Bad Debt Expense account is closed at the end of each accounting period along with the other expense accounts. The credit in the above journal entry was made to a **contra account** titled "Allowance for Doubtful

Accounts.''[3] Accounts Receivable cannot be credited because there is no way of knowing which account receivable is involved. The balance in Allowance for Doubtful Accounts **always** is a subtraction from the balance of Accounts Receivable. The two accounts would be reported in the current asset section of the balance sheet as follows:

CAMPUS CORNER
Balance Sheet (partial)
At December 31, 19F

Current assets:
Cash $34,000
Accounts receivable $100,000
    Less: Allowance for doubtful accounts . . .   2,400 *   97,600

* This amount assumes a balance of $2,000 carried forward prior to the above entry.

Allowance for Doubtful Accounts has a cumulative credit balance. It is not closed at the end of the accounting period because it is a balance sheet account. The balance of the allowance account is an approximation of the total amount of the accounts receivable that is estimated to be uncollectible. The difference between the balances of Accounts Receivable and the allowance account measures the **estimated net realizable** value of accounts receivable. In the above example, the difference between the two accounts—$97,600—represents the **estimated net realizable value** of accounts receivable (also called the book value of accounts receivable).

The bad debt estimate should be based only on credit sales. Sometimes, a company bases the estimate on total sales (i.e., cash plus credit sales). This practice may lead to poor estimates because (1) it is impossible to have a bad debt loss on a cash sale and (2) a shift in the relative proportion between cash and credit sales would affect the accuracy of the estimate. The total amount of credit sales for each period can be determined (because these transactions are recorded in Accounts Receivable as debits); therefore, there is no reason for not using credit sales as the base for the estimate.

Aging Accounts Receivable. As an alternative to the percent of credit sales method, some companies use the average age that accounts receivable have been outstanding as the basis for estimating bad debt expense. Usually as an account receivable gets older, there is an increase in the probability that the account will be uncollectible. The amount estimated to be uncollectible under the aging method is the balance that should be in the Allowance for Doubtful Accounts at the end of the period. The difference between the actual balance in the account and the estimated balance is the bad debt expense for the period.

---

[3] Other acceptable titles for this account are Allowance for Bad Debts and Allowance for Uncollectible Accounts.

To illustrate the aging method, we will consider a new company. The general ledger for Macon Appliance Store reflected the following account balances on December 31, 19B:

Accounts receivable . . . . $ 40,000 (debit balance)
Allowance for doubtful accounts . . . .   900 (credit balance)
Sales on credit for 19B 200,000

Macon developed the following aging analysis of accounts receivable:

MACON APPLIANCE STORE
Aging Analysis of Accounts Receivable, December 31, 19B

Customer	Total	Not Yet Due	1–30 Days Past Due	31–60 Days Past Due	61–90 Days Past Due	Over 90 Days Past Due
Adams, A. K.	$ 600	$ 600				
Baker, B. B.	1,300	300	$ 900	$ 100		
Cox, R. E.	1,400			400	$ 900	$ 100
Day, W. T.	3,000	2,000	600	400		
Zoe, A. B.	900					900
Total	$40,000	$17,200	$12,000	$8,000	$1,200	$1,600

Management of Macon **estimated** the following probable bad debt loss rates: not yet due, 1%; 1–30 days past due, 3%; 31–60 days, 6%; 61–90 days, 10%; over 90 days, 25%. The following estimating schedule can be prepared:

MACON APPLIANCE STORE
Estimate of Probable Uncollectible Accounts, December 31, 19B

Age	Amount of Receivable	Percent Estimated to Be Uncollectible	Balance Needed in Allowance for Doubtful Accounts
Net yet due	$17,200	1	$ 172
1–30 days past due	12,000	3	360
31–60 days past due	8,000	6	480
61–90 days past due	1,200	10	120
Over 90 days past due	1,600	25	400
Total	$40,000		$1,532

The amount of bad debt expense for the period is the difference between the estimated uncollectible accounts (calculated above) and the current balance of the Allowance for Doubtful Accounts:

Computation:
Estimated balance $1,532
Current balance   900
Bad debt expense . . . . . . $ 632

The adjusting entry on December 31, 19B, for Macon Appliance is:

Dec. 31 Bad debt expense 632
           Allowance for doubtful accounts   632
        To adjust Allowance for Doubtful Accounts to the estimated balance
        needed.

The aging accounts receivable method can produce an excellent estimate of the realizable value of accounts receivable. Short-term creditors often prefer the aging method because of their interest in the amount of cash that can be collected from the current assets of a company. While the aging method focuses on a balance sheet valuation (accounts receivable), the percent of credit sales method focuses on an income statement valuation (bad debt expense). Some accountants prefer the percent of credit sales method because they believe that it is more consistent with the matching principle (i.e., bad debt expense is estimated directly from the sales revenue of the period). Both methods are acceptable under GAAP and are widely used in practice.

Writing Off a Bad Debt

When a specific customer's account receivable is determined to be uncollectible (e.g., due to personal bankruptcy), the amount should be removed from the Accounts Receivable account with an offsetting reduction of the allowance account. This entry does not record a bad debt expense because the estimated expense was recorded with an adjusting entry in the period of sale, and the related allowance account was established. Let's return to the Campus Corner illustration. Assume Campus Corner sold J. Doe merchandise on credit in 19D amounting to $100 (which was properly credited to 19D Sales Revenue and debited to Accounts Receivable). At the end of 19F, Campus Corner decided that it would never collect the $100. The journal entry to record the write-off is:

December 31, 19F:

Allowance for doubtful accounts 100
       Accounts receivable (J. Doe)   100
    To write off a receivable from J. Doe determined to be uncollectible.

Notice that the above journal entry did not affect any income statement accounts. The expense already had been recorded when the adjusting entry was made at the end of 19D. Also, the entry did not change the **net realizable value** (i.e., the book value) of Accounts Receivable. The difference between Accounts Receivable and the allowance account is the same as before the entry:

	Before write-off	After write-off
Accounts receivable	$100,000	$99,900
Less: Allowance for doubtful accounts	2,400	2,300
Difference—estimated net realizable value	$ 97,600	$97,600

Actual write-offs compared with estimates

The amount of uncollectible accounts actually written off seldom will equal the estimated amounts previously recorded. If the accounts actually written off are less than the estimated amount, the Allowance for Doubtful Accounts will continue with a credit balance.[4]

Under unusual circumstances, it may be necessary to restore a previously written off account. In these cases, the journal entry to write off the account is reversed and the collection of cash recorded.

Assume on June 1, 19G, J. Doe paid $100 on the account that was written off (shown above). The entry to record the collection is:

June 1, 19G

```
Accounts receivable . . . . . . . . . . . . . . . . . . . . . . . . . . . . . . . . . . . 100
    Allowance for doubtful accounts . . . . . . . . . . . . . . . . . . . . . .        100
    To reinstate the account.

Cash . . . . . . . . . . . . . . . . . . . . . . . . . . . . . . . . . . . . . . . . . . 100
    Accounts receivable . . . . . . . . . . . . . . . . . . . . . . . . . . . . . .        100
    To record cash collection.
```

Terminology

The caption "Accounts receivable" often appears on the balance sheet under current assets without additional descriptive terms; however, a more descriptive phrase such as "Receivables from trade customers" is preferable. Receivables from other than the regular trade customers, such as loans to officers or employees, should not be included in the accounts receivable category. Instead, such nontrade receivables should be reported as separate items.

---

[4] On the other hand, if the amount written off is more than the allowance balance, there will be a temporary debit balance in the allowance account. This situation will be resolved when the next adjusting entry is made. It indicates that the estimated loss rate used may be too low.

Sales Returns and Allowances

Many businesses let customers return unsatisfactory or damaged merchandise and receive a refund. In some cases, rather than taking back such merchandise, an adjustment may be given to the customer. To measure correctly sales revenue, returns and adjustments are recorded by reversing the original sales entry. Although the Sales account could be debited (i.e., reduced) to record these reductions in sales, a separate account called Sales Returns and Allowances often is used. This account has an important purpose because it informs management of the volume of returns and allowances. The Sales Returns and Allowances account is a contra revenue account; therefore, it is a deduction from gross sales revenue (as shown in Exhibit 6–1). Assume a customer, F. Fox, bought five new lamps from Campus Corner for $500. Fifteen days after payment, Fox returned one damaged lamp. The sequence of journal entries by Campus Corner is:

Date of sale:

```
Accounts receivable (F. Fox) . . . . . . . . . . . . . . . . . . . . . . . . . . . . . 500
    Sales revenue . . . . . . . . . . . . . . . . . . . . . . . . . . . . . . . . . . .        500
    To record sale.
```

Date of sale return:

```
Sales returns and allowances  . . . . . . . . . . . . . . . . . . . . . . . . . . . 100
    Cash* . . . . . . . . . . . . . . . . . . . . . . . . . . . . . . . . . . . . . . . .      100
    To record sale return, one unit.
    * If payment had not been made, this credit would be to Accounts Receivable.
```

PART B—ACCOUNTING FOR COST OF GOODS SOLD

Nature of Cost of Goods Sold

Cost of goods sold (CGS) is a major expense item for most nonservice businesses and is directly related to sales revenue. The amount of sales revenue during an accounting period is the number of units sold multiplied by the sales price. Cost of goods sold is the same number of units multiplied by their unit cost and includes the cost of all merchandise sold during the period. The cost of all merchandise remaining on hand at the end of the accounting period (i.e., the ending merchandise inventory) is excluded from cost of goods sold. The measurement of cost of goods sold is an excellent example of the application of the matching principle.

A business starts each accounting period with a stock of merchandise on hand for resale called the **beginning inventory (BI).** The merchandise on hand at the end of an accounting period is called the **ending inventory (EI).** The ending inventory for one accounting period automatically becomes the beginning inventory for the next period.

During the accounting period, the beginning inventory is increased by the purchase or manufacture of more merchandise. The sum of the beginning inventory and the **purchases (P)** during the period represents the **goods available for sale** during that period. If all of the goods available for sale were sold during the period, there would be no ending inventory. Typically, not all of the goods available for sale are sold, and there is an ending inventory for the period. From these relationships, we can compute cost of goods sold as follows:

$$BI + P - EI = CGS$$

To illustrate, Campus Corner reported cost of goods sold of $60,000 (Exhibit 6–1), which was computed as follows:

Beginning inventory (January 1, 19F)	$40,000
Add purchases of merchandise during 19F	55,000
Goods available for sale	95,000
Deduct ending inventory (December 31, 19F)	35,000
Cost of goods sold	$60,000

Two Different Inventory Systems

To compute cost of goods sold, three amounts must be known: (1) beginning inventory, (2) purchases of merchandise during the period, and (3) ending inventory. The beginning inventory of one accounting period is the ending inventory of the previous period. The amount of purchases for the period is accumulated in the accounting system. The amount of the ending inventory can be determined by using one of two different inventory systems:

1. **Periodic inventory system.**   Under this system, no up-to-date record of inventory is maintained during the year. An actual physical count of the goods remaining on hand is required at the **end of each period.** The number of units of each type of merchandise on hand is multiplied by their unit cost to compute the dollar amount of the ending inventory. Thus, the amount of inventory is not known until the last day of the period when the inventory count is done. Also, the amount of cost of goods sold cannot be determined until the inventory count is done.

2. **Perpetual inventory system.**   This system involves the maintenance of up-to-date inventory records in the accounting system during the period. For each type of merchandise stocked, a detailed record is maintained that shows (*a*) units and cost of the beginning inventory, (*b*) units and cost of each purchase, (*c*) units and cost of the goods for each sale, and (*d*) the units and cost of the goods on hand at any point in

time. This up-to-date record is maintained on a transaction-by-transaction basis throughout the period. **Thus, the inventory record gives both the amount of ending inventory and the cost of goods sold amount at any point in time.** Under this system, a physical count must be performed from time to time to assure accurate records in case errors or theft of merchandise occurred.

Periodic Inventory System

The periodic inventory system requires an actual count of the goods on hand at the end of the period and valuation of the units at their purchase cost. The primary reasons for using the periodic inventory system are low cost and convenience. Consider the expense and difficulty associated with a store attempting to keep track of the number of units sold and the cost of each purchase and sale for thousands of items. In many stores, no record is made at the cash register of the cost and quantity of each item sold. Instead, only the total sales price is entered into the cash register. The primary disadvantage of a periodic inventory system is the lack of inventory information. Managers are not provided with any information concerning low stock or overstocked situations.[5]

A periodic inventory system calculates the cost of goods sold as follows:

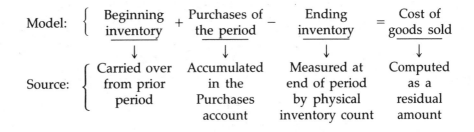

A periodic inventory system may be outlined sequentially as follows:

1. **Record all purchases.**   During the period, the cost of all goods purchased is recorded in an account called Purchases (or Merchandise Purchases). A purchase is recorded as follows:

January 14, 19F:

Purchases 9,000
       Accounts payable (or Cash)   9,000

---

[5] Because of this important disadvantage, many stores now have computerized perpetual inventory systems tied in directly to the cash registers. When grocery stores use scanning devices at the checkout, managers can easily be provided with up-to-date information concerning stock levels. This information facilitates reordering merchandise.

2. **Record all sales.**   During the period, the sales price received for all goods sold is recorded in a Sales Revenue account. A sale is recorded as follows:

January 30, 19F:

```
Accounts receivable (or Cash) . . . . . . . . . . . . . . . . . . . . . . . 8,000
      Sales revenue . . . . . . . . . . . . . . . . . . . . . . . . . . . . . . .        8,000
```

3. **Count the number of units on hand.**   At the end of each accounting period, the Inventory account balance still shows the ending inventory amount carried over from the prior period because **no journal entries** are made to the Inventory account during the period. To measure the ending inventory for the current period, a physical inventory count must be made. A physical count is needed because under the periodic inventory system, a transaction-by-transaction record is not maintained in the Inventory account.

4. **Compute the dollar valuation of the ending inventory.**   The dollar amount of the ending inventory quantities is computed by multiplying the number of units on hand by their unit purchase cost. The dollar amounts of all of the types of goods stocked are summed to determine the total ending inventory valuation for the company.

5. **Compute cost of goods sold.**   After the ending inventory valuation is determined, cost of goods sold for the period is computed. The calculation of cost of goods sold for Campus Corner is shown below.

CAMPUS CORNER
Schedule of Cost of Goods Sold
For the Year Ended December 31, 19F

```
Beginning inventory (carried over from the last period in the
   Inventory account) . . . . . . . . . . . . . . . . . . . . . . . . . . . . . . . . . . . . . . $40,000
Add purchases for the period (accumulated balance in the
   Purchases account) . . . . . . . . . . . . . . . . . . . . . . . . . . . . . . . . . . .   55,000
Goods available for sale . . . . . . . . . . . . . . . . . . . . . . . . . . . . . . . .   95,000
Less ending inventory (determined by physical count, per above) . . . . .   35,000
         Cost of goods sold (as shown in Exhibit 6–1) . . . . . . . . . . . . . $60,000
```

Perpetual Inventory System

A perpetual inventory system typically involves a large amount of clerical effort. However, the maintenance of a separate inventory record for each type of goods stocked on a transaction-by-transaction basis usually is desirable for control purposes. To minimize clerical difficulties, most perpetual inventory systems are computerized. Whether the accounting system is manual, mechanical, or computerized, the data that are recorded and reported are the same. Assume, for this illustration only, that Campus Corner stocks and sells only one item called Super X. The following events apply to 19F:

Exhibit 6-2 Perpetual inventory record

		PERPETUAL INVENTORY RECORD								
Item	Super X			Code	No. 33			Minimum stock	10	
Location	Storage No. 4			Valuation basis Cost				Maximum stock	20	

		Goods Purchased			Goods Sold			Balance on Hand		
Date	Explanation	Units Rec'd	Unit Cost	Total Cost	Units Sold	Unit Cost	Total Cost	Units	Unit Cost	Total Cost
Jan. 1	Beginning inventory							8	$5,000	$40,000
July 14	Purchase	11	$5,000	$55,000				19	5,000	95,000
Nov. 30	Sale				13	$5,000	$65,000	6	5,000	30,000
Dec. 31	Return sale				(1)	5,000	(5,000)	7	5,000	35,000
Recap: Total purchases		11		55,000						
Total cost of goods sold					12		60,000			
Ending inventory								7		35,000

Jan.   1   Beginning inventory—8 units, at unit cost of $5,000.
July 14   Purchased—11 additional units, at unit cost of $5,000.
Nov. 30   Sold—13 units, at unit sales price of $8,333.
Dec. 31   Return sale—1 unit (returned to stock and refunded sales price).

The perpetual inventory record for the Super X item is shown in Exhibit 6-2.[6] When the perpetual inventory system is computerized, the computer does exactly what was done manually in Exhibit 6-2. Computers overcome many of the clerical difficulties associated with the perpetual system. Computers permit large, medium, and small companies to use the perpetual system.

A perpetual inventory system may be outlined sequentially as follows:

1. **Record all purchases.** During the period, the cost of all goods purchased is recorded in the **Inventory account** and is entered in a detailed perpetual inventory record (Exhibit 6-2). A purchase of goods for resale is recorded as follows:

---

[6] Measuring inventories and cost of goods sold when there are different unit purchase costs is deferred to Chapter 7.

July 14, 19F:

```
Inventory* (Super X, code 33)  . . . . . . . . . . . . . . . . . . . . 55,000
     Accounts payable (or Cash)  . . . . . . . . . . . . . . . . . .        55,000
```
* Also entered in the perpetual inventory record as shown in Exhibit 6–2.

2. **Record all sales.**   During the period, each sale is recorded using **two companion journal entries.** One entry is to record the sales revenue, and the other entry is to record the cost of goods sold. A sale is recorded as follows (refer to data presented in Exhibit 6–2):

   a. To record the sales revenue at the sales price of $8,333 per unit:

   ```
   Accounts receivable (or Cash) . . . . . . . . . . . . . . . . . . 108,329
        Sales revenue (13 units @ $8,333) . . . . . . . . . . . .      108,329
   ```

   b. To record the cost of goods sold (at cost per the perpetual inventory record—Exhibit 6–2):

   ```
   Cost of goods sold*  . . . . . . . . . . . . . . . . . . . . . . . 65,000
        Inventory (13 units @ $5,000) . . . . . . . . . . . . . .      65,000
   ```
   * Also entered in the perpetual inventory record as shown in Exhibit 6–2.

3. **Record all returns.**   During the period, the costs of both **purchase returns and sales returns** are recorded in the Inventory account and on the perpetual inventory record. The return by a customer of one unit of Super X on December 31 requires companion journal entries to reverse the two entries made on the date of sale (but only for the number of units returned). The return is recorded as follows:

   a. To record the sales return at sale price (one unit):

   ```
   Sales returns and allowances (one unit @ $8,333) . . . . . .      8,333
        Accounts receivable (or Cash) . . . . . . . . . . . . . .          8,333
   ```

   b. To record the return of the unit to inventory at cost:

   ```
   Inventory (one unit @ $5,000)  . . . . . . . . . . . . . . . .     5,000 *
        Cost of goods sold  . . . . . . . . . . . . . . . . . . . .        5,000
   ```
   * This amount was provided by the perpetual inventory record; also it is restored to the perpetual inventory record as shown in Exhibit 6–2.

4. **Use cost of goods sold and inventory amounts.**   At the end of the accounting period, the balance in the Cost of Goods Sold account is the amount of that expense reported on the income statement. It is not necessary to compute cost of goods sold because under the perpetual inventory system the Cost of Goods Sold account is up-to-date. Also, the Inventory account shows the ending inventory amount reported on the balance sheet. The sum of all the inventory balances in the various perpetual inventory records should equal the balance in the Inventory account in the ledger at any point in time.

When a perpetual inventory system is used, it is not necessary to take a physical inventory count to measure the inventory and cost of goods sold. However, because clerical errors, theft, and spoilage may occur, a physical inventory should be taken from time to time to check on the accuracy of the perpetual inventory records. If an error is found, the perpetual inventory records and the Inventory account must be changed to agree with the physical count.

Comparison of Periodic and Perpetual Systems

There are two basic differences between the periodic and perpetual inventory systems:

1. **Inventory account:**
   a. Periodic system.   During the period, the balance in the Inventory account is not changed; thus, it reflects the beginning inventory amount. During the period, each purchase is recorded in the Purchases account. Therefore, the ending inventory for each accounting period must be measured by physical count, then valued at unit purchase cost.
   b. Perpetual system.   During the period, the Inventory account is increased for each purchase and decreased (at cost) for each sale. At any point during the period, it measures the correct amount of inventory.
2. **Cost of Goods Sold account:**
   a. Periodic system.   During the period, no entry is made for cost of goods sold. At the end of the period, after the physical inventory count, cost of goods sold is calculated as follows:

$$\frac{\text{Beginning}}{\text{inventory}} + \text{Purchases} - \frac{\text{Ending}}{\text{inventory}} = \frac{\text{Cost of}}{\text{goods sold}}$$

   b. Perpetual system.   During the period, cost of goods sold is recorded at the time of each sale, and the Inventory account is reduced (at cost). This system directly measures the amount of cost of goods sold for the period.

The perpetual inventory system provides the following advantages over the periodic inventory system:

1. It gives up-to-date inventory amounts (units and dollar cost for each item).
2. It gives the cost of goods sold amount without having to take a periodic inventory count.

3. It gives continuing information needed to keep minimum and maximum inventory levels by appropriate timing of purchases.
4. It gives a basis for measuring the amount of theft.
5. It is adaptable for use by computers that quickly process inventory data.

For these reasons there has been an increase in the use of the perpetual inventory system and a decrease in use of the periodic inventory system.

Taking a Physical Inventory

A physical inventory count must be taken from time to time. When a **periodic** inventory system is used, a physical inventory must be taken at the **end of each period** because the financial statements cannot be prepared without this key amount. When a perpetual inventory system is used, the inventory count should be scheduled at various times to verify the perpetual inventory records. The two steps in taking a **physical inventory** are:

1. **Quantity count.** The **count** of merchandise is made after the close of business on the inventory date because it would be difficult to count the goods during business hours when sales activities are taking place. A physical count is made of all items of merchandise on hand and entered on an appropriate form. An inventory form, such as the one shown in Exhibit 6–3, may be used. All of the merchandise owned by the business, wherever located, must be included. All items for which the business does not have legal ownership should be excluded. Sometimes, a business will have possession of goods it does not own (see discussion of consignments in Chapter 7).
2. **Inventory costing.** After the physical count of goods on hand has been completed, each kind of merchandise must be assigned a **unit cost.** The quantity of each item is multiplied by the unit cost to derive the inventory amount. The sum of the inventory amounts for all merchandise on hand is the total ending inventory amount for the business. Exhibit 6–3 shows computation of the ending inventory shown in the income statement for Campus Corner. To determine the value of inventory, the cost principle is applied. A problem arises if there are different unit costs for inventory items that are the same. This problem is discussed in Chapter 7.

Management must deal with complex problems associated with planning and control of inventories. An excessive amount of inventory may tie up cash that could be used more effectively in other ways in the business. Insufficient inventory often results in lost sales and unhappy customers. Decisions must be made concerning maximum and minimum levels of inventory that should be

Exhibit 6–3 Physical inventory form

Campus Corner
PHYSICAL INVENTORY SHEET

Date of Inventory _12/31/90_ Department _4(2nd last)_ Taken by _M. R._

Location	Identification of Merchandise	Quantity on Hand	Date Purchased	Unit Cost	Unit Market Price*	Unit Cost (LCM)	Inventory Amount
1	Headsets #8-16	20	12/2/90	$ 20	$ 21	$ 20	$ 400
2	Television sets #17-961	7	11/5/90	300	300	300	2,100
2	Radios #23-72	4	10/26/90	52	50	50	200
	Total Department Inventory						6,000
	TOTAL INVENTORY VALUE—ALL DEPARTMENTS 12/31/90						$ 35,000

* Replacement cost that would have to be paid if the item were being purchased on the inventory date (see lower-of-cost-or-market discussion in Chapter 7).

kept; when to reorder; how much to reorder; and the characteristics of the items to stock, such as size, color, style, and specifications. Because of the importance of good inventory management, explanatory footnotes related to inventories are included in the financial reports.

Inventory Shrinkage

Inventory shrinkage occurs because of theft, breakage, spoilage, and incorrect measurements. The measurement of inventory shrinkage is important for internal control purposes and, if large, is a major concern for investors and creditors. The dollar amount of shrinkage is reported on **internal** financial statements, but seldom are such amounts significant enough to be reported **separately** on **external** financial statements. Accurate measurement of this loss is related directly to the inventory system used.

When a **periodic inventory** is used, measurement of inventory shrinkage often is difficult, and may be impossible. The inventory, as counted at the end of the period, does not give a basis for measurement of shrinkage. An implicit assumption underlying the calculation of cost of goods sold (i.e., Beginning inventory + Purchases − Ending inventory = Cost of goods sold) is that if an item is not in ending inventory, it must have been sold. Therefore, under the periodic inventory system, cost of goods sold includes inventory shrinkage.

In contrast, a perpetual inventory system gives data on shrinkage loss. The inventory record gives both cost of goods sold and the ending inventory. These data make it possible to measure shrinkage loss. Assume the perpetual inventory records showed ending inventory of seven units, $35,000, but an inventory count at the end of the period showed six units on hand. An inventory shrinkage would be reported as one unit, and the loss amount would be $5,000 (assuming no insurance recovery). The journal entry to record the shrinkage, using a perpetual inventory system, is:

```
Inventory shrinkage* . . . . . . . . . . . . . . . . . . . . . . . . . . . . . . . . . . . . 5,000
    Inventory  . . . . . . . . . . . . . . . . . . . . . . . . . . . . . . . . . . . . . . .          5,000
* Closed to Income Summary.
```

Additional Issues in Measuring Purchases

A purchase of goods is recorded at the date that **ownership** passes from the seller to the buyer. Ownership usually passes when the goods are received and not when the purchase order is placed. Goods purchased should be recorded at their **cash equivalent cost** in conformity with the cost principle. Cost includes the cash equivalent price paid to the vendor plus other amounts paid for transportation and handling in order to get the goods into location and condition for intended use. Cost does not include interest paid on cash borrowed to make the purchase. Many of the problems associated with accounting for purchases are the same as those discussed in Part A of this chapter from the perspective of the seller.

Purchase Returns and Allowances

Goods purchased may be returned to the vendor if they do not meet specifications, arrive in damaged condition, or otherwise are unsatisfactory. When the goods are returned or when the vendor makes an allowance because of the circumstances, the effect on the cost of purchases must be measured. The purchaser normally will receive a cash refund or a reduction in the liability to the vendor when there is a return. Assume Campus Corner returned unsatisfactory goods that cost $1,000 to Company B. The return is recorded by Campus Corner (which uses the periodic system) as follows:

```
Accounts payable (or cash)  . . . . . . . . . . . . . . . . . . . . . . . . . . . . . 1,000
    Purchase returns and allowances* . . . . . . . . . . . . . . . . . . . . . .          1,000
* Inventory is credited when the perpetual inventory system is used.
```

Purchase returns and allowances are accounted for as a deduction from the cost of purchases.

Transportation-In

The **purchase cost** of goods acquired for resale should include all freight and other transportation-in costs incurred by the purchaser. When a perpetual inventory system is used, transportation costs paid on goods purchased should be apportioned to each inventory item and included in the inventory cost amount entered in the perpetual inventory. When a periodic inventory system is used, such costs should be recorded as a debit (i.e., increase) to the Purchases account. For control purposes, some companies enter the amount of the bill in a separate account called Transportation-In or Freight-In to classify separately this significant cost. The journal entry to record a payment for transportation charges is:

Jan. 17	Transportation-in	3,000
	Cash	3,000

At the end of the accounting period, the balance in the Transportation-In account is reported as an addition to the cost of purchases.

Assuming transportation-in and purchase returns, cost of goods sold may be shown as follows on the income statement when periodic inventory procedures are used:

Cost of goods sold:		
Beginning inventory		$40,000
Purchases	$53,000	
Add: Transportation-in	3,000	
Deduct: Purchase returns and allowances	(1,000)	
Net purchases		55,000
Goods available for sale		95,000
Less: Ending inventory		35,000
Cost of goods sold		$60,000

Purchase Discounts

Cash discounts must be accounted for by both the seller and the buyer (accounting by the seller was discussed in Part A of this chapter). When merchandise is bought on credit, terms such as 2/10, n/30 sometimes are specified. This means that if payment is made within 10 days from date of purchase, a 2% cash discount is granted. If payment is not made within the discount period, then the full invoice cost is due 30 days after purchase. Assume on January 17, Campus Corner bought goods that had a $1,000 invoice price with terms 2/10, n/30. The purchase should be recorded on the net basis by Campus Corner as follows:[7]

---

[7] Some accountants prefer to record the transaction at the date of purchase at the gross amount, that is, at $1,000. In this instance, payment within the discount period would result in credit to an account called Purchase Discounts, $20. The purchase discount credit is reported as a revenue, or as a deduction from purchases. This credit is not revenue and if deducted in full from purchases on the income statement would tend to misstate both inventory and purchases. In contrast, the net basis has the distinct advantage in that recording the **purchase discount lost** calls direct attention to inefficiency—failure to take the discount.

January 17—date of purchase:

Purchases*   980
    Accounts payable   980
* Inventory is debited when a perpetual inventory system is used.

January 26—date of payment, within the discount period:

Accounts payable   980
    Cash   980

If for any reason Campus Corner did not pay within the 10-day discount period, the following entry would be needed:

Feb. 1   Accounts payable   980
        Purchase discounts lost (or Interest expense)   20
           Cash   1,000

Purchase discounts lost should be reported on the income statement along with interest expense because it basically reflects the cost of borrowing money by delaying payment to the vendor.

Closing Entries for Sales Revenue, Cost of Goods Sold, and Merchandise Inventory

Closing the Sales Revenue and Bad Debt Expense Accounts

All revenue and expense accounts are temporary accounts that must be closed at the end of the accounting period. These accounts may be closed directly to Retained Earnings, but many companies use another temporary account called Income Summary. After all of the revenue and expense accounts have been closed to Income Summary, the balance in the account is net income, which is then closed to Retained Earnings. Exhibit 6–4 shows how some of the revenue and expense accounts discussed in this chapter are closed to Income Summary. The closing entries are boxed. A single closing entry can be prepared as follows:

Sales revenue   10,000
Sales discount revenue   800
    Bad debt expense   1,100
    Sales returns and allowances   350
    Income summary   9,350

The closing entries for cost of good sold and inventory depend on whether the periodic or perpetual system is used.

Closing Entries When a Periodic Inventory System Is Used

When a periodic inventory syst m is used, there is no Cost of Goods Sold account in the ledger. Two closing entries affect the Merchandise Inventory account: (1) an entry to transfer the **beginning inventory** amount to the Income

Exhibit 6–4 Closing Sales Revenue and Bad Debt Expense accounts

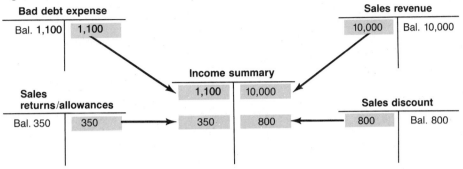

Summary account and (2) an entry to transfer the **ending inventory** amount from the Income Summary account to the Merchandise Inventory account. A third entry is needed to close the Purchases account. Campus Corner would make closing entries for the merchandise inventories as follows:

December 31, 19F:

a. To transfer the **beginning** merchandise inventory amount into Income Summary:

Income summary 40,000
    Merchandise inventory (beginning) 40,000

b. To transfer the **ending** merchandise inventory amount from the Income Summary account to the Merchandise Inventory account:

Merchandise inventory (ending) 35,000
    Income summary 35,000

The effects of these two journal entries are (a) to replace the beginning inventory amount in the Merchandise Inventory account with the ending inventory amount, (b) to enter the beginning inventory amount in the Income Summary account as an **expense** (a debit), and (c) to remove the ending inventory amount from the Income Summary account (a credit) as a cost transfer to the asset account Merchandise Inventory.

c. In addition, the Purchases account is closed to Income Summary as follows:

Income summary 55,000
    Purchases 55,000

Any accounts related to purchases (e.g., Purchase Returns and Allowances) also should be closed to Income Summary.

After completion of the closing entries, the accounts for Campus Corner would appear as follows:

PERIODIC INVENTORY SYSTEM

Merchandise Inventory

12/31/19E (beginning)	40,000	(*a*) Transfer to income summary	40,000
(*b*) 12/31/19F (ending)	35,000		

Purchases

12/31/19F (balance)	55,000	(*c*) To close	55,000

Income Summary

Operating expenses (not shown)		Revenues (not shown)	
(*a*) 12/31/19E (beginning inventory)	40,000	(*b*) 12/31/19F (ending inventory)	35,000
(*c*) (purchases)	55,000		

(Note that these three amounts net to $60,000, the amount of cost of goods sold.)

The reason for this sequence of closing entries can be understood if you study the Income Summary account. Under the periodic system, cost of goods sold is calculated as beginning inventory plus purchases minus ending inventory. Notice that these closing entries perform the cost of goods sold calculation in the Income Summary account. Also notice that the balance in the Merchandise Inventory account has been updated to reflect the ending inventory amount.[8]

Closing Entries When a Perpetual Inventory System Is Used

When a perpetual inventory system is used, the Merchandise Inventory account and Cost of Goods Sold account always show the correct up-to-date balance. Therefore, no adjusting entries are needed for the Merchandise Inventory account; it shows the ending inventory amount that will be reported on the balance sheet. Because the Cost of Goods Sold account is an expense account, it will be closed. Campus Corner would record the following closing entry under the perpetual inventory system:

Income summary 60,000
　　　Cost of goods sold . . . .　　　 60,000

---

[8] There are several mechanical variations in how the closing entries can be made; all of them give the same end results. For example, some persons prefer to use a temporary Cost of Goods Sold account in the closing process under a periodic inventory system; in this approach, the two inventory amounts and purchases are first transferred to the Cost of Goods Sold account, which is then closed to Income Summary.

Financial Statement Analysis

Cost of goods sold is a major expense for most nonservice companies, and most companies must invest large amounts of money in inventory to meet the needs of their customers. As a result, users of financial statements are particularly interested in the topics that were discussed in this chapter.

Analysts often calculate an amount called **gross margin on sales,**[9] which is the difference between net sales revenue and cost of goods sold. This amount may be reported on the income statement (Exhibit 6–1). Gross margin reflects the total amount of markup on all goods sold during the period. It can be expressed as a dollar amount (gross margin for Campus Corner was $40,000) or as a ratio called the gross margin ratio. The gross margin ratio is calculated as Gross margin ÷ Net sales revenue (the ratio for Campus Corner was 40% = $40,000 ÷ $100,000).[10] The ratio for Campus Corner (40%) is typical for a full-service department store. The ratio for a discount store is usually much less.

Anaysts use the gross margin ratio to compare similar companies. If a major competitor to Campus Corner reported a gross margin ratio of 25%, analysts would attempt to determine the cause of the difference. Perhaps the competitor has adopted an aggressive pricing policy and intends to sell its merchandise at a discount below the prices charged by Campus Corner. This example illustrates how analysts can use accounting information to gain additional insight into the operation and competitiveness of a company. We will discuss ratio analysis in additional detail in Chapter 16.

DEMONSTRATION CASE

(Try to resolve the requirements before proceeding to the suggested solution that follows.)

Rote Appliance Store has been operating for a number of years. It is a relatively small but profitable retail outlet for major appliances, such as refrigerators and air conditioners. Approximately 40% of the sales are on short-term credit. This case has been simplified to demonstrate information processing when there are significant selling activities (the service activities have been deleted). The case shows the application of both perpetual and periodic inventory systems with the same data. The annual accounting period ends December 31, 19D. Two independent cases will be assumed:

---

[9] This often is called gross profit on sales or simply gross margin or gross profit. In the *Accounting Terminology Bulletins,* the AICPA recommended against use of the term **profit** in this context.

[10] This percent is based on sales revenue rather than cost. The markup percent on **cost** would be $40,000 ÷ $60,000 = 66⅔%.

Case A—perpetual inventory system.

Case B—periodic inventory system.

The trial balance at December 31, 19D, was:

	Unadjusted trial balance			
	Case A—perpetual inventory system used		Case B—periodic inventory system used	
Account titles	**Debit**	**Credit**	**Debit**	**Credit**
Cash	$ 34,100		$ 34,100	
Accounts receivable	5,000		5,000	
Allowance for doubtful accounts		$ 1,000		$ 1,000
* Merchandise inventory:				
January 1, 19D			20,000	
December 31, 19D	16,000			
Store equipment	30,000		30,000	
Accumulated depreciation		9,000		9,000
Accounts payable		8,000		8,000
Income taxes payable				
Capital stock (par $10)		40,000		40,000
Retained earnings, January 1, 19D		9,000		9,000
Sales revenue		102,000		102,000
Sales returns and allowances	2,000		2,000	
* Cost of goods sold	60,000			
* Purchases			57,000	
* Purchase returns and allowances				1,000
Expenses (not detailed)	21,900		21,900	
Depreciation expense				
Income tax expense				
Totals	$169,000	$169,000	$170,000	$170,000

* These account balances are different between the two cases because of the effects of the two inventory systems used.

Data developed by Rote as a basis for the adjusting entries at December 31, 19D, were:

a. Credit sales in 19D were $40,000; the average loss rate for bad debts is estimated to be 0.25% of credit sales.

b. The store equipment is depreciated on the basis of an estimated 10-year useful life with no residual value.

c. On December 31, 19D, the periodic inventory count of goods remaining on hand was $16,000.

d. The average income tax rate is 20%.

e. The beginning inventory, January 1, 19D, was as shown on the trial balance (Case B).

Required:

a. Based on the above data, complete a worksheet at December 31, 19D, similar to that shown in Exibit 5–3. You may omit the columns for Adjusted Trial Balance. **Prepare a separate worksheet for each separate case.**

b. Based on the completed worksheets, present an income statement for each case. Use a single-step format for Case A and a multiple-step format for Case B.

c. Based on the two worksheets, present in parallel columns the adjusting entries for each case at December 31, 19D.

d. Based on the two worksheets, present in parallel columns the closing entries for each situation at December 31, 19D.

In preparing the worksheet when a **perpetual inventory** system is used, no new complications are presented. The inventory amount is extended across the worksheet as an asset because the balance in the Merchandise Inventory account reflects the ending inventory when a perpetual inventory system is used. The expense—cost of goods sold—is extended to the Income Summary debit column along with the other expenses. See Exhibit 6–5.

In preparing the worksheet with a **periodic inventory system,** both the beginning and ending inventory amounts must be used. First, the beginning inventory amount must be extended horizontally as a debit to the Income Statement column (because it now is an expense). A special line, "Merchandise inventory, ending," is added to the bottom of the worksheet, and the ending inventory amount is entered on this line under Income Statement credit. This amount also is listed on the same line under Balance Sheet, debit.[11]

---

[11] There are several mechanical ways of handling the inventories on the worksheet when a periodic inventory system is used. Some accountants view the inventory entries as closing rather than adjusting entries. The various approaches arrive at the same net result, and each has its particular mechanical advantages and disadvantages.

Suggested Solution   *Requirement a:*

Exhibit 6–5 Worksheets compared for perpetual and periodic inventory systems

ROTE APPLIANCE STORE
Worksheet for the Year Ended December 31, 19D
Case A—Assuming Perpetual Inventory System Is Used

Account Titles	Trial Balance Debit	Trial Balance Credit	Adjusting Entries* Debit	Adjusting Entries* Credit	Income Statement Debit	Income Statement Credit	Retained Earnings Debit	Retained Earnings Credit	Balance Sheet Debit	Balance Sheet Credit
Cash	34,100								34,100	
Accounts receivable	5,000								5,000	
Allowance for doubtful accounts		1,000		(a) 100						1,100
Merchandise inventory, Dec. 31, 19D	16,000								16,000	
Store equipment	30,000								30,000	
Accumulated depreciation		9,000		(b) 3,000						12,000
Accounts payable		8,000								8,000
Income taxes payable				(c) 3,000						3,000
Capital stock (par $10)		40,000								40,000
Retained earnings, Jan. 1, 19D		9,000						9,000		
Sales revenue		102,000				102,000				
Sales returns and allowances	2,000				2,000					
Cost of goods sold	60,000				60,000					
Expenses (not detailed)	21,900		(a) 100		22,000					
Depreciation expense			(b) 3,000		3,000					
	169,000	169,000			87,000	102,000				
Income tax expense†			(c) 3,000		3,000					
Net income					12,000			12,000		
			6,100	6,100	102,000	102,000	–0–	21,000		
Retained earnings, Dec. 31, 19D							21,000			21,000
							21,000	21,000	85,100	85,100

* Note that a **simplifying mechanical change** is used—the "Adjusting Entries" total is not entered until **after** the income tax is computed and entered.
† ($102,000 − $87,000) × 20% = $3,000 income tax expense.

Requirement a (concluded):

Exhibit 6–5 (Concluded)

ROTE APPLIANCE STORE
Worksheet for the Year Ended December 31, 19D
Case B—Assuming Periodic Inventory System Is Used

Account Titles	Trial Balance Debit	Trial Balance Credit	Adjusting Entries* Debit	Adjusting Entries* Credit	Income Statement Debit	Income Statement Credit	Retained Earnings Debit	Retained Earnings Credit	Balance Sheet Debit	Balance Sheet Credit
Cash	34,100								34,100	
Accounts receivable	5,000								5,000	
Allowance for doubtful accounts		1,000		(a) 100						1,100
Merchandise inventory, Jan. 1, 19D	20,000				20,000					
Store equipment	30,000								30,000	
Accumulated depreciation		9,000		(b) 3,000						12,000
Accounts payable		8,000								8,000
Income taxes payable				(c) 3,000						3,000
Capital stock (par $10)		40,000								40,000
Retained earnings, Jan. 1, 19D		9,000						9,000		
Sales revenue		102,000				102,000				
Sales returns and allowances	2,000				2,000					
Purchases	57,000				57,000					
Purchase returns and allowances		1,000				1,000				
Expenses (not detailed)	21,900		(a) 100		22,000					
Depreciation expense			(b) 3,000		3,000					
Merchandise inventory, Dec. 31, 19D						16,000			16,000	
	170,000	170,000			104,000	119,000				
Income tax expense†			(c) 3,000		3,000					
Net income					12,000			12,000		
			6,100	6,100	119,000	119,000	–0–	21,000		
Retained earnings, Dec. 31, 19D							21,000			21,000
							21,000	21,000	85,100	85,100

* Note that a **simplifying mechanical change** is used—the "Adjusting Entries" total is not entered until after the income tax is computed and entered.
† ($119,000 − $104,000) × 20% = $3,000 income tax expense.

Requirement b:

ROTE APPLIANCE STORE
Income Statement
For the Year Ended December 31, 19D
Case A—Perpetual Inventory System and Single-Step Format

Revenues:
Gross sales revenue	$102,000	
Less: Sales returns and allowances	2,000	
Net sales revenue		$100,000

Expenses:
Cost of goods sold	60,000	
Expenses (not detailed for case purposes)	22,000	
Depreciation expense	3,000	85,000
Pretax income		15,000
Income tax expense ($15,000 × 20%)		3,000
Net income		$ 12,000
EPS ($12,000 ÷ 4,000 shares)		$3.00

ROTE APPLIANCE STORE
Income Statement
For the Year Ended December 31, 19D
Case B—Periodic Inventory System and Multiple-Step Format

Gross sales revenue		$102,000
Less: Sales returns and allowances		2,000
Net sales revenue		100,000
Cost of goods sold:		
Inventory, January 1, 19D	$ 20,000	
Purchases	57,000	
Purchase returns and allowances	(1,000)	
Goods available for sale	76,000	
Less: Inventory, December 31, 19D	16,000	
Cost of goods sold		60,000
Gross margin on sales		40,000
Operating expenses:		
Expenses (not detailed for case purposes)	22,000	
Depreciation expense	3,000	25,000
Pretax income		15,000
Income tax expense ($15,000 × 20%)		3,000
Net income		$ 12,000
EPS ($12,000 ÷ 4,000 shares)		$3.00

Requirement c:

Adjusting Entries
December 31, 19D

	Case A		Case B	
	Perpetual inventory		**Periodic inventory**	
a. Expenses (estimated bad debt loss)	100		100	
Allowance for doubtful accounts		100		100
Bad debt loss estimated, $40,000 × 0.25% = $100.				
b. Depreciation expense	3,000		3,000	
Accumulated depreciation		3,000		3,000
Depreciation for one year, $30,000 ÷ 10 years = $3,000.				
c. Income tax expense	3,000		3,000	
Income taxes payable		3,000		3,000
Income tax for year, $15,000 × 20% = $3,000.				

Requirement d:

Closing Entries
December 31, 19D

	Case A		Case B	
	Perpetual inventory		**Periodic inventory**	
1. Sales revenue	102,000		102,000	
Sales returns and allowances .		2,000		2,000
Income summary		100,000		100,000
To transfer the revenue amounts to Income Summary.				
2. Income summary	(Not applicable)		56,000	
Purchase returns and allowances .			1,000	
Purchases				57,000
To transfer purchase amounts to Income Summary.				
3. Income summary	(Not applicable)		20,000	
Merchandise inventory (beginning)				20,000
To transfer beginning inventory to Income Summary.				
4. Merchandise inventory (ending) .	(Not applicable)		16,000	
Income summary				16,000
To transfer ending inventory from Income Summary.				

Requirement d (Concluded):

Closing Entries
December 31, 19D

	Case A		Case B	
	Perpetual inventory		**Periodic inventory**	
5. Income summary	60,000		(Not applicable)	
Cost of goods sold		60,000		
6. Income summary	28,000		28,000	
Expenses (not detailed)		22,000		22,000
Depreciation expense		3,000		3,000
Income tax expense		3,000		3,000
To transfer expense amounts				
to Income Summary.				
7. Income summary	12,000		12,000	
Retained earnings		12,000		12,000
To transfer net income				
to Retained Earnings.				

SUMMARY OF CHAPTER

This chapter discussed the measuring, recording, and reporting of the effects on income of the selling and purchasing activities of various types of businesses.

In conformity with the matching principle, the total cost of the goods sold during the period must be matched with the sales revenue earned during the period. The Cost of Goods Sold account measures the **cost** of merchandise that was sold while the Sales revenue account measures the **selling price** of the same merchandise. When cost of goods sold is deducted from sales revenue for the period, the difference is called gross margin on sales. From this amount, the remaining expense must be deducted to derive income.

This chapter also discussed the effect on cost of goods sold of the beginning and ending inventory amounts. The ending inventory of one period is the beginning inventory of the next period. Two inventory systems were discussed for measuring the ending inventory and cost of goods sold for the period: (1) the perpetual inventory system, which is based on the maintenance of detailed and continuous inventory records for each kind of merchandise stocked; and (2) the periodic inventory system, which is based on a physical inventory count of ending inventory and the costing of those goods to determine the proper amounts for cost of goods sold and ending inventory.

CHAPTER SUPPLEMENT 6A

Control Accounts and Subsidiary Ledgers

Control accounts and subsidiary ledgers facilitate keeping records in situations where a large number of similar transactions occur. Their use does not involve accounting theory, principles, or standards but involves only the mechanics of data processing. The use of control accounts and subsidiary ledgers will be explained for accounts receivable; however, the procedure also is applicable in any situation that involves numerous transactions that are similar and require detailed records, such as accounts payable and operational assets.

Some businesses carry thousands of individual customers on a credit status. If a separate Accounts Receivable account was kept in the general ledger for each customer, there would be thousands of receivable accounts in the general ledger.

Instead, most large businesses keep a **single control account** in the general ledger for Accounts Receivable and a **separate subsidiary ledger** that carries an individual account for each credit customer and may include several thousand **individual receivable accounts.** The **sum** of the individual account balances in the receivable subsidiary ledger always should equal the single balance in the Accounts Receivable control account in the general ledger. The individual customer accounts, as subdivisions of the control account, are subsidiary to the control account; thus, they are called subsidiary ledgers.

To illustrate the use of a control account with a subsidiary ledger for Accounts Receivable, we will assume several transactions for the Mayo Department Store. Mayo uses a manual system, but control accounts and subsidiary ledgers also are used extensively with computerized systems. Credit sales could be recorded in the general journal as follows:

GENERAL JOURNAL   Page 1

Date	Account Titles and Explanation	Folio	Debit	Credit
Jan. 5	Accounts receivable	102	2,400	
	Sales revenue	610		2,400
	To record the following credit sales:			
	Adams, J. K. . . . . $ 740	102.1		
	Baker, B. B. 570	102.2		
	Ford C. E. 340	102.3		
	Moore, W. E. 320	102.4		
	Price, V. T. 430	102.5		
	Total $2,400			

Exhibit 6–6 General and subsidiary ledgers for Mayo Department Store

GENERAL LEDGER

Date /9A	Cash #101	Folio	Debit	Credit	Balance
Jan. 12		3	1 000		

	Accounts Receivable Control #102				
Jan 5		1	2 400		2 400
7		2		140	2 260
12		3		1 000	1 260

	Sales #610				
Jan 5		1		2 400	2 400

	Sales Returns #620				
Jan 7		2	140		140

Posting of the journal entry on page 271 to the control account in the general ledger is indicated by entering the Accounts Receivable and Sales Revenue **account numbers** in the Folio column in the usual manner. Posting to the individual customer accounts in the subsidiary ledger is indicated by entering an individual customer's account number in the Folio column of the journal. Notice Exhibit 6–6. The total amount ($2,400) was posted to the control account, Accounts Receivable, and the several single amounts were posted to the subsidiary ledger. The debit-credit-balance form is used in the Mayo subsidiary ledger rather than the T-account form that often is used for instructional purposes.

On January 7, one customer, J. K. Adams, returned some unsatisfactory merchandise purchased on January 5. Mayo accepted the goods and gave Adams credit on his account. The journal entry is shown at the bottom of page 273:

Exhibit 6–6 (Concluded)

SUBSIDIARY LEDGER

		Adams, J. K. 102.1					
Jan.	5		1	740			740
	7	Return	2		140		600
	12		3		400		200

		Baker, B. B. 102.2					
Jan.	5		1	570			570

		Ford, C. E. 102.3					
Jan.	5		1	340			340
	12		3		340		–0–

		Moore, W.E. 102.4					
Jan.	5		1	320			320
	12		3		220		100

		Price, V. T. 102.5					
Jan.	5		1	430			430
	12		3		40		390

		Ward, B. L. 102.6					
Jan.	5		1	450			450

GENERAL JOURNAL   Page 2

Date	Account Titles and Explanation	Folio	Debit	Credit
Jan. 7	Sales returns	620	140	
	Accounts receivable	102		140
	To record the return of goods:			
	Adams, J. K. $140	102.1		

The Folio column shows that the above entry has been posted in total to the control account in the general ledger. Also, the single amount has been posted to the individual customer account in the subsidiary ledger (Exhibit 6–6).

Cash collections from customers are recorded in the journal entry given below. The Folio column shows that the entry has been posted in total to the control account and each single amount to the individual customer accounts in the subsidiary ledger (Exhibit 6–6).

GENERAL JOURNAL   Page 3

Date	Account Titles and Explanation	Folio	Debit	Credit
Jan. 12	Cash	101	1,000	
	Accounts receivable	102		1,000
	To record collections on accounts as follows:			
	Adams, J. K. . . . . $ 400	102.1		
	Ford, C. E. 340	102.3		
	Moore, W. E. 220	102.4		
	Price, V. T. 40	102.5		
	Total $1,000			

The subsidiary ledger should be reconciled frequently with the control account to determine whether errors were made in posting. This reconciliation is accomplished by summing the balances in the subsidiary ledger to determine whether that total agrees with the total shown by the control account in the general ledger. A reconciliation schedule for Mayo follows:

MAYO DEPARTMENT STORE
Schedule of Accounts Receivable
January 28, 19A

Account		Amount
No.	Customer	(per subsidiary)
102.1	Adams, J. K.	$ 200
102.2	Baker, B. B.	570
102.4	Moore, W. E.	100
102.5	Price, V. T.	390
102	Total accounts receivable (per control account)	$1,260

The subsidiary ledger total should agree with the balance in the control account. If there is disagreement, one or more errors are indicated; however, agreement does not necessarily mean there are no errors. A transaction could be posted to the wrong customer's account, and the two ledgers would still reconcile in total.

The **Sales Revenue** account also could be established as a control account. This account would be supported by a subsidiary ledger that would contain separate accounts for the sales of **each department** or for **each product.** Another common application of control accounts relates to **accounts payable** when there are numerous purchases on credit.

Control accounts are also useful when accounting for **operational assets.** For example, the Office Equipment account usually is included in the general ledger as a control account. This control account is supported by a subsidiary ledger of office equipment that has an account for each different kind of office equipment, such as copiers, typewriters, calculators, and furniture. These examples show that the control account/subsidiary ledger procedure is an important element of the accounting information processing system of most enterprises.

One advantage of the use of subsidiary ledgers in a manual system is that it facilitates the subdivision of work. A person can be trained in a short time to maintain a subsidiary ledger because a knowledge of the broad field of accounting is not needed for such routine bookkeeping tasks.

In the journal entries given above, the individual amounts relating to each individual customer account were listed in the Explanation column of the journal and then were posted to the subsidiary ledger. There are two approaches to simplifying this phase of the bookkeeping. Amounts could be transferred directly from the charge tickets to the subsidiary ledger accounts and thus avoid the detailed listing in the journal entry. This approach is used sometimes by small companies. Another simplifying approach involves the use of a related procedure known as **special journals.** This procedure is explained in Chapter Supplement 8B.

Although our illustration used a manual approach to show subsidiary ledgers, most companies apply the procedure using computers. The computer can be programmed to process credit sales, returns, collections on account, reconciliation of account balances, and a printout of monthly bills to be mailed to the customers.

IMPORTANT TERMS DEFINED IN THIS CHAPTER

Aging Accounts Receivable Method to estimate uncollectible accounts based on the age of each account receivable. *p. 245*

Bad Debt Allowance Method Method that bases bad debt expense on an estimate of uncollectible accounts. *p. 244*

Bad Debt Loss Expense associated with estimated uncollectible accounts receivable. *p. 243*

Gross Margin on Sales As a dollar amount, net sales minus cost of goods sold; as a ratio, gross margin divided by net sales revenue. *p. 263*

Gross Method to Record Revenue Sales revenue is recorded without deducting the authorized cash discount. *p. 242*

Inventory Shrinkage Missing inventory caused by theft, breakage, spoilage, and incorrect measurements. *p. 257*

Markup The difference between sales revenue and cost of goods sold. *p. 263*

Net Method to Record Revenue Sales revenue is recorded after deducting the amount of any authorized cash discount. *p. 242*

Periodic Inventory System   Ending inventory and cost of goods sold are determined at the end of the accounting period. *p. 251*

Perpetual Inventory System   A detailed inventory record is maintained continuously during the accounting period. *p. 252*

Physical Inventory Count   Actual count of units in inventory. *p. 256*

Purchase Discount   Cash discount received for prompt payment of an account payable. *p. 259*

Purchase Returns and Allowances   A deduction from the cost of purchases associated with unsatisfactory goods. *p. 258*

Sales Discount   Cash discount offered to encourage prompt payment of an account receivable. *p. 241*

Sales Returns and Allowances   A contra revenue account that is associated with unsatisfactory goods. *p. 249*

Subsidiary Ledgers   A group of subaccounts that provides more detail than the general ledger control account. *p. 271*

Trade Discount   A discount that is deducted from list price to derive the actual sales price. *p. 243*

QUESTIONS

Part A: Questions 1–12

1. The **quantity** of goods included in sales revenue also must be included in a particular **expense** amount. Explain the basis for this statement.
2. Explain the difference between gross sales and net sales.
3. What is gross margin on sales? How is the gross margin ratio computed (in your explanation, assume that net sales revenue was $100,000 and cost of goods sold was $60,000)?
4. What is a sales discount? Use 1/10, n/30 in your explanation.
5. When merchandise invoiced at $1,000 is sold on terms 2/10, n/30, the vendor must make the following entry:

    Accounts receivable . . . .
       Sales revenue   . . . .

    What amounts should be used in this entry under the net method of recording sales discounts? Why is the net method preferred over the gross method?
6. A sale is made for $500; terms are 2/10, n/30. At what amount should the sale be recorded under the net method of recording sales discounts? Give the required entry with an explanation. Also, give the collection entry assuming it is after the discount period.

7. Because the actual time of cash collection is not relevant in determining the date on which a sale should be given accounting recognition, what factor is relevant?

8. Why is an estimate, instead of the actual amount of bad debts, used as a measure of periodic bad debt expense?

9. What is a contra account? Give two examples.

10. Define the book value of accounts receivable.

11. Why should estimated bad debt losses be based on credit sales rather than on total sales for the period?

12. What is the distinction between sales allowances and sales discounts?

Part B: Questions 13–23

13. Define goods available for sale. How does it differ from cost of goods sold?

14. Define beginning inventory and ending inventory.

15. Briefly distinguish between the perpetual and periodic inventory systems. How does each measure *(a)* inventory and *(b)* cost of goods sold?

16. Describe the calculation of cost of goods sold under the periodic inventory system.

17. Why is it necessary to take an actual physical inventory count at the end of the period when the periodic inventory system is used?

18. Under the cost principle, at what amount should a purchase be recorded? Be specific.

19. What is the purpose of a perpetual inventory record for each item stocked?

20. What accounts are debited and credited for a purchase of goods for resale *(a)* when a perpetual inventory system is used and *(b)* when a periodic inventory system is used?

21. What accounts are debited and credited for a sale of goods on credit *(a)* when a perpetual inventory system is used and *(b)* when a periodic inventory system is used?

22. Why is there no purchases account when the perpetual inventory system is used?

23. Why is transportation-in considered to be a cost of purchasing merchandise?

EXERCISES

Part A: Exercises 6–1 to 6–10

E6–1 (Match Definitions with Terms)
Match each definition with its related term by entering the appropriate letter in the space provided.

Terms	Definitions

Terms

_____ (1) Cost of goods sold

_____ (2) Trade discount

_____ (3) Bad debt loss

_____ (4) Sales returns and allowances

_____ (5) Gross margin on sales

_____ (6) Inventory shrinkage

_____ (7) Aging accounts receivable

_____ (8) Periodic inventory system

_____ (9) Physical inventory count

_____ (10) Markup

_____ (11) Purchase returns and allowances

_____ (12) Net method to record revenue

_____ (13) Perpetual inventory method

_____ (14) Bad debt allowance method

_____ (15) Gross method to record revenue

_____ (16) Sales discount

_____ (17) Subsidiary ledger

_____ (18) Purchase discount

Definitions

A. Analysis of the elements of individual accounts receivable according to the time elapsed after the dates of billing.

B. Use of this method establishes a contra account called Allowance for Doubtful Accounts, which is considered a subtraction from the balance of the Accounts Receivable account.

C. Receivables determined to be uncollectible.

D. Synonym for gross profit.

E. Method of recording revenue which, without adjusting entries, may overstate both accounts receivable and sales revenue.

F. The difference between the value of inventory if there were no theft, breakage, or clerical errors; and the value of inventory when it is physically counted.

G. A percentage often reported as the gross margin ratio.

H. The preferred method for recording sales on credit.

I. Method where the cost of goods sold is computed periodically by relying solely on physical counts and not keeping any day-to-day records.

J. A system that keeps a continuous record that tracks inventories and cost of goods sold on a day-to-day basis.

K. A process that involves two steps: (1) a quantity count and (2) an inventory costing.

L. A cash discount received by a credit customer for prompt payment.

M. Products returned by the customer, or a reduction in the selling price resulting in a deduction from the cost of purchases.

N. A price concession offered by a seller to a customer for prompt payment.

O. A contra revenue account used to record goods returned by customers.

P. A supporting ledger that provides details for specific accounts in the general ledger.

Q. A price concession often offered on volume orders that applies a reduction to the list price resulting in a lower invoice price.

R. Beginning inventory + Purchases − Ending inventory.

E6-2 **(Analysis of Income Statement Relationships)**
Supply the missing dollar amounts for the 19B income statement of High Fashion Company for each of the following independent cases:

	Case A	Case B	Case C	Case D	Case E
Sales revenue	$1,000	$800	$800	$?	$?
Selling expense	?	200	80	120	200
Cost of goods sold	?	480	?	500	610
Income tax expense	?	30	30	40	30
Gross margin	400	?	?	?	390
Pretax income	100	40	?	180	?
Administrative expense	100	?	60	100	80
Net income	80	?	120	?	80

E6-3 **(Preparation of an Income Statement Using the Gross Margin)**
The following data were taken from the records of Kelli Appliances, Incorporated, at December 31, 19D:

Sales revenue $150,000
Administrative expense 15,000
Selling (distribution) expense 20,000
Income tax rate 30%
Gross margin ratio 40%
Shares of stock outstanding   2,000

Required:
Prepare a complete income statement for the company. Show all computations. (Hint: Set up side captions starting with sales revenue and ending with earnings per share; rely on the percents given.)

E6-4 **(Preparation of a Multiple-Step Income Statement)**
The following data were taken from the records of Metro Corporation at December 31, 19B:

Gross margin (30% ratio) $24,000
Selling (distribution) expense   9,000
Administrative expense . . . .   ?
Pretax income   10,000
Income tax rate, 25%.
Shares of stock outstanding   3,000

Required:
Prepare a complete multiple-step income statement for the company. Show all computations. (Hint: Set up the side captions starting with sales revenue and ending with earnings per share; rely on the percents given.)

E6–5   (Preparation of a Multiple-Step Income Statement and Analysis of Gross Margin)
The following data were taken from the records of Richard Corporation on December 31, 19B:

Sales of merchandise for cash	$150,000
Sales of merchandise for credit	257,000
Sales returns and allowances	7,000
Selling expense	100,000
Cost of goods sold	242,000
Administrative expense	42,000

Items not included in above amounts:
   Estimated bad debts loss, 1% of net credit
      sales.
   Average income tax rate, 20%.
   Number of shares of common stock outstand-
      ing, 10,000.

Required:

a. Based on the above data, prepare a multiple-step income statement. There were no extraordinary items. Include a Percentage Analysis column.

b. How much was the gross margin? What was the gross margin ratio? Explain what these two amounts mean.

E6–6   (Preparation of a Multiple-Step Income Statement and Analysis of Gross Margin)
The following summarized data were provided by the records of Baldwin, Incorporated, for the year ended December 31, 19B:

Sales of merchandise for cash	$126,000
Sales of merchandise on credit	80,000
Cost of goods sold	120,000
Selling expense	30,800
Administrative expense	20,000
Sales returns and allowances	6,000

Items not included in above amounts:
   Estimated bad debt loss, 2% of credit sales.
   Average income tax rate, 25%.
   Number of shares of common stock
      outstanding, 4,000.

Required:

a. Based on the above data, prepare a multiple-step income statement. Include a Percentage Analysis column.

b. What was the amount of gross margin? What was the gross margin ratio? Explain.

E6–7   (Recording Sales Revenue Using the Net Method)
During the months of January and February, Silver Corporation sold goods to three customers. The sequence of events was as follows:

Jan.   6   Sold goods for $800 to J. Doe and billed that amount subject to terms 2/10, n/30.
      6   Sold goods to R. Roe for $600 and billed that amount subject to terms 2/10, n/30.
   14   Collected cash due from J. Doe.
Feb.   2   Collected cash due from R. Roe.
   28   Sold goods for $500 to B. Moe and billed that amount subject to terms 2/10, n/45.

Required:

a. Give the appropriate journal entry for each date. Assume a periodic inventory system is used and that the net method is used to record sales revenue.

b. Explain how each account balance as of February 28 should be reported, assuming that this is the end of the accounting period.

E6–8   (Using the Net Method to Record Sales Revenue)

The following transactions were selected from among those completed by Prentice Retailers:

Nov. 25 Sold 20 items of merchandise to Customer A at an invoice price of $2,000 (total); terms 3/10, n/30.

28 Sold 10 items of merchandise to Customer B at an invoice price of $4,000 (total); terms 3/10, n/30.

30 Customer B returned one of the items purchased on the 28th; the item was defective, and credit was given to the customer.

Dec. 6 Customer B paid the account balance in full.

30 Customer A paid in full for the invoice of November 25, 19B.

Required:

a. Give the appropriate journal entry for each of the above transactions assuming the company uses the periodic inventory system and records sales revenue under the net method.

b. Assume it is December 31, 19B, end of the accounting period. Show how the various account balances would be reported on the balance sheet and the income statement.

E6–9   (Accounting for Bad Debts Using the Allowance Method)

Martin Company started business on January 1, 19A. During the year 19A, the company's records indicated the following:

Sales on cash basis	$300,000
Sales on credit basis	100,000
Collections on accounts receivable	75,000

The manager of the company is concerned about accounting for the bad debts. At December 31, 19A, although no accounts were considered bad, several customers were considerably overdue in paying their accounts. A friend of the manager suggested a 1% bad debt rate on sales, which the manager decided to use at the start.

Required:

a. You have been employed on a part-time basis to assist with the recordkeeping for the company. The manager told you to set up bad debt expense of $4,000. Give the required entry.

b. You are concerned about how the $4,000 was determined, and the manager told you it was from another manager "who knew his business" and used 1% of sales. Do you agree with the estimate of bad debts? If you disagree, give the correct entry and explain the basis for your choice.

c. Show how the various accounts related to credit sales should be shown on the December 31, 19A, income statement and balance sheet.

E6–10   (Analysis and Evaluation of a Bad Debt Estimate)

During 19G, Mike's Bike Shop had sales revenue of $110,000, of which $45,000 was on credit. At the start of 19G, Accounts Receivable shows an $8,000 debit balance, and the Allowance for Doubtful Accounts shows a $600 credit balance. Collections on accounts receivable during 19G amounted to $33,000.

Data during 19G:

1. On December 31, 19G, an account receivable (J. Doe) of $800 from a prior year was determined to be uncollectible; therefore, it was written off immediately as a bad debt.

2. On December 31, 19G, on the basis of experience, a decision was made to continue the accounting policy of basing estimated bad debt losses on 2% of credit sales for the year.

Required:

a. Give the required journal entries for the two items on December 31, 19G (end of the accounting period).

b. Show how the amounts related to accounts receivable and bad debt expense would be reported on the income statement and balance sheet for 19G. Disregard income tax considerations.

c. On the basis of the data available, does the 2% rate appear to be reasonable? Explain.

Part B: Exercises 6–11 to 6–19

E6–11   (Analysis of Income Statement Relationships)

Supply the missing dollar amounts for the 19B income statement of Andrew Retailers for each of the following independent cases:

Cases	Sales Revenue	Beginning Inventory	Purchases	Total Available	Ending Inventory	Cost of Goods Sold	Gross Margin	Expenses	Pretax Income or (Loss)
A	$ 900	$100	$700	$?	$200	$?	$?	$200	$?
B	900	180	750	?	?	?	?	100	0
C	?	140	?	?	300	650	350	100	?
D	1,050	?	600	?	210	?	?	250	100
E	1,000	?	650	900	?	?	200	?	(50)

E6–12   **(Finding Missing Amounts Based on Income Statement Relationships)**
Supply the missing dollar amounts for the 19D income statement of Lakeway Company for each of the following independent cases:

	Case A	Case B	Case C
Sales revenue	$ 6,000	$ 6,000	$?
Sales returns and allowances	150	?	100
Net sales revenue	?	?	5,920
Beginning inventory	9,000	9,500	8,000
Purchases	5,000	?	5,300
Transportation-in	?	120	120
Purchase returns	40	30	?
Goods available for sale	?	14,790	13,370
Ending inventory	10,000	9,000	?
Cost of goods sold	?	?	5,400
Gross margin	?	110	?
Expenses	690	?	520
Pretax income	1,000	(500)	–0–

E6–13   **(Accounting for Sales and Purchases Using the Periodic Inventory System)**
The following transactions involving University Book Store were selected from the records of January 19B:

1. Sales: cash, $150,000; and on credit, $40,000 (terms n/45).
2. Some of the merchandise sold on credit in 1 was subsequently returned for credit, $1,000.
3. Purchases: cash, $80,000; and on credit, $15,000 (terms n/60).
4. Some of the merchandise purchased was subsequently returned for credit, $700.
5. Shipping costs paid in cash on the merchandise purchased, $600 (debit Transportation-In).
6. On the basis of experience, bad debt losses are estimated to be 2% of credit sales net of sales returns and allowances.
7. An account receivable amounting to $500 was written off as uncollectible. The sale was made two years earlier.

Required:
a. Give the journal entry that would be made for each transaction, assuming the company uses a periodic inventory system.
b. Prepare an income statement for January 19B through the caption "Gross margin on sales" and show the details of cost of goods sold. The December 31, 19A, inventory of merchandise was $75,000; and the physical inventory count of merchandise taken on January 31, 19B, amounted to $90,000.

E6–14   **(Recording Sales and Purchases Using the Net Method)**
The Sport Shop sells merchandise on credit terms of 2/10, n/30. A sale invoiced at $1,000 was made to Wendy Hillyer on February 1, 19B. The company uses the net method of recording sales discounts.

Required:

a. Give the journal entry to record the credit sale.

b. Give the journal entry assuming the account was collected in full on February 9, 19B.

c. Give the journal entry assuming, instead, the account was collected in full on March 2, 19B.

On March 4, 19B, the company purchased sporting goods from a supplier on credit, invoiced at $6,000; the terms were 1/15, n/30. The company uses the net method to record purchases.

Required:

d. Give the journal entry to record the purchase on credit. Assume the periodic inventory system.

e. Give the journal entry assuming the account was paid in full on March 12, 19B.

f. Give the journal entry assuming, instead, the account was paid in full on March 28, 19B.

E6–15   (Accounting for Inventory Using the Perpetual Inventory System)
Gerald Company uses a perpetual inventory system. Because it is a small business and sells only five different high-cost items, a perpetual inventory record is maintained for each item. The following selected data relate to Item A for the month of January:

1. Beginning inventory—quantity 5, cost $77 each.
2. Purchased—quantity 4, cost $72 each; paid $20 total freight.
3. Sold—quantity 6, sales price $150 each.
4. Returns—three units sold in 3 were returned for full credit.

Required:

a. Give the journal entries for the above transactions assuming a perpetual inventory system and cash transactions.

b. Prepare the perpetual inventory record for Item A.

c. For January, give the following amounts for Item A:

> a. Sales revenue . . . . $_____
> b. Cost of goods sold . . . . . . $_____
> c. Gross margin on sales . . . . . $_____
> d. Ending inventory . . . . $_____

d. Is it possible to determine if there were any inventory shrinkage? Explain.

E6–16   (Accounting for Sales and Purchases under the Perpetual Inventory System)
Sullivan Company uses a perpetual inventory system that provides amounts for the period for (a) cost of goods sold and (b) ending inventory. Physical inventory counts are made from time to time to verify the perpetual inventory records. On December 31, 19B, the end of the accounting year, the perpetual inventory record for Item 18 showed the following (summarized):

	Units	Unit cost	Total cost
Beginning inventory	500	$2	$1,000
Purchases during the period	900	2	1,800
Sales during the period (sales price $4)	800		

Required:

a. Give the journal entry to record the purchase of 900 units for cash during the period.

b. Give the journal entry to record the sales for cash during the period.

c. Assume a physical inventory count was made after the above transactions, and the count shows 595 units of Item 18 on hand. Give any journal entry required.

d. Give the following amounts for 19B related to Item 18:

      1. Ending inventory . . . . units _____ $ _____
      2. Cost of goods sold . . . . units _____ $ _____
      3. Shrinkage loss . . . . units _____ $ _____

e. As a manager, what would you investigate in this situation? How?

E6–17   (Comparison of the Periodic and Perpetual Inventory Systems)

During 19B, Wayne Corporation's records reflected the following for one product stocked:

    1. Beginning inventory . . 1,000 units, unit cost $2
    2. Purchases . . . . 8,000 units, unit cost $2
    3. Sales . . . . 7,000 units, unit sales price $4
    4. Purchase returns . . . .   10 units, for $2 per unit refund from the supplier
    5. Sales returns . . . . . .   5 units, for $4 per unit refund to the customer

Required:

a. All transactions were in cash; give the journal entries for the above transactions assuming:

    Case A—perpetual inventory system.

    Case B—periodic inventory system.

b. How would the amount of cost of goods sold be determined in each case?

c. Would you expect the cost of goods sold amount to be the same for Case A as for Case B? Why?

E6–18   (Use of a Worksheet; Periodic Inventory System)

The trial balance for Mountain Store, Incorporated, at December 31, 19B (the end of the accounting year), is given below. Only selected accounts are given to shorten the case. The company uses a periodic inventory system. With the exception of the ending inventory, all of the accounts (before adjusting and closing entries) that you will need are listed in the trial balance.

Data developed as a basis for the adjusting entries at December 31, 19B, were:

a. Estimated bad debt expense for 19B was 1% of net credit sales of $12,000.

b. An inventory of store supplies on hand taken at December 31, 19B, reflected $50.

c. Depreciation on the store equipment is based on an estimated useful life of 10 years and no residual value.

d. Wages earned through December 31, 19B, not yet paid or recorded amounted to $500.

e. The beginning inventory is shown in the trial balance. A physical inventory count of merchandise on hand and unsold at December 31, 19B, reflected $2,000.

f. Assume an average income tax rate of 20%.

Required:

Prepare a worksheet similar to the one in the demonstration case. If desired, you may omit columns for Adjusted Trial Balance and Retained Earnings. Enter the trial balance, adjusting entries, ending inventory, and complete the worksheet.

Debits		**Credits**	
Cash	$ 8,000	Allowance for doubtful	
Accounts receivable	3,000	accounts	$ 150
Merchandise inventory,		Accumulated depreciation	900
January 1, 19B	4,000	Accounts payable	5,000
Store supplies inventory	250	Wages payable	
Store equipment	3,000	Income taxes payable	
Sales returns	150	Capital stock (par $10)	6,000
Purchases	6,000	Retained earnings	1,870
Bad debt expense		Sales revenue	13,000
Depreciation expense		Purchase returns	480
Transportation-in (on purchases)	100		
Income tax expense			
Other operating expenses	2,900		
	$27,400		$27,400

E6–19   (Use of a Worksheet; Perpetual Inventory System)

The trial balance for Nonex, Incorporated, at December 31, 19B (end of the accounting year), is given below. Only selected items have been used to shorten the case. The company uses a perpetual inventory system. All of the accounts you will need are listed in the trial balance.

NONEX, INCORPORATED
Trial Balance
December 31, 19B

Account titles	Debit	Credit
Cash	$ 10,000	
Accounts receivable	13,000	
Allowance for doubtful accounts		$ 700
Merchandise inventory, ending	64,000	
Operational assets	40,000	
Accumulated depreciation		16,200
Accounts payable		8,000
Income taxes payable		
Capital stock (par $10)		60,000
Retained earnings, January 1, 19B		14,300
Sales revenue		105,000
Sales returns and allowances	1,200	
Cost of goods sold	56,000	
Expenses (not detailed)	20,000	
Bad debt expense		
Depreciation expense		
Income tax expense		
Totals	$204,200	$204,200

Additional Data Developed for the Adjusting Entries:

a. Estimated bad debt expense is 2% of net credit sales. Net credit sales for 19B amounted to $35,000.

b. The operational assets are being depreciated $4,000 each year.

c. The average income tax rate is 20%.

Required:

Prepare a worksheet similar to the one in the demonstration case. If desired, you may omit columns for Adjusted Trial Balance and Retained Earnings. Enter the trial balance, adjusting entries, and complete the worksheet.

PROBLEMS

Part A: Problems 6–1 to 6–6

P6–1 **(Understanding the Income Statement)**

The following data were taken from the year-end records of Qwest Company. You are to fill in all of the missing amounts. Show computations.

		Independent cases		
Income statement items		**Case A**		**Case B**
Gross sales revenue		$110,000		$212,000
Sales returns and allowances		?		12,000
Net sales revenue		?		?
Cost of goods sold . . . . (62%)		?		?
Gross margin on sales		?	(30%)	?
Operating expenses		18,000		?
Pretax income		?		15,000
Income tax expense (20%)		?		?
Income before extraordinary items		?		?
Extraordinary items . . . . (gain)	5,000	(loss)	1,000
Less: Income tax (20%)		?		?
Net income		?		?
EPS (10,000 shares)		2.00		?

P6–2 **(Preparation of a Multiple-Step Income Statement)**

Home Company, Inc., sells heavy construction equipment. There are 10,000 shares of capital stock outstanding. The annual fiscal period ends on December 31. The following condensed trial balance was taken from the general ledger on December 31, 19D:

Account titles	**Debit**	**Credit**
Cash	$ 22,500	
Accounts receivable	20,000	
Allowance for doubtful accounts		$ 1,000
Inventory, ending	90,000	
Operational assets	40,000	
Accumulated depreciation		12,000
Liabilities		17,000
Capital stock		105,000
Retained earnings, January 1, 19D		20,000
Sales revenue		208,000
Sales returns and allowances	8,000	
Cost of goods sold	110,000	
Selling expense	37,000	
Administrative expense	20,000	
Interest expense	3,000	
Extraordinary loss, unusual and infrequent		
storm damage	5,000	
Income tax expense*	7,500	
Totals	$363,000	$363,000

* Assume a 30% average tax rate on both operations and the extraordinary loss.

Required:

a. Prepare a multiple-step income statement.

b. Prepare the following ratio analyses:
   (1) Gross margin on sales ratio.
   (2) Profit margin ratio (Chapter 2).
   (3) Return on investment; use owners' equity (Chapter 2).

c. To compute (*b2*) and (*b3*), what amount did you use as the numerator? Explain why.

d. Briefly explain the meaning of each of the three ratios computed in (*b*).

P6–3 **(Preparation and Analysis of a Multiple-Step Income Statement)**
Fat Alport Corporation is a local grocery store organized seven years ago as a corporation. At that time, a total of 5,000 shares of common stock was issued to the three organizers. The store is in an excellent location, and sales have increased each year. At the end of 19G, the bookkeeper prepared the following statement (assume all amounts are correct; also note the inappropriate terminology and format):

FAT ALPORT CORPORATION
Profit and Loss
December 31, 19G

	Debit	Credit
Sales		$305,000
Cost of goods sold	$169,500	
Sales returns and allowances	5,000	
Selling expense	60,000	
Administrative and general expense	30,000	
Interest expense	500	
Extraordinary loss	4,000	
Income tax expense (on operations, $12,000 less		
$1,200 saved on the extraordinary loss)	10,800	
Net profit	25,200	
Totals	$305,000	$305,000

Required:

a. Prepare a multiple-step income statement. Assume an average 30% income tax rate.

b. Prepare the following ratio analyses:
   (1) Profit margin on sales ratio (Chapter 2).
   (2) Gross margin on sales ratio.
   (3) Return on investment; use owners' equity of $200,000 (Chapter 2).

c. In computing ratios (*b1*) and (*b3*), what amount did you use for income? Explain why.

d. Generally, it is conceded that of the three ratios in (*b*), return on investment has the highest information content for the typical investor. Why?

P6–4   (Recording Sales, Returns, and Bad Debts)

The data below were selected from the records of Deere Company for the year ended December 31, 19C.

Balances January 1, 19C:
Accounts receivable (various customers) $100,000
Allowance for doubtful accounts   7,000

Transactions during 19C:

1. Sold merchandise for cash, $350,000. In the order given below, sold merchandise and made collections on credit terms 2/10, n/30 (assume a unit sales price of $1,000 in all transactions and use the net method to record sales revenue):

2. Sold merchandise to T. Smith; invoice price, $18,000.

3. Sold merchandise to K. Jones; invoice price, $30,000.

4. Two days after purchase date, T. Smith returned one of the units purchased in 2 above and received account credit.

5. Sold merchandise to B. Sears; invoice price, $20,000.

6. T. Smith paid his account in full within the discount period.

7. Collected $92,000 cash from customer sales on credit in prior year, all within the discount periods.

8. K. Jones paid the invoice in 3 above within the discount period.

9. Sold merchandise to R. Roy; invoice price, $10,000.

10. Three days after paying the account in full, K. Jones returned two defective units and received a cash refund.

11. After the discount period, collected $5,000 cash on an account receivable on sales in a prior year.

12. The company wrote off a 19A account of $2,500 after deciding that the amount would never be collected.

13. The estimated bad debt rate used by the company is 1% of **net** credit sales.

Required:

a. Give the journal entries for the above transactions, including the write-off of the uncollectible account and the adjusting entry for estimated bad debts. Assume a periodic inventory system. Show computations for each entry. (Hint: Set up T-accounts on scratch paper for Cash, Accounts Receivable by customer, Allowance for Doubtful Accounts, Sales Revenue, Sales Returns, Sales Discount Revenue, and Bad Debt Expense [this will provide the data needed for the next requirement].)

b. Show how the accounts related to the above sale and collection activities should be reported on the 19C income statement and balance sheet.

P6–5 **(Comparison of the Net and Gross Methods Using the Periodic Inventory System)**
The following transactions were selected from the records of Eldon Company:

July 15 Sold merchandise to Customer A at an invoice price of $4,000; terms 2/10, n/30.
   20 Sold merchandise to Customer B at an invoice price of $3,000; terms 2/10, n/30.
   21 Purchased inventory from Alpha Supply Company at an invoice price of $2,000; terms 3/10, n/45.
   22 Purchased inventory from Beta Supply Company at an invoice price of $1,000; terms 1/20, n/30.
   23 Received payment from Customer A within the discount period.
   25 Paid invoice from Alpha Supply Company within the discount period.
Aug. 25 Received payment from Customer B after the discount period.
   26 Paid invoice from Beta Supply Company, after the discount period.

Required:
a. Give the appropriate journal entry for each of the above transactions. Assume that the company uses the periodic inventory system and records sales and purchases using the net method.
b. Give the appropriate journal entry for each of the above transactions. Assume that the company uses the periodic inventory system and records sales and purchases using the gross method.

P6–6 **(Bad Debt Expense Based on Aging Analysis)**
Farmer Equipment Company uses the aging approach to estimate bad debt expense at the end of each accounting year. Credit sales occur frequently on terms n/60. The balance of each account receivable is aged on the basis of three time periods as follows: (a) not yet due, (b) up to one year past due, and (c) more than one year past due. Experience has shown that for each age group the average loss rate on the amount of the receivable at year-end due to uncollectibility is (a) 1%, (b) 5%, and (c) 40%.

At December 31, 19F (end of the current accounting year), the Accounts Receivable balance was $50,500 and the Allowance for Doubtful Accounts balance was $1,500. To simplify, only five customer accounts are used; the details of each on December 31, 19F, follow:

A. Able—Account Receivable

Date	Explanation	Debit	Credit	Balance
3/11/19E	Sale	15,000		15,000
6/30/19E	Collection		5,000	10,000
1/31/19F	Collection		3,000	7,000

C. Carson—Account Receivable

2/28/19F	Sale	21,000		21,000
4/15/19F	Collection		10,000	11,000
11/30/19F	Collection		3,000	8,000

M. May—Account Receivable

11/30/19F	Sale	18,000		18,000
12/15/19F	Collection		8,000	10,000

T. Tyler—Account Receivable

3/2/19D	Sale	5,000		5,000
4/15/19D	Collection		5,000	–0–
9/1/19E	Sale	12,000		12,000
10/15/19E	Collection		10,000	2,000
2/1/19F	Sale	19,000		21,000
3/1/19F	Collection		1,000	20,000
12/31/19F	Sale	1,500		21,500

Z. Ziltch—Account Receivable

12/30/19F	Sale	4,000		4,000

Required:

a. Set up an aging analysis schedule and complete it.

b. Compute the estimated uncollectible amount for each age category and in total.

c. Give the adjusting entry for bad debt expense at December 31, 19F.

d. Show how the amounts related to accounts receivable should be presented on the 19F income statement and balance sheet.

Part B: Problems 6–7 to 6–16

P6–7 **(Accounting for Cash Discounts by the Vendor and the Purchaser)**
Assume the following summarized transactions between Company A, the vendor, and Company B, the purchaser. Use the letters to the left as the date notations. Assume each company uses a periodic inventory system and each uses the net method to record sales revenue and purchases.

1. Company A sold Company B merchandise for $10,000; terms 2/10, n/30.

2. Prior to payment, Company B returned $1,000 (one tenth) of the merchandise for credit because it did not meet B's specifications.

Required:
Give the following journal entries in parallel columns for each party:

a. The sale/purchase transaction.

b. The return transaction.

c. Payment in full assuming it was made within the discount period.

d. Payment in full assuming, instead, it was made after the discount period.

Use a form similar to the following:

		Co. A—Vendor		Co. B—Purchaser	
Date	Accounts	Debit	Credit	Debit	Credit

P6–8 (Recording Sales and Purchases Using the Net Method)

Prep Shop, Incorporated, is a student co-op. On January 1, 19X, the beginning inventory was $200,000; the Accounts Receivable balance was $3,000; and the Allowance for Doubtful Accounts had a credit balance of $600. A periodic inventory system is used, and purchases are recorded using the net method.

The following transactions (summarized) have been selected from 19X for case purposes:

1. Merchandise sales for cash $325,000
2. Merchandise returned by customers as unsatisfactory, for cash refund   1,400
   Merchandise purchased from vendors on credit; terms 2/10, n/30:
3.   May Supply Company invoice price before deduction of cash discount   4,000
4.   Other vendors, invoice price, before deduction of cash discount 115,000
5. Purchased equipment for use in the store; paid cash   1,800
6. Purchased office supplies for future use in the store; paid cash   600
7. Freight on merchandise purchased; paid cash (set up a separate account for
     this item)   500
   Accounts payable paid in full during the period as follows:
8.   May Supply Company, paid after the discount period   4,000
9.   Other vendors, paid within the discount period 98,000

Required:

a. Prepare journal entries for each of the above transactions.

b. Give the closing entry required at December 31, 19X, for:
   (1) Beginning inventory.
   (2) Ending inventory (assume $130,000).

c. Prepare a partial income statement through gross margin on sales.

d. Explain why it was preferable to record purchases using the net method.

P6–9 (Reporting Sales Transactions on the Financial Statements)

The transactions listed below were selected from those occurring during the month of January 19D for Pete's Store, Incorporated. A wide line of goods is offered for sale. Credit sales are extended to a few select customers; the usual credit terms are n/EOM.

1. Sales to customers:
     Cash $350,000
     On credit 40,000
2. Unsatisfactory merchandise returned by customers:
     Cash   4,000
     Credit   1,000
   Merchandise purchased from vendors on credit; terms 2/10, n/30:
3.   AB Supply Company, amount billed, before deduction of cash discount   1,000
4.   From other vendors, amount billed, before deduction of cash discount 120,000
5. Freight paid on merchandise purchased; paid cash (set up a separate account for
     this item)   2,000
6. Collections on accounts receivable 17,000

The accounts payable were paid in full during the period as follows:

7. AB Supply Company, paid after the discount period   1,000
8. Other vendors, paid within the discount period   117,600
9. Purchased two new typewriters for the office; paid cash   900
10. An account receivable from a customer from a prior year amounting to $300 was determined to be uncollectible and was written off.
11. At the end of January the adjusting entry for estimated bad debts is to be made. The loss rate, based on experience, is 1% of net credit sales for the period (i.e., on credit sales less credit returns).

Relevant account balances on January 1, 19D, were Accounts Receivable, $3,200 (debit); and Allowance for Doubtful Accounts, $1,000 (credit). Total assets at the end of the period, $250,000.

Required:

a. Prepare journal entries for the above transactions assuming a periodic inventory system is in use and record purchases using the net method.

b. Show how the following amounts should be reported on the January 19D income statement and balance sheet. Show computations.
   (1) Bad debt expense.
   (2) Balance in accounts receivable.
   (3) Balance in allowance for doubtful accounts.

c. Explain why bad debt expense should not be debited for the $300 uncollectible account written off in January.

P6–10   (Application of the Perpetual Inventory System)

Fargo Company uses a perpetual inventory system for the items it sells. The following selected data relate to Item 10, a small but high-cost item stocked during the month of January 19B.

1. Beginning inventory—quantity, 60; cost, $50 each.

2. Purchases—quantity, 90; cost, $48 each plus $180 for transportation on the purchases.

3. Sales—quantity, 120; sale price, $95 each.

4. Returns—the company accepted a return of two of the items sold in 3 because they were not needed by the customer and they had not been used.

5. At the end of January 19B, a physical inventory count showed 30 items remaining on hand.

Required (assume all transactions were cash):

a. Prepare the perpetual inventory record for Item 10.

b. Give journal entries for each of the above transactions.

c. Prepare the income statement for January 19B through gross margin on sales as it related to Item 10. What was the gross margin ratio?

d. As the responsible manager, would you investigate the inventory shrinkage? How?

e. Assume that you observe quite often that the required items are out of stock. How can a perpetual inventory system be helpful in avoiding this problem?

P6–11   **(Use of the Perpetual Inventory System and Analysis of Shrinkage)**
Black Company uses a perpetual inventory system. During the month of January 19D, the perpetual inventory record for Item A, which is one of the 23 items stocked, is shown below (summarized):

PERPETUAL INVENTORY RECORD

Date	Explanation	Goods Purchased Units	Goods Purchased Total Cost	Goods Sold Units	Goods Sold Total Cost	Balance Units	Balance Total Cost
1	Beginning inventory					40	$3,200
2	Purchase (at $80 each)	20					
3	Sale (sales price $150 each)			31			
4	Purchase return (one unit)						
5	Purchase (at $80 each)	30					
6	Sales return (one unit)						
7	Sale (sales price $150 each)			29			
8	Inventory shortage (four units)						

Required:

a. Complete the perpetual inventory record.
b. Give the journal entry for each transaction reflected in the perpetual inventory record (assume transactions are cash).
c. Complete the following tabulation:

> **Income statement:**
> Sales . . . . $ _____
> Cost of goods sold . . . .   _____
> Gross margin on sales . . . . . .   _____
> Gross margin ratio . . . .   _____
> **Balance sheet:**
> Inventory . . . .   _____

d. Explain how the inventory shortage should be reported.
e. As the responsible manager, would you investigate this situation? How?
f. Assume stockout has been a problem. What would you recommend?

P6–12   **(Comparison of Periodic and Perpetual Inventory Systems)**
During January, the following transactions relating to one product sold by McDonald
Company were completed in the order given:

a. Purchased—quantity, 120; cost, $20 each.

b. Sold—quantity, 110; $40 each.

c. Purchase return—returned two of the units purchased in (a) because they were the
wrong size.

d. Sales return—accepted one unit from a customer that was sold in (b). The customer did not need it, and it was not damaged.

e. Inventories:

Beginning inventory, January 1—30 units at total cost of $600.

Ending inventory, January 31—per periodic inventory count, 39 units
@ $20 = $780.

Required:
Give the journal entries for the above transactions assuming that Case A—a perpetual
inventory system is used and Case B—a periodic inventory system is used. To do this, set
up the following form (assume cash transactions):

		Perpetual		Periodic	
Date	**Explanation**	**Debit**	**Credit**	**Debit**	**Credit**
a.	To record the purchase				
b.	To record the sale				
c.	To record the purchase return				
d.	To record the sales return				
e.	To record the closing entries for inventories				
f.	To record the closing entry for cost of goods sold				
g.	To close purchases and purchase returns				

P6–13   **(Completion of a Worksheet)**

Quality Retailers, Inc., is completing the accounting information processing cycle for the
year ended December 31, 19D. The worksheet given below has been completed through
the adjusting entries. (An optional column called Adjusted Trial Balance may be helpful
in completing the requirements.)

Required:

a. Complete the following worksheet (periodic inventory system is used). Assume an
average income tax rate of 20%.

b. Give the closing journal entries at December 31, 19D. Close all revenue and expense accounts to Income Summary.

QUALITY RETAILERS, INC.
Worksheet for the Year Ended December 31, 19D

Account Titles	Trial Balance Debit	Trial Balance Credit	Adjusting Entries Debit	Adjusting Entries Credit	Income Statement Debit	Income Statement Credit	Retained Earnings Debit	Retained Earnings Credit	Balance Sheet Debit	Balance Sheet Credit
Cash	27,200									
Accounts receivable	12,000									
Allowance for doubtful accounts		300		(a) 400						
Merchandise inventory, Jan. 1, 19D	30,000									
Equipment	22,500									
Accumulated depreciation, equipment		9,000		(b) 1,500						
Other assets	20,000									
Accounts payable		8,000								
Interest payable				(c) 300						
Note payable, long term (12%)		10,000								
Capital stock (par $10)		50,000								
Contributed capital in excess of par		7,500								
Retained earnings, Jan. 1, 19D		13,000								
Dividends declared and paid (19D)	6,000									
Sales revenue		95,000								
Sales returns and allowances	1,000									
Purchases	52,000									
Transportation-in	2,000									
Purchase returns and allowances		1,100								
Operating expenses (not detailed)	20,300									
Bad debt expense			(a) 400							
Depreciation expense			(b) 1,500							
Interest expense	900		(c) 300							
Merchandise inventory, Dec, 31, 19D ($32,000)										
	193,900	193,900								
Income tax expense										
Income taxes payable										
Net income										
Retained earnings, Dec. 31, 19D										

P6–14   (Related to Chapter Supplement 6A; Use of Subsidiary Ledgers)

Hillard Store, Incorporated, is a large department store that carries top brands and attempts to appeal to "quality customers." Approximately 80% of the sales are on credit. As a consequence, there is a significant amount of detailed recordkeeping related to credit sales, returns, collections, and billings. The accounts receivable records are maintained manually; however, the store is considering computerizing this phase of the accounting information system. Included in the general ledger is a control account for Accounts Receivable. Supporting the control account is an accounts receivable subsidiary ledger that has individual accounts for more than 20,000 customers. For case purposes, a few accounts and transactions with simplified amounts have been selected.

On January 1, 19F, the Accounts Receivable control account (No. 52) in the general ledger shows a debit balance of $4,000, and the subsidiary ledger shows the following balances:

52.1	Akins, A. K.	$400
52.2	Blue, V. R.	700
52.3	Daley, U. T.	900
52.4	Evans, T. V.	300
52.5	May, O. W.	800
52.6	Nash, G. A.	100
52.7	Roth, I. W.	600
52.8	Winn, W. W.	200

During the month of January, the following transactions and events relating to sales activities occurred (use the notation at the left for date):

a. Sales of merchandise on credit.

Akins, A. K.	$300
Blue, V. R.	250
Winn, W. W.	730
May, O. W.	140
Daley, U. T.	500
Roth, I. W.	370
Evans, T. V.	410

b. Unsatisfactory merchandise returned by customers:

Roth, I. W.	$30
Winn, W. W.	70

c. Collections on accounts receivable:

Winn, W. W.	$800
May, O. W.	940
Akins, A. K.	200
Roth, I. W.	700
Blue, V. R.	750
Daley, U. T.	600

d. The account for G. A. Nash has been inactive for several years. After an investigation, the management decided that it was uncollectible; therefore, it is to be written off immediately.

e. The estimated loss rate is 1% of net credit sales (i.e., credit sales less returns for credit).

Required:

a. Set up the general ledger control account for Accounts Receivable. Also, set up the general ledger account for Allowance for Doubtful Accounts (No. 53) with a credit balance of $600. Indicate the beginning balance as "Bal." and for convenience use T-accounts for these two accounts.

b. Set up an accounts receivable subsidiary ledger; use three columns—Debit, Credit, and Balance. Enter the beginning balances with the notation "Bal."

c. Prepare journal entries for each of the above transactions.

d. Post the entries prepared in (c) to the Accounts Receivable control account, Allowance for Doubtful Accounts, and the subsidiary ledger. Use folio numbers.

e. Prepare a schedule of accounts receivable to show how much each customer owed at the end of January.

f. Show how accounts receivable and the related allowance amounts would be reported in the January balance sheet.

P6–15 **(Review of Chapters 3, 4, 5, and 6)**

Discount Furniture Store, Inc., has been in operation for a number of years and has been quite profitable. The losses on uncollectible accounts and on merchandise returns are about the same as for other furniture stores. The company uses a perpetual inventory system. The annual fiscal period ended December 31, 19B, and the end-of-period accounting information processing cycle has been started. The following trial balance was derived from the general ledger at December 31, 19B:

Account titles	Debit	Credit
Cash	$ 28,880	
Accounts receivable	36,000	
Allowance for doubtful accounts		$ 4,600
Merchandise inventory, ending	110,000	
Store equipment	22,000	
Accumulated depreciation		10,000
Accounts payable		10,000
Income taxes payable		
Interest payable		
Notes payable, long term (12%)		50,000
Capital stock (par $10)		70,000
Retained earnings, January 1, 19B		11,400
Sales revenue		441,000
Sales returns and allowances	25,000	
Cost of goods sold	223,350	
Selling expense	102,700	
Administrative expense	49,070	
Bad debt expense		
Depreciation expense		
Interest expense		
Totals	$597,000	$597,000
Income tax expense		
Net income		

Data for adjusting entries:

a. The bad debt losses due to uncollectible accounts are estimated to be $6,000.

b. The store equipment is being depreciated over an estimated useful life of 11 years with no residual value.

c. The long-term note of $50,000 was for a two-year loan from a local bank. The interest rate is 12%, payable at the end of each 12-month period. The note was dated April 1, 19B. (Hint: Accrue interest for nine months.)

d. Assume an average 20% corporate income tax rate.

Required:

a. Based on the above data, complete a worksheet similar to the one illustrated in the chapter for the demonstration case. If you prefer, you may omit columns for Adjusted Trial Balance and Retained Earnings.

b. Based on the completed worksheet, prepare a multiple-step income statement and classified balance sheet.

c. Based on the completed worksheet, prepare the adjusting and closing journal entries for December 31, 19B. Close all revenue and expense accounts to Income Summary.

P6–16   (Review of Chapters 3, 4, 5, and 6)

Northwest Appliances, Incorporated, is owned by six local investors. It has been operating for four years and is at the end of the 19D fiscal year. For case purposes, certain accounts have been selected to demonstrate the information processing activities at the end of the year for a corporation that sells merchandise rather than services. The following trial balance, assumed to be correct, was taken from the ledger on December 31, 19D. The company uses a periodic inventory system.

Debits		**Credits**	
Cash	$ 18,000	Allowance for doubtful	
Accounts receivable	28,000	accounts	$ 600
Merchandise inventory,		Accumulated depreciation	12,000
January 1, 19D	80,000	Accounts payable	15,000
Prepaid insurance	300	Notes payable,	
Store equipment	40,000	long term (12%)	30,000
Sales returns and		Capital stock (par $10)	40,000
allowances	3,000	Retained earnings,	
Purchases	250,000	January 1, 19D	2,000
Transportation-in	11,000	Sales revenue	400,000
Operating expenses	76,300	Purchase returns	7,000
Total	$506,600	Total	$506,600

Additional data for adjusting entries:

a. Credit sales during the year were $100,000; based on experience, a 1% loss rate on credit sales has been established.

b. Insurance amounting to $100 expired during the year.

c. The store equipment is being depreciated over a 10-year estimated useful life with no residual value.

d. The long-term note payable for $30,000 was dated May 1, 19D, and carries a 12% interest rate per annum. The note is for three years, and interest is payable on April 30 each year.

e. Assume an average income tax rate of 30%.

f. Inventories:

Beginning inventory, January 1, 19D (per above trial balance) $80,000.

Ending inventory, December 31, 19D (per physical inventory count), $75,000.

Required:

a. Prepare a worksheet at December 31, 19D, similar to the one shown in the demonstration problem in the chapter. If you prefer, you may omit columns for Adjusted Trial Balance and Retained Earnings. To save time and space, all operating expenses have been summarized. However, you should set up additional expense accounts for depreciation, bad debts, interest, and income tax. Also, you will need additional liability accounts for interest payable and income taxes payable.

b. Based on the completed worksheet, prepare a multiple-step income statement and classified balance sheet.

c. Based on the completed worksheet, prepare the adjusting and closing journal entries at December 31, 19D. Close all revenue and expense accounts to Income Summary.

CASES

C6–1 **(Analysis of the Impact of Uncollectible Accounts)**
A recent annual report for Sears, Roebuck and Company contained the following information at the end of their fiscal year:

	Year 1	Year 2
Accounts receivable	$7,022,075,000	$7,336,308,000
Allowance for doubtful accounts	(86,605,000)	(96,989,000)
	$6,935,470,000	$7,239,319,000

A footnote to the financial statements disclosed that uncollectible accounts amounting to $55,000,000 were written off as bad during year 1 and $69,000,000 during year 2. Assume that the tax rate for Sears was 30%.

Required:

a. Determine the bad debt expense for year 2 based on the facts given above.

b. Working capital is defined as current assets minus current liabilities. How was Sears' working capital affected by the write-off of $69,000,000 in uncollectible accounts during year 2? What impact did the recording of bad debt expense have on working capital in year 2?

c. How was net income affected by the $69,000,000 write-off during year 2? What impact did the recording of bad debt expense have on net income for year 2?

C6–2 **(Analysis of Sales Revenue and Cost of Goods Sold for an Actual Company)**
JCPenney   Refer to the financial statements of J.C. Penney Company, Inc. given in the appendix immediately preceding the index.

1. What is the amount of the Allowance for Doubtful Accounts for the current year?

2. What amount of bad debt was written off during the current year?

3. Is the amount of bad debt expense reported in the notes to the statement? If not, can it be calculated?

4. The company includes occupancy, buying, and warehousing costs with cost of goods sold. Assume that cost of goods sold (without the additional costs) was $10,000 million. Determine the cost of goods purchased during the year.

SEVEN

COSTING METHODS FOR MEASURING INVENTORY AND COST OF GOODS SOLD

PURPOSE

Chapter 6 discussed accounting for sales revenue and cost of goods sold. You were introduced to the periodic and perpetual inventory systems. In Chapter 6, we assumed that the cost of items purchased for inventory did not change over time. In reality, however, the unit cost of inventory items often will change each time a new purchase order is placed. In this chapter, we will discuss accounting for inventory and cost of goods sold when unit costs are changing.

The example on the opposite page shows how inventory is reported on the balance sheet. The note provides additional information concerning inventory.

LEARNING OBJECTIVES

1. Analyze the effects of inventory errors.
2. Identify what items should be included in inventory.
3. Describe and use the four inventory costing methods with the periodic and perpetual inventory systems.
4. Explain the comparability principle.
5. Apply the lower-of-cost-or-market (LCM) rule.
6. Estimate ending inventory and cost of goods sold.
7. Expand your accounting vocabulary by learning the "Important Terms Defined in This Chapter."
8. Apply the knowleldge learned from this chapter by completing the homework assigned by your instructor.

ORGANIZATION

Part A—measuring ending inventory and cost of goods sold with a periodic inventory system
1. Inventory effects on the measurement of income.
2. Measuring inventory cost.
3. Application of the inventory costing methods with the periodic inventory system.

Part B—application of a perpetual inventory system and selected inventory costing problems
1. Application of the inventory costing methods with a perpetual inventory system.
2. Lower of cost or market; damaged goods; estimating ending inventory and cost of goods sold; impact of errors in measuring ending inventory.

CORPORATION

Statements of Consolidated Financial Condition

Thousands of Dollars	December 31	
ASSETS	**1987**	1986
Current Assets		
Cash and short-term investments	$ 14,980	$ 40,786
Amount due on disposition of business		31,985
Accounts receivable, less allowance—(1987–$3,278; 1986–$3,861)	204,523	192,232
Inventories	260,772	240,505
Deferred income taxes	31,603	29,555
Other current assets	10,489	16,511
Total current assets	522,367	551,574

Notes to Consolidated Financial Statements

Inventories

Inventories consist of the following:

In thousands	1987	1986
Finished appliances	$144,305	$144,656
Work in process	42,784	44,954
Materials and supplies	73,683	50,895
	$260,772	$240,505

If the first-in, first-out (FIFO) method of inventory accounting, which approximates current cost, had been used, inventory would have been $65,000,000 and $60,800,000 higher than reported at December 31, 1987 and 1986, respectively.

PART A—MEASURING ENDING INVENTORY AND COST OF GOODS SOLD WITH A PERIODIC INVENTORY SYSTEM

Items Included in Inventory

Usually, inventory includes tangible property that (1) is held for sale in the normal course of business or (2) will be used in producing goods or services for sale. Inventory is reported on the balance sheet as a current asset because it usually will be used or converted into cash within one year or within the next operating cycle of the business, whichever is the longer. Because inventory is less liquid (i.e., less readily convertible to cash) than accounts receivable, it is listed below accounts receivable on the balance sheet.

The kinds of inventory normally held depend on the characteristics of the business:[1]

Retail or Wholesale Business

Merchandise inventory—goods (or merchandise) held for resale in the normal course of business. The goods usually are acquired in a finished condition and are ready for sale without further processing.

Manufacturing Business[2]

Finished goods inventory—goods manufactured by the business, completed and ready for sale.

Work in process inventory—goods in the process of being manufactured but not yet completed as finished goods. When completed, work in process inventory becomes finished goods inventory.

Raw materials inventory—items acquired by purchase, growth (such as food products), or extraction (natural resources) for processing into finished goods. Such items are accounted for as raw materials inventory until used. When used, their cost is included in the work in process inventory (along with other processing costs such as direct labor and factory overhead). The flow of inventory costs in a manufacturing environment can be diagrammed as shown in Exhibit 7–1.

The work in process inventory includes (1) the cost of raw materials used, (2) the **direct** labor incurred in the manufacturing process, and (3) the factory overhead costs. Direct labor cost represents the earnings of employees who work directly on the products being manufactured. Factory overhead costs include all manufacturing costs that are not raw material or direct labor costs. For example, the salary of the plant supervisor is included in factory overhead.

---

[1] Supplies on hand usually are reported as prepaid expenses.

[2] Subsequent accounting courses present a complete discussion of inventory measurement and accounting in a manufacturing environment.

Exhibit 7–1 Flow of inventory costs for a manufacturing business

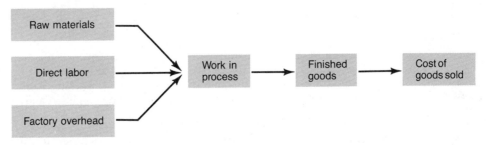

When counting the **physical quantity** of goods in the inventory, a company should include all items to which it has **ownership,** regardless of their locations. In sales transactions, inventory accounting focuses on the passage of ownership. Usually when ownership passes, goods should be included in the inventory of the purchaser and not in the inventory of the seller. In a sales transaction, the basic guideline is that ownership to the goods passes at the **time intended by the parties** to the transaction. Usually, ownership passes when the seller gives the goods to the buyer; however, there are situations in which this is not the case.

When the intentions of the parties concerning the passage of ownership are not clear, all of the circumstances must be assessed. A judgment must be made concerning when the buyer and seller intended ownership to pass. For example, the buyer may ask the seller to hold the goods pending shipping instructions. In this instance, ownership has passed, regardless of the delivery date. A similar problem arises when a third party has physical possession of the goods for a period of time. For example, an independent transportation company may move the goods from the seller's location to the buyer's location. If the terms of the sale provide that the buyer must pay the transportation charges (known as FOB shipping point), then ownership usually passes when the seller delivers the goods to the transportation agent. However, if the terms of the sale are FOB destination (i.e., the seller must pay the freight), ownership passes when the goods are delivered to the buyer at destination. FOB stands for "free on board" and is used in business to indicate who is responsible for paying transportation charges. FOB destination means that the seller pays the freight; FOB shipping point means that the buyer pays the freight.

When a company has possession of goods that it does not own, it should exclude those goods from the inventory. This situation often occurs when goods are on **consignment** for sale on a commission basis. The supplier (called the consignor) legally retains ownership to the goods on consignment, although the goods are in the physical possession of the party that will sell them (called the consignee). The consignor should include the goods in the ending inventory, while the consignee should exclude them from the ending inventory.

The passage-of-ownership guideline that is used in accounting for inventory is consistent with the revenue principle (Exhibit 4–5). The revenue principle states that revenue from a sales transaction should not be recorded until ownership is transferred.

Measuring Inventory Cost

Goods in inventory are recorded in conformity with the **cost principle** as follows:

> The primary basis of accounting for inventory is cost, which is the price paid or consideration given to acquire an asset. As applied to inventories, cost means, in principle, the sum of the applicable expenditures and charges directly or indirectly incurred in bringing an article to its existing condition and location.[3]

Indirect expenditures related to the purchase of goods, such as freight, insurance, and storage, theoretically should be included in measuring the purchase cost of the goods acquired. However, because these incidental costs often are not **material in amount** (see the materiality constraint, Exhibit 4–5), they do not have to be assigned to the inventory cost. Thus, for practical reasons, some companies use the **net invoice price** to assign a unit cost to goods and record the indirect expenditures as a separate cost that is reported as an expense.

Chapter 6 discussed the assignment of **dollar cost** to (*a*) the ending inventory and (*b*) cost of goods sold in situations in which unit purchase (or manufacturing) cost remained constant. This chapter expands those discussions to the typical situation in which the purchase cost per unit changes during the accounting period.

Two alternative inventory systems are used to accumulate data to facilitate determination of the amount (expressed in dollars) of (*a*) the ending inventory and (*b*) cost of goods sold:

1. **Periodic inventory system.** This system accumulates total merchandise acquisition cost (including the beginning inventory). At the **end of the accounting period,** the ending inventory is measured by means of a physical inventory count of all goods remaining on hand. The units counted on hand then are valued in dollars by using appropriate unit purchase costs. The periodic inventory system measures **cost of goods sold** as a residual amount; that is:

$$BI + P - EI = CGS$$

2. **Perpetual inventory system.** This system keeps a detailed daily inventory record throughout the period for each item stocked. This record includes (*a*) the beginning inventory; (*b*) each purchase; (*c*) each issue (i.e., sales); and (*d*) a continuous balance of the inventory. This system measures cost of goods sold and ending inventory without the requirement of a physical inventory count at the end of each accounting period.

---

[3] AICPA, *Accounting Research Bulletin No. 43* (New York, 1961), chap. 4, statement 3.

In this part of the chapter, we discuss several alternative inventory costing methods using the **periodic inventory system.** Part B of this chapter discusses these methods with a perpetual inventory system.

Purpose of Inventory Costing Methods

There are four generally accepted inventory costing methods:

1. Weighted average.
2. First-in, first-out (FIFO).
3. Last-in, first-out (LIFO).
4. Specific identification.

If unit costs of items purchased for inventory did not change, there would be no need for alternative inventory costing methods. When unit costs change, an accounting method is needed to assign the various costs to units in the ending inventory and to the units that have been sold. Consider Witt, Inc. (Exhibit 7–2). The total cost of goods available for sale is $3,630. There are four different unit costs ($6, $7, $8, and $9). The dollar amounts of ending inventory and cost of goods sold depend on the costing method that is selected.

The four inventory costing methods are **alternative allocation methods** for assigning the total dollar amount of goods available for sale (BI + P) between (a)

Exhibit 7–2 Illustrative inventory data

WITT, INC.
19A Illustrative Data—Beginning Inventory, Purchases, and Sales

Transactions	Symbol	Number of units	Unit cost	Total cost	
Beginning inventory, January 1, 19A (carried over from last period)	BI	100	$6		$ 600
Purchases during 19A:					
January 3, first purchase	P	50	7	$ 350	
June 12, second purchase	P	200	8	1,600	
December 20, third purchase	P	120	9	1,080	
Total purchases during 19A		370			3,030
Goods available for sale during the year . . .		470			3,630
Goods sold during 19A:					
January 6 (unit sales price, $10)	S	40			
June 18 (unit sales price, $12)	S	220			
December 24 (unit sales price, $14)	S	60			
Total sales during 19A		320			?
Ending inventory, December 31, 19A (units 470 − 320)	EI	150			?

Exhibit 7–3 Illustration of cost allocation

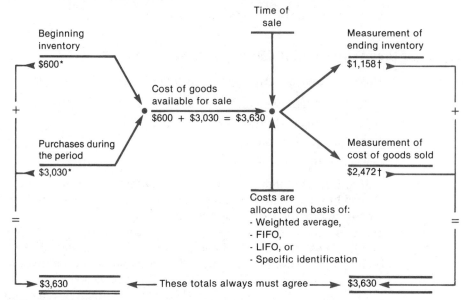

* Data from Exhibit 7–2.
† Based on the weighted-average cost method.

ending inventory (reported as an asset at the end of the period) and *(b)* cost of goods sold (reported as an expense of the period). Refer to the data for Witt, Inc., given in Exhibit 7–2. The two allocated amounts were calculated using the weighted-average inventory costing method, as shown below. At this point you need not be concerned about how the two amounts were calculated.

	Units	Amount
Goods available for sale (total amount to be allocated)	470	$3,630
Cost allocation:		
Ending inventory (determined by inventory count and then costed at weighted-average unit cost)	150	1,158
Cost of goods sold (residual amount)	320	$2,472

The amount of **goods available for sale** ($3,630) was allocated between **ending inventory** ($1,158) and **cost of goods sold** ($2,472). The sum of these two amounts (and the related units) must be the same as goods available for sale. This cost allocation procedure also is shown graphically in Exhibit 7–3.

Inventory Costing Methods Illustrated

The choice among the four inventory costing methods is not based on the physical flow of goods on and off the shelves. For most companies, the actual **physical flow** of goods is first-in, first-out (FIFO). Regardless of the physical flow of goods, a company can use any of the inventory costing methods. Generally accepted accounting principles (GAAP) only require that the inventory costing method used be rational and systematic.

A company is not required to use the same inventory costing method for all inventory items, and no particular justification is needed for the selection of one or more of the acceptable methods. However, a change in method is significant and needs special disclosures in the notes to the financial statements.

Weighted-Average Inventory Costing Method

The weighted-average method requires computation of the weighted-average unit cost of the goods available for sale.[4] In a periodic inventory system, the computed unit cost is multiplied by the **number of units** in inventory to derive the total cost of ending inventory. Cost of goods sold is determined by subtracting the ending inventory amount from the amount of goods available for sale. For example, the weighted-average method would be applied by Witt (Exhibit 7–2) as follows using a **periodic** inventory system.[5]

Step 1.   Computation of the weighted-average unit cost for the period:

$$\frac{\text{Total goods available for sale—at cost}}{\text{Total goods available for sale—units}} = \frac{\$3,630}{470} = \$7.72 \left\{ \begin{array}{l} \text{Weighted-} \\ \text{average} \\ \text{cost per} \\ \text{unit for} \\ \text{the period} \end{array} \right.$$

Step 2.   Allocation of the cost of goods available for sale under the periodic inventory system:

	Units	Amount
Goods available for sale (Exhibit 7–2)	470	$3,630
Ending inventory (150 units × $7.72)	150	1,158*
Cost of goods sold (residual amount)	320	$2,472†

* Reported on the balance sheet.
† Reported as an expense on the income statement.

The weighted-average cost method is representative of costs during the entire period including the beginning inventory rather than of the cost only at the

---

[4] A weighted-average unit cost rather than a simple average of the unit costs must be used. For example, ($6 + $7 + $8 + $9) ÷ 4 = $7.50 would be incorrect because it does not consider the number of units at each unit cost.

[5] When an average cost is used, uneven unit cost amounts usually are rounded to the nearest cent. The rounded unit cost amount is used to compute the ending inventory amount, which allocates any rounding error to cost of goods sold. Under the perpetual inventory system, a moving average unit cost (rather than the weighted-average unit cost) usually is used (see Part B).

beginning, end, or at one point during the period. Representative costs are reported on both the balance sheet (ending inventory) and the income statement (cost of goods sold).

First-In, First-Out Inventory Costing Method

The first-in, first-out method, frequently called **FIFO,** assumes that the oldest units (i.e., the first costs in) are the first units sold (i.e., the first costs out). The units in the beginning inventory are treated as if they were sold first. Then the units from the first purchase are sold next, and so on until the units left in the ending inventory all come from the most recent purchases. FIFO allocates the oldest unit costs to cost of goods sold and the most recent unit costs to the ending inventory.

Often, FIFO is justified because it is consistent with the actual physical flow of the goods. In most businesses, the first goods placed in stock are the first goods sold. However, FIFO can be used regardless of the actual physical flow of goods.

FIFO is applied by Witt (Exhibit 7–2) as follows under a **periodic** inventory system:

	Units	Unit cost	Total cost
Goods available for sale (Exhibit 7–2)	470		$3,630
Valuation of ending inventory (FIFO):			
At latest unit costs, 150 units:			
From December 20 purchase (latest)	120	$9	$1,080
From June 12 purchase (next latest)	30	8	240
Valuation, FIFO basis	150		1,320
Cost of goods sold (residual FIFO amount) . . .	320		$2,310

On the balance sheet, the FIFO ending inventory amount is valued on the basis of the most recent unit costs. It is likely to provide a realistic valuation prevailing at the balance sheet date. In contrast, on the income statement, cost of goods sold is valued at the oldest unit costs, which may not reflect the current cost of items that were sold.

Last-In, First-Out Inventory Costing Method

The last-in, first-out method, often called **LIFO,** assumes that the most recently acquired goods are sold first. Regardless of the physical flow of goods, LIFO treats the costs of the most recent units purchased as cost of goods sold. Therefore, the unit costs of the beginning inventory and the earlier purchases remain in the ending inventory. The LIFO flow assumption is the exact opposite of the FIFO flow assumption.

Under a **periodic** inventory system, LIFO is applied by Witt (Exhibit 7–2) as follows:

	Units	Unit cost	Total cost
Goods available for sale (Exhibit 7–2)	470		$3,630
Valuation of ending inventory (LIFO):			
At older unit costs, 150 units:			
From beginning inventory (oldest)	100	$6	$600
From January 3 purchase (next oldest)	50	7	350
Valuation, LIFO basis	150		950
Cost of goods sold (residual LIFO amount) . . .	320		$2,680

LIFO can be manipulated by buying (or not buying) goods at the end of a period when unit costs have changed. By this action, it is possible to manipulate cost of goods sold and, hence, reported income. On the income statement, LIFO cost of goods sold is based on the latest unit costs, which is a realistic measurement of the current cost of items that were sold. In contrast, on the balance sheet, the ending inventory amount is based on the oldest unit costs, which may be an unrealistic valuation.[6]

Specific Identification Inventory Costing Method

When the specific identification method is used, the cost of each item sold is individually identified and recorded as cost of goods sold. This method requires keeping track of the purchase cost of each item. This is done either by (1) coding the purchase cost on each unit before placing it in stock or (2) keeping a separate record of the unit and identifying it with a serial number. If the 40 units sold by Witt (Exhibit 7–2) on January 6 were selected from the units that were purchased at $6 each, the cost of goods sold amount for that sale would be measured as 40 units × $6 = $240. Alternatively, if 20 of the units were selected from those that cost $6 each and the other 20 from those that cost $7 each, cost of goods sold would be measured as (20 units × $6) + (20 units × $7) = $260.

The specific identification method is tedious and impractical when a large number of different items are stocked. On the other hand, when there are big ticket items such as automobiles and expensive jewelry, this method is appropriate because each item tends to be different from the other items. In such situations, the selling price of an item usually is based on a markup over its cost. However, the method may be manipulated when the units are identical because one can affect the cost of goods sold and the ending inventory accounts by "picking and choosing" from among the several available unit costs, even though the goods are identical in other respects.

---

[6] This discussion assumes an item-by-item application of LIFO and costing of goods sold currently throughout the period. For income tax purposes, LIFO costing must be done at the end of the taxable year. Although the concepts are the same, many companies use a method known as dollar-value LIFO, and the costing is at the end of the year. These complexities are beyond the scope of this course.

Comparison of the Inventory Costing Methods

Each of the four alternative inventory costing methods is in conformity with GAAP. However, each method may produce significantly different income and asset (i.e., ending inventory) amounts. To illustrate this difference, the comparative results for Witt, Inc., are as follows:

	Sales revenue	Cost of goods sold	Gross margin	Balance sheet (inventory)
Weighted average	$3,880	$2,472	$1,408	$1,158
FIFO	3,880	2,310	1,570	1,320
LIFO (end of period) . . .	3,880	2,680	1,200	950

Notice that the difference in **the gross margin** among each of the methods is the same as the difference in the inventory amounts. The method that gives the highest ending inventory amount also gives the highest income amount and vice versa. The weighted-average cost method will give income and inventory amounts that are between the FIFO and LIFO extremes.

Note in the comparison above that unit costs were **increasing. When unit costs are rising, LIFO produces lower income and a lower inventory valuation than FIFO. Conversely, when unit costs are declining, LIFO produces higher income and higher inventory valuation than FIFO.** These effects occur because LIFO will cause the new unit costs to be reflected on the income statement, whereas FIFO will cause the older unit costs to be reflected on the income statement.

Impact of Alternative Inventory Costing Methods on Financial Statement Analysis

Some individuals are critical of the accounting profession for permitting alternative accounting methods to be used. The case of Witt, Inc., demonstrates that accounting alternatives can result in large differences in the amounts reported on the financial statements. For example, ending inventory for Witt was 39% more under FIFO than under LIFO ($1,320 compared to $950). Differences of this magnitude clearly cause problems for statement users when they attempt to compare companies that use different accounting methods. Critics charge that the existence of alternative accounting methods is inconsistent with the **comparability quality** (Exhibit 4–5), which states that accounting concepts, principles, and methods should be applied in a similar way from one period to the next and by different entities. This quality is needed so that analysts can compare information for a company with the results from previous accounting periods and compare the current results with other companies for the same time period. These types of comparisons are more difficult if different accounting methods are used.

The Financial Accounting Standards Board (FASB) does in fact attempt to limit the number of acceptable accounting alternatives whenever a "best" approach can be identified. Unfortunately, no single inventory costing method can be considered best. Some financial statement users prefer LIFO because it allocates the most current purchase costs to cost of goods sold. These individuals believe that the current cost of an item determines its selling price; therefore, accounting should match current costs with revenues. The LIFO method does the best job of matching current costs and revenue.

Other financial statement users place more emphasis on the balance sheet and prefer to see the inventory valuation reflect current costs. FIFO does the best job of allocating current costs to inventory.

Some analysts prefer to avoid the extremes of LIFO and FIFO. The weighted-average inventory method usually produces results that are less extreme than LIFO and FIFO.

Because no inventory costing method can be considered "best," the accounting profession has been unwilling to require all companies to follow a single method. As a result, users of financial statements must be knowledgeable about alternative accounting methods and how they affect statements. Users must be certain that their decisions are based on real differences and not artificial differences created by alternative accounting methods.

To enhance comparability, accounting rules require companies to apply their accounting methods on a consistent basis. A company is not permitted to use LIFO one period, FIFO the next, and then go back to LIFO. A change in method is allowed only if the change will improve the measurement of financial results and financial position. Changing from one inventory costing method to another is a significant event. Such a change requires full disclosure about the reason for the change and the accounting effects.

Income Tax Effects Related to Inventory Methods

The selection of an inventory costing method often has a significant impact on income taxes that must be paid. The various inventory costing methods produce different amounts of pretax income among accounting periods. When prices are rising, **LIFO** often is preferred for income tax purposes because it results in a lower pretax income and a lower tax obligation.

In recent years, many businesses have adopted LIFO because prices were rising, and with rising prices, LIFO allocates higher costs to cost of goods sold. This in turn reduces pretax income so the income tax bill is lower. Of course, if prices should decline at some future date, those businesses may want to change from LIFO to FIFO to minimize income taxes on the downward trend of prices. In many cases, it is difficult to get permission from the Internal Revenue Service to change the inventory costing method.[7]

---

[7] The internal revenue code specifies a LIFO conformity rule: If LIFO is used on the income tax return, it must also be used to calculate inventory and cost of goods sold for the financial statements. This conformity rule is unusual because a business typically may use one set of accounting procedures for financial reports and a different set of procedures for preparing the tax return.

Exhibit 7–4   Income tax effects illustrated—Young Corporation

---

A. **Fact situation for 19B (when prices increased rapidly):**

    a. Sales revenue $900,000
    b. Cost of goods sold:
        FIFO basis 400,000
        LIFO basis 600,000
    c. Remaining expenses (excluding income taxes) 250,000
    d. Average income tax rate 30%

B. **Effect on income tax expense:**

	Inventory costing method	
	FIFO	**LIFO**
Sales revenue	$900,000	$900,000
Cost of goods sold	400,000	600,000
Gross margin	500,000	300,000
Less: Remaining expenses (except income taxes)	250,000	250,000
Pretax income	250,000	50,000
Income tax expense (30% rate)	75,000	15,000
Net income	$175,000	$ 35,000
EPS (100,000 shares common stock outstanding)	$1.75	$0.35

Reduction in income tax expense ($75,000 − $15,000) = $60,000.
Cash saved ($75,000 − $15,000) = $60,000.

    The income tax effects associated with LIFO and FIFO are illustrated in Exhibit 7–4 for the Young Corpration. In this situation, ending inventory, cost of goods sold, and pretax income were different by $200,000, which was caused by the differences between the FIFO and LIFO methods. Costs were rising, and there was a significant difference between the "old" and "new" unit costs. When multiplied by the 30% income tax rate, the $200,000 difference indicates a cash saving of $60,000 in 19B. LIFO cannot provide permanent tax savings because (*a*) when inventory levels drop or (*b*) costs drop, the income effect reverses and the income taxes deferred will have to be paid. The only advantage of deferring income taxes in such situations is due to the fact that interest can be earned on the money that otherwise would be paid as taxes for the current year.

PART B—APPLICATION OF A PERPETUAL INVENTORY SYSTEM AND SELECTED INVENTORY COSTING PROBLEMS

    This part of the chapter discusses **application of each of the inventory costing methods with a perpetual inventory system.** Separate discussion of the two inventory systems is essential because:

a. The periodic inventory system costs inventory units at the end of the period; the perpetual inventory system costs units on a day-to-day basis. This can cause differences in reported amounts for inventory and cost of goods sold.

b. The accounting entries vary between the two systems.

Application of the Inventory Costing Methods with a Perpetual Inventory System

A perpetual inventory system requires the maintenance of a day-to-day **perpetual inventory record** for each kind of goods or merchandise. This record shows units, unit costs, and dollar amounts for (a) beginning inventory, (b) goods received (purchases), (c) goods sold (issues), and (d) balance of goods on hand (ending inventory). Each purchase and each sale transaction is entered in the perpetual inventory record when it occurs. The perpetual inventory record is designed so that cost of goods sold and the ending inventory are measured on a perpetual or continuous basis. An example of a perpetual inventory record is shown in Exhibit 7–5.

In the following discussions, we will use the data for Witt, Inc., given in Exhibit 7–2. The beginning inventory of 100 units at a unit cost of $6 has been carried over in the records from the prior period. Each purchase is recorded as follows and at the same time entered on the perpetual inventory record (Exhibit 7–5):

Jan. 3	Inventory (50 units × $7)	350
	Cash (or accounts payable)	350

A sale generates two companion entries when a perpetual inventory system is used; one at sales price and one at cost:

Jan. 6	Cash	400
	Sales revenue (40 units × $10)	400
	Cost of goods sold (FIFO basis)	240
	Inventory (40 units × $6)	240

Weighted-Average Inventory Costing Method

Under the perpetual inventory system, cost of goods sold is measured and recorded at the time of each sale. When the weighted-average cost method is used with a perpetual system, a **moving** weighted-average unit cost must be computed after each purchase. It is impossible to use an annual weighted average because the recording of cost of goods sold would be delayed until year-end, which is the only time an annual average cost can be computed.

A perpetual inventory record on a moving weighted-average basis for Witt, Inc., is shown in Exhibit 7–5. The moving weighted-average unit cost was recomputed three times during the period because there were three purchases. Units sold are removed from the inventory record at the current moving average

Exhibit 7–5 Moving weighted-average method—perpetual inventory system

PERPETUAL INVENTORY RECORD

Item ___ Item A ___   Cost basis ___ Moving average ___

Location ___ 320 ___   Minimum level ___ 100 ___

Code ___ 13 ___   Maximum level ___ 300 ___

Date	Received (purchases) Units	Unit Cost	Total Cost	Issued (sales) Units	Unit Cost	Total Cost	Inventory Balance Units	Unit Cost	Total Cost
1/1 bal.							100	$6.00	$ 600
1/3	50	$7.00	$ 350				150	6.33	950
1/6				40	$6.33	$ 253	110	6.33	697
6/12	200	8.00	1,600				310	7.41*	2,297
6/18				220	7.41	1,630	90	7.41	667
12/20	120	9.00	1,080				210	8.32*	1,747
12/24				60	8.32	499	150	8.32	1,248
Total cost of goods sold						2,382			
Total ending inventory									1,248

* New moving weighted-average unit cost computed.

unit cost. For example, the moving weighted-average unit cost was computed on the date of the first purchase as follows:

	Units	Cost
Beginning inventory	100	$600
Purchase, January 3	50	350
Totals	150	$950

Moving average unit cost:
$950 ÷ 150 units = $6.33 per unit.

The companion journal entries for the sale on January 6 would reflect sales revenue of $400 and cost of goods sold of $253 (from the perpetual inventory record) as follows:

```
Jan. 6   Cash . . . . . . . . . . . . . . . . . . . . . . . . . . . . . . . . . . 400
                Sales revenue (40 units × $10) . . . . . . . . . . . . . . . . . . . .        400

         Cost of goods sold (moving average basis) . . . . . . . . . . . . . . . . 253
                Inventory . . . . . . . . . . . . . . . . . . . . . . . . . . . . . . .        253
         From Exhibit 7–5, 40 units × $6.33 = $253.
```

FIFO Inventory Costing Method

When the FIFO method is applied with a perpetual inventory system, the remaining units on hand after each sale must be layered by the different unit costs. These layers are called **inventory cost layers.** The identification of inventory cost layers is necessary because goods are removed from the perpetual inventory record in FIFO order; that is, the oldest unit cost is taken out first. The perpetual inventory record on a FIFO basis for Witt, Inc., is shown in Exhibit 7–6. Each purchase and each sale of goods is entered in the inventory record at the time of the transaction. At each transaction date, the Balance column on the perpetual inventory record is restated to show the units and amount on hand for each different unit cost. At the same time, each transaction is recorded in the journal. The two companion journal entries to record the sales of June 18 are:

```
June 18   Cash . . . . . . . . . . . . . . . . . . . . . . . . . . . . . . . . . . 2,640
                 Sales revenue (220 units × $12) . . . . . . . . . . . . . . . . .       2,640

          Cost of goods sold (FIFO basis) . . . . . . . . . . . . . . . . . . . . 1,590
                 Inventory . . . . . . . . . . . . . . . . . . . . . . . . . . . . . .       1,590
          From Exhibit 7–6, $360 + $350 + $880 = $1,590.
```

LIFO Inventory Costing Method

When the LIFO method is used with a perpetual inventory system, the inventory cost layers must be identified separately on the perpetual inventory record, as was the case with FIFO. This identification is necessary so that the units (and their costs) can be removed at the time of sale from the inventory record in the opposite order that they came in. Unit costs are removed from the perpetual inventory record at the time of each issue, which means that the **timing of costing is during the period rather than at the end of the period.** The perpetual inventory record on a LIFO basis for Witt, Inc., is shown in Exhibit 7–7.

Specific Identification Inventory Costing Method

When the specific identification method is applied with a perpetual inventory system, the item-by-item choice (for entry in the perpetual inventory record and in the accounts) should be made at the time of sale. Use of the specific identifica-

Exhibit 7–6 FIFO method—perpetual inventory system

PERPETUAL INVENTORY RECORD

Item _____ Item A _____   Cost basis _____ FIFO _____

Location _____ 320 _____   Minimum level _____ 100 _____

Code _____ 13 _____   Maximum level _____ 300 _____

Date	Received (purchases)			Issued (sales)			Inventory Balance*		
	Units	Unit Cost	Total Cost	Units	Unit Cost	Total Cost	Units	Unit Cost	Total Cost
1/1 bal.							100	$6	$ 600
1/3	50	$7	$ 350				100	6	600
							50	7	350
1/6				40	$6	$ 240	60	6	360
							50	7	350
6/12	200	8	1,600				60	6	360
							50	7	350
							200	8	1,600
6/18				60	6	360			
				50	7	350			
				110	8	880	90	8	720
12/20	120	9	1,080				90	8	720
							120	9	1,080
12/24				60	8	480	30	8	240
							120	9	1,080
Total cost of goods sold						2,310			
Total ending inventory									1,320

* Maintained by FIFO unit cost inventory layers.

Exhibit 7–7 LIFO method, costed currently—perpetual inventory system

PERPETUAL INVENTORY RECORD									

Item **Item A** Cost basis **LIFO**

Location **320** Minimum level **100**

Code **13** Maximum level **300**

Date	Received (purchases)			Issued (sales)			Inventory Balance*		
	Units	Unit Cost	Total Cost	Units	Unit Cost	Total Cost	Units	Unit Cost	Total Cost
1/1 bal.							100	$6	$ 600
1/3	50	$7	$ 350				100	6	600
							50	7	350
1/6				40	$7	$ 280	100	6	600
							10	7	70
6/12	200	8	1,600				100	6	600
							10	7	70
							200	8	1,600
6/18				200	8	1,600			
				10	7	70			
				10	6	60	90	6	540
12/20	120	9	1,080				90	6	540
							120	9	1,080
12/24				60	9	540	90	6	540
							60	9	540
Total cost of goods sold						2,550			
Ending inventory									1,080

* Maintained by LIFO unit cost inventory layers.

tion costing method with a perpetual inventory system is done in a manner like that shown in the preceding illustrations.

Comparison of Periodic and Perpetual Inventory Systems

The periodic and perpetual inventory systems often produce different valuations of cost of goods sold and ending inventory because of differences in the timing of the costing of cost of goods sold and inventory. The **periodic** inventory system costs ending inventory and cost of goods sold at the **end** of the accounting period. The **perpetual** inventory system costs inventory and cost of goods sold **throughout** the accounting period.

The FIFO inventory method gives identical valuations of ending inventory and cost of goods sold under both the periodic and perpetual inventory systems. The results are identical because of the basic FIFO assumption that the first goods into inventory are the first goods taken out of inventory, and that order is always maintained. Compare the following FIFO results for Witt, Inc.:

FIFO	Perpetual inventory system	Periodic inventory system
Source	Exhibit 7–6	Page 310
Ending inventory	$1,320	$1,320
Cost of goods sold	2,310	2,310
Total goods available	$3,630	$3,630

In contrast, results typically will be different under periodic and perpetual systems when either the LIFO or the average inventory costing method is used. The results will be different under the **average cost** method because the **periodic** inventory system applies an **annual** weighted average for cost allocation, whereas the **perpetual** inventory system applies a series of **moving** averages throughout the accounting period.

Results will be different under the **LIFO** method because the **periodic** inventory system allocates the most recent purchase cost to cost of goods sold at the end of the accounting period. In contrast, the **perpetual** system allocates the most recent purchase costs to cost of goods sold **during** the accounting period on the date that each sales transaction occurs.

To show the differences that can occur between LIFO and weighted average, compare the following results for Witt, Inc.:

LIFO	Perpetual inventory system	Periodic inventory system
Source	Exhibit 7–7	Page 311
Ending inventory	$1,080	$ 950
Cost of goods sold	2,550	2,680
Total goods available	$3,630	$3,630

Weighted Average		
Source	Exhibit 7–5	Page 308
Ending inventory	$1,248	$1,158
Cost of goods sold	2,382	2,472
Total goods available	$3,630	$3,630

To summarize, the four **inventory costing methods** (weighted average, FIFO, LIFO, and specific identification) are alternative methods of measuring the valuation of ending inventory and cost of goods sold. Each method assumes a different flow of unit costs during the accounting period; therefore, each method produces different results. The **periodic** and **perpetual inventory systems** are two different accounting approaches for applying the inventory costing methods to measure cost of goods sold and ending inventory. The periodic inventory system allocates costs at the end of the accounting period (using one of the four inventory costing methods). The perpetual inventory system allocates costs currently during the accounting period (again, using one of the inventory costing methods). Because of these two different timing assumptions, the two systems give different valuations of ending inventory and cost of goods sold under the weighted average, LIFO, and specific identification costing methods. Valuations are always the same under FIFO.

Selected Inventory Topics

The remaining discussions in this chapter relate to four problems that may affect accounting for inventories. They are (a) lower-of-cost-or-market (LCM) valuation, (b) damaged goods, (c) estimating ending inventory and cost of goods sold, and (d) impact of errors in measuring ending inventory.

Inventories at Lower of Cost or Market (LCM)

Inventories should be measured at their purchase cost in conformity with the cost principle. However, when the goods remaining in the ending inventory can be replaced with identical goods at a lower cost, the lower cost should be used as the inventory valuation. This rule is known as measuring inventories on a **lower-of-cost-or-market (LCM) basis.** It is a departure from the cost principle because of the conservatism constraint (Exhibit 4–5) that requires special care to avoid overstating assets and income. Under LCM, a "holding" loss is recognized in the period in which the replacement cost of an item dropped, rather than in the period in which the item is sold. The holding loss is the difference between purchase cost and the subsequent lower replacement cost. To illustrate, assume that an office equipment dealer has 10 new electronic calculators in the 19B ending inventory. The calculators were bought for $450 each and were marked to sell at $499.95. At the end of the year, the same new calculators can be purchased for $400 and will be marked to sell for $429.95. The 10 calculators should be costed in the ending inventory at the lower of cost ($450) or current market ($400). Under LCM, the ending inventory should be costed at $400 per unit. Several effects are caused by using a replacement cost of $400 instead of the original purchase cost of $450. By costing the calculators at $50 per unit below their purchase cost, 19B pretax income will be $500 less (i.e., 10 × $50) than it would have been had they been costed in the inventory at $450 per unit. This $500 loss in the value of the inventory (i.e., the holding loss) was due to a decline in the replacement cost. Pretax income is reduced by $500 in the period in which

Exhibit 7–8   Effect of inventory measurement at LCM

	Cost (FIFO)	LCM
	Inventory measured at—	
Sales revenue	$41,500	$41,500
Cost of goods sold:		
Beginning inventory . . . . $ 5,000		$ 5,000
Add purchases 20,000		20,000
Goods available for sale 25,000		25,000
Less ending inventory (10 calculators):		
At purchase cost of $450 4,500		
At LCM of $400		4,000
Cost of goods sold	20,500	21,000
Gross margin on sales	21,000	20,500
Expenses	15,000	15,000
Pretax income	$ 6,000	$ 5,500

the replacement cost dropped (19B) rather than in the later period when the goods actually are sold. The $500 loss also reduces the amount of inventory that is reported on the 19B balance sheet. These effects are shown in Exhibit 7–8. LCM usually is applied to all inventories on an item-by-item basis rather than on the aggregate inventory as a whole.[8]

Damaged and Deteriorated Goods

Merchandise on hand that is damaged, obsolete, or shopworn should not be reported at original cost. Instead this merchandise should be reported at its present **net realizable value** when it is below cost. Net realizable value is the **estimated amount** that will be realized when the goods are sold in their deteriorated condition, less all repair and sale costs.

Assume a retail store has on hand two television sets that have been used as demonstrators and cannot be sold as new because they are shopworn. When purchased, the sets cost $300 each. Based on their present condition, realistic estimates are:

	Per set
Estimated sales price in present condition	$175
Estimated repair costs of $20 and sales costs of $15	35
Estimated net realizable value	$140

---

[8] In contrast, if the replacement cost had increased to $500 each, there would have been a **holding gain** of 10 units × $50 = $500. Recognition of holding gains is not permitted by GAAP because revenue is recognized only at date of sale of the goods.

The two television sets should be included in inventory at $140 each, rather than at the original cost of $300 each. Net realizable value is used, rather than cost, because it records the loss in the period in which it occurred rather than in the period of sale. This method also avoids overstatement of the asset on the balance sheet in conformity with the conservatism constraint.

If a **periodic** inventory system is used, the item is included in the ending inventory of **damaged goods** at its estimated net realizable value. The loss is reflected in cost of goods sold. However, if a **perpetual** system is used, the following entry would be made:

Inventory of damaged goods (2 × $140)	280	
Loss on damaged goods (an expense) ($600 − $280)	320	
Inventory (2 × $300)		600

The perpetual inventory record also would be changed to show this entry.[9]

Estimating Ending Inventory and Cost of Goods Sold

When a periodic inventory system is used, a physical inventory count must be taken to determine the amount of ending inventory and to compute cost of goods sold. Because taking a physical inventory is a time-consuming task, many businesses take inventories only once a year. Nevertheless, managers may want financial statements for internal use on a monthly or quarterly basis. Some businesses **estimate** the ending inventory for the monthly or quarterly financial statements rather than taking a physical inventory when a periodic inventory system is used. The **gross margin method** is used for this purpose. The method uses an estimated gross margin ratio.

The gross margin ratio is calculated by dividing gross margin (sales revenue minus cost of goods sold) by net sales revenue. Because cost of goods sold for the current period cannot be determined without taking an inventory, it is impossible to calculate the gross margin ratio for the current period. Therefore, the average gross margin ratio for one or more prior periods is used as an estimate of the ratio for the current period.

We will illustrate the use of the gross margin method with the following data from Patz Company:

---

[9] The subsequent entries may be as follows:

  a. To record actual repair costs of $25:

Inventory of damaged goods	25	
Cash		25

  b. To record sale of the two sets for $360 (less actual selling costs of $15):

Cash ($360 − $15)	345	
Selling expense	15	
Inventory ($280 + $25)		305
Gain on sale of damaged goods		55

PATZ COMPANY
Income Statement
For the Month Ended January 31, 19D

Sales revenue	$100,000*
Cost of goods sold:	
Beginning inventory $15,000*	
Add purchases 65,000*	
Goods available for sale 80,000	
Less ending inventory . . . . ?	
Gross margin on sales	?
Expenses	30,000*
Pretax income	$?

* Provided by the accounts.

The January ending inventory is to be **estimated** rather than determined by physical count. The yearly net sales for 19C amounted to $1,000,000, and gross margin was $400,000; therefore, the actual gross margin ratio for 19C was $400,000 ÷ $1,000,000 = 0.40. Management has decided that this ratio is a realistic estimate for use during 19D. Using the 0.40 as our estimate for 19D, we can compute an **estimated** inventory valuation. The computational steps, in lettered sequence, are shown below:

PATZ COMPANY
Income Statement
For the Month Ended January 31, 19D (estimated)

		Computations (sequence a, b, c)
Sales revenue	$100,000	Per accounts
Cost of goods sold:		
Beginning inventory $15,000		Per accounts
Add purchases 65,000		Per accounts
Goods available for sale 80,000		
Less ending inventory 20,000		c. $ 80,000 − $60,000 = $20,000
Cost of goods sold	60,000	b. $100,000 − $40,000 = $60,000*
Gross margin on sales	40,000	a. $100,000 × 0.40 = $40,000
Expenses	30,000	Per accounts
Pretax income	$ 10,000	

* Or alternatively, $100,000 × (1.00 − 0.40) = $60,000.

The balance sheet can be completed by reporting the $20,000 estimated ending inventory account as a current asset.

The gross margin method has other uses. Auditors and accountants may use this method to test the reasonableness of the amount of the inventory determined by other means. If the current gross margin ratio has changed materially from the recent past, it may suggest an error in the ending inventory. The method also is used in the case of a casualty loss when an inventory of goods is destroyed or stolen and its valuation must be estimated for settlement purposes with an insurance company.

Errors in Measuring Ending Inventory

A direct relationship exists between ending inventory and cost of goods sold. When the periodic inventory system is used, items not in the ending inventory are assumed to have been sold. Thus, the measurement of ending inventory affects both the balance sheet (assets) and the income statement (cost of goods sold and net income). The measurement of ending inventory affects not only the net income for that period but also the net income for the **next accounting period.** This two-period effect occurs because the ending inventory for one period is the beginning inventory for the next accounting period. The 19A and 19B income statements for SAL Company are shown in panel A of Exhibit 7–9. The reported 19A ending inventory was $10,000. Notice that this amount is shown as the beginning inventory for 19B.

An error in measuring the 19A ending inventory would affect both 19A and 19B income. For example, if the 19A ending inventory for SAL Company should have been $11,000 (i.e., $1,000 more than reported), both 19A and 19B income would be incorrect by $1,000. The restated income statements for SAL Company are shown in Panel B of Exhibit 7–9. The various accounts that are affected by the $1,000 error are identified in Panel C. Two generalizations can be made concerning the impact of an inventory error:

1. **In the period of the change.**   An increase in the amount of the ending inventory for a period decreases cost of goods sold by the same amount, which in turn increases pretax income for that period by the same amount. A decrease in the amount of ending inventory increases cost of goods sold, which in turn decreases pretax income for that period by the same amount.
2. **In the next period.**   An increase in the amount of the ending inventory for a period increases the beginning inventory for the next period. The increase in beginning inventory increases cost of goods sold, which decreases the pretax income of the **next period** by the same amount. In contrast, a decrease in the amount of the ending inventory for a period decreases cost of goods sold of the next period, which increases pretax income of the **next period** by the same amount.

An error in measuring ending inventory is caused by either incorrectly counting the inventory or by using an incorrect unit cost to value the inventory. Accountants use great care in counting and valuing inventory, but errors do occur. For example, several years ago the financial statements of Lafayette Radio Electronics Corporation had the following note:

> Subsequent to the issuance of its financial statements the company discovered a computational error in the amount of $1,046,000 in the calculation of its year-end inventory which resulted in an overstatement of ending inventory.

Exhibit 7–9 Impact of error in measuring inventory

Panel A:

SAL COMPANY
Income Statement (as reported)

	19A		19B
Sales revenue		$100,000	$110,000
Cost of goods sold			
Beginning inventory	$ –0–		$10,000
Purchases	70,000		58,000
Goods available for sale	70,000		68,000
Ending inventory	10,000		–0–
Cost of goods sold		60,000	68,000
Gross margin		40,000	42,000
Expenses		35,000	35,500
Pretax income		$ 5,000	$ 6,500

Panel B:

SAL COMPANY
Income Statement (corrected)

	19A		19B
Sales revenue		$100,000	$110,000
Cost of goods sold:			
Beginning inventory	$ –0–		$11,000
Purchases	70,000		58,000
Goods available for sale	70,000		69,000
Ending inventory	11,000		–0–
Cost of goods sold		59,000	69,000
Gross margin		41,000	41,000
Expenses		35,000	35,500
Pretax income		$ 6,000	$ 5,500

Panel C—comparison:

		As reported	Corrected
19A	Ending inventory	$10,000	$11,000
19A	Cost of goods sold	60,000	59,000
19A	Gross margin	40,000	41,000
19A	Pretax income	5,000	6,000
19B	Beginning inventory	10,000	11,000
19B	Goods available for sale	68,000	69,000
19B	Gross margin	42,000	41,000
19B	Pretax income	6,500	5,500

DEMONSTRATION CASE A

(Try to resolve the requirements before proceeding to the suggested solution that follows.)

Metal Products, Incorporated, has been operating for three years as a distributor of a line of metal products. It is now the end of 19C, and for the first time the company will undergo an audit by an independent CPA. The company uses a **periodic** inventory system. The annual income statements prepared by the company were:

	19B	19C
	For the year ended December 31	
Sales revenue	$750,000	$800,000
Cost of goods sold:		
Beginning inventory	45,000	40,000
Add purchases	460,000	484,000
Goods available for sale	505,000	524,000
Less ending inventory	40,000	60,000
Cost of goods sold	465,000	464,000
Gross margin on sales	285,000	336,000
Operating expenses	275,000	306,000
Pretax income	10,000	30,000
Income tax expense (20%)	2,000	6,000
Net income	$ 8,000	$ 24,000

During the early stages of the audit, the independent CPA discovered that the ending inventory for 19B was understated by $15,000.

Required:
a. Based on the above income statement amounts, compute the gross margin ratio on sales for each year. Do the results suggest an inventory error? Explain.
b. Reconstruct the two income statements on a correct basis.
c. Answer the following questions:
   (1) What are the correct gross margin ratios?
   (2) What effect did the $15,000 understatement of the ending inventory have on 19B pretax income? Explain.
   (3) What effect did the inventory error have on 19C pretax income? Explain.
   (4) How did the inventory error affect income tax expense?

Suggested Solution

Requirement a—Gross Margin Ratios as Reported:

$$19B: \$285,000 \div \$750,000 = 0.38$$
$$19C: \$336,000 \div \$800,000 = 0.42$$

The change in the gross margin ratio from 0.38 to 0.42 suggests the possibility of an inventory error in the absence of any other explanation.

Requirement b—Income Statements Corrected:

	For the year ended December 31	
	19B	**19C**
Sales revenue	$750,000	$800,000
Cost of goods sold:		
Beginning inventory	45,000	55,000*
Add purchases	460,000	484,000
Goods available for sale	505,000	539,000
Less ending inventory	55,000*	60,000
Cost of goods sold	450,000	479,000
Gross margin on sales	300,000	321,000
Operating expenses	275,000	306,000
Pretax income	25,000	15,000
Income tax expense (20%)	5,000	3,000
Net income	$ 20,000	$ 12,000

* Increased by $15,000.

Requirement c:

1. Correct gross margin ratios:

$$19B: \quad \$300,000 \div \$750,000 = 0.400$$
$$19C: \quad \$321,000 \div \$800,000 = 0.401$$

The inventory error of $15,000 was responsible for the difference in the gross margin ratios reflected in Requirement *(a)*. The error in the 19B ending inventory affected gross margin for both 19B and 19C—in the opposite direction but by the same amount ($15,000).

2. Effect on pretax income in 19B: **Ending inventory understatement** **($15,000)** caused an **understatement of pretax income** by the **same amount.**

3. Effect on pretax income in 19C: Beginning inventory **understatement** (by the same $15,000 since the inventory amount is carried over from the prior period) caused an **overstatement** of pretax income by the same amount.

4. Total income tax expense for 19B and 19C combined was the same ($8,000) regardless of the error. However, there was a shift of $3,000 ($15,000 × 20%) income tax expense from 19B to 19C.

Observation—An ending inventory error in one year affects pretax income by the amount of the error and in the next year affects pretax income again by the same amount but in the opposite direction.

DEMONSTRATION CASE B

(Try to resolve the requirements before proceeding to the suggested solution that follows.)

This case compares a **periodic** inventory system with a **perpetual** inventory system assuming the LIFO inventory costing method is applied in each system.

Balent Appliances distributes a number of high-cost household appliances. One product, microwave ovens, has been selected for case purposes. Assume the following summarized transactions were completed during the accounting period in the order given below (assume all transactions are cash):

	Units	Unit cost
a. Beginning inventory	11	$200
b. Sales (selling price, $420)	8	?
c. Sales returns (can be resold as new)	1	200
d. Purchases	9	220
e. Purchase returns (damaged in shipment)	1	220

Required:

a. Compute the following amounts assuming application of the LIFO inventory costing method:

	Ending inventory		Cost of goods sold	
	Units	Dollars	Units	Dollars
(1) Periodic inventory system (costed at end of period)	____	____	____	____
(2) Perpetual inventory system (costed during period)	____	____	____	____

b. Give the indicated journal entries for transactions (b) through (e) assuming:

(1) Periodic inventory system.
(2) Perpetual inventory system.

Suggested Solution

Requirement a:

	Ending inventory		Cost of goods sold	
	Units	Dollars	Units	Dollars
1. Periodic inventory system (costed at end of the period)	12	$2,420	7	$1,540
2. Perpetual inventory system (costed during the period)	12	2,560	7	1,400

Computations:
  Goods available for sale: (11 units × $200 = $2,200) + (8 units × $220 = $1,760) = $3,960.
  1. Periodic LIFO inventory (costed at end):
     Ending inventory: (11 units × $200 = $2,200) + (1 unit × $220 = $220) = $2,420.
     Cost of goods sold: (Goods available, $3,960) − (Ending inventory, $2,420) = $1,540.
  2. Perpetual LIFO inventory (costed during period):
     Ending inventory: (8 units × $220 = $1,760) + (4 units × $200 = $800) = $2,560.
     Cost of goods sold: 7 units × $200 = $1,400.

Requirement b—Journal Entries:

1. Periodic Inventory System	2. Perpetual Inventory System
b. Sales: Cash (8 × \$420) . . . . 3,360 Sales revenue 3,360	Cash . . . . 3,360 Sales revenue . . . . 3,360 Cost of goods sold . . . . 1,600 Inventory (8 × \$200) 1,600
c. Sales returns: Sales returns . . . . 420 Cash (1 × \$420) 420	Sales returns . . . . 420 Cash . . . . 420 Inventory (1 × \$200) . . . . 200 Cost of goods sold 200
d. Purchases: Purchases . . . . 1,980 Cash (9 × \$220) 1,980	Inventory . . . . 1,980 Cash 1,980
e. Purchase return: Cash . . . . 220 Purchase returns 220	Cash . . . . 220 Inventory 220

SUMMARY OF CHAPTER

This chapter focused on the problem of measuring cost of goods sold and ending inventory when unit costs change during the period. Inventory should include all the items for resale to which the entity has ownership. Costs flow into inventory when goods are purchased (or manufactured) and flow out (as expense) when the goods are sold or disposed of otherwise. When there are different unit cost amounts representing the inflow of goods for the period, a rational and systematic method must be used to allocate costs to the units remaining in inventory and to the units sold. The chapter discussed four different inventory costing methods and their applications in both a perpetual and a periodic inventory system. The methods discussed were weighted-average cost, FIFO, LIFO, and specific identification. Each of the inventory costing methods is in conformity with GAAP. The selection of a method of inventory costing is important because it will affect reported income, income tax expense (and hence cash flow), and the inventory valuation reported on the balance sheet. In a period of rising prices, FIFO gives a higher income than does LIFO; in a period of falling prices, the opposite result occurs.

Damaged, obsolete, and deteriorated items in inventory should be assigned a unit cost that represents their current estimated net realizable value. Also, the ending inventory of new items (not damaged, deteriorated, or obsolete) should be measured on the basis of the lower of actual cost or replacement cost (i.e., LCM basis).

This chapter explained another fundamental accounting concept (Exhibit 4–5) known as the comparability quality, which means that all accounting concepts, principles, and measurement approaches should be applied in a consistent manner from period to period.

IMPORTANT TERMS DEFINED IN THIS CHAPTER

Comparability Quality Accounting methods should be consistently applied from one period to the next. *p. 312*

Consignments Goods in possession of a seller, but legal title is retained by the supplier. *p. 305*

Finished Goods Inventory Manufactured goods that are completed and ready for sale. *p. 304*

First-In, First-Out Inventory costing method that assumes the oldest units are the first units sold. *p. 310*

Gross Margin Method Method to estimate ending inventory based on the gross margin ratio. *p. 323*

Last-In, First-Out Inventory costing method that assumes the newest units are the first units sold. *p. 310*

Lower of Cost or Market Departure from cost principle that serves to recognize a "holding" loss when replacement cost drops below cost. *p. 321*

Merchandise Inventory Goods held for resale in the ordinary course of business. *p. 304*

Moving Weighted Average Weighted-average inventory costing method applied in the perpetual inventory system. *p. 315*

Net Realizable Value Estimated amount to be realized when goods are sold, less repair and disposal costs. *p. 322*

Periodic Inventory System Ending inventory and cost of goods sold are determined at the end of the accounting period; a physical inventory count must be taken. *p. 306*

Perpetual Inventory System A detailed daily inventory record is updated continuously during the accounting period; provides ending inventory and cost of goods sold. *p. 306*

Raw Materials Inventory Items acquired for the purpose of processing into finished goods. *p. 304*

Specific Identification   Inventory costing method that identifies the cost of the specific item that was sold. *p. 311*

Weighted Average   Inventory costing method used with a periodic inventory system that averages all purchase costs to calculate a weighted-average unit cost on an annual basis. *p. 309*

Work in Process Inventory   Goods in the process of being manufactured that are not yet complete. *p. 304*

QUESTIONS

Part A: Questions 1–14

1. Match the type of inventory with the type of business in the following matrix:

Type of Inventory	Type of Business	
	Trading	Manufacturing
Merchandise		
Finished goods		
Work in process		
Raw materials		

2. Why is inventory an important item to both internal management and external users of financial statements?

3. What are the general guidelines for deciding which items should be included in inventory?

4. In measuring cost of goods sold and inventory, why is passage of ownership an important issue? When does ownership to goods usually pass? Explain.

5. Identify the two parties to a consignment. Which party should include the goods on consignment in inventory? Explain.

6. Explain the application of the cost principle to an item in the ending inventory.

7. When a perpetual inventory system is used, unit costs of the items sold are known at the date of each sale. In contrast, when a periodic inventory system is used, unit costs are known only at the end of the accounting period. Why are these statements correct?

8. The periodic inventory calculation is BI + P − EI = CGS. The perpetual inventory calculation is BI + P − CGS = EI. Explain the significance of the difference between these two calculations.

9. The chapter discussed four inventory costing methods. List the four methods and briefly explain each.

10. The four inventory costing methods may be applied with either a periodic inventory system or a perpetual inventory system. Briefly explain how the methods are applied in each system.

11. Explain how income can be manipulated when the specific identification inventory costing method is used.

12. Contrast the effects of LIFO versus FIFO on reported assets (i.e., the ending inventory) when (*a*) prices are rising and (*b*) prices are falling.

13. Contrast the income statement effect of LIFO versus FIFO (i.e., on pretax income) when (*a*) prices are rising and (*b*) prices are falling.

14. Contrast the effects of LIFO versus FIFO on cash outflow and inflow.

Part B: Questions 15–22

15. What is the purpose of a perpetual inventory record? List the four main column headings and briefly explain the purpose of each.

16. When a perpetual inventory system is used, a moving weighted average is used. In contrast, when a periodic inventory system is used, an annual weighted average is used. Explain why the different averages are used.

17. The weighted-average inventory costing method usually produces different results when a perpetual inventory system is used rather than a periodic inventory system. Explain why.

18. Explain briefly application of the LCM concept to the ending inventory and its effect on the income statement and balance sheet when market is lower than cost.

19. When should net realizable value be used in costing an item in the ending inventory?

20. The chapter discussed the gross margin method to estimate inventories. Briefly explain this method and indicate why it is used.

21. Briefly explain the comparability quality. How might it relate to the inventory costing methods?

22. Assume the 19A ending inventory was understated by $100,000. Explain how this error would affect the 19A and 19B pretax income amounts. What would be the effects if the 19A ending inventory were overstated by $100,000 instead of understated?

EXERCISES

Part A: Exercises 7–1 to 7–8

E7–1 **(Match Definitions with Terms)**
Match each definition with its related term by entering the appropriate letter in the space provided.

Terms

_____ (1) Specific identification

_____ (2) Work in process inventory

_____ (3) Merchandise inventory

_____ (4) Periodic inventory system

_____ (5) Last-in, first-out

_____ (6) Weighted average

_____ (7) Finished goods inventory

_____ (8) Comparability quality

_____ (9) Perpetual inventory system

_____ (10) Gross margin method

_____ (11) First-in, first-out

_____ (12) Net realizable value

_____ (13) Lower of cost or market

_____ (14) Raw materials inventory

_____ (15) Moving weighted average

_____ (16) Consignment

Definitions

A. Prevents arbitrary changes from one accounting or measurement approach to another from one period to another.

B. Goods held on this basis should be excluded from inventory because legal title still resides with the consignor.

C. An account reported on the balance sheet as a current asset; represents goods completed in the manufacturing process.

D. An inventory costing method that assumes that those items which have been in inventory the longest are sold first.

E. Uses a ratio derived by dividing the gross margin amount by the net sales revenue to compute estimates for CGS, gross margin on sales, and ending inventory.

F. An inventory method that assumes that the units acquired most recently are sold first.

G. Recognizes a holding loss when replacement cost drops below cost.

H. The inventory of a retailer or wholesaler.

I. An inventory costing method in which a new average unit cost is computed at the time of each new purchase.

J. Estimated selling price of a product in the ordinary course of business, less reasonably predictable costs of completion and disposal.

K. Requires computation of the ending inventory by means of a physical count of the goods remaining on hand; CGS is computed as a residual amount.

L. System that maintains a detailed daily inventory record throughout the period for each item stocked.

M. Those items acquired by purchase, growth, or extraction of natural resources for further processing into finished goods.

N. An inventory costing method that may be appropriate for big ticket items but may be impractical when unit costs are low.

O. An inventory costing method that weights the number of units purchased and unit costs that prevailed during the period; used in conjunction with a periodic inventory system.

P. An asset that includes the cost of raw materials used, the direct labor incurred in the manufacturing process, and factory overhead costs.

E7–2 (Use of a Periodic Inventory System)

Anita Fashions purchased 100 new shirts and recorded a total cost of $2,840 determined as follows:

Invoice cost	$2,000
Less: Cash discount 3%	
Shipping charges	530
Import taxes and duties	110
Interest paid in advance (10%) on $2,000	
borrowed to finance the purchase	200
	$2,840

Give the journal entry(s) to record this purchase assuming a periodic inventory system. Show computations.

E7–3 (Use of the Four Inventory Methods)

The records at the end of January 19B for Quality Company showed the following for a particular kind of merchandise:

Transactions	Units	Total cost
Inventory, December 31, 19A	30	$390
Purchase, January 9, 19B	60	900
Sale, January 11, 19B (at $36 per unit)	50	
Purchase, January 20, 19B	35	490
Sale, January 27, 19B (at $37 per unit)	41	

Required:

Assuming a periodic inventory system, compute the amount of (1) goods available for sale, (2) ending inventory, and (3) cost of goods sold at January 31, 19B, under each of the following inventory costing methods (show computations and round to the nearest dollar):

a. Weighted-average cost.
b. First-in, first-out.
c. Last-in, first-out.
d. Specific identification (assume the sale on January 11 was identified with the purchase of January 9, the sale of January 27 was identified with the purchase of January 20, and any excess identified with the beginning inventory).

E7–4 (Comparison of Alternative Inventory Methods)

Solar Company uses a periodic inventory system. At the end of the annual accounting period, December 31, 19B, the accounting records provided the following information for Product 2:

Transactions	Units	Unit cost
1. Inventory, December 31, 19A	2,000	$20
For the year 19B:		
2. Purchase, April 11	2,000	22
3. Sale, May 1 (@ $55 each)	3,000	
4. Purchase, June 1	6,000	24
5. Sale, July 3 (@ $55 each)	4,000	
6. Operating expenses (excluding income tax expense), $150,000.		

Required:

a. Prepare a separate income statement through pretax income that details cost of goods sold for:

Case A—annual weighted average.

Case B—FIFO.

Case C—LIFO.

Case D—specific identification assuming two thirds of the first sale was selected from the beginning inventory and one third was selected from the items purchased on April 11, 19B. The second sale was selected from the purchase of June 1, 19B.

For each case, show the computation of the ending inventory. (Hint: Set up adjacent columns for each case.)

b. For each case, compare the pretax income and the ending inventory amounts. Explain the similarities and differences.

E7–5   (Comparison of LIFO and FIFO)
Use the data given in Exercise 7–3 for this exercise (assume cash transactions and a periodic inventory system).

Required:

a. Compute (1) goods available for sale, (2) cost of goods sold, and (3) ending inventory for Case A—FIFO and Case B—LIFO.

b. In parallel columns, give the journal entries for each purchase and sale transaction, assuming a periodic inventory system is used for each case. Set up captions as follows:

	FIFO		LIFO	
Accounts	Debit	Credit	Debit	Credit

c. Prepare an income statement through gross margin and explain why the FIFO and LIFO ending inventory, cost of goods sold, and gross margin amounts are different.

d. Which inventory costing method may be preferred for income tax purposes? Explain.

E7–6   (Comparison of Cash Flow and Income Effects of LIFO and FIFO)
During January 19B, Merkur Company reported sales revenue of $400,000 for the one item stocked. The inventory for December 31, 19A, showed 7,500 units on hand with a cost of $165,000. During January 19B, two purchases of the item were made: the first was for 1,500 units at $24 per unit; and the second was for 7,600 units at $25 each. The periodic inventory count reflected 8,600 units remaining on hand on January 31, 19B. Total operating expense for the month was $84,900.

Required:

a. On the basis of the above information, complete the 19B summary income statements under FIFO and LIFO. Use a single list of side captions including computation of cost of goods sold. Set up three separate column headings as follows: Units, FIFO, and LIFO. Show your computations of the ending inventory.

b. Which method gives the higher pretax income? Why?

c. Which method gives the more favorable cash flow effects? By how much, assuming a 30% tax rate?

E7–7 **(Comparison of Alternative Inventory Methods Using the Periodic Inventory System)**

Janice Company uses a periodic inventory system. Data for 19B were: beginning merchandise inventory (December 31, 19A), 1,600 units @ $15; purchases, 6,000 units @ $18; expenses (excluding income taxes), $54,000; ending inventory per physical count at December 31, 19B, 1,500 units; sales price per unit, $40; and average income tax rate of 30%.

Required:

a. Prepare income statements under the FIFO, LIFO, and weighted-average costing methods. Use a format similar to the following:

		Inventory costing method		
Income statement	Units	FIFO	LIFO	Weighted average
Sales revenue	———	$ ——	$ ——	$ ——
Cost of goods sold:				
Beginning inventory	———	———	———	———
Purchases	———	———	———	———
Goods available for sale . . .	———	———	———	———
Ending inventory	———	———	———	———
Cost of goods sold	———	———	———	———
Gross margin	———	———	———	———
Expenses	———	———	———	———
Pretax income		———	———	———
Income tax expense		———	———	———
Net income		══	══	══

b. Comparing FIFO and LIFO, which method is preferable in terms of (1) net income and (2) cash flow? Explain.

c. What would be your answer to Requirement *(b)* assuming prices were falling? Explain.

E7–8 **(Analysis of Cash Flow Effects of Alternative Inventory Methods)**

Following is partial information for the income statement of White Company under three different inventory costing methods assuming a periodic inventory system:

	FIFO	LIFO	Weighted average
Unit sales price, $30.			
Cost of goods sold:			
Beginning inventory (480 units) . . .	$ 9,600	$ 9,600	$ 9,600
Purchases (520 units)	13,000	13,000	13,000
Goods available for sale			
Ending inventory (530 units) . . .			
Cost of goods sold			
Expenses, $1,200			

Required:

a. Compute cost of goods sold under the FIFO, LIFO, and weighted-average inventory costing methods.

b. Prepare an income statement through pretax income for each method.

c. Rank the three methods in order of favorable cash flow and explain the basis for your ranking.

Part B: Exercises 7–9 to 7–17

E7–9 **(Use of FIFO with a Perpetual Inventory System)**
Westport Company uses a perpetual inventory system and FIFO. The inventory records reflected the following for January 19B:

Transactions	Units	Unit cost
Beginning inventory, January 1	80	$1.00
Purchase, January 6	200	1.10
Sale, January 10 (at $2.75 per unit)	100	
Purchase, January 14	100	1.30
Sale, January 29 (at $3 per unit)	160	

Required:

a. Prepare the perpetual inventory record for January.

b. Give journal entries indicated by the above data for January (assume cash transactions).

c. Prepare a summary income statement for January through gross margin.

E7–10 **(Comparison of Periodic and Perpetual Inventory Systems Using LIFO)**
At the end of the accounting period, the inventory records of Gulfport Company reflected the following:

Transactions (in order of date)	Units	Unit cost
Beginning inventory	500	$10
1. Purchase No. 1	600	12
2. Sale No. 1 (@ $25 per unit)	(700)	
3. Purchase No. 2	800	13
4. Sale No. 2 (@ $25 per unit)	(500)	
Ending inventory	(700)	

Required:

a. Compute goods available for sale in units and dollars.

b. Compute the (1) ending inventory valuation and (2) cost of goods sold assuming a periodic inventory system under the LIFO inventory costing method.

c. For comparative purposes compute the (1) ending inventory valuation and (2) cost of goods sold assuming a perpetual inventory system under the LIFO inventory costing method. To do this, prepare a perpetual inventory record and cost each sale when made.

d. Compare the results of (b) and (c) and explain why the valuations of ending inventory and cost of goods sold are different as between the periodic and perpetual inventory systems.

E7–11   **(Analysis of the Moving Weighted-Average Cost Inventory Method)**
Use the data given in Exercise 7–3 for this exercise (assume cash transactions).

Required:
a. Prepare the perpetual inventory record for January on a moving weighted-average basis. Round to the nearest cent on unit costs and the nearest dollar on total cost.
b. Give the journal entry to record the purchase of January 9.
c. Give the journal entries to record the sale on January 11.
d. Prepare a summarized income statement through gross margin for January.
e. Explain why a moving weighted average rather than a weighted average for the period was used.
f. When the weighted-average cost method is used, would the ending inventory and cost of goods sold amounts usually be different between periodic and perpetual inventory systems? Explain why.

E7–12   **(Comparison of FIFO, Periodic and FIFO, Perpetual)**
Haven Company uses a perpetual inventory system and applies FIFO inventory costing. The data below were provided by the accounting records for 19B:

Transactions (in order of date)	Units	Unit cost	Total cost
Beginning inventory	125	$10	$1,250
1. Purchase No. 1	300	12	3,600
2. Sale No. 1 (@ $23 each)	(275)		
3. Purchase No. 2	400	13	5,200
4. Sale No. 2 (@ $23 each)	(200)		
Ending inventory	350		

Required:
a. Compute the valuation of (1) cost of goods sold and (2) ending inventory assuming a perpetual inventory system and application of the FIFO inventory costing method.
b. Give the journal entries to record transactions 1 and 2 assuming FIFO:

   Case A—perpetual inventory system.
   Case B—periodic inventory system.

   Use adjacent amount columns for each system and assume cash transactions.
c. Explain why the journal entries are different between the perpetual and periodic inventory systems.

E7–13   **(Accounting for Damaged Goods under a Perpetual Inventory System)**
Redd Company is preparing the annual financial statements at December 31, 19D. Two different types of tape recorders that were used as demonstrators remained on hand at year-end. These items will be sold as damaged (used) merchandise; therefore, they must

be removed from the ending inventory of new merchandise. The company uses a perpetual inventory system. These items will be included in the inventory of damaged goods. Data on the tape recorder models are:

	Model 2—206	Model 112A
Quantity damaged	1	2
Actual unit cost	$400	$300
Regular sales price	700	600
Estimated unit market value in present condition	380	300
Estimated unit cost to sell	80	50

Required:

a. Compute the valuation of each item that should be used for 19D inventory purposes. Show computations.

b. Give the required journal entry(s) to reflect the appropriate inventory valuations in the accounts.

E7–14   (Alternative Applications of LCM)

Mill Company is preparing the annual financial statements dated December 31, 19B. Ending inventory information about the five major items stocked for regular sale is:

	Ending inventory, 19B	
Item	Quantity on hand	Unit cost when acquired (FIFO)	Replacement cost (market) at year-end
---	---	---	---
A . . .	40	$20	$18
B . . .	100	45	45
C . . .	20	60	62
D . . .	40	40	40
E . . .	500	10	8

Required:

a. Compute the valuation that should be used for the 19B ending inventory using the LCM rule applied on an item-by-item basis. (Hint: Set up columns for Item, Quantity, Total cost, Total market, and LCM valuation).

b. Compute the valuation of ending inventory using the LCM rule applied to total cost and total market value of the inventory.

c. Which method (a) or (b) is preferable? Why?

E7–15   (Estimating Ending Inventory)

Young Company prepares annual financial statements each December 31. The company uses a periodic inventory system. This sytem requires an annual detailed inventory count on all items on the store shelves and items stored in a separate warehouse. However, the management also desires quarterly financial statements but will not take a physical inventory count four times during the year. Accordingly, they use the gross margin method to estimate the ending inventory for the first three quarters.

At the end of the first quarter, March 31, 19D, the accounting records provided the following information:

1. Beginning inventory, January 1, 19D . . . . $ 60,000

Data for the first quarter of 19D:
2. Sales revenue 425,000
3. Sales returns 5,000
4. Purchases 296,000
5. Transportation-in 4,000
6. Operating expenses (excluding income tax expense) 60,000
7. Estimated average income tax rate, 25%.
8. Estimated gross margin ratio, 30%.

Required:

Based on the above information, prepare a detailed income statement for the first quarter of 19D. Show all computations.

E7–16   (Estimating Inventory Based on Partial Records)

On November 2, 19C, a fire destroyed the inventory of College Book Store. The accounting records were not destroyed; therefore, they provided the following information:

	19A	19B	19C to date of fire
Sales revenue	$120,000	$142,000	$120,000
Cost of goods sold	73,200	85,200	?
Gross margin on sales	46,800	56,800	?
Expenses	34,800	42,800	35,000
Pretax income	$ 12,000	$ 14,000	?
Ending inventory	$ 20,000	$ 22,000	?
Purchases during year	70,000	87,200	75,000

Required:

a. Based on the data available, prepare an estimated income statement for 19C up to the date of the fire. Show details for the cost of goods sold. Disregard income taxes and show computations.

b. What amount of loss on the inventory should be submitted to the insurance company (a casualty loss insurance policy is in effect)? Write a brief statement in support of the amount of indemnity claimed.

E7–17   (Analysis of the Impact of an Inventory Error)

Houston Corporation prepared the two income statements that follow (simplified for illustrative purposes):

	First quarter 19B		Second quarter 19B	
Sales revenue		$11,000		$13,000
Cost of goods sold:				
Beginning inventory	$ 2,000		$ 3,000	
Purchases	9,000		10,000	
Goods available for sale	11,000		13,000	
Ending inventory	3,000		4,000	
Cost of goods sold		8,000		9,000
Gross margin		3,000		4,000
Expenses		1,000		1,000
Pretax income		$ 2,000		$ 3,000

During the third quarter it was discovered that the ending inventory for the first quarter should have been $3,200.

Required:

a. What effect did this error have on the combined pretax income of the two quarters? Explain.

b. Did this error affect the EPS amounts for each quarter? Explain.

c. Prepare corrected income statements for each quarter.

d. Set up a schedule that reflects the comparative effects of the correct and incorrect amounts.

PROBLEMS

Part A: Problems 7–1 to 7–6

P7–1   **(Analysis of Possible Inventory Errors)**

Archie Company has just completed a physical inventory count at year-end, December 31, 19B. Only the items on the shelves, in storage, and in the receiving area were counted and costed on a FIFO basis. The inventory amounted to $80,000. During the audit, the independent CPA developed the following additional information:

a. Goods costing $400 were being used by a customer on a trial basis and were excluded from the inventory count at December 31, 19B.

b. Goods in transit on December 31, 19B, from a supplier, with terms FOB destination, cost, $700. Because these goods had not arrived, they were excluded from the physical inventory count.

c. On December 31, 19B, goods in transit to customers, with terms FOB shipping point, amounted to $900 (expected delivery date January 10, 19C). Because the goods had been shipped, they were excluded from the physical inventory count.

d. On December 28, 19B, a customer purchased goods for cash amounting to $1,500 and left them "for pickup on January 3, 19C." Archie Company had paid $800 for the goods and, because they were on hand, included the latter amount in the physical inventory count.

e. On the date of the inventory, the company received notice from a supplier that goods ordered earlier, at a cost of $2,400, had been delivered to the transportation company on December 27, 19B; the terms were FOB shipping point. Because the shipment had not arrived by December 31, 19B, it was excluded from the physical inventory.

f. On December 31, 19B, the company shipped $750 worth of goods to a customer, FOB destination. The goods are expected to arrive at their destination no earlier than January 8, 19C. Because the goods were not on hand, they were not included in the physical inventory count.

g. One of the items sold by the company has such a low volume that the management planned to drop it last year. To induce Archie Company to continue carrying the item, the manufacturer-supplier provided the item on a consignment basis. At the end of each month, Archie Company (the consignee) renders a report to the manufacturer on the number sold and remits cash for the cost. At the end of December 19B, Archie Company had four of these items on hand; therefore, they were included in the physical inventory count at $2,000 each.

Required:

Begin with the $80,000 inventory amount and compute the correct amount for the ending inventory. Explain the basis for your treatment of each of the above items. (Hint: Set up three columns: Item, Amount, and Explanation.)

P7–2   **(Use of Four Alternative Inventory Methods with the Periodic System)**
Glowlite Company uses a periodic inventory system. At the end of the annual accounting period, December 31, 19E, the accounting records for the most popular item in inventory showed:

Transactions	Units	Unit cost
Beginning inventory, January 1, 19E	300	$20
Transactions during 19E:		
1. Purchase, February 20	500	22
2. Sale, April 1 (@ $40 each)	(600)	
3. Purchase, June 30	400	25
4. Sale, August 1 (@ $40 each)	(200)	
5. Sales return, August 5 (related to transaction 4)	10	

Required:

Compute the amount of (1) goods available for sale, (2) ending inventory, and (3) cost of goods sold at December 31, 19E, under each of the following inventory costing methods (show computations and round to the nearest dollar):

a. Weighted-average cost.

b. First-in, first-out.

c. Last-in, first-out.

d. Specific identification, assuming the April 1, 19E, sale was selected one third from the beginning inventory and two thirds from the purchase of February 20, 19E. Assume the sale of August 1, 19E, was selected from the purchase of June 30, 19E.

P7–3   **(Analysis and Use of Alternative Inventory Methods)**
At the end of January 19B, the records at Detroit Company showed the following for a particular item that sold at $25 per unit:

Transactions	Units	Amount
Inventory, January 1, 19B	700	$4,200
Sale, January 10	(600)	
Purchase, January 12	600	4,200
Sale, January 17	(550)	
Purchase, January 26	310	2,790
Purchase return, January 28	(10)	Out of Jan. 26 purchase

Required:

a. Assuming a periodic inventory system, prepare a summarized income statement through gross margin on sales under each method of inventory: (1) weighted-average cost, (2) FIFO, (3) LIFO, and (4) specific identification. For specific identification, assume the first sale was out of the beginning inventory and the second sale was out of the January 12 purchase. Show the inventory computations in detail.

b. Between FIFO and LIFO, which method will derive the higher pretax income? Which would derive the higher EPS?

c. Between FIFO and LIFO, which method will derive the lower income tax expense? Explain, assuming a 30% average tax rate.

d. Between FIFO and LIFO, which method will produce the more favorable cash flow? Explain.

P7–4   (Manipulation of Income under the LIFO Inventory Method)
Overseas Company sells large computers that it acquires from a foreign source. During the year 19W, the inventory records reflected the following:

	Units	Unit cost	Total cost
Beginning inventory	20	$25,000	$500,000
Purchases	30	20,000	600,000
Sales (35 units @ $50,000) . . .			

The company uses the LIFO inventory costing method. On December 28, 19W, the unit cost of the computer was decreased to $18,000. The cost will be decreased again during the first quarter of the next year.

Required:

a. Complete the following income statement summary using the LIFO method and the periodic inventory system (show computations):

```
Sales revenue . . . . . . . . . $ _____
Cost of goods sold . . . . . . .   _____
Gross margin . . . . . . . . . .   _____
Expenses  . . . . . . . . . . .   400,000
Pretax income . . . . . . . . . $ _____
Ending inventory . . . . . . . $ _____
```

b. The management, for various reasons, is considering buying 20 additional units before December 31, 19W, at $18,000 each. Restate the above income statement (and ending inventory) assuming this purchase is made on December 31, 19W.

c. How much did pretax income change because of the decision on December 31, 19W? Is there any evidence of income manipulation? Explain.

P7–5   (Change in Inventory Method from FIFO to LIFO)
Northland Corporation reported the following summarized annual data at the end of 19X:

	(millions)
Sales revenue	$950
Cost of goods sold*	500
Gross margin	450
Expenses	240
Pretax income	$210

* Based on ending FIFO inventory of $140 million. On a LIFO basis this ending inventory would have been $80 million.

Before issuing the preceding statement, the company decided to change from FIFO to LIFO for 19X because "it better reflects our operating results." The company has always used FIFO.

Required:

a. Restate the summary income statement on a LIFO basis.

b. How much did pretax income change due to the LIFO decision for 19X? What caused the change in pretax income?

c. If you were a stockholder, what would be your reaction to this change? Explain.

P7-6 **(Comparison of LIFO and FIFO when Costs Are Rising and Falling)**
Income to be evaluated under four different situations as follows:

Prices are rising:

Situation A—FIFO is used.

Situation B—LIFO is used.

Prices are falling:

Situation C—FIFO is used.

Situation D—LIFO is used.

The basic data common to all four situations are sales, 600 units for $6,000; beginning inventory, 500 units; purchases, 500 units; ending inventory, 400 units; and operating expenses, $3,000. The following tabulated income statements for each situation have been set up for analytical purposes:

	Prices rising		Prices falling	
	Situation A FIFO	Situation B LIFO	Situation C FIFO	Situation D LIFO
Sales revenue	$6,000	$6,000	$6,000	$6,000
Cost of goods sold:				
Beginning inventory	1,000	?	?	?
Purchases	1,500	?	?	?
Goods available for sale	2,500	?	?	?
Ending inventory	1,200	?	?	?
Cost of goods sold	1,300	?	?	?
Gross margin	4,700	?	?	?
Expenses	3,000	3,000	3,000	3,000
Pretax income	1,700	?	?	?
Income tax expense (30%)	510	?	?	?
Net income	$1,190			

Required:

a. Complete the above tabulation for each situation. In Situations A and B (prices rising), assume the following: beginning inventory, 500 units @ $2 = $1,000; and purchases, 500 units @ $3 = $1,500. In Situations C and D (prices falling), assume the opposite; that is, beginning inventory, 500 units @ $3 = $1,500; and purchases, 500 units @ $2 = $1,000. Use periodic inventory procedures.

b. Analyze the relative effects on pretax income and on net income as demonstrated by Requirement (*a*) when prices are rising and when prices are falling.

c. Analyze the relative effects on the cash position for each situation.

d. Would you recommend FIFO or LIFO? Explain.

Part B: Problems 7–7 to 7–15

P7–7 (Analysis of Inventory Errors)

The income statements for four consecutive years for Slade Company reflected the following summarized amounts:

	19A	19B	19C	19D
Sales revenue	$60,000	$60,000	$78,000	$65,000
Cost of goods sold	36,000	38,300	50,100	39,000
Gross margin	24,000	21,700	27,900	26,000
Expenses	15,000	16,700	17,200	15,800
Pretax income	$ 9,000	$ 5,000	$10,700	$10,200

Subsequent to development of the above amounts, it has been determined that the physical inventory taken on December 31, 19B, was understated by $4,000.

Required:

a. Recast the above income statements to reflect the correct amounts, taking into consideration the inventory error.

b. Compute the gross margin ratio for each year (1) before the correction and (2) after the correction. Do the results lend confidence to your corrected amounts? Explain.

c. What effect would the error have had on the income tax expense assuming a 30% average rate?

P7–8 (Analysis of the Effects of Damaged Goods in Inventory)

Carolina Company has completed taking the periodic inventory count of merchandise remaining on hand at the end of the fiscal year, December 31, 19D. Questions have arisen concerning inventory costing for five different items. The inventory reflected the following:

	Units	Original unit cost
Item A—The two units on hand are damaged because they were used as demonstrators. The company estimated that they will be sold at 25% below cost and that disposal costs will amount to $60 each.	2	$260
Item B—Because of a drop in the market, this item can be replaced from the original supplier at 10% below the original cost. The sale price also was reduced.	20	70

	Units	Original unit cost
Item C—Because of style change, it is highly doubtful that the four units can be sold; they have no scrap value.	4	80
Item D—This item no longer will be stocked; as a consequence it will be marked down from the regular sale price of $110 to $50. Cost of selling is estimated to be 20% of the original cost.	3	80
Item E—Because of high demand and quality, the cost of this item has been raised from $120 to $150; hence, all replacements for inventory in the foreseeable future will be at the latter price.	15	120

The remaining items in inventory pose no valuation problems: their costs sum to $40,000.

Required:

Compute the total amount of the ending inventory including the damaged goods. List each of the above items separately and explain the basis for your decision with respect to each item.

P7–9 **(Comparison of LIFO and FIFO Using a Perpetual Inventory System)**

Baylor Hardware Store uses a perpetual inventory system. This problem will focus on one item stocked, designated as Item A. The beginning inventory was 2,000 units @ $4. During January, the following transactions occurred that affected Item A:

Jan 5 Sold 500 units at $15 per unit.
    10 Purchased 1,000 units at $5 per unit.
    16 Sold 1,800 units at $15 per unit.
    18 Purchased 2,300 units for $13,800.
    24 Sold 500 units at $15 per unit.

Required (assume cash transactions):

a. Prepare a perpetual inventory record for January on (1) a FIFO basis and (2) a LIFO basis.

b. Give the journal entry for each basis for the purchase on January 10.

c. Give the journal entries for each basis for the sale on January 16.

d. Complete the following financial statement amounts for each basis:

	January	
	FIFO	LIFO
Income statement:		
Sales revenue . . . . $	?	$?
Cost of goods sold	?	?
Gross margin	?	?
Expenses	15,000	15,000
Pretax income	?	?
Balance sheet:		
Current assets:		
Merchandise inventory	?	?

e. Which method gives the higher pretax income? Under what conditions would this comparative effect be the opposite?

    f. Assuming a 30% average tax rate, which method would provide the more favorable cash position? By how much? Explain.

    g. Which basis would you recommend for the company? Why?

P7–10   (Use of a Perpetual Inventory Record)

Ellsworth Company uses a perpetual inventory system. Below is a perpetual inventory record for the period for one product sold at $6 per unit.

PERPETUAL INVENTORY RECORD

Date									
a.							400		1,200
b.	800	3.30				1,200			
c.				500		1,600	700		2,240
d.	300		1,050						3,290
e.				200			800		2,632
f.				600		1,974	200		
g.	500	3.60							

Required:

1. Complete the column captions for the perpetual inventory record.
2. What inventory costing method is being used?
3. Enter all of the missing amounts on the perpetual inventory records.
4. Complete the following tabulation:

	Units	Per unit	Amount
a. Beginning inventory	_____	_____	_____
b. Ending inventory	_____	_____	_____
c. Total purchases	_____	_____	_____
d. Total cost of goods sold	_____	_____	_____

5. Give the journal entry(s) for date (*b*).
6. Give the journal entry(s) for date (*c*).
7. Assume a periodic inventory taken at the end of the period reflected 680 units on hand. Give any journal entry(s) required.
8. Disregard Requirement 7 and assume that on date (*h*), 10 units of the beginning inventory were returned to the supplier and a cash refund of $2 per unit was recovered. Give the required entry.

P7–11   (Comparison of FIFO and LIFO Using a Perpetual Inventory System)

Delta Company executives are considering their inventory policies. They have been using the moving weighted-average method with a perpetual inventory system. They have requested an "analysis of the effects of using FIFO versus LIFO." Selected financial statement amounts (rounded) for the month of January 19B, based on the moving weighted-average method, are as follows:

	Units	Amounts
Income statement:		
Sales revenue	180	$10,800
Cost of goods sold	180	5,710
Gross margin on sales		5,090
Less: Expenses		1,500
Pretax income		$ 3,590
Balance sheet:		
Merchandise inventory . . .		$ 2,620

Transactions during the month were:

Beginning inventory 50 units @ $30.

Jan.   6   Sold 40 units @ $60.
       9   Purchased 100 units @ $32.
      16   Sold 80 units @ $60.
      20   Purchased 110 units @ $33.
      28   Sold 60 units @ $60.

Required:

a. Copy the above statement data and extend each item to the right by adding columns for FIFO and LIFO using a perpetual inventory system. This statement will provide one basis for analyzing the different results among the three inventory costing methods.

b. Which inventory costing method produces the highest pretax income? Explain.

c. Between FIFO and LIFO, which inventory costing method provides the more favorable cash position for 19B? Explain.

P7–12   (Use of LCM under the Periodic Inventory System)
Sharp Company prepared their annual financial statements dated December 31, 19B. The company uses a periodic inventory system and applies the FIFO inventory costing method; however, the company neglected to apply LCM to the ending inventory. The preliminary 19B income statement is summarized below:

Sales revenue		$310,000
Cost of goods sold:		
Beginning inventory	$ 40,000	
Purchases	206,000	
Goods available for sale	246,000	
Ending inventory (FIFO cost)	53,000	
Cost of goods sold		193,000
Gross margin		117,000
Operating expenses		52,000
Pretax income		65,000
Income tax expense (30%)		19,500
Net income		$ 45,500

Assume you have been asked to restate the 19B financial statements to incorporate LCM. You have developed the following data relating to the 19B ending inventory:

Item	Quantity	Acquisition cost Unit	Acquisition cost Total	Current replacement unit cost (market)
A	2,000	$ 2	$ 4,000	$ 4
B	3,000	6	18,000	5
C	4,000	4	16,000	5
D	1,000	15	15,000	12
			$53,000	

Required:

a. Restate the above income statement to reflect LCM valuation of the 19B ending inventory. Apply LCM on an item-by-item basis and show computations.

b. Compare and explain the LCM effect on each amount that was changed in (*a*).

c. What is the conceptual basis for applying LCM to merchandise inventories?

d. Thought question: What effect did LCM have on the cash flow of 19B? What will be the long-term effect on cash flow?

P7–13   **(Estimating the Amount of Inventory Damaged in a Flood for Insurance Purposes)**
On April 15, 19B, Import Company suffered a major flood that damaged their entire merchandise inventory. Fortunately, the company carried a casualty insurance policy that covered floods. The company uses the periodic inventory system. The accounting records were not damaged; therefore, they provided the following information for the period January 1 through April 14, 19B:

Merchandise inventory,
   December 31, 19A . . . . $ 21,000
Transactions through April 14, 19B:
   Purchases   70,000
   Purchase returns   2,000
   Transportation-in   1,000
   Sales 103,000
   Sales returns   3,000

Required:
For insurance indemnity purposes you have been asked to estimate the amount of the inventory loss. Your analysis to date indicates that (*a*) a 40% gross margin rate is reasonable and (*b*) the damaged merchandise can be sold to a local salvage company for approximately $6,000 cash.

What amount should be presented to the insurance company as a claim for insurance indemnity? Show computations.

P7–14   **(Preparing an Interim Income Statement Without Taking an Inventory Count)**
The president of Sydney Company has been presented with the March 19B financial statements. They reflect data for three months as summarized below:

Income statements

	January	February	March	Quarter
Sales revenue	$100,000	$106,000	$90,000	$296,000
Cost of goods sold	61,000	59,360	?	?
Gross margin on sales	39,000	46,640	?	?
Expenses	32,000	33,500	32,000	97,500
Pretax income	$ 7,000	$ 13,140	$?	$?
Gross margin ratio	0.39	0.44	0.42 (estimated)	
Ending inventory	$ 14,000	$ 16,000		

The company uses a periodic inventory system. Although monthly statements are prepared, a monthly inventory count is not made. Instead, the company uses the gross margin method for monthly inventory purposes.

Required:

a. Complete computations in the following tabulation to estimate the results for March:

	Amounts	Computations
Cost of goods sold:		
Beginning inventory	$20,000	From records
Purchases	51,000	From records
Goods available for sale	?	?
Ending inventory	?	?
Cost of goods sold	?	

b. Complete the income statements given above (March and Quarter). Disregard income tax.

c. What level of confidence do you think can be attributed to the results for March? Explain.

d. Would you recommend continued use of the gross margin method for the company? Explain.

P7–15   **(Analysis and Correction of an Error in Ending Inventory)**
The income statement for Forest Company summarized for a four-year period shows the following:

	19A	19B	19C	19D
Sales revenue	$1,000,000	$1,200,000	$1,300,000	$1,500,000
Cost of goods sold	600,000	610,000	870,000	975,000
Gross margin	400,000	590,000	430,000	525,000
Expenses	300,000	328,000	362,000	360,000
Pretax income	100,000	262,000	68,000	165,000
Income tax expense (30%)	30,000	78,600	20,400	49,500
Net income	$ 70,000	$ 183,400	$ 47,600	$ 115,500

An audit revealed that in determining the above amounts, the ending inventory for 19B was overstated by $30,000. The company uses a periodic inventory system.

Required:

a. Recast the above income statements on a correct basis.

b. Did the error affect cumulative net income for the four-year period? Explain.

c. Did the error affect cash inflows or outflows? Explain.

CASES

C7–1   (Analysis of the Effects of a Reduction in the Amount of LIFO Inventory)

An annual report of Standard Oil Company (Indiana) contained the following footnote:

> During this year and last year, the company reduced certain inventory quantities that were valued at lower LIFO costs prevailing in prior years. The effect of these reductions was to increase aftertax earnings this year by $71 million, or $0.24 per share, and $74 million, or a $0.25 per share last year.

Required:

a. Explain why the reduction in inventory quantity increased aftertax earnings (net income) for Standard Oil.

b. If Standard Oil had used FIFO, would the reductions in inventory quantity during the two years have increased aftertax earnings? Explain.

C7–2   (Analysis of the Effect of an Inventory Error Disclosed in an Actual Note to a Financial Statement)

Several years ago, the financial statements of Lafayette Radio Electronics Corporation contained the following footnote:

> Subsequent to the issuance of its financial statements, the company discovered a computational error in the amount of $1,046,000 in the calculation of its year-end inventory which resulted in an overstatement of ending inventory.

> Assume that Lafayette reported an incorrect net income amount of $3,101,000 for the year in which the error occurred and that the income tax rate is 40%.

Required:

a. Compute the amount of net income that Lafayette should report after correcting the inventory error. Show computations.

b. Assume that the inventory error had not been discovered. Identify the financial statement accounts that would have been incorrect for the year the error occurred and for the subsequent year. State whether each account was understated or overstated.

C7–3   (Analysis of LIFO and FIFO Based on an Actual Note to the Financial Statements)

An annual report for General Motors Corporation included the following footnote:

> Inventories are stated generally at cost, which is not in excess of market. The cost of substantially all domestic inventories was determined by the last-in, first-out (LIFO) method. If the first-in, first-out (FIFO) method of inventory valuation had

been used by the Corporation for U.S. inventories, it is estimated that they would be $2,077.1 million higher at the end of this year, compared with $1,784.5 million higher at the end of last year.

For the year, GM reported net income (after taxes) of $320.5 million. At year-end, the balance of the GM retained earnings account was $15,340 million.

Required:

a. Determine the amount of net income that GM would have reported for the year if the FIFO method had been used (assume a 30% tax rate).

b. Determine the amount of retained earnings that GM would have reported at year-end if the FIFO method had always been used (assume a 30% tax rate).

c. Use of the LIFO method reduced the amount of taxes that GM had to pay for the year compared with the amount that would have been paid if FIFO had been used. Calculate the amount of this reduction (assume a 30% tax rate).

C7-4

JCPenney

(Analysis of Inventory and Cost of Goods Sold for an Actual Company) Refer to the financial statements of J.C. Penney Company, Inc. given in the appendix immediately preceding the index.

1. What method does the company use to determine the cost of its inventory?

2. Determine the amount of inventory for the current year, assuming the company used FIFO.

3. Determine the cost of goods sold for the first quarter of 1988. (Hint: Use the gross margin percent to calculate cost of goods sold.)

4. Why did the gross margin improve in 1988?

EIGHT

CASH, SHORT-TERM INVESTMENTS IN SECURITIES, AND RECEIVABLES

PURPOSE

The discussions in the two preceding chapters have focused primarily on the income statement. In this chapter, the focus will shift to the balance sheet. Our discussion of balance sheet classifications will begin with the most liquid (or current) assets: cash, short-term investments, and receivables. In the previous chapter, we discussed accounting for another important current asset, inventories.

Because of the importance of accounts receivable and the related bad debt expense, many financial statements contain supplemental notes similar to the one on the opposite page.

LEARNING OBJECTIVES

1. Identify internal control procedures for cash.
2. Perform a bank reconciliation.
3. Apply the lower-of-cost-or-market (LCM) rule to short-term investments.
4. Calculate interest on receivables.
5. Account for a discounted note receivable.
6. Compare different types of receivables.
7. Expand your accounting vocabulary by learning the "Important Terms Defined in this Chapter."
8. Apply the knowledge learned from this chapter by completing the homework assigned by your instructor.

ORGANIZATION

Part A—safeguarding and reporting cash
1. Internal control of cash.
2. Bank reconciliation.

Part B—measuring and reporting short-term investments
1. Definition of short-term investments.
2. Lower-of-cost-or-market (LCM) rule.

Part C—measuring and reporting receivables
1. Classification of receivables.
2. Interest on receivables.

Sears

Notes to Consolidated Financial Statements

Credit operations in the United States continued to be a significant contributor to the Group's results.

$ millions	1987	1986	1985
Customer receivable balances at Dec. 31	$13,227.1	11,714.3	11,539.3
Balances sold at Dec. 31	831.5	2,247.3	2,361.5
Average account balance (dollars)	515	497	495
Finance charge revenues	2,010.8	2,068.5	2,097.8
Credit sales as percentage of gross sales	58.6%	60.6	62.0
Yield on receivables	17.4%	17.6	17.7
Provision for uncollectible accounts	291.3	349.8	224.2
Ratio to credit sales	1.75%	2.08	1.35
Ratio of net charged-off accounts to credit sales	1.69%	1.62	1.24
Percentage of accounts delinquent three or more months to total	1.02%	1.26	1.18
Interest expense	776.5	819.0	872.8
Credit income	263.1	253.2	293.5
Ratio to credit sales	1.6%	1.5	1.8

Finance charge revenues decreased 2.8 and 1.4 percent in 1987 and 1986, respectively. The decline in both years was primarily due to lower average receivable balances owned.

The provision for uncollectible accounts decreased 16.7 percent in 1987 because of an improvement in delinquencies. This reversed the trend from 1986 when greater numbers of delinquencies required a 56.0 percent increase in the provision in 1986. Lower effective interest rates and a decrease in the debt necessary to finance the receivable balances reduced interest expense by 5.2 percent. The same trend produced a decrease of 6.2 percent in 1986. The effective income tax rate decreased to 43.2 percent in 1987 from 49.6 percent the prior year due to the reduction in federal income tax rates under the Tax Reform Act of 1986. Receivables were not sold in 1987, while in 1986 and 1985 the after-tax gains on the sale of receivables were $38.8 and $33.3 million, respectively.

Credit income increased 3.9 percent for 1987 principally because of the decreases in the provision for uncollectible accounts, interest expense and income tax expense. The decline of 13.7 percent in Credit net income for 1986 was attributable to the substantial increase in the provision for uncollectible accounts and a slight drop in finance charge revenues, partially offset by lower interest expense.

PART A—SAFEGUARDING AND REPORTING CASH

Cash Defined

Cash is defined as money and any instrument that banks will accept for deposit and immediate credit to the depositor's account, such as a check, money order, or bank draft. Cash **excludes** such items as notes receivable, IOUs, and postage stamps (a prepaid expense). Cash usually is divided into three categories: cash on hand, cash deposited in banks, and other instruments that meet the definition of cash. All cash accounts are combined as one amount for financial reporting purposes, even though a company may have several bank accounts.

Many businesses receive a large amount of cash from their customers each day. Cash can be spent by anyone, so management must develop procedures to safeguard the cash that is used in the business. Effective cash management involves more than protecting cash from theft, fraud, or loss through carelessness. Other cash management responsibilities are:

1. Accurate accounting so that relevant reports of cash inflows, outflows, and balances may be prepared periodically.
2. Control to assure that enough cash is on hand to meet (*a*) current operating needs, (*b*) maturing liabilities, and (*c*) unexpected emergencies.
3. Planning to prevent excess amounts of idle cash from accumulating. Idle cash produces no revenue; therefore, it often is invested in securities to get a return (i.e., revenue) pending future need for the cash.

Internal Control of Cash

Internal control refers to policies and procedures that are designed to properly account for and safeguard all of the **assets** of the enterprise. Internal control procedures should extend to all assets—cash, receivables, investments, operational assets, and so on.

Because cash is the asset most vulnerable to theft and fraud, a significant number of internal control procedures should focus on cash. You have already observed internal control procedures for cash, although you may not have known it at the time. At most movie theaters, one employee sells tickets and another employee collects the tickets. It would be less expensive to have one employee do both jobs, but it would be easier for an employee to steal cash.

Effective internal control of cash should include:

Separation of duties:

1. Complete separation of the jobs of receiving cash and disbursing cash.
2. Complete separation of the **procedures** of accounting for cash receipts and cash disbursements.

3. Complete separation of the **physical** handling of cash and all phases of the **accounting** function.

Responsibilities assigned to individuals:

4. Require that all cash receipts be deposited in a bank daily. Keep any cash held on hand (for making change) under strict control.
5. Require that all cash payments be made by prenumbered checks with a separate approval of the expenditures and separate approval of the checks in payment.
6. Assign the cash payment approval and check signing responsibilities to different individuals.

The separation of individual responsibilities and the use of prescribed policies and procedures are important phases in the control of cash. Separation of duties deters theft because collusion would be needed among two or more persons to steal cash and then conceal the theft in the accounting records. Prescribed procedures are designed so that the work done by one individual is checked by the results reported by other individuals.

To show how easy it is to hide cash theft when internal control is lacking, two examples are provided:

Case 1—an employee handles both cash receipts and the recordkeeping. Cash amounting to $100 was collected from J. Moss in payment of an account receivable. An employee pocketed the cash and wrote off the account by making an entry for $100 crediting Accounts Receivable (J. Moss) and debiting Allowance for Doubtful Accounts.

Case 2—occasionally an employee with cash payment authority would send a fictitious purchase invoice through the system. The check, payable to a fictitious person, was not mailed but was cashed by the employee.

In each case, the accounting records did not reveal the theft. Also, the financial statements did not provide any evidence that theft had occurred. The thefts could have been prevented with simple internal control procedures.

All cash disbursements should be made with prenumbered checks. Cash payments should involve separate responsibilities for (1) payment approvals, (2) check preparation, and (3) check signing. When procedures similar to these are followed, it is difficult to conceal a fraudulent cash disbursement without the collusion of two or more persons. The level of internal control, which is reviewed by the outside independent auditor, increases the reliability of the financial statements of the business.

Cash Accounts in the Ledger

The amount of cash reported on a balance sheet is the **total amount** of cash at the end of the last day of the accounting period. The total amount of cash reported on the balance sheet includes:

1. Cash on deposit in all checking accounts subject to current checking privileges (offset by any overdrafts).[1]
2. Cash on hand (not yet taken to a bank for deposit).
3. All petty cash funds.

A company will have a separate account in the **ledger** for each bank account.[2] Often companies keep a small amount of **cash on hand.** Such amounts may be included in the balance of the **regular Cash account** or kept in a separate account. In either case, this amount will be included in the total cash balance reported on the balance sheet. Cash on hand includes: (*a*) amounts of cash received since the last deposit was made and (*b*) a stable amount of cash needed for making change to start the next day.

Often, a **petty cash system** is kept to make **small cash payments** (not to make change) in lieu of writing a separate check for each such item. This system necessitates the use of another separate cash account, usually called Petty Cash (discussed later).

Cash Over and Short

Errors in handling cash inevitably occur. These errors cause cash shortages or cash overages when the cash is counted and compared with the cash records for the day. Cash overages and shortages must be recorded in the accounts. If the count of cash from sales amounted to $1,347 but the cash register tapes for sales totaled $1,357, a **cash shortage** of $10 is indicated. The sales for the day should be recorded as follows:

```
Cash . . . . . . . . . . . . . . . . . . . . . . . . . . . . . . . . . . 1,347.00
Cash over and short . . . . . . . . . . . . . . . . . . . . . . . .     10.00
  Sales  . . . . . . . . . . . . . . . . . . . . . . . . . . . . . . . .            1,357.00
    To record cash sales and cash shortage.
```

In the case of a **cash overage,** the Cash Over and Short account is credited. Sales revenue should be recorded for the correct amount shown on the register tapes regardless of any cash overage or shortage. At the end of the period, a debit balance in the Cash Over and Short account usually is reported as miscellaneous expense. If a credit balance exists, it is reported as miscellaneous revenue.

Both cash overages and cash shortages, if significant in amount, should be investigated by management to determine the cause of the error.

---

[1] Adjusted for deposits in transit and outstanding checks (discussed later).

[2] Larger companies often carry one Cash control account in the ledger, which is supplemented with a series of separate cash subsidiary accounts for the depository banks. Refer to Chapter Supplement 6A.

Petty Cash

Disbursements of cash should be made by **prenumbered checks.** However, many businesses find it inconvenient and expensive to write checks for small payments for items such as taxi fares, newspapers, and small amounts of supplies. To avoid this inconvenience and expense, businesses often set up a **petty cash fund** to handle small miscellaneous cash payments.

To set up a petty cash fund, a check should be drawn "Pay to the order of Petty Cash" for the amount needed in the fund and cashed. Small cash payments, supported by written receipts, are made from this fund, and no journal entry is made at the time of payment. When the petty cash fund gets low and at the end of each accounting period, the expenditures from the fund are summarized and a journal entry is made to reflect the payments from the fund (debits to expenses) and to record the check written to reimburse the fund for the total amount spent (credit to Cash). For balance sheet reporting, the amount in the Petty Cash account must be added to the other cash balances. The details of accounting for a petty cash fund are discussed in Chapter Supplement 8A.

Bank Statements to Depositors

Proper use of the bank accounts of a business can be an important internal control procedure for cash. Each month, the bank provides the depositor with a **bank statement** that lists (1) each deposit recorded by the bank during the period, (2) each check cleared by the bank during the period, and (3) the balance of the depositor's account. The bank statement also shows the bank charges or deductions (such as service charges) made directly to the depositor's account by the bank. The bank statement may include copies of the deposit slips and all checks that cleared through the bank during the period covered by the statement. A typical bank statement (excluding the deposit slips and canceled checks) is shown in Exhibit 8–1.

Example of a Bank Statement

Exhibit 8–1 lists three items that need explanation. Notice that on June 20, listed under "Checks and Debits," there is a deduction for $18 coded with "NC."[3] A check for $18 was received from a customer, R. Roe, which then was deposited by J. Doe Company with its bank, the Texas Commerce Bank. The bank processed the check through banking channels to Roe's bank. Roe's account did not have sufficient funds to cover it; therefore, Roe's bank returned it to the Texas Commerce Bank which then charged it back to J. Doe Company. This type of check often is called an **NSF check** (not sufficient funds). The NSF check is now a

---

[3] These codes vary among banks.

Exhibit 8–1   Example of a bank statement

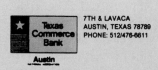

		7TH & LAVACA
Texas Commerce Bank		AUSTIN, TEXAS 78789
		PHONE: 512/476-6611

ACCOUNT NUMBER	STATEMENT DATE	PAGE NO.
877-95861	6-30-90	1

J. Doe Company
1000 Blank Road
Austin, Texas   78703

STATEMENT OF ACCOUNT

Please examine statement and checks promptly. If no error is reported within ten days, the account will be considered correct. Please report change of address.
For questions or problems
call TCB-Austin's Hotline · 476-6100

ON THIS DATE	YOUR BALANCE WAS	DEPOSITS ADDED		CHECKS AND DEBITS SUBTRACTED		SERVICE COST	RESULTING BALANCE
		NO.	AMOUNT	NO.	AMOUNT		
6-1-90	7 762 40	5	4 050 00	23	3 490 20	6 00	8 322 20

CHECKS AND DEBITS				DEPOSITS	DATE	DAILY BALANCE
					6-1-90	7 762 40
				3 000 00	6-2-90	10 762 40
500 00					6-4-90	10 262 40
55 00	5 00		40 00		6-5-90	10 162 40
100 00				500 00	6-8-90	10 562 40
8 20	16 50		160 00		6-10-90	10 377 70
2 150 00	10 00			*100 00CM	6-12-90	8 317 70
7 50	15 30				6-16-90	8 294 90
35 00	1 50			150 00	6-17-90	8 408 40
40 20	15 00		6 00		6-18-90	8 347 20
*18 00NC					6-20-90	8 329 20
125 50	80 00		2 00		6-21-90	8 121 70
18 90				300 00	6-24-90	8 402 80
7 52	19 60				6-27-90	8 375 68
15 00	32 48				6-28-90	8 328 20
*6 00SC					6-30-90	8 322 20

Code:
   CM-Credit Memo-Customer note collected
   NC-Not sufficient funds
   SC-Service charge

MEMBER F.D.I.C.   IMPORTANT: SEE REVERSE SIDE OF STATEMENT.

receivable; consequently, J. Doe Company must make an entry to debit Receivables (R. Roe) and credit Cash for the $18.

Notice the $6 listed on June 30 under "Checks and Debits" and coded "SC." This is the code for **bank service charges.** The bank statement included a memo by the bank explaining this service charge (which was not documented by a check). J. Doe Company must make an entry to reflect this $6 decrease in the bank balance as a debit to an appropriate expense account, such as Bank Service Expense, and a credit to Cash.

Notice the $100 listed on June 12 under "Deposits" and coded "CM" for "credit memo." The bank collected a note receivable owned by Doe and increased the depositor account of J. Doe Company. The bank service charge (SC) included the collection service cost. J. Doe Company must record the collection by making an entry to debit Cash and credit Note Receivable for the $100 (assume interest on the note had been recorded).

Bank Reconciliation

A **bank reconciliation** is the process of comparing (reconciling) the **ending** cash balance in the company's records and the **ending** cash balance reported by the bank on the monthly **bank statement.** A bank reconciliation should be completed for each separate checking account (i.e., for each bank statement received from each bank) at the end of each month.

Usually, the ending cash balance as shown on the bank statement does not agree with the ending cash balance shown by the related Cash ledger account on the books of the depositor. For example, the Cash ledger account at the end of June of J. Doe Company showed the following (Doe has only one checking account):

Cash

June 1	Balance	7,010.00	June	Checks written	3,800.00
June	Deposits	5,750.00			

(Ending balance, $8,960.00)

The $8,322.20 **ending cash balance** shown on the **bank statement** (Exhibit 8–1) is different from the $8,960.00 **ending book balance** of cash shown on the books of the J. Doe Company. This difference exists because (1) some transactions affecting cash were recorded in the books of depositor Doe but were not shown on the bank statement and (2) some transactions were shown on the bank statement but had not been recorded in the books of the depositor, Doe. The most common causes of differences between the ending bank balance and the ending book balance of cash are:

1. **Outstanding checks**—checks written by the depositor and recorded in the depositor's ledger as credits to the Cash account. These checks have not cleared the bank (they are not shown on the bank statement as a deduction from the bank balance). The outstanding checks are identified by comparing the canceled checks that the bank returned with the record of checks (such as the check stubs) maintained by the depositor.

2. **Deposits in transit**—deposits sent to the bank by the depositor and recorded in the depositor's ledger as debits to the Cash account. These deposits have not been recorded by the bank (they are not shown on the bank statement as an increase in the bank balance). Deposits in transit usually happen when deposits are made one or two days before the close of the period covered by the bank statement. Deposits in

transit are determined by comparing the deposits listed on the bank statement with the copies of the deposit slips retained by the depositor.

3. **Bank service charges**—an expense for bank services; listed on the bank statement. This expense must be recorded in the depositor's ledger by making a debit to an appropriate expense account, such as Bank Service Expense, and a credit to Cash.

4. **NSF checks**—a "bad check" that was deposited and must be deducted from the depositor's account. The depositor must make a journal entry to debit a receivable and credit Cash.

5. **Credit memo**—a note receivable collected by the bank for the depositor. It is recorded by making a debit to Cash and credits to Notes Receivable and Interest Revenue.

6. **Errors**—both the bank and the depositor may make errors, especially when the volume of cash transactions is large.

A **bank reconciliation** should be made by the depositor immediately after each bank statement is received. A bank reconciliation is an important element of internal control and is needed for accounting purposes. To encourage bank reconciliation by depositors, many banks provide a form on the back of the bank statement for this purpose. A typical form is shown in Exhibit 8–2.

Bank Reconciliation Illustrated

The bank reconciliation for the month of June prepared by J. Doe Company to reconcile the **ending bank balance** (Exhibit 8–1, $8,322.20) with the **ending book balance** ($8,960) is shown in Exhibit 8–3. On the completed reconciliation, Exhibit 8–3, the **correct** cash balance is $9,045. This balance is different from both the reported bank and book balances before the reconciliation.

The format of a bank reconciliation can vary. A simple and flexible one uses a balancing format with the "Depositor's Books" and the "Bank Statement" identified separately. This format starts with two different amounts: (1) the **ending balance per books** and (2) the **ending balance per bank statement.** Space is provided for additions to, and subtractions from, each balance so that the last line shows the same correct cash balance (for the bank and the books). This correct balance is the amount that should be shown in the Cash account **after the reconciliation.** In this example it is also the correct amount of cash that should be reported on the balance sheet (J. Doe Company has only one checking account and no cash on hand or petty cash system). J. Doe Company followed these steps in preparing the bank reconciliation:

1. **Identify the outstanding checks.** A comparison of the canceled checks returned by the bank with the records of the company of all checks drawn showed the following checks still outstanding (not cleared) at the end of June:

Exhibit 8–2 Sample form and instructions for a bank reconciliation

	CHEQUES OUTSTANDING	
	NO.	AMOUNT

THIS IS PROVIDED TO HELP YOU BALANCE
YOUR BANK STATEMENT

BANK BALANCE
SHOWN ON THIS STATEMENT $_____

ADD + (IF ANY)
DEPOSITS NOT SHOWN
ON THIS STATEMENT _____

TOTAL _____

SUBTRACT - (IF ANY)
CHEQUES OUTSTANDING _____

TOTAL

BALANCE $_____
SHOULD AGREE WITH YOUR CHEQUEBOOK BALANCE

THIS IS PROVIDED TO HELP YOU BALANCE
YOUR CHEQUEBOOK

CHEQUEBOOK BALANCE
$_____

SUBTRACT - (IF ANY)
ACTIVITY CHARGE _____

SUB-TOTAL _____

SUBTRACT - (IF ANY)
OTHER BANK CHARGES _____

BALANCE $_____
SHOULD AGREE WITH YOUR STATEMENT BALANCE.

IF YOUR ACCOUNT DOES NOT BALANCE
PLEASE CHECK THE FOLLOWING CAREFULLY

☐ HAVE YOUR CORRECTLY ENTERED THE AMOUNT OF
EACH CHEQUE ON YOUR CHEQUEBOOK STUB?

☐ ARE THE AMOUNTS OF YOUR DEPOSIT ENTERED ON
CHEQUEBOOK STUBS THE SAME AS IN YOUR STATE-
MENT?

☐ HAVE ALL CHEQUES BEEN DEDUCTED FROM YOUR
STUBS?

☐ HAVE YOU DEDUCTED ALL BANK CHARGES FROM YOUR
STUBS?

☐ HAVE YOU CARRIED THE CORRECT BALANCE FORWARD
FROM ONE CHEQUEBOOK STUB TO THE NEXT?

☐ HAVE YOU CHECKED ALL ADDITIONS AND SUBTRAC-
TIONS ON YOUR CHEQUEBOOK STUBS?

Exhibit 8–3 Bank reconciliation illustrated

J. DOE COMPANY
Bank Reconciliation
For the Month Ending June 30, 1990

Depositor's Books			Bank Statement		
Ending cash balance per books		$8,960.00	Ending cash balance per bank statement		$ 8,322.20
Additions:			Additions:		
Proceeds of customer note collected by bank		100.00	Deposit in transit		1,800.00
Error in recording check No. 137		9.00			
		9,069.00			10,122.20
Deductions:			Deductions:		
NSF check of R. Roe	$18.00		Outstanding checks		1,077.20
Bank service charges	6.00	24.00			
Ending correct cash balance		$9,045.00	Ending correct cash balance		$ 9,045.00

Check No.	Amount
101	$ 145.00
123	815.00
131	117.20
Total	$1,077.20

This total was entered on the reconciliation as a **deduction** from the bank account. These checks will be deducted by the bank when they clear the bank.

2. **Identify the deposits in transit.**   A comparison of the deposit slips on hand with those listed on the bank statement revealed that a deposit made on June 30 for $1,800 was not listed on the bank statement. This amount was entered on the reconciliation as an **addition** to the bank account. It will be added by the bank when the deposit is recorded by the bank.

3. **Record bank charges and credits:**
   a. Proceeds of note collected, $100—entered on the bank reconciliation as an **addition** to the book balance; it already has been included in the bank balance. A journal entry is needed to debit Cash and credit Note Receivable.
   b. NSF check of R. Roe, $18—entered on the bank reconciliation as a **deduction** from the book balance; it has been deducted from the bank statement balance. A journal entry is needed to credit Cash and to debit a receivable account.
   c. Bank service charges, $6—entered on the bank reconciliation as a **deduction** from the book balance; it has been deducted from the bank balance. A journal entry is needed to credit Cash and to debit an expense account.

4. **Determine the impact of errors.**   At this point, J. Doe Company found that the reconciliation did not balance by $9. Because this amount is divisible by 9, they suspected a transposition. (A transposition, such as writing 27 for 72, always will cause an error that is exactly divisible by 9.) Upon checking the journal entries made during the month, they found that a check was written for $56 to pay an account payable. The check was recorded in the company's accounts as $65. The incorrect entry made was a debit to Accounts Payable and a credit to Cash for $65 (instead of $56). Therefore, $9 (i.e., $65 − $56) must be **added** to the book cash balance on the reconciliation; the bank cleared the check for the correct amount, $56. The following correcting entry must be made in the accounts: Cash, debit $9; and Accounts Payable, credit $9.

Note in Exhibit 8–3 that the "Depositor's Books" and the "Bank Statement" parts of the bank reconciliation now agree at a **correct cash balance** of $9,045. This amount will be reported as cash on a balance sheet prepared at the end of the period. If the company had petty cash or cash on hand for making change, it would be added to the $9,045, and the total would be reported on the balance sheet.

A bank reconciliation as shown in Exhibit 8–3 accomplishes two major objectives:

1. Checks the accuracy of the bank balance and the company cash records, which involves development of the **correct cash balance.** The correct cash balance (plus petty cash and cash on hand, if any) is the amount of cash that is reported on the balance sheet.

2. Identifies any previously unrecorded transactions or changes that are necessary to cause the company's Cash account(s) to show the **correct cash balance.** These transactions or changes need journal entries. The explanations given above of the development of the bank reconciliation of J. Doe Company cite such transactions and changes. Therefore, the entries shown in Exhibit 8–4, taken directly from the "Depositor's

Exhibit 8–4 Entries from bank reconciliation (Exhibit 8–3)

Accounts of J. Doe Company:

a. Cash	100	
Note receivable		100
To record note collected by bank.		
b. Accounts receivable	18	
Cash		18
To record NSF check.		
c. Bank service expense	6	
Cash		6
To record service fees charged by bank.		
d. Cash	9	
Accounts payable (name)		9
To correct error made in recording a check payable to a creditor.		

Cash account of J. Doe Company:

The Cash account prior to reconciliation was given earlier in the chapter. After the above journal entries are posted, the Cash account is as follows:

Cash (after recording results of bank reconciliation)

June 1	Balance	7,010.00	June	Checks written	3,800.00
June	Deposits	5,750.00	June 30	NSF check*	18.00
June 30	Note collected*	100.00	June 30	Bank service charge*	6.00
June 30	Correcting entry*	9.00			

(Correct cash balance, $9,045.00)

* Based on the bank reconciliation.

Books" side of the bank reconciliation (Exhibit 8–3), must be entered into the company's records.

Notice that all of the additions and deductions on the "Depositor's Books" side of the reconciliation need journal entries to update the Cash account. The additions and deductions on the "Bank Statement" side do **not** need journal entries because they will work out automatically when they clear the bank. The cash amount reported on the balance sheet and reflected in the Cash account will be the **correct cash balance** only if the proper journal entries are made after the bank reconciliation is completed.

Compensating Balances

A **compensating balance** exists when the bank requires a business to keep a minimum amount in its bank account. A compensating balance may be required by the bank explicitly (by a loan agreement) or implicitly (by informal understanding) as part of a credit-granting arrangement. Information on compensating balances is important to statement users because of two major effects on the business: (1) a compensating balance requirement imposes a restriction on the amount of cash readily available; and (2) if it arises in connection with a loan, the compensating balance increases the real rate of interest on the loan because not all of the cash borrowed can be used (i.e., the minimum must remain on deposit).

Information concerning a compensating balance must be reported in the notes to the financial statements because of its relevance to statement users.

PART B—MEASURING AND REPORTING SHORT-TERM INVESTMENTS

Most businesses hold extra cash in addition to the minimum required for normal daily transactions. This extra cash may be held to meet unexpected needs or may be the result of normal seasonal variations in the level of business operations. Cash that is deposited in many checking accounts earns a low rate of interest. A company can earn more revenue by investing such idle cash in short-term investments. These investments include savings accounts and certificates of deposit, commercial paper (short-term debt issued by corporations), bonds, and capital stock. Investments in commercial paper, bonds, and stock can be quickly converted into cash because they can be sold on stock exchanges such as the New York Stock Exchange.

When bonds of another company are acquired, the purchaser becomes a creditor of the issuing company because bonds represent debt owed by the other company similar to a long-term note payable. The holder of a bond is entitled to receive interest on the principal of the bond and the principal if held to maturity. In contrast, the purchaser of capital stock becomes one of the owners of the company that issued the stock. As an owner, the stockholder receives dividends when they are paid by the other company. Most capital stock confers voting rights, which means a stockholder can exercise some **control** over the issuing company. The degree of control depends on the number of voting shares owned by the stockholder in relation to the total number of such shares of stock outstanding.

Investments made by one company in the equity securities (stocks) or debt securities (bonds) of another company may be either (1) short-term investments (also called marketable securities) or (2) long-term investments. This chapter discusses the reporting of short-term investments; long-term investments are discussed in Chapter 13.

Short-Term Investments Defined

To be classified as a short-term investment, a security must meet a twofold test of (1) marketability and (2) an expected short-term holding period. **Marketability** means that the security must be readily convertible into cash or it must be traded regularly on the market so that it easily can be converted to cash. Short-term investments usually must be listed on an established stock exchange. A short-term holding period means that it must be the **intention** of the management to convert the investment into cash in the near future for normal operating purposes.[4] Short term refers to the longer of the normal operating cycle of the business or one year (as specified in the definition of current assets). The distinction between short-term and long-term investments is important because (1) accounting for the two types of investments is different; and (2) short-term investments are classified as a current asset, and long-term investments are classified as a noncurrent asset.

Measurement of Short-Term Investments

In conformity with the **cost principle,** short-term investments are initially recorded at their acquisition cost. Cost includes the market price paid plus all additional costs incurred to buy the security. Assume that in December 19A, Brown Corporation purchased 1,000 shares of Fetter Corporation stock for $56,000, including all broker's fees, transfer costs, and taxes related to the purchase. This transaction is recorded as follows:

```
Short-term investments (1,000 shares @ $56) . . . . . . . . . . . . . . . . . . 56,000
    Cash  . . . . . . . . . . . . . . . . . . . . . . . . . . . . . . . . . . . . . . .     56,000
    Purchase of 1,000 shares of Fetter stock at $56 as a
    short-term investment.
```

When a cash dividend is received, Cash is debited for the amount received, and a revenue account, such as Investment Revenue, is credited for the same

---

[4] Long-term investments also include marketable securities. The basic distinction between short-term and long-term investments hinges primarily on the intention of management in respect to their expected disposal date. As a result, the same kind of security may be a short-term investment in one company and a long-term investment in another company, depending on the intentions of the respective managements.

amount. Assume Brown Corporation received a cash dividend of $0.70 per share on the Fetter stock on February 2, 19B. This transaction is recorded as follows:

```
Cash . . . . . . . . . . . . . . . . . . . . . . . . . . . . . . . . . . . . . .    700
    Investment revenue . . . . . . . . . . . . . . . . . . . . . . . . . . .           700
    Cash dividend of $0.70 per share on short-term investment,
    $0.70 × 1,000 shares = $700.
```

For reporting purposes, the current market value of a short-term investment should be shown parenthetically or in a note to the financial statements. If a short-term investment is sold, any gain or loss on the sale must be recognized. The difference between the sale price of the security and its original cost is the amount of the gain or loss. Assume that Brown Corporation sold 250 shares of Fetter stock at $58 per share. The transaction would be recorded as follows:

```
Cash . . . . . . . . . . . . . . . . . . . . . . . . . . . . . . . . . . . . 14,500
    Short-term investments (250 shares @ $56) . . . . . . . . . . . . . .        14,000
    Gain on sale of investments . . . . . . . . . . . . . . . . . . . . . .          500
    Sale of 250 shares of Fetter stock at $58 per share = $14,500.
```

When a company owns short-term equity securities in several other companies, the securities held are referred to collectively as a **short-term portfolio of equity securities.** If debt securities also are held, they are considered to be a separate **portfolio of debt securities.** Each portfolio of short-term investments is managed (i.e., acquired, held, and sold) with the objective of maximizing the return while minimizing the risk. Thus, each **investment portfolio** is accounted for as a whole rather than as a number of separate investments.

Short-Term Investments Valued at Lower of Cost or Market (LCM)

Short-term investments are usually reported at cost. There is an exception related **only** to equity securities. The exception occurs when the **current** market value of the **short-term portfolio of equity securities** drops below the recorded acquisition cost.[5]

Chapter 7 discussed the lower-of-cost-or-market (LCM) basis for inventory. A similar rule applies to the **short-term portfolio of equity securities.** When the market value of a short-term portfolio of equity securities drops below cost, an **unrealized loss** should be recognized in the period in which the price drop occurred. However, an unrealized holding gain is **not** recorded when the current market value is **above** the acquisition cost. The LCM basis is an exception to the **cost principle** because the **conservatism exception** (Exhibit 4–5) overrides the cost principle. The LCM rule does not have to be applied to short-term investments in **debt** securities. They are accounted for at cost (with parenthetical disclosure of their current market value).

---

[5] FASB, *Statement of Accounting Standards No. 12,* "Accounting for Certain Marketable Securities" (Stamford, Conn., December 1975). The procedures and accounting entries in this section specifically follow the **requirements** of *FASB Statement 12.* This statement **does not apply LCM to investments in debt securities.**

Exhibit 8–5 Recording and reporting short-term equity investments at LCM

Journal entry:

December 31, 19B (end of accounting period)—Fetter common stock held as a short-term investment; 750 shares, cost $56, current market, $55 per share.

Unrealized loss on short-term investments 750*		
Allowance to reduce short-term investments to market		750

Computation:

Cost (750 shares @ $56)	$42,000	
Market (750 shares @ $55)	41,250	
Unrealized loss	$ 750	

Financial statements:

Balance sheet at December 31, 19B:

Current assets:

Short-term investments (at cost)	$42,000	
Less: Allowance to reduce short-term investments		
to market	750	$41,250

or alternatively:

Current assets:

Short-term investment, at LCM (cost $42,000)	$41,250

Income statement for year ended December 31, 19B:

Expenses:

Unrealized loss on short-term investments	$750

An unrealized loss on short-term investments in equity securities is recorded as a debit to an **expense** account called Unrealized Loss on Short-Term Investments and a credit to an **asset contra** account called Allowance to Reduce Short-Term Investments to Market. This entry records the holding loss as an expense in the period in which the market dropped and revalues the short-term investment on an LCM basis.

At the end of 19B, Brown Corporation still owned 750 shares of the Fetter common stock acquired at $56 per share (i.e., total cost is $42,000). At the end of 19B, the Fetter stock was selling on the stock exchange at $55 per share, which was $1 per share less than its cost. Therefore, the LCM rule must be applied. An **unrealized** loss of $750 must be recorded and reported as shown in Exhibit 8–5.

When investments that were written down to a lower market (i.e., LCM) are **sold,** the **realized gain or loss** is recognized as the difference between the sale price and the original cost regardless of any balance in the allowance account. The balance in the allowance account at the end of the accounting period is adjusted (up or down) to reflect any difference between total portfolio cost and a lower total portfolio market of the short-term investments held at the end of the accounting period.

Assume that Brown Corporation sold its entire portfolio on January 15, 19C, for $41,250 cash. The transaction is recorded as follows:

```
Cash (750 shares × $55) . . . . . . . . . . . . . . . . . . . . . . . . . .    41,250
Loss on sale of short-term investments  . . . . . . . . . . . . . . . . .       750
    Short-term investments (at cost)   . . . . . . . . . . . . . . . . . .            42,000
```

At the end of the accounting period, Brown Corporation must make an adjusting entry to update the balance in the Allowance to Reduce Short-Term Investments to Market. Because Brown does not own any short-term investments at the end of the year, the allowance account should have a zero balance. Brown would make the following adjusting entry on December 31, 19C:

```
Allowance to reduce short-term investments to market . . . . . . . . . . . . .    750
    Recovery of unrealized loss  . . . . . . . . . . . . . . . . . . . . . . . .          750
```

The recovery of unrealized loss is an income statement account that offsets the loss that was recorded when Brown sold the securities on January 15, 19C.[6] Notice that there is no effect on net income for the year in which the securities are sold because the recovery of $750 offsets the realized loss of $750. Instead, the net income for 19B is reduced when the unrealized loss is recorded. The LCM rule records the loss in the year that the value of the securities falls rather than the year in which the securities are sold.

Brown Corporation had only one stock in the investment portfolio. Often the portfolio includes several different equity securities. In such cases, LCM is applied by comparing the **total portfolio cost and the total portfolio market value** rather than on an item-by-item basis. To illustrate, assume Cox Company has three separate stocks, A, B, and C, in its short-term investment portfolio. The measurement at the end of the accounting period was:

Security	Acquisition cost	Current market	LCM applied item by item*
A Company common stock	$10,000	$ 9,000	$ 9,000
B Company preferred stock	23,000	22,000	22,000
C Company common stock	7,000	8,000	7,000
Total portfolio	$40,000	$39,000	$38,000

* Not an accepted method.

The LCM rule is applied on a portfolio basis, which means that total cost ($40,000) is compared to total market ($39,000). Under LCM, the short-term investment account for Cox Company would be written down to $39,000 and a $1,000 unrealized holding loss would be recorded as follows:

```
Unrealized loss on short-term investments  . . . . . . . . . . . . . . . . . . . .  1,000
    Allowance to reduce short-term investments to market  . . . . . . . . . .           1,000
```

---

[6] The account title "Recovery of Unrealized Loss" is confusing to most people. Unfortunately, it is widely used in practice. You should focus on the purpose of the account (explained above) instead of its name.

If the LCM rule were to be applied on an item-by-item basis, the resulting valuation would be either the same as or lower than the portfolio basis. Thus, applying LCM on a portfolio basis is usually **less** conservative than the item-by-item basis ($39,000 versus $38,000 in the case of Cox Company). The FASB's decision to require the less conservative portfolio approach for LCM surprised some people who assumed that accountants always adopted the most conservative method. The **conservatism constraint** (Exhibit 4–5) states that special care must be exercised to avoid overstating assets. Conservatism does not mean that assets should be arbitrarily understated. The LCM rule is applied to the total portfolio because the portfolio is typically managed as a single diversified investment instead of several individual investments with different objectives. Furthermore, if Cox Company sold the entire portfolio, they would receive $39,000 (not the $38,000 that resulted from applying LCM on an item-by-item basis).[7]

LCM Applied in Subsequent Accounting Periods

If a company continues to hold short-term investments in subsequent accounting periods, it must apply the LCM rule at the end of each accounting period. First, acquisition cost is compared to market. The difference is then compared to the current balance of the Allowance to Reduce Short-Term Investments to Market, and an appropriate adjusting entry is made to update the allowance account. To illustrate, assume Brown Corporation (Exhibit 8–5) continued to own Fetter stock on December 31, 19C, when the market value of the stock was $50. The total cost of Fetter stock was $42,000 (750 shares × $56), and the total market value is $37,500 (750 shares × $50). An unrealized loss on short-term investments must be recorded. The amount of the loss is the difference between LCM applied on December 31, 19C ($42,000 − $37,500 = $4,500), and the balance in the allowance account ($750; see Exhibit 8–5). Brown would make the following adjusting entry:

December 31, 19C

Unrealized loss on short-term investments ($4,500 − $750) 3,750
    Allowance to reduce short-term investments to market   3,750

Notice that the total unrealized loss on Fetter stock is $4,500; a portion of the loss ($750) occurred in 19B and another portion ($3,750) occurred in 19C.

A different adjusting entry must be prepared if the market value of the stock increases from one accounting period to the next. Now assume that on December 31, 19C, the Fetter stock had increased in value to $56. In this case, the market value equals cost, so it might appear that no adjusting entry is required on December 31, 19C. Remember it is necessary to compare the difference between cost and market with the current balance of the allowance account

---

[7] In contrast, LCM is applied to inventories on an item-by-item basis because the merchandise is viewed as separate items rather than a portfolio.

(which is $750 on December 31, 19C). Because there is no difference between cost and market, the allowance account should have a zero balance. Brown would make the following adjusting entry:

December 31, 19C

Allowance to reduce short-term investment to market	750	
Recovery of unrealized loss		750

After the adjusting entry, Brown would report their short-term investment on the balance sheet at cost ($42,000) because the allowance account has a zero balance.

Under no circumstances can the total of the Recovery of Unrealized Loss exceed the total of the Unrealized Losses. In other words, if the market value of the stock exceeds cost, the Recovery of Unrealized Loss is limited to the amount necessary to reduce the allowance account to zero, but no further. In the Brown Corporation example, the adjusting entry would be the same as shown above if the Fetter stock had increased in value to $59 on December 31, 19C.

Certificates of Deposit

A commonly used short-term investment is called a **certificate of deposit** (CD). A CD is an investment contract (a certificate is received) that may be purchased from a bank for cash. The contract specifies (1) a limited period of time for the investment, such as 90 days, 6 months, 1 year, and so on; and (2) a guaranteed interest rate. Usually, a higher interest rate is available for large investments and for longer time periods to maturity. CDs and similar commercial paper often are used for the short-term investment of idle cash because of the relatively high interest return and the liquidity factor.

CDs are accounted for on the cost basis (not LCM) because they are **debt** securities. At the end of the accounting period, an **adjusting entry** is made for any accrued interest earned but not yet collected. The interest earned is reported on the income statement as **investment revenue.** CDs are reported on the balance sheet as a current asset.

Adjusting Entries for Investment Revenue

At the end of the accounting period, **no adjusting entry is made for dividend revenue** on capital stock held as an investment because dividends (1) do not accrue on the basis of time and (2) are not paid unless formally declared by the board of directors of the issuing corporation. In contrast, when CDs, bonds, or other **debt securities are held, an adjusting entry is needed** for accrued interest revenue because interest is a legal liability that increases in amount with the passage of time. Accrual of interest is illustrated in Part C of this chapter.

PART C—MEASURING AND REPORTING RECEIVABLES

Receivables Defined

Receivables include all claims of the entity against other entities or persons for money, goods, or services. In most businesses, there are two types of receivables: trade receivables and special (nontrade) receivables. Either type may include both short-term receivables and long-term receivables. For example, a balance sheet may report the following receivables:

```
Current assets:
    Trade accounts receivable . . . . . . . . . . . $40,000
        Less: Allowance for doubtful accounts . . .   3,000   $37,000
    Trade notes receivable, short term  . . . . .               5,000
    Special receivables:
        Due from employees . . . . . . . . . . . .                400
        Equipment note receivable, short term . . .               600
Long-term investments:
    Note receivable, long term . . . . . . . . . .             10,000
    Special receivable, long term . . . . . . . . .             8,000
Others assets:
    Utility deposits . . . . . . . . . . . . . . . . .          2,000
    Due from company officers . . . . . . . . . .              1,000
```

Trade Receivables

Trade receivables include **accounts receivable** and trade notes receivable. Either may be short term or long term, although the latter is rare. Trade receivables arise from the normal operating activities of the business, that is, from the sale of merchandise and services.

Many businesses **sell** their accounts receivable instead of holding them until they are collected. Factoring is a term used for the **sale** of accounts receivable to a financial institution. Factoring is used widely because the company immediately receives the cash for sales. The rate of interest for factoring arrangements is high. A discussion of the detailed accounting involved for factoring is included in advanced accounting courses.

Special Receivables

Special (or nontrade) receivables arise from transactions other than the normal sale of merchandise and/or services. Special receivables may be short term or long term and should be given descriptive titles. They should not be included in the caption "Accounts receivable." Other than for appropriate classification on the balance sheet, special receivables seldom involve unusual accounting problems.

Notes Receivable

Notes receivable may be either **trade** notes receivable or **special** notes receivable, depending on the source of the note. A note is an unconditional promise in writing (i.e., a formal document) to pay (1) a specified sum of money on demand or at a definite future date known as the maturity date and (2) specified interest at one or more future dates. The person who signs a note is called the **maker.** The person to whom payment is to be made is known as the **payee.** The maker views the note as a note payable, whereas the payee views the note as a note receivable. A note involves two distinctly different amounts: (1) **principal,** which is the amount that the interest rate is based on; and (2) **interest,** which is the specified amount charged for use of the principal. The **face amount** of a note is the amount that is payable at maturity.

Interest Calculations on Notes

Interest represents the cost of using money over time. To the payee of a note, interest is **revenue,** while to the maker it is **expense.** The formula for computing interest is:

$$\text{Principal} \times \text{Annual rate of interest} \times \text{Fraction of year} = \text{Interest amount}$$

Interest rates are quoted on an **annual basis** and must be restated for time periods of less than one year. Thus, the interest on a $10,000, 12%, 90-day note is calculated as follows:

$$\$10,000 \times 12\% \times 90/360 = \$300$$

When a note specifies a number of days, the exact days must be counted on the calendar to determine the due date and then related to the number of days in the year. For simplicity, sometimes it is assumed that the year has 360 days. Therefore, each day's interest is $1/360$ of a year rather than $1/365$. This simplification has the effect of making the actual interest cost for a short-term loan slightly higher than the stated amount of interest.[8]

All commercial notes have interest, either explicitly or implicitly, because money borrowed or loaned has a value that cannot be ignored.[9]

---

[8] Most lending institutions use 365 days in the calculations.

[9] An **interest-bearing note** explicitly specifies a stated rate of interest (such as 12%) on the face of the note, and the interest is to be paid in addition to the **face amount** of the note. In contrast, a **noninterest-bearing note** does not explicitly state an interest rate on the note because the interest charge is included in the face amount of the note (i.e., the interest is implicit).

Accounting for Notes Receivable

Notes receivable usually arise when a business sells merchandise or services. Although most businesses use open accounts (i.e., accounts receivable), those selling high-priced items on credit often require notes from their customers. To illustrate, assume Jackson Company received a $10,000, 12% interest-bearing note from a customer as a result of the sale of goods; the payee would record it on the date of the sale as follows:

Notes receivable (trade)	10,000	
Sales revenue		10,000
To record 90-day, 12% interest-bearing note received from customer.		

When **collection** is made at **maturity date** 90 days later, the entry to record the principal amount and the interest is:

Cash	10,300	
Notes receivable (trade)		10,000
Interest revenue		300
To record collection of a 90-day, 12% interest-bearing note receivable		
of $10,000 plus interest ($10,000 $\times$ 12% $\times$ $^{90}/_{360}$ = $300).		

Default of a Note Receivable

A note receivable that is not collected at maturity is **defaulted** on by the maker. Immediately after default, an entry should be made by the payee transferring the amount due from the Notes Receivable account to a special account such as Special Receivable—Defaulted Trade Notes. The maker is responsible for both the unpaid principal and the unpaid interest. The receivable account should reflect the full amount owed to the payee. If the above note receivable was defaulted by the maker, the entry made by the payee is:[10]

Special receivable—defaulted trade notes	10,300	
Notes receivable (trade)		10,000
Interest revenue		300
To record the principal and interest earned on defaulted note.		

Special Receivable—Defaulted Trade Notes is reported as a current or non-current asset depending on the probable collection date.

---

[10] From date of default, the amount due at that date (principal plus interest) continues to draw interest either at the stipulated rate or the legal rate as specified by the law of the state. There may be a question about the propriety of recognizing the interest revenue before collection is made when there is a reasonable probability that collection will not be made.

Discounting a Note Receivable

A note receivable often can be sold to a financial institution, such as a bank, to get needed cash before the maturity date. Selling a note receivable to a financial institution is called **discounting** a note receivable.

A **negotiable instrument** has a maker and a payee. It can be transferred to a third party by the endorsement of the payee (there are other technical legal requisites for negotiability). The most common negotiable instrument is a check. Notes and a number of other instruments can be transferred by endorsement (i.e., signature of the holder). The note may be negotiated **with recourse,** which means that the endorser is liable for repayment if the maker defaults. An endorsement may be made without recourse by writing this phrase on the instrument before the endorsement signature. **Without recourse** means that the endorser cannot be held contractually liable in the case of default by the maker. Most banks, businesses, and individuals will not accept endorsements without recourse. As a result, financial institutions can rely on both the maker and the endorser. An endorsement with recourse makes the endorser **contingently liable.** If the maker does not pay the note at maturity, the endorser pays. The **full-disclosure principle** (Exhibit 4–5) requires that such contingent liabilities be reported as a note to the financial statements.

The sale of a note receivable gives the payee immediate cash and causes the transfer of the note receivable to the lender. Often there will be a difference between the interest rate specified on the note and the interest rate charged by the purchaser of the note.

For example, assume that Jackson Company held a $10,000, 10%, 90-day interest-bearing note receivable for 30 days, then sold it with recourse to the First National Bank at an interest rate of 12%. The bank's interest rate is applied to the **maturity value** of the note (that is, the principal amount of the note **plus** the amount of interest due at maturity). The bank's rate of interest is charged for the number of days the bank will hold the note (in this case, 60 days). Computation of the amount of cash the bank will pay for the note is:

Discounting a note receivable (Jackson Company):

Note: Principal, $10,000; annual interest rate, 10%; term, 90 days.
Discounted: Thirty days after date; discount rate, 12% per year.

Principal amount	$10,000.00
Plus: Interest due at maturity ($10,000 × 10% × 90/360)	250.00
Maturity value—amount subject to discount rate	10,250.00
Less: Discount—interest charged by bank ($10,250 × 12% × 60/360)	205.00
Cash proceeds—amount the bank pays for the note	$10,045.00

The discounting of the note receivable is recorded by Jackson Company as follows:[11]

---

[11] The credit of $45 to Interest Revenue may be explained as follows: Had the note been held to maturity, the payee would have earned $250 interest revenue; however, the bank charged interest amounting to $205. The difference is $45, which is the net interest earned by the payee for holding it 30 of the 90 days. The discount rate is applied to the maturity value of the note because that is the amount the bank will advance, less the interest required by the bank.

Cash 10,045.00
    Notes receivable (trade) 10,000.00
    Interest revenue 45.00
  To record discounting of note receivable.

Even though the note was sold, the bank had recourse against the endorser in case of default by the maker. Therefore, Jackson Company has a **contingent liability** that must be disclosed in a note to the financial statements similar to the following:

Note: At December 31, 19B, the company was contingently liable for notes receivable discounted in the amount of $10,250.

DEMONSTRATION CASE

(Try to resolve the requirements before proceeding to the suggested solution that follows.)

Dotter Equipment Company has been selling farm machinery for more than 30 years. A wide range of farm equipment, including trucks, is sold. Credit terms with varying conditions are typical. Although most of the credit granted is carried by several financial institutions, Dotter will carry the credit in special circumstances. As a result, the company occasionally accepts a promissory note and keeps it to maturity. However, if a cash need arises, some of these notes may be discounted to the local bank. This case focuses on two farm equipment notes that were received during 19D. The accounting period ends December 31, 19D.

The series of transactions with respect to the two notes follows:

Equipment Note No. 1:

19D
Jan. 15 Sold a farm tractor to S. Scott for $20,000 and received a 25% cash down payment plus a $15,000 equipment note receivable for the balance. The note was due in nine months and was interest bearing at 12% per annum. A mortgage on the tractor was executed as a part of the agreement.

Apr. 15 The Scott equipment note was sold to the local bank at the 13% per annum discount rate. Dotter endorsed the note, with recourse, and the proceeds were deposited in Dotter's checking account.

Oct. 15 Scott paid the bank the face amount of the note plus the interest, $15,000 + ($15,000 × 12% × %12) = $16,350.

Required:

    a. Give appropriate journal entries for Dotter Equipment Company on each of the three dates. Show the interest computations and give an explanation for each entry.

    b. Assume that instead of payment on October 15, 19D, S. Scott defaulted on the note. When notified by the bank, Dotter paid the note and interest in full. Give the appropriate entry for this assumption and one for the further assumption that Scott later paid Dotter in full on December 1, 19D.

Equipment Note No. 2:

19D

Oct. 1 Sold a farm truck to B. Day for $7,000; received a down payment of $1,000 and set up an account receivable for the balance; terms n/30.

Nov. 1 Day came in and wanted an extension on the account receivable "until he sold some equipment." After some discussion it was agreed to settle the account receivable with a six-month, 12% interest-bearing note. Day signed the $6,000 note and a mortgage on this date.

Dec. 31 End of the accounting period. An adjusting entry is required.

19E

Jan. 1 Start of the new accounting period.

May 1 On this due date, Day paid the face amount of the note plus interest in full. The note was marked paid, and the mortgage was canceled by Dotter.

Required:

    c. Give appropriate journal entries on each date, including any adjusting entries at year-end and the entry on maturity date. Omit closing entries at year-end. Explain what could be done on January 1, 19E, to simplify subsequent accounting. Provide a brief explanation with each entry.

Suggested Solution

The solutions for Requirements (*a*), (*b*), and (*c*) are given in Exhibits 8–6 and 8–7.

Exhibit 8–6 Accounting for discounted and defaulted notes receivable illustrated

Requirement *a*—Equipment Note No. 1:

January 15, 19D—note executed:

Cash	5,000.00	
Equipment notes receivable	15,000.00	
Sales revenue		20,000.00

Sale of tractor to S. Scott for cash and equipment note; terms of note, nine months, 12% interest, including a mortgage.

April 15, 19D—note discounted:

Cash	15,287.25	
Equipment notes receivable		15,000.00
Interest revenue		287.25

Discounted Scott equipment note receivable at bank discount rate of 13%.

Proceeds computed:

Principal amount	$15,000.00
Interest to maturity ($15,000 × 12% × 9/12)	1,350.00
Maturity value	16,350.00
Discount ($16,350 × 13% × 6/12)	(1,062.75)
Cash proceeds	$15,287.25

October 15, 19D—maturity date of note:

No entry required; Scott paid the bank that owned the note. During the period from April 15, 19D, until the note was paid, Dotter was contingently liable for the note because of the possibility that Scott would default.

Requirement *b*—note defaulted:

October 15, 19D—Under the assumption that Scott defaulted on the note on due date, Dotter would have to pay the principal plus interest in full.

Special receivable (defaulted note—S. Scott)	16,350.00	
Cash		16,350.00

Scott note defaulted; payment to bank of the $15,000 principal plus interest ($15,000 × 12% × 9/12 = $1,350).

December 1, 19D—Scott paid Dotter the full amount of the note plus interest.

Cash	16,350.00	
Special receivable (defaulted note, S. Scott)		16,350.00

Payment received in full on Scott note in default.

Note: In most states, Dotter could have assessed Scott interest at the **legal** rate on the $16,350 amount overdue; in this case, there would be a credit to Interest Revenue.

Exhibit 8–7 Accounting for interest accrual on notes receivable illustrated

Requirement c—Equipment Note No. 2:

October 1, 19D—sale:

Cash	1,000	
Accounts receivable	6,000	
Sales revenue		7,000

Sold truck to B. Day; terms of the receivable, n/30.

November 1, 19D—note executed:

Equipment notes receivable	6,000	
Accounts receivable		6,000

Settled account receivable with a six-month, 12% interest-bearing note.

December 31, 19D—accrual (end of accounting period):

Interest receivable	120	
Interest revenue		120

Adjusting entry for two months' interest accrued at 12% on Day equipment note ($6,000 × 12% × 2/12 = $120).

January 1, 19E—start of next accounting period:

No entry is required on this date; however, a **reversal** of the adjusting entry could be made to facilitate the subsequent entry when the interest is collected on April 30, 19E. The **optional reversing entry** would be (see Chapter Supplement 5A):

Interest revenue	120	
Interest receivable		120

Reversing entry on Day note.

April 30, 19E—maturity date (assuming **no** reversing entry was made on January 1, 19E):

Cash $6,000 + ($6,000 × 12% × 6/12)	6,360	
Note receivable (principal amount)		6,000
Interest revenue ($6,000 × 12% × 4/12)		240
Interest receivable		120

SUMMARY OF CHAPTER

This chapter discussed cash, short-term investments, and receivables. Cash is the most liquid of all assets, and it flows continually into and out of a business. As a result, cash presents some of the most critical control problems facing the managers. Also, cash may be of critical importance to decision makers who rely on financial statements for relevant information. The measurement and reporting of cash includes such problems as controlling and safeguarding cash, reconciling bank balances, accounting for petty cash, and recording the cash inflows and outflows.

The use of short-term investments to employ idle cash was discussed. Marketability and the length of the expected holding period are fundamental in the classification of an investment as short term as opposed to long term. Short-term investments are accounted for in conformity with the **cost principle;** however, in conformity with the conservatism constraint, the LCM rule is applied to the short-term investment portfolio of **equity securities** at the end of each accounting period. **Debt securities** held as short-term investments are accounted for at **cost** (not LCM). Long-term investments are discussed in Chapter 13.

Receivables include trade receivables (usually called accounts receivable), special receivables, and notes receivable. Each of these should be accounted for separately. Interest calculations and discounting of notes receivable were discussed.

The chapter emphasized the importance of careful measurement of these liquid assets and the importance of examining their characteristics before classifying them as current assets for reporting purposes. Financial statement users often are faced with decisions in which these liquid assets are critical; therefore, they should be measured properly and reported adequately.

CHAPTER SUPPLEMENT 8A

Petty Cash

A petty cash fund is established to avoid the inconvenience and cost of writing checks for the many small payments that occur daily in some businesses. This supplement discusses the detailed accounting and recordkeeping for a petty cash fund (also called an imprest fund).

Establishing the Petty Cash Fund

To establish a petty cash fund, a check should be written for the estimated amount needed to meet the expected payments, say, for an average month. The check, made payable to "Petty Cash," is cashed. The money is kept in a safe place under the direct control of a **designated individual** known as the **custodian.** The entry to set up a **separate Cash account** and to record the initial check is:

Petty cash	100	
Cash		100

To record establishment of a petty cash fund.

Disbursements from the Petty Cash Fund

The custodian should keep a perpetual record of all disbursements and the amount of cash on hand. No entry is made in the regular ledger accounts at the time each payment is made from the petty cash fund. Instead, the custodian keeps a separate **petty cash record** in which each disbursement is recorded when made. This record is supported by documentation, such as a signed bill, voucher, or receipt for each payment made. As an internal control feature, occasional surprise audits of the fund and the records of disbursements should be conducted. "Borrowing" from the fund by the custodian or others should not be allowed. Careless handling of petty cash often leads to theft.

Replenishment of the Petty Cash Fund

When the amount of cash held by the custodian gets low, and at the end of each accounting period, the fund should be reimbursed (or replenished) with an amount of cash sufficient to restore it to the original amount (to $100 in the example). Reimbursement is made by having the custodian submit the petty cash record and the supporting documents to the accountants. On the basis of these records, a check to "Petty Cash" is written for the amount of cash needed for replenishment which is the same as the sum of the expenditures reported by the custodian. The check is cashed, and the money is given to the custodian, which increases the cash held by the custodian to the original amount. A journal entry is made to credit Cash for the amount of the check and to debit expenses. The petty cash documents turned in by the custodian provide the underlying support for this journal entry.

To illustrate, assume that by the end of the month there was $8.50 petty cash on hand. This means that cash expenditures by the custodian were $91.50 for the month. Assuming no shortage or overage, the bills, vouchers, and receipts accumulated by the custodian should equal this amount. These documents provide support for the additional check to petty cash for $91.50.

The detailed data for recording the replenishment check in the following journal entry are based on the supporting documents:

Telephone expense	12.40	
Office supplies expense	6.32	
Postage expense	21.45	
Delivery expense	6.33	
Taxi fare expense	14.87	
Repair expense, office equipment	15.00	
Coffee expense	10.04	
Miscellaneous expenses	5.09	
Cash		91.50

Notice that the Petty Cash account is debited **only** when the petty cash fund is first established and when the fund amount is increased on a permanent basis. The Petty Cash account shows a stable balance at all times ($100 in the above example). Expense accounts, not Petty Cash, are debited, and the **regular** Cash account is credited when the fund is replenished. Therefore, there will be no further entries in the Petty Cash account once it is established unless management increases or decreases the original amount on a permanent basis. The fund must be replenished (*a*) when the balance of cash in the fund is low; and (*b*) always at the end of the accounting period, whether low or not. Replenishment at the end of the accounting period is necessary to (*a*) record the expenses incurred by the fund up to the date of the financial statements and (*b*) have the amount of petty cash on hand that is shown in the Petty Cash account. The petty cash fund should be subject to rigid internal control procedures to remove all temptations to misuse it.

CHAPTER SUPPLEMENT 8B

Special Journals

In the preceding chapters, the **general journal** was used to record all transactions in chronological order (i.e., by order of date). The general journal can be used to record any transaction. However, it is inefficient if used for recording transactions that occur frequently, such as credit sales, credit purchases, cash receipts, and cash payments. The **general journal** is inefficient in three ways: (1) the same journal entry must be recorded repeatedly (except for changed amounts), (2) a large number of journal entries must be posted to the ledger, and (3) division of labor is difficult with a single journal. Special journals are designed to reduce these inefficiencies.

No new accounting principles or concepts are involved with special journals. They involve only the mechanics of data processing. Special journals should be designed to meet a special need when a particular type of data processing problem arises. We will limit this discussion to the four special journals that often are used: credit sales, credit purchases, cash receipts, and cash payments.

Credit Sales Journal

This journal is designed to accommodate **only credit sales.** Cash sales are entered in the cash receipts journal as explained below. Recall that the journal entry to record a credit sale (assuming a periodic inventory system) is:[12]

Jan. 3	Accounts receivable (customer's name) 100	
	Sales	100
	To record credit sale; Invoice No. 324; terms n/30.	

The credit sales journal is designed to simplify (1) recording this kind of entry and (2) subsequent posting to the ledger. The design of a credit sales journal is

---

[12] For instructional purposes, we will utilize simplified amounts, a limited number of transactions and customers, T-accounts, and a manual system. In many companies these procedures are computerized.

Exhibit 8–8 Credit sales journal and accounts receivable subsidiary ledger illustrated

CREDIT SALES JOURNAL					Page 9
Date	Customer	Terms	Invoice Number	Folio	Amount
Jan. 3	Adams, K. L.	n/30	324	34.1	100
4	Small, C. C.	n/30	325	34.6	60
6	Baker, C. B.	n/30	326	34.2	110
10	Roe, R. R.	n/30	327	34.5	20
11	Mays, O. L.	n/30	328	34.3	200
16	Roe, R. R.	n/30	329	34.5	90
18	Null, O. E.	n/30	330	34.4	30
20	Baker, C. B.	n/30	331	34.2	180
21	Small, C. C.	n/30	332	34.6	150
31	Null, O. E.	n/30	333	34.4	260
	Total				1,200
	Posting				(34) (81)

ACCOUNTS RECEIVABLE SUBSIDIARY LEDGER

Adams, K. L.			34.1
Jan. 3		9	100

Baker, C. B.				34.2
Jan. 6		9	110	
20		9	180	290

Mays, O. L.			34.3
Jan. 11		9	200

Null, O. E.				34.4
Jan. 18		9	30	
31		9	260	290

Roe, R. R.				34.5
Jan. 10		9	20	
16		9	90	110

Small, C. C.				34.6
Jan. 4		9	60	
21		9	150	210

GENERAL LEDGER

Accounts Receivable (control)			34
Jan. 31	9	1,200	

Sales Revenue			81
	Jan. 31	9	1,200

shown in Exhibit 8–8. Notice the **saving** in space, time, and accounting expertise required to journalize a credit sale.

Posting the Credit Sales Journal

Posting the special credit sales journal involves two distinct phases. First, the **individual charges** (i.e., debits) must be posted daily to the customers' individual accounts in the accounts receivable subsidiary ledger. This task may be divided among several employees. Second, periodically (usually weekly or monthly), the **totals** are posted to the **general ledger** accounts—Accounts Receivable (debit) and Sales Revenue (credit). There is a significant saving in time compared with posting each transaction to the general ledger.

Posting on a daily basis to the **subsidiary ledger,** as shown in Exhibit 8–8, is indicated in the Folio column by entering the account number for each individual customer. Daily posting to the subsidiary ledger is necessary because customers may, on any day, want to pay the current balance of their accounts.

The second phase in posting the sales journal is to transfer to the general ledger the total credit sales for the month. Thus, the $1,200 total will be posted to the general ledger as (1) a debit to the Accounts Receivable **control account** and (2) a credit to the Sales Revenue account. This posting is shown in Exhibit 8–8; note in the credit sales journal that two ledger account numbers were entered for the $1,200 total to indicate the posting procedure.

The credit sales journal can be adapted readily to fill special needs. For example, sales taxes could be recorded by adding a column headed "Sales Taxes Payable," and separate sales columns can be added to accumulate sales by department or product. You should observe the following efficiencies: (1) recording in the credit sales journal is much less time consuming than separately entering each credit sale in the general journal, (2) posting is reduced by transferring the **total** to the general ledger instead of posting separate debits and credits for each sales transaction, (3) the opportunity for division of labor, and (4) additional information (such as sales revenue by department) can be recorded easily.

Credit Purchases Journal

Following the same pattern as described above, a credit purchases journal may be designed to record the entry common to all purchases on credit:

Jan. 8 Purchases* 392
        Accounts payable, C. B. Smith   392
        To record purchase on credit from C. B. Smith, Purchase Order
        No. 139; invoice dated January 5, 19B; terms 2/10, n/30. Recorded
        net of discount, $400 $\times$ 0.98 = $392.

     * This debit assumes a periodic inventory system; if a perpetual system is used this account would be Merchandise Inventory.

Exhibit 8-9 Credit purchases journal illustrated

CREDIT PURCHASES JOURNAL						Page 4
Date	Creditor's Account	Purchase Order No.	Date of Invoice	Terms	Folio	Amount
Jan. 8	Smith, C. B. Etc.	139	Jan. 5	2/10, n/30	51.8	392
	Total					784
	Posting					(6) (51)

Only credit purchases are recorded in the credit purchases journal. Cash purchases are entered in the cash payments journal as illustrated later. The design of a purchases journal is as shown in Exhibit 8-9.

Notice that purchases are recorded net of the purchase discount (as explained in Chapter 6). The cash payments journal will be used to record the subsequent payment of cash for the purchase including situations where the purchase discount is lost.

Exhibit 8-9 was not completed in detail for illustrative purposes because it follows the same pattern already shown for the credit sales journal. Daily posting would involve transfer to the creditors' individual accounts in the **accounts payable subsidiary ledger.** Periodically, the total would be posted to the **general ledger** as (1) a debit to the Purchases account and (2) a credit to the Accounts Payable control account. The efficiencies cited for the sales journal also are realized by a purchases journal.

Cash Receipts Journal

All cash receipts can be recorded in the cash receipts journal, but no other transactions can be recorded in it. The design of a special journal to accommodate **cash receipts** is more complex because there are many different accounts that are **credited individually** when the Cash account is debited. To resolve this problem, more than one **credit** column is needed to record the various credits. The number and designation of the debit and credit columns depends on the character of the repetitive cash receipts transactions in the particular business.

A typical cash receipts journal with some usual transactions recorded is shown in Exhibit 8-10. Notice that there are separate debit and credit sections. Each column is used as follows:

Exhibit 8–10 Cash receipts journal illustrated

Date		Explanation	DEBITS	CREDITS				
			Cash	Account Title	Folio	Accounts Receivable	Sundry Accounts	Cash Sales
Jan	2	Cash sales	1,237					1,237
	3	Cash sales	1,482					1,482
	4	Sale of land	2,500	Land	43		2,000	
				Gain on sale of land	91		500	
	4	Cash sales	992					992
	6	Invoice #324	100	Adams, K.L.	341	100		
	6	Cash sales	1,570					1,570
	10	Bank loan, 12%	1,000	Notes payable	54		1,000	
	15	Invoice #328	200	Mays, O.L.	343	200		
	26	Cash sales	1,360					1,360
	31	Invoice #326	110	Baker, C.B.	342	110		
	31	Cash sales	1,810					1,810
		Totals	12,361			410	3,500	8,451
		Posting	(12)			(34)	(NP)	(81)

CASH RECEIPTS JOURNAL   Page 14

1. **Cash debit.** This column is used for **each** debit to cash. The column is totaled at the end of the month and posted as one debit amount to the Cash account in the general ledger. The posting number at the bottom indicates the total was posted to account number "12," which is the Cash account.[13]

2. **Accounts Receivable credit.** This column is used to enter the individual amounts collected on trade accounts that must be posted to the individual customer accounts in the **accounts receivable subsidiary ledger** (as indicated by the posting numbers in the Folio columns). The **total** of this column is posted at the end of the month as a credit to the Accounts Receivable **control** account in the general ledger as indicated by the posting number "34."

3. **Sundry Accounts credit.** This column is used for recording credits to all accounts other than those for which special credit columns are provided (in this example Accounts Receivable and Sales Revenue). The titles of the accounts to be credited are entered in the Account Title column. Because the Sundry Accounts column represents a number of **accounts,** the **total** is not posted; rather, each individual amount must

---

[13] This design assumes that the company correctly records credit sales at net of discounts. If credit sales are recorded at "gross," then a Sales Discount debit column also would be needed in this special journal.

be posted as a credit directly to the indicated general ledger account. Account numbers entered in the related Folio column indicate the posting.

4. **Cash Sales credit.**   This column is used to record **all cash sales.** The total at the end of the month is posted as a credit to the Sales Revenue account in the general ledger.

Posting the cash receipts journal involves the same two phases explained previously for the credit sales and credit purchases journals. The **daily posting** phase involves posting the individual credits to the accounts receivable subsidiary ledger. The **second phase** involves posting the totals periodically to the accounts in the general ledger, with the exception of the column total for Sundry Accounts, as explained above.

The individual accounts shown in the Sundry Accounts column can be posted daily or at the end of the month. Posting through January is indicated by account code numbers in the illustrated cash receipts journal.

The representative entries shown in the illustrated cash receipts journal are summarized in Exhibit 8–11, in **general journal form,** for convenience in assessing the increased efficiencies of the cash receipts journal approach in journalizing and posting a large number of individual cash transactions.

Other debit and credit columns can be added to the cash receipts journal to accommodate repetitive transactions that also involve cash receipts.

Cash Payments Journal

The special cash payments journal (often called the check register) is designed to accommodate efficiently the recording of **all cash payments.** Only cash payments can be recorded in the cash payments journal. The basic credit column is for Cash; columns for debits are incorporated into the format to accommodate repetitive transactions that involve cash payments. The cash payments journal also must include a column for Sundry Accounts, Debits to accommodate the nonrecurring transactions involving cash payments for which a special debit column is not provided.

A typical cash payments journal with some usual transactions recorded is shown in Exhibit 8–12. Notice that there are separate debit and credit sections. Each column illustrated is used as follows:

1. **Cash credit.**   This column is for **every credit** to the Cash account. The column is totaled at the end of the month and posted as a credit to the Cash account in the general ledger.

2. **Accounts Payable debit.**   This column is used to enter the individual amounts paid on accounts payable. The individual amounts are posted as debits to the **accounts payable subsidiary ledger** (as indicated by the account numbers under folio), and the total at the end of the month is

Exhibit 8–11 Journal entries for cash receipts

Jan. 2 Cash 1,237		
Sales revenue	1,237	
To record total cash sales for the day.		
3 Cash 1,482		
Sales revenue	1,482	
To record total cash sales for the day.		
4 Cash 2,500		
Land	2,000	
Gain on sale of land	500	
To record sale of land for $2,500 that originally cost $2,000.		
4 Cash 992		
Sales revenue	992	
To record total cash sales for the day.		
6 Cash 100		
Accounts receivable	100	
To record total collection of K. L. Adams account for Invoice No. 324 (no discount).		
6 Cash 1,570		
Sales revenue	1,570	
To record total cash sales for the day.		
10 Cash 1,000		
Notes payable	1,000	
To record bank loan, 90-day, 12%.		
15 Cash 200		
Accounts receivable	200	
To record collection of O. L. Mays account for Invoice No. 328 (no discount).		
26 Cash 1,360		
Sales revenue	1,360	
To record total cash sales for the day.		
31 Cash 110		
Accounts receivable	110	
To record total collection of C. B. Baker account for Invoice No. 326 (no discount).		
31 Cash 1,810		
Sales revenue	1,810	
To record total cash sales for the day.		

Exhibit 8–12 Cash payments journal illustrated

			CREDITS	DEBITS					
Date	Check No.	Explanation	Cash	Account Title	Folio	Accounts Payable	Sundry Accounts	Cash Purchases
Jan 2	101	Purchased mdse.	1,880					1,880
4	102	Invoice #37	2,970	Ray Mfg. Co.	51.3	2,970		
5	103	Jan. rent	1,200	Rent expense	71		1,200	
8	104	Purchased mdse.	250					250
10	105	Freight on mdse.	15	Freight in	63		15	
14	106	Invoice #42	980	Bows Supply Co.	51.1	980		
15	107	Paid note, plus	2,200	Notes payable	54		2,000	
		interest		Interest expense	79		200	
20	108	Insurance premium	600	Prepaid insurance	19		600	
26	109	Purchased mdse.	2,160					2,160
29	110	Invoice #91 - after	500	Myar Corp.	51.2	490		
		discount period		Discount lost	80		10	
31	111	Wages	1,000	Wage expense	76		1,000	
		Totals	13,755			4,440	5,025	4,290
		Posting	(12)			(51)	(NP)	(61)
Feb. 1		Etc.						

posted as a debit to the Accounts Payable control account in the general ledger.

3. **Sundry Accounts debit.**   This column is used to record all accounts debited for which special columns are not provided (in this example Accounts Payable and Purchases are provided). The titles of the accounts to be debited are entered in the Account Titles column. Because this column represents a number of accounts, the total cannot be posted; rather, each individual amount is posted as a debit directly to the indicated general ledger account.

4. **Cash Purchases debit.**   All cash purchases are entered in this column. The total at the end of the month is posted as a debit to the Purchases account in the ledger.

Posting the cash payments journal involves two phases: (1) **daily posting** of the individual credit amounts to the **accounts payable subsidiary ledger;** and (2) **periodic posting** of the totals to the **general ledger,** with the exception of the total of Sundry Accounts. The posting of the individual amounts in the Sundry Accounts column can be done during the period, say, daily.

The illustrative transactions entered in the cash payments journal (Exhibit 8–12) were:

Jan. 2 Issued Check No. 101 for cash purchase of merchandise costing $1,880.

4 Issued Check No. 102 to pay account payable owed to Ray Manufacturing Company within the discount period. Discount allowed, 1%; Invoice No. 37, $3,000.

5 Issued Check No. 103 to pay January rent, $1,200.

8 Issued Check No. 104 for cash purchase of merchandise costing $250.

10 Issued Check No. 105 for transportation-in on merchandise purchased, $15.

14 Issued Check No. 106 to pay account payable owed to Bows Supply Company within the discount period. Discount allowed, 2%; Invoice No. 42, $1,000.

15 Issued Check No. 107 to pay $2,000 note payable plus 10% interest for one year.

20 Issued Check No. 108 to pay three-year insurance premium, $600.

26 Issued Check No. 109 for cash purchase of merchandise costing $2,160.

29 Issued Check No. 110 to pay account payable to Myar Corporation; terms 2/10, n/30; Invoice No. 91, $500. Therefore, accounts payable to Myar was credited for $490 at the purchase date (Chapter 6). The payment was made after the discount period; hence, the full invoice price of $500 was paid and purchase discount lost of $10 was recorded.

31 Issued Check No. 111 to pay wages amounting to $1,000.

Additional debit and credit columns can be added to the cash payments journal to accommodate other repetitive transactions involving cash disbursements.

Many companies control expenditures with a **voucher system** rather than using the credit purchases and the cash payments journals. A voucher system is adaptable to computerized accounting and gives tight control mechanisms on the sequence of events for each transaction from incurrence until final cash payment. The voucher system is explained and illustrated in Chapter 10.

In summary, special journals do not involve new accounting principles or concepts. Rather, they represent a mechanical technique designed to increase efficiency in the data processing cycle. Special journals are not standardized. They should be designed to fit each situation. Although a manual approach has been illustrated for instructional purposes, many companies have computerized the procedures represented by special journals. In computerized systems, essentially the same mechanics illustrated for the manual system are accomplished by the computer.

CHAPTER SUPPLEMENT 8C

Ethics

Ethics is a system of moral principles. It deals with examining human conduct with respect to the rightness or wrongness of certain actions. Ultimately, ethics involves a series of individual decisions that we must each make with respect to the type of life that we want to lead.

Each of us faces ethical decisions in daily life. In some cases, it is easy to determine the "correct" action. For example, while many of us are tempted to cheat on examinations, we all agree that cheating is improper and unethical. In other cases, the situations that confront us involve more subtle ethical issues, and selecting the "correct" action is more difficult. We agree that cheating on an examination is wrong, but most of us have observed cheating without trying to do anything to stop it (such as talking to the person who cheated or informing the teacher). The decision not to act when observing cheating involves an ethical choice. The person who fosters an environment in which cheating can take place is probably as guilty of unethical behavior as the person who cheats.

Business and Ethics

As you begin your business careers, you will be exposed to complex situations that pose increasingly difficult ethical dilemmas. Unfortunately, recent newspaper stories concerning illegal insider trading on Wall Street, payment of bribes to government officials to secure large contracts, and dumping unsafe products in less developed countries may suggest ethics is not part of business. Fortunately, such is not the case. Most major corporations have strong, formal codes of conduct that are strictly enforced. In a sense, ethical behavior is simply good business. As world markets become more competitive, customers, suppliers, and employees have more choices concerning the type of organization with which they want to do business. Organizations that stress quality, value, and fairness will be more successful in the long run than organizations that are interested in short-term gains associated with unethical behavior. Nevertheless, it would be naive to assume that you will not face many important and difficult ethical decisions during your career.

Ethics and Accounting

Accounting serves a variety of objectives within an organization. One of these objectives is to help employees make good ethical decisions. For example, Chapter 8 discusses internal control of cash. These accounting procedures are designed to lessen the opportunities for employee theft and to increase the likelihood of discovery if theft occurs. These procedures exist not because management assumes that all employees are dishonest, but because it is important to establish high standards for ethical conduct. When unethical behavior is tolerated, it often becomes an accepted value ("I cheated because I knew everyone was cheating"). An accounting system that establishes proper control over an organization's resources is one of the tools managers use to help insure that employees are making ethical decisions.

Significant ethical issues may also arise when management selects from among acceptable accounting alternatives. An example may be drawn from the discussion in Chapter 7 of alternative costing methods for measuring inventory and cost of goods sold. During a period of rising prices, LIFO produces lower net income than FIFO. At first, the selection of LIFO or FIFO might not seem to involve any ethical issues, but most managers' compensation is affected by the reported profits of their companies. The use of LIFO may be in the best interests of a corporation because LIFO often reduces its corporate tax liability (for an explanation, see the discussion in Chapter 7). But FIFO may favor the manager because higher reported profits may result in increased compensation. Clearly a manager who selects an accounting method that is not optimal for the company, solely in order to increase his or her own compensation, has engaged in questionable ethical behavior.

It may seem surprising that an accounting procedure acceptable under GAAP, when used in a specific situation, could be ethically questionable. In fact, any application of a general law, rule, or regulation requires judgment. What is very sound practice in most situations may be unacceptable under certain facts and circumstances. It is the ability to make appropriate (and ethical) decisions that separates respected professionals from technicians.

You will not be able to avoid confronting difficult ethical issues during your career. You should continually work to develop, examine, and modify your own ethical philosophy so that you will be prepared to deal with these difficult situations when they occur.

IMPORTANT TERMS DEFINED IN THIS CHAPTER

Bank Reconciliation Process of verifying the accuracy of both the bank statement and the cash accounts of the business. *p. 361*

Bank Statement Monthly report from a bank that shows deposits recorded, checks cleared, and a running bank balance. *p. 359*

Cash Money and any instrument that banks will accept for immediate increase in depositor's checking account. *p. 356*

Cash Over and Short Difference between the amount of cash held at a particular time and the amount the cash records call for. *p. 358*

Certificates of Deposit A CD; an investment contract that can be purchased from banks; specifies amount, time, and interest rate. *p. 372*

Compensating Balances Exists when a bank requires that a specified minimum cash balance must be maintained in the depositor's account. *p. 366*

Contingent Liability An endorser (on a negotiable instrument) is liable for its payment if the maker defaults; a contingent liability exists for the endorser. *p. 376*

Default of Note Receivable   Failure of the maker (payor) of a note to pay it by its maturity date. *p. 375*

Deposits in Transit   Deposits made by a depositor that have not yet been reported on the bank statement. *p. 361*

Discounting a Note Receivable   Sale of a note receivable to another party prior to its maturity date. *p. 376*

Internal Control   Policies and procedures of a business designed to safeguard the assets of the business. *p. 356*

Investment Portfolio   A group of securities (stock or bonds) held as an investment; grouped to be accounted for as one unit. *p. 368*

Lower of Cost or Market   Valuation of an investment at either *(a)* original cost or *(b)* current market whichever is lower. *p. 368*

Negotiable Instrument   A formal (written) instrument that specifies the terms of a debt; it is **transferable by endorsement.** *p. 376*

Notes Receivable   A written promise that requires another party to pay the business under specified conditions (amount, time, interest). *p. 374*

Outstanding Checks   Checks written by a depositor that have not yet been cleared (cashed) by the depositor's bank. *p. 361*

Petty Cash   A small amount of cash set aside for making small cash payments instead of writing checks. *p. 359*

Receivables, Short Term   Short-term notes and accounts owed to the business by regular trade customers. *p. 373*

Short-term Investment   An investment that *(a)* is marketable and *(b)* will have a short-term holding period. *p. 367*

Special Receivables   Receivables that arise from transactions other than merchandise and services sold. *p. 373*

Trade Receivables   Another name for accounts receivable; open accounts owed to the business by trade customers. *p. 373*

Unrealized Loss   Difference between original purchase cost of an investment and its current market value; if market value is **lower,** there is an unrealized loss (if not sold). *p. 369*

QUESTIONS

Part A: Questions 1–6

1. Define cash in the context of accounting and indicate the types of items that should be included and excluded. Identify typical categories of cash.

2. Summarize the primary characteristics of an effective internal control system for cash.

3. Why should cash-handling and cash-recording activities be separated? How is this separation accomplished?

4. What are the purposes of a bank reconciliation? What balances are reconciled?

5. Briefly explain how the total amount of cash reported on the balance sheet is computed.

6. What is the purpose of petty cash? How is it related to the regular Cash account?

Part B: Questions 7–11

7. Define a short-term investment. What is the twofold test for classification of an investment as short term?

8. Is a marketable security always classified as a short-term investment? Explain.

9. How does the cost principle apply in accounting for short-term investments in (*a*) debt securities and (*b*) equity securities?

10. What is the rationale for application of the LCM rule to the short-term investment portfolio of equity securities?

11. Explain the purpose of the Allowance to Reduce Short-Term Investments to Market account.

Part C: Questions 12–18

12. Distinguish between accounts receivable and special receivables.

13. Define a promissory note indicating the designation of the parties and explain what is meant by principal, maturity date, face amount, and interest rate.

14. Distinguish between an interest-bearing and noninterest-bearing note.

15. What is a negotiable note?

16. What is a defaulted note? Who is responsible for its payment? Explain.

17. What is meant by discounting a note receivable?

18. What is a contingent liability? How does one arise with respect to a note receivable?

EXERCISES

Part A: Exercises 8–1 to 8–6

E8–1 **(Match Definitions with Terms)**
Match each definition with its related term by entering the appropriate letter in the space provided.

	Terms		Definitions
____	(1) Bank statement	A.	An analysis that explains any differences existing between the cash balance shown by the depositor and that shown by the bank.
____	(2) Short-term investment		
____	(3) Cash over and short	B.	Provided by the bank to the depositor each month listing deposits, checks cleared, and running balance.
____	(4) Petty cash		
____	(5) Compensating balances	C.	Examples of this, by definition, are currency, checks, money orders, or bank drafts.
____	(6) Contingent liability	D.	Account to record errors that occur inevitably when a large number of cash transactions is involved.
____	(7) Bank reconciliation		
____	(8) Special receivables		
____	(9) Internal control	E.	Required minimum cash balances on deposit.
____	(10) Cash	F.	A potential liability that depends on a future event arising out of a past transaction.
____	(11) Deposits in transit		
____	(12) Notes receivable	G.	A note receivable not collected at maturity.
____	(13) Discounting a note receivable	H.	Deposits recorded in the depositor's ledger as debits to cash that have not been recorded by the bank.
____	(14) Negotiable instrument		
____	(15) Outstanding checks	I.	Selling a negotiable note receivable before its maturity date to obtain cash.
____	(16) Default of note receivable	J.	Methods and procedures concerned with the accuracy of financial records.

K. The most common example of this is a check.

L. Promissory notes that are evidence of a debt and state the terms of payment.

M. Checks not listed on the bank's statement.

N. Currency used for disbursements that are usually relatively minor and conveniently made from cash on hand.

O. A temporary investment in marketable securities.

P. Receivables, short or long term, that arise from transactions other than the sale of goods and/or services.

E8–2   (Reporting Cash When There Are Several Bank Accounts)

Gettler Corporation has manufacturing facilities in several cities and has cash on hand at several locations as well as in several bank accounts. The general ledger at the end of 19A showed the following accounts: Petty Cash—Home Office, $500; City Bank—Home Office, $57,300; Cash Held for Making Change, $200 (included in the regular Cash Account balance); Petty Cash—Location A, $100; National Bank—Location A, $4,458; Petty Cash—Location B, $200; Southwest Bank—Location B; $864; Petty Cash—Location C, $100; State Bank—Location C, $965; Metropolitan Bank—Savings account, $8,700; and postdated checks held that were received from two regular customers, $750.

The four bank balances given represent the current cash balances as reflected on the bank reconciliations.

Required:

What cash amount should be reported on the company's 19A balance sheet? Explain the basis for your decisions on any questionable items.

E8–3   (Analysis of Items to Determine Correct Cash Balance)

Avery Company prepared a December 31, 19B, balance sheet that reported cash, $8,225. The following items were included in the reported cash balance:

	Balance per bank statement at City Bank	$5,125*
a.	A deposit made to the local electric utility	500
b.	Postage stamps on hand	80
c.	Check signed by a customer, returned NSF	30
d.	Petty cash on hand	150
e.	IOUs signed by employees	125
f.	Check signed by the company president for an advance to him; to be held until he "gives the word to cash it"	2,000
g.	Money orders on hand (received from customers)	45
h.	A signed receipt from a freight company that involved a $10 overpayment to them. They have indicated a "check will be mailed shortly"	10
i.	A money order obtained from the post office to be used to pay for a special purchase upon delivery; expected within the next five days	160
	Total cash shown on the 19B balance sheet	$8,225

* Items not considered: deposit in transit, $500; checks outstanding, $175; and cash held for making change, $400 (all included in the regular Cash account).

Required:

a. The reported cash balance is not correct. Compute the correct cash amount that should be reported on the balance sheet. Give appropriate reporting for any items that you exclude. (Hint: Set up a form similar to the above.)

b. Assume the company carries two cash accounts in the general ledger—Cash and Petty Cash. What is the correct balance that should be reflected in each cash account at December 31, 19B (end of the accounting period)? Show computations.

E8–4   (Bank Reconciliation, Entries, and Reporting)

Case Company has the June 30, 19B, bank statement and the June ledger accounts for cash, which are summarized below:

Bank Statement

	Checks	Deposits	Balance
Balance, June 1, 19B			$ 5,900
Deposits during June		$17,000	22,900
Checks cleared through June	$17,700		5,200
Bank service charges	75		5,125
Balance, June 30, 19B			5,125

Cash

June 1	Balance	5,400	June	Checks written	18,100
June	Deposits	19,000			

Petty Cash

June 30 Balance	200		

Required:

a. Reconcile the bank account. A comparison of the checks written with the checks that have cleared the bank show outstanding checks of $900. Some of the checks that cleared in June were written prior to June. There were no deposits in transit carried over from May, but there is a deposit in transit at the end of June.

b. Give any journal entries that should be made as a result of the bank reconciliation.

c. What is the balance in the Cash account after the reconciliation entries?

d. What total amount of cash should be reported on the balance sheet at June 30?

E8–5   **(Bank Reconciliation, Entries, and Reporting)**

The September 30, 19D, bank statement for Dean Company and the September ledger accounts for cash are summarized below:

Bank Statement

	Checks	Deposits	Balance
Balance, September 1, 19D			$ 5,100
Deposits recorded during September . . .		$27,000	32,100
Checks cleared during September	$27,300		4,800
NSF check—Sally Jones	200		4,600
Bank service charges	100		4,500
Balance, September 30, 19D			4,500

Cash

Sept. 1 Balance	5,100	Sept. Checks written	27,800
Sept. Deposits	29,500		

Petty Cash

Sept. 30 Balance	450		

There were no outstanding checks and no deposits in transit carried over from August; however, there are deposits in transit and checks outstanding at the end of September.

Required:

a. Reconcile the bank account.

b. Give any journal entries that should be made as a result of the bank reconciliation.

c. What should be the balance in the Cash account after the reconciliation entries?

d. What total amount of cash should the company report on the September 30 balance sheet?

E8–6 **(Bank Reconciliation with an Overage or Shortage)**

The March 31, 19C, bank statement for Town Company and the March ledger accounts for cash are summarized below:

Bank Statement

	Checks	Deposits	Balance
Balance, March 1, 19C			$ 9,900
Deposits during March		$28,000	37,900
Note collected for depositor			
(including $100 interest)		1,060	38,960
Checks cleared during March	$32,200		6,760
Bank service charges	50		6,710
Balance, March 31, 19C			6,710

Cash

Mar.	1	Balance	9,300	Mar.	Checks written	32,500
Mar.		Deposits	31,000			

Petty Cash

Mar. 31	Balance	400	

A comparison of March deposits recorded with deposits on the bank statement showed deposits in transit of $3,000. Outstanding checks at the end of March were determined to be $900.

Required:

a. Prepare a bank reconciliation for March. The bank figures have been verified as correct.

b. Give any journal entries that should be made by the company based on the reconciliation.

c. What amount should be shown as the ending balance in the Cash account after the reconciliation entries? What total amount of cash should be reported on the company's balance sheet at the end of March?

Part B: Exercises 8–7 to 8–10

E8–7 **(Recording and Reporting Short-Term Investments)**

In July 19B, Green Company had accumulated excess cash that would not be needed for 10 to 15 months. To employ the idle cash profitably, the management decided to purchase some shares of stock as a short-term investment. The following transactions occurred:

19B

July 30 Purchased 10,000 shares of the common stock of Sharp Corporation. The cash price, including fees and transfer costs, was $40,000.

Dec. 15 Received a cash dividend of $0.40 per share on the Sharp shares.

30 Sold 1,000 of the Sharp shares at $5 per share.

Required:

a. Give the journal entries that Green Company should make on each date for this short-term investment. Their accounting period ends on December 31.

b. Show how this short-term investment should be reported on the balance sheet at December 31, 19B. Assume the market value of the Sharp stock was $5 per share on December 31, 19B.

E8–8   **(Recording and Reporting a Single Equity Security)**
Norwok Company purchased some common stock in Bay Corporation as a short-term investment. The following related transactions occurred:

19B
Feb.   1   Purchased 10,000 shares of Bay Corporation common stock for $60,000 cash.
Aug. 15   Received a cash dividend on the Bay stock of $0.50 per share.
Dec. 30   Sold 3,000 shares of the Bay stock at $5.80 per share.
       31   End of the accounting year. Bay stock was selling at $5 per share.

Required:

a. Give the journal entries for Norwok Company on each date (including December 31) for the investment in Bay stock. The company had no other short-term investments.

b. Show how the effects of this short-term investment should be reported on the financial statements at December 31, 19B.

c. Give the entry on January 15, 19C, assuming the remaining shares were sold at $4.50 per share.

d. Explain what Norwok Company should do about the allowance account on December 31, 19C, assuming no short-term investments are held on that date.

E8–9   **(Recording and Reporting a Short-Term Investment in Several Securities)**
During March 19B, Johnson Company acquired 200 shares of common stock in each of three corporations at the following costs: Corporation A, $8,000; Corporation B, $6,000; and Corporation C, $12,000. At the end of the annual accounting period, December 31, 19B, the quoted market prices per share were Corporation A, $40; Corporation B, $25; and Corporation C, $61.

Required:

a. Give the journal entry to record the acquisition of these short-term investments.

b. Give the entry to record cash dividends of $2,400 received on the short-term investments in November 19B.

c. Give the entry to reflect the investments at LCM at December 31, 19B. Show computations.

d. Show how the investments would be reported on the financial statements at December 31, 19B.

e. Give the entry on January 5, 19C, assuming all of the shares were sold for $24,000 cash.

f. Give any entry required at December 31, 19C, assuming no short-term equity investments are held at that time (disregard any closing entries).

E8–10   **(Accounting for an Investment in a Debt Security)**
On October 1, 19B, Hadaway Company purchased a debt security as a short-term investment for $24,000 cash. The security (due in 12 months) earns 10% annual interest on its principal amount of $24,000, payable on the date of maturity. At the end of the annual accounting period (December 31), the same security could be purchased for $22,800 cash.

Required:

a. Give all of the journal entries for the following dates and provide an explanation for each date:
   (1) October 1, 19B.
   (2) December 31, 19B.
   (3) September 30, 19C.

b. Show how the security would be reported on the 19B financial statements.

Part C: Exercises 8–11 to 8–14

E8–11   **(Accounting for a Credit Sale through Accounts Receivable, to Notes Receivable, to Final Collection)**
Approximately 40% of the merchandise sold by Martin Company is sold on credit. Accounts receivable that are overdue, if material in amount, are converted to notes receivable when possible. The related transactions during 19B were:

Jan. 10   Sold merchandise on account to B. A. Cable for $10,000; terms n/30.
Mar. 1   The account was unpaid. The company asked Cable to sign a six-month, 12% interest-bearing note for the account. Cable executed the note on this date.
Aug. 31   Cable paid the principal of the note plus interest.

Required:

a. Give the journal entry that the company should make on each of the three dates.

b. Give the journal entry that should be made on September 1, 19B, assuming Cable defaulted.

c. Give the journal entry assuming the default in (b) and also that Cable paid the note in full on September 15, 19B (no additional interest was paid).

E8–12   **(Accounting for a Credit Sale with a Note Payable)**
White Company sells a line of products that has a high unit sales price. Credit terms are traditional in the industry. The company frequently takes a promissory note for the sale price. The accounting year ends December 31. The transactions and events were:

19B
Dec. 1   Sold merchandise to B. T. Hamm on a three-month, 8% interest-bearing note for $15,000.
     31   End of accounting year.

19C
Jan. 1   Start of new accounting period.
Mar. 1   Collected the note plus interest.

Required:

a. Give the journal entries for the company at each of the four dates; if none, so
   state.

b. With respect to the note, what item(s) and amount(s) should be reported on the
   19B income statement?

c. With respect to the note, what item(s) and amount(s) should be reported on the
   balance sheet at December 31, 19B?

E8–13   (Accounting for a Defaulted Note)

Davidson Company frequently sells merchandise on a promissory note. These notes
frequently are sold (i.e., discounted) to the local bank to obtain cash needed before
maturity date. The following transactions relate to one note:

19B
Apr. 1   Sold merchandise for $6,000 to R. C. Day; took a six-month, 12% interest-bearing
         note.
June 1   Discounted the note at the local bank at a 10% discount rate.
Oct. 1   Due date of the note plus interest.

Required:

a. Give the journal entries of the three dates, assuming Day paid the bank for the
   note on due date.

b. Give the journal entry on October 1, 19B, assuming Day defaulted on the note and
   the company had to make payment plus a $50 protest fee. This protest fee will be
   charged to Day.

c. Give the journal entry assuming Day paid in full on October 5, 19B (no additional
   interest was paid).

E8–14   (Based on Chapter Supplement 8A—Accounting and Reporting Petty Cash)

On January 1, 19B, Bay Company established a petty cash fund of $400 by writing a check
to Petty Cash. The fund was assigned to J. Wright, an employee, to administer as
custodian. At the end of January, $60 cash remained in the fund. Signed receipts for
expenditures during January were summarized as follows: postage, $63; office supplies,
$28; transportation, $101; newspapers, $34; and miscellaneous (coffee for the office), $14.

Required:

a. Give the journal entry to establish the petty cash fund on January 1, 19B.

b. Give the journal entry to replenish the fund on January 31, 19B.

c. What balance would be shown in the Petty Cash account in the ledger at January
   31? Explain.

d. How would petty cash be reported on the balance sheet at January 31,19B?

e. Explain how the petty cash fund affected the January 19B income statement?

f. Assume it is January 5, 19C, and the management has decided to decrease the
   petty cash fund to $250. Give the required journal entry.

PROBLEMS

Part A: Problems 8-1 to 8-4

P8-1 (Analysis of Internal Control)

Pedernales Company has one trusted employee who, as the owner said, "handles all of the bookkeeping and paperwork for the company." This employee also is responsible for counting, verifying, and recording cash receipts and payments, such as making the weekly bank deposit, preparing checks for major expenditures (signed by the owner), making small expenditures from the cash register for daily expenses, and collecting accounts receivable. The owners asked the local bank for a $25,000 loan. The bank asked that an audit be performed covering the year just ended. The independent auditor (a local CPA), in a private conference with the owner, presented some evidence of the following activities of the trusted employee during the past year:

1. Cash sales sometimes were not entered in the cash register, and the trusted employee pocketed approximately $40 per month.
2. Cash taken from the cash register (and pocketed by the trusted employee) was replaced with expense memos with fictitious signatures (approximately $10 per day).
3. A $500 collection on an account receivable of a valued out-of-town customer was pocketed by the trusted employee and was covered by making a $500 entry as a debit to Sales Returns and a credit to Accounts Receivable.
4. A $700 collection on an account receivable from a local customer was pocketed by the trusted employee and was covered by making a $700 entry as a debit to Allowance for Doubtful Accounts and a credit to Accounts Receivable.

Required:

a. What was the approximate amount stolen during the past year?
b. What would be your recommendations to the owner?

P8-2 (Prepare a Bank Reconciliation and Related Journal Entries)

The bookkeeper at Baker Company has not reconciled the bank statement with the Cash account, saying, "I don't have time." You have been asked to prepare a reconciliation and review the procedures with the bookkeeper.

The April 30, 19D, bank statement and the April ledger accounts for cash showed the following (summarized):

Bank Statement

	Checks	Deposits	Balance
Balance, April 1, 19D			$23,550
Deposits during April		$38,000	61,550
Note collected for depositor			
(including $90 interest)		1,090	62,640
Checks cleared during April	$44,200		18,440
NSF check—A. B. Cage	140		18,300
Bank service charges	100		18,200
Balance, April 30, 19D			18,200

Cash

Apr. 1	Balance	22,750	Apr.	Checks written	44,500
Apr.	Deposits	42,000			

Petty Cash

Apr. 30	Balance	200	

A comparison of checks written before and during April with the checks cleared through the bank showed outstanding checks at the end of April of $1,100. No deposits in transit were carried over from March, but there was a deposit in transit at the end of April.

Required:

a. Prepare a detailed bank reconciliation for April.

b. Give any required journal entries as a result of the reconciliation. Why are they necessary?

c. What were the balances in the cash accounts in the ledger on May 1, 19D?

d. What total amount of cash should be reported on the balance sheet at the end of April?

P8–3 **(Compute Outstanding Checks and Deposits in Transit; Prepare a Bank Reconciliation and Journal Entries)**

The August 19B bank statement for Mindy Company and the August 19B ledger accounts for cash are given below:

Bank Statement

Date		Checks	Deposits	Balance
Aug. 1				$16,000
2	$ 300			15,700
3			$7,000	22,700
4		400		22,300
5		200		22,100
9		900		21,200
10		300		20,900
15			9,000	29,900
21		700		29,200
24		21,000		8,200
25			8,000	16,200
30		800		15,400
30			2,180*	17,580
31		150†		17,430

* $2,000 note collected plus interest.
† Bank service charge.

Cash

Aug. 1 Balance	15,100	Checks written:	
Deposits:		Aug. 2	300
Aug. 2	7,000	4	900
12	9,000	15	850
24	8,000	17	550
31	6,000	18	800
		18	700
		23	21,000

Petty Cash

Aug. 31 Balance	250

Outstanding checks at the end of July were $200, $400, and $300. There were no deposits in transit at the end of July.

Required:

a. Compute the deposits in transit at the end of August.

b. Compute the outstanding checks at the end of August.

c. Prepare a bank reconciliation for August.

d. Give any journal entries that should be made as a result of the bank reconciliation by the company. Why are they necessary?

e. After the reconciliation journal entries are posted, what balances would be reflected in the cash accounts in the ledger?

f. What total amount of cash should be reported on the August 31, 19B, balance sheet?

P8–4 **(Compute Outstanding Checks and Deposits in Transit; Prepare Bank Reconciliation)**

The December 31, 19B, bank statement for Mork Company and the December 19B ledger accounts for cash are given below.

Bank Statement

Date	Checks	Deposits	Balance
Dec. 1			$41,000
2	$400, 150	$16,000	56,450
4	7,000, 80		49,370
6	120, 180, 1,500		47,570
11	900, 1,200, 90	21,000	66,380
13	450, 700, 1,900		63,330
17	17,000, 2,000		44,330
23	40, 23,500	36,000	56,790
26	1,800, 2,650		52,340
28	2,200, 4,800		45,340
30	13,000, 1,890, 200*	19,000	49,250
31	1,650, 1,200, 125‡	6,360 †	52,635

* NSF check, J. Doe, a customer.
† Note collected, principal, $6,000 plus interest.
‡ Bank service charge.

Cash

Dec. 1 Balance	55,700	Checks written during December:		
Deposits:		40	5,000	2,650
Dec. 11	21,000	13,000	4,800	1,650
23	36,000	700	1,890	2,200
30	19,000	4,400	1,500	7,000
31	18,000	1,200	120	150
		180	80	450
		17,000	23,500	2,000
		90	900	1,900
		1,800	1,200	

Petty Cash

Dec. 31 Balance	200	

The November 19B bank reconciliation showed the following: correct cash balance at November 30, $55,700; deposits in transit on November 30, $16,000; and outstanding checks on November 30, $400 + $900 = $1,300.

Required:

a. Compute the deposits in transit December 31, 19B.

b. Compute the outstanding checks at December 31, 19B.

c. Prepare a bank reconciliation at December 31, 19B.

d. Give any journal entries that should be made as a result of the bank reconciliation made by the company. Why are they necessary?

e. After the reconciliation journal entries, what balances would be reflected in the cash accounts in the ledger?

f. What total amount of cash should be reported on the December 31, 19B, balance sheet?

Part B: Problems 8–5 to 8–7

P8–5 **(Accounting for a Portfolio of Short-Term Investments; Use of LCM)**

Landmark Company usually acquires common stocks as a short-term investment. This problem focuses on the purchase of three different common stocks during 19B. The annual accounting period ends December 31. The sequence of transactions was:

19B
Apr. 2 Purchased (with cash) the following common stocks as a short-term investment:

Corporation	Number of shares	Total price per share
X	300	$50
Y	400	70
Z	200	90

Sept. 8 Received a cash dividend of $2 per share on Corporation Z stock.

Dec. 10 Sold the stock of Corporation Y for $72 per share.

     31 Quoted market prices on this date were Corporation X stock, $53; Corporation Y stock, $75; and Corporation Z stock, $80.

Required:

a. Give the journal entry for the company on each date.

b. How would the effects of these investments be shown on the 19B income statement and the balance sheet at December 31, 19B?

c. What was the amount of the 19B unrealized loss? Explain what this means.

d. Assume it is December 31, 19C, and that all of the X and Z shares still are held and that their market values per share are X, $51; and Z, $80. Give the required LCM entry.

(Hint: Leave the correct balance in the Allowance account.)

P8–6 (Accounting for Short-Term Investments in Debt Securities)

On July 1, 19D, South Company purchased, as a short-term investment, ten $1,000, 10% bonds of Lowe Corporation at par (i.e., at $1,000 each). The bonds mature on June 30, 19G. Annual interest is payable on June 30 each year. The accounting period for the company ends on December 31.

Required:

a. Give the journal entries required for the company on the following dates (if no entry is required, explain why): July 1, 19D, and December 31, 19D.

b. At the end of 19D, the bonds were quoted on the market at $960 each. Give any LCM basis journal entry required on December 31, 19D. If none is required, explain why.

c. Show how this investment should be reported on the 19D balance sheet and income statement.

d. Give the journal entry required on June 30, 19E.

P8–7 (Accounting for Short-Term Investments in Equity and Debt Securities; Use of LCM)

Woody Company produces and sells one main product. Demand is seasonal, and the unit sales price is high. The company's accounting year ends December 31. Typically, in the busy months of the demand cycle, the company collects large amounts of cash, which is not needed during the slow months. The company often purchases short-term investments to earn a return on idle cash. Recently, the company purchased 1,000 shares of common stock in each of two other corporations—Corporations A and B. The prices per share, including fees and related costs, were A, $30; and B, $70. In addition, the company purchased a $10,000 bond of James Corporation. The bond pays 10% annual interest on each March 31. The bond was purchased for $10,000 cash (i.e., at par).

The sequence of transactions was:

19B

Apr. 1 Purchased the common stock and the bond. (Hint: Account for the stock and bond portfolios separately.)

Oct. 3 Received a cash dividend of $2 per share on the stock of Corporation B.

Nov. 30   Sold 600 shares of the stock of Corporation A at $26 per share and 600 shares of the stock of Corporation B at $75 per share.

Dec. 31   End of the accounting period. The market prices on this date were A stock, $28; B stock, $68; and James bonds, 100 (i.e., at par). (Hint: Do not overlook accrued interest.)

Required:

a. Give the journal entries for the company at each of the four dates given above. Omit any closing entries.

b. Show how the effects of the investment should be reported on the balance sheet at December 31, 19B.

c. What items and amounts should be reported on the 19B income statement?

Part C: Problems 8–8 to 8–10

P8–8   **(Accounting for Accounts Receivable and Notes Receivable)**

Plaza Company sells approximately 80% of its merchandise on credit; terms n/30. Occasionally, a note will be received as a part of the collection process of a delinquent account. The annual accounting period ends December 31. The sequence of transactions was:

Note No. 1:

19B

Feb. 15   Sold merchandise for $5,000 to A. B. Lee; received $2,000 cash, and the balance was debited to Accounts Receivable.

Apr. 1   Received a 12% interest-bearing note in settlement of the overdue account of Lee. The note is due in four months.

July 31   Due date for note; Lee defaulted.

Oct. 1   Lee paid the defaulted note plus interest, plus 8% interest on the defaulted amount for the period July 31–October 1. The 8% is the legal rate of interest on overdue obligations.

Note No. 2:

19B

Oct. 1   Sold merchandise for $4,000 to J. K. Pope on account.

Nov. 1   Received a 12% interest-bearing note in settlement of the overdue account from Pope. The note is due in three months.

Dec. 31   End of accounting period.

19C

Jan. 1   Start of new accounting period.

     30   Maturity date of the note. Pope paid the principal plus interest.

Required:

a. Note No. 1—Give the journal entries for the company on each date. Show interest calculations. Omit any closing entries.

b. Note No. 2—Give the journal entries for the company on each date. Show interest calculations. Omit any closing entries.

c. Note No. 2—How much interest revenue should the company report on the 19B income statement?

d. Note No. 2—How will this note affect the 19B balance sheet of the company?

P8-9 (Accounting for Notes Receivable, Including Discounting)

Deere Company sells heavy machinery. Credit terms are customary and usually involve promissory notes and a mortgage on the machinery sold. The annual accounting period ends December 31. The transactions involving notes were:

Note No. 1:

19B

Feb. 1 Sold equipment to W. D. Fort for $40,000; received a $16,000 down payment and a four-month, 12% interest-bearing note for the balance.

Mar. 1 Sold the note to the local bank at a 10% discount rate.

June 1 Due date of the note plus interest; Fort paid the note and interest in full.

Required:

a. Give the journal entry for the company on each of the three dates. Show interest computations. Assume that Fort paid the bank the principal plus interest on the due date.

b. Give the journal entry on the due date, June 1, 19B, assuming instead that Fort defaulted on the note and the company paid the local bank the face amount of the note plus interest, and a $25 protest fee.

c. How much interest revenue should be reported on the 19B income statement for Note No. 1?

Note No. 2:

19B

Dec. 1 Sold equipment to W. T. Owens for $30,000; received $12,000 cash down payment and a three-month, 12% interest-bearing note for the balance.

31 End of accounting period.

19C

Jan. 1 Start of new accounting period.

Mar. 1 Due date of the principal plus interest; Owens paid the note plus interest in full.

Required:

d. Give the journal entry for the company on each of the four dates (omit any closing entries). State any assumptions you make.

e. How much interest revenue (Note No. 2) should be reported on the 19B income statement?

f. Show how Note No. 2 should be reported on the balance sheet at December 31, 19B.

P8-10   **(Based on Chapter Supplement 8B—Use of Control Accounts and Subsidiary Ledgers)**

New Company completes a variety of transactions each year. A number of them are repetitive in nature; therefore, the company maintains five different journals: general, credit sales, credit purchases, cash receipts, and cash payments. Selected transactions are listed below that are to be appropriately entered in these journals. To shorten this problem, amounts have been simplified and the number of transactions limited. All credit sales and credit purchases are recorded net of discount.

Selected transactions are listed below (use the letter to the left in lieu of the date and use the letter *v* for the last day of the period):

a. Sold merchandise to K. K. May at invoice cost of $250; terms 2/10, n/20; Invoice No. 38.

b. Received merchandise from Sable Company at invoice cost of $300; credit terms 1/10, n/20; Purchase Order No. 17.

c. Sold merchandise to B. B. Wise for $200 on credit; terms 2/10, n/20; Invoice No. 39.

d. Received merchandise from Rex Supply Company at an invoice cost of $200 on credit; terms 1/10, n/20; Purchase Order No. 18.

e. Sold merchandise to A. B. Cox for $750.

f. Received merchandise from Baker Manufacturing Company at a cost of $360; paid cash (number the checks consecutively starting with No. 81).

g. Purchased an operational asset (machinery) at a cost of $5,000; gave a 90-day, 12% interest-bearing note payable for the purchase price.

h. Sold a tract of land for $9,000 that previously was used by the company as a parking lot and originally cost $4,000; collected cash.

i. Collected the account receivable from B. B. Wise within the discount period; Invoice No. 39.

j. Paid $600 for a three-year insurance policy on operational assets.

k. Obtained a $5,000 bank loan; signed a one-year, 12% interest-bearing note payable.

l. Paid the account payable to Rex Supply Company within the discount period.

m. Paid monthly rent, $1,200.

n. Sold merchandise for cash, $1,400.

o. Purchased merchandise for cash, $980.

p. Sold merchandise on credit to C. C. Coe for $700; terms 2/10, n/20; Invoice No. 40.

q. Purchased merchandise on credit from Stubbs Company at an invoice cost of $400; terms 2/10/, n/30; Purchase Order No. 19.

r. Collected the account receivable from K. K. May after the discount period.

s. Paid the account payable to Sable Company after the discount period.

t. Paid monthly salaries, $2,400.

u. By year-end, six months of the prepaid insurance had expired.

Use the following general ledger account code numbers for posting: Cash, 11; Accounts Receivable, 14; Prepaid Insurance, 16; Machinery, 17; Land, 19; Accounts Payable, 21;

Notes Payable, 22; Purchases, 31; Purchase Discounts Lost, 33; Sales Revenue, 41; Sales Discount Revenue, 43; Expenses, 51; and Gain on Sale of Operational Assets, 53. For journals, use the following page numbers: General, 15; Credit Sales, 18; Credit Purchases, 14; Cash Receipts, 21; and Cash Payments, 34.

Required:

1. Draft a format for each of the five journals, including a general journal, following the illustrations included in Chapter Supplement 8B. Include Folio columns.

2. Set up separate T-accounts for each of the general ledger accounts listed above.

3. Set up separate T-accounts (with account numbers) for the subsidiary ledgers as follows:

Accounts receivable (14)	Accounts payable (21)
Coe—14.1	Stable—21.1
May—14.2	Stubbs—21.2
Wise—14.3	Rex—21.3

4. Enter each transaction in the appropriate journal.

5. Indicate all postings to the subsidiary ledgers by entering appropriate account numbers in the Folio columns.

6. Total each money column in the special journals and indicate all postings to the general ledger accounts by entering the account code numbers in the Folio columns and below total amounts posted. Use the account code numbers given above.

CASES

C8–1 (Analysis and Evaluation of Internal Controls)

Hall Manufacturing Company is a relatively small local business that specializes in the repair and renovation of antique jewelry, brass objects, and silverware. The owner is an expert craftsman. Although a number of skilled workers are employed, there is always a large backlog of work to be done. A long-time employee, who serves as clerk-book-keeper, handles cash receipts, keeps the records, and writes checks for disbursements. The checks are signed by the owner. Small amounts are paid in cash by the clerk-bookkeeper, subject to a month-end review by the owner. Approximately 100 regular customers regularly are extended credit that typically amounts to less than $500. Although credit losses are small, in recent years the bookkeeper had established an Allowance for Doubtful Accounts, and all write-offs were made at year-end. During January 19E (the current year), the owner decided to start construction as soon as possible of a building for the business that would provide many advantages over the presently rented space and would have space usable for expansion of facilities. As a part of the considerations in financing, the financing institution asked for "19D audited financial statements." The company statements never had been audited. Early in the audit, the independent CPA found numerous errors and one combination of amounts, in particular, that caused concern.

There was some evidence that a $1,500 job completed by Hall had been recorded as a receivable (from a new customer) on July 15, 19D. The receivable was credited for a $1,500 cash collection a few days later. The new account never was active again. The auditor also observed that shortly thereafter three write-offs of Accounts Receivable balances had been made to Allowance for Doubtful Accounts as follows: Jones, $250; Adams, $750; and Coster, $500—all of whom were known as regular customers. These write-offs drew the attention of the auditor.

Required:

a. What caused the CPA to be concerned? Explain. Should the CPA report the suspicions to the owner?

b. What recommendations would you make in respect to internal control procedures for this company?

C8–2 **(Analysis of Cash and Short-Term Investments for an Actual Company)**

JCPenney   Refer to the financial statements of J.C. Penney Company, Inc. given in the appendix immediately preceding the index.

1. How much cash does the company hold at the end of the current year?

2. What types of securities are included in short-term investments?

3. How is income on short-term investments reported? What was the amount of income on short-term investments for the current year?

4. How does the company anticipate that the major portion of its cash requirements during the next few years will be met?

NINE

OPERATIONAL ASSETS— PROPERTY, PLANT, AND EQUIPMENT; NATURAL RESOURCES; AND INTANGIBLES

PURPOSE

The operation of a business requires a combination of assets that are classified on a balance sheet as current, investments, operational, and other. The purpose of this chapter is to discuss operational assets. These assets usually are called property, plant, and equipment and intangible assets (and sometimes fixed assets). **Operational assets are the noncurrent assets that a business retains more or less permanently (not for sale) to carry on its continuing operations.** Operational assets include land, buildings, equipment, fixtures, natural resources, and certain intangible assets (such as a patent). Operational assets are important in carrying out the normal profit-making activities of a business.

Disclosures concerning property, plant, and equipment are illustrated on the opposite page.

LEARNING OBJECTIVES

1. Define, classify, and explain the nature of operational assets.

2. Apply the cost principle to measure and record operational assets.

3. Apply the matching principle to record and report depreciation and depletion.

4. Define, record, and amortize intangible operational assets.

5. Expand your accounting vocabulary by learning the "Important Terms Defined in This Chapter."

6. Apply the knowledge learned from this chapter by completing the homework assigned by your instructor.

ORGANIZATION

Part A—property, plant, and equipment, including depreciation
1. Measuring and recording acquisition cost.
2. Depreciation concepts and methods.
3. Effects of depreciation on the financial statements.
4. Depreciation and cash flows.

Part B—repairs and maintenance, natural resources, and intangible assets
1. Repairs, maintenance, and additions.
2. Natural resources and depletion.
3. Intangible assets and amortization.
4. Disposal of operational assets.

CONSOLIDATED BALANCE SHEETS

(thousands)	January 3, 1988	December 28, 1986
Assets		
Current Assets		
Cash	$ 4,673	$ 5,047
Certificates of deposit	803	6,401
Marketable securities	42,156	28,067
Receivables—trade and other (net of allowance for		
doubtful accounts, 1987—$842,000 and 1986—$752,000)	41,704	32,960
Inventories	59,779	50,058
Deferred income taxes	6,691	5,622
Other	5,229	6,831
Total current assets	161,035	134,986
PROPERTY, PLANT AND EQUIPMENT–NET	58,133	54,939
OTHER ASSETS	4,664	3,446
TOTAL	$223,832	$193,371

NOTES TO CONSOLIDATED FINANCIAL STATEMENTS

PROPERTY, PLANT AND EQUIPMENT — NET:
  Property, plant and equipment—net consists of the following:

(thousands)	January 3, 1988	December 28, 1986
Land	$ 2,228	$ 2,220
Buildings and improvements	29,945	29,923
Machinery and equipment	107,511	101,101
Construction in progress	7,226	3,037
Total	146,910	136,281
Less accumulated depreciation	88,777	81,342
TOTAL	$ 58,133	$ 54,939

Classification of Operational Assets

Operational assets have different characteristics depending on the nature of the business. Operational assets are classified as follows:

1. **Tangible assets**—the operational assets that have **physical substance;** that is, they are tangible. This classification usually is called property, plant, and equipment. There are three kinds of tangible assets:
   a. Land—held for use in operations; it is **not** subject to depreciation.
   b. Buildings, fixtures, equipment; subject to **depreciation.**
   c. Natural resources; subject to **depletion.**
2. **Intangible assets**—the operational assets that do not have physical substance that are held by the business because of the **use rights** they confer to the owner. Examples are patents, copyrights, franchises, licenses, and trademarks. Intangible assets are subject to periodic **amortization.**

Accounting Concepts Applied to Accounting for Operational Assets

The life span of operational assets owned by a business extends over many accounting periods. The following accounting concepts must be applied (refer to Exhibit 4–5):

1. **Cost principle**—at purchase date, each operational asset is recorded at its **cash-equivalent** cost.
2. **Matching principle**—during the period from acquisition date to disposal date, the expense of using each asset is recorded in a way to match this expense with the revenues that the asset helped to earn.
3. **Recognition of gain or loss**—at disposal date of operational assets.

This chapter discusses the application of these accounting principles to long-term assets.

PART A—PROPERTY, PLANT, AND EQUIPMENT, INCLUDING DEPRECIATION

Measuring and Recording Acquisition Cost

Under the **cost principle,** all reasonable and necessary costs incurred in **acquiring** an operational asset, **placing** it in its operational setting, and **preparing** it for use should be recorded in a designated asset account. Cost is measured as the **net cash equivalent** amount paid or to be paid. **Acquisition cost** must be determined when an operational asset is purchased for cash. The acquisition cost of a machine on January 1, 19A, may be measured as follows:

```
Invoice price of the machine  . . . . . . . . . . . . . . . . . . .   $10,000
    Less: Cash discount allowed ($10,000 × 2%)  . . . . . . . .       200
Net cash invoice price . . . . . . . . . . . . . . . . . . . . .      9,800
Add: Transportation charges paid by purchaser  . . . . . . . .         150
     Installation costs paid by purchaser . . . . . . . . . . .        200
     Sales tax paid ($10,000 × 2%) . . . . . . . . . . . . . .         200
Cost—amount debited to the Machinery account  . . . . . . .        $10,350
```

The seller agreed to give a 2% discount for immediate cash payment. Even if the $200 discount is not taken, it still is deducted from the acquisition cost of the machine because the extra amount paid is a cost of credit, not a part of the cost of the machine. The $200 is recorded as interest expense. Notice that the cost includes transportation, installation, and sales tax. The journal entry to record the purchase of this machine is:[1]

January 1, 19A:

```
Machinery . . . . . . . . . . . . . . . . . . . . . . . . . . . . . . .   10,350
    Cash  . . . . . . . . . . . . . . . . . . . . . . . . . . . . . . .            10,350
```

When a **noncash** consideration is included in the purchase of an asset, the cash equivalent cost is measured as any cash paid plus the **current market value** of the noncash consideration given. Alternatively, if the market value of the noncash consideration given cannot be determmined, the current market value of the asset purchased is used for measurement purposes. Assume a tract of timber was acquired by Fast Corporation. Payment in full was made as follows: $28,000 cash plus 2,000 shares of Fast Corporation capital stock (nopar).[2] At the date of the purchase, Fast stock was selling at $12 per share. The cost of the tract would be measured as follows:

```
Cash paid . . . . . . . . . . . . . . . . . . . . . . . . . . . . . . . . . . . . .  $28,000
Market value, noncash consideration given (2,000 shares nopar stock × $12) . . . . . .   24,000
                                                                                         52,000
Title fees, legal fees, and other costs paid in cash (incidental to the acquisition) . . . .   1,000
Cost—amount debited to the asset account  . . . . . . . . . . . . . . . . . . . . .  $53,000
```

The journal entry to record the acquisition of this natural resource is:

January 1, 19A:

```
Timber tract (No. 12) . . . . . . . . . . . . . . . . . . . . . . . . . . .   53,000
    Cash  . . . . . . . . . . . . . . . . . . . . . . . . . . . . . . . . .            29,000
    Capital stock, nopar (2,000 shares × $12) . . . . . . . . . . . . . . .            24,000
```

---

[1] If the invoice is not paid immediately, this entry would be:

```
Machinery . . . . . . . . . . . . . . . . . . . . . . . . . . . . . . . . . .   10,350
Interest expense  . . . . . . . . . . . . . . . . . . . . . . . . . . . . . .      200
    Liability, equipment purchase . . . . . . . . . . . . . . . . . . . . . .            10,000
    Cash ($150 + $200 + $200)  . . . . . . . . . . . . . . . . . . . . . .                  550
```

[2] See Chapter 12 for discussion of capital stock.

When land is purchased, all of the incidental costs paid by the purchaser, such as title fees, sales commissions, legal fees, title insurance, delinquent taxes, and surveying fees, should be included in the cost of the land. Because land is **not** subject to depreciation, it must be recorded and reported as a separate operational asset.

Sometimes, an **old** building or used machinery is purchased for operational use in the business. Renovation and repair cost incurred by the purchaser **prior to use** should be included in the asset account as a part of the cost of the asset. Ordinary repair costs incurred **after** the asset is placed in use are normal operating expenses when incurred.

Basket Purchases of Assets

When several operational assets are acquired in a single transaction and for a single lump sum, the cost of each asset must be **measured and recorded separately.** When a building and the land on which it is located are purchased for a lump sum, two separate accounts must be established. One is for the building (which is subject to depreciation), and one is for the land (which is not subject to depreciation). The purchase price must be apportioned between the land and the building on a **rational** basis.

Relative market value of the several assets at the date of acquisition is the most logical basis on which to allocate the single lump sum. Appraisals or tax assessments often have to be used as indications of the market values. Assume Fox Company paid $300,000 cash to purchase a building and the land on which the building is located. The separate, true market values of the building and land were not known; therefore, a professional appraisal was obtained. This appraisal showed the following estimated market values: building, $189,000; and land, $126,000 (apparently the buyer got a good deal). The apportionment of the $300,000 purchase price and the journal entry to record the acquisition are shown in Exhibit 9–1.

Matching Costs with Revenues Generated from Operational Assets

In conformity with the **matching principle,** the costs of using an operational asset must be matched with revenues earned each accounting period. The costs of using an operational asset include: (1) depreciation, depletion, and amortization (discussed in Part A of this chapter); and (2) repairs and maintenance (discussed in Part B).

Nature of Depreciation, Depletion, and Amortization

An operational asset that has a limited useful life represents the **prepaid cost** of a bundle of **future** services or benefits that will help earn future revenues. The **matching principle** (Exhibit 4–5) requires that the cost of operational assets (other than land) be **allocated** as expense to the periods in which revenue is earned as a result of using those assets. Thus, the cost of operational assets is

Exhibit 9–1 Recording a basket purchase of assets

Situation:

Fox Company purchased a building and the related land for $300,000 cash. Estimated current market values: building, $189,000; and land, $126,000.

Allocation of acquisition cost:

	Appraised value		Apportionment of lump-sum acquisition cost	
Asset	Amount	Ratio	Computation	Apportioned cost
Building	$189,000	0.60*	$300,000 × 0.60 =	$180,000
Land	126,000	0.40†	300,000 × 0.40 =	120,000
	$315,000	1.00		$300,000

* $189,000 ÷ $315,000 = 0.60.
† $126,000 ÷ $315,000 = 0.40.

Entry to record the acquisition:

```
Plant building . . . . . . . . . . . . . . . . . . . . . . . . . . . . . . . . .   180,000
    Land—plant site . . . . . . . . . . . . . . . . . . . . . . . . . .   120,000
        Cash  . . . . . . . . . . . . . . . . . . . . . . . . . . . . . . .               300,000
```

matched in a systematic and rational manner in the future with the future revenues.

Three different terms are used to identify the allocation of costs required by the matching principle. These terms are:

1. **Depreciation**—the systematic and rational allocation of the acquisition cost of **tangible** operational assets, other than natural resources, to future periods in which the assets contribute services or benefits to help earn revenue. Example—depreciation of the $10,350 cost of a machine over its estimated useful life of 10 years and no residual value. The accounting year ends December 31, and it is the end of 19B (the second year after purchase).[3]

   December 31, 19B (adjusting entry):

   ```
   Depreciation expense ($10,350 ÷ 10 years)  . . . . . . . . . . . . . .   1,035
       Accumulated depreciation, machinery  . . . . . . . . . . . . . .            1,035
   ```

2. **Depletion**—the systematic and rational allocation of the acquisition cost of **natural resources** to future periods in which the use of those natural resources contributes to revenue. Example—depletion of the $53,000

---

[3] Adjusting entries made at the end of 19A would be the same as the following three entries because the allocation shown uses a straight-line assumption.

cost of timber tract over the estimated period of cutting based on "cutting" rate of approximately 20% per year:

December 31, 19B (adjusting entry):

Depletion expense ($53,000 × 20%) 10,600
    Timber tract (No. 12)   10,600

Note: A contra account could be used, such as Accumulated Depletion.

3. **Amortization**—the systematic and rational allocation of the acquisition cost of **intangible** assets to future periods in which the benefits contribute to revenue. Example—amortization of the $8,500 purchase cost of a patent over its estimated economic useful life to the entity of 17 years:

December 31, 19B (adjusting entry):

Patent expense ($8,500 ÷ 17 years)   500
    Patents   500

Note: A contra account, such as Accumulated Patent Amortization, could be used for the credit.

The three terms—depreciation, depletion, and amortization—relate to the same basic objective; that is, the allocation of the acquisition cost of an operational asset to the future periods in which the benefits of its use contribute to earning revenue.

The amounts of depreciation, depletion, and amortization recorded during each period are reported as expenses for the period. The amounts of depreciation, depletion, and amortization **accumulated since acquisition** date are reported on the balance sheet as deductions from the assets to which they pertain. An operational asset, such as the machine illustrated above, would be reported on the balance sheet (at the end of the second year in the example) as follows:

Balance Sheet
At December 31, 19B

Property, plant, and equipment:
  Machinery $10,350
    Less: Accumulated depreciation 2,070 $8,280*

or

Machinery (less accumulated depreciation, $2,070) $8,280*

* Called book value or carrying value.

The amounts for operational assets reported on the balance sheet do not represent their market values at the balance sheet date. The balance sheet amounts are called book, or carrying, values. The **book value** of an operational asset is its acquisition cost, less the accumulated depreciation, depletion, or amortization from acquisition date to the date of the balance sheet. Depreciation is a process of **cost allocation.** It is not a process of determining the current market value of the asset. Under the **cost principle,** the cost of an operational asset is recorded at acquisition date at its current market value. The cost is not remeasured on a market value basis at subsequent balance sheet dates. Instead, the acquisition cost is reduced by the accumulated depreciation, depletion, or amortization.

Depreciation Concepts

Tangible operational assets, except land, are subject to depreciation because they have limited economic lives. Usually, land is not subject to depreciation because it does not wear out and has an unlimited life.

Tangible operational assests (except land) decrease in economic utility to the user because of a number of **causative factors,** such as wear and tear, the passage of time, effects of the elements (such as the weather), obsolescence, technological changes, and inadequacy. These causative factors affect such assets during the periods in which the assets are being used to earn revenues. Thus, under the **matching principle,** at the end of each accounting period an **adjusting entry** is needed to record these expense-causing factors. In developing the adjusting entry, accounting principles require the use of a rational and systematic allocation to match the acquisition cost of tangible operational assets with the revenue earned each period.

The calculation of depreciation expense requires three amounts for each asset: (1) **acquisition cost,** (2) **estimated residual value,** and (3) **estimated useful life.** Of these three amounts, two are **estimates** (residual value and useful life). Therefore, depreciation expense is an **estimate.** Depreciation expense may be measured as follows:

Acquisition cost	$625
Less: Estimated residual value	25
Amount to be depreciated over useful life	$600
Estimated useful life	3 years
Annual depreciation expense: $600 ÷ 3 =	$200

Estimated residual value[4] must be deducted from acquisition cost to compute depreciation expense. It represents that part of the acquisition cost that is expected to be recovered by the user upon disposal of the asset at the end of its estimated useful life to the entity. **Residual value** is the estimated amount to be recovered **less** any estimated costs of dismantling, disposal, and selling. Disposal costs may approximately equal the gross residual amount recovered. Therefore, many depreciable assets are assumed to have no residual value. The estimated net residual value is not necessarily the value of the asset as salvage or scrap. Rather, it may be the value to another user at the date on which the

---

[4] Residual value also is called scrap value or salvage value; however, the term **residual value** is more descriptive because the asset may not be scrapped or sold as salvage upon disposition—a subsequent buyer may renovate it and reuse it for many years.

current owner intends to dispose of it. A company whose policy is to replace all trucks at the end of three years normally would use a higher estimated residual value than would a user of the same kind of truck whose policy is to replace the trucks at the end of five years.

Estimated useful life represents the useful **economic** life to the **present owner** rather than the total economic life to all potential users. In the example above, for accounting purposes, one owner would use a three-year estimated useful life, and the other owner would use a five-year estimated useful life.

The determination of estimated useful life of an operational asset must conform to the **continuity assumption** (Exhibit 4–5). This assumption holds that the business will continue indefinitely to pursue its commercial objectives and will not liquidate in the foreseeable future. A business should not estimate the life of an operational asset to be less than its potential life because of some conjecture that the business will liquidate in the near future.

Depreciation Methods

The depreciation methods commonly used for **accounting purposes** are discussed in this section.[5] The different depreciation methods are based on the same concept; each method allocates a portion of the cost of a depreciable asset to each future period in a systematic and rational manner. Nevertheless, each method allocates to each period a different portion of the cost to be depreciated. The discussions that follow focus on the following depreciation methods:

1. Straight line (SL).
2. Productive output (PO) (units of production).
3. Accelerated depreciation methods:
    a. Sum-of-the-years' digits (SYD).
    b. Declining balance (DB).

The common set of facts and notations shown in Exhibit 9–2 will be used to illustrate these methods.

Straight-Line (SL) Method

Most companies use the straight-line (SL) method in their financial statements. Under the SL method, an **equal portion** of the acquisition cost less the estimated residual value is allocated to each accounting period during the estimated useful life. The annual depreciation expense is measured as follows (refer to Exhibit 9–2):

---

[5] The internal revenue code specifies a different depreciation method (Accelerated Cost Recovery System) that should be used in preparing a corporation's federal income tax return.

Exhibit 9–2 Illustrative data for depreciation

DEP CORPORATION	
Acquisition cost of an operational asset	$ 62,500
Estimated net residual value at end of useful life	2,500
Estimated life in years	3
Estimated life in units of production	100,000

$$\text{Depreciation expense} = \frac{\text{Cost } - \text{ Residual value}}{\text{Life in years}}$$

$$\$20,000 = \frac{\$62,500 - \$2,500}{3 \text{ years}}$$

Depreciation expense for DEP Corporation would be $20,000 per year if the SL method is used. A depreciation schedule for the entire useful life of the machine is:

Depreciation Schedule—Straight-Line Method

Year	Depreciation expense (income statement)	Accumulated depreciation (balance sheet at year end)	Book value (at year end)
At acquisition . . .			$62,500
1	$20,000	$20,000	42,500
2	20,000	40,000	22,500
3	20,000	60,000	2,500

The adjusting entry to record depreciation expense on the machine is the same for each of the three years of the useful life:

	Year 1	Year 2	Year 3
Adjusting entry			
Depreciation expense	20,000	20,000	20,000
Accumulated depreciation, machinery	20,000	20,000	20,000

Notice that (*a*) depreciation expense is a constant amount for each year, (*b*) accumulated depreciation increases by an equal amount each year, and (*c*) book value decreases by the same amount each year. This is the reason for the designation, straight line.

Evaluation. The SL method is simple, rational, and systematic. It is appropriate when the asset is used at about the same rate each period. It implies an approximately equal decline in the economic usefulness of the asset each period. For these reasons, the SL method is used more often than all of the other methods combined.

Productive-Output (PO) Method

The productive-output (PO) method relates depreciable cost to the total estimated productive output. A depreciation rate per **unit of output** is computed as follows (refer to Exhibit 9–2):

$$\text{Depreciation rate} = \frac{\text{Cost} - \text{Residual value}}{\text{Life in units of output}}$$

$$\$0.60 = \frac{\$62,500 - \$2,500}{100,000 \text{ units}}$$

For every unit produced by the machine, DEP Corporation will record depreciation expense of $0.60. Depreciation expense each year is calculated as follows:

Depreciation expense = Depreciation rate × Units of output for the year

Assume output of 30,000 units in year 1, 50,000 units in year 2, and 20,000 units in year 3. Depreciation expense each year would be:

Year	Rate	×	Units	=	Depreciation expense
1	$0.60	×	30,000	=	$18,000
2	0.60	×	50,000	=	30,000
3	0.60	×	20,000	=	12,000

The depreciation schedule for DEP Corporation under the productive-output method is:

Depreciation Schedule—Productive-Output Method

Year	Depreciation expense (income statement)	Accumulated depreciation (balance sheet at year end)	Book value (at year end)
At acquisition ...			$62,500
1	$18,000	$18,000	44,500
2	30,000	48,000	14,500
3	12,000	60,000	2,500

The adjusting entry for productive-output depreciation at the end of each year is:

	Year 1	Year 2	Year 3
Adjusting entry			
Depreciation expense	18,000	30,000	12,000
Accumulated depreciation, machinery	18,000	30,000	12,000

Notice that depreciation expense, accumulated depreciation, and book value vary from period to period directly with the units produced. When the productive-output method is used, depreciation expense is said to be a **variable** expense because it varies directly with production.

Evaluation. The productive-output method is based on the assumption that the revenue-generating benefits derived from a depreciable asset are related directly to the periodic **output** of the asset. Many accountants believe that such equipment as a machine should be depreciated on the basis of units produced each period rather than on the passage of time as is assumed by the SL method. These accountants believe that many productive assets contribute to the earning of revenues only when they are used productively, not because time has passed.

The productive-output method is simple, rational, and systematic. It is appropriate if **output** of the asset can be measured realistically. Also, it is appropriate when the economic utility of the asset to the entity decreases with productive use rather than with the passage of time. When the productive use varies significantly from period to period, a more realistic **matching** of expense with revenue is attained. Despite these conceptual and practical advantages, it is not widely used, primarily because of the problems associated with measuring output.

Accelerated Depreciation—Concepts

Accelerated depreciation means that in the early years of the useful life of an asset, depreciation expense amounts are higher, and the amounts are correspondingly lower in the later years. Accelerated depreciation is supported by the following arguments:

1. A depreciable asset produces more revenue in its early life because it is more efficient in the early years than in the later years.
2. Repair costs increase in later years; therefore, **total use cost** per period should include decreasing depreciation expense to "offset" the increasing repair expense each period.

The relationship between accelerated depreciation expense, repair expense, and total use expense can be illustrated as follows for DEP Corporation:

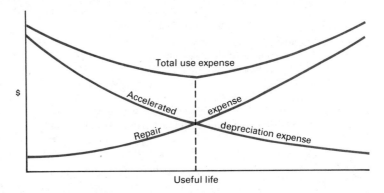

Accelerated methods are not often used for financial reporting purposes. However, the two methods used more frequently than others are the sum-of-the-years'-digits (SYD) method and the declining-balance (DB) method.

Sum-of-the-Years'-Digits (SYD) Method

Under the SYD method, depreciation expense is computed for each accounting year by multiplying the acquisition cost, less estimated residual value, by a fraction that is successively **smaller** each year. Each of the decreasing fractions is determined by using the sum of the digits that make up the estimated useful life as the denominator. The numerator is the specific year of life in **inverse order.** Using the data given in Exhibit 9–2, the computations are:

1. Compute the annual depreciation fraction:

    Denominator—sum of digits in useful life: [6] $1 + 2 + 3 = \underline{\underline{6}}$.

    Numerators—digits (specific year of life) in inverse order: $\underline{\underline{3}}$, $\underline{\underline{2}}$, $\underline{\underline{1}}$.

    Depreciation fractions—year 1, ³⁄₆; year 2, ²⁄₆; year 3, ¹⁄₆ (total, %).

2. Use the annual depreciation fractions as follows:

Year	Fraction	×	Cost less residual value	=	Depreciation expense
1	³⁄₆	×	$60,000	=	$30,000
2	²⁄₆	×	60,000	=	20,000
3	¹⁄₆	×	60,000	=	10,000

The depreciation schedule for DEP Corporation under the SYD method is:

Depreciation Schedule—Sum-of-the-Years'-Digits Method

Year	Depreciation expense (income statement)	Accumulated depreciation (balance sheet at year end)	Book value (at year end)
At acquisition . . .			$62,500
1	$30,000	$30,000	32,500
2	20,000	50,000	12,500
3	10,000	60,000	2,500

The adjusting entry for SYD depreciation expense by year is:

	Year 1		Year 2		Year 3	
Adjusting entry						
Depreciation expense	30,000		20,000		10,000	
Accumulated depreciation, machinery		30,000		20,000		10,000

---

[6] The denominator (i.e., sum of the digits) can be computed by using the formula:

$$\text{SYD} = n\left(\frac{n + 1}{2}\right)$$

For example, a five-year life would be:

$$\text{SYD} = 5\left(\frac{5 + 1}{2}\right) = 15$$

Notice that, compared to straight-line results, depreciation expense under the SYD method is higher in the earlier years and lower in the later years. The total amount of depreciation expense over the entire life of the asset is the same under both methods.

Evaluation. The SYD method is used because it produces a significant accelerated effect and is simple to apply, rational, and systematic. However, the SYD method is criticized because it often does not relate depreciation expense to use or output. In such cases, its conformity to the **matching** principle is questionable. SYD is not widely used.

Declining-Balance (DB) Method

There are several variations of the declining-balance (DB) method. One variation is based on an acceleration rate applied to the SL rate. The **declining-balance (DB) rate** is found by (1) computing the SL rate, ignoring residual value, then (2) multiplying that SL rate by a **selected acceleration rate** which may not exceed 200%. Assuming a five-year estimated useful life, the SL rate, excluding residual value, is:

$$1 \text{ period of life} \div 5 \text{ total periods} = 20\%$$

Computation of the DB rate for three different acceleration rates (for illustrative purposes):

SL rate (excluding RV)	×	Selected acceleration rate	=	DB rate
Case A, 20%	×	200%	=	40%
Case B, 20%	×	175%	=	35%
Case C, 20%	×	150%	=	30%

To calculate depreciation expense under the DB method, the book value of the asset is multiplied by the DB rate. Notice at this stage of the calculation, residual value is ignored (i.e., it is **not** subtracted from book value).

Computation of DB depreciation expense is illustrated below using the data given in Exhibit 9–2 and assuming an acceleration rate of 200%:

1. Compute the DB rate:

$$SL \text{ rate} = 1 \text{ year} \div 3 \text{ years}$$
$$= 33\frac{1}{3}\%$$
$$DB \text{ rate} = \text{Acceleration} \times SL \text{ rate}$$
$$= 200\% \times 33\frac{1}{3}\%$$
$$= 66\frac{2}{3}\%$$

2. Compute depreciation expense. Use a depreciation schedule to calculate the book value that is required for computation of depreciation expense under the DB method.

Depreciation Schedule—Declining-Balance Method

Year	Depreciation expense* (income statement)	Accumulated depreciation (balance sheet at year end)	Book value (at year end)
At acquisition ..			$62,500
1	$41,667	$41,667	20,833
2	13,889	55,556	6,944
3	4,444†	60,000	2,500

* Computations:

Year	Book value	×	DB rate	=	Depreciation expense
1	$62,500	×	66⅔%	=	$41,667
2	20,833	×	66⅔%	=	13,889
3	6,944	×	66⅔%	=	4,629†

† See explanation below.

Notice that the calculated depreciation expense for year 3 ($4,629) is not the same as the amount actually reported on the income statement ($4,444). An asset should never be depreciated below its residual value. The asset owned by the DEP Corporation has an estimated residual value of $2,500. If depreciation expense were recorded in the amount of $4,629, the book value of the asset would be less than $2,500. The correct depreciation expense for year 3 is the amount that will reduce the book value to exactly $2,500. Thus, while residual value is ignored in the computation of depreciation expense under the DB method, it is necessary to check each year to be certain that the calculated amount of depreciation expense does not reduce the book value of the asset below its estimated residual value. In cases where this would occur, depreciation expense is limited to the amount that reduces book value to the exact amount of the estimated residual value.

The adjusting entries to record depreciation expense are:

	Year 1	Year 2	Year 3
Adjusting entry			
Depreciation expense	41,667	13,889	4,444
Accumulated depreciation, machinery	41,667	13,889	4,444

Evaluation. This method began because it was acceptable for income tax purposes. The method is criticized because the **selected acceleration rate** is subjectively determined for accounting purposes. Income tax provisions have been changed; therefore, this method is not widely used.

Partial Year Depreciation

The preceding examples assumed that assets were acquired on the first day of the year and depreciated for the entire year. In practice, assets are purchased at various times during the year. Rather than establishing a large number of depreciation schedules based on small differences in the dates of purchase for the assets, most companies adopt a policy to cover partial year depreciation. Some typical policies are:

1. Depreciate for a full month all assets acquired before the 15th of the month. There is no depreciation for the month on assets acquired after the 15th.
2. Depreciate for a full year all assets acquired before July 1. There is no depreciation for the year on assets acquired after July 1.
3. Take one-half year depreciation in the year of acquisition of the asset without regard to the month in which the asset was actually purchased.

More precise methods for calculating partial year depreciation are discussed in advanced accounting courses.

Changes in Depreciation Estimates

Depreciation is based on two estimates—useful life and residual value. These estimates are made at the time a depreciable asset is acquired. One, or both, of these initial estimates may have to be revised as experience with the asset accumulates. When it is clear that either estimate should be revised (to a material degree), the undepreciated asset balance, less any residual value, at that date should be apportioned, based on the new estimate, over the **remaining** estimated life. This is called a **change in estimate.**

Assume the following for a machine:

Cost of machine when acquired	$33,000
Estimated useful life	10 years
Estimated residual value	$ 3,000
Accumulated depreciation through year 6 (assuming the SL method is used); ($33,000 − $3,000) × 6/10	$18,000

Shortly after the start of year 7, the initial estimates were changed to the following:

Revised estimated total life	14 years
Revised estimated residual value	$ 1,000

No entry is needed when this decision is reached. However, the **adjusting entry at the end of year 7** would be:

Depreciation expense	1,750	
Accumulated depreciation		1,750

Computation:

Acquisition cost	$33,000
Accumulated depreciation, years 1–6	18,000
Undepreciated balance	15,000
Less: Revised residual value	1,000
Balance to be depreciated	$14,000

Annual depreciation:

$14,000 ÷ (14 years − 6 years)	$ 1,750

Under GAAP, changes in accounting estimates and depreciation methods should be made only when the new estimate or accounting method "better measures" the periodic income of the business. The **characteristic of comparability** (Exhibit 4–5) requires that accounting information reported in the financial statements should be comparable across accounting periods and among similar entities. This principle has a significant constraint on changing depreciation estimates and methods unless the effect is to improve the measurement of depreciation expense and net income.

Financial Statement Analysis

Each of the depreciation methods reports a different amount of depreciation expense each year during the life of an asset. The **total** amount of depreciation reported over the life of an asset is the same under each method. Exhibit 9–3 illustrates how the pattern of depreciation varies with each method. The accelerated methods report higher depreciation during the early years of the life of an asset and therefore report lower net income. As the age of the asset increases, this effect reverses; therefore, companies that use accelerated depreciation report lower depreciation expense and higher net income during the later years of an asset's life. Users of financial statements must understand the impact of differences in the methods of accounting for depreciation and how the passage of time affects those differences. Significant differences in the reported net incomes of companies can be caused by differences in depreciation methods rather than real economic differences.

Depreciation alternatives also affect the balance sheet because accumulated depreciation (a balance sheet account) reflects an accumulation of previously reported depreciation expense on the assets that are held. Accelerated depreciation results in a lower book value of assets because higher depreciation expense was recorded.

GAAP requires that the depreciation method that is used by a company must be "rational and systematic." Most companies use the SL method for financial reporting because it is easy to use and understand. Some managers prefer the SL method because it permits their companies to report higher net income.

Most companies use an accelerated method for tax reporting because it results in lower net income and, therefore, a lower tax liability. Companies attempt to minimize or delay to future periods the payment of federal taxes because it permits them to earn money on the cash that is saved. Depreciation for tax purposes is discussed in Chapter Supplement 9C.

Depreciation and Cash Flows

Depreciation expense does not directly affect cash flows because it is a **noncash expense.** The cash outflow associated with depreciation occurred when the related asset was acquired. Each period when depreciation is recorded, no cash payment is made (i.e., there is not a credit to Cash related to recording depreciation expense). Most other expenses cause an immediate or subsequent outflow

Exhibit 9–3 Depreciation methods compared

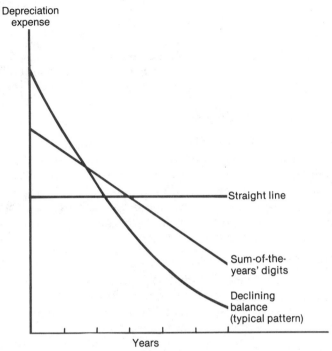

Some analysts misinterpret the meaning of a noncash expense and often say that "cash is provided by depreciation." Depreciation is not a source of cash. Cash from operations can only be provided by selling goods and services. A company with a large amount of depreciation expense does not generate more cash compared with a company that reports a small amount of depreciation expense (assuming that they are exactly the same in every other respect). While depreciation expense reduces the amount of reported net income for a company, it does not reduce the amount of cash generated by the company because it is a noncash expense.

PART B—REPAIRS AND MAINTENANCE, NATURAL RESOURCES, AND INTANGIBLE ASSETS

Repairs, Maintenance, and Additions

Subsequent to the acquisition of a tangible operational asset, related expenditures often must be made for ordinary repairs and maintenance, major repairs, replacements, and additions. Certain expenditures should be recorded as expenses of the period when incurred, while others should be recorded as assets (i.e., as a prepayment) to be matched with **future** revenues.

Expenditures made after the acquisition date are called either revenue expenditures or capital expenditures. A **revenue expenditure is recorded as expense when incurred. A capital expenditure is recorded as an asset when incurred.**[7] This section discusses various types of revenue and capital expenditures.

Ordinary Repairs and Maintenance

Ordinary repairs and maintenance are expenditures for normal maintenance and upkeep of operational assets that are necessary to keep the assets in their usual condition. These expenditures are recurring in nature, involve small amounts at each occurrence, and do not directly lengthen the useful life of the asset. Ordinary repairs and maintenance are **revenue expenditures.** They are recorded as expense in the accounting period in which incurred.

Extraordinary Repairs

Extraordinary repairs are classified as **capital expenditures.** An extraordinary repair is debited to the related asset account and depreciated over the **remaining life** of that asset. **Extraordinary repairs** seldom occur, involve large amounts of money, and increase the economic usefulness of the asset in the future because of either greater efficiency or longer life. Examples are major overhauls, complete reconditioning, and major replacements and improvements. The complete replacement of a roof on the factory building is an extraordinary repair. Patching the old roof is an ordinary repair.

To illustrate the accounting for extraordinary repairs, assume a machine that originally cost $40,000 is being depreciated on a straight-line basis over 10 years with no estimated residual value. At the beginning of the seventh year, a major reconditioning was finished that cost $12,700. The estimated useful life changed from 10 years to 13 years (i.e., a change in estimate). A typical sequence of entries is:

At acquisition date:

Machinery	40,000	
Cash		40,000
Purchase of machinery.		

End of each accounting period (depreciation):

Depreciation expense	4,000	
Accumulated depreciation, machinery		4,000
Adjusting entry to record annual depreciation ($40,000 ÷ 10 years).		

---

[7] The term **revenue** expenditure is widely used. It suggests that the expenditure is to be deducted in the current period from revenue in deriving income. However, a term such as **expense expenditure** would be more descriptive.

Extraordinary repair—at the start of year 7:

Machinery[8] 12,700
    Cash   12,700
  Capital expenditure.

Revised annual depreciation, years 7–13:

Depreciation expense 4,100
    Accumulated depreciation, machinery   4,100
  Adjusting entry to record annual depreciation.

Computation:
  Original cost $40,000
  Depreciation, years 1–6   24,000
  Book value remaining $16,000
  Extraordinary repair   12,700
  Balance to be depreciated over remaining life . . . $28,700

Annual depreciation: $28,700 ÷ (13 − 6 years) = $4,100.

Additions

Additions are extensions to, or enlargements of, existing assets, such as the addition of a wing to a building. These additions are **capital expenditures;** therefore, the cost of additions should be debited to the existing account for the asset and depreciated over the remaining life of the asset to which the cost is related. However, if the life of the addition is shorter than the life of the related asset, the addition should be depreciated over its remaining useful life (less its residual value).

Natural Resources

Natural resources, such as a mineral deposit, oil well, or timber tract, are often called wasting assets because they are **depleted** (i.e., physically used). When acquired or developed, a natural resource is recorded in conformity with the **cost principle.** As a natural resource is used up, its acquisition cost, in conformity with the **matching principle,** must be apportioned among the various periods in which the resulting revenues are earned. The term **depletion** describes the process of periodic cost allocation over the economic life of a natural resource. A **depletion rate** is computed by dividing the total acquisition and development cost (less any estimated residual value, which is rare) by the **estimated units** that can be withdrawn economically from the resource. The depletion rate is multiplied each period by the **actual** number of units withdrawn during the accounting period. This procedure is the same as the productive-output method of calculating depreciation.

To illustrate accounting for a natural resource, assume that a gravel pit was developed that cost $80,000. A reliable estimate was made that 100,000 cubic

---

[8] Alternatively, the debit could be made to the account for accumulated depreciation; the result would be the same.

yards of gravel could be economically withdrawn from the pit. The **depletion rate per unit** is computed as follows (assuming no residual value):

$80,000 ÷ 100,000 cubic yards = $0.80 per cubic yard (depletion rate per unit)

Assuming 5,000 cubic yards of gravel were withdrawn and sold during the year, depletion expense for the first year is recorded by making the following adjusting entry.[9]

Depletion expense	 4,000	
Gravel pit	. . . .	4,000
Depletion for the year, 5,000 cubic yards × $0.80 = $4,000.		

At the end of the first year, this natural resource should be reported as follows:

Balance Sheet

Operational assets:
Gravel pit $76,000

Since it is difficult to estimate the recoverable units from a natural resource, the depletion rate often must be revised. This is a **change in estimate;** therefore, the undepleted acquisition cost is spread over the estimated remaining recoverable units by computing a new depletion rate. Assume in year 2 that the estimate of recoverable units remaining was changed from 95,000 to 150,000 cubic yards. The depletion rate to be applied to the cubic yards of gravel withdrawn in year 2 is:

($80,000 − $4,000) ÷ 150,000 cubic yards = $0.51 per cubic yard

When buildings and similar improvements are acquired for the development and exploitation of a natural resource, they should be recorded in separate asset accounts and **depreciated**—not depleted. Their estimated useful lives cannot be longer than the time needed to exploit the natural resource unless they have a significant use after the source is depleted.

Intangible Assets

An intangible asset, like any other asset, has value because of certain rights and privileges conferred by law on the owner of the asset. However, an intangible asset has **no material or physical substance** as do tangible assets such as land

---

[9] Consistent with the procedure for recording depreciation, an Accumulated Depletion account may be used. However, as a matter of precedent, the asset account itself usually is credited directly for the periodic depletion. Either procedure is acceptable. The same is true for intangible assets, discussed in the next section.

and buildings. Examples of intangible assets are patents, copyrights, franchises, licenses, trademarks, and goodwill. An intangible asset should be recorded in conformity with the **cost principle.** Subsequently, it is recorded at cost less accumulated amortization in conformity with the matching principle.

Each kind of intangible asset should be recorded in a separate asset account. Assume that on January 1, 19A, Mason Company bought a patent from its developer, J. Doe, at a cash price of $17,000. The acquisition of this intangible asset is recorded as follows:

January 1, 19A:

```
Patents . . . . . . . . . . . . . . . . . . . . . . . . . . . . . . . . . . . . . . . . . . 17,000
    Cash  . . . . . . . . . . . . . . . . . . . . . . . . . . . . . . . . . . . . . . . .          17,000
  Bought a patent from J. Doe.
```

Under the cost principle, although an intangible right or privilege may have value, it is not recorded unless there has been an identifiable expenditure of resources to acquire or develop it. A brand name may have considerable value in the market (i.e., goodwill), but it cannot be recorded as an asset unless a cost was incurred to acquire it in a purchase transaction.

Research and development (R&D) costs are recorded as expenses in the period incurred, even though they sometimes result in the development of a patent that has future value.

Amortization of Intangible Assets

Intangible assets normally have limited lives because the **rights or privileges** that help earn revenues terminate or disappear. Therefore, in conformity with the **matching principle,** the acquisition cost of an intangible asset must be apportioned to the various periods it helps produce revenue. This apportionment is called **amortization.** *APB Opinion 17* states that for accounting purposes, the estimated useful life of an intangible asset cannot exceed 40 years. The *Opinion* does not permit an arbitrary life for an intangible asset. These rules are intended to avoid income manipulation.

An intangible asset may be amortized by using any "systematic and rational" method that reflects the actual expiration of its economic usefulness. However, the straight-line method is used almost exclusively. The primary intangible assets are discussed below.

Patents

A patent is an exclusive right, recognized by law, that enables the owner to use, manufacture, and sell the subject of the patent, and the patent itself. A patent that is **purchased** is recorded at its cash-equivalent cost. An **internally developed** patent is recorded at only its registration and legal cost. GAAP requires the immediate expensing of research and development costs. In conformity with the **matching principle,** the capitalized cost of a patent must be amortized over the **shorter** of its economic life or its remaining legal life (of the 17 years from date of grant). Assume the patent acquired by Mason Company had an estimated 10-year remaining economic life. At the end of 19A, the **adjusting entry** to record amortization for one year is (see footnote 9):

December 31, 19A:

Patent expense 1,700
    Patents 1,700
  Adjusting entry to record amortization of patent over the estimated
  economic life of 10 years ($17,000 ÷ 10 years = $1,700).

The amount of patent amortization expense recorded for 19A is reported on the income statement as an operating expense. The patent would be reported on the December 31, 19A, balance sheet as follows:

Intangible assets:
    Patents (cost, $17,000, less amortization) . . . $15,300

Copyrights

A copyright is similar to a patent. A copyright gives the owner the exclusive right to publish, use, and sell a literary, musical, or artistic piece of work for a period not exceeding 50 years after the author's death. The same principles, guidelines, and procedures used in accounting for the cost of patents also are used for copyrights.

Franchises and Licenses

Franchises and licenses frequently are granted by governmental and other units for a specified period and purpose. A city may grant one company a franchise to distribute gas to homes for heating purposes, or a company may sell franchises, such as the right for a local outlet to operate a Kentucky Fried Chicken restaurant. Franchises and licenses usually require an investment by the franchisee to acquire them; therefore, they represent intangible assets that should be accounted for as shown above for patents.

Leaseholds

Leasing is a common type of business contract. For a consideration called rent, the owner (lessor) extends to another party (lessee) certain rights to use specified property (leasehold). Leases may vary from simple arrangements, such as the month-to-month lease of an office or the daily rental of an automobile, to long-term leases having complex contractual arrangements.

Long-term leases sometimes require a lump-sum advance rental payment by the lessee. In such cases, the lessee should record the advance payment as a debit to an intangible asset account (usually called Rent Paid in Advance or Leaseholds). This cost should be amortized to expense based on the lease contract (e.g., the cost may apply to the last month's rent). Assume Favor Company leased a building for its own use on January 1, 19A, under a five-year contract that required in addition to the monthly rental payments of $2,000, a single payment in advance of $20,000. The advance payment is recorded as follows:

January 1, 19A:

```
Leasehold (or Rent paid in advance) . . . . . . . . . . . . . . . . . . . . . . 20,000
    Cash  . . . . . . . . . . . . . . . . . . . . . . . . . . . . . . . . . . . . .         20,000
    Rent paid in advance.
```

According to the lease contract, the advance payment is to be considered a part of each year's rent expense. At the end of each year, 19A through 19E, the following **adjusting entry** is made to amortize the cost of this intangible asset:

December 31, 19A:

```
Rent expense  . . . . . . . . . . . . . . . . . . . . . . . . . . . . . . . . . . 4,000
    Leasehold  . . . . . . . . . . . . . . . . . . . . . . . . . . . . . . . . . .        4,000
    Adjusting entry to record amortization of leasehold over five
    years ($20,000 ÷ 5 years = $4,000).
```

The $2,000 monthly rental payments would be debited to Rent Expense when paid each month. Thus, the 19A income statement would report rent expense of $28,000 [i.e., ($2,000 × 12) + $4,000 = $28,000]. The December 31, 19A, balance sheet would report an asset, Leasehold, of $16,000 (i.e., Cost, $20,000 − Amortization, $4,000 = $16,000).

Leasehold Improvements

In most cases, when buildings, improvements, or alterations are built by the **lessee** on leased property, such assets legally belong to the owner of the property at the end of the lease. The lessee has full use of such improvements during the term of the lease. Therefore, the cost should be recorded as an intangible asset, Leasehold Improvements. These expenditures should be amortized over the estimated useful life of the related improvements or the remaining life of the lease, whichever is shorter.

Goodwill

Often when a successful business is sold, the price will be higher than the fair market value of its recorded assets less its liabilities. A business may command a higher price because an intangible asset called goodwill is attached to a successful business.

Goodwill represents the potential of a business to earn above a normal rate of return on its assets. Goodwill arises from such factors as customer confidence, reputation for dependability, efficiency and internal competencies, quality of goods and services, and financial standing. From the date of organization, a successful business continually builds goodwill. In this context, the goodwill is said to be "internally generated at no identifiable cost." On the other hand, when a business is purchased as an entity, the purchase price may include a payment for any goodwill that exists at that time. **In conformity with the cost principle, goodwill is recorded as an intangible asset only when it actually is purchased at a measurable cost.**

Assume Roe Company purchased the College Men's Store on January 1, 19A, for $200,000 cash. At the date of purchase, the recorded assets had a total **market**

value of $160,000, comprised of the market values of inventory, $110,000; fixtures, $35,000; prepaid rent, $1,000; and remaining assets, $14,000. There were no liabilities for College Men's Store. The purchase is recorded by Roe as follows:

January 1, 19A:

Inventory	110,000	
Furniture and fixtures	35,000	
Prepaid rent	1,000	
Remaining assets	14,000	
Goodwill	40,000	
Cash		200,000
Purchase of College Men's Store.		

The intangible asset—goodwill—must be amortized to expense over its estimated economic life not to exceed 40 years (*APB Opinion 17*). Assuming a 20-year economic life, the amortization for 19A is recorded in an **adjusting entry** as follows:

December 31, 19A:

Goodwill amortization (expense)	2,000	
Goodwill		2,000
Adjusting entry to record goodwill amortization for one year based on 20-year economic life ($40,000 ÷ 20 years = $2,000).		

Deferred Charges

An asset category called **deferred charges** may be reported on the balance sheet. A deferred charge, like a prepaid expense, is an **expense paid in advance.** That is, goods or services were acquired that will be used later to earn future revenues. A deferred charge is a **long-term** prepaid expense. Therefore, it cannot be classified as a current asset. A prepaid expense is a short-term prepayment and is classified as a current asset. Thus, the only difference between the two is time. For example, a $1,000 insurance premium for five years' coverage paid in advance at the start of year 1 would be reported as follows at the end of year 1:

Income statement:
Insurance expense ($1,000 ÷ 5 years) $200

Balance sheet:
Current assets:
Prepaid insurance ($1,000 ÷ 5 years) 200
Deferred charges:
Insurance premium paid in advance ($1,000 × 3/5) . . . 600

Common examples of deferred charges are bond issuance costs (Chapter 11), start-up costs, organization costs, and plant rearrangement costs. In conformity with the **matching principle,** deferred charges are amortized to expense each period over the future periods benefited.

Exhibit 9–4 Disposal of an operational asset

Panel A—situation of Bye Company:

January 1, 19A—purchased a heavy-duty truck for $38,000 cash; estimated useful life eight years and $6,000 residual value (straight-line depreciation).

December 31—end of accounting year.

June 30, 19D—The truck was wrecked, and the insurance company paid a claim of $21,000 (i.e., the replacement cost of the truck at the date of the wreck).

Panel B—entries during the life of the truck:

January 1, 19A—to record purchase of the truck:

Truck 38,000	
Cash	38,000

December 31—to record annual depreciation 19A–19C:

	19A	**19B**	**19C**
Depreciation expense 4,000		4,000	4,000
Accumulated depreciation	4,000	4,000	4,000

Computation: ($38,000 − $6,000) ÷ 8 years = $4,000.

Panel C—June 30, 19D—entries on date of disposal (wreck):

1. To record depreciation for six months (to date of wreck):

Depreciation expense 2,000	
Accumulated depreciation	2,000

Computation: $4,000 × 6/12 = $2,000.

2. To record the involuntary disposal of the asset and the insurance indemnity:

Cash (insurance indemnity) 21,000	
Accumulated depreciation ($4,000 × 3) + $2,000 14,000	
Casualty loss on operational assets 3,000	
Truck	38,000

Panel D—reporting (by year):

	19A	**19B**	**19C**	**19D**
Income statement (for the year):				
Depreciation expense	$ 4,000	$ 4,000	$ 4,000	$2,000
Loss on disposal				3,000
Balance sheet (at December 31):				
Truck	$38,000	$38,000	$38,000	$ –0–
Accumulated depreciation	(4,000)	(8,000)	(12,000)	–0–
Book value	$34,000	$30,000	$26,000	$ –0–

Disposal of Operational Assets

Operational assets may be disposed of in two ways: **voluntarily** by sale, trade-in, or retirement; or **involuntarily** as a result of a casualty, such as a storm, fire, or accident. Whatever the nature of the disposal, the cost of the asset and any accumulated depreciation, depletion, or amortization must be removed from the accounts at the date of disposal. The difference between any resources received on disposal of an operational asset and the **book or carrying value** of the asset at the date of disposal is a **gain or loss on disposal of operational assets.** This gain (or loss) is reported on the income statement. However, it is not revenue (or expense) because it is from "peripheral or incidental" activities rather than from normal operations (Exhibit 4–5). Assume a machine is sold for $3,500 cash when the account balances showed Machine, $10,000; and Accumulated Depreciation, Machine, $7,000 (i.e., a book value of $3,000). The entry to record this disposal is:

```
Cash . . . . . . . . . . . . . . . . . . . . . . . . . . . . . . . . . . . . . .   3,500
Accumulated depreciation, machine  . . . . . . . . . . . . . . . . . . . . .   7,000
    Machine . . . . . . . . . . . . . . . . . . . . . . . . . . . . . . . . .          10,000
    Gain on disposal of operational asset  . . . . . . . . . . . . . . . . . .             500

Gain computed:
  Sale price  . . . . . . . . . . . . . . . . . . . . . .   $3,500
  Book value at date of sale ($10,000 − $7,000)  . . .    3,000
    Difference, gain  . . . . . . . . . . . . . . . . . .   $  500
```

Disposals of operational assets seldom occur on the last day of the accounting period. Therefore, the depreciation, depletion, or amortization must be updated to the date of disposal. The disposal of a depreciable operational asset usually requires two entries: (1) an adjusting entry to update the depreciation expense and accumulated depreciation accounts and (2) an entry to record the disposal. Exhibit 9–4 illustrates a typical disposal. Panel A gives the situation, Panels B and C show the journal entries, and Panel D presents the reporting of a disposal.

A gain or loss on disposal occurs because (1) depreciation expense is based on estimates that may differ from actual experience and (2) depreciation is based on original cost, not current market values.

DEMONSTRATION CASE

(Resolve the requirements before proceeding to the suggested solution that follows.)

Diversified Industries has been operating for a number of years. It started as a residential construction company. In recent years it expanded into heavy construction, ready-mix concrete, sand and gravel, construction supplies, and earth-moving services.

The transactions below were selected from those completed during 19D. They focus on the primary issues discussed in this chapter. Amounts have been simplified for case purposes.

19D

Jan. 1 The management decided to buy a building that was about 10 years old. The location was excellent, and there was adequate parking space. The company bought the building and the land on which it was situated for $305,000 cash. A reliable appraiser provided the following market values: land, $126,000; and building, $174,000.

12 Paid renovation costs on the building of $38,100.

June 19 Bought a third location for a gravel pit (designated No. 3) for $50,000 cash. The location had been carefully surveyed. It was estimated that 100,000 cubic yards of gravel could be removed from the deposit.

July 10 Paid $1,200 for ordinary repairs on the building.

Aug. 1 Paid $10,000 for costs of preparing the new gravel pit for exploitation.

December 31, 19D (end of the annual accounting period)—the following data were developed as a basis for the adjusting entries:

a. The building will be depreciated on a straight-line basis over an estimated useful life of 30 years. The estimated residual value is $35,000.

b. During 19D, 12,000 square yards of gravel were removed and sold from gravel pit No. 3.

c. The company owns a patent right that is used in operations. On January 1, 19D, the Patent account had a balance of $3,300. The patent has an estimated remaining useful life of six years (including 19D).

Required:

1. Give the journal entries for the five transactions completed during 19D.
2. Give the adjusting entries on December 31, 19D.
3. Show the December 31, 19D, balance sheet classification and amount for each of the following items: land, building, gravel pit, and patent.

Suggested Solution:

Requirement 1—Entries during 19D:

January 1, 19D:

Land (building site)	128,100	
Building	176,900	
Cash		305,000

Allocation of cost (based on appraisal):

Item	Appraisal value	Percent		Computation		Allocation
Land	$126,000	42	×	$305,000	=	$128,100
Building	174,000	58	×	305,000	=	176,900
Totals	$300,000	100				$305,000

January 12, 19D:

Building	38,100	
Cash		38,100
Renovation costs on building prior to use.		

June 19, 19D:

Gravel pit (No. 3)	50,000	
Cash		50,000
Purchased gravel pit; estimated production, 100,000 cubic yards.		

July 10, 19D:

Repair expense	1,200	
Cash		1,200
Ordinary repairs.		

August 1, 19D:

Gravel pit (No. 3)	10,000	
Cash		10,000
Preparation costs.		

Requirement 2—Adjusting Entries:

December 31, 19D:

a. Depreciation expense, building 6,000

    Accumulated depreciation   6,000

Computation:
Cost ($176,900 + $38,100) $215,000
Less: Residual value   35,000
Cost to be depreciated $180,000

Annual depreciation: $180,000 ÷ 30 years = $6,000.

b. Depletion expense 7,200

    Gravel pit (No. 3)   7,200

Computation:
Cost ($50,000 + $10,000) $60,000
Depletion rate:
  $60,000 ÷ 100,000 cubic yards = $0.60
Depletion expense: $0.60 × 12,000 cubic yards = $7,200

c. Patent expense 550

    Patent   550

Computations:
  $3,300 ÷ 6 years = $550.

Requirement 3—Balance Sheet, December 31, 19D:

Assets

Operational assets:			
Land		$128,100	
Building	$215,000		
Less: Accumulated depreciation . . .	6,000	209,000	
Gravel pit		52,800	
Total operational assets			$389,900
Intangible assets:			
Patent ($3,300 − $550)			2,750

SUMMARY OF CHAPTER

This chapter discussed accounting for operational assets. These are the noncurrent assets that a business retains for long periods of time for use in the course of normal operations rather than for sale. They include tangible assets and intangible assets. At acquisition, an operational asset is recorded at cost. Cost includes the cash equivalent purchase price plus all reasonable and necessary expenditures made to acquire and prepare the asset for its intended use.

An operational asset represents a bundle of future services and benefits that have been paid for in advance. As an operational asset is used, this bundle of services gradually is used to earn revenue. Therefore, in conformity with the **matching principle,** cost (less any estimated residual value) is allocated to periodic expense over the periods benefited. In this way, the expense associated with the use of operational assets is matched with the revenues earned. This allocation process is called **depreciation** in the case of property, plant, and equipment; **depletion** in the case of natural resources; and **amortization** in the case of intangibles.

Four methods of depreciation are used widely: straight line, productive output, sum-of-the-years' digits, and declining balance.

Expenditures related to operational assets are classified as:

1. **Capital expenditures**—those expenditures that provide benefits for one or more accounting periods beyond the current period; therefore, they are debited to appropriate asset accounts and depreciated, depleted, or amortized over their useful lives; or

2. **Revenue expenditures**—those expenditures that provide benefits during the current accounting period only; therefore, they are debited to appropriate current expense accounts when incurred.

Ordinary repairs and maintenance costs are revenue expenditures. Extraordinary repairs and asset additions are capital expenditures.

Operational assets may be disposed of voluntarily by sale or retirement, or involuntarily through casualty, such as storm, fire, or accident. Upon disposal, such assets must be depreciated, depleted, or amortized up to the date of disposal. The disposal transaction is recorded by removing the cost of the old asset and the related accumulated depreciation, depletion, or amortization amount from the accounts. A gain or loss on disposal of an operational asset will result when the disposal price is different from the book value of an old asset. Special rules apply to the trade in of an asset as all, or part, of the consideration given for another asset (trade-ins are discussed in Chapter Supplement 9B).

CHAPTER SUPPLEMENT 9A

Capitalization of Interest as a Cost of Operational Assets

When an operational asset is purchased, the cost of the asset does not include interest expense that was incurred to finance the purchase. However, *FASB*

Statement 34 provides an exception to this principle. The cost of an asset that is constructed for a company's internal use must include interest cost during the period of construction. Interest is included in the cost of the asset (*a*) **only** during the construction or acquisition period and (*b*) not in excess of total interest cost for all borrowings by the entity during the period. It is not necessary that the debts of the company be related to the construction of the operational asset.

To illustrate capitalization of interest during construction, assume that on January 1, 19A, Byers Corporation signed a contract that required Dow Construction Company to build a new plant building at a contract price of $1,000,000. The construction period started March 1, 19A, and the building was substantially complete and ready for its intended use on December 31, 19A (end of the 10-month construction period). Byers Corporation was required to make the following quarterly cash progress payments on the contract during 19A:

Date of payment	Amount
a. March 31, 19A	$ 120,000
b. June 30, 19A	220,000
c. September 30, 19A	480,000
d. December 31, 19A	180,000
Total	$1,000,000

To make the progress payments, Byers Corporation borrowed 60% of each payment from a financial institution at 10% annual interest; the remaining cash needed was from within Byers Corporation. Total interest cost incurred by Byers during the period was $70,000 (at an average rate of 10%).

Upon completion, December 31, 19A, Byers Corporation should reflect the following acquisition cost in the operational asset account, Plant Building:

Contract price (paid in full)		$1,000,000
Add interest during the construction period:		
a. $120,000 × 10% × 9/12	$ 9,000	
b. $220,000 × 10% × 6/12	11,000	
c. $480,000 × 10% × 3/12	12,000	
d. $180,000—no interest	–0–	32,000*
Total acquisition cost		$1,032,000

* Note that this amount was not based on the specific borrowings of 60% but on the expenditures. This amount cannot exceed the $70,000 total interest cost for the period (19A).

This example provides the following guidelines that must be observed.

1. Interest is capitalized **only** during the construction period.
2. Interest is computed on the average **expenditures** during the construction period.
3. The applicable **borrowing interest rate** for the company is used.
4. Interest is computed **regardless of the source** of the funds (which may be borrowed or obtained from normal operations of the entity).

5. Interest added to the cost of the operational assets **cannot exceed** the total amount of total interest cost incurred by the entity in that period (for all purposes).

CHAPTER SUPPLEMENT 9B

Trading in Assets

It is not unusual when acquiring an asset to trade in another asset. Although there may be a direct trade of two assets, the typical case involves the trading in of an old asset plus the payment of cash for the difference. In such transactions, the asset acquired must be recorded in the accounts, and the old asset is removed from the accounts.

Accounting for the exchange of one asset for another asset depends on two factors:

1. Whether the two assets are similar or dissimilar.
2. Whether cash for the difference is paid or received.

The trading in of an old truck for a new truck would involve similar assets. In contrast, the trading in of a plot of land for a new truck would involve dissimilar assets.

The basic principle for recording the exchange of assets can be stated as follows: If the assets exchanged are similar, the exchange should be recorded on a **book value** basis because there is no completed earning process.[10] If the assets exchanged are dissimilar, the exchange should be recorded on a **market value** basis because there is a completed earning process (for the old asset).

Exhibit 9–5 illustrates accounting for the acquisition of an asset when another asset is given as a trade-in. Four independent cases are illustrated:

Case	**Situations**
A	Similar assets are exchanged; no cash is paid.
B	Dissimilar assets are exchanged; no cash is paid.
C	Similar assets are exchanged; cash is paid.
D	Dissimilar assets are exchanged; cash is paid.

In the illustration in Exhibit 9–5, the market value of old Asset O was $200 in excess of its book value [i.e., $2,200 − ($5,000 − $3,000)]. Therefore, in Cases B and D (relating to dissimilar assets), this amount was recorded as a gain. In contrast, if the market value of old Asset O had been $1,900 (i.e., $100 below book value), a loss of $100 would be reported in Cases B and D. A loss would be

---

[10] In an exchange of similar productive assets, because the asset acquired performs essentially the same productive function as the asset given up, the exchange is only one step in the earning process. The earning process in these situations is completed when the goods or services are sold that the similar productive assets helped to produce. In contrast, in the case of an exchange of dissimilar productive assets, the earning process is completed because the productive function of the productive asset given up is terminated. The asset acquired serves a different economic purpose for the entity and begins a new earning process of its own.

Exhibit 9–5   Trading in used assets illustrated

Situation of Company T:

Transaction: Company T acquired Asset N and traded in Asset O. At the date of the transaction, the accounts of Company T reflected the following:

> **Asset O:**
> Cost when acquired $5,000
> Accumulated depreciation   3,000
> Estimated market value   2,200
>
> **Asset N:**
> Market value   2,250

Case A—similar assets are exchanged; no cash paid.

Principle applied: The asset acquired is recorded at the **book value** of the asset traded in.

Asset N 2,000
Accumulated depreciation, Asset O 3,000
   Asset O   5,000

Case B—dissimilar assets are exchanged; no cash paid.

Principle applied: The asset acquired is recorded at the **market value** of the asset traded in.

Asset N 2,200
Accumulated depreciation, Asset O 3,000
   Asset O   5,000
   Gain on disposal of operational asset   200

Case C—similar assets are exchanged; $60 cash is paid.

Principle applied: The asset acquired is recorded at the **book value** of the asset traded in **plus the cash** paid.

Asset N ($2,000 + $60) 2,060*
Accumulated depreciation, Asset O 3,000
   Asset O   5,000
   Cash   60

Case D—dissimilar assets are exchanged; $60 cash is paid.

Principle applied: The asset acquired is recorded at the **market value** of the asset traded in **plus the cash** paid.

Asset N 2,250*
Accumulated depreciation, Asset O 3,000
   Asset O   5,000
   Cash   60
   Gain on disposal of operational assets   190

* Calculation: $2,200 + $60, but this amount cannot exceed the market value of the asset acquired, $2,250.

recorded for Cases A and C (similar assets) when the market value of either asset is below book value because an acquired asset cannot be recorded at an amount greater than its market value.

CHAPTER SUPPLEMENT 9C

Depreciation and Federal Income Tax

In the chapter, we discussed depreciation for financial reporting purposes in conformity with GAAP. This supplement discusses depreciation for federal income tax purposes in conformity with the internal revenue code. The objectives of GAAP and the internal revenue code are different. The objective of financial reporting (Exhibit 4–5) is to provide economic information about a business that is useful in projecting the future cash flows of a business. The objective of the internal revenue code is to raise sufficient revenues to pay for the expenditures of the federal government. In addition, many provisions of the internal revenue code are designed to encourage certain behaviors that are thought to benefit our society (e.g., contributions to charities are tax deductible to encourage people to support worthy programs).

Because of the different objectives of GAAP and the internal revenue code, there are many significant differences in the accounting methods that are acceptable for financial reporting and federal income tax reporting. Most large corporations maintain separate accounting records and methods to comply with the different reporting requirements associated with GAAP and the internal revenue code.

Some of the depreciation methods discussed in the previous section are not acceptable for federal income tax reporting. Most corporations use the Modified Accelerated Cost Recovery System (MACRS) for calculating depreciation expense for their tax statement. MACRS specifies various classes of assets and establishes a depreciation rate for each class. It is similar to the declining balance method, but the rates do not have to be calculated. They are published as part of the internal revenue service regulations.

The basic classes of assets specified under MACRS are[11]: (1) 3-year property, which includes tractors that are used on the open roads; (2) 5-year property, which includes computers, copiers, cars, and light-duty trucks; (3) 7-year property, which includes office furniture and fixtures; (4) 10-year property, which includes water transportation equipment; (5) 15-year property, which includes certain telephone equipment; and (6) 20-year property, which includes certain railroad equipment. Real property (e.g., buildings) is depreciated on a straight-line basis over either 27½ or 31½ years (depending on the type of property).

Exhibit 9–6 shows depreciation rates for the basic classes of assets. Depreciation expense under MACRS is calculated by multiplying the depreciable cost of

---

[11] Internal revenue service regulations are subject to constant change. This discussion focuses on the basic concepts of MACRS rather than the complexities of recent changes. The information in this chapter pertains to assets placed in service after 1986.

Exhibit 9–6   Depreciation rates for the Modified Accelerated Cost Recovery System (MACRS)

Year	3-year property	5-year property	7-year property	10-year property	15-year property	20-year property
				Asset class		
1	33.33%	20.00%	14.29%	10.00%	5.00%	3.750%
2	44.45	32.00	24.49	18.00	9.50	7.219
3	14.81	19.20	17.49	14.40	8.55	6.677
4	7.41	11.52	12.49	11.52	7.70	6.177
5		11.52	8.93	9.22	6.93	5.713
6		5.76	8.92	7.37	6.23	5.285
7			8.93	6.55	5.90	4.888
8			4.46	6.55	5.90	4.522
9				6.56	5.91	4.462
10				6.55	5.90	4.461
11				3.28	5.91	4.462
12					5.90	4.461
13					5.91	4.462
14					5.90	4.461
15					5.91	4.462
16					2.95	4.461
17						4.462
18						4.461
19						4.462
20						4.461
21						2.231

an asset by the rate for the appropriate year of the asset's life. For example, depreciation under MACRS for a $10,000 car (five-year property class) in the third year of the asset's life is $1,920 (19.2% × $10,000).

MACRS does not attempt to match the cost of an asset with the revenue it produces over its useful life in conformity with the matching principle (Exhibit 4–5). MACRS provides for rapid depreciation of an asset over a life that is usually much shorter than its estimated useful life. The intent of MACRS is to provide an incentive for corporations to invest in modern property, plant, and equipment in order to be competitive in world markets. The high depreciation expense reported under MACRS reduces a corporation's taxable income and therefore the amount it must pay in taxes. MACRS is not used for financial reporting purposes.

IMPORTANT TERMS DEFINED IN THIS CHAPTER

Accelerated Depreciation   Higher depreciation expense in early years, and lower in later years of an operational asset's life. *p. 425*

Acquisition Cost   Net cash equivalent amount paid for an asset. *p. 416*

Amortization Systematic and rational allocation of the cost of an intangible asset over its useful life. *p. 420*

Basket Purchase Acquisition of two or more assets in a single transaction for a single lump sum. *p. 418*

Book (or Carrying) Value Acquisition cost of an operational asset less accumulated depreciation, depletion, or amortization. *p. 420*

Capital Expenditures Expenditures that are debited to an asset account; the acquisition of an asset. *p. 432*

Capitalization of Interest Interest expenditures included in the cost of an operational asset; interest capitalized during construction period. *p. 443*

Copyright Exclusive right to publish, use, and sell a literary, musical, or artistic work. *p. 436*

Declining Balance Depreciation An accelerated depreciation method based on a multiple of the SL rate; it disregards residual value. *p. 427*

Deferred Charges An expense paid in advance of usage of the goods or services; long-term prepayment. *p. 438*

Depletion Systematic and rational allocation of the cost of a natural resource over the period of exploitation. *p. 433*

Depreciation Systematic and rational allocation of the cost of property, plant, and equipment (but not land) over its useful life. *p. 419*

Estimated Useful Life Estimated service life of an operational asset to the present owner. *p. 421*

Extraordinary Repairs Major, high cost, and long-term repairs; debited to an asset account (or accumulated depreciation); a capital expenditure. *p. 432*

Goodwill Acquisition cost of the purchase of a business that is in excess of the market value of the other assets of the business purchased. *p. 437*

Intangible Assets Assets that have special rights but not physical substance. *p. 434*

Leasehold Improvements Expenditures by the lessee on leased property that have use value beyond the current accounting period. *p. 437*

Leaseholds Rights granted to a lessee under a lease contract that have been paid for. *p. 436*

Natural Resources Mineral deposits, timber tracts, oil, and gas. *p. 433*

Operational Assets Tangible and intangible assets owned by a business and used in its operations. *p. 416*

Productive-Output Depreciation Cost of an operational asset is allocated over its useful life based on the periodic output related to total estimated output. *p. 424*

Repairs and Maintenance Expenditures for normal operating upkeep of operational assets; debit expense for ordinary repairs. *p. 431*

Residual Value Estimated amount to be recovered, less disposal costs, at the end of the estimated useful life of an operational asset. *p. 421*

Revenue Expenditures Expenditures that are debited to an expense account; the incurrence of an expense. *p. 432*

Straight-Line Depreciation Cost of an operational asset is allocated over its useful life in equal periodic amounts. *p. 422*

Sum-of-the-Years'-Digits Depreciation Cost of an operational asset is allocated over its useful life based on a fraction when the denominator is the total of all of the useful years and the numerator is the year of life in inverse order. *p. 426*

Tangible Assets Assets that have physical substance. *p. 416*

QUESTIONS

Part A: Questions 1–14

1. Define operational assets. Why are they considered a "bundle of future services?"
2. What are the classifications of operational assets? Explain each.
3. Relate the cost principle to accounting for operational assets.
4. Describe the relationship between the matching principle and accounting for operational assets.
5. Define and calculate the book value of a three-year-old operational asset that cost $11,500, has an estimated residual value of $1,500, and an estimated useful life of five years. Relate book value to carrying value and market value.
6. Under the cost principle, what amounts usually should be included in the acquisition cost of an operational asset?
7. What is a basket purchase? What measurement problem does it pose?
8. Distinguish between depreciation, depletion, and amortization.
9. In computing depreciation, three values must be known or estimated; identify and explain the nature of each.
10. Estimated useful life and residual value of an operational asset relate to the current owner or user rather than to all potential users. Explain this statement.
11. What kind of a depreciation-expense pattern is provided under the straight-line method? When would its use be appropriate?
12. What kind of depreciation-expense pattern emerges under the productive-output method? When would its use be appropriate?
13. What are the arguments in favor of accelerated depreciation?
14. Explain how monthly depreciation should be computed when the sum-of-the-year's-digits method is used for an asset having a 10-year life.

Part B: Questions 15–24

15. Distinguish between capital expenditures and revenue expenditures.
16. Distinguish between ordinary and extraordinary repairs. How is each accounted for?

17. Over what period should an addition to an existing operational asset be depreciated? Explain.
18. Define an intangible asset.
19. What period should be used to amortize an intangible asset?
20. Define goodwill. When is it appropriate to record goodwill as an intangible asset?
21. Distinguish between a leasehold and a leasehold improvement.
22. Over what period should a leasehold improvement be amortized? Explain.
23. Compare the accounting for a prepaid expense with accounting for a deferred charge.
24. When an operational asset is disposed of during the accounting period, two separate entries usually must be made. Explain this statement.

EXERCISES

Part A: Exercises 9–1 to 9–8

E9–1 (Match Allocation Terms with Assets)

For each asset listed below, enter a code letter to the left to indicate the allocation terminology for each asset. Use the following letter codes:

Allocation Term

A—Amortization   P—Depletion
D—Depreciation   N—None of these

Assets

_____ (1) Patent	_____ (11) Copyright
_____ (2) Land	_____ (12) Investment in common stock
_____ (3) Building	_____ (13) Mineral deposit
_____ (4) Cash	_____ (14) Machinery
_____ (5) Oil well	_____ (15) License right
_____ (6) Trademark	_____ (16) Deferred charge
_____ (7) Goodwill	_____ (17) Inventory of goods
_____ (8) Stamps	_____ (18) Timber tract
_____ (9) Franchise	_____ (19) Tools
_____ (10) Plant site in use	_____ (20) Gravel pit

E9–2   (Match Definitions with Terms)

Match each definition with its related term by entering the appropriate letter in the space provided.

Terms	Definitions
_____ (1) Acquisition cost	A. Assets that have physical substance.
_____ (2) Depreciation	B. Declining expense; numerator year of life in inverse order.
_____ (3) SL depreciation	
_____ (4) Productive-output depreciation	C. Use cost is the same amount per year during useful life.
_____ (5) Tangible assets	D. Estimated recovery less costs of disposal.
_____ (6) Natural resource	E. Cash equivalent amount.
_____ (7) Useful life	F. Periodic expense fluctuates with actual output.
_____ (8) Depletion	G. A timber tract.
_____ (9) Basket purchase	H. Estimated productive life to the current user.
_____ (10) Book value	I. Systematic allocation of the cost of a natural resource.
_____ (11) SYD depreciation	
_____ (12) Residual value	J. Must allocate a single purchase cost to two or more assets.
	K. Systematic allocation of the cost of a tangible operational asset.
	L. Acquisition cost minus accumulated allocation of original cost.

E9–3   (Record Asset Acquisition and Straight-Line Depreciation; Basket Purchase)

Tiger Company bought a building and the land on which it is located for a total cash price of $197,000. Also, the company paid transfer costs of $3,000. Renovation costs on the building were $16,000. An independent appraiser provided market values of building, $145,152; and land, $56,448.

Required:

a. Apportion the cost of the property on the basis of the appraised values. Show computuations.

b. Give the journal entry to record the purchase of the property, including all expenditures. Assume that all transactions were for cash and that all purchases occurred at the start of year 1.

c. Give the journal entry to record straight-line depreciation at the end of one year assuming an estimated 15-year useful life and a $10,000 estimated residual value.

d. What would be the book value of the property at the end of year 2?

E9–4   (Apply Cost Principle and Record Straight-Line Depreciation)

A machine was purchased by Foster Company on March 1, 19A, at an invoice price of $25,000. On date of delivery, March 2, 19A, the company paid $10,000 on the machine, and the balance was on credit at 12% interest. On March 3, 19A, $150 was paid for freight on the machine. On March 5, installation costs relating to the machine were paid amounting to $1,000. On October 1, 19A, the company paid the balance due on the machine plus the interest.

Required (round all amounts to the nearest dollar):

a. Give the journal entries on each of the above dates through October 19A.

b. Give the adjusting entry for straight-line depreciation at the end of 19A, assuming an estimated useful life of 10 years and an estimated residual value of $6,150. Depreciate to the nearest month. The accounting period ends December 31, 19A.

c. What would be the book value of the machine at the end of 19B?

E9–5   **(Compute Depreciation for Four Years Using Four Different Depreciation Methods)** Mario Corporation bought a machine at a cost of $5,400. The estimated useful life was four years, and the residual value, $600. Assume that the estimated productive life of the machine is 60,000 units and each year's production was year 1, 24,000 units; year 2, 20,000 units; year 3, 10,000 units; and year 4, 6,000 units.

Required:

a. Determine the amount for each cell in the following schedule. Show your computations, and round to the nearest dollar.

	Depreciation Expense			
Year	Straight Line	Productive Output	Sum-of-the-Years' Digits	150% Declining Balance
1				
2				
3				
4				
Totals				

b. Assuming the machine was used directly in the production of one of the products manufactured and sold by the company, what factors might be considered in selecting a preferable depreciation method in conformity with the matching principle?

E9–6   **(Compute Depreciation and Book Value for Two Years Using Four Depreciation Methods)** Slade Company bought a machine for $35,000. The estimated useful life was five years, and the estimated residual value, $5,000. Assume the estimated useful life in productive units is 75,000. Units actually produced were year 1, 15,000; and year 2, 20,000.

Required:

a. Determine the appropriate amounts to complete the schedule below. Show computations, and round to the nearest dollar.

	Depreciation expense		Book value at end of	
Method of depreciation	Year 1	Year 2	Year 1	Year 2
Straight line	⸻	⸻	⸻	⸻
Productive output	⸻	⸻	⸻	⸻
Sum-of-the-years' digits	⸻	⸻	⸻	⸻
150% declining balance	⸻	⸻	⸻	⸻

b. Which method would result in the lowest EPS for year 1? For year 2?

E9–7   (Monthly Depreciation Using Two Depreciation Methods; Effect on Income Statement)

Monroe Company acquired, and paid for, a machine that cost $5,300 on July 1, 19B. The estimated useful life is four years, and the estimated residual value is $500. The accounting period ends December 31.

Required:

a. Compute monthly depreciation expense for July 19B and July 19C assuming (*a*) the straight-line method and (*b*) the SYD method.

b. Assume revenues of $75,000 and expenses other than depreciation of $40,000 for the year 19B and an income tax rate of 25%. Complete the following tabulation for 19B:

	Straight Line	Sum-of-the-Years' Digits
Revenues		
Expenses		
Depreciation expense		
Pretax income		
Income tax expense		
Net income		

c. Which method produced the higher net income? By how much? Why do the net incomes differ (use amounts)?

E9–8 **(Record and Explain Change in Useful Life and Residual Value)**
Lutz Company owns the office building occupied by its administrative office. The office building was reflected in the accounts at the end of last year as follows:

Cost when acquired $250,000
Accumulated depreciation (based on straight-line depreciation, an
  estimated life of 30 years, and a $40,000 residual value) 105,000

During January of this year, on the basis of a careful study, the management decided that the total estimated useful life should be changed to 25 years (instead of 30) and the residual value reduced to $30,000 (from $40,000). The depreciation method will not be changed.

Required:
a. Give the adjusting entry (or entries) related to depreciation at the end of the year in which the change is made. Show computations.
b. Explain the basis for the entry (or entries) that you gave in (a).

Part B: Exercises 9–9 to 9–20

E9–9 **(Identify Capital and Revenue Expenditures)**
For each item listed below, enter the correct letter to the left to show the type of expenditure. Use the following:

Type of Expenditure

A—Capital expenditure
B—Revenue expenditure
C—Neither

Transactions

_____ (1) Paid $500 for ordinary repairs.
_____ (2) Paid $6,000 for extraordinary repairs.
_____ (3) Addition to old building; paid cash, $10,000.
_____ (4) Routine maintenance; cost, $300; on credit.
_____ (5) Purchased a machine, $6,000; gave long-term note.
_____ (6) Paid $2,000 for organization costs.
_____ (7) Paid three-year insurance premium, $600.
_____ (8) Purchased a patent, $3,400 cash.
_____ (9) Paid $10,000 for monthly salaries.
_____ (10) Paid cash dividends, $15,000.

E9–10   (Match Definitions with Terms)

Match each definition with its related term by entering the appropriate letter in the space provided.

	Terms	Definitions

Terms

_____ (1) Patents

_____ (2) Goodwill

_____ (3) Leaseholds

_____ (4) Amortization

_____ (5) Copyright

_____ (6) Capitalization of interest

_____ (7) Intangible assets

_____ (8) Deferred charges

_____ (9) Ordinary repairs and maintenance

_____ (10) Additions (to assets)

_____ (11) Leasehold improvements

_____ (12) Franchise

_____ (13) Gain (loss) on disposal of an operational asset

_____ (14) Lessor

_____ (15) Extraordinary repairs

Definitions

A. The owner of leased property.

B. Ownership right to publish, use, or sell a literary, musical, or artistic work.

C. An expense paid in advance that represents a long-term payment.

D. Long-term, major, high-cost repairs.

E. Price paid for a business in excess of the market value of the net assets.

F. Assets used in the operations of a business because of their special rights.

G. Rights granted to a lessee that have been paid for.

H. An exclusive ability to use, manufacture, and sell a right that is protected by law.

I. Time cost of money allocated as a part of the cost of an operational asset.

J. A right granted by a governmental or business entity to offer services or products under a contract.

K. Costs expended by a lessee on leased property (e.g., a building on leased land).

L. Difference between consideration received and book value of an operational asset disposed of.

M. Systematic and rational allocation of the cost of an intangible asset.

N. Normal low cost, regularly recurring expenditures for upkeep of operational assets.

O. Extensions to, or enlargements of, an operational asset; a capital expenditure.

E9–11   (Record Depreciation, Repairs, and Amortization)

Waverly Company operates a small manufacturing facility as a supplement to its regular service activities. At the beginning of 19L, an operational asset account for the company showed the following balances:

Manufacturing equipment $70,000
Accumulated depreciation through 19K . . .   48,400

During 19L, the following expenditures were incurred for repairs and maintenance:

1. Routine maintenance and repairs on the equipment . . . $ 750
2. Major overhaul of the equipment   5,200

The equipment is being depreciated on a straight-line basis over an estimated life of 15 years and a $4,000 estimated residual value. The annual accounting period ends on December 31.

Required:

a. Give the adjusting entry for depreciation on the manufacturing equipment that was made at the end of 19K. Starting with 19L, what is the remaining estimated life?

b. Give the journal entries to record the two expenditures for repairs and maintenance during 19L.

c. Give the adjusting entry that should be made at the end of 19L for depreciation of the manufacturing equipment assuming no change in the estimated life or residual value. Show computations.

E9–12 (Record Depreciation; Extraordinary Repairs; Change in Estimated Useful Life and Residual Value)

At the end of the annual accounting period, December 31, 19C, the records of Viva Company reflected the following:

> Machine A:
> Cost when acquired $34,000
> Accumulated depreciation . . . 12,000

During January 19D, the machine was renovated, including several major improvements at a cost of $10,000. As a result, the estimated life was increased from 8 years to 12 years, and the residual value was increased from $2,000 to $5,000.

Required:

a. Give the journal entry to record the renovation. How old was the machine at the end of 19C?

b. Give the adjusting entry at the end of 19D to record straight-line depreciation for the year.

c. Explain the rationale for your entries in (a) and (b).

E9–13 (Record Acquisition and Depletion of a Natural Resource)

In February 19A, Dyno Extractive Industries paid $500,000 for a mineral deposit. During March, $140,000 was spent in preparing the deposit for exploitation. It was estimated that 800,000 total cubic yards could be extracted economically. During 19A, 70,000 cubic yards were extracted. During January 19B, another $16,000 was spent for additional developmental work. After conclusion of the latest work, the estimated remaining recovery was increased to one million cubic yards over the remaining life. During 19B, 40,000 cubic yards were extracted.

Required:

Give the appropriate journal entry on each of the following dates:

a. February 19A, for acquisition of the deposit.

b. March 19A, for developmental costs.

c. Year 19A, for annual depletion assuming the company uses a contra account (show computations).

d. January 19B, for developmental costs.

e. Year 19B, for annual depletion (show computations).

E9–14   **(Record Acquisition, Amortization, and Reporting of Three Different Intangible Assets)**
Hyatt Company had three intangible operational assets at the end of 19F (end of the accounting year):

1. Patent—purchased from J. Ray on January 1, 19F, for a cash cost of $4,260. Ray had registered the patent with the U.S. Patent Office five years earlier on January 1, 19A. Amortize over the remaining legal life.

2. A franchise acquired from the local community to provide certain services for 10 years starting on January 1, 19F. The franchise cost $40,000 cash.

3. On January 1, 19F, the company leased some property for a five-year term and immediately spent $5,200 cash for long-term improvements (estimated useful life, eight years, and no residual value). At the termination of the lease, there will be no recovery of these improvements.

Required:

a. Give the journal entry to record the acquisition of each intangible asset. Provide a brief explanation with the entries.

b. Give the adjusting journal entry at December 31, 19F, for amortization of each intangible. Show computations. The company does not use contra accounts.

c. Show how these assets, and any related expenses, should be reported on the financial statements for 19F.

E9–15   **(Record a Patent, Copyright, and Goodwill and Amortize Each)**
Disney Company acquired three intangible operational assets during 19F. The relevant facts were:

1. On January 1, 19F, the company purchased a patent from J. Doe for $4,800 cash. Doe had developed the patent and registered it with the Patent Office on January 1, 19A. Amortize over the remaining legal life.

2. On January 1, 19F, the company purchased a copyright for a total cash cost of $12,000, and the remaining legal life was 25 years. The company executives estimated that the copyright would have no value by the end of 20 years.

3. The company purchased another company in January 19F at a cash cost of $150,000. Included in the purchase price was $40,000 for goodwill; the balance was for plant, equipment, and fixtures (no liabilities were assumed). Amortize the goodwill over the maximum period permitted.

Required:

a. Give the journal entry to record the acquisition of each intangible asset.

b. Give the adjusting journal entry that would be required at the end of the annual accounting period, December 31, 19F, for each intangible asset. The company uses contra accounts. Include a brief explanation and show computations.

c. What would be the book (carrying) value of each intangible asset at the end of 19G?

E9–16   (Record and Amortize Rent Paid in Advance, Leasehold Improvements, and Periodic Rent)

Baylor Company conducts operations in several different sites. To expand into still another city, the company obtained a 10-year lease, starting January 1, 19D, on a downtown location. Although there was a serviceable building on the property, the company had to build an additional structure to be used for storage. The 10-year lease required a $10,000 cash advance payment, plus cash payments of $3,000 per month during occupancy. During January 19D, the company spent $75,000 cash building the structure. The new structure has an estimated life of 14 years with no residual value (straight-line depreciation).

Required:

  a. Give the journal entries for the company to record the payment of the $10,000 advance on January 1, 19D, and the first monthly rental.

  b. Give the journal entry to record the construction of the new structure.

  c. Give any adjusting entries required at the end of the annual accounting period on December 31, 19D, in respect to (1) the advance payment and (2) the new structure. Show computations.

  d. What is the total amount of expense resulting from the lease for 19D?

E9–17   (Reporting Intangible Assets on the Balance Sheet)

Lutz Company is in the process of preparing the balance sheet at December 31, 19B. The following are to be included:

Prepaid insurance	$ 1,200
Long-term investment in common stock of	
X Corporation, at cost (market, $10,600)	10,000
Patent (at cost)	3,400
Accumulated amortization, patent	1,000
Accounts receivable	24,000
Allowance for doubtful accounts	700
Franchise (at cost)	1,000
Accumulated amortization, franchise	600
Land—site of building	40,000
Building	400,000
Accumulated depreciation, building	160,000

Required:

Show how each of the above assets would be reflected on the company's balance sheet at December 31, 19B. Use the following subcaptions: Current assets, Investments and funds, Tangible operational assets, and Intangible assets. The company uses the "accumulated" accounts as listed above.

E9–18   (Record the Disposal of an Asset at Three Different Assumed Sale Prices)

Brokaw Company sold a small truck that had been used in the business for three years. The records of the company reflected the following:

Delivery truck	$22,000
Accumulated depreciation . . .	17,000

Required:

a. Give the journal entry for the disposal of the truck assuming the sales price was $5,000.

b. Give the journal entry for the disposal of the truck assuming the sales price was $5,400.

c. Give the journal entry for the disposal of the truck assuming the sales price was $4,400.

d. Summarize the effects of the disposal of the asset under the three different situations above.

E9–19   (Record the Disposal of an Operational Asset; Compute Estimated Life)

The records of Maloy Company on December 31, 19D, showed the following data about a particular machine:

> Machine, original cost $27,000
> Accumulated depreciation . . .   16,000*
>
> * Based on a six-year estimated useful
> life, a $3,000 residual value, and
> straight-line depreciation.

On April 1, 19E, the machine was sold for $12,000 cash. The accounting period ends on December 31.

Required:

a. How old was the machine on January 1, 19E? Show computations.

b. Give the journal entry, or entries, related to the sale of the machine.

E9–20   (Record Accident and Insurance Indemnity on an Operational Asset)

On August 31, 19C, a delivery truck owned by King Corporation was a total loss as a result of an accident. On January 1, 19C, the records showed the following:

> Truck (estimated residual value, $1,000) $10,000
> Accumulated depreciation (straight line, two years)   3,000

The truck was insured; therefore, the company collected $5,800 cash from the insurance company on October 5, 19C.

Required:

a. Based on the data given, compute the estimated useful life and the estimated residual value of the truck.

b. Given all of the journal entries with respect to the truck from January 1 through October 5, 19C. Show computations.

PROBLEMS

Part A: Problems 9–1 to 9–7

P9–1   **(Apply the Cost Principle to Determine the Cost of an Operational Asset)**
On January 1, 19A, Brown Company bought a machine for use in operations. The machine has an estimated useful life of 10 years and an estimated residual value of $1,000. The expenditures given below were provided by the company:

a. Invoice price of the machine, $60,000.
b. Less: Cash discount of 2% on all cash paid by January 10.
c. Freight paid by the vendor per sales agreement, $1,000.
d. Installation costs, $1,200.
e. Payment of the $60,000 was made on January 15, 19A, as follows:

> Brown common stock, par $1; 3,000 shares (market value, $4 per share).
>
> Note payable, $30,000, 10% due April 16, 19A (principal plus interest).
>
> Balance of the invoice price settled with cash.

Required:
Compute the cost of the machine that the company should record. Explain the basis you used for any questionable items.

P9–2   **(Basket Purchase Allocation; Record Cost and Depreciation—Three Methods)**
George Company bought three used machines from J. Doe for a cash price of $48,000. Transportation costs on the machines were $2,000. The machines immediately were overhauled, installed, and started operating. The machines were different; therefore, each had to be recorded separately in the accounts. An appraiser was employed to estimate their market values at date of purchase (prior to the overhaul and installation). The book values shown on Doe's books also are available. The book values, appraisal results, installation costs, and renovation expenditures were:

	Machine A	Machine B	Machine C
Book value—Doe	$6,000	$10,000	$7,000
Appraisal value	7,200	24,400	8,400
Installation costs	300	500	200
Renovation costs prior to use	1,000	600	400

Required:
a. Compute the cost of each machine by making a supportable allocation. Explain the rationale for the allocation basis used.
b. Give the journal entry to record the purchase of the three machines assuming all payments were cash. Set up a separate asset account for each machine.
c. Give the entry to record depreciation expense at the end of year 1, assuming:

		Estimates	
Machine	Life	Residual value	Depreciation method
A	6	$1,300	Straight-line
B	4	1,600	SYD
C	4	1,100	200% DB

P9–3   **(Compute and Record Depreciation Using Four Methods; Explain Effect of Depreciation on Cash Flow and EPS)**

Van Company bought a machine that cost $34,375. The estimated useful life is 10 years, and the estimated residual value is $1,375. The machine has an estimated useful life in productive output of 100,000 units. Actual output was year 1, 15,000; and year 2, 10,000.

Required:

a. Determine the appropriate amounts for the table below. Show your computations.

Depreciation method	Depreciation expense Year 1	Year 2	Book value at end of Year 1	Year 2
Straight line	$_____	$_____	$_____	$_____
Productive output	_____	_____	_____	_____
Sum-of-the-years' digits	_____	_____	_____	_____
200% declining balance	_____	_____	_____	_____

b. Give the adjusting entries for years 1 and 2 under each method.

c. In selecting a depreciation method, some companies assess the comparative effect on **cash flow** and **EPS.** Briefly comment on the depreciation methods in terms of effects on cash flow and EPS.

P9–4   **(Compute Depreciation Expense and Accumulated Depreciation for Four Depreciation Methods; Also a Change in Useful Life and Residual Value)**

On January 1,19A, Ajax Company bought a special heavy-duty truck that cost $28,500. The truck has an estimated five-year life and a $6,000 residual value. Estimated total mileage by disposal date is 50,000. Actual mileage was: year A, 12,000; year B, 14,000; year C, 16,000; year D, 6,000; and year E, 3,000.

Required:

a. Complete the following comparative depreciation schedule:

Depreciation Method	Year A	B	C	D	E

1. Straight line (SL):
  Depreciation expense
  Accumulated depreciation
	$	$	$	$	$

2. Sum-of-the-years' digits (SYD):
  Depreciation expense
  Accumulated depreciation					

3. Productive output (PO):
  Depreciation expense
  Accumulated depreciation					

4. Declining balance, 150% (DB):
  Depreciation expense
  Accumulated depreciation					

b. The interim depreciation expense for January 19A would be: SL, $_____; SYD, $_____; PO, $_____; and DB, $_____.

c. Assume that at the start of 19D, the estimates were changed; total life, seven years; residual value, $3,000. Give all related entries for 19D, for the SL method.

P9–5   (Compute and Analyze Net Cash Flow)
Tiana Corporation bought an operational asset on January 1, 19A, at a cash cost of $34,000. The estimated useful life is five years, and the estimated residual value is $4,000. Assume a constant 30% income tax rate; all paid in cash.

The company is deciding whether to use either straight-line (SL) depreciation or 200% declining-balance (DB) depreciation for both accounting and income tax purposes. The five-year projected all-cash incomes (before depreciation and income tax) are shown in the second column below.

Schedule to Compare Projected SL and DB Results

Year	Income (all cash) before Depreciation and Income Tax	Depreciation Expense (dollars) SL	200% DB	Income Tax Expense (dollars) SL	200% DB	Net Income (dollars) SL	200% DB	Net Cash Inflow (dollars) SL	200% DB
1	$ 40,000	6,000	13,600	10,200	7,920	23,800	18,480	29,800	32,080
2	40,000								
3	40,000								
4	40,000								
5	40,000								
Totals	200,000	30,000		51,000		119,000		149,000	

Required:

a. Complete the above schedule. Round to the nearest dollar. (Hint: Use the total line to prove your computations.)

b. Respond to each of the following items, based on your answer in (*a*):
(1) Total depreciation under each method.
(2) Explain the periodic depreciation amounts of SL versus DB.
(3) Total income tax under each method.
(4) Explain the periodic income tax amounts of SL versus DB.
(5) Total net income under each method.
(6) Explain the periodic net income under each method.
(7) Total cash flow under each method.
(8) Explain the periodic cash flow amounts in terms of DB and SL.

P9–6   (Analyze and Give Entries Related to a Change in Estimated Life and Residual Value)
Antonio Company owns an existing building that was built at an original cost of $500,000. It is being depreciated on a straight-line basis over a 20-year estimated useful life and has a $60,000 estimated residual value. At the end of 19H, the building had been depreciated

for a full eight years. In January 19I, a decision was made, on the basis of new information, that a total estimated useful life of 25 years, and a residual value of $86,000 would be more realistic. The accounting period ends December 31.

Required:

a. Compute (1) the amount of depreciation expense recorded in 19H and (2) the book value of the building at the end of 19H.

b. Compute the amount of depreciation that should be recorded in 19I. Show computations.

c. Give the adjusting entry for depreciation at December 31, 19I.

P9–7   **(This Problem Relates to Chapter Supplement 9A; It Requires Computation of Interest that Must be Capitalized on an Operational Asset)**
On January 1, 19A, Elliot Corporation bought land at a cost of $120,000 and paid transfer fees of $6,000. Clearing the land and planning for the building construction was started immediately. Construction of an office building for company use was started on April 1, 19A. The company borrowed about 80% of the funds to purchase the land and construct the office building at an 8% interest rate. The remaining cash needed was paid from company funds. Total interest cost for 19A was $25,000. The company made the following cash expenditures at the dates indicated:

January 1, 19A, down payment on the land (20%)	$ 24,000
January 1, 19A, transfer costs on the land	6,000
March 1, 19A, fees for preliminary surveys and work prior to start of construction	12,000
Progress payments to contractor for construction costs:	
May 31, 19A, No. 1	200,000
August 31, 19A, No. 2	300,000
November 30, 19A, No. 3 (end of the construction period)	200,000

Required:

a. Compute the cost of the tangible operational asset with separate amounts for the land and building. Assume the construction period started on April 1, 19A. Show computations.

b. How much interest expense should be reported on the 19A income statement?

Part B: Problems 9–8 to 9–16

P9–8   **(Recording Repairs and an Addition)**
Page Company made extensive repairs on its existing building and added a new wing. The existing building originally cost $360,000; and by the end of 19J (10 years) it was half depreciated on the basis of a 20-year estimated useful life and no residual value. During 19K, the following expenditures were made that were related to the building:

1. Ordinary repairs and maintenance expenditures for the year, $12,000 cash.

2. Extensive and major repairs to the roof of the building, $21,000 cash. These repairs were completed on June 30, 19K.

3. The new wing was completed on June 30, 19K, at a cash cost of $150,000. The wing had an estimated useful life of 10 years and no residual value.

Required:

a. Give the journal entry to record each of the 19K transactions.

b. Give the adjusting entry that would be required at the end of the annual accounting period, December 31, 19K, for the building after taking into account your entries in (*a*) above. Assume straight-line depreciation. The company computes depreciation based on the nearest month.

c. Show how the assets would be reported on the December 31, 19K, balance sheet.

P9–9 **(Analyze, Record, Give Adjusting Entries, and Compute Book Value Related to Five Different Intangible Assets)**

Long Company has five different intangible assets to be accounted for and reported on the financial statements. The management is concerned about the amortization of the cost of each of these intangibles. Facts about each intangible are:

1. **Patent.** The company purchased a patent at a cash cost of $45,500 on January 1, 19E. The patent had a legal life of 17 years from date of registration with the U.S. Patent Office, which was January 1, 19A. Amortize over the remaining legal life.

2. **Copyright.** On January 1, 19E, the company purchased a copyright for $20,000 cash. The legal life remaining from that date is 30 years. It is estimated that the copyrighted item will have no value by the end of 25 years.

3. **Franchise.** The company obtained a franchise from X Company to make and distribute a special item. The franchise was obtained on January 1, 19E, at a cash cost of $15,000 and covered a 10-year period.

4. **License.** On January 1, 19D, the company secured a license from the city to operate a special service for a period of four years. Total cash expended to obtain the license was $8,000.

5. **Goodwill.** The company started business in January 19C by purchasing another business for a cash lump sum of $400,000. Included in the purchase price was "Goodwill, $80,000." Company executives stated that "the goodwill is an important long-term asset to us." Amortize over the maximum period permitted.

Required:

a. Analyze each intangible asset and give the journal entry to record each of the five acquisitions.

b. Give the adjusting entry for each intangible asset that would be necessary at the end of the annual accounting period, December 31, 19E. Provide a brief explanation and show computations. If no entry is required for a particular item, explain the basis for your conclusion.

c. Give the book value of each intangible on January 1, 19G.

P9–10 **(Record the Purchase of a Business Including Goodwill; Depreciation of Assets Acquired and Amortization of Goodwill)**

On January 1, 19A, Investor Corporation was organized by five individuals to purchase and operate a successful business known as Amy's. The name was retained, and all of the assets, except cash, were purchased for $300,000 cash. The liabilities were not assumed by Investor Corporation. The transaction was closed on January 5, 19A, at which time the balance sheet of Amy's reflected the book values shown below:

AMY'S
January 5, 19A

	Book value	Market value*
Accounts receivable (net)	$ 30,000	$ 30,000
Inventory	180,000	175,000
Operational assets (net)	19,000	40,000
Other assets	1,000	5,000
Total assets	$230,000	
Liabilities	$ 80,000	
Owners' equity	150,000	
Total liabilities and owners' equity	$230,000	

* These values for the assets purchased were provided to Investor Corporation by an independent appraiser.

Required:

a. Give the journal entry by Investor Corporation to record the purchase. Include goodwill. (Hint: Record the assets at market value in conformity with the cost principle.)

b. Give the adjusting entries that would be made by Investor Corporation at the end of the annual accounting period, December 31, 19A, for:
    (1) Depreciation of the operational assets (straight line) assuming an estimated remaining useful life of 20 years and no residual value.
    (2) Amortization of goodwill assuming the maximum amortization period is used.

P9–11   (Record the Disposal of Three Operational Assets)

During 19K, Marwick Company disposed of three different assets. On January 1, 19K, prior to their disposal, the accounts reflected the following:

Assets	Original cost	Residual value	Estimated life	Accumulated depreciation (straight line)
Machine A	$20,000	$2,000	10 years	$12,600 (7 years)
Machine B	35,400	3,000	9 years	21,600 (6 years)
Machine C	65,200	6,400	14 years	46,200 (11 years)

The machines were disposed of in the following ways:

Machine A—sold on January 1, 19K, for $8,500 cash.

Machine B—sold on May 1, 19K, for $12,000; received cash, $2,000, and a $10,000 interest-bearing (12%) note receivable due at the end of 12 months.

Machine C—July 2, 19K, this machine suffered irreparable damage from an accident. On July 10, 19K, it was given to a salvage company at no cost. The salvage company agreed to remove the machine immediately at no cost. The machine was insured, and $19,500 cash was collected from the insurance company.

Required:

Give all journal entries related to the disposal of each machine. Explain the accounting rational for the way that you recorded each disposal.

P9–12 **(Analyze Five Transactions to Give Original Entry and Any Related Depreciation and Amortization Adjusting Entries)**

During the 19X5 annual accounting period, McAdams Company completed the following transactions:

1. On January 10, 19X5, paid $6,000 for a complete reconditioning of each of the following machines acquired on January 1, 19X1 (total cost, $12,000):

   Machine A—original cost, $23,000; accumulated depreciation to December 31, 19X4, $16,000 (straight-line, $3,000 residual value).

   Machine B—original cost, $28,000; accumulated depreciation, $12,000 straight-line ($4,000 residual value).

2. On July 1, 19X5, purchased a patent for $17,500 cash (estimated useful life, seven years).

3. On January 1, 19X5, purchased another business for cash $50,000 including $12,000 for goodwill. No liabilities were assumed by the company.

4. On September 1, 19X5, constructed a storage shed on some land leased from J. Doe. The cost was $9,200; the estimated useful life was 5 years with no residual value. The company uses straight-line depreciation. The lease will expire at the end of 19X8.

5. Total expenditures during 19X5 for ordinary repairs and maintenance were $3,200.

6. On July 1, 19X5, sold Machine A for $5,500 cash.

Required (compute depreciation to the nearest month):

a. For each of the above transactions, give the entry (or entries) that should be made during 19X5.

b. For each of the above transactions, give any adjusting entry that should be made at December 31, 19X5.

P9–13 **(A Challenging Analytical Problem; Different Situations Are Analyzed—Two Involve Accounting Errors, One Involves a Basket Purchase, and One Involves Some Noncash Payments; Related Entries Are Required)**

It is the end of the annual accounting period, December 31, 19F, for Post Company. The following items must be resolved before the financial statements can be prepared:

1. On January 1, 19F, a used machine was bought for $5,000 cash. This amount was properly debited to an operational asset account, Machinery. Prior to use, cash was spent for (*a*) major overhauling the machine, $600, and (*b*) for installation, $150; both of these amounts were debited to Expense. The machine has an estimated remaining useful life of five years and a 10% residual value. Straight-line depreciation will be used.

2. A small warehouse (and the land on which it is located) was purchased on January 1, 19F, at a cash cost of $40,000 which was debited in full to an operational asset account, Warehouse. The property was appraised for tax purposes near the end of 19E as follows: warehouse, $21,250; and land, $8,250. The warehouse has an estimated remaining useful life of 10 years and a 10% residual value; 150% declining balance depreciation will be used.

3. During the year 19F, usual recurring repair costs of $1,200 were paid. During January 19F, major repairs (on the warehouse purchased in 2 above) of $1,000 were paid. Repair expense was debited $2,200, and Cash was credited.

4. On June 30, 19F, the company purchased a patent for use in the business at a cash cost of $6,000. The patent was dated July 1, 19A. The Patent account was debited for the full amount.

5. On December 31, 19F, the company acquired a new truck that had a list price of $15,000 (estimated life, five years; residual value, $2,000). The company paid for the truck with cash, $7,000, and issued to the seller 600 shares of its own capital stock, par $8. The market value of the stock was $14 per share. This purchase has not been recorded.

Required:

a. Give the journal entry or entries that should be made to correct the accounts at December 31, 19F, before the adjusting entries are made. If none is required, so state.

b. Give the adjusting journal entries at December 31, 19F, after the corrections in Requirement (*a*) have been made.

P9–14   (A Challenging Problem; Focuses on the Cash Flow Effects of Income Tax for Straight-Line Depreciation versus Accelerated Depreciation)
On January 1, 19A, Paris Corporation bought a special machine for use in the business for $33,000. The machine has a three-year useful life and a residual value of $3,000. The company is considering using either the straight-line method or the 200% declining balance method of depreciation. Assume an average income tax rate of 30% (for both accounting and income tax purposes) and that it is paid in full in cash.

Required:

a. Prepare an anaysis of the effects of SL versus 200% DB depreciation on the projected financial statements and cash flows over the life of the machine (19A–19C). Complete the following schedules—one set based on straight-line depreciation and another set based on 200% declining balance depreciation:

	Year 1	Year 2	Year 3
Income statements:			
Revenues (all cash)	$90,000	$95,000	$99,000
Expenses (all cash)	(60,000)	(62,000)	(63,000)
Depreciation expense			
Pretax income			
Income tax expense			
Net income			
EPS (5,000 shares)			
Balance sheets:			
Operational assets:			
Machine			
Accumulated depreciation			
Book value			
Cash flows:			
Revenues			
Expenses			
Depreciation expense			
Income tax			
Net cash inflow			

b. Complete the following summary of **relevant comparisons** based on your answer to Requirement (*a*):

Items Compared	Year 1		Year 2		Year 3		Total (each method)
	SL	200% DB	SL	200% DB	SL	200% DB	
1. Net income							
2. Machine, book value							
3. Net cash inflow							

c. List, and explain, any generalizations that you can make about the three items summarized in Requirement (*b*): (1) net income, (2) book value, and (3) net cash inflow.

d. Which method would you recommend? Explain the basis for your recommendation.

P9–15 **(This Problem Relates to Chapter Supplement 9B; Record the Sale of an Operational Asset under Two Assumptions: All Cash and Exchange)**
Big Company operates a number of machines. One particular group of machines has five identical machines acquired on the same date. At the beginning of 19G, the operational asset account for the five machines showed the following:

> Machinery (Type A, five machines) $300,000
> Accumulated depreciation (Type A machines) 168,000*
>
> * Based on 10-year estimated useful life and $4,000 residual value per machine and straight-line depreciation.

One of the machines (Type A) was disposed of on October 1, 19G.

Required:

a. How old were the Type A machines at January 1, 19G? Show computations.

b. What was the book value of the machine sold (at date of disposal)? Show computations. The company computes depreciation to the nearest full month.

c. Give all journal entries to record the disposal of the machine under two independent assumptions:
   (1) It was sold outright for $20,000 cash.
   (2) It was exchanged for a new similar machine having a list price of $47,000; however, it was determined that it could be purchased for $44,000 cash. The old machine was traded in, and $30,000 was paid in cash. Assume the machines were similar. No reasonable market value was determinable for the old machine.

P9–16　**(This Problem Relates to Chapter Supplement 9B; Record Exchanges of Similar and Dissimilar Machine, with and without a Cash Difference)**

Ben Company owned a particular machine (designated Machine O for case purposes) which no longer met their needs. On December 31, 19F, the records reflected the following:

> Machine O:
> Original cost $30,000
> Accumulated depreciation 17,000

On January 3, 19G, the company acquired another machine (Machine N) and traded in Machine O. On this date, a reliable estimate of the market value of Machine O was $16,000.

Required:

a. Give the journal entry to record the transaction completed on January 3, 19G, for each of the following independent cases:

> Case A—The machines were similar, and no cash difference was paid or received.
>
> Case B—The machines were dissimilar, and no cash difference was paid or received.

For each case, explain the underlying reasons for the amount that you recorded as the cost of Machine N.

b. Use the facts and requirements given above, except that for each case assume the company paid a $2,000 cash difference and that the market value of Machine N was $18,200.

CASES

C9–1　**(Comprehensive Case; Involves Computation and Evaluation of Cash Flow Effects for 10 Years for Three Different Depreciation Methods)**

Slick Corporation acquired a large machine for use in its productive activities at a cash cost of $189,000. The machine was acquired on January 1, 19A, at which time its estimated useful life was 500,000 units of output over a period of 10 years. The estimated residual value was $24,000. Assume a 40% income tax rate for Slick for both accounting and income tax purposes.

The management of Slick is considering using either straight-line (SL), productive-output (PO), or sum-of-the-years'-digits (SYD) depreciation. The management also is developing a 10-year profit plan. The 10-year projected all-cash incomes (before depreciation and income tax) are shown in the first column below.

Required:

a. Complete the following tabulation (round to nearest $1):

Year	Income (all cash) before Depreciation and Income Tax		Depreciation Expense (dollars)			Income Tax Expense (dollars)			Net Income (loss) (dollars)		
	Units	Dollars	SL	PO	SYD	SL	PO	SYD	SL	PO	SYD
1	70,000	96,500	16,500	23,100	30,000	32,000	29,360	26,600	48,000	44,040	39,900
2	75,000	103,400									
3	80,000	102,300									
4	75,000	103,400									
5	60,000	82,700	16,500	19,800	18,000	26,480	25,160	25,880	39,720	37,740	38,820
6	60,000	82,700									
7	50,000	69,000									
8	20,000	27,600	16,500	6,600	9,000	4,440	8,400	7,440	6,660	12,600	11,160
9	8,000	11,000									
10	2,000	2,400	16,500	660	3,000	(5,640)	696	(240)	(8,460)	1,044	(360)
Σ	500,000	681,000	165,000	165,000	165,000	206,400	206,400	206,400	309,600	309,600	309,600

    b. List and explain any generalizations that you can make from the columns for (1) depreciation expense, (2) income tax expense, and (3) net income.

    c. Which method would you recommend in this situation? Explain the basis for your recommendation.

C9–2 **(Analysis of Depreciation and Property, Plant, and Equipment for an Actual**
JCPenney **Company)**
Refer to the financial statements of J.C. Penney Company, Inc. given in the appendix immediately preceding the index.

1. What method of depreciation is used by the company?
2. For depreciation purposes, what is the expected life of the buildings owned by the company?
3. What was the original cost of the properties reported on the J.C. Penney balance sheet at the end of the current year?
4. What is the cost of the land included in properties reported on the J.C. Penney balance sheet at the end of the current year?
5. How much was expended during the current year to acquire fixtures and equipment?
6. Were any fixtures and equipment disposed of during the current year?

TEN

MEASURING AND REPORTING LIABILITIES

PURPOSE

A business generates or receives resources from three sources: (*a*) capital contributed by owners, (*b*) income from operations, and (*c*) borrowing from creditors. **Creditors** provide resources by making cash loans and by selling property, goods, and services on credit. For users of financial statements, the liabilities reported on the balance sheet and the related interest expense reported on the income statement are important factors in evaluating the financial performance of a business. The purpose of this chapter is to discuss the measurement, recording, and reporting of liabilities and the related interest expense.

As the balance sheet on the opposite page illustrates, most companies have many different types of liabilities.

LEARNING OBJECTIVES

1. Define and classify liabilities.

2. Record and report current liabilities.

3. Apply deferred income tax allocation.

4. Record and report contingent liabilities.

5. Apply the concepts of the future and present values of a single amount.

6. Apply annuity concepts to liabilities.

7. Expand your accounting vocabulary by learning the "Important Terms Defined in This Chapter."

8. Apply the knowledge learned from this chapter by completing the homework assigned by your instructor.

ORGANIZATION

Part A—measuring, accounting, and reporting liabilities

1. Liabilities defined and classified.

2. Measuring liabilities.

3. Current liabilities.

4. Long-term liabilities.

5. Contingent liabilities.

6. Controlling expenditures with a voucher system.

Part B—future value and present value concepts

1. Concepts.

2. Future and present values of a single amount.

3. Future and present values of an annuity.

4. Present value concepts and lease liabilities.

UNITED AIRLINES

(In Thousands, Except Share Data)	1987	December 31 1986
Liabilities and Shareholders' Equity		
Current liabilities:		
Short-term borrowings	$1,010,311	$ 747,698
Long-term debt maturing within one year	27,233	26,586
Current obligations under capital leases	19,965	21,275
Advance ticket sales	581,333	561,322
Accounts payable	496,216	474,970
Accrued salaries, wages and benefits	536,291	438,931
Accrued income taxes	261,862	28,827
Other accrued liabilities	476,650	277,084
	3,409,861	2,576,693
Long-term debt	996,553	663,010
Long-term obligations under capital leases	430,742	450,725
Other liabilities and deferred credits:		
Other liabilities	350,411	285,635
Deferred income taxes	17,658	91,105
Other deferred credits	95,936	63,614
	464,005	440,354
Redeemable preferred stock:		
5½% cumulative prior preferred stock, $100 par value	3,021	3,498
Common stock and other shareholders' equity:		
Common stock, $5 par value; authorized, 125,000,000 shares; issued, 58,470,707 shares in 1987 and 50,223,688 shares in 1986	292,354	251,118
Additional capital invested	1,678,306	1,260,595
Retained earnings	1,073,760	780,535
Common stock held in treasury — 1,730,400 shares	(122,333)	—
	2,922,087	2,292,248
Commitments and contingent liabilities (See note on contingencies and commitments)		
	$8,226,269	$6,426,528

PART A—MEASURING, RECORDING, AND REPORTING LIABILITIES

Liabilities Defined and Classified

Liabilities are **defined** as probable future sacrifices of economic benefits. Liabilities **arise** from present obligations of an entity to transfer assets or provide services to other entities in the future as a result of past transactions or events. Liabilities often are called debts or obligations.

Usually a business has several kinds of liabilities and a wide range of creditors. Users of financial statements rely on the statements for relevant information about the kinds and amounts of liabilities owed by the entity. Liabilities usually are classified on the balance sheet as follows:

1. Current liabilities:
    a. Accounts payable.
    b. Short-term notes payable.
    c. Other short-term obligations.
2. Long-term liabilities:
    a. Long-term notes payable and mortgages.
    b. Bonds payable.
    c. Other long-term obligations.

Bonds payable will be discussed in Chapter 11. The other classifications will be discussed in this chapter.

Measuring Liabilities

A liability usually involves the payment of two different amounts: (*a*) the **principal** of the debt and (*b*) the **interest** on the principal. Assume that you borrowed $1,000 cash on January 1, 19A, and signed a $1,000 note payable that specified 10% interest and a time to maturity (repayment) of one year. You would receive $1,000 cash and repay $1,100 ($1,000 principal plus $100 interest). This liability would be recorded on January 1, 19A, at its principal amount. The transaction is recorded as follows:

January 1, 19A:

Cash	1,000	
Note payable		1,000

Liabilities are measured in conformity with the **cost principle.** When initially incurred, the amount of a liability is equivalent to the current market value of the resources received when the transaction occurred. In most cases, liabilities are recorded at their **principal** amounts.[1] This amount usually is the same as the face amount or maturity value. However, there are two exceptions:

---

[1] The principal amount of a debt does not include interest because interest is an expense that is incurred only after a debt is incurred (i.e., after the passage of time).

1. **Noninterest-bearing notes.** Some notes do not specify a rate of interest but have **implicit** interest. Assume you borrow $1,000 cash on January 1, 19A, and agree to repay $1,100 in one year. You sign a $1,100 note that does not specify an interest rate (called a noninterest-bearing note). The difference between the cash you repay and the cash you borrow ($1,100 − $1,000 = $100) is implicit interest expense.

2. **Liabilities with an unrealistic interest rate.** In some cases, the **stated** interest rate is higher or lower than the **effective** (or true) interest rate for the transaction.[2] For example, the stated rate on the above note may have been 6%, although its effective rate was 10%. Measuring liabilities with an effective interest rate that is different than the stated interest requires application of present value concepts (discussed in Part B of this chapter).

In most cases, the stated and effective interest rates for liabilities will be the same; in these cases, the liabilities are measured at their **principal** amounts.

Current Liabilities

Current liabilities are defined as **short-term obligations that will be paid within the current operating cycle of the business or within one year of the balance sheet date, whichever is longer.** This definition presumes that current liabilities will be paid with assets that are classified as current assets on the same balance sheet.[3]

Current liabilities include trade accounts payable, short-term notes payable, accrued expenses (such as wages payable, taxes payable, and interest payable), cash dividends payable, the current portion of long-term debt, and revenues collected in advance (also called deferred or unearned revenues).

Accounts Payable

Trade accounts payable are created by purchases of goods for resale and services received in the normal course of business. The term **accounts payable** is used in accounting to mean trade accounts payable. Typical journal entries for an account payable are:

March 6, 19B (purchase on credit; terms 2/10, n/30; periodic inventory system):

Purchases	980	
Accounts payable		980
Purchase of merchandise on credit; terms 2/10, n/30. (Invoice price, $1,000 × 0.98 = $980.)		

---

[2] The effective rate of interest also is called the **going** or **market** rate of interest. As discussed later, interest expense is based on the effective rate, rather than the stated rate, when the two rates are different.

[3] The AICPA Committee on Accounting Procedure defined current liabilities as follows: The term **current liabilities** is used principally to designate obligations whose liquidation is reasonably expected to require the use of existing resources properly classifiable as current assets, or the creation of other current liabilities.

March 11, 19B (payment of liability):

Accounts payable	980	
Cash		980

Payment of account payable within the discount period.

If payment is made after the discount period, the entry is:

April 1, 19B:

Accounts payable	980	
Purchase discounts lost	20	
Cash		1,000

Accrued Expenses

Accrued expenses (also called accrued liabilities) arise when expenses have been incurred but have not yet been paid at the end of the accounting period. These liabilities are recorded as **adjusting entries.** To illustrate an accrued expense, assume that on December 31, 19B, the annual amount of property taxes for 19B was $1,600, which had not been paid or recorded. At the end of the accounting period, December 31, 19B, the expense and related liability must be recorded. Therefore, the following **adjusting entry** must be made:

December 31, 19B (adjusting entry):

Property tax expense	1,600	
Property taxes payable		1,600

Adjusting entry to record property taxes incurred in 19B not yet recorded or paid.

The entry in 19C for payment of the above liability would be:

January 15, 19C:

Property taxes payable	1,600	
Cash		1,600

Payment of liability for property taxes accrued in 19B.

Payroll Liabilities

When employees perform services, the employer incurs an obligation that is not settled until the employees are paid on a weekly or monthly payroll basis. In previous chapters, accounting for wage and salary expense was simplified by ignoring payroll taxes and payroll deductions; we will now discuss these complications.

Besides the obligation to the employee for salary or wages, the employer incurs other liabilities that are related directly to the payment of salaries and wages. These liabilities usually arise as a result of federal and state laws (e.g., social security taxes), and contractual obligations (such as pension plans and union dues). Some of these liabilities are paid by the **employees** through the employer (as payroll deductions); others must be paid by the **employer** and thus are additional expenses to the business.

The take-home pay of most employees is considerably less than the gross salary or wages. This difference is caused by **payroll deductions** for employee income taxes withheld, social security taxes (known as FICA taxes) that must be paid by the employee, and other employee deductions such as insurance and union dues. The employer must pay the amounts deducted from the wages to the designated governmental agencies and other organizations such as the union. From the date of the payroll deduction until the date of payment to the agencies or organizations, the employer must record the **current liabilities** associated with the payroll deductions. A typical journal entry for a $100,000 payroll is as follows:

January 31, 19B:

Salary and wage expense	100,000	
Liability for income taxes withheld—employees		21,000
Liability for union dues withheld—employees		400
FICA taxes payable—employees		7,150
Cash (take-home pay)		71,450
To record the payroll including employee deductions.		

Besides the payroll taxes that the **employees** must pay through the employer, the **employer** is required by law to pay additional specified payroll taxes. These taxes include the employer's share of social security taxes (FICA) and Federal Unemployment Compensation (FUTA). These taxes are an operating expense for the business. Therefore, a second entry related to the payroll is needed to record the payroll taxes to be paid by the **employer**. A typical entry related to the above payroll is as follows:

January 31, 19B:

Payroll tax expense	10,550*	
FICA taxes payable—employer (matching)		7,150
FUTA taxes payable—employer		700
State unemployment taxes payable—employer		2,700
Employer payroll taxes for January payroll.		

* Total payroll expense: $100,000 + $10,550 = $110,550.

The six current liabilities recorded in the two entries immediately above will be paid in the near future. At that time, the company remits the requisite amounts of cash to the appropriate taxing agencies and other parties. Payroll accounting does not entail any new accounting concepts or principles; however, much clerical detail is involved. Details involved in payroll accounting are discussed in Chapter Supplement 10A.

Deferred Revenues

When a company collects cash before the related revenue has been earned (e.g., a magazine subscription may be paid a year in advance), this cash is called **deferred revenues** (or unearned revenues or revenues collected in advance). Deferred revenues arise when revenues are collected during the current period that will not be earned until a **later** accounting period. Under the revenue principle (Exhibit 4–5), revenue cannot be recorded until it has been earned.

Deferred revenues are a liability because cash has been collected but the related revenue has not been earned by the end of the accounting period. There is a **current obligation** to provide the services or goods in the future. For example, on November 15, 19B, rent revenue of $6,000 was collected. This amount was recorded as a debit to Cash and a credit to Rent Revenue. At the end of 19B, $2,000 of this amount was for January 19C rent. Thus, there is a current liability of $2,000 for deferred rent revenue that must be recognized. The sequence of entries for this case is as follows:

November 15, 19B (collection of rent revenue):

Cash	6,000	
Rent revenue		6,000
Collection of revenue.[4]		

December 31, 19B (adjusting entry for unearned rent revenue):

Rent revenue	2,000	
Rent revenue collected in advance (deferred revenue)		2,000
Adjusting entry to record unearned rent revenue at the end of the accounting period.		

Long-Term Liabilities

Long-term liabilities include all obligations of the entity not classified as current liabilities. Long-term liabilities often are incurred when purchasing operational assets or borrowing large amounts of cash for major expansions of the business. Long-term liabilities usually are represented by long-term **notes payable** or **bonds payable.** A long-term liability may be supported by a mortgage on specified assets **pledged** by the borrower as security for the liability. A liability supported by a mortgage is a "**secured** debt." An **unsecured** debt is one for which the creditor relies primarily on the integrity and general earning power of the borrower.

Long-term liabilities are reported on the balance sheet (immediately following current liabilities) under a separate caption "Long-term liabilities." As a long-term debt approaches the maturity date, the part of it that is to be paid from current assets is reclassified as a current liability. For example, a five-year note payable of $50,000 was signed on January 1, 19A. Repayment is in two install-

---

[4] On November 15, 19B, the $6,000 credit could have been made to Rent Revenue Collected in Advance. In that case, the adjusting entry to give the same results on December 31, 19B, is:

Rent revenue collected in advance	4,000	
Rent revenue		4,000

ments as follows: December 31, 19D, $25,000; and December 31, 19E, $25,000. The December 31, 19B, 19C, and 19D balance sheets would report the following:

December 31, 19B:
  Long-term liabilities:
    Note payable $50,000
December 31, 19C:
  Current liabilities:
    Maturing portion of long-term note . . . 25,000
  Long-term liabilities:
    Long-term note 25,000
December 31, 19D:
  Current liabilities:
    Maturing portion of long-term note . . . 25,000

Notes payable may be either short term or long term. A short-term note payable usually has a maturity date within one year from the balance sheet date. Short-term notes often arise as a result of borrowing cash or from purchasing merchandise or services on credit. Bonds payable (discussed in Chapter 11) always are long-term liabilities, except for any currently maturing portion as shown above for the long-term note payable.

Notes Payable

A note payable is a written promise to pay a stated sum at one or more specified future dates called the maturity date. A note payable may require a single-sum payment at the maturity date or it may call for installment payments (called an annuity). A typical car loan and home mortgage are examples of installment loans that require the periodic payment of principal and interest.

Notes payable require the payment of interest and the periodic recording of interest expense. Interest expense is incurred on liabilities because of the **time value of money.** The word **time** is significant because the longer borrowed money is held, the larger is the total dollar amount of interest expense. There is more interest for a two-year loan of a given amount, at a given **interest rate,** than for a one-year loan. To the **borrower, interest is an expense;** to the **creditor, interest is a revenue.**

To calculate interest, three variables must be considered: (1) the principal, (2) the interest rate, and (3) the duration of time. The interest formula is:

$$\text{Interest} = \text{Principal} \times \text{Rate} \times \text{Time}$$

Accounting for an Interest-Bearing Note
On November 1, 19A, Baker Company borrowed $10,000 cash on a six-month, 12% interest-bearing note payable. The interest is payable at the maturity date of the note. The computation of interest expense would be: $10,000 \times 12\% \times 6/12 = $600. The note is recorded in the accounts as follows:

November 1, 19A:

```
Cash . . . . . . . . . . . . . . . . . . . . . . . . . . . . . . . . . . . . . . . . . . 10,000
      Note payable, short term . . . . . . . . . . . . . . . . . . . . . . . . .              10,000
   Borrowed on short-term note; terms, six months at 12% per
   annum; interest is payable at maturity.
```

Interest is an expense of the period when the money is used; therefore, it is recorded on a **time basis** rather than when the cash actually is paid. This concept is based on legal as well as on economic considerations. For example, if the $10,000 loan cited above was paid off four months early (i.e., in two months instead of in six months), interest amounting to $10,000 $\times$ 12% $\times$ $\frac{2}{12}$ = $200 would have to be paid.

The **adjusting entry** for accrued interest is made at the end of the accounting period on the basis of time expired from the last interest date or from the date of the note. Assume the accounting period for Baker Company ends December 31, 19A. Although the $600 interest for the six months will not be paid until April 30, 19B, two months' unpaid interest (i.e., November and December 19A) must be **accrued** by means of the following adjusting entry by Baker Company:

December 31, 19A:

```
Interest expense  . . . . . . . . . . . . . . . . . . . . . . . . . . . . . . .     200
      Interest payable . . . . . . . . . . . . . . . . . . . . . . . . . . . . .              200
   Adjusting entry to accrue two months' interest ($10,000 ×
   12% × ²⁄₁₂ = $200).
```

At maturity date, the payment of principal plus interest for six months is recorded as follows:

April 30, 19B:

```
Note payable, short term  . . . . . . . . . . . . . . . . . . . . . . . . . . 10,000
Interest payable (per prior entry) . . . . . . . . . . . . . . . . . . . . .        200
Interest expense ($10,000 × 12% × ⁴⁄₁₂) . . . . . . . . . . . . . . . . .            400
      Cash ($10,000 + $600 interest)  . . . . . . . . . . . . . . . . . . . .            10,600
   To record payment of note payable including interest.
```

Accounting for a note payable is the same whether it is classified as a current or as a long-term liability; and it is the same regardless of the purpose for which the note was executed.

Accounting for a Noninterest-Bearing Note

A noninterest-bearing note includes the interest amount in the face amount of the note. This causes a difference in the accounting entries. For example, if the Baker note above was noninterest bearing, its face amount would be $10,600 (i.e., the principal amount plus interest). The journal entry to record the note is:

November 1, 19A:

```
Cash . . . . . . . . . . . . . . . . . . . . . . . . . . . . . . . . . . . . . . . . . 10,000
Discount on note payable . . . . . . . . . . . . . . . . . . . . . . . . . .        600
      Note payable . . . . . . . . . . . . . . . . . . . . . . . . . . . . . . . . . .            10,600
```

The Discount on Note Payable is a contra liability account. It is reported on the balance sheet immediately after the Note Payable account and reduces the book value of the note. The $10,600 balance in Note Payable includes principal and interest. The contra account Discount on Note Payable reduces the amount in the Note Payable account by the amount of interest expense that has not yet accrued. On November 1, 19A, there is no accrued interest. As a result, the book value of the note should be $10,000 ($10,600 − $600).

The adjusting entry to record interest expense on December 31, 19A, is:

December 31, 19A:

Interest expense ($10,000 × 12% × 2/12)	200	
Discount on note payable		200

The adjusting entry records interest expense and reduces the Discount on Note Payable account for the amount of interest that has accrued. The book value of the note on December 31, 19A, is $10,200 ($10,600 − $400), which reflects the $10,000 that was borrowed plus $200 interest that has accrued.

The entry to record the payment of the note is as follows:

April 30, 19B:

Note payable	10,600	
Interest expense	400	
Discount on note payable		400
Cash		10,600

Accounting for a noninterest-bearing note may seem confusing. It is somewhat less confusing if you observe an important concept: accounting focuses on the economic substance of a transaction and not the mere form of the transaction. A "noninterest-bearing" note is actually a misnomer because interest is charged in all business transactions. Accounting ignores the misleading name of the note and measures the true interest cost that is implicit in the transaction. Notice that given the same basic facts, $600 interest expense is recorded for both an interest-bearing and a noninterest-bearing note.

Deferred Income Tax

Usually corporations must pay federal income tax. The basic entry to record income tax debits Income Tax Expense and credits Income Taxes Payable. However, in many cases, a taxable revenue or a tax-deductible expense may occur in one accounting period but its tax effect is reported in another accounting period. In these cases, tax expense is not equal to income taxes payable, which causes a **deferred income tax** amount.

Deferred income tax is recognized **only** for those few transactions when a taxable revenue or tax-deductible expense must be reported on the income statement and on the income tax return in different accounting years. In these cases, the amount of the taxable revenue or tax-deductible expense is called a **temporary difference.** For example, at the end of 19A, DIT Corporation has a $10,000 taxable revenue and a 30% income tax rate. This revenue must be reported on the 19A income statement (in conformity with GAAP), but the income tax laws require that it must be reported in the 19B income tax return. This means that there is a temporary difference of $10,000, and the **income tax effect** is $10,000 × 30% = $3,000.

Application of the Deferred Income Tax Concept

Under this concept (*a*) income tax **expense** is calculated based on the numbers reported on the income statement and (*b*) income taxes **payable** is calculated based on numbers reported on the income tax return.

Each temporary difference will **always reverse** (or turn around) at some time(s) in the future. Each temporary difference **initially** occurs in one or more accounting period(s) and then **reverses** in one or more future accounting period(s). The time between the initial and reversing periods is called the **tax deferral time.** A tax deferral may start with either a credit (a liability) or a debit (an asset). During the reversing periods, these debits or credits will be the opposite so that at the end of the tax deferral time the deferred tax account will have a zero balance. Permanent differences do not cause deferred taxes.

When there are temporary differences, **income tax expense** must be computed each year-end as follows:

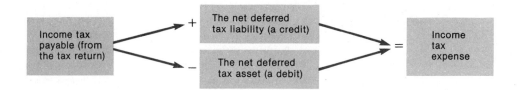

The primary problem in deferred tax accounting is to properly identify and measure each **temporary difference.** To illustrate, return to the DIT Corporation case given above. There was a 19A taxable revenue of $10,000, reported on the 19B tax return at a 30% rate. The following steps illustrate accounting for deferred taxes:

Step 1.   Determine if any temporary differences exist.

In the case of DIT Corporation, the $10,000 revenue is a temporary difference because it must be reported on the income statement and the income tax return in different years.

Step 2.   Determine the income taxes payable (based on the numbers reported on the tax return) and the tax effects associated with the temporary differences. The tax effects are determined by applying the provisions of enacted tax laws.

For DIT Coporation, assume the 19A income taxes payable is $20,000. The tax effect of the temporary difference is $3,000 (which is the temporary difference, $10,000, multiplied by the tax rate, 30%.)

Step 3. Record the originating entry:

December 31, 19A—originating entry:

a. Income tax expense ($b + c$) 23,000
b.   Deferred income tax liability (computed)*   3,000
c.   Income taxes payable (from tax return)   20,000

* $10,000 × 30% = $3,000. This is a liability (credit) because the income tax on the $10,000
temporary difference must be recognized on the 19B tax return—to be paid in the future.

Step 4. In subsequent accounting periods, record the reversing of deferred
taxes:

Assume income taxes payable for DIT Corporation is $22,000 in
19B.

December 31, 19B—reversing of deferred taxes:

a. Income tax expense ($c - b$)   19,000
b. Deferred income tax (computed)   3,000
c.   Income taxes payable (from tax return)   22,000

The income tax expense associated with the temporary difference is matched
with the $10,000 revenue reported on the 19A income statement instead of
reporting it in the year that the tax obligation was paid (19B). Deferred tax
accounting is a good example of an application of the matching principle (Exhibit
4–5). Examples of temporary differences are discussed in Chapter Supplement
10–D.

Contingent Liabilities

The basic definition of a liability is a "**probable** future sacrifice of economic
benefits." In some situations, a transaction or event may occur that creates a
potential (but not probable) future sacrifice of economic benefits. These situations create a **contingent liability,** which is a potential liability that has arisen
because of an event or transaction that already has occurred. The conversion of a
contingent liability to a recorded liability depends on one or more future events.
A situation that causes a contingent liability also causes a contingent loss.

Whether a situation causes a recorded or a contingent liability depends on the
probability of the future economic sacrifice. There are three classes of proba-
bilities:

a. **Probable**—the future event or events are likely to occur.
b. **Reasonably possible**—the chance of the occurrence of the future event
or events is more than remote but less than likely.
c. **Remote**—the chance of occurrence of the future event or events is
slight.

At the end of the accounting period, the company must determine whether
the **amount** of any contingent liability can be **"reasonably estimated."** The
general accounting guidelines are (1) a contingent liability that is both **probable**

and can be **reasonably estimated** must be **recorded** and reported in the financial statements, (2) a contingent liability that is **reasonably possible** (whether it can be estimated or not) must be **disclosed** in a note in the financial statements, and (3) remote contingencies are not disclosed. For example, during 19B, Baker Company was sued for $200,000 damages based on an accident involving one of the trucks owned by the company. The suit is scheduled to start during March 19C. Whether there is an effective (i.e., enforceable) liability at the end of 19B (end of the accounting period) depends on a future event—the decision of the court at the end of the trial.

Case A. Baker Company and its legal counsel determine that (1) it is probable that damages will be assessed and (2) a reasonable estimate is $150,000. Therefore, Baker must make the following entry:

December 31, 19B:

```
Loss due to accident . . . . . . . . . . . . . . . . . . . . . . . . . . . . . . . . .   150,000
    Estimated liability due to accident  . . . . . . . . . . . . . . . . . . . .              150,000
```

The loss is reported on the 19B income statement, and the liability is reported on the 19B balance sheet.

Case B. Baker Company determines that (1) it is reasonably possible that damages will be assessed and (2) a reasonable estimate cannot be made. Therefore, Baker must disclose the contingency by a note in the 19B balance sheet similar to the following:

> The company was sued for $200,000 based on an accident involving a company vehicle. Legal counsel believes that it is reasonably possible that some damages will be assessed. The amount cannot be reasonably estimated at this date. The trial is scheduled for March 19C.

Published financial statements seldom reflect an admission of guilt when discussing contingent liabilities associated with litigation. To do so would insure loss of the lawsuit.

Controlling Expenditures with a Voucher System

Most companies make a large number of cash payments on liabilities. Proper control over cash expenditures can prevent the misapplication of cash in the cash-disbursement process. In a small business, it is possible for the owner to give personal attention to each transaction. This personal attention may assure that the business is getting what it pays for, that cash is not being disbursed carelessly, and that there is no theft or fraud involving cash.

As a business grows and becomes more complex, the owner or top executive cannot devote personal attention to each transaction involving the processing of cash disbursements. In such cases, these activities must be assigned to various employees. The assignment of these responsibilities to others creates a need for systematic procedures for the control of cash expenditures. This facet is important in the internal control of a well-designed accounting system.

Chapter 8 discussed the essential features of effective **internal control.** The emphasis was on the control of cash receipts. Similar internal control procedures were discussed for cash disbursements—the separation of duties, disbursement of cash by check, and the use of petty cash. In larger companies, the method usually used for maintaining control over cash expenditures is the **voucher system.** This system replaces the cash disbursements journal that was explained in Chapter Supplement 8B.

A voucher system establishes strict control over transactions that create a legal obligation for an **expenditure of cash.** The system requires that a **written authorization,** called a **voucher,** be approved by one or more designated managers at the time each such transaction occurs. A voucher system can be used for transactions involving the purchase of merchandise and services, the acquisition of operational assets, the payment of a liability, and for investments. The system permits checks to be issued only in payment of properly prepared and approved vouchers. Check writing is kept separate from the voucher-approval, check-approval, and check-distribution procedures.

The voucher system requires that every obligation be supported by a previously approved voucher and that each transaction be recorded when incurred. The incurrence of each obligation is treated as an independent transaction. Also, each payment of cash is treated as another independent transaction. This sequence of voucher approval, followed by payment by check, is required even if there is an immediate payment of cash. A **cash** purchase of merchandise for resale would be recorded under the voucher system as follows:

1. To record the incurrence of an obligation (with a periodic inventory system):

Purchases	1,000	
Vouchers payable		1,000

2. To record payment of the obligation by check (immediately thereafter):

Vouchers payable	1,000	
Cash		1,000

In a voucher system, **Vouchers Payable** replaces the account entitled Accounts Payable in the ledger, but the designation on the balance sheet continues to be "Accounts Payable." The incurrence entries (1 above) are entered in a **voucher register,** and the payment entries (2 above) are entered in a **check register.**

The primary objective of the voucher system is to have continuous control over each step in an expenditure from the incurrence of an obligation to the final disbursement of cash to satisfy the obligation. Each transaction is reviewed systematically and is subjected to an approval system based on separately designated responsibilities. Chapter Supplement 10B discusses the **mechanics** of the voucher system.

Financial Statement Analysis

The distinction between short-term and long-term liabilities is an important one for financial analysts. Many companies go bankrupt each year because they are unable to pay their creditors on time. Analysts are particularly interested in short-term liabilities because these obligations are due within one year or one operating cycle, whichever is longer. One tool for bankruptcy prediction is to assess the probability that a company will be able to pay its short-term liabilities.

When evaluating a company, analysts often calculate the current ratio (Current assets ÷ Current liabilities). This relationship can also be expressed as a dollar amount called *working capital* (current assets − current liabilities). A current ratio of 2 means that a company has $2 of current assets for every $1 of current liabilities. Analysts compare the current ratio for a company with other similar companies. The current ratio for an electric utility is often as low as 1.0 because cash flows for electric utilities are very stable. An airline may have a current ratio as high as 2.0 because of highly variable cash flows.

Analysts also compare current ratios over time for a company. A deterioration of the ratio is often an early warning of financial difficulties.

To properly use the current ratio, analysts must understand the accounting for the various elements that make up the ratio. For example, the reclassification of the current maturing portion of long-term debt (discussed in this chapter) may have different analytical importance than new short-term borrowing.

PART B—FUTURE VALUE AND PRESENT VALUE CONCEPTS

Concepts

Accounting for liabilities often involves the concepts of present value and future value. These concepts also are used in accounting for long-term investments in bonds, leases, and pension plans. Most of these applications involve either measurement of a liability or a receivable, or the establishment of a fund of cash to be used in the future for some special purpose (such as for the retirement of debt).

The concept of future value (FV) and present value (PV) focus on the time value of money, which is another name for interest. A dollar received today is worth more than a dollar received one year from today (or at any other future date) because it can be used to earn interest. If a dollar received today can be invested at 10%, it will increase to $1.10 in one year. In contrast, if the dollar is to be received one year from today, the opportunity to earn the $0.10 interest revenue for the year is lost. The difference between the $1 and $1.10 is interest that can be earned during the year. Interest is the cost of the use of money for a specific period of time, just as rent represents the cost for use of a tangible asset for a period of time. Interest may be stated explicitly, as in the case of an interest-bearing note; or it may be unspecified, as in a noninterest-bearing note (but interest is still paid).

Exhibit 10–1   Four types of future and present value problems

Payment or Receipt	Symbol	
	Future Value	Present Value
Single amount	f	p
Annuity (equal payments or receipts for a series of equal time periods)	F	P

There are four different types of problems related to the time value of money; they are identified in Exhibit 10–1. Each type of problem is based on the interest formula that was discussed in Part A of this chapter:

$$\text{Interest} = \text{Principal} \times \text{Rate} \times \text{Time}$$

In **future value** problems, you will be given the amount of cash (principal) to be invested at the current date and you will be asked to use the basic interest formula to calculate the amount of principal plus interest that will be available at some **future date.** In contrast, **present value** problems involve a rearrangement of the basic interest formula. In present value problems, you will be given the amount that will be available at some **future date** (principal plus interest) and you will be asked to calculate the **current** cash equivalent of that amount.

Tables are used to avoid the detailed arithmetic calculations that are required in future value and present value computations. These tables (Tables 10–1 to 10–4) give values for each of the four types of problems for different periods of time (*n*) and at different rates of interest (*i*). The values given in the tables are based on payments of $1. If a problem involves payments other than $1, it is necessary to multiply the value from the table by the amount of the payment.[5] We will examine each of the four types of present value and future value problems.

Future and Present Values of a Single Amount

Future Value of a Single Amount (f)

The future value of a single amount (i.e., the principal) is the sum to which that amount will increase at *i* interest rate for *n* periods. The future sum will be the **principal plus interest.** The future value concept is based on compound interest.

---

[5] Present value and future value problems assume cash flows. The basic concepts are the same for cash inflows (receipts) and cash outflows (payments). Thus, there are no fundamental differences between present value and future value calculations for cash payments versus cash receipts.

Table 10–1 Future value of $1, $f = (1 + i)^n$

Periods	2%	3%	3.75%	4%	4.25%	5%	6%	7%	8%
0	1.	1.	1.	1.	1.	1.	1.	1.	1.
1	1.02	1.03	1.0375	1.04	1.0425	1.05	1.06	1.07	1.08
2	1.0404	1.0609	1.0764	1.0816	1.0868	1.1025	1.1236	1.1449	1.1664
3	1.0612	1.0927	1.1168	1.1249	1.1330	1.1576	1.1910	1.2250	1.2597
4	1.0824	1.1255	1.1587	1.1699	1.1811	1.2155	1.2625	1.3108	1.3605
5	1.1041	1.1593	1.2021	1.2167	1.2313	1.2763	1.3382	1.4026	1.4693
6	1.1262	1.1941	1.2472	1.2653	1.2837	1.3401	1.4185	1.5007	1.5869
7	1.1487	1.2299	1.2939	1.3159	1.3382	1.4071	1.5036	1.6058	1.7138
8	1.1717	1.2668	1.3425	1.3686	1.3951	1.4775	1.5938	1.7182	1.8509
9	1.1951	1.3048	1.3928	1.4233	1.4544	1.5513	1.6895	1.8385	1.9990
10	1.2190	1.3439	1.4450	1.4802	1.5162	1.6289	1.7908	1.9672	2.1589
20	1.4859	1.8061	2.0882	2.1911	2.2989	2.6533	3.2071	3.8697	4.6610

Periods	9%	10%	11%	12%	13%	14%	15%	20%	25%
0	1.	1.	1.	1.	1.	1.	1.	1.	1.
1	1.09	1.10	1.11	1.12	1.13	1.14	1.15	1.20	1.25
2	1.1881	1.2100	1.2321	1.2544	1.2769	1.2996	1.3225	1.4400	1.5625
3	1.2950	1.3310	1.3676	1.4049	1.4429	1.4815	1.5209	1.7280	1.9531
4	1.4116	1.4641	1.5181	1.5735	1.6305	1.6890	1.7490	2.0736	2.4414
5	1.5386	1.6105	1.6851	1.7623	1.8424	1.9254	2.0114	2.4883	3.0518
6	1.6771	1.7716	1.8704	1.9738	2.0820	2.1950	2.3131	2.9860	3.8147
7	1.8280	1.9487	2.0762	2.2107	2.3526	2.5023	2.6600	3.5832	4.7684
8	1.9926	2.1436	2.3045	2.4760	2.6584	2.8526	3.0590	4.2998	5.9605
9	2.1719	2.3579	2.5580	2.7731	3.0040	3.2519	3.5179	5.1598	7.4506
10	2.3674	2.5937	2.8394	3.1058	3.3946	3.7072	4.0456	6.1917	9.3132
20	5.6044	6.7275	8.0623	9.6463	11.5231	13.7435	16.3665	38.3376	86.7362

Therefore, the amount of interest for each period is calculated by multiplying the interest rate by the principal plus any interest that accrued in prior interest periods but was not paid out.

To illustrate, on January 1, 19A, $1,000 was deposited in a savings account at 10% annual interest, compounded annually. At the end of three years, the $1,000 originally deposited would increase to $1,331 as follows:

Year	Amount at start of year	+	Interest during the year	=	Amount at end of year
1	$1,000	+	$1,000 × 10% = $100	=	$1,100
2	1,100	+	1,100 × 10% = 110	=	1,210
3	1,210	+	1,210 × 10% = 121	=	1,331

We can avoid the detailed arithmetic by referring to Table 10–1, **Future value of $1** (f). For $i = 10\%$; $n = 3$, we find the value 1.331. We can compute the balance at the end of year 3 as $1,000 × 1.331 = $1,331. The increase of $331 was due to

Table 10–2 Present value of $1, $p = \dfrac{1}{(1 + i)^n}$

Periods	2%	3%	3.75%	4%	4.25%	5%	6%	7%	8%
1	0.9804	0.9709	0.9639	0.9615	0.9592	0.9524	0.9434	0.9346	0.9259
2	0.9612	0.9426	0.9290	0.9246	0.9201	0.9070	0.8900	0.8734	0.8573
3	0.9423	0.9151	0.8954	0.8890	0.8826	0.8638	0.8396	0.8163	0.7938
4	0.9238	0.8885	0.8631	0.8548	0.8466	0.8227	0.7921	0.7629	0.7350
5	0.9057	0.8626	0.8319	0.8219	0.8121	0.7835	0.7473	0.7130	0.6806
6	0.8880	0.8375	0.8018	0.7903	0.7790	0.7462	0.7050	0.6663	0.6302
7	0.8706	0.8131	0.7728	0.7599	0.7473	0.7107	0.6651	0.6227	0.5835
8	0.8535	0.7894	0.7449	0.7307	0.7168	0.6768	0.6274	0.5820	0.5403
9	0.8368	0.7664	0.7180	0.7026	0.6876	0.6446	0.5919	0.5439	0.5002
10	0.8203	0.7441	0.6920	0.6756	0.6595	0.6139	0.5584	0.5083	0.4632
20	0.6730	0.5534	0.4789	0.4564	0.4350	0.3769	0.3118	0.2584	0.2145

Periods	9%	10%	11%	12%	13%	14%	15%	20%	25%
1	0.9174	0.9091	0.9009	0.8929	0.8850	0.8772	0.8696	0.8333	0.8000
2	0.8417	0.8264	0.8116	0.7972	0.7831	0.7695	0.7561	0.6944	0.6400
3	0.7722	0.7513	0.7312	0.7118	0.6931	0.6750	0.6575	0.5787	0.5120
4	0.7084	0.6830	0.6587	0.6355	0.6133	0.5921	0.5718	0.4823	0.4096
5	0.6499	0.6209	0.5935	0.5674	0.5428	0.5194	0.4972	0.4019	0.3277
6	0.5963	0.5645	0.5346	0.5066	0.4803	0.4556	0.4323	0.3349	0.2621
7	0.5470	0.5132	0.4817	0.4523	0.4251	0.3996	0.3759	0.2791	0.2097
8	0.5019	0.4665	0.4339	0.4039	0.3762	0.3506	0.3269	0.2326	0.1678
9	0.4604	0.4241	0.3909	0.3606	0.3329	0.3075	0.2843	0.1938	0.1342
10	0.4224	0.3855	0.3522	0.3220	0.2946	0.2697	0.2472	0.1615	0.1074
20	0.1784	0.1486	0.1240	0.1037	0.0868	0.0728	0.0611	0.0261	0.0115

the time value of money. It is interest revenue to the owner of the savings account and interest expense to the savings institution. A convenient format to display the computations for this problem is: $\$1{,}000 \times f_{i=10\%;\, n=3}$ (Table 10–1; 1.3310) = $1,331. Exhibit 10–2 gives a summary of this future value concept.

Present Value of a Single Amount (p)

Present value of a single amount is the value now of an amount to be received at some date in the future. To compute the present value of a sum to be received in the future, the sum is subjected to compound **discounting** at *i* interest rate for *n* periods. In compound discounting, the interest is subtracted rather than added (as in compounding). To illustrate, assume today is January 1, 19A, and you will receive $1,000 cash on December 31, 19C; that is, three years from now. With an interest rate of 10% per year, how much would the $1,000 be worth on January 1, 19A? We could set up a discounting computation, year by year, that would be

Table 10–3 Future value of annuity of $1 (ordinary), $F = \dfrac{(1 + i)^n - 1}{i}$

Periods*	2%	3%	3.75%	4%	4.25%	5%	6%	7%	8%
1	1.	1.	1.	1.	1.	1.	1.	1.	1.
2	2.02	2.03	2.0375	2.04	2.0425	2.05	2.06	2.07	2.08
3	3.0604	3.0909	3.1139	3.1216	3.1293	3.1525	3.1836	3.2149	3.2464
4	4.1216	4.1836	4.2307	4.2465	4.2623	4.3101	4.3746	4.4399	4.5061
5	5.2040	5.3091	5.3893	5.4163	5.4434	5.5256	5.6371	5.7507	5.8666
6	6.3081	6.4684	6.5914	6.6330	6.6748	6.8019	6.9753	7.1533	7.3359
7	7.4343	7.6625	7.8386	7.8983	7.9585	8.1420	8.3938	8.6540	8.9228
8	8.5830	8.8923	9.1326	9.2142	9.2967	9.5491	9.8975	10.2598	10.6366
9	9.7546	10.1591	10.4750	10.5828	10.6918	11.0266	11.4913	11.9780	12.4876
10	10.9497	11.4639	11.8678	12.0061	12.1462	12.5779	13.1808	13.8164	14.4866
20	24.2974	26.8704	29.0174	29.7781	30.5625	33.0660	36.7856	40.9955	45.7620

Periods*	9%	10%	11%	12%	13%	14%	15%	20%	25%
1	1.	1.	1.	1.	1.	1.	1.	1.	1.
2	2.09	2.10	2.11	2.12	2.13	2.14	2.15	2.20	2.25
3	3.2781	3.3100	3.3421	3.3744	3.4069	3.4396	3.4725	3.6400	3.8125
4	4.5731	4.6410	4.7097	4.7793	4.8498	4.9211	4.9934	5.3680	5.7656
5	5.9847	6.1051	6.2278	6.3528	6.4803	6.6101	6.7424	7.4416	8.2070
6	7.5233	7.7156	7.9129	8.1152	8.3227	8.5355	8.7537	9.9299	11.2588
7	9.2004	9.4872	9.7833	10.0890	10.4047	10.7305	11.0668	12.9159	15.0735
8	11.0285	11.4359	11.8594	12.2997	12.7573	13.2328	13.7268	16.4991	19.8419
9	13.0210	13.5795	14.1640	14.7757	15.4157	16.0853	16.7858	20.7989	25.8023
10	15.1929	15.9374	16.7220	17.5487	18.4197	19.3373	20.3037	25.9587	33.2529
20	51.1601	57.2750	64.2028	72.0524	80.9468	91.0249	102.4436	186.6880	342.9447

* There is one payment each period.

the **inverse** to the tabulation shown above for the future value.[6] However, to facilitate the computation, we can refer to the **Present value of $1 table** (p), Table 10–2. For $i = 10\%$; $n = 3$, we find the present value of $1 is 0.7513. The $1,000, to be received at the end of three years has a **present value** (today) of $1,000 × 0.7513 = $751.30. The difference (i.e., the discount) of $248.70 is interest. A convenient format to display the computations for this problem is $1,000 ×

---

[6] The detailed discounting would be as follows:

Periods	Interest for the year	Present value*
1 . . .	$1,000 − ($1,000 × 1/1.10) = $90.91	$1,000 − $90.91 = $909.09
2 . . .	$909.09 − ($909.09 × 1/1.10) = $82.65	$909.09 − $82.65 = 826.44
3 . . .	$826.44 − ($826.44 × 1/1.10) = $75.14	$826.44 − $75.14 = 751.30

* Verifiable in Table 10–2.

Table 10–4 Present value of annuity of $1 (ordinary), $P = \dfrac{1 - \dfrac{1}{(1 + i)^n}}{i}$

Periods*	2%	3%	3.75%	4%	4.25%	5%	6%	7%	8%
1	0.9804	0.9709	0.9639	0.9615	0.9592	0.9524	0.9434	0.9346	0.9259
2	1.9416	1.9135	1.8929	1.8861	1.8794	1.8594	1.8334	1.8080	1.7833
3	2.8839	2.8286	2.7883	2.7751	2.7620	2.7232	2.6730	2.6243	2.5771
4	3.8077	3.7171	3.6514	3.6299	3.6086	3.5460	3.4651	3.3872	3.3121
5	4.7135	4.5797	4.4833	4.4518	4.4207	4.3295	4.2124	4.1002	3.9927
6	5.6014	5.4172	5.2851	5.2421	5.1997	5.0757	4.9173	4.7665	4.6229
7	6.4720	6.2303	6.0579	6.0021	5.9470	5.7864	5.5824	5.3893	5.2064
8	7.3255	7.0197	6.8028	6.7327	6.6638	6.4632	6.2098	5.9713	5.7466
9	8.1622	7.7861	7.5208	7.4353	7.3513	7.1078	6.8017	6.5152	6.2469
10	8.9826	8.5302	8.2128	8.1109	8.0109	7.7217	7.3601	7.0236	6.7101
20	16.3514	14.8775	13.8962	13.5903	13.2944	12.4622	11.4699	10.5940	9.8181

Periods*	9%	10%	11%	12%	13%	14%	15%	20%	25%
1	0.9174	0.9091	0.9009	0.8929	0.8850	0.8772	0.8696	0.8333	0.8000
2	1.7591	1.7355	1.7125	1.6901	1.6681	1.6467	1.6257	1.5278	1.4400
3	2.5313	2.4869	2.4437	2.4018	2.3612	2.3216	2.2832	2.1065	1.9520
4	3.2397	3.1699	3.1024	3.0373	2.9745	2.9137	2.8550	2.5887	2.3616
5	3.8897	3.7908	3.6959	3.6048	3.5172	3.4331	3.3522	2.9906	2.6893
6	4.4859	4.3553	4.2305	4.1114	3.9975	3.8887	3.7845	3.3255	2.9514
7	5.0330	4.8684	4.7122	4.5638	4.4226	4.2883	4.1604	3.6046	3.1611
8	5.5348	5.3349	5.1461	4.9676	4.7988	4.6389	4.4873	3.8372	3.3289
9	5.9952	5.7590	5.5370	5.3282	5.1317	4.9464	4.7716	4.0310	3.4631
10	6.4177	6.1446	5.8892	5.6502	5.4262	5.2161	5.0188	4.1925	3.5705
20	9.1285	8.5136	7.9633	7.4694	7.0248	6.6231	6.2593	4.8696	3.9539

* There is one payment each period.

$P_{i=10\%;\ n=3}$ (Table 10–2; 0.7513) = \$751.30. The concept of the present value of \$1 is summarized in Exhibit 10–2.

Future and Present Values of an Annuity

An annuity means that instead of a single amount, there is a **series of consecutive payments** characterized by:

1. An equal dollar amount each interest period.
2. Interest periods of equal length (year, semiannual, or month).
3. An equal interest rate each interest period.

Examples of annuities include monthly payments on an automobile or a home, yearly contributions to a savings account, and monthly retirement benefits received from a pension fund.

Exhibit 10–2 Overview of future and present value determinations

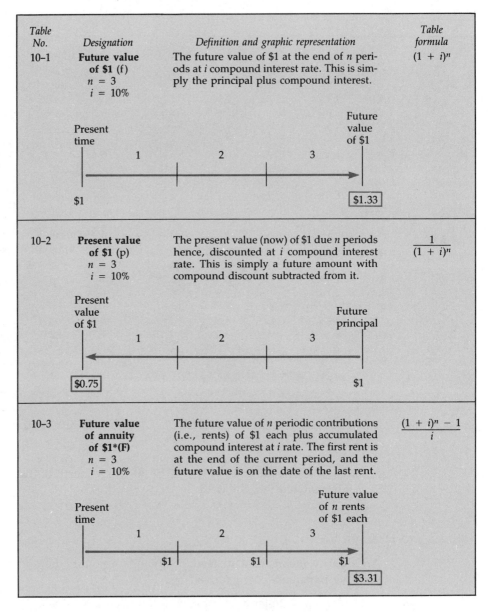

Table No.	Designation	Definition and graphic representation	Table formula
10–1	**Future value of $1** (f) $n = 3$ $i = 10\%$	The future value of $1 at the end of n periods at i compound interest rate. This is simply the principal plus compound interest.	$(1 + i)^n$
10–2	**Present value of $1** (p) $n = 3$ $i = 10\%$	The present value (now) of $1 due n periods hence, discounted at i compound interest rate. This is simply a future amount with compound discount subtracted from it.	$\dfrac{1}{(1 + i)^n}$
10–3	**Future value of annuity of $1*(F)** $n = 3$ $i = 10\%$	The future value of n periodic contributions (i.e., rents) of $1 each plus accumulated compound interest at i rate. The first rent is at the end of the current period, and the future value is on the date of the last rent.	$\dfrac{(1 + i)^n - 1}{i}$

Future Value of an Annuity (F)

The future value of an annuity includes **compound interest** on each payment from the date of payment to the end of the term of the annuity. Each payment accumulates less interest than the prior payments only because the number of periods that it accumulates interest will be less. To illustrate, you deposit $1,000

Exhibit 10–2 *(concluded)*

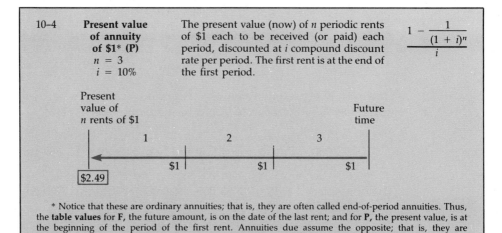

| 10–4 | **Present value of annuity of $1* (P)** $n = 3$ $i = 10\%$ | The present value (now) of n periodic rents of $1 each to be received (or paid) each period, discounted at i compound discount rate per period. The first rent is at the end of the first period. | $$1 - \dfrac{\dfrac{1}{(1 + i)^n}}{i}$$ |

Present value of n rents of $1

Future time

1   2   3

$1 $1 $1

$2.49

* Notice that these are ordinary annuities; that is, they are often called end-of-period annuities. Thus, the **table values** for **F**, the future amount, is on the date of the last rent; and for **P**, the present value, is at the beginning of the period of the first rent. Annuities due assume the opposite; that is, they are "beginning-of-period" annuities. Ordinary annuity values can be converted to annuities due simply by multiplication of $(1 + i)$.

cash in a savings account each year for three years at 10% interest per year (i.e., a total principal of $3,000). The first $1,000 deposit is made on December 31, 19A; the second one on December 31, 19B; and the third and last one on December 31, 19C. The first $1,000 deposit would earn compound interest for two years (for a total principal and interest of $1,210); the second deposit would earn interest for one year (for a total principal and interest of $1,100); and the third deposit would earn no interest because it was made on the day that the balance is computed. Thus, the total amount in the savings account at the end of three years would be $3,310 ($1,210 + $1,100 + $1,000). We could compute the interest on each deposit to derive the future value of this annuity. However, we can refer to Table 10–3, **Future value of annuity of $1 (F)** for $i = 10\%$; $n = 3$, to find the value 3.3100. The total of your three deposits of $1,000 each increased to $1,000 × 3.31 = $3,310 by December 31, 19C. The increase of $310 was due to interest. A convenient format for this problem is $1,000 × $F_{i=10\%;\ n=3}$ (Table 10–3; 3.3100) = $3,310. This concept is summarized in Exhibit 10–2.

Present Value of an Annuity (P)

The present value of an annuity is the value now of a series of equal amounts to be received each period for some specified number of periods in the future. It involves compound **discounting** of each of the equal periodic amounts.

To illustrate, assume it now is January 1, 19A, and you are to receive $1,000 cash on each December 31, 19A, 19B, and 19C. How much would the sum of these three $1,000 future amounts be worth now, on January 1, 19A, assuming an interest rate of 10% per year? We could use Table 10–2 values to calculate the present value as follows:

Year	Amount	Value from Table 10–2, $i = 10\%$	Present value
1	$1,000	× 0.9091 ($n = 1$) =	$ 909.10
2	1,000	× 0.8264 ($n = 2$) =	826.40
3	1,000	× 0.7513 ($n = 3$) =	751.30
	Total present value		$2,486.80

However, the present value of this annuity can be more easily computed by using one PV amount from Table 10–4 as follows:

$$\$1,000 \times \mathbf{P}_{i=10\%;\ n\ =\ 3} \text{ (Table 10–4; 2.4869)} = \$2,487 \text{ (rounded).}$$

The difference of $513 (i.e., $3,000 − $2,487) is interest. This concept is summarized in Exhibit 10–2.

Interest Rates and Interest Periods

Notice that the preceding illustrations assumed annual interest rates and annual periods for compounding and discounting. While interest rates almost always are quoted on an annual basis, interest compounding periods often are less than one year (such as semiannually or quarterly). When interest periods are less than a year, the values of n and i must be restated to be consistent with the length of the interest period. To illustrate, 12% interest compounded annually for five years requires use of $n = 5$ and $i = 12\%$. If compounding is quarterly, the interest period is one quarter of a year (i.e., four periods per year), and the quarterly interest rate would be one quarter of the annual rate (i.e., 3% per quarter); therefore, 12% interest compounded quarterly for five years requires use of $n = 20$ and $i = 3\%$.

Accounting Applications of Future and Present Values

There are many transactions when the concepts of future and present value must be used for accounting measurements. Four such cases are presented below:

Case A:

On January 1, 19A, Company A set aside $200,000 cash in a special building fund (an asset) to be used at the end of five years to construct a new building. The fund is expected to earn 10% interest per year, which will be added to the fund balance each year-end. On the date of deposit, the company made the following entry:

January 1, 19A:

Special building fund	200,000	
Cash		200,000

1. What will the balance of the fund be at the end of the fifth year?

    Answer: This case requires application of the future value of a single amount as follows:

$$\$200,000 \times f_{i=10\% \; ; \; n=5;} \text{ (Table 10–1; 1.6105)} = \underline{\underline{\$322,100}}$$

2. How much interest revenue was earned on the fund during the five years?

    Answer:

$$\$322,100 - \$200,000 = \underline{\underline{\$122,100}}$$

3. What entry would be made on December 31, 19A, to record the interest revenue for the first year?

    Answer: Interest for one year on the fund balance is added to the fund and is recorded as follows:

    December 31, 19A:

Special building fund	20,000	
Interest revenue ($200,000 × 10%)		20,000

4. What entry would be made on December 31, 19B, to record interest revenue for the second year?

    Answer:

    December 31, 19B:

Special building fund	22,000	
Interest revenue		22,000
($200,000 + $20,000) × 10% = $22,000.		

Case B:

On January 1, 19A, Company B bought a new machine that had a list price of $20,000. A $20,000, two-year noninterest-bearing note payable was signed by Company B. The $20,000 is to be paid on December 31, 19B. The market interest rate for this note was 12%.

1. How should the accountant record the purchase?

    Answer: This case requires application of the present value of a single amount. In conformity with the **cost principle,** the cost of the machine is its current cash equivalent price, which is the present value of the future payment. The present value of the $20,000 is computed as follows:

$$20,000 \times p_{i=12\% \; ; \; n=2} \text{ (Table 10–2; 0.7972)} = \underline{\underline{\$15,944}}$$

Therefore, the journal entry is as follows:

January 1, 19A:

```
Machinery . . . . . . . . . . . . . . . . . . . . . . . . . . . . . . . . . . . .  15,944
    Note payable . . . . . . . . . . . . . . . . . . . . . . . . . . . .              15,944
```

2. What journal entry would be made at the end of the first and second years for interest expense?

   Answer: Interest expense for each year on the amount in the Note Payable account would be recorded in an adjusting entry, as follows:

   December 31, 19A:

```
Interest expense . . . . . . . . . . . . . . . . . . . . . . . . . . . . . . .  1,913
    Note payable . . . . . . . . . . . . . . . . . . . . . . . . . . . .           1,913
$15,944 × 12% = $1,913.
```

   Note: The note payable would be reported on the 19A balance sheet at $15,944 + $1,913 = $17,857.

   December 31, 19B:

```
Interest expense . . . . . . . . . . . . . . . . . . . . . . . . . . . . . . .  2,143
    Note payable . . . . . . . . . . . . . . . . . . . . . . . . . . . .           2,143
    ($15,944 + $1,913) × 12% = $2,143.
```

3. What journal entry should be made on December 31, 19B, to record payment of the debt?

   Answer: At this date the amount to be paid is the balance of Note Payable, which is the same as the maturity amount on the due date, that is, $15,944 + $1,913 + $2,143 = $20,000.[7]

   The journal entry to record full payment of the debt would be:

   December 31, 19B:

```
Note payable . . . . . . . . . . . . . . . . . . . . . . . . . . . . . . . . .  20,000
    Cash . . . . . . . . . . . . . . . . . . . . . . . . . . . . . . . . . . .      20,000
```

---

[7] The following entries also could be made with the same results:

January 1, 19A:

```
Machinery . . . . . . . . . . . . . . . . . . . . . . . . . . . . . . . . . . .  15,944
Discount on note payable . . . . . . . . . . . . . . . . . . . . . . . . . . .   4,056
    Note payable . . . . . . . . . . . . . . . . . . . . . . . . . . . . . . .      20,000
```

December 31, 19A:

```
Interest expense ($15,944 × 12%) . . . . . . . . . . . . . . . . . . . . . . .   1,913
    Discount on note payable . . . . . . . . . . . . . . . . . . . . . . . . .      1,913
```

At the end of 19A, the liability would be reported at net as $20,000 − $2,143 = $17,857.

December 31, 19B:

```
Interest expense ($17,857 × 12%) . . . . . . . . . . . . . . . . . . . . . . .   2,143
Note payable . . . . . . . . . . . . . . . . . . . . . . . . . . . . . . . . .  20,000
    Cash . . . . . . . . . . . . . . . . . . . . . . . . . . . . . . . . . . .      20,000
    Discount on note payable . . . . . . . . . . . . . . . . . . . . . . . . .       2,143
```

Case C:

Company C will make five equal annual payments of $30,000 each with a financial institution to accumulate a debt retirement fund. The payments will be made each December 31, starting December 31, 19A. The fifth and last payment will be made December 31, 19E. The financial institution will pay 8% annual compound interest, which will be added to the fund at the end of each year.

1. What entry should be made to record the first payment?

   Answer:

   December 31, 19A:

   Debt retirement fund 30,000
       Cash 30,000

2. What will be the balance in the fund immediately after the fifth and last payment (i.e., on December 31, 19E)?

   Answer: This case requires application of future value of an annuity as follows:

   $$\$30,000 \times F_{i\ =\ 8\%;\ n\ =\ 5}\ (\text{Table 10–3; 5.8666}) = \underline{\$175,998}$$

3. What entries would be made at the end of 19B?

   Answer:
   a. Interest for one year on the fund balance is added to the fund and recorded as follows:

   December 31, 19B:

   Debt retirement fund 2,400
       Interest revenue ($30,000 × 8%) 2,400

   b. The second payment would be recorded as follows:

   December 31, 19B:

   Debt retirement fund 30,000
       Cash 30,000

4. What is the amount of interest revenue that should be recorded at the end of 19C?

   Answer: Interest would be computed on the increased fund balance as follows:

   $$(\$30,000 + \$2,400 + \$30,000) \times 8\% = \underline{\$4,992}$$

   December 31, 19C:

   Debt retirement fund 4,992
       Interest revenue 4,992

5. Prepare a fund accumulation schedule that shows the entry for each deposit and the increasing balance in the fund.

Fund Accumulation Schedule

Date	Cash payment (credit)	Interest revenue (prior balance × 8%) (credit)	Fund increase (debit)	Fund balance
12/31/19A	$ 30,000		$ 30,000	$ 30,000
12/31/19B	30,000	$ 30,000 × 8% = $ 2,400	32,400[(a)]	62,400[(b)]
12/31/19C	30,000	62,400 × 8% = 4,992	34,992	97,392
12/31/19D	30,000	97,392 × 8% = 7,791	37,791	135,183
12/31/19E	30,000	135,183 × 8% = 10,815	40,815	175,998
Total	$150,000	$25,998	$175,998	

Computations:
(a) $30,000 + $2,400 = $32,400, etc.
(b) $30,000 + $32,400 = $62,400, etc.

Case D:

On January 1, 19A, Company D bought a new machine that cost $40,000. The company was short of cash so it signed a $40,000 note payable, to be paid off in three equal annual installments. Each installment includes principal plus interest on the unpaid balance at 11% per year. The equal annual installments are due on December 31, 19A, 19B, and 19C. The acquisition was recorded as follows:

January 1, 19A:

Machinery	40,000	
Note payable		40,000

1. What is the amount of each equal annual installment?

   Answer: The $40,000 is the amount of the debt today. Therefore, $40,000 is the present value of the debt, $i = 11\%$ and $n = 3$. This is an **annuity** because payment is made in three equal installments. The amount of each equal annual payment is computed by **dividing** the amount of the debt by the present value of an annuity of $1 as follows:

$$\$40,000 \div P_{i\ =\ 11\%;\ n\ =\ 3}\ \text{(Table 10–4; 2.4437)} = \underline{\$16,369}$$

2. What was the total amount of interest expense in dollars?

   Answer:

$$\$16,369 \times 3 = \$49,107 - \$40,000 = \underline{\$9,107}$$

3. What journal entry should be made at the end of each year to record the payment on this $40,000 note payable?

Answer:

a. To record the first installment payment on the note:

December 31, 19A:

```
Note payable . . . . . . . . . . . . . . . . . . . . . . . . . . . . . . . 11,969
Interest expense ($40,000 × 11%) . . . . . . . . . . . . . . . . .  4,400
        Cash (computed above) . . . . . . . . . . . . . . . . . . . .        16,369
```

b. To record the second installment payment on the note:

December 31, 19B:

```
Note payable . . . . . . . . . . . . . . . . . . . . . . . . . . . . . . . 13,285
Interest expense [($40,000 − $11,969) × 11%] . . . . . . . . .  3,084
        Cash (computed above) . . . . . . . . . . . . . . . . . . . .        16,369
```

c. To record final installment payment on the note:

December 31, 19C:

```
Note payable . . . . . . . . . . . . . . . . . . . . . . . . . . . . . . . 14,746
Interest expense . . . . . . . . . . . . . . . . . . . . . . . . . . . .  1,623
        Cash (computed above) . . . . . . . . . . . . . . . . . . . .        16,369
    Interest: ($40,000 − $11,969 − $13,285) × 11% = $1,623
    (rounded to accommodate rounding errors).
```

4. Prepare a **debt payment schedule** that shows the entry for each payment and the effect on interest expense and the unpaid amount of principal each period.

Debt Payment Schedule

Date	Cash payment (credit)	Interest expense (prior balance × 11%) (debit)		Principal decrease (debit)	Unpaid principal
1/1/A					$40,000
12/31/A	$16,369	$40,000 × 11% =	$4,400	$11,969[a]	28,031[b]
12/31/B	16,369	28,031 × 11% =	3,084	13,285	14,746
12/31/C	16,369	14,746 × 11% =	1,623*	14,746	–0–
Total	$49,107		$9,107	$40,000	

* To accommodate rounding error.

Computations:
(*a*) $16,369 − $4,400 = $11,969, etc.
(*b*) $40,000 − $11,969 = $28,031, etc.

Notice in the debt payment schedule that of each successive payment an increasing amount is payment on principal and a decreasing amount is interest expense. This effect occurs because the interest each period is based on a lower amount of unpaid principal. When an annuity is involved, schedules such as this one often are essential.

Present Value Concepts and Lease Liabilities

A lease is a contract that specifies that a particular asset will be leased by the owner (i.e., the lessor) to another party (i.e., the lessee) under certain agreements. For accounting purposes, leases are classified as **operating leases** (usually short term) or **capital leases** (usually long term).

Significantly different accounting approaches are required for operating leases than for capital leases. Because of the importance of these differences, the FASB established four criteria to differentiate capital leases from operating leases. If **any one** of the four criteria is met by the lease contract, the lease **must** be accounted for as a **capital** lease; all other leases must be accounted for as **operating** leases. The four criteria for a **capital lease** are: (1) the leased property transfers to the lessee by the end of the term of the lease, (2) the lessee can purchase the asset at a bargain price at the end of the term of the lease, (3) the lease term is at least 75% of the estimated useful life of the lease asset, and (4) the present value of the minimum lease payments is at least 90% of the market value of the leased asset on the date of the lease contract.

Basically, accounting for an **operating** lease requires a journal entry for each rental payment (the lessee makes a debit to Rent Expense and a credit to Cash). In contrast, accounting for a **capital** lease assumes that the lessor sold the leased asset and the lessee purchased it. This assumption means that when the lease contract is signed, the lessee debits an asset and credits a long-term lease liability.

A typical operating and a typical capital lease are shown in Exhibit 10–3. On January 1, 19A, Daly Construction Company must acquire a heavy-duty machine ready to operate. The machine has a cash price of $100,000, and it has a five-year estimated useful life and no residual value. Daly's top management is considering acquiring the machine from one of three vendors. Each vendor sells exactly the same machine, but each offers a different way to acquire it. The three alternatives are:

Alternative *a*. Purchase the machine and sign a two-year interest-bearing note; 15% interest and principal payable each month-end (i.e., 24 equal payments). On January 1, 19A, Daly would record the purchase at cost and a liability as illustrated in Exhibit 10–3. Equal monthly payments of principal plus interest ($4,849) are to be made; the journal entry to record the first payment is illustrated in Exhibit 10–3. Under this alternative, Daly would own the machine. Therefore, Daly would record depreciation expense, and all other expenses incurred, such as maintenance, insurance, and taxes.

Alternative *b*. Lease the machine on a month-to-month lease that qualifies as an **operating lease**. The monthly rental of $6,000 is payable at each month-end. Under this alternative, Daly would not own the machine. Therefore, the only journal entries to be recorded by Daly would be for the monthly rental payments as illustrated in Exhibit 10–3. Under this alternative, Daly

Exhibit 10-3   Operating lease and capital lease compared

Situation:

    Daly Construction Company intends to acquire a heavy-duty machine that will cost $100,000 cash equivalent price. Estimated useful life of the machine is five years and no residual value. Daly is considering three alternatives: *(a)* purchase by signing note, *(b)* rent on an operating lease, and *(c)* rent on a capital lease.

Alternative *a:*

    On January 1, 19A, purchased the machine for $100,000 and signed a two-year, 15% note that requires equal month-end payments (24) of $4,849.

    Journal entries:

    Purchase, January 1, 19A:

Machinery	100,000	
Note payable, long term		100,000

    Payment on note, January 31, 19A:

Interest expense ($100,000 × 1¼%)	1,250	
Note payable ($4,849 − $1,250)	3,599	
Cash (per note)		4,849

Alternative *b:*

    Lease on a month-to-month **operating lease;** month-end rental payments of $6,000, as required by lessor.

    Journal entries:

    January 31, 19A:

Machinery rental expense	6,000	
Cash (per lease agreement)		6,000

Alternative *c:*

    Lease on a **capital lease** that requires month-end payments of $3,321 for 36 months (the implied interest rate is 12%). Daly is required by the lease to pay all ownership costs.

    Journal entries:

    January 1, 19A—inception date of the lease (record as a purchase):

Machinery (under capital lease)	100,000	
Liability, capital lease		100,000

    Computation:
      Present value = Payments × Table 10-4 (*i* = 1%; *n* = 36)
             = $3,321 × 30.0175*
             = $100,000 (rounded)

    January 31, 19A, first monthly rental payment:

Interest expense ($100,000 × 1%)	1,000	
Liability, capital lease ($3,321 − $1,000)	2,321	
Cash (per lease contract)		3,321

* This value is given for illustrative purposes. Table 10-4 does not contain values for 36 periods.

would have to continue lease payments as long as the machine is used and would never own the machine.

Alternative *c*. Lease the machine on a three-year lease that qualifies as a **capital lease.** The contract requires Daly to pay 36 month-end rentals of $3,321. The lessee learned that the rental of $3,321 was based on 12% interest; therefore, the **lessee** computed the **present value** of the future lease rentals as follows:

$$
\begin{aligned}
\text{Present value} &= \text{Payments} \times (\text{Table 10--4, } i = 1\%; \, n = 36)\\
&= \$3{,}321 \times 30.1075 \text{ (given; Table 10--4 does not contain}\\
&\quad \text{values for 36 periods)}\\
&= \$100{,}000 \text{ (rounded)}
\end{aligned}
$$

In accounting, a **capital lease** is a sale of the asset by the lessor to the lessee. Daly (the lessee) would record a purchase of the machine on the date of the lease contract for $100,000 (its present value).

On January 1, 19A, Daly would debit Machinery and credit a lease liability for $100,000 as shown in Exhibit 10–3. Each of the 36 month-end lease payments would be recorded, in part as payment of principal and in part as payment of interest expense. Exhibit 10–3 shows entries at the inception of the lease (i.e., a "purchase" of the machine is recorded) and the first interest payment on January 31, 19A.

Because Daly is assumed to own the machine during the lease term, Daly will record depreciation expense and all other "ownership" expenses incurred, such as maintenance, insurance, and taxes. Under this alternative, Daly will own the machine after the last rental payment with no further obligations to the lessor.

The above example does not suggest which alternative is the best for Daly. Such a determination would need more information than given. Rather, it is intended to differentiate between the required accounting approaches for an operating lease versus a capital lease. The basic difference requires the application of **present value** determination for a **capital lease.**

SUMMARY OF CHAPTER

Liabilities are obligations of either a known or estimated amount. Detailed information about the liabilities of an entity is important to many decision makers, whether internal or external to the enterprise, because liabilities represent claims against the resources of an entity. The existence and amount of liabilities sometimes are easy to conceal from outsiders. The accounting model and the verification by an independent CPA are the best assurances that all liabilities are disclosed.

Current liabilities are obligations that will be paid from the resources reported on the same balance sheet as current assets. They are short-term obligations that will be paid within the coming year or within the normal operating cycle of the business, whichever is longer. All other liabilities (except contingent liabilities) are reported as **long-term liabilities.** A **contingent liability** is a potential claim due to some event or transaction that has happened, but whether it will materialize as an effective liability is not certain because that depends on some future event or transaction. At the end of the accounting period, a contingent liability must be recorded (as a debit to a loss account and a credit to a liability account) if (*a*) it is **probable** that a loss will occur and (*b*) if the amount of the loss can be estimated reasonably. Contingent liabilities that are **reasonably possible** must be disclosed in the notes to the financial statements.

Future and present value concepts often must be applied in accounting for liabilities. These concepts focus on the time value of money (i.e., interest). Future value is the amount that a principal amount will increase to in the future due to compound interest. Present value is the amount that a future principal amount will decrease to due to compound discounting. Future and present values are related to (*a*) a single amount or (*b*) a series of equal periodic amounts (called annuities). Typical applications of future and present values are to create a fund, determine the cost of an asset, account for notes payable, and account for installment debts and receivables.

CHAPTER SUPPLEMENT 10A

Payroll Accounting

Payroll accounting does not involve any new accounting concepts or principles. However, payroll accounting needs additional discussion because it is necessary to pay employees for their services promptly and correctly. Also, detailed payroll accounting is necessary to fulfill legal requirements under federal and state laws concerning withholding taxes, social security taxes, and unemployment taxes. Further, the management of an enterprise, for planning and control purposes, needs detailed and accurate cost figures for wages and salaries. Often, salaries and wages constitute the largest category of expense in an enterprise. Because a large amount of detailed recordkeeping is required, payroll accounting often is computerized, including the production of individual checks for the employees.

A detailed payroll record must be kept for each employee. The payroll record varies with the circumstances in each company; however, it must include for each individual such data as social security number, number of dependents (for income tax withholding), rate of pay, a time record (for hourly paid employees), and deductions from gross pay.

In payroll accounting, a distinction must be made between (1) payroll deductions and taxes that must be paid by the **employee** (i.e., deducted from the employee's gross earnings) and (2) payroll taxes that must be paid by the **employer.** Both types of payroll amounts must be remitted to the governmental unit or other party to whom the amounts are owed. Payroll taxes and deductions apply only in cases where there is an employer-employee relationship. Independent contractors that are not under the direct supervision of the employer, such as outside lawyers, independent accountants, consultants, and building contractors, are not employees; hence, amounts paid to them are not subject to payroll taxes and related deductions.

An employee usually receives take-home pay that is much less than the gross earnings for the period. This is due to two types of payroll deductions:

1. Required deductions for taxes that must be paid by the employee as specified by state and federal laws.
2. Optional deductions authorized by the employee for special purposes.

Required Deductions

There are two categories of taxes that the employee must pay and thus must be deducted from the employee's gross earnings. They are income taxes and social security taxes. The employer must remit the total amount deducted to the appropriate government agency.

Employee Income Taxes

Most employees must prepare an annual federal income tax return. Wages and salaries earned during the year must be reported on the income tax return as income. Federal laws require the employer to deduct an appropriate amount of income tax each perod from the gross earnings of each employee. The amount of the deduction for income tax is obtained from a tax table (provided by the Internal Revenue Service) based on the earnings and number of exemptions (for self and dependents) of the employee. The amount of income tax withheld from the employee's wages is recorded by the employer as a current liability between the date of deduction and the date the amount withheld is remitted to the government. The total amount withheld must be paid to the Internal Revenue Service within a specified short period of time. A form that accompanies each remittance is provided by the Internal Revenue Service. The form identifies the employees and the amounts withheld. Some states also require withholding for state income tax.

Employee FICA Taxes

The social security taxes paid by the employee are called FICA taxes because they are required by the Federal Insurance Contributions Act. This act provides that persons who are **qualified** under the provisions of the act, upon reaching age 62, may retire and receive the minimum monthly benefits for life, plus certain medical benefits after age 65. Retirement at age 65 provides maximum pension benefits. It also provides benefits for the family of a deceased person who was qualified.

The funds required by the government to provide the benefits under the Social Security Act are obtained by payroll taxes, which are imposed in equal amounts on **both the employee and the employer.**[8] Effective January 1, 1989, the FICA rate was 7.51% on the first $48,000 paid to each employee during the year.

At the end of each year, the employer is required to give each employee a **Withholding Statement, Form W-2,** which reports to the employee (1) gross earnings for the year, (2) earnings subject to FICA taxes, (3) income taxes withheld, and (4) FICA taxes withheld. A copy of this form also is sent to the Internal Revenue Service.

Optional Deductions

Many companies encourage programs of voluntary deductions from earnings by employees. These voluntary deductions include savings funds, insurance premiums, charitable contributions, supplementary retirement programs, repayment of loans, stock purchase plans, and the purchase of U.S. savings bonds. The employer agrees to make these deductions, subject to employee authorization, as a convenience to the employees. The amounts deducted are remitted in a short time to the organization or agency in whose behalf the deduction was authorized. Another type of deduction is for union dues as specified in the union contract. In some states, this deduction may not be voluntary. The employer is required to remit the deductions, along with the employee list, to the union each month.

Accounting for Employee Deductions

The employer must keep detailed and accurate records of all deductions from the earnings of each employee. From the employer's viewpoint, the employee deductions are **current liabilities** from the date of the payroll deduction to the date of remittance to the government or other entity.

To illustrate the basic accounting entry for the payment of a payroll and the accrual of liabilities for the **employee deductions,** assume that Real Company accumulated the following data in the detailed payroll records for the month of January 19B:

> Gross earnings:
> Salaries $60,000
> Wages (hourly paid employees) 40,000
> Income taxes withheld 21,000
> Union dues withheld 400
> FICA taxes (assume no maximums were exceeded
> in January, $100,000 × 7.51%) 7,510

The entry to record the payroll and employee deductions would be:

---

[8] The amount of benefits and the FICA tax deductions are frequently changed by the U.S. Congress.

January 31, 19A:

```
Salary and wage expense  . . . . . . . . . . . . . . . . . . . . . . . . . . . 100,000
        Liability for income taxes withheld—employees . . . . . . . . . . . .         21,000
        Liability for union dues withheld—employees . . . . . . . . . . . . .            400
        FICA taxes payable—employees . . . . . . . . . . . . . . . . . . . . .          7,510
        Cash (take-home pay) . . . . . . . . . . . . . . . . . . . . . . . . . .        71,090
    Payroll for January, including employee payroll deductions.
```

Accounting for Employer Payroll Taxes

Remember that the payroll taxes illustrated above are those levied on the **employees.** The employer simply acts as a tax collector. Also, specific payroll taxes are levied on the employer. These taxes represent **operating expenses** of the business. The liability for these taxes is settled when the taxes are paid to the designated agencies of the state and federal governments. Usually, three different payroll taxes must be paid by the employer—FICA taxes, FUTA taxes, and state unemployment compensation taxes.

Employer FICA Taxes

The employer must pay an additional FICA tax equal to the amount withheld from the employee's wages. Thus, the FICA tax paid by the employer is at the same rate as the FICA employee tax and on the same amount of wages.

Employer FUTA Taxes

The Social Security Act provides for another program known as unemployment compensation. This program derives its monetary support under the provisions of the Federal Unemployment Tax Act. The FUTA, or unemployment tax, is paid **only by the employer.** Currently, the federal tax amounts to 6.2% of the first $7,000 in wages paid to each employee during the year. Employers who participate in a state unemployment compensation plan are entitled to a reduction in the amount that must be paid to the federal government.

The unemployment program specified in the Federal Unemployment Tax Act is a joint federal-state program. Therefore, each state participates in the program by sharing both in providing benefits and in funding the program through payroll taxes. Although state laws vary in some respects, a minimum of 0.8% is payable to the Federal Treasury (i.e., on the first $7,000 wages paid). Taxes in excess of this minimum are paid to the state government. Most states have a merit-rating plan that provides for a reduction in the tax rate for employers that establish a record of stable employment over a period of time.

Payroll taxes paid by the employer are debited to an expense account and credited to a current liability when the payroll is paid each period. Assuming $800 in FUTA taxes are payable to the federal government and $2,600 to the state government, the January entry for the employer's payroll taxes for Real Company (data shown above) is:

Payroll tax expense	10,910	
FICA taxes payable—employer ($100,000 × 7.51% matching)		7,510
FUTA taxes payable—employer		800
State unemployment taxes payable—employer		2,600
To record employer payroll taxes.		

When the taxes are remitted to the government, the liability accounts are debited, and Cash is credited.

CHAPTER SUPPLEMENT 10B

The Voucher System

The voucher system is designed to attain strict control over cash expenditures from the point an obligation is incurred (by means of purchase of merchandise for resale, services, operational assets, investments, etc.) through the payment of cash. The incurrence of an obligation and the payment of cash to satisfy it are viewed as separate and independent transactions. When a voucher system is used, an account called **Vouchers Payable** replaces the account called **Accounts Payable** in the ledger. Similarly, a **voucher register** and a **check register** replace the purchases journal and the cash disbursements journal, respectively (Chapter Supplement 8B).

The basic document in the voucher system is the **voucher.** A voucher is a form, prepared and used within the business, on which a transaction is (1) summarized and supported, (2) approved, (3) analyzed for recording, and (4) approved for payment. Thus, it is a comprehensive document that follows a transaction from the transaction date to the final cash payment. A voucher is prepared for **each** transaction involving the payment of cash, such as the purchase of assets, the use of services, the incurrence of expenses, and the payment of debt. The form of a voucher varies between companies because it is designed to meet the specific internal requirements of the individual company. For control purposes, all voucher forms and checks should be numbered consecutively when printed.

After approval, each voucher is entered in the voucher register numerically. The voucher register is designed to record the basic data from the voucher, including the accounts to be debited and credited.

To illustrate the mechanics of a voucher system, we will follow a purchase of merchandise for resale through the system from the **order date** to the final cash payment date. Each step in the sequence may be illustrated and explained as follows:

19A

Jan. 10 Merchandise ordered from Box Supply Company, cost $1,000; terms n/15. A purchase order is prepared and approved.

12 Merchandise ordered from Box Supply Company on January 10 is received; invoice is received. Voucher No. 47 is drawn, and the pur-

Exhibit 10–4   Voucher format

	Voucher No. 47

MAY DEPARTMENT STORE
Boston, Mass.

Date of Voucher _____ *Jan. 12, 19A* _____   Date Paid _____ *Jan. 27, 19A* _____

Pay to: *Box Supply Company* _____   Check No. _____ *90* _____

1119 Brown Street

Philadelphia, Pa.

For the following goods or services: (attach all supporting documents)

Date Incurred	Terms	Explanation of Details	Amount
Jan. 12	*n/15*	*Merchandise, Dept. 8*	*1,000.00*
		Invoice No. 17-8132	
		Receiving Report No. 123	
		Net payable	*1,000.00*

Approvals:

Voucher Approval: Date   *1/12/A*   Signature   *R. C. Roe* _____

Payment Approval: Date   *1/26/A*   Signature   *A. B. Doe* _____

Accounting Analysis:

Account Debited:	Acct. No.	Amount
Purchases	*91*	*1,000.00*
Office Supplies		
Sales Salaries		
Operational Assets		
Etc.		
Total, Voucher Payable Credit *41*		*1,000.00*

Exhibit 10–5 Voucher register

Date	Vou. No.	Payee	Payment Date	Payment Check No.	Vouchers Payable (Credit)	Purchases (Debit)	Selling Expense Control Account Code	Selling Expense Control Folio	Selling Expense Control Amount (Debit)	Adm. Expense Control Account Code	Adm. Expense Control Folio	Adm. Expense Control Amount (Debit)	Other Accounts to Be Debited Account Name	Other Accounts to Be Debited Folio No.	Other Accounts to Be Debited P	Other Accounts to Be Debited Amount (Debited)
Jan 12	47	Box Supply Co	1/27	90	1,000.00	1,000.00										
Jan. 14	48	John Day-salary	1/15	89	600.00		64	✓	600.00							
Jan. 31	98	Capital Natl			2,160.00								Notes payable	44	✓	2,000.00
		Bank-note											Interest expense	82	✓	160.00
		Totals			27,605.00	14,875.00			7,410.00			3,160.00				2,160.00
		Posting notations			(41)	(91)			(60)			(70)				(✓)

Exhibit 10–6 Check register

Date	Payee	Voucher No. Paid	Check No.	Vouchers Payable (Debit)*	Cash (Credit)*
Jan. 15	John Day	48	89	600.00	600.00
27	Box Supply Co.	47	90	1,000.00	1,000.00
31	Totals			18,751.00	18,751.00
	Posting notation			(41)	(11)

* These two columns could be combined.

chase order is attached (Exhibit 10–4). Goods are checked for quantity and condition; a receiving report is prepared.

12 Receiving report and invoice sent to accounting department; they are attached to the voucher. Voucher is approved, and then recorded in the voucher register (Exhibit 10–5).

26 Voucher is approved by designated manager for payment on January 27 and sent to disbursements department; Check No. 90 is prepared.

27 Check No. 90 is signed by treasurer and mailed.

28 The accounting department enters Check No. 90 in the check register (Exhibit 10–6); enters payment notation in the voucher register (Exhibit 10–5); and files the voucher in the **Vouchers Paid File.**

For illustrative purposes, two more transactions are recorded in the voucher register, one of which is unpaid.

At the end of the month, the voucher register and the check register are totaled, and the equality of the debits and credits is verified. Posting to the ledger from these two special journals follows the same pattern as for the special journals explained in Chapter Supplement 8B. Posting involves two separate phases:

1. **Current posting.** During the period, and even daily, the details in the Voucher Register columns are posted to (*a*) the selling expense subsidiary ledger (under the selling expense control), (*b*) the administrative expense subsidiary ledger (under the administrative expense control), and (*c*) other accounts to be debited. No current posting is required from the check register as illustrated.

2. **Monthly posting.** The totals from the voucher register, except for the "Other Accounts to Be Debited," are posted at the end of each month. The account number to which each total is posted is entered below the amount. The column for "Other Accounts to Be Debited" was posted individually; hence, the total should not be posted. The totals from the check register are posted to the accounts at the end of each month as shown by the account numbers entered below the total.

The balance in the ledger account Vouchers Payable is reported on the balance sheet as a liability and is designated as Accounts Payable. The amount should be allocated and classified between current and long-term liabilities, depending on due dates.

The Vouchers Payable account is a control account. Its balance represents all of the **unpaid** vouchers for any given time. The total of all vouchers in the **Unpaid Voucher File** must agree with the balance of the Vouchers Payable account; therefore, the Vouchers Payable account replaces the Accounts Payable control account in the ledger (Chapter Supplement 6A).

In studying the mechanics of the voucher system, you should not overlook its most important aspect—the high degree of **internal control** attained through formalization of the sequence of acquiring operational assets, services, and merchandise, and in making the cash payments. The internal control feature rests on (1) clear-cut separation and designation of specific approval responsibilities, (2) a prescribed routine for carrying out these responsibilities, and (3) accounting for the results.

Although a manual approach was illustrated, these routines can be adapted easily for the computer. A computer program can be designed to accomplish the same steps and procedures illustrated above. Most companies have a computerized voucher system to attain a high degree of control over expenditures and to accelerate the processing of a large volume of transactions, including cash disbursements.

CHAPTER SUPPLEMENT 10C

Ordinary Annuities and Annuities Due

There are two kinds of annuities, called ordinary annuities and annuities due. The only difference between them is the timing of the periodic payments. **Ordinary annuities** assume that the periodic payments are made at the **end of each interest period**. This chapter illustrates ordinary annuities only. **Annuities due** assume that the periodic payments are made at the **beginning of each interest period**. Therefore, an annuity due involves one more interest period (but the same number of payments) as an ordinary annuity. The **table value** for an annuity due can be readily computed as: Ordinary annuity value (Table 10–3 or 10–4) × (1 × *i*) = Annuity due value. Ordinary annuities (often called end-

Exhibit 10–7   Ordinary annuities and annuities due compared

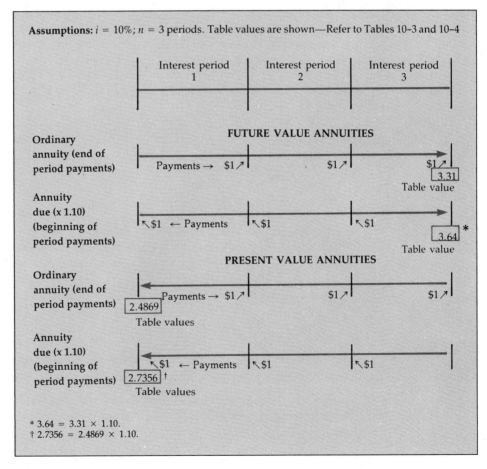

of-period annuities) and annuities due (often called beginning-of-period an-nuities) may be compared as shown in Exhibit 10–7. The homework for this chapter uses only ordinary annuities.

CHAPTER SUPPLEMENT 10D

Federal Income Tax Concepts

A business may be organized as a sole proprietorship, partnership, or corpora-tion. Sole proprietorships and partnerships are not required to pay federal income taxes, but their owners must report and pay taxes on their personal tax returns. Corporations, as separate legal entities, are required to pay income taxes.

Corporations must prepare a U.S. Corporate Tax Return (Form 1120) as shown in Exhibit 10–8. The amount of the tax that is payable is based on the taxable income reported on the tax return. Taxable income is usually different than the income reported on the income statement because the income state-ment is prepared in conformity with GAAP and the tax return is prepared in conformity with tax regulations issued by the Internal Revenue Service.

Calculation of Taxes Payable

To determine a corporation's tax obligation, the taxable income is multiplied by the following rates:

Taxable income	Tax rate
$1–$50,000	15%
$50,001–$75,000	25
Over $75,000	34

There is a 5% tax surcharge applied to taxable income over $100,000. This surcharge is designed to phase out the benefit of lower tax rates. The surcharge maximum is $11,750 (i.e., it applies only to income between $100,000 and $335,000). As a result, large corporations effectively pay a 34% tax rate on all taxable income. Exhibit 10–9 illustrates the calculation of taxes payable.

Revenue and Expense Recognition for Income Tax Purposes

There are several differences between GAAP and the rules that govern the preparation of the income tax return. Common examples are:

1. Interest revenue on state and municipal bonds is generally excluded from taxable income, although it is included in accounting income.
2. Revenue collected in advance (e.g., rent revenue) is included in taxable income when it is collected but is included in accounting income when it is earned.

Exhibit 10–8 U.S. Corporation income tax return

The Tax Form Library, 518 W. Main St., Louisville, Ky., 40202, (502) 589-7466

Form **1120**

Department of the Treasury
Internal Revenue Service

U.S. Corporation Income Tax Return

For calendar year 1990 or tax year beginning _____, 1990, ending _____, 19 ____

▶ For Paperwork Reduction Act Notice, see page 1 of the instructions.

OMB No. 1545-0123

1990

Check if a—			
A Consolidated return ☐	Use IRS label. Other-wise, please print or type.	Name	**D** Employer identification number
B Personal holding co. ☐		Number and street (or P.O. box number if mail is not delivered to street address)	**E** Date incorporated
C Personal service corp.(as defined in Temp. Regs. sec. 1.441-4T—see instructions)		City or town, state, and ZIP code	**F** Total assets (See Specific Instructions.) Dollars / Cents

G Check applicable boxes: (1) ☐ Initial return (2) ☐ Final return (3) ☐ Change in address $

Income	**1a** Gross receipts or sales _____ **b** Less returns and allowances _____ **c** Bal ▶		**1c**
	2 Cost of goods sold and/or operations (Schedule A)		**2**
	3 Gross profit (line 1c less line 2)		**3**
	4 Dividends (Schedule C, line 19)		**4**
	5 Interest		**5**
	6 Gross rents		**6**
	7 Gross royalties		**7**
	8 Capital gain net income (attach separate Schedule D)		**8**
	9 Net gain or (loss) from Form 4797, Part II, line 18 (attach Form 4797)		**9**
	10 Other income (see instructions—attach schedule)		**10**
	11 Total income—Add lines 3 through 10 and enter here . . . . ▶		**11**

Deductions (See Instructions for limitations on deductions.)	**12** Compensation of officers (Schedule E)		**12**
	13a Salaries and wages _____ **b** Less jobs credit _____ **c** Balance ▶		**13c**
	14 Repairs		**14**
	15 Bad debts		**15**
	16 Rents		**16**
	17 Taxes		**17**
	18 Interest		**18**
	19 Contributions (**see instructions for 10% limitation**)		**19**
	20 Depreciation (attach Form 4562) **20**		
	21 Less depreciation claimed in Schedule A and elsewhere on return . . **21a**		**21b**
	22 Depletion		**22**
	23 Advertising		**23**
	24 Pension, profit-sharing, etc., plans		**24**
	25 Employee benefit programs		**25**
	26 Other deductions (attach schedule)		**26**
	27 Total deductions—Add lines 12 through 26 and enter here. . . . . . . ▶		**27**
	28 Taxable income before net operating loss deduction and special deductions (line 11 less line 27) .		**28**
	29 Less: a Net operating loss deduction (see instructions) **29a**		
	b Special deductions (Schedule C, line 20) **29b**		**29c**

Tax and Payments	**30** Taxable income (line 28 less line 29c)		**30**
	31 Total tax (Schedule J)		**31**
	32 Payments: a 1989 overpayment credited to 1990 **32a**		
	b 1990 estimated tax payments . . **32b**		
	c Less 1990 refund applied for on Form 4466 **32c** (_____) **d** Bal ▶ **32d**		
	e Tax deposited with Form 7004 . . . . . . **32e**		
	f Credit from regulated investment companies (attach Form 2439) . . **32f**		
	g Credit for Federal tax on fuels (attach Form 4136) . . **32g**		**32h**
	33 Enter any **penalty** for underpayment of estimated tax—check ▶ ☐ if Form 2220 is attached .		**33**
	34 Tax due—If the total of lines 31 and 33 is larger than line 32h, enter amount owed		**34**
	35 Overpayment—If line 32h is larger than the total of lines 31 and 33, enter amount overpaid . .		**35**
	36 Enter amount of line 35 you want: **Credited to 1991 estimated tax** ▶ _____ **Refunded** ▶		**36**

Please Sign Here

Under penalties of perjury, I declare that I have examined this return, including accompanying schedules and statements, and to the best of my knowledge and belief, it is true, correct, and complete. Declaration of preparer (other than taxpayer) is based on all information of which preparer has any knowledge.

▶ _____ Signature of officer   Date   ▶ _____ Title

Paid Preparer's Use Only

Preparer's signature ▶	Date	Check if self-employed ☐	Preparer's social security number
Firm's name (or yours if self-employed) and address ▶		E.I. No. ▶	
		ZIP code ▶	

Exhibit 10–9 Calculation of taxes payable

Case A—taxable income, $90,000:

Computation:

15% of first $50,000	$ 7,500
25% of next $25,000	6,250
34% of $15,000	5,100
Taxes payable	$18,850

Case B—taxable income, $150,000:

Computation:

15% of first $50,000	$ 7,500
25% of next $25,000	6,250
34% of $75,000	25,500
5% of $50,000 ($150,000 − $100,000)	2,500
Taxes payable	$41,750

Case C—taxable income, $400,000:

Computation:

15% of first $50,000	$ 7,500
25% of next $25,000	6,250
34% of $325,000	110,500
5% of $235,000*	11,750
Taxes payable	$136,000†

* Surcharge applies to taxable income from $100,000 to $335,000 only.
† Notice this is the same as 34% of $400,000. The surcharge effectively phases out the benefit of the lower tax rate.

3. Proceeds from life insurance policies (e.g., "key executive" insurance) is excluded from taxable income but is included in accounting income.

4. Corporations that own less than 20% of another corporation's stock may exclude 70% of the dividends received from taxable income, although all the dividends are included in accounting income. The exclusion is 80% if the corporation owns more than 20% of the other corporation's stock.

5. Amortization of purchased goodwill is not deductible when computing taxable income, although it is deductible when computing accounting income (goodwill is discussed in Chapter 14).

6. Depreciation expense for tax purposes is generally based on the Accelerated Cost Recovery System (ACRS) if the assets were placed in service after 1980 and before 1987, or the Modified Accelerated Cost Recovery System (MACRS) if the assets were placed in service after 1986. These methods were discussed in Chapter 9.

Tax Minimization versus Tax Evasion

Most large corporations spend considerable time and money developing strategies that minimize the amount of federal income taxes that must be paid. There is nothing wrong with this approach because courts have stated that there is no legal obligation to pay more taxes than the law demands. Even if you do not major in accounting, you will probably want to take a course in federal income taxation because knowledge of Internal Revenue Service regulations is important for most executives. This knowledge offers opportunities to save significant amounts of money.

In contrast, tax evasion involves illegal means to avoid paying taxes which are due. Use of accelerated depreciation is an example of tax minimization; failure to report revenue that was collected in cash is an example of tax evasion. While efforts at tax minimization represent good business practice, tax evasion is morally and legally wrong. Individuals who evade taxes run the risk of severe financial penalties including the possibility of being sent to jail.

IMPORTANT TERMS DEFINED IN THIS CHAPTER

Accrued Expenses Expenses that have been incurred but have not yet been paid at the end of the accounting period; a liability. *p. 476*

Annuities Due Beginning-of-period annuities; payments are assumed to be on the first day of each interest period. *p. 511*

Annuity A series of periodic cash receipts or payments that are equal in amount each interest period. *p. 491*

Capital Lease A lease that is viewed as a purchase/sale, for accounting purposes. *p. 500*

Contingent Liability Potential liability that has arisen as the result of a past event; not an effective liability until some future event occurs. *p. 483*

Current Liabilities Short-term obligations that will be paid within the current operating cycle or one year, whichever is longer. *p. 475*

Current Ratio The ratio of total current assets divided by total current liabilities; also known as the working capital ratio. *p. 486*

Deferred Income Tax Difference between income tax expense and income tax liability; caused by temporary differences; may be a liability or an asset. *p. 481*

Deferred Revenues Revenues that have been collected but not earned; a liabiity until the goods or services are provided. *p. 477*

Future Value The sum to which an amount will increase as the result of compound interest. *p. 487*

Interest-Bearing Note A note that explicitly gives a stated rate of interest. *p. 479*

Liabilities Probable future sacrifices of economic benefits that arise from past transactions. *p. 474*

Long-Term Liabilities All obligations that are not properly classified as current liabilities. *p. 478*

Noninterest-Bearing Note A note that does not explicitly state a rate of interest but has implicit interest; interest is included in the face amount of the note. *p. 475*

Operating Lease A rental agreement between a lessor and lessee that is not viewed as a purchase/sale in accounting. *p. 500*

Ordinary Annuities End-of-period annuities; payments are assumed to be on the last day of each interest period. *p. 511*

Permanent Difference An income tax difference that does not cause deferred taxes. *p. 482*

Present Value The current value of an amount to be received in the future; a future amount discounted for compound interest. *p. 489*

Temporary Difference An income tax difference that causes deferred taxes; will reverse or turn around in the future. *p. 481*

Time Value of Money Interest that is associated with the use of money over time. *p. 479.*

Working Capital The dollar difference between total current assets and total current liabilities. *p. 486*

QUESTIONS

Part A: Questions 1–14

1. Define a liability. Distinguish between a current liability and a long-term liability.
2. How can external parties be informed about the liabilities of a business?
3. Liabilities are measured and reported at their current cash equivalent amount. Explain.
4. A liability is a known obligation of either a definite or estimated amount. Explain.
5. Define working capital. How is it computed?
6. What is the current ratio? How is the current ratio related to the classification of liabilities?
7. Define an accrued liability. What kind of an entry usually reflects an accrued liability?
8. Define a deferred revenue. Why is it a liability?
9. Define a note payable. Distinguish between a secured and an unsecured note.
10. Distinguish between an interest-bearing note and a noninterest-bearing note.

11. Define deferred income tax. Explain why deferred income tax "reverses, or turns around," in subsequent periods.
12. What is a contingent liability? How is a contingent liability reported?
13. Explain the primary purpose of a voucher system.
14. Compute 19A interest expense for the following note: face, $6,000; 10% interest; date of note, April 1, 19A.

Part B: Questions 15–22

15. Explain the time value of money.
16. Explain the basic difference between future value and present value.
17. If you deposited $10,000 in a savings account that would earn 10%, how much would you have at the end of 10 years? Use a convenient format to display your computations.
18. If you hold a valid contract that will pay you $10,000 cash 10 years hence and the going rate of interest is 10%, what is its present value? Use a convenient format to display your computations.
19. What is an annuity?
20. Complete the following schedule:

Concept	Symbol	Table Values		
		$n = 4; i = 5\%$	$n = 7; i = 10\%$	$n = 9; i = 15\%$
FV of $1 *PV* of $1 *FV* of annuity of $1 *PV* of annuity of $1				

21. If you deposit $1,000 for each of 10 interest periods (ordinary annuity) that would earn 10% interest, how much would you have at the end of period 10? Use a convenient format to display your computations.
22. You purchased an XIT auto for $20,000 by making a $5,000 cash payment and six semiannual installment payments for the balance at 10% interest. Use a convenient format to display computation of the amount of each payment.

EXERCISES

Part A: Exercises 10–1 to 10–11

E10–1   (Match Definitions with Terms)

Match each definition with its related term by entering the appropriate letter in the space provided.

Terms	Definitions
_____ (1) Liabilities	A. Provides resources to a business by selling its goods and services on credit.
_____ (2) Interest expense	
_____ (3) Current ratio	B. Probable future sacrifices of economic benefits.
_____ (4) Full-disclosure principle	C. The two major classifications of liabilities on a balance sheet.
_____ (5) Interest-bearing note	D. All liabilities must be reported in conformity with this principle.
_____ (6) Secured debt	E. A liability requires the payment of these two different amounts.
_____ (7) Short term and long term	F. Interest payable on a noninterest-bearing note.
_____ (8) Deferred revenues	G. Current assets divided by current liabilities.
_____ (9) Principal and interest	H. A liability that represents trade accounts payable only.
_____ (10) Working capital	I. A liability that is supported by a mortgage on specified assets.
_____ (11) Noninterest-bearing note	J. A note that does not specify a stated rate of interest but interest nevertheless is paid.
_____ (12) Accounts payable	K. Unearned revenues or revenues collected in advance.
_____ (13) Accrued expenses	
_____ (14) Creditors	L. Principal × Rate × Time, related to a liability.
_____ (15) Implicit interest	M. Expenses incurred by the end of the period but not yet paid.
	N. Current assets minus current liabilities.
	O. A note that specifies a stated rate of interest on the principal amount.

E10–2   (Match Definitions with Terms)

Match each definition with its related term by entering the appropriate letter in the space provided.

Terms	Definitions
_____ (1) A temporary difference	A. Amount of the difference between income tax expense and income taxes payable.
_____ (2) A permanant tax difference	B. A potential liability from an event that has already happened but depends on a future event.
_____ (3) A contingent liability that must be recorded as a loss and a liability	C. A contingent liability that is reasonably possible.
	D. A system used to attain control over cash expenditures.

	Terms	
____	(4) Voucher system	
____	(5) Contingent liability	
____	(6) Deferred income tax	
____	(7) Current ratio	
____	(8) A contingent liability that must be reported only in a footnote	
____	(9) An unsecured debt	
____	(10) Cost principle	

Definitions

E. A deferred income tax item that will "reverse or turn around."

F. A liability that is not supported by a mortgage on specific assets.

G. All liabilities are measured in conformity with this principle.

H. A contingent liability that is probable and can be reasonably estimated.

I. Current assets divided by current liabilities.

J. An income tax difference that will never "reverse or turn around."

E10–3   (Compute Owners' Equity, Working Capital, and Interest Expense; Provide an Adjusting Entry)

Nair Corporation is preparing its 19B balance sheet. The company records show the following related amounts at the end of the accounting period, December 31, 19B:

Total current assets	$160,100
Total all remaining assets	665,000
Liabilities:	
Note payable (12%, due in 5 years)	24,000
Accounts payable	50,000
Income taxes payable	15,000
Liability for withholding taxes	2,000
Rent revenue collected in advance	3,000
Bonds payable (due in 15 years)	200,000
Wages payable	4,900
Property taxes payable	1,000
Note payable (10%; due in 6 months)	8,000
Interest payable	200

Required:

a. Compute total owners' equity.

b. Compute (1) working capital and (2) the current ratio (show computations).

c. Compute the amount of interest expense for 19B on the long-term note. Assume it was dated October 1, 19B.

d. Give any adjusting entry required for the long-term note payable on December 31, 19B.

E10–4   (Accounting for, and Reporting, Accrued Expenses and Deferred Revenue)

During 19B, the two transactions given below were completed by Brookline Company. The annual accounting period ends December 31.

1. Wages paid and recorded during 19B were $120,000; however, at the end of December 19B, there were three days' wages unpaid and unrecorded because the weekly payroll will not be paid until January 6, 19C. Wages for the three days were $3,500.

2. On December 10, 19B, the company collected rent revenue of $1,500 on office space that it rented to another party. The rent collected was for 30 days from December 10, 19B, to January 10, 19C, and was credited in full to Rent Revenue.

Required:

a. Give (1) the adjusting entry required on December 31, 19B, and (2) the January 6, 19C, journal entry for payment of any unpaid wages from December 19B.

b. Give (1) the journal entry for the collection of rent on December 10, 19B, and (2) the adjusting entry on December 31, 19B.

c. Show how any liabilities related to the above transactions should be reported on the company's balance sheet at December 31, 19B.

E10–5   (Accounting for an Interest-Bearing Note Payable through Its Time to Maturity)
On November 1, 19A, Baxter Company borrowed $60,000 cash from the City Bank for working capital purposes and gave an interest-bearing note with a face amount of $60,000. The note was due in six months. The interest rate was 12% per annum payable at maturity. The accounting period ends December 31.

Required:

a. Give the journal entry to record the note on November 1.

b. Give any adjusting entry that would be required at the end of the annual accounting period.

c. Give the journal entry to record payment of the note and interest on the maturity date, April 30, 19B.

E10–6   (Record a Payroll, Including Deductions)
Lakeview Company has completed the payroll for January 19B, reflecting the following data:

> Salaries and wages earned $78,000
> Employee income taxes withheld . . .   9,000
> Union dues withheld   1,000
> FICA payroll taxes*   5,720
> FUTA payroll taxes   560
> State unemployment taxes   2,160
>
> * Assessed on both employer and employee (i.e., $5,720 each).

Required:

a. Give the journal entry to record payment of the payroll and employee deductions.

b. Give the journal entry to record employer payroll taxes.

c. What was the amount of additional labor expense to the company due to tax laws? What was the amount of the employees' take-home pay?

d. List the liabilities, and their amounts, that are reported on the company's January 31, 19B balance sheet.

E10–7   (Accounting for Accounts Payable and an Interest-Bearing Note Payable)
Cole Company sells a wide range of goods through two retail stores that are operated in adjoining cities. Most purchases of goods for resale are on invoices with credit terms of

3/10, n/30. Occasionally, a short-term note payable is used to obtain cash for current use. The following transactions were selected from those occurring during 19B:

1. On January 10, 19B, purchased merchandise on credit, $20,000; terms 3/10, n/30. Record at net (Chapter 6); the company uses a periodic inventory system.
2. On March 1, 19B, borrowed $60,000 cash from Town Bank and gave an interest-bearing note payable: face amount, $60,000; due at the end of six months, with an annual interest rate of 10% payable at maturity.

Required:

a. Give the journal entry for each of the above transactions. Record purchases and accounts payable at net.

b. Give the journal entry if the account payable of January 10, 19B, was paid within the discount period.

c. Give the journal entry if the account payable of January 10, 19B, was paid after the discount period.

d. Give the journal entry for the payment of the note payable plus interest on its maturity date.

E10–8   (Accounting for a Noninterest-Bearing Note Payable)

On September 1, 19A, Clayton Company borrowed $30,000 and signed a one-year note payable for $33,000. The accounting period ends December 31.

Required:

a. What kind of note was involved? Explain.

b. How much interest should be recorded? What was the implicit interest rate?

c. Give the required entries (if any) on the following dates: September 1, 19A, December 31, 19A, and August 31, 19B. Assume that reversing entries are not used.

E10–9   (Deferred Income Tax; One Temporary Difference)

The comparative income statements of Rowan Corporation at December 31, 19B, showed the following summarized pretax data:

	Year 19A	Year 19B
Sales revenue	$50,000	$61,000
Expenses (excluding income tax) . . .	40,000	48,000
Pretax income	$10,000	$13,000

Included in the above 19B data is a $2,000 expense that was deductible only in the 19A income tax return (rather than in 19B). The average income tax rate was 30%. Taxable income from the income tax returns were 19A, $9,000; and 19B, $12,300.

Required:

a. For each year compute (1) income taxes payable and (2) deferred income tax. Is the deferred income tax a liability or an asset? Explain.

b. Give the journal entry for each year to record income taxes payable, deferred income tax, and income tax expense.

c. Show what amounts, related to income taxes, should be reported each year on the income statement and balance sheet. Assume income tax is paid on April 15 of the next year.

E10–10   **(Deferred Income Tax; One Temporary Difference)**

The comparative income statement for Nader Corporation at the end of December 31, 19B, provided the following summarized pretax data:

	Year 19A	Year 19B
Revenues	$90,000	$94,000
Expenses (excluding income tax)	75,000	78,000
Pretax income	$15,000	$16,000

Included in the above 19B data is a $6,000 revenue that was taxable only in the 19A income tax return (rather than in 19B). The average income tax rate was 32%. Taxable income shown in the tax returns were 19A, $14,000; and 19B, $15,500.

Required:

a. For each year compute (1) income taxes payable and (2) deferred income tax. Is the deferred income tax a liability or an asset? Explain.

b. Give the journal entry for each year to record income taxes payable, deferred income tax, and income tax expense.

c. Show what amounts, related to income taxes, should be reported each year on the income statement and balance sheet. Assume income tax is paid on April 15 of the next year.

E10–11   **(Deferred Income Tax; Depreciation)**

Green Corporation reported the following summarized pretax data at the end of each year:

	Income statement at December 31		
	19A	19B	19C
Revenues	$150,000	$160,000	$175,000
Expenses (including depreciation)*	110,000	106,000	115,000
Pretax income	$ 40,000	$ 54,000	$ 60,000

* Depreciation expense on the income statement was straight line, on a machine purchased January 1, 19A, for $60,000. The machine has a three-year estimated life and no residual value. The company used accelerated depreciation on the income tax return as follows: 19A, $30,000; 19B, $20,000; and 19C, $10,000. The average income tax rate is 30% for the three years.

Taxable income from the income tax return was as follows: 19A, $28,000; 19B, $53,000; and 19C, $82,000.

Required:

a. For each year compute (1) income taxes payable and (2) deferred income tax. Is the deferred income tax a liability or an asset? Explain.

b. Give the journal entry for each year to record income taxes payable, deferred income tax, and income tax expense.

c. Show what amounts, related to income taxes, should be reported each year on the income statement and balance sheet.

Part B: Exercises 10–12 to 10–19

E10–12   (Match Definitions with Terms)

Match each definition with its related term by entering the appropriate letter in the space provided.

Terms	Definitions
_____ (1) Interest	A. Future value of a single amount at 10% interest for five interest periods.
_____ (2) Principal × Rate × Time	B. A series of consecutive equal payments each interest period.
_____ (3) $f_{i=10;\ n=5} = 1.6105$	C. Time cost of using money.
_____ (4) Balance in a fund for $i = 8\%; n = 4$	D. Present value of a series of equal payments at 10% interest for five periods.
_____ (5) $P_{i=10\%;\ n=5} = 3.7908$	E. Formula for computing interest.
_____ (6) Ordinary annuity	F. A beginning-of-period annuity.
_____ (7) $F_{i=10\%;\ n=5} = 6.1051$	G. Value today of a single future amount.
_____ (8) Annuity	H. $30,000 \times f_{i=8\%;\ n=4} (1.3605) = \$40,815$.
_____ (9) Future value of 1	I. An end-of-period annuity.
_____ (10) Table value for an annuity due	J. Future value of a series of equal payments at 10% interest for five periods.
_____ (11) Annuity due	K. Value in the future of a single present amount.
_____ (12) $P_{i=10\%;\ n=5} = 0.6209$	L. Present value of a single amount at 10% interest for five interest periods.
_____ (13) Balance in a fund with equal payments for $i = 8\%; n = 4$	M. $\$20,000 \div P_{i=12\%;\ n=3} (2.4018) = \$8,327$.
_____ (14) Present value of 1	N. Table value of an ordinary annuity × $(1 + i)$.
_____ (15) Periodic payments on a debt, $i = 12\%; n = 3$	O. $\$5,000 \times P_{i=8\%;\ n=4} (4.5061) = \$22,531$.

E10–13   (Application of the Four Kinds of Present and Future Values)

On January 1, 19A, Stanley Company completed the following transactions (assume a 12% annual interest rate):

1. Deposited $15,000 in a fund (designated Fund A).
2. Established a fund (designated Fund B) by making six equal annual deposits of $3,000 each.
3. Established a fund (designated Fund C) by depositing a single amount that will increase to $50,000 by the end of year 7.
4. Decided to deposit a single sum in a fund (designated Fund D) that will provide 10 equal annual year-end payments of $10,000 to a retired employee (payments starting December 31, 19A).

Required (show computations and round to the nearest dollar):

a. What will be the balance of Fund A at the end of year 9?
b. What will be the balance of Fund B at the end of year 6?
c. What single amount must be deposited in Fund C on January 1, 19A?
d. What single sum must be deposited in Fund D on January 1, 19A?

E10–14   **(Accounting for a Savings Account; a Single Amount)**

On January 1, 19A, you deposited $8,000 in a savings account. The account will earn 8% annual compound interest, which will be added to the fund balance at the end of each year.

Required (round to the nearest dollar):

a. What will be the balance in the savings account at the end of 10 years?

b. What is the time value of the money in dollars for the 10 years?

c. How much interest revenue did the fund earn in 19A? 19B?

d. Give the journal entry to record interest revenue at the end of 19A and 19B.

E10–15   **(Compute Deposit Required and Account for a Single-Sum Savings Account)**

On January 1, 19A, Tom Fox decided to deposit an amount in a savings account that will provide $40,000 four years later to send his son to college. The savings account will earn 9%, which will be added to the fund each year-end.

Required (show computations and round to the nearest dollar):

a. How much must Tom deposit on January 1, 19A?

b. Give the journal entry that Tom should make on January 1, 19A.

c. What is the time value of the money for the four years?

d. Give the journal entry that Tom should make on (1) December 31, 19A, and (2) December 31, 19B.

E10–16   **(Accounting for a Savings Account with Equal Periodic Payments)**

On each December 31, you plan to deposit $1,500 in a savings account. The account will earn 8% annual interest, which will be added to the fund balance at year-end. The first deposit will be made December 31, 19A (end of period).

Required (show computations and round to the nearest dollar):

a. Give the required journal entry on December 31, 19A.

b. What will be the balance in the savings account at the end of the 10th year (i.e., 10 deposits)?

c. What is the time value of money in dollars for the 10 deposits?

d. How much interest revenue did the fund earn in 19B? 19C?

e. Give all required journal entries at the end of 19B and 19C.

E10–17   **(Accounting for a Savings Fund with Periodic Rents)**

You have planned to take a trip around the world upon graduation, four years from now (now it is January 1, 19A). Your grandfather wants to deposit sufficient funds for this trip in a savings account for you. On the basis of a budget, you estimate the trip now would cost $12,000. To be generous, your grandfather decided to deposit $2,800 in the fund at the end of each of the next four years, starting on December 31, 19A. The savings account will earn 7% annual interest, which will be added to the savings account at each year-end.

Required (show computations and round to the nearest dollar):

a. What journal entry should your grandfather make on December 31, 19A, to record the first deposit.

b. How much money will you have for the trip at the end of year 4 (i.e., after four deposits)?

c. What is the time value of the money for the four years?

d. How much interest revenue did the fund earn in 19A, 19B, 19C, and 19D?

e. Give the journal entries at the end of 19B and 19C. Yes, you left on January 1, 19E.

E10–18 (Valuation of an Asset Based on Present Value)

You have the chance to purchase the royalty interest in an oil well. Your best estimate is that the net royalty income will average $35,000 per year for five years. There will be no residual value at that time. Assume the cash inflow is at each year-end and that, considering the uncertainty in your estimates, you expect to earn 14% per year on the investment.

Required (show computations and round to the nearest dollar):

a. What should you be willing to pay for this investment on January 1, 19A?

b. Give the required journal entry (cash paid in full for the royalty interest) on January 1, 19A.

c. Give the required journal entries on December 31, 19A, assuming the net cash received was equal to your estimate. Assume the cost of the royalty interest is depleted on a straight-line basis.

E10–19 (Accounting for Interest-Bearing and Noninterest-Bearing Notes Compared)

Assume you needed to borrow $3,500 cash for one year. The City Bank charges 10% interest per annum on such loans. Answer the following questions (show computations):

Required:

a. What would be the face amount of the note assuming the bank agreed to accept an interest-bearing note?

b. What would be the face amount of the note assuming the bank insisted on a non-interest-bearing note?

c. Give the journal entries to record the note in (a) and (b). Set the entries in parallel columns.

d. Give the journal entries at date of maturity in (a) and (b).

PROBLEMS

Part A: Problems 10–1 to 10–9

P10–1 (Record and Report Five Current Liabilities)

Hill Company completed the transactions listed below during 19B. The annual accounting period ends December 31, 19B.

Jan. 8 Purchased merchandise for resale at an invoice cost of $12,000; terms 2/10, n/60. Record at net (Chapter 6); assume a periodic inventory system.

17 Paid invoice of January 8.

Apr. 1 Borrowed $50,000 from the National Bank for general use; executed a 12-month, 12% interest-bearing note payable.

June 3 Purchased merchandise for resale at an invoice cost of $20,000; terms 1/20, n/30; record at net.

July 5 Paid invoice of June 3.

Aug. 1 Rented two rooms in the building owned by the company and collected six months' rent in advance amounting to $4,800. Record the collection in a way that will not require an adjusting entry at year-end.

Dec. 20 Received a $200 deposit from a customer as a guarantee to return a large trailer "borrowed" for 30 days.

     31 Wages earned but not paid on December 31 of $7,500 (disregard payroll taxes).

Required:

a. Prepare journal entries for each of the above transactions.

b. Prepare all adjusting entries required on December 31, 19B.

c. Show how all of the liabilities arising from the above transactions would be reported on the balance sheet at December 31, 19B.

P10–2 (Accounting for an Interest-Bearing Note, with Adjusting Entries)

On April 1, 19A, Alpert Company bought equipment for $150,000. A cash down payment of $50,000 was made. A $100,000 interest-bearing note (including a mortgage on the equipment) was given for the balance. The note specified 10% annual interest. Two payments on principal of $50,000 each, plus interest on the unpaid balance on March 31, 19B, and March 31, 19C, are required—these will be unequal cash payments. The accounting period ends December 31.

Required:

a. Give all of the related journal entries for the terms of this note. Do not use reversing entries.

b. Show how the liabilities should be reported on the company's 19A and 19B balance sheets.

P10–3 (Accounting for Interest-Bearing and Noninterest-Bearing Notes, Including Adjusting Entries)

During 19A, Conrad Company completed two transactions that involved notes payable. The accounting period ends December 31. The company does not use reversing entries.

May 1, 19A—borrowed $36,000 cash and signed a one-year interest-bearing note. The interest rate specified on the note was 10%. The principal and interest are payable on the maturity date, April 30, 19B.

September 1, 19A—borrowed $30,000 cash and signed a six-month noninterest-bearing note for $31,500. The note did not give a stated rate of interest. The face amount is payable at maturity date, February 28, 19B.

Required:

a. Give all of the entries related to the $36,000 note from May 1, 19A, through April 30, 19B.

b. Give all of the entries related to the $31,500 note from September 1, 19A, through maturity date, February 28, 19B.

c. Show how the liabilities related to the two notes should be reported on the 19A balance sheet.

P10–4 **(Purchase of a Noncash Asset with a Noninterest-Bearing Note; Including Adjusting Entries)**

On August 1, 19A, Deming Company purchased a machine that cost $23,000. The company paid cash $3,000 and signed a six-month noninterest-bearing note with a face amount of $21,200. The note did not specify a stated rate of interest. The accounting period ends December 31.

Required:

a. Compute the implicit rate of interest.

b. Give all entries related to the note from August 1, 19A, through the maturity date, February 1, 19B. Do not use reversing entries.

c. Show how the note should be reported on the 19A balance sheet.

P10–5 **(Record and Report Five Liabilities Including an Interest-Bearing Note and a Noninterest-Bearing Note)**

Robo Company completed the transactions listed below during 19A. The annual accounting period ends December 31.

May   1   Purchased an operational asset (fixtures) for $40,000; paid $10,000 cash and signed a 12-month, 10% interest-bearing note payable for the balance.

June   5   Purchased an operational asset (machine) at an invoice cost of $12,000; terms 2/10, n/60.

    14   Paid invoice of June 5.

Sept. 1   Collected rent revenue on office space rented to another company; the rent of $6,000 was for the next six months. Record the collection in a way to avoid an adjusting entry at the end of 19A.

Nov.   1   Borrowed $30,000 cash and signed a noninterest-bearing note for $31,800. The note matures on April 30,19B.

Dec. 31   Received a tax bill for property tax for 19A in the amount of $1,200; the taxes are payable no later than March 1, 19B.

Required:

a. Give the 19A journal entries for each of the above transactions.

b. Prepare any required adjusting entries on December 31, 19A.

c. Show how all liabilities arising from the above transactions would be reported on the 19A balance sheet.

P10–6 **(Deferred Income Tax; Two Temporary Differences)**

The records of Radney Corporation provided the following summarized data for 19D and 19E:

	Year-end December 31	
	19D	**19E**
a. Income statement:		
Revenues	$180,000	$190,000
Expenses (excluding income tax)	120,000	125,000
Pretax income	$ 60,000	$ 65,000

b. Income tax rate, 35%. Assume income taxes payable is paid 75% in the current year and 25% on April 15 of the next year.

c. Temporary differences:
  (1) The 19E expenses include a $6,000 expense that must be deducted only in the 19D tax return.
  (2) The 19E revenues include a $4,000 revenue that was taxable only in 19F.
d. Taxable income shown in the tax returns were 19D, $62,000; and 19E, $65,000.

Required:

a. For each year compute (1) income taxes payable and (2) deferred income tax. Is each deferred income tax a liability or an asset? Explain.

b. Give the journal entry for each year to record income taxes payable, deferred income tax, and income tax expense.

c. Show what amounts, related to income taxes, should be reported each year on the income statement and balance sheet.

P10-7   (Deferred Income Tax; Depreciation)

At December 31, 19A, the records of Laymon Corporation provided the following information:

1. Income statement:

Revenues	$ 150,000*
Depreciation expense (straight line)	(13,000)†
Remaining expenses (excluding income tax) . . .	(100,000)
Pretax income	$ 37,000

  * These revenues include $20,000 interest on tax-free municipal bonds.
  † Equipment depreciated—acquired January 1, 19A, cost $52,000; estimated useful life, four years and no residual value. Accelerated depreciation is used on the tax return as follows: 19A, $20,800; 19B, $15,600; 19C, $10,400; and 19D, $5,200.

2. Income tax rate, 35%. Assume 75% is paid in year incurred.

3. Taxable income from the 19A income tax return, $90,000.

Required:

a. Compute income taxes payable and deferred income tax for 19A. Is the deferred income tax a liability or an asset? Explain.

b. Give the journal entry to record income taxes for 19A.

c. Show what amounts, related to 19A income taxes, should be reported on the income statement and balance sheet.

P10-8   (Based on Chapter Supplement 10A; Accounting for Payroll Costs)

McNair Company completed the salary and wage payroll for March 19A. Details provided by the payroll were:

Salaries and wages earned	$210,000
Employee income taxes withheld	42,000
Union dues withheld	2,000
Insurance premiums withheld	900
FICA taxes*	15,015
FUTA taxes	1,470
State unemployment taxes	5,670

  * Equal amount for employer and employees.

Required:

a. Give the journal entry to record the payroll for March, including employee deductions.

b. Give the journal entry to record the employer's payroll taxes.

c. Give a combined journal entry to show the payment of amounts owed to governmental agencies and other organizations.

d. What was the total labor cost for the company? Explain. What percent of the payroll was take-home pay?

P10–9 (Based on Chapter Supplement 10B: Application of a Voucher System to Control Cash Expenditures)

Charles Company uses a voucher system to control cash expenditures. The following transactions have been selected from December 19B for case purposes. The accounting year ends December 31.

Design a voucher register and a check register similar to those shown in Chapter Supplement 10B. The transactions that follow will be entered in these two special journals.

Dec. 2 Purchased merchandise from AB Wholesalers for resale, $2,000; terms 2/10, n/30; record purchases at net and assume a periodic inventory system (Chapter 6); Invoice No. 14; start with Voucher No. 11.

7 Approved contract with Ace Plumbing Company for repair of plumbing, $450; account, Building Repairs, No. 77.

11 Paid Voucher No. 11; start with Check No. 51.

22 Purchased store supplies for future use from Crown Company; Invoice No. 21 for $90; account, Store Supplies Inventory, No. 16.

23 Advertising for pre-Christmas sale, $630; bill received from Daily Press and payment processed immediately; account, Advertising Expense, No. 54.

31 Monthly payroll voucher, total $2,500; $1,500 was selling expense (Sales Salaries, No. 52), and $1,000 was administrative expense (Administrative Salaries, No. 62). The voucher was supported by the payroll record; therefore, one voucher was prepared for the entire payroll. The voucher was approved for immediate payment. Six checks with consecutive numbers were issued.

Required:

a. Enter the above transactions in the voucher register and the check register.

b. Total the special journals and check the equality of the debits and credits. Set up T-accounts and post both registers. Complete all posting notations. The following accounts may be needed:

Account titles	Account No.
Cash	01
Store supplies inventory	16
Vouchers payable	30
Purchases	40
Selling expense control	50
Subsidiary ledger:	
Sales salaries	52
Advertising expense	54
Administrative expense control . . .	60

	Account
Account titles	No.
Subsidiary ledger:	
Administrative salaries	62
Building repairs	77

c. Reconcile the Vouchers Payable account balance with the Unpaid Vouchers File at the end of December.

Part B: Problems 10–10 to 10–17

P10–10   (Application of Four PV and FV Concepts)

On January 1, 19A, Dodge Company completed the following transactions (use a 10% annual interest rate for all transactions):

1. Deposited $60,000 in a debt retirement fund. Interest will be computed at six-month intervals and added to the fund at those times (i.e., semiannual compounding). (Hint: Think carefully about *n* and *i*).

2. Established a plant addition fund of $200,000 to be available at the end of year 5. A single sum will be deposited on January 1, 19A, that will grow to the $200,000.

3. Established a pension retirement fund of $400,000 to be available by the end of year 6 by making six equal annual deposits each at year-end, starting on December 31,19A.

4. Purchased a $120,000 machine on January 1, 19A, and paid cash, $40,000. A three-year note payable is signed for the balance. The note will be paid in three equal year-end payments starting on December 31, 19A.

Required (show computations and round to the nearest dollar):

a. In transaction 1 above, what will be the balance in the fund at the end of year 4? What is the total amount of interest revenue that will be earned?

b. In transaction 2 above, what single sum amount must the company deposit on January 1, 19A? What is the total amount of interest revenue that will be earned?

c. In transaction 3 above, what is the required amount of each of the six equal annual deposits? What is the total amount of interest revenue that will be earned?

d. In transaction 4 above, what is the amount of each of the equal annual payments that will be paid on the note? What is the total amount of interest expense that will be incurred?

P10–11   (Accounting for a Fund; Fund Accumulation Schedule and Entries)

On January 1, 19A, Turbo Company decided to accumulate a fund to build an addition to its plant. The company will deposit $250,000 in the fund at each year-end, starting on December 31 ,19A. The fund will earn 8% interest which will be added to the fund at each year-end. The accounting period ends December 31.

Required:

a. What will be the balance in the fund immediately after the December 31, 19C, deposit?

b. Complete the following fund accumulation schedule:

Date	Cash Payment	Interest Revenue	Fund Increase	Fund Balance
12/31/19A				
12/31/19B				
12/31/19C				
Total				

c. Give journal entries on December 31, 19A, 19B, and 19C.

d. The plant addition was completed on January 1, 19D. The total cost was $825,000. Give the entry assuming this amount is paid in full to the contractor.

P10–12 (Accounting for a Plant Fund; a Single Amount)

Bridge Company will build another plant during 19C estimated to cost $900,000. At the present time, January 1, 19A, the company has excess cash, some of which will be set aside in a savings account to cover the plant cost. The savings account will earn 10% annual interest which will be added to the savings account each year-end.

Required (show computations and round to the nearest dollar):

a. What single amount must be deposited in the savings account on January 1, 19A, to create the desired amount by the end of 19C?

b. What will be the time value of the money by the end of 19C?

c. How much interest revenue will be earned each year (19A through 19C)?

d. Give the following journal entries:
   (1) Establishment of the fund.
   (2) Interest earned at each year-end.
   (3) Use of the fund and other cash needed to pay for the plant (completed December 31, 19C, at a cost of $940,000).

P10–13 (Accounting for a Debt Retirement Fund; a Single Amount)

On January 1, 19A, Young Company set aside a fund to provide cash to pay off the principal amount of a $100,000 long-term debt that will be due at the end of five years. The single deposit will be made with an independent trustee. The fund will earn 7% annual interest which will be added to the fund balance at each year-end.

Required (show computations and round to the nearest dollar):

a. How much must be deposited as a single sum on January 1, 19A, to pay off the debt?

b. What is the time value of the money in dollars for the five years?

c. How much interest revenue will the fund earn in 19A? 19B?

d. Give journal entries for the company to record:
   (1) The deposit on January 1, 19A.
   (2) The interest revenue for 19A and 19B (separately).
   (3) Payment of the maturing liability at the end of the fifth year.

e. Show how the effects of the fund will be reported on the 19B income statement and balance sheet.

P10–14   (Accounting for a Debt Fund; Equal Periodic Rents)

On December 31, 19A, Cartwright Company set aside, in a fund, cash to pay the principal amount of a $120,000 debt due on December 31, 19D. The company will make four equal annual deposits on each December 31, 19A, 19B, 19C, and 19D. The fund will earn 8% annual interest, which will be added to the balance of the fund at each year-end. The fund trustee will pay the loan principal (to the creditor) upon receipt of the last fund deposit. The company's accounting period ends December 31.

Required (show computations and round to the nearest dollar):

a. How much must be deposited each December 31?
b. What will be the time value of the money in dollars for the fund?
c. How much interest revenue will the fund earn in 19A, 19B, 19C, and 19D?
d. Give journal entries for the company on the following dates:
    (1) For the first deposit on December 31, 19A.
    (2) For all amounts at the ends of 19B and 19C.
    (3) For payment of the debt on December 31, 19D.
e. Show how the effect of the fund will be reported on the December 31, 19B, income statement and balance sheet.

P10–15   (Debt Paid in Equal Installments; Debt Payment Schedule and Entries)

On January 1, 19A, Big Company sold a new machine to Small Company for $50,000. A cash down payment of $20,000 was made by Small Company. A $30,000, 12% note was signed by Small Company for the balance due. The note is to be paid off in three equal installments due on December 31, 19A, 19B, and 19C. Each payment is to include principal plus interest on the unpaid balance. The purchase was recorded by Small as follows:

January 1, 19A:

Machine 50,000		
Cash		20,000
Note payable		30,000

Required (show computations and round to the nearest dollars):

a. What is the amount of the equal annual payment that must be made by Small Company?
b. What was the time value of the money, in dollars, on the note?
c. Complete the following debt payment schedule:

Date	Cash Payment	Interest Expense	Principal Decrease	Unpaid Principal
1/1/19A				
12/31/19A				
12/31/19B				
12/31/19C				
Totals				

d. Give the journal entries for each of the three payments.

e. Explain why interest expense decreased in amount each year.

P10–16   **(Payment for Auto in Equal Periodic Installments; Prepare Debt Payment Schedule; Entries)**

On January 1, 19A, you bought a new XR4TI automobile for $21,000. You paid a $6,000 cash down payment and signed a $15,000 note, payable in four equal intallments on each December 31, the first payment to be made on December 31, 19A. The interest rate is 14% per year on the unpaid balance. Each payment will include payment on principal plus the interest.

Required:

a. Compute the amount of the equal payments that you must make.

b. What is the time value of the money in dollars for the installment debt?

c. Complete a schedule using the format below.

DEBT PAYMENT SCHEDULE

Date	Cash Payment	Interest Expense	Reduction of Principal	Unpaid Principal
1/1/A				
12/31/A				
12/31/B				
12/31/C				
12/31/D				
Totals				

d. Explain why the amount of interest expense decreases each year.

e. Give the journal entries on December 31, 19A, and 19B.

P10–17   **(Accounting for a Noninterest-Bearing Note; Time to Maturity, Two Years)**

On January 1, 19A, Solly Company borrowed $50,000 cash from Mellon Financial Corporation and signed a two-year noninterest-bearing note. The note plus all interest are payable on the maturity date December 31, 19B. The market rate of interest for this risk level was 12%. The accounting period ends December 31.

Required (show computations and round all amounts to the nearest dollar):

a. Compute the face amount of the note.

b. Give journal entries for the company at the following dates:
   (1) January 1, 19A, date of loan.
   (2) December 31, 19A, end of accounting period.
   (3) December 31, 19B, end of accounting period.
   (4) December 31, 19B, maturity date.

c. Show how this note should be reported on the company's December 31, 19A, balance sheet.

CASES

C10-1   (Accounting for Warranty Expense and Warranty Liability; a Challenging Case)

Sound Warehouse sells television sets, stereos, and other related items. This case relates to stereos. During 19A, the company sold stereos for $180,000 cash; the related cost of goods sold was $70,000. Each stereo is guaranteed for one year for defective parts. In case of a defective part, the part is replaced and the labor cost of replacing it involves no cost to the customer. Experience by the manufacturer shows that the average cost to make good the warranty is approximately 4% of cost of goods sold. The company uses a perpetual inventory system and the accounting period ends December 31.

Actual expenditures for warranties (i.e., replacement parts and labor) during 19A was $2,100. During 19A, this amount was debited to an account called Warranty Expense and credited to Cash. Stereo sales were much higher during December than in any other prior month.

Required:

a. Give the two summary journal entries for the company to record the sales of stereos during 19A.

b. Explain why the company debited the actual 19A warranty expenditures to warranty expense.

c. Explain the nature of any liability that the company should record at the end of 19A related to the warranties.

d. Compute the estimated amount of any warranty liability that exists at December 31, 19A.

e. Give any entry needed based on your answer to Requirement (d).

f. Show how warranty expense and any warranty liability should be reported in the 19A income statement and balance sheet.

C10-2   (Hidden Interest in a Real Estate Deal; PV)

Jack Laymon, a home builder, distributed an advertisement that offered "a $180,000 house with a zero interest rate mortgage for sale." If the purchaser made monthly payments of $3,000 for five years ($180,000 ÷ 60 months), there would be no additional charge for interest. When the offer was made, mortgage interest rates were 12%. Present value for $n = 60$, and $i = 1\%$ is 44.9550.

Required:

a. Did the builder actually provide a mortgage at zero interest?

b. Estimate the true price of the home that was advertised. Assume that the monthly payment was based on an implicit interest rate of 12%.

C10-3   (Alternative Choices Involving Leases; Challenging)

Several years ago, Payne Company borrowed $10 million from First American Bank. At the time the loan was approved, the company agreed not to borrow any additional money from any other sources until at least half of the First American loan was repaid. As the result of continued growth, the company must acquire a large computer during the current year. Unfortunately, the company does not have sufficient cash to purchase the computer or to repay the loan to First American. You have been engaged as a consultant.

The president of the company, Allison Payne, described the problem during your first meeting:

> We need a new IBM computer. The computer can be purchased from Super Computer Company for $500,000, but we don't have the cash and the bank won't let us borrow any more money. However, Jackson Leasing Company has agreed to lease the computer to us on a 10-year lease, which is the expected useful life of the computer (no residual value). Annual lease payments of $81,372 would be paid based on an interest rate of 10%. I think that this lease deal will solve our problem because we will not violate our agreement with First American as long as we don't report any additional debt on the balance sheet. We must work this out without recording any debt. What do you think?

To help the president understand the required accounting treatment, the president should consider three alternatives as follows:

Alternative No. 1—The company can purchase the computer but would have to borrow $500,000 with a note payable to the computer company at 10% interest for 10 years. Annual year-end payments for principal and interest amount to $81,372.

Alternative No. 2—The company could rent the computer on a lease basis. The terms of the lease cause it to be considered an operating lease. Annual rent payments would be $100,000 at each year-end for 10 years.

Alternative No. 3—The company could acquire the computer on a long-term lease basis. At the expiration date of the lease, the computer would be retained by the company for no additional cost. The terms of the lease cause it to be accounted for as a capital lease. Annual lease payments would be $81,372 for 10 years.

Required:

a. Assume that the computer was acquired on January 1, 19D, which is the beginning of the accounting period. Prepare journal entries to record the acquisition of the computer under each of the three alternatives.

b. Assume the company makes cash payments under each alternative on December 31 of each year. Prepare the required journal entries on December 31, 19D (include adjusting entries, if required). The company uses straight-line depreciation for all assets.

c. Would the capital lease alternative, described by the president, permit the company to acquire the computer, and conform to GAAP? Would a capital lease violate the agreement with the bank?

d. What are the primary problems of Alternatives 1 and 2?

C10–4   **(Analysis of Liabilities for an Actual Company)**

JCPenney   Refer to the financial statements of J.C. Penney Company, Inc. given in the appendix immediately preceding the index.

1. What is the amount of accounts payable at the end of the current year?
2. What is the average interest rate on short-term debt for the current year?
3. What is the present value of commitments under capital leases at the end of the current year?
4. What is the amount of deferred taxes reported on the balance sheet at the end of the current year?
5. What amount of interest was paid in cash during the current year?

ELEVEN

MEASURING AND REPORTING BONDS PAYABLE

PURPOSE

Chapter 10 discussed current liabilities and the concepts of future and present value. This chapter discusses bonds payable. Bonds are long-term debt instruments that are an important source of funds which are primarily used to pay for noncurrent assets. When bonds are issued (i.e., sold), they represent an investment for the buyer and a liability for the issuer. Accounting for bonds involves some complexities. The purpose of this chapter is to discuss measuring, recording, and reporting the financial effects of bonds payable. Because of the importance of long-term debt, most companies provide supplemental disclosures similar to the note on the opposite page. Notice the extensive use of foreign debt by this company.

LEARNING OBJECTIVES

1. Define and classify bonds payable.
2. Record and report bonds payable, with discount and premium amortization.
3. Record and report bond sinking funds.
4. Account for debt retirement funds.
5. Expand your accounting vocabulary by learning the "Important Terms Defined in This Chapter."
6. Apply the knowledge learned from this chapter by completing the homework assigned by your instructor.

ORGANIZATION

Part A—fundamentals of measuring, recording, and reporting bonds payable
1. Characteristics of bonds payable.
2. Measuring bonds payable and interest expense.
3. Accounting for bonds sold at par, discount, and premium.
4. Advantages and disadvantages of issuing bonds.
5. Financial leverage.

Part B—additional topics in accounting for bonds payable
1. Effective-interest amortization of bond discount and premium.
2. Accounting for bonds sold between interest dates.
3. Accounting for bonds with different interest and accounting period dates.
4. Bond sinking funds.

Disney

Borrowings

(In millions)	1987	1986
Commercial paper	**$195.0**	$ 15.0
4.75% Swiss franc bonds due October, 1996	**64.7**	
9.125% ECU notes due March, 1995, principal payable in annual installments of $12.5 commencing March, 1991	**62.4**	62.4
Borrowings from limited partnership, net of unamortized discount, due in varying amounts through 1989	**59.9**	111.1
8.75% ECU notes due February, 1994, principal payable in annual installments of $5.4 commencing February, 1990, with balance due at maturity	**54.1**	54.1
14.50% Australian dollar notes due May, 1990	**52.4**	
6.625% Euroyen notes due February, 1996	**49.5**	49.5
9.32% pounds sterling term loan due September, 1996, principal and interest payable in varying semi-annual installments	**29.7**	31.5
12.50% Eurodollar notes		150.0
6.40% yen term loan		47.5
Other	**16.8**	26.1
	$584.5	$547.2

Borrowings have the following scheduled maturities (in millions): $55.0 in 1988, $9.2 in 1989, $60.3 in 1990; $37.4 in 1991; $21.1 in 1992; and $401.5 thereafter.

The Company has available through 1990 unsecured revolving lines of bank credit of up to $385 million for general corporate purposes, including the support of commercial paper borrowings. The Company has the option to borrow at various interest rates not to exceed LIBOR. As of September 30, 1987 and 1986, the interest rates associated with commercial paper borrowings were 7.6% and 5.9%, respectively.

The Company entered into forward exchange agreements which converted the 4.75% Swiss franc bonds and the 14.50% Australian dollar notes into Japanese yen equivalents with effective interest rates of 6.05% and 4.25%, respectively. The 9.125% and the 8.75% ECU notes were converted into Japanese yen equivalents in 1986 with effective interest rates of 6.565% and 7.065%, respectively. The Company has hedged its yen borrowings and a portion of its cumulative yen royalties from Tokyo Disneyland and other Japanese royalty sources, thus offsetting the effects of fluctuations in the exchange rate.

The Company capitalizes interest on assets constructed for its theme park and resort developments, and on theatrical and television productions in process. In 1987, 1986 and 1985, respectively, total interest costs incurred were $52.7, $67.1 and $86.2 million, of which $23.6, $23.0 and $31.6 million were capitalized.

PART A—FUNDAMENTALS OF MEASURING, RECORDING, AND REPORTING BONDS PAYABLE

Characteristics of Bonds Payable

Funds needed for long-term purposes, such as the acquisition of high-cost machinery or the construction of a new plant, often are obtained by issuing long-term debt instruments. These instruments usually are long-term notes payable (discussed in Chapter 10) and bonds payable. Bonds payable may be **secured** by a mortgage on specified assets, or the bonds may be **unsecured.** Bonds usually are issued in denominations of $1,000 or $10,000, and sometimes in denominations of $100,000. They usually are negotiable (i.e., transferable by endorsement). The bonds of most large companies are bought and sold daily by investors on the major stock exchanges.

The **principal** of a bond is the amount (*a*) payable at the maturity date and (*b*) on which the periodic cash interest payments are computed. It does not change. The principal is also called the par value, face amount, and maturity value. A bond will always specify a **stated rate of interest** and when **periodic cash interest payments** must be paid—usually annually or semiannually. Each periodic interest payment is computed as **principal times the stated interest rate.** The selling price of a bond does not affect the periodic **cash** payment for interest. For example, a $1,000, 8% bond always pays cash interest of (*a*) $80 on an annual basis or (*b*) $40 on a semiannual basis.

A company that wants to sell a bond issue must prepare a **bond indenture** (or bond contract) that states the legal provisions of the bonds. These provisions include the maturity date, rate of interest to be paid, date of each interest payment, and any conversion privileges (explained later). When a bond is issued, the investor receives a **bond certificate.** All of the bond certificates for a single bond issue are identical. The face of each certificate shows the same maturity date, interest rate, interest dates, and other provisions. Usually when a company issues bonds, an **underwriter** is engaged to sell the bonds to the public. A third party, called the **trustee,** usually is appointed to represent the bondholders. The duties of an independent trustee are to ascertain whether the issuing company fulfills all of the provisions of the bond indenture.

Special Characteristics of Bonds

Each bond issue has characteristics that are specified in the bond indenture. The issuing company often will add special characteristics to a bond issue to make the bond more attractive to investors who normally have a large number of investment alternatives to select from. Bonds may be classified in different ways, depending on their characteristics. Typical bond characteristics and their related classifications are shown in Exhibit 11–1.

Exhibit 11–1 Bond characteristics and classifications of bonds

Bond classification	Bond characteristic
1. On the basis of collateral (assets):	
a. Unsecured bonds (often called debentures).	*a.* Bonds that do **not** include a mortgage or pledge of specific assets as a guarantee of repayment at maturity.
b. Secured bonds (often designated on the basis of the type of asset pledged, such as a real estate mortgage).	*b.* Bonds that include the pledge of specific assets as a guarantee of repayment at maturity.
2. On the basis of repayment of principal:	
a. Ordinary or single-payment bonds.	*a.* The principal is payable in full at a single specified maturity date in the future.
b. Serial bonds.	*b.* The principal is payable in installments on a series of specified maturity dates in the future.
3. On the basis of early retirement:	
a. Callable bonds.	*a.* Bonds that may be called for early retirement at the option of the **issuer.**
b. Redeemable bonds.	*b.* Bonds that may be turned in for early retirement at the option of the **bondholder.**
c. Convertible bonds.	*c.* Bonds that may be converted to other securities of the issuer (usually common stock) at the option of the **bondholder.**
4. On the basis of payment of interest:	
a. Registered bonds.	*a.* Payment of interest is made by check and mailed **direct** to the bondholder whose name must be on file (i.e., in the bond register).
b. Coupon bonds.	*b.* Bonds with a printed coupon attached for each interest payment. The bondholder "clips" the coupon on the interest date and deposits it in a bank like a check, or mails it to the issuing company. Then the company mails the interest check direct to the person and address shown on the completed coupon. The interest rate on coupon bonds often is called the coupon rate.

Advantages of Issuing Bonds

A corporation often uses long-term debt to get additional cash rather than by selling its capital stock. The primary advantages of using bonds rather than capital stock are:

1. Ownership and control of the company are not diluted—in contrast to stockholders, bondholders do not participate in the management (by voting) and accumulated earnings of the company.
2. Cash payments to the bondholders are limited to the specified interest payments and the principal of the debt.
3. The net interest cost of borrowed funds often is less because **interest expense** reduces taxable income. Dividends paid to stockholders are not tax deductible.
4. **Positive financial leverage** often occurs. This occurs when the **net interest rate** on debt is less than the interest rate earned by the company on its total assets. For example, if a company borrows funds for an after-tax interest rate of 5.4% and earns 15% on its total assets, the difference, 9.6%, is called positive financial leverage because the company earns more on total invested funds than it pays out to borrow funds. Therefore, the stockholders had a significant benefit because of the relatively low cost of the borrowed cash. **Financial leverage is measured as the difference between the return on stockholders' equity and the return on total assets.**[1]

Disadvantages of Issuing Bonds

The primary disadvantages of using bonds are that (*a*) the required interest payments must be made each interest period and (*b*) the large principal amount must be paid at maturity date. Sound financing of a business requires a realistic **balance** between the amounts of debt and owners' equity. Interest payments to bondholders are **fixed charges,** which increase the risk of business. Interest payments legally must be paid each period, whether the corporation earns income or incurs a loss. In contrast, dividends usually are paid to stockholders only if earnings are satisfactory. Each year, some companies go bankrupt because of their inability to make their required interest payments to creditors.

Measuring Bonds Payable and Interest Expense

A bond may sell at its par value, at a discount (below par), or at a premium (above par). The selling price of a bond is **determined by the difference between its stated interest rate and its market rate of interest.** The market rate of interest is the interest rate that investors (i.e., bond buyers) require to adequately

---

[1] Financial leverage is discussed in Chapter 16.

compensate them for the risks related to the bonds. If the stated and market rates are the same, a bond will sell at par; if the market rate is higher than the stated rate, a bond will sell at a discount; and if the market rate is lower than the stated rate, the bond will sell at a premium. These relationships can be understood in commonsense terms. If a bond pays an interest rate that is less than investors demand, they will not buy the bond unless a discount is provided. If the stated interest rate is more than investors demand, they will be willing to pay a premium to buy the bond. The amount of the premium or discount is determined with present value calculations that are explained later in this chapter.

There are several names that are used for bond interest rates. The stated rate is also called a coupon or contract rate. The market rate is also called a yield, effective, or true rate. Even though there are a variety of names for bond interest rates, there are only two relevant rates: the rate specified in the bond contract (the stated rate) and the rate demanded by investors (the market rate).

When a bond is issued at par, the issuer receives cash equal to the par value of the bond. When a bond is issued at a discount, the issuer receives less cash than the par value of the bond. When a bond is issued at a premium, the issuer receives more cash than the par value.

Each accounting period, bond interest expense is recorded in conformity with the **matching principle.** At the end of each period, the amount of interest unpaid must be accrued and reported as expense so that it will be matched with the revenues in the period in which it was incurred. Accounting for interest on bonds is similar to interest on notes receivable and notes payable. However, when bonds are issued at a premium or discount, an additional measurement problem occurs because (*a*) interest expense is based on the market rate of interest and (*b*) interest paid is based on the stated rate of interest.

Accounting for Bonds Illustrated

Three different cases of accounting for bonds payable are illustrated in Exhibit 11–2: (1) bonds issued at par, (2) bonds issued at a discount, and (3) bonds issued at a premium. In each of these cases, the bonds are sold on the authorization date, January 1, 19A.

Bonds Issued at Par

Bonds sell at their par value when buyers are willing to invest in them at the stated interest rate on the bond. For example, on January 1, 19A, Mason Corporation issued 10% bonds with a par value of $400,000 and received $400,000 in cash. The bonds were dated to start interest on January 1, 19A. The entry by Mason Corporation to record the issuance of these bonds is given in Exhibit 11–2, Case A. In this case, the bonds sold at par because the stated rate and the effective (market) rate were the same.

Subsequent to the sale of the bonds, interest at 5% (i.e., 10% per year) on the par value of the bonds must be paid each June 30 and December 31 until

Exhibit 11–2 Accounting for bonds payable illustrated

Situation:

Mason Corporation approved a bond issue on January 1, 19A: bonds payable authorized, 400 bonds, $1,000 par per bond, 10% interest (payable semiannually each June 30 and December 31), maturity in 10 years on December 31, 19J. Mason's accounting period ends December 31.

Case A—bonds issued at par:

On January 1, 19A, Mason issued 400 bonds at par (i.e., an effective rate of 10%) for $400,000 cash.

Entries during 19A:

January 1, 19A—To record issuance of the bonds at par:
Cash (400 bonds × $1,000) 400,000
   Bonds payable (400 bonds)   400,000

Interest payments during 19A:

	June 30, 19A	December 31, 19A
Bond interest expense	20,000	20,000
Cash ($400,000 × 5%)	20,000	20,000

Financial statements for 19A:

Income statement:
Bond interest expense . . . . $ 40,000

Balance sheet:
Long-term liabilities:
   Bonds payable, 10% (due December 31, 19J) 400,000

---

maturity. The entries to record the interest payments during 19A are given in Exhibit 11–2, Case A.

At the end of the accounting period, December 31, 19A, the financial statements must report bond interest expense and a long-term liability, as shown in Exhibit 11–2, Case A.

In this case, Mason Corporation received $1,000 cash for each $1,000 bond sold and will pay back $1,000; principal + ($50 × 20 semiannual interest payments) = $2,000. The $1,000 difference is the amount of interest expense for the 10 years. Because the effective-interest rate and the stated rate are the same, interest expense and cash interest paid are the same amount each year.

The $1,000 cash that Mason Corporation received when each bond was sold is the present value of the future cash flows associated with the bond. This is computed as follows:

		Present value
a.	Principal: $1,000 × $p_{n=20;\ i=5\%}$ (Table 10–2; 0.3769)	$ 377
b.	Interest: $50 × $P_{n=20;\ i=5\%}$ (Table 10–4; 12.4622)	623
	Issue price of one Mason bond	$1,000

Exhibit 11–2 *(continued)*

Case B—bonds issued at a discount:

On January 1, 19A, Mason issued 400 ($400,000 par) of the bonds at an effective interest rate of 12% (i.e., at price of 88.5) for $354,000 cash.

Entries during 19A:

January 1, 19A—To record issuance of the bonds at a discount:

Cash (400 bonds × $885)	354,000	
Discount on bonds payable [400 bonds × ($1,000 − $885)]	46,000*	
Bonds payable (400 bonds × $1,000)		400,000*

* Note: In effect, the bonds are recorded at their **issue price** because the liability is reported on the balance sheet net of these two balances.

Interest payments during 19A:

	June 30, 19A	December 31, 19A
Bond interest expense (cash interest plus amortized discount)	22,300	22,300
Discount on bonds payable, straight-line amortization ($46,000 ÷ 20 periods)	2,300	2,300
Cash ($400,000 × 5%)	20,000	20,000

Financial statements for 19A:

Income statement:

Bond interest expense ($22,300 × 2)	$ 44,600

Balance sheet:

Long-term liabilities:

Bonds payable, 10%, due December 31, 19J	$400,000	
Less unamortized discount	41,400*	358,600†

Or, alternatively:

Bonds payable, 10%, due December 31, 19J (maturity amount, $400,000, less unamortized discount)	358,600†

* $46,000 − $2,300 − $2,300 = $41,400.
† This amount is called the carrying value or net liability.

When the effective rate of interest is equal to the stated rate of interest, the present value of the future cash flows associated with a bond **always** will equal the bond's par amount. It is important to remember that the selling price of a bond is determined by the present value of its future cash flows, not the par value. Also, bond liabilities are initially recorded at the present value of future cash flows on date of issue, not par value.

Bonds Issued at a Discount

Bonds sell at a discount when the buyers are willing to invest in them only at a market rate of interest that is **higher** than the stated interest rate on the bonds.

EXHIBIT 11–2 *(concluded)*

Case C—bonds issued at a premium:

On January 1, 19A, Mason issued 400 ($400,000 par) of the bonds at an effective-interest rate of 8½% (i.e., at a price of 110) for $440,000 cash.

Entries during 19A:

January 1, 19A—To record issuance of the bonds at a premium:
Cash (400 bonds × $1,100) 440,000
    Premium on bonds payable [400 bonds × ($1,100 − $1,000)]   40,000
    Bonds payable (400 bonds × $1,000)   400,000

Interest payments during 19A:

	June 30, 19A	December 31, 19A
Bond interest expense (cash interest less amortized premium) 18,000		18,000
Premium on bonds payable, straight-line amortization ($40,000 ÷ 20 periods) 2,000		2,000
Cash ($400,000 × 5%)	20,000	20,000

Financial statements for 19A:

Income statement:
Bond interest expense ($18,000 × 2) . . . . $ 36,000

Balance sheet:
Long-term liabilities:
    Bonds payable, 10% (due December 31, 19J) $400,000
    Add unamortized premium . . . .   36,000 *   436,000†

Or, alternatively:
Bonds payable, 10%, due December 31, 19J (maturity amount, $400,000, plus
    unamortized premium) . . . . 436,000†

  * $40,000 − $2,000 − $2,000 = $36,000.
  † This amount is called the carrying value or net liability.

Payment of principal (face) amount at maturity date (all three situations):

December 31, 19J:

Bonds payable 400,000
    Cash   400,000

Case B (Exhibit 11–2) assumes a 12% market rate of interest for the 10-year Mason bonds. The bonds have a stated rate of 10%, payable semiannually. Therefore, the bonds sold at a **discount.** To compute the cash issue price of one bond requires computation of its present value, at the **market rate,** of the future cash flows specified on the bond: (*a*) the principal (*n* = 20, *i* = 6%) and (*b*) the cash interest paid each semiannual interest period (*n* = 20, *i* = 6%). Thus, the cash issue price of one Mason bond is computed as follows:

**Present
value**

a. Principal: $1,000 $\times$ $p_{n=20;\ i=6\%}$ (Table 10–2; 0.3118) $312

b. Interest: $50 $\times$ $P_{n=20;\ i=6\%}$ (Table 10–4; 11.4699) . . . . <u>573</u>

      Issue (sale) price of one Mason bond . . . . <u><u>$885*</u></u>

* Thus, the issue price was 88.5% of par value. Discount: $1,000 − $885 = $115.

The cash issue price of the 400 bonds issued by Mason would be $354,000 (i.e., 400 bonds $\times$ $885).

When a bond is sold at a discount, the Bonds Payable account is credited for the par amount and the **discount is recorded as a debit to Discount on Bonds Payable.** The issuance of the bonds of Mason Company at a discount is recorded as shown in Exhibit 11–2, Case B.

The journal entry to record the issuance of the bonds (Exhibit 11–2) shows the discount in a separate contra liability account (Discount on Bonds Payable) as a **debit.** The balance sheet reports the bonds payable at their **carrying value** (maturity amount less any **unamortized** discount).

Measuring and Recording Interest on Bonds Issued at a Discount

In Exhibit 11–2, Case B, the issue price of each bond was $885. During the 10-year term of the bonds, Mason must make 20 semiannual cash interest payments of $50 each (i.e., $50 $\times$ 20 = $1,000) and at maturity pay back the $1,000 cash principal. Therefore, in addition to the cash interest of $1,000, $115 more cash per bond is paid back than was borrowed (i.e., $1,000 − $885). This $115 discount on each bond causes the effective-interest rate to be 12% (instead of the 10% stated on the bonds). The discount is an adjustment of the amount of interest expense that will be **reported** each accounting period on the income statement. Bond discount represents an **increase in bond interest expense.** The bond discount must be apportioned to each semiannual interest period as an increase in interest expense from the date of issuance to maturity date. There are two methods for doing this: (1) **straight-line amortization** and (2) **effective-interest amortization.** Straight-line amortization is easy to compute. The effective-interest method is discussed later in this chapter.

Straight-Line Amortization. To amortize the $46,000 bond discount over the life of the bond on a straight-line basis, an equal dollar amount is allocated to each interest period. The Mason bonds have 20 six-month interest periods. Therefore, the computation is $46,000 ÷ 20 periods = $2,300 amortization on each semiannual interest date. The interest payment on the bonds during 19A would be recorded as shown in Exhibit 11–2, Case B.

Bonds payable should be reported on the balance sheet at their **net liability amount;** that is, the maturity amount less any unamortized bond discount or plus any unamortized bond premium. Therefore, at the end of the accounting period, December 31, 19A, the financial statements would report interest expense and bonds payable as shown in Exhibit 11–2, Case B.

Each succeeding year the unamortized discount will **decrease** by $4,600; therefore, the net liability will **increase** each year by $4,600. At the maturity date of the bonds, the unamortized discount (i.e., the balance in the Discount on Bonds Payable account) will be **zero.** At that time the maturity amount of the bonds and the current net liability amount will be the same (i.e., $400,000).

When straight-line amortization of bond discount is used, **interest expense** is computed as the **sum** of interest paid or accrued plus the amount of discount amortized (see Exhibit 11–2).

Bonds Issued at a Premium

Bonds sell at a premium when the buyers are willing to invest in bonds at a market rate of interest that is **lower** than the stated interest rate on the bonds. For example, the capital market established an 8½% market rate of interest for the 10-year Mason bonds (Exhibit 11–2, Case C, stated rate, 10%, payable on semiannual basis), which means the bonds sold at a **premium.** The cash issue price of one Mason bond is computed as follows:

	Present value
a. Principal: $1,000 × $p_{n=20;\ i=4\frac{1}{4}\%}$ (Table 10–2; 0.4350)	$ 435
b. Interest: $50 × $\mathbf{P}_{n=20;\ i=4\frac{1}{4}\%}$ (Table 10–4; 13.2944)	665
Issue (sale) price of one Mason bond	$1,100

The cash issue price of the 400 bonds issued by Mason would be $440,000 (i.e., 400 bonds × $1,100).

When a bond is sold at a premium, the Bonds Payable account is credited for the par amount, and the **premium is recorded as a credit to Premium on Bonds Payable.** The issuance of the bonds of Mason Company at a premium is recorded as shown in Exhibit 11–2, Case C.

Measuring and Recording Interest Expense on Bonds Issued at a Premium

The premium of $40,000 recorded by Mason must be apportioned to each of the 20 interest periods. Either the effective-interest method or the straight-line method may be used. Using the straight-line method, the amortization of premium each semiannual interest period would be $40,000 ÷ 20 periods = $2,000. Therefore, the payments of interest on the bonds during 19A would be recorded as shown in Exhibit 11–2, Case C.

In the journal entry to record the issuance of the bonds by Mason, the premium was recorded in a separate account, **Premium on Bonds Payable, as a credit.** Amortization of the premium **decreases** interest expense. Notice in Exhibit 11–2, Case C, that the $20,000 cash paid each period includes $18,000 interest expense and $2,000 of premium amortization. Thus, the cash payment to the investors includes the current interest they have earned plus a return of part of the premium they paid when they bought the bonds. At the end of 19A,

Exhibit 11-3 Amortization of bond discount and premium compared

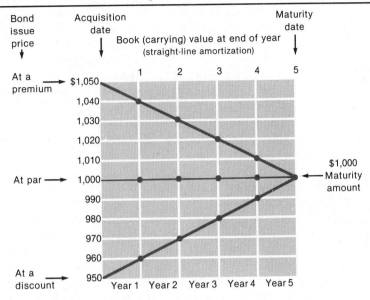

Amortization of bond discount and premium compared

the financial statements of Mason Company would report interest expense and bonds payable as shown in Exhibit 11–2, Case C.

When straight-line amortization of bond premium is used, **interest expense** is computed as interest paid or accrued **minus** the amount of premium amortized (see Exhibit 11–2).

At maturity date, after the last interest payment, the bond premium of $40,000 will be fully amortized, and the maturity amount of the bonds and the current net liability of the bonds will be the same (i.e., $400,000). At maturity, December 31, 19J, the bonds will be paid off in full, resulting in the same entry whether the bond was originally sold at par, a discount, or a premium.

The effect of amortization of bond discount and bond premium on a $1,000 bond is shown graphically in Exhibit 11–3.

PART B—ADDITIONAL TOPICS IN ACCOUNTING FOR BONDS PAYABLE

This part of the chapter discusses four problems commonly encountered in accounting for bonds payable. These poblems are (1) effective-interest amortization of bond discounts and premiums, (2) accounting for bonds sold between interest dates, (3) adjusting entries for accrued bond interest, and (4) bond sinking funds.

Effective-Interest Amortization of Bond Discounts and Premiums

The straight-line method for amortizing a bond discount or premium was discussed in Part A of this chapter. The only advantage of the straight-line method is calculational simplicity. Under GAAP, the straight-line method may be used only if the reported results are not materially different than the effective-interest method. The effective-interest method is conceptually superior, and it provides a better basis for understanding why the amortization of a bond discount or premium is an adjustment to interest expense.

Interest expense is the cost of borrowing money. Interest expense is correctly measured by multiplying the "true" interest rate times the amount of money that was actually borrowed. The "true" interest rate associated with a bond is the market rate of interest that existed on the date the bond was issued because it is the rate that is used to determine the present value of the bond. The actual amount borrowed is the issue price of the bond (i.e., its present value) not the par value of the bond.

According to GAAP, interest expense for a bond should be measured by multiplying the current unpaid balance (i.e., the carrying value of the bond) times the market rate of interest (i.e., the "true" interest rate). The periodic amortization of a bond premium or discount is then calculated as the difference between interest expense (market rate times unpaid balance) and the amount of cash paid or accrued (stated rate times principal).

Exhibit 11–4 illustrates the effective-interest method. West Corporation sold bonds with a stated interest rate of 8% when the market rate was 12%, which resulted in a discount. The entry to record the sale is shown in the exhibit. The present value of the bond is $8,558, which is the actual amount borrowed.

The West Corporation bonds pay interest once per year on December 31. The interest expense at the end of the first year is calculated by multiplying the amount that was actually borrowed by the market rate of interest ($8,558 × 12% = $1,027). The amount of cash that is paid is calculated by multiplying the principal by the stated rate of interest ($10,000 × 8% = $800). The difference between the interest expense and the cash paid (or accrued) is the amount of discount that has been amortized ($1,027 − $800 = $227). The journal entry to record interest expense on December 31, 19A, is:

```
Interest expense . . . . . . . . . . . . . . . . . . . . . . . . . . . . . . . . . . . 1,027
    Discount on bonds payable . . . . . . . . . . . . . . . . . . . . . . . . . .          227
    Cash . . . . . . . . . . . . . . . . . . . . . . . . . . . . . . . . . . . . . .          800
```

The Discount on Bonds Payable account is a contra liability with a debit balance. The credit amount ($227) in the previous entry reduces the balance of the Discount on Bonds Payable account. A reduction of a contra liability account increases the book value of the liability, as shown below:

	January 1, 19A	**December 31, 19A**
Bonds payable	$10,000	$10,000
Discount on bonds payable . . .	1,442	1,215*
Book value	$ 8,558	$ 8,785

* $1,442 − $227 = $1,215.

Exhibit 11–4 Effective-interest amortization on bond discount

---

Situation: West Corporation sold ten, $1,000 bonds as follows:

Bonds payable authorized (10 bonds at $1,000 par each)	$10,000
Date printed on each bond	January 1, 19A
Maturity date (five-year term from January 1, 19A)	December 31, 19E
Interest, **cash payable per annum** each December 31, 8%	$800
Issued (sold) all of the bonds	January 1, 19A
Market interest rate	12%
Sale price (at a discount)	$8,558*
End of the accounting period for West	December 31

* Issue price computed as follows:
$10,000 × $P_{n=5; \; i=12\%}$ (Table 10–2; 0.5674) = $5,674
$800 × $P_{n=5; \; i=12\%}$ (Table 10–4; 3.6048) = 2,884
$8,558

Entry to record issuance (sale) of the bonds at a discount:

January 1, 19A:

Cash (computed above)	8,558	
Discount on bonds payable ($10,000 − $8,558)	1,442	
Bonds payable (10 bonds × $1,000 par)		10,000

Bond payment schedule, effective-interest amortization:

(a)	(b)	(c)	(d)	(e)
	Cash Interest Paid on Each Interest Date	Interest Expense (based on beginning unpaid liability at market rate	Effective-Interest Amortization (increase of	Net Liability (unpaid
Date	($10,000 × 8%)	of 12%)	liability)*	balance)
1/1/19A				$ 8,558
12/31/19A	$ 800	$8,558 × 12% = $1,027	$ 227	8,785
12/31/19B	800	8,785 × 12% = 1,054	254	9,039
12/31/19C	800	9,039 × 12% = 1,085	285	9,324
12/31/19D	800	9,324 × 12% = 1,119	319	9,643
12/31/19E	800	9,643 × 12% = 1,157	357	10,000
Subtotal	4,000	$5,442	1,442	
12/31/19E	$10,000†		$10,000	–0–

* Adjusts the net liability to the maturity amount.
† Payment of principal.

Each period the amortization of the bond discount increases the book value (or unpaid balance) of the bond. The $227 amortization of bond discount can be thought of as interest that was earned by the bondholders but not paid to them. During 19A, the bondholders earned interest of $1,027 but only $800 was paid in cash. The additional $227 was added to the principal of the bond and will be paid when the bond matures.

Interest expense at the end of 19B must reflect the change in the unpaid balance of bonds payable that occurred with the amortization of the bond discount. The interest expense for 19B is calculated by multiplying the unpaid balance at the end of 19A by the market rate of interest ($8,785 × 12% = $1,054). The entry to record interest expense on December 31, 19B, is:

Interest Expense	1,054	
Discount on bonds payable		254
Cash		800

Notice that interest expense for 19B is greater than the amount for 19A. This is logical because West Corporation effectively borrowed more money in 19B (i.e., the $227 unpaid interest).

An organized approach for applying the effective-interest amortization method is a debt payment schedule shown in Exhibit 11–4. The amounts needed for recording interest expense each period are shown in columns *b, c,* and *d.* The book value (unpaid balance) of the liability each year is shown in column *e.*

While the effective-interest method is preferred conceptually, some companies use the straight-line method because of the materiality constraint (Exhibit 4–5). Accounting for various transactions should be in conformity with generally accepted accounting principles (GAAP) unless the amounts involved are immaterial and will not affect the decisions made by users of the statements. The straight-line method is permitted when the difference in periodic amortization between the two methods is not material in amount.

Accounting for Bonds Sold between Interest Dates

Although bonds may be sold on an interest date, most are sold **between interest dates.** The exact amount of interest stated on the bond certificate for each interest date will be paid, regardless of when the bond is sold. Therefore, when bonds are sold between two interest dates, the buyer must pay the interest that has **accrued since the last interest date** in addition to the market price of the bond. The amount of the next interest payment will be for a **full interest period;** therefore, the accrued interest is returned to the buyer. The net effect is that the investor will realize interest revenue only for the number of months the bonds were held from the date of sale. Similarly, the issuing corporation will incur interest expense for the same period. This case presents two complexities in accounting for bonds: (1) the amount of accrued interest charged to the buyer must be included in the journal entry of the issuer to record the sale of bonds; and (2) any premium or discount must be amortized by the issuer over the remaining period that the bonds will be outstanding, that is, the period from date of sale to date of maturity of the bonds.

To illustrate accounting for bonds sold between interest dates, we will use data for Mendez Corporation (Exhibit 11–5). When Mendez sold the bonds on August 1, 19A, it received cash for the sale price of the bonds, plus two months' accrued interest (June 1, 19A, to July 31, 19A), computed as follows:

Exhibit 11–5 Accounting for bonds sold between interest dates

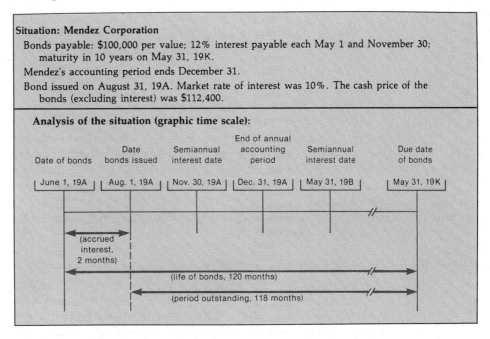

Situation: Mendez Corporation

Bonds payable: $100,000 per value; 12% interest payable each May 1 and November 30; maturity in 10 years on May 31, 19K.

Mendez's accounting period ends December 31.

Bond issued on August 31, 19A. Market rate of interest was 10%. The cash price of the bonds (excluding interest) was $112,400.

Analysis of the situation (graphic time scale):

			End of annual		
Date of bonds	Date bonds issued	Semiannual interest date	accounting period	Semiannual interest date	Due date of bonds
June 1, 19A	Aug. 1, 19A	Nov. 30, 19A	Dec. 31, 19A	May 31, 19B	May 31, 19K

(accrued interest, 2 months)

(life of bonds, 120 months)

(period outstanding, 118 months)

Market price	$112,400
Add accrued interest for 2 months (June and July):	
$100,000 × 12% × 2/12	2,000
Total cash received	$114,400

The bond investors must pay two months' accrued interest to Mendez because the bond contract requires that Mendez pay a full six months of interest on each interest date. On the first interest date, the bonds will have been outstanding for only four months (August 1 through November 30). Therefore, on November 30, 19A, the investors have earned only four months' interest revenue, but Mendez must pay six months' interest in cash. Payment by the investor to the issuer of two months' accrued interest when the bonds are purchased is an offset that causes interest to be adjusted to a four-month basis for both the investor and the issuer.

To record the sale of the bonds on August 1, 19A, Mendez would make the following journal entry:

Cash	114,400	
Bonds payable		100,000
Interest payable		2,000
Premium on bonds payable		12,400

On the date of the first interest payment, Mendez will record interest expense for only four months because the debt has been outstanding for less than a full interest period. Under the effective-interest method, the calculation is as follows:

$$\frac{\text{Unpaid balance}}{\$112,400} \times \frac{\text{Market rate}}{10\%} \times \frac{\text{Time}}{4/12} = \frac{\text{Interest expense}}{\$3,747}$$

The journal entry to record interest expense is:

Interest expense	3,747	
Interest payable	2,000	
Premium on bonds payable ($4,000 − $3,747)	253	
Cash		6,000

The amortization of bond premium is the difference between the interest expense for four months and the cash interest that accrued for four months ($4,000 − $3,747 = $253). If the straight-line method were used, it would be necessary to amortize the premium over the actual time the bond is outstanding (118 months). The straight-line amortization would be $420 ($12,400 × 4/118 months), and interest expense would be $3,580 ($4,000 − $420).

Adjusting Entry for Accrued Bond Interest

In Chapter 10, we discussed the adjusting entry that must be made for any accrued interest expense at the end of an accounting period. The same adjustment procedure must be applied to bonds payable. In the case of bonds, the adjusting entry must include **both the accrued interest and amortization of any bond discount or premium.** Mendez Corporation (Exhibit 11–5) recorded an interest payment on November 30, 19A. Therefore, on December 31, 19A, there is accrued interest for one month. Bond premium also must be amortized for one more month. Under the effective-interest amortization method, interest expense is always calculated by multiplying the unpaid balance of the liability at the beginning of the interest period by the market rate of interest on the date of issuance. The unpaid balance for Mendez is the sale price minus the premium that was amortized on November 30, 19A ($112,400 − $253 = $112,147). Accrued interest expense is $935 ($112,147 × 10% × 1/12). The adjusting entry for Mendez is:

Interest expense	935	
Premium on bonds payable ($1,000 − $935)	65	
Interest payable ($100,000 × 12% × 1/12)		1,000

The demonstration case illustrates accounting for accrued interest under the straight-line method.

Bond Sinking Funds

On the maturity date of bonds payable, the issuing company must have available a large amount of cash to pay off the bondholders. A demand for a large amount of cash might place the issuing company in a financial strain. To avoid this situation, some companies create a separate **cash fund** by making **equal** annual **contributions** over a period of time in advance of the bond maturity date.

Exhibit 11-6 Accounting for a bond sinking fund

Situation:

Mendez Corporation plans to accumulate a bond sinking fund sufficient to retire the $100,000 bond issue outstanding on maturity date, May 31, 19K (Exhibit 11-5). Five equal annual deposits are to be made on each May 31, starting in 19G. Expected earning rate on the fund is 8%.

Computation of periodic deposits ($n = 5$, years G through K; $i = 8\%$):

Computation (application of future value of annuity of $1):
Future value = Periodic payment $\times$ F$_{n=5;\ i=8\%}$
Substituting:
$100,000 = $? $\times$ 5.8666 (Table 10–3)
Periodic payment = $100,000 \div 5.8666$
= $\underline{\$\ 17,046}$

Entries—for first year of the fund and the second deposit:

May 31,19G—To record the first deposit by Mendez:

Bond sinking fund	17,046	
Cash (computed above)		17,046

May 31, 19H—to record interest revenue for one year added to the fund:

Bond sinking fund (notice, not the Cash account)	1,364	
Interest revenue ($17,046 $\times$ 8%)		1,364

May 31, 19H—to record the second deposit by Mendez:

Bond sinking fund	17,046	
Cash (computed above)		17,046

Entry at maturity date (May 31, 19K) to retire the bonds:

Bonds payable	100,000	
Bond sinking fund		100,000

Sinking fund accumulation schedule (deposits, $17,046; $n = 5$; $i = 8\%$):

Date	Cash Deposit (credit Cash)	Interest Revenue (credit)	Fund Increase (debit Fund)	Accumulated Fund Balance
5/31/19G	$17,046[a]		$ 17,046	$ 17,046
5/31/19H	17,046	$17,046 $\times$ 8% = $ 1,364[b]	18,410[c]	35,456[d]
5/31/19I	17,046	35,456 $\times$ 8% = 2,836	19,882	55,338
5/31/19J	17,046	55,338 $\times$ 8% = 4,427	21,473	76,811
5/31/19K	17,046	76,811 $\times$ 8% = 6,143*	23,189	100,000
Totals	$85,230	$14,770	$100,000	

* Rounded $2 to accommodate prior rounding errors.
[a] Computed above.
[b] Interest earned on beginning balance in the fund each period at 8%.
[c] Periodic deposit ($17,046) plus interest earned ($1,364) = $18,410 (etc.)
[d] Prior balance ($17,046) plus increase in fund ($18,410) = $35,456 (etc.).

This separate cash fund is called a **bond sinking fund.** A bond sinking fund is an asset that is invested pending the due date of the bonds. It is reported on the balance sheet under the caption "Investments and funds."

A bond sinking fund also reduces the risk of nonpayment for the bondholders. It assures them that funds will be available for retirement of the bonds at their maturity date. Each cash contribution to the fund is deposited with an **independent trustee** (a designated third party such as a bank or another financial institution). The trustee invests the funds and adds the fund earnings to the fund balance each year. Interest earned on a sinking fund is recorded as an increase in the fund balance (a debit) and as interest revenue (a credit). Thus, a bond sinking fund has the characteristics of a savings account as shown in Chapter 10, Part B. At the maturity date of the bonds, the balance of the fund is used to pay the bondholders. Any excess cash is returned to the issuing corporation, or in the case of a deficit, it is made up by the issuer.

Exhibit 11–6 illustrates a bond sinking fund for Mendez Corporation. The fund will be built up over the last five years that the bonds are outstanding by making five equal annual deposits each May 31, starting in 19G. The sinking fund contributions will be deposited with City Bank, as trustee, which will pay 8% annual interest on the fund balance each May 31. The amount of each deposit required can be calculated using the time value of money concepts discussed and illustrated in Chapter 10, Part B. If the fund earned no interest, each deposit would have to be $20,000 (i.e., $100,000 ÷ 5 contributions = $20,000). Instead of $20,000, the annual deposit required is **less** than $20,000 because the interest earned each year will be added to the fund balance. The $17,046 required annual deposit was computed as shown in Exhibit 11–6.

The journal entries for May 31, 19G, and 19H, for the sinking fund are shown in Exhibit 11–6. Notice that the fund is increased by both the annual deposits and the accumulation of interest. Identical journal entries with different interest amounts would be made for each of the five years of the accumulation period. The interest amounts increase each year because of the increasing balance in the fund. At the maturity date of the bonds, payment will be made to the bondholders using the cash accumulated in the sinking fund. The journal entry to retire the bonds payable is shown in the exhibit.

Often it is useful to prepare a fund accumulation schedule as shown in Exhibit 11–6. Notice that the schedule provides data for (1) the entry on each interest date and (2) the buildup of the fund to maturity date.

DEMONSTRATION CASE

(Try to resolve the requirements before proceeding to the suggested solution that follows.)

To raise funds to build a new plant, the management of Reed Company issued bonds. A bond indenture was approved by the board of directors. Some provisions in the bond indenture and specified on the bond certificates were:

Par value of the bonds ($1,000 bonds), $600,000

Date of bond issue—February 1, 19A; due in 10 years on January 31, 19K.

Interest—10% per annum, payable 5% on each July 31 and January 31.

All of the bonds were sold on June 1, 19A, at 102½, plus accrued interest. The annual accounting period for Reed Company ends on December 31.

Required:

    a. How much cash was received by Reed Company from the sale of the bonds payable on June 1, 19A? Show computations.

    b. What was the amount of premium on the bonds payable? Over how many months should it be amortized?

    c. Compute the amount of amortization of premium per month and for each six-month interest period; use straight-line amortization. Round to the nearest dollar.

    d. Give the journal entry on June 1, 19A, to record the sale and issuance of the bonds payable.

    e. Give the journal entry for payment of interest and amortization of premium for the first interest payment on July 31, 19A.

    f. Give the adjusting entry required on December 31, 19A, at the end of the accounting period.

    g. Give the journal entry to record the second interest payment and the amortization of premium on January 31, 19B.

    h. Show how bond interest expense and bonds payable are reported on the financial statements at December 31, 19A.

Suggested Solution

Requirement a:

Sale price of the bonds: ($600,000 × 102.5%)	$615,000
Add accrued interest for four months (February 1 to May 31)	
($600,000 × 10% × 4/12)	20,000
Total cash received for the bonds	$635,000

Requirement b:

Premium on the bonds payable ($600,000 × 2.5%)	$ 15,000
Months amortized: From date of sale, June 1, 19A, to maturity date,	
January 31, 19K (120 months − 4 months)	116 months

Requirement c:

Premium amortization: $15,000 ÷ 116 months = $129 per month, or $774 each six-month interest period (straight line).

Requirement d:
June 1, 19A (issuance date):

Cash (per Requirement [a] above)	635,000	
Premium on bonds payable (per Requirement [b] above)		15,000
Interest expense (per Requirement [a] above)		20,000
Bonds payable		600,000

To record sale of bonds payable at 102½ plus accrued interest for four
months, February 1 to May 31, 19A.

Requirement e:
July 31, 19A (first interest payment date):

Bond interest expense ($30,000 − $258)	29,742	
Premium on bonds payable ($129 × 2 months)	258	
Cash ($600,000 × 5%)		30,000

To record payment of semiannual interest and to amortize
premium for two months, June 1 to July 31, 19A.

Requirement f:
December 31, 19A (end of the accounting period):

Bond interest expense	24,355	
Premium on bonds payable ($129 × 5 months)	645	
Bond interest payable ($600,000 × 10% × 5/12)		25,000

Adjusting entry for five months' interest accrued plus amortization
of premium, August 1 to December 31, 19A.

Requirement g:
January 31, 19B (second interest date):

Bond interest payable	25,000	
Premium on bonds payable	129	
Bond interest expense	4,871	
Cash		30,000

To record payment of semiannual interest.

Requirement h:

Interest expense reported on the 19A income statement should be for the period
outstanding during the year (i.e., for seven months, June 1 through December
31). Interest expense, per the above entries, is $29,742 + $24,355 − $20,000 =
$34,097; or alternatively, ($600,000 × 10% × 7/12 = $35,000) − ($129 × 7
months = $903) = $34,097.

Income statement for 19A:
Interest expense $34,097

Balance sheet, December 31, 19A:
Long-term liabilities:
Bonds payable, 10% (due January 31, 19K) . . . $600,000
Add unamortized premium* . . . . <u>14,097</u>   614,097

* $15,000 − ($258 + $645) = $14,097.

SUMMARY OF CHAPTER

This chapter discussed bonds payable, which represent a primary way to obtain funds to acquire long-term assets and to expand a business. An important advantage of bonds payable is that the **cost** of borrowing the funds—interest expense—is deductible for income tax purposes which reduces the interest cost to the business.

Bonds may be sold at their par amount, at a premium, or at a discount, depending on the stated interest rate on the bonds compared with the market rate of interest. In each case, bonds are recorded at the present value of their future cash flows. The price of a bond varies based on the relationship between the market and stated rates of interest. If the market rate is higher than the stated rate on the bond, the bonds will sell at a discount. Conversely, if the market rate is lower than the stated rate on the bond, the bonds will sell at a premium.

Discounts and premiums on bonds payable are adjustments to interest expense for the issuing company during the term of the bonds. Therefore, discount or premium on bonds payable is amortized over the period outstanding from issue date to maturity date.

To assure that funds are available to retire bonds payable at maturity, a company may set aside cash in advance by means of periodic contributions to a bond sinking fund. Such a fund is like a savings account. The bond sinking fund usually is administered by an independent trustee. Interest earned on the fund balance is added to the fund each period. At the maturity date of the bonds, the fund is used to pay the bondholders. The fund is reported on the balance sheet under the caption "Investments and funds." Interest earned on the fund is reported on the income statement as "Interest revenue."

IMPORTANT TERMS DEFINED IN THIS CHAPTER

Bond Certificate The bond document; each bondholder receives a bond certificate. *p. 538*

Bond Discount A bond that is sold for less than par is sold at a discount; the difference between selling price and par. *p. 543*

Bond Premium A bond that is sold for more than par is sold at a premium; the difference between selling price and par. *p. 546*

Bond Principal The amount payable at the maturity of the bond; face amount. *p. 538*

Bond Sinking Fund A cash fund accumulated for payment of a bond at maturity. *p. 552*

Callable Bond A bond that may be called for early retirement at the option of the issuer. *p. 539*

Convertible Bond A bond that may be converted to other securities of the issuer (usually common stock). *p. 539*

Coupon Rate of Interest The stated rate of interest on coupon bonds. *p. 541*

Debenture An unsecured bond; no assets are specifically pledged to guarantee repayment. *p. 539*

Effective-Interest Amortization Theoretically preferred method to amortize a bond discount or premium; interest expense is based on the effective-interest rate. *p. 548*

Effective-Interest Rate Another name for the market rate of interest on a bond when issued; also called the yield rate. *p. 541*

Face Amount Another name for principal or the principal amount of a bond. *p. 538*

Financial Leverage Use of borrowed funds to increase the rate of return on owners' equity; occurs when the interest rate on debt is lower than the earnings rate on total assets. *p. 540*

Indenture A bond contract that specifies the legal provisions of a bond issue. *p. 538*

Market Interest Rate Current rate of interest on a debt when incurred; also called yield or effective rate. *p. 540*

Net Interest Cost Interest cost, less any income tax savings associated with interest expense. *p. 540*

Par Value Another name for bond principal or the maturity amount of a bond. *p. 538*

Redeemable Bond Bond that may be turned in for early retirement at the option of the bondholder. *p. 539*

Stated Rate The rate of cash interest per period specified in the bond contract. *p. 541*

Straight-Line Amortization Simplified method to amortize a bond discount or premium. *p. 545*

Trustee An independent party appointed to represent the bondholders. *p. 538*

Yield Interest Rate Another name for the market rate of interest on a bond. *p. 541*

QUESTIONS

Part A: Questions 1–14

1. What are the primary characteristics of a bond? For what purposes are bonds usually issued?
2. What is the difference between a bond indenture and a bond certificate?
3. Distinguish between secured and unsecured bonds.
4. Distinguish among callable, redeemable, and convertible bonds.

5. Distinguish between registered and coupon bonds.

6. From the perspective of the issuer, what are some advantages of issuing bonds, as compared with issuing capital stock?

7. As the tax rate increases, the net cost of borrowing money decreases. Explain.

8. Explain financial leverage. Can financial leverage be negative?

9. At the date of issuance, bonds are recorded at their current cash equivalent amount. Explain.

10. What is the nature of the discount and premium on bonds payable? Explain.

11. What is the difference between the stated interest rate and the effective-interest rate on a bond?

12. Distinguish between the stated and effective rates of interest on a bond (*a*) sold at par, (*b*) sold at a discount, and (*c*) sold at a premium.

13. Why are bond discounts and premiums amortized over the outstanding life of the related bonds payable rather than the period from the date of the bonds to their maturity date?

14. What is the carrying value of a bond payable?

Part B: Questions 15–18

15. Why is the lender (i.e., the purchaser of a bond) charged for the accrued interest from the last interest date to the date of purchase of the bonds?

16. If a 10-year bond dated January 1, 19A, is sold on April 1, 19B, how many months are used as the period outstanding for amortizing any bond premium or discount?

17. What is a bond sinking fund? How should a bond sinking fund be reported in the financial statements?

18. Explain the basic difference between straight-line amortization and effective-interest amortization of bond discount or premium. Explain when each method should, or may, be used.

EXERCISES

Part A: Exercises 11–1 to 11–7

E11–1 **(Match Definitions with Terms)**
Match each definition with its related term by entering the appropriate letter in the space provided.

Terms	Definitions
_____ (1) Secured bonds	A. Amount payable at due date (other than interest).
_____ (2) Principal of a bond	
_____ (3) Stated interest rate on a bond	B. An individual or company that is engaged by bond issuers to sell bonds.
_____ (4) Trustee (related to a bond issue)	C. Arises when a bond is sold for less than its par amount.

Terms	Definitions
_____ (5) Par value of a bond	D. Bond supported by a mortgage on specified assets.
_____ (6) Bond premium	E. Same as the face or maturity amount of a bond.
_____ (7) Carrying value of a bond	F. The amount of cash interest that must be paid regardless of its issue price.
_____ (8) Bond indenture	G. An independent party appointed to represent bondholders.
_____ (9) Underwriter	H. Same as the market or yield rate of interest on a bond.
_____ (10) Bond discount	I. Arises when a bond is sold for more than its par amount.
_____ (11) Financial leverage	
_____ (12) Primary disadvantage of bonds payable	J. A contract that specifies the legal provisions of a bond issue.
_____ (13) Present and par value of a bond are the same	K. Present value of the future cash flows related to a bond.
	L. A bond sold at its par value.
_____ (14) Effective-interest rate	M. Issue price of a bond less any amortized premium or plus any amortized discount.
_____ (15) Bond issue or selling price	N. Net interest rate on debt is different from interest rate earned on total assets.
	O. Cash payments of interest and principle required, regardless of income or loss.

E11–2 (Match Bond Characteristics with Bond Classifications)

Match each bond characteristic with its related bond classification by entering the answer code in the space provided.

Bond classification	Bond characteristics
_____ (1) Serial bonds	A. Bonds with parts attached that are turned in to receive interest.
_____ (2) Unsecured bonds	B. Bonds that are retired early on request of the issuer.
_____ (3) Convertible bonds	C. The principal amount is payable at a single maturity date.
_____ (4) Ordinary bonds	D. Bonds that may be turned in for early retirement at the option of the bondholders.
_____ (5) Coupon bonds	E. Principal amount is payable in installments.
_____ (6) Redeemable bonds	F. Do not include a mortgage on specific assets.
_____ (7) Registered bonds	G. Bonds that include pledged assets to assure payment at maturity.
_____ (8) Callable bonds	H. Bonds that may be exchanged for other securities at the option of the bondholder.
_____ (9) Secured bonds	I. Interest payments are made by check directly to the bondholders on each interest date.

E11–3   **(Compute Issue Prices of Bonds for Three Cases; Record Bond Issuances)**
Katt Corporation is planning to issue $100,000, five-year, 10% bonds. Interest is payable semiannually each June 30 and December 31. All of the bonds will be sold on January 1, 19A. The bonds mature on December 31, 19E.

Required:

a.   Compute the issue (sale) price on January 1, 19A, for each of the following three independent cases (show computations):

   Case A—market (yield) rate, 10%.

   Case B—market (yield) rate, 8%.

   Case C—market (yield) rate, 12%.

b.   Give the journal entry to record the issuance for each case.

E11–4   **(Record Bond Issue and First Interest Payment, with Discount; Verify Issue Price)**
On January 1, 19A, Fair Corporation sold a $300,000, 7% bond issue (8% market rate). The bonds were dated January 1, 19A, and pay interest each December 31. The bonds mature 10 years from January 1, 19A.

Required:

a.   Give the journal entry to record the issuance of the bonds.

b.   Give the journal entry to record the interest payment on December 31, 19A. Assume straight-line amortization.

c.   Show how the bond interest expense and the bonds payable should be reported on the December 31, 19A, annual financial statements.

E11–5   **(Record Bond Issue and First Interest Payment, with Premium; Show Reporting and Verify the Issue Price)**
Market Corporation sold a $150,000, 10% bond issue on January 1, 19A, at a market rate of 9%. The bonds were dated January 1, 19A, and interest is paid each December 31. The bonds mature 10 years from January 1, 19A.

Required:

a.   Give the journal entry to record the issuance of the bonds.

b.   Give the journal entry for the interest payment on December 31, 19A. Assume straight-line amortization.

c.   Show how the bond interest expense and the bonds payable should be reported on the December 31, 19A, annual financial statements.

E11–6   **(Analysis to Determine Bond Issue Price and Stated Interest Rate; Entries for Issuance and Interest)**
Mopac Corporation had $200,000, 10-year coupon bonds outstanding on December 31, 19A (end of the accounting period). Interest is payable each December 31. The bonds were issued (sold) on January 1, 19A. The 19A annual financial statements showed the following:

> **Income statement:**
> Bond interest expense (straight-line amortization)   . . . $ 18,800
> **Balance sheet:**
> Bonds payable (net liability)   192,800

Required (show computations):

a. What was the issue price of the bonds? Give the issuance entry.

b. What was the coupon rate on the bonds? Give the entry to record 19A interest.

E11–7   (Cash Borrowed; Analyze Financing Cost (Net of Tax) and Determine Financial Leverage)

On January 1, 19A, Rockpoint Corporation borrowed $200,000 on a three-year note payable. The interest rate is 10% per annum, payable each year-end. The company computed its return on total assets [i.e., Net income ÷ (Liabilities + Owners' equity)] to be 20%. The average income tax rate for the company is 30%.

Required:

a. What amount of interest would be paid for 19A?

b. Considering the effect of income tax, what would be the net interest cost and the net interest rate (net of income tax)?

c. Would financial leverage be present in this situation? Explain.

d. List two primary advantages to the company in favor of the note payable versus selling more of its unissued capital stock to obtain needed funds.

Part B: Exercises 11–8 to 11–14

E11–8   (Accrued Interest on Bond Issue Date; Record Issuance; Reporting at Year-End)

Windsor Corporation authorized the issuance of $300,000, 10-year, 9% bonds. The bonds are dated January 1, 19A. The interest is payable each June 30 and December 31.

On September 1, 19A, the company issued (sold) $200,000 of the bonds at 98 plus any accrued interest. The accounting period ends December 31.

Required:

a. How much cash did the company receive on September 1, 19A? Show computations.

b. Give the journal entry to record the issuance.

c. How much interest expense should be reported on the 19A income statement? Use straight-line amortization.

d. Show how the bonds should be reported on the 19A balance sheet.

E11–9   (Accrued Interest on Bond Issue Date; Straight-Line Amortization; Reporting)

Yale Corporation issued the following bonds:

> Bonds payable authorized $60,000
> Date on each bond . . . . Jan. 1, 19A
> Maturity date (10 years) . . . . Dec. 31, 19J
> Interest, 10% per year, payable each December 31.

The company sold all of the bonds on April 1, 19A, and received $63,255 cash which included the accrued interest.

Required:

a. What was the amount of accrued interest and the discount or premium on issuance date?

b. Over what period of time should the discount or premium be amortized?

c. What would be the amortization amount per month assuming straight-line amortization?

d. Give the journal entry to record the issuance.

e. Give the journal entry on first interest payment date.

f. What amount should be reported as interest expense for 19A?

g. What amount of net liability should be shown on the balance sheet at December 31, 19A?

E11–10   (Effective-Interest Amortization of a Bond Discount)

Bay Corporation issued $10,000, 9% bonds dated April 1, 19A. The market rate of interest was 10%. Interest is paid each March 31. The bonds mature in three years on March 31, 19D. The accounting period ends each December 31.

Required:

a. Give the journal entry to record the bond issuance on April 1, 19A.

b. Give the adjusting entry required on December 31, 19A. Use effective-interest amortization.

c. Show how the bonds should be reported on the balance sheet at December 31, 19A?

d. Give the journal entry to record the first interest payment on March 31, 19B.

E11–11   (Accounting and Reporting for a Bond Sinking Fund; Compute the Annual Contribution Needed)

Pike Corporation has a $100,000 bond issue outstanding that is due four years hence. It wants to set up a bond sinking fund for this amount by making five equal annual contributions. The first contribution will be made immediately (December 31, 19A), and the last one on the due date (i.e., an ordinary annuity). The corporation will deposit the annual contributions with a trustee who will increase the fund at the end of each year at 8% on the fund balance that existed at the beginning of the year.

Required:

a. Compute the required annual contribution to the fund.

b. Give the journal entry for the first and second contributions, including interest.

c. Show how the effects of the fund would be reported on the financial statements at the end of the second year.

d. Give the entry to pay the bondholders at maturity date assuming the bond sinking fund has the exact amount needed.

E11–12   (Accounting and Reporting for a Bond Sinking Fund; Fund Accumulation Schedule; Entries)

Grant Company has a $90,000 debt that will be due at the end of three years. The management will deposit three equal year-end amounts in a debt retirement fund (i.e., an ordinary annuity). The fund balance will earn 8% interest which will be added to the fund at each year-end.

Required:

a. Prepare a fund accumulation schedule as shown in the chapter. Round to the nearest dollar and show computations.

b. Give the journal entry(s) at the end of the second year to record the increase in the fund.

c. Did the earnings on the fund increase the balance of the company's Cash account? Explain.

E11–13   **(Analyze a Bond Amortization Schedule; Reporting Bonds Payable)**
Collins Corporation issued a $1,000 bond on January 1, 19A. The bond specified an interest rate of 8% payable at the end of each year. The bond matures at the end of 19C. It was sold at a market rate of 9% per year. The following schedule was completed:

	Cash	Interest	Amortization	Balance
January 1, 19A (issuance) . . .				$ 975
End of year A	$80	$88	$8	983
End of year B	80	88	8	991
End of year C	80	89	9	1,000

Required:

a. What was the issue price of the bond?

b. Did the bond sell at a discount or a premium? How much was the premium or discount?

c. What amount of cash was paid each year for bond interest?

d. What amount of interest expense should be shown each year on the income statement?

e. What amount(s) should be shown on the balance sheet for bonds payable at each year-end (for year C, show the balance just before retirement of the bond)?

f. What method of amortization was used?

g. Show how the following amounts were computed for year B: (1) $80, (2) $88, (3) $8, and (4) $991.

h. Is the method of amortization that was used preferable? Explain why.

E11–14   **(Prepare a Debt Payment Schedule with Effective-Interest Amortization; Entries)**
Butle Company issued a $10,000, three-year, 11% bond on January 1, 19A. The bond interest is paid each December 31. The bond was sold to yield 10%.

Required:

a. Complete a bond payment schedule. Use the effective-interest method.

b. Give the interest and amortization entry at the end of 19A, 19B, and 19C.

PROBLEMS

Part A: Problems 11-1 to 11-6

P11-1   **(Bonds Issued at Par, Discount, and Premium Compared; Entries and Reporting)**
Woody Corporation, whose annual accounting period ends on December 31, issued the following bonds:

Date of bonds: January 1, 19A.

Maturity amount and date: $100,000 due in 10 years (December 31, 19J).

Interest: 11% per annum payable each December 31.

Date sold: January 1, 19A.

Required:

a. Give the journal entry to record the issuance and the first two interest payments under each of the three different independent cases (assume straight-line amortization):

Case A—bonds sold at par.

Case B—bonds sold at 98.

Case C—bonds sold at 104.

b. Provide the following amounts to be reported on the 19A financial statements:

	Case A	Case B	Case C
1. Interest expense	$ _____	$ _____	$ _____
2. Bonds payable	_____	_____	_____
3. Unamortized premium or discount . . .	_____	_____	_____
4. Net liability	_____	_____	_____
5. Stated rate of interest	_____	_____	_____
6. Cash interest paid	_____	_____	_____

c. Explain why Items 1 and 6 are different in Requirement (b).

P11-2   **(Compute Issue Price of Bonds; Record Issuance and Interest Payments; Reporting)**
Ward Company issued bonds with the following provisions:

Maturity value: $500,000.

Interest: 11% per annum payable semiannually each June 30 and December 31.

Terms: Bonds dated January 1, 19A, due five years from that date.

The annual accounting period ends December 31. The bonds were sold on January 1, 19A, at a 10% market rate.

Required:

a. Compute the issue (sale) price of the bonds (show computations).

b. Give the journal entry to record issuance of the bonds.

c. Give the journal entries at the following dates (use straight-line amortization): June 30, 19A; December 31, 19A; and June 30, 19B.

d. How much interest expense would be reported on the income statement for 19A? Show how the liability related to the bonds should be reported on the December 31, 19A, balance sheet.

P11-3   **(A Comprehensive Analysis of the Issuance of Bonds at Par, Discount, and Premium; No Entries)**

On January 1, 19A, Commonwealth Corporation sold and issued $100,000, five-year, 8% bonds. The bond interest is payable annually each December 31. Assume the bonds were sold under three separate and independent cases: Case A, at par; Case B, at 95; and Case C, at 105.

Required:

a. Complete a schedule similar to the following for each separate case assuming straight-line amortization of discount and premium. Disregard income tax. Give all dollar amounts in thousands.

	At Start of 19A	At End of 19A	At End of 19B	At End of 19C	At End of 19D	At End of 19E Prior to Payment of Principal	At End of 19E Payment of Principal
Case A—sold at par (100): Pretax cash inflow	$	$	$	$	$	$	$
Pretax cash outflow							
Interest expense on income statement							
Net liability on balance sheet							
Case B—sold at a discount (95): Pretax cash inflow							
Pretax cash outflow							
Interest expense on income statement							
Net liability on balance sheet							
Case C—sold at a premium (105): Pretax cash inflow							
Pretax cash outflow							
Interest expense on income statement							
Net liability on balance sheet							

   b. For each separate case, calculate each of the following:
   (1) Total pretax cash outflow.
   (2) Total pretax cash inflow.
   (3) Difference—net pretax cash outflow.
   (4) Total pretax interest expense.
   c. (1) Explain why the net pretax cash outflows differ among the three cases.
   (2) For each case, explain why the net pretax cash outflow is the same amount as total interest expense.

P11–4   (Analysis of Differences among Bonds Issued at Par, Discount, and Premium; Issuance and Interest Entries)
Jentz Corporation sold a $200,000, 8% bond issue on January 1, 19A. The bonds pay interest each December 31 and will mature 10 years from January 1, 19A. For comparative study and analysis, assume three separate cases. Use straight-line amortization and disregard income tax unless specifically required.

   Case A—bonds sold at par.

   Case B—bonds sold at 97.

   Case C—bonds sold at 103.

Required:
a. Complete the following schedule to analyze the differences among the three cases.

	Case A (par)	Case B (at 97)	Case C (at 103)
1. Cash inflow at issue (sale) date			
2. Total cash outflow through maturity date			
3. Difference—total interest expense			
Income statement for 19A:			
4. Bond interest expense, pretax			
Balance sheet at December 31, 19A:			
Long-term liabilities:			
5. Bonds payable, 8%			
6. Unamortized discount			
7. Unamortized premium			
8. Net liability			
9. Stated interest rate			
10. Total interest expense, net of income tax (30% tax rate)			

   b. Give the journal entries for each case on January 1, 19A, and December 31, 19A (excluding closing entries).
   c. For each case, explain why the amounts in Items 3, 4, and 10 of Requirement (*a*) are the same, or different.

P11–5   (Computation and Explanation of Financial Leverage)
The 19A financial statements of Provo Corporation provided the following data:

Balance sheet:
Total assets $100,000
Total liabilities (average interest rate is 10%) .   60,000
Total stockholders' equity   40,000

Income statement:

Total revenues $150,000
Total expenses (including pretax interest) . . . 135,000

Pretax income 15,000

Income tax ($15,000 × 30%) 4,500

Net income . . . . $ 10,500

Required:

a. Compute the following:
   (1) Return on stockholders' equity.
   (2) Return on total assets.
   (3) Financial leverage.

b. Is the financial leverage positive or negative? Explain.

P11–6   **(Compute, Interpret, and Compare Financial Leverage for Two Companies in the Same Industry)**

The information given below is from the 19B annual financial statements of two competing companies in the same industry. Each company had 50,000 shares of common stock outstanding.

	Thousands of dollars	
	Company A	Company B
Balance sheet:		
Total assets	$900	$900
Total liabilities (10% interest)	400	600
Income statement:		
Total revenues	480	421
Total expenses (including income tax) . . .	300	400
Income tax rate	40%	20%

Required:

a. Complete a tabulation similar to the following (show computations):

Item	Company A	Company B
Earnings per share		
Return on stockholders' equity		
Return on total assets		
Financial leverage		

b. Interpret and compare the financial leverage figures for the two companies.

Part B: Problems 11–7 to 11–14

P11–7   **(Recording and Reporting Bonds Issued between Interest Dates)**

On January 1, 19A, Porter Corporation authorized $500,000, five-year, 10% bonds payable. The bonds are dated January 1,19A, and pay semiannual interest each June 30 and December 31. The accounting period ends December 31.

On March 31, 19A, $400,000 of the bonds were sold at 103.

Required (round to the nearest dollar):

a. Give the journal entry to record the issuance of the bonds on March 31, 19A.

b. Give all of the interest entries (excluding closing entries) required during 19A. Use straight-line amortization.

c. Give the amounts that should be reported on the 19A financial statements for:
   (1) Interest expense.
   (2) Bonds payable.
   (3) Unamortized discount or premium.
   (4) Net liability.

d. What would be the 19A aftertax net interest cost (dollars) assuming a 30% income tax rate?

P11-8   (Bonds Sold at Par, Discount, and Premium between Interest Dates; Compare Cash Flows and Reporting)

Warde Corporation authorized a $300,000, 10-year bond issue dated July 1, 19A. The bonds pay 10% interest each June 30. The accounting period ends December 31. Assume the bonds were sold on August 1, 19A, under three different cases as follows:

> Case A—sold at par.
>
> Case B—sold at 98.
>
> Case C—sold at 102.

Required:

Complete a schedule similar to the following assuming straight-line amortization. Show computations.

	Case A par	Case B 98	Case C 102
1. Cash received at issuance (sale) date . . . . $ ___		$ ___	$ ___
2. Cash received for accrued interest at issuance date . . . ___		___	___
3. Amount of premium or discount at issuance date . . . . ___		___	___
4. Stated rate of interest (annual) . . . . ___%		___%	___%
5. Net cash interest paid during 19A . . . . $ ___		$ ___	$ ___
6. Interest expense reported for 19A . . . . ___		___	___
7. Bonds payable reported at end of 19A . . . . ___		___	___
8. Unamortized premium or discount reported at end of 19A . . . . ___		___	___
9. Net liability (carrying value) reported at end of 19A . . . . ___		___	___
10. Interest payable reported at end of 19A . . . . ___		___	___

P11-9   (Recording and Reporting Bonds Issued between Interest Dates and the Interest Period, Not at the End of the Accounting Year)

Fama Corporation issued bonds with the following provisions and dates:

> Maturity amount: $100,000
> Interest: 8%, payable each December 31
> Dates: Bonds dated January 1, 19A
>   Bonds sold, $60,000 at 103 on May 1, 19A
>   End of accounting period, June 30
>   Maturity date, December 31, 19E (5 years)

Required: (round to the nearest dollar):

a. Give the journal entry to record the issuance of the bonds.

b. Give all 19A entries related to the interest on the bonds. Use straight-line amortization and exclude closing entries.

c. Complete the following for the year ending June 30, 19A:

Income statement:
  Interest expense

Balance sheet:
  Current liabilities
  Long-term liabilities

P11–10   (Recording and Reporting Bonds Issued between Interest Dates and Interest Period, Not at the End of the Accounting Period)

To expand to a new region, Waverly Company decided to build a new plant and warehouse. Approximately 60% of the resources required would be obtained through a $600,000 bond issue. The company developed and approved a bond indenture with the following provisions:

> Date of bonds . . . . . . March 1, 19A, due in 10 years
> Amount authorized . . . $600,000 (par amount)
> Interest . . . . 12% per annum, payable 6%
>   each Feb. 28 and Aug. 31

The annual accounting period ends on December 31. The bonds were issued (sold) on May 1, 19A, at 102.36.

Required:

a. How much cash was received by the company on May 1, 19A?

b. What was the amount of the premium? Over how many months will it be amortized?

c. Give journal entries, if any, at each of the following dates: May 1, 19A; August 31, 19A; December 31, 19A; and February 28, 19B. Do not use a reversing entry on January 1, 19B.

d. As to the financial statements for December 31, 19A:
  (1) How much interest expense should be reported on the income statement?
  (2) Show how the liabilities related to the bonds should be reported on the balance sheet.

P11–11   (Accounting for a Bond Sinking Fund; Compute Deposits; Entries)

On December 31, 19F, Hogan Company had outstanding bonds of $120,000, par (8% annual interest payable each December 31). The bonds will mature at the end of 19J Anticipating the maturity date, the maturity amount, and some possible miscellaneous related costs, the company decided to accumulate a bond sinking fund of $122,102 so that cash will be available to pay the bonds on maturity date. The company will make five equal annual deposits on December 31, 19F, G, H, I, and J. The trustee will handle the fund and will increase its balance by 10% at each year-end starting in 19G.

Required:

a. Compute the amount of each of the five equal deposits that the company must make to accumulate $122,102.

b. Give the journal entry to record the first deposit (December 31, 19F).

c. Prepare a fund accumulation schedule for the five annual deposits.

d. Give the journal entry that the company should make on December 31,19G.

e. Assume it is December 31, 19J.

(1) Give the journal entry that the company should make to record the payment of the bond principal.

(2) What balance remains in the bond sinking fund? What disposition should the company make of this amount?

P11–12   (Accounting for Bonds and Related Bond Sinking Funds; Compute Fund Deposits)
On January 1, 1975, Levin Corporation issued $500,000, 6% bonds due at the end of 20 years (December 31, 1994). The bonds specified semiannual interest payments on each June 30 and December 31. The bonds originally sold at par. The bond indenture called for the establishment of a bond sinking fund to be accumulated over the last five years by making five equal annual deposits on each December 31, starting in 1990. Interest on the fund balance at 8% will be added to the fund at year-end.

Required:

a. Give the journal entry for issuance of the bonds on January 1,1975.

b. Give the journal entry for the semiannual interest payment on the bonds on June 30, 1990.

c. Give the journal entry on December 31, 1990, for the first $85,228 contribution of cash to the sinking fund. Show how this amount was computed.

d. Give the sinking fund entry that will be made at the end of 1991.

e. Prepare a fund accumulation schedule.

f. Give the journal entry to record retirement of the bonds at maturity assuming the total bond sinking fund accumulation is $500,000.

P11–13   (Effective-Interest Amortization of Bond Premium; Completion and Analysis of an Amortization Schedule)
Stanford Corporation issued bonds and received cash in full for the issue price. The bonds were dated and issued on January 1, 19A. The stated interest rate was payable at the end of each year. The bonds mature at the end of four years. The following schedule has been completed:

Date	Cash	Interest	Amortization	Balance
January 1, 19A				$5,173
End of year 19A	$350	$310	$40	5,133
End of year 19B	350	?	?	5,091
End of year 19C	350	?	?	?
End of year 19D	350	?	?	5,000

Required:

a. Complete the amortization schedule.

b. What was the maturity amount of the bonds?

c. How much cash was received at date of issuance (sale) of the bonds?

d. Was there a premium or a discount? If so, which and how much?

e. How much cash will be disbursed for interest each period and in total for the full life of the bond issue?

f. What method of amortization is being used? Explain.

g. What is the stated rate of interest?

h. What is the effective rate of interest?

i. What amount of interest expense should be reported on the income statement each year?

j. Show how the bonds should be reported on the balance sheet at the end of each year (show the last year immediately before retirement of the bonds).

k. Why is the method of amortization being used preferable to other methods? When must it be used?

P11–14   **(Straight-Line versus Effective-Interest Methods of Amortizing Bond Discount and Premium)**

Sterling Corporation manufactures electronic equipment. The board of directors of the company authorized a bond issue on January 1, 19A, with the following terms:

Maturity (par) value: $500,000.

Interest: 9% per annum payable each December 31.

Maturity date: December 31, 19E.

The bonds were sold at an effective-interest rate of 13%.

Required:

a. Compute the bond issue price. Explain why both the stated and effective-interest rates are used in this computation.

b. Give the entry to record this bond issue.

c. Assume the company used the straight-line approach to amortize the discount on the bond issue. Compute the following amounts for each year (19A–E):

(1) Cash payment for bond interest.

(2) Amortization of bond discount or premium.

(3) Bond interest expense.

(4) Interest rate indicated (Item 3 ÷ $500,000).

(5) The straight-line rate is theoretically deficient when interest expense, (4) above, is related to the net liability (i.e., carrying value of the debt). Explain.

d. Assume instead that the company used the effective-interest method to amortize the discount. Prepare an effective-interest bond amortization schedule similar to the one in the text.

   The effective-interest method provides a constant interest rate when interest expense is related to the net liability. Explain by referring to the bond amortization schedule.

e. Which method should be used by the company to amortize the bond discount?

CASES

C11–1   **(Demonstration of Financial Leverage; Computation and Interpretation)**
The financial statements of June Corporation for 19A showed the following:

Income Statement

Revenues	$200,000
Expenses	(139,000)
Interest expense	(1,000)
Pretax income	60,000
Income tax (30%)	(18,000)
Net income	$ 42,000

Balance Sheet

Assets	$150,000
Liabilities (average interest rate, 10%)	$ 10,000
Common stock, par $10	100,000
Retained earnings	40,000
	$150,000

Notice in the above data that the company had a debt of only $10,000 compared with common stock outstanding of $100,000. A consultant recommended the following: debt, $60,000 (at 10%) instead of $10,000 and common stock outstanding of $50,000 (5,000 shares) instead of $100,000 (10,000 shares). That is, the company should have more debt and less owner contributions to finance the business.

Required (round to nearest percent):

a. You have been asked to develop a comparison between the (1) actual results and (2) results had the consultant's recommendation been followed. To do this you decided to develop the following schedule:

Item	Actual results for 19A	Results with an increase in debt of $50,000
a. Total debt		
b. Total assets		
c. Total stockholders' equity		
d. Interest expense (total at 10%)		
e. Net income		
f. Return on total assets		
g. Earnings available to stockholders:		
(1) Amount		
(2) Per share		
(3) Return on stockholders' equity		
h. Financial leverage		

b. Based on the completed schedule in (a), provide a comparative analysis and interpretation of the actual results and the recommendation.

C11–2   (Analysis of Zero Coupon Bonds)

Early in 1981, J.C. Penney Company issued zero coupon bonds with a face (maturity value) of $400 million due in 1989 (eight years after issuance). When the bonds were sold to the public, similar bonds paid 15% effective interest. An article in *Forbes* magazine (May 25, 1981) discussed the J.C. Penney bonds and stated: "It's easy to see why corporations like to sell bonds that don't pay interest. But why would anybody want to buy that kind of paper (bond)?"

Required:

a. Explain why an investor would buy a J.C. Penney bond with a zero interest rate. If investors could earn 15% on similar investments, how much should they be willing to pay for a J.C. Penney bond with a par value of $1,000 (due eight years after issuance)?

b. Assume that J.C. Penney sold the $400 million bond issue on May 1, 1981, the first day of the term (life) of the bond issue. Give the journal entry to record the sale of the bonds for cash.

c. Assume that the accounting period for J.C. Penney ends on December 31 each year. Give the journal entry required on December 31, 1981, to record accrued interest expense. If none is required, explain.

d. Give the entry on maturity date to pay the bondholders. How much cash interest was paid on the bonds? Explain.

C11–3   (Analysis of Long-Term Debt for an Actual Company)

JCPenney   Refer to the financial statements of J.C. Penney Company, Inc. given in the appendix immediately preceding the index.

1. What is the amount of amortization of discount (on long-term bonds) reported by the company for the current year?

2. What is the amount of long-term debt due in the year 1992?

3. The long-term debt includes "zero coupon notes." Is there any interest expense associated with a zero coupon note?

4. What was the amount of interest expense on long-term debt for the current year?

TWELVE

MEASURING AND REPORTING OWNERS' EQUITY

PURPOSE

The two previous chapters discussed accounting for funds provided by creditors. This chapter will examine measuring and reporting funds provided by the owners of a business. Accounting for owners' equity is affected by the type of business. Owners' equity appears somewhat differently on the balance sheets of sole proprietorships, partnerships, and corporations. However, given the same set of transactions, the total amount of owners' equity on a given date will be the same (except for income tax effects) for every type of business. This chapter will focus primarily on the corporate form, the most prominent type of business. In addition to the three basic financial statements, some corporations prepare a statement of stockholders' equity similar to the one shown on the opposite page.

LEARNING OBJECTIVES

1. Describe the basic nature of a corporation.
2. Compare and contrast the various types of capital stock.
3. Record transactions involving treasury stock.
4. Account for dividends on common and preferred stock.
5. Record stock dividends and stock splits.
6. Measure and report retained earnings.
7. Expand your accounting vocabulary by learning the "Important Terms Defined in This Chapter."
8. Apply the knowledge learned from this chapter by completing the homework assigned by your instructor.

ORGANIZATION

Part A—stockholders' equity
1. Nature and structure of a corporation.
2. Accounting for various types of capital stock.
3. Treasury stock.

Part B—accounting for dividends, retained earnings, and unincorporated businesses
1. Dividends defined.
2. Dividends on preferred stock.
3. Stock dividends and stock splits.
4. Reporting retained earnings.
5. Unincorporated businesses.

CONSOLIDATED STATEMENT OF STOCKHOLDERS' EQUITY

(in thousands except per share amounts)

Three years ended December 31, 1987	Common stock	Capital in excess of par value	Retained earnings	Treasury stock	Total
Balance at December 31, 1984	$ 29,570	$117,643	$215,322	$ (767)	$361,768
Issuance of common stock and warrants for acquistion of TranStar (Note 2)	793	25,365	—	767	26,925
Issuance of common stock upon conversion of debentures	1,891	32,158	—	—	34,049
Cash dividends, $.13 per share	—	—	(4,016)	—	(4,016)
Net income — 1985	—	—	47,278	—	47,278
Balance at December 31, 1985	32,254	175,166	258,584	—	466,004
Proceeds from issuance of common stock	—	4	—	—	4
Cash dividends, $.13 per share	—	—	(4,193)	—	(4,193)
Net income — 1986	—	—	50,035	—	50,035
Balance at December 31, 1986	32,254	175,170	304,426	—	511,850
Purchase of treasury stock	—	—	—	(13,627)	(13,627)
Issuance of treasury stock upon exercise of stock options	—	—	(14)	79	65
Cash dividends, $.13 per share	—	—	(4,165)	—	(4,165)
Net income — 1987	—	—	20,155	—	20,155)
Balance at December 31, 1987	$ 32,254	$175,170	$320,402	$(13,548)	$514,278

PART A—STOCKHOLDERS' EQUITY

Nature of a Corporation

A corporation is a separate legal entity that is created by law. It has many of the same rights and duties as individuals. A corporation may be owned by a number of persons and perhaps other business entities. Ownership in the corporation is evidenced by shares of capital stock that typically are traded on established stock exchanges (such as the New York Stock Exchange). The life of a corporation is indefinite and is not affected by changes in the group of individuals, or other entities, that own it.

In terms of volume of business, the corporation is the dominant type of business organization in the United States. This popularity can be attributed to three important advantages that a corporation has over the sole proprietorship and the partnership. First, the corporate form facilitates the bringing together of large amounts of funds through the sale of ownership interests (capital stock) to the public. Second, it facilitates the transfer of separate ownership interests because the shares can be transferred easily to others. Third, it provides the stockholder with limited liability.[1]

The corporation is the only business form that is recognized in law as a separate legal entity. As a distinct entity, the corporation enjoys a continuous existence separate and apart from its owners. It may own assets, incur liabilities, expand and contract in size, sue others, be sued, and enter into contracts independently of the stockholder owners.

Structure of a Corporation

Ownership of a corporation is evidenced by shares of **capital stock** that are freely transferable without affecting the corporation. The owners of a corporation are known as **stockholders** or **shareholders.**

Each state has different laws that govern the organization and operation of corporations within their boundaries. To create a corporation, an **application for a charter** must be submitted to the appropriate state official. The application must specify the name of the corporation, the purpose (type of business), kinds and amounts of capital stock **authorized,** and a minimum amount of capital that must be invested by the owners at the date of organization. Most states require a minimum of three stockholders when the corporation is formed. Upon approval of the application, the state issues a **charter** (sometimes called the **articles of incorporation**). The governing body of a corporation is the **board of directors,** which is elected by the stockholders.

---

[1] In case of insolvency of a corporation, the creditors have recourse for their claims only to the assets of the corporation. Thus, the stockholders stand to lose, as a maximum, only their equity in the corporation. In the case of a partnership or sole proprietorship, creditors have recourse to the personal assets of the owners if the assets of the business are insufficient to meet the outstanding debts of the business.

Exhibit 12–1 Typical organizational structure of a corporation

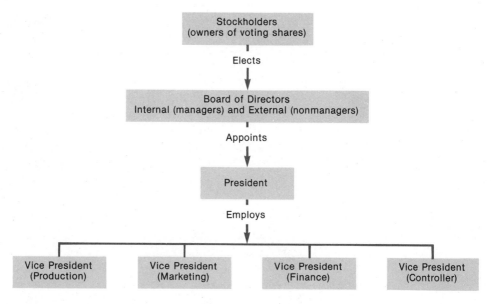

When a person acquires shares of capital stock, a **stock certificate** is issued as evidence of an ownership interest in the corporation. The certificate states the name of the stockholder, date of purchase, type of stock, number of shares represented, and the characteristics of the stock. The back of the certificate has instructions and a form to be completed when the shares are sold or transferred to another party.

Stockholders have the following basic rights:

1. Vote in the stockholders' meeting (or by proxy) on major issues concerning management of the corporation.[2]
2. Participate proportionately with other stockholders in the distribution of profits of the corporation.
3. Share proportionately with other stockholders in the distribution of corporate assets upon liquidation.
4. Purchase shares of any new issues of common stock on a pro rata basis in order to maintain their percentage of ownership.

Stockholders exercise their control of a corporation by voting in the annual meeting of the stockholders. The usual organizational structure of a corporation is shown in Exhibit 12–1.

---

[2] A voting proxy is a written authority given by a stockholder that gives another party the right to vote the stockholder's shares in the annual meeting of the stockholders. Typically, proxies are solicited by, and given to, the president of the corporation.

Authorized, Issued, and Outstanding Capital Stock

The corporate charter states the maximum number of shares of capital stock the corporation can issue. This maximum is called the **authorized** number of **shares.** The number of shares issued and the number of shares outstanding are determined by the stock transactions of the corporation. Shares of stock that never have been sold to the public are called unissued shares. In some situations, shares of stock may be sold on credit. These shares are called subscribed stock, which will not be issued until cash is collected from the investor. Exhibit 12–2 defines and illustrates the five terms usually used in respect to corporate shares.

Typically, the corporate charter authorizes a larger number of shares than the corporation expects to issue after its organization. This strategy provides future flexibility for the issuance of additional shares without amending the charter.

Exhibit 12–2 Authorized, issued, and outstanding shares

Definitions	Illustrations
Authorized number of shares: The **maximum** number of shares that can be issued as specified in the **charter** of the corporation.	Charter of Tye Corporation specifies "authorized capital stock, **100,000 shares,** par value $1 per share."
Issued number of shares: The total cumulative number of shares that has been issued to date by the corporation.	To date, Tye Corporation has sold and issued **30,000** shares of its capital stock.
Unissued number of shares: The number of authorized shares that have never been issued to date.	Authorized shares . . . . 100,000 Issued shares . . . . 30,000 Unissued shares **70,000**
Subscribed number of shares: Shares of authorized stock sold on credit and not yet issued.	Tye Corporation sold 1,000 shares on credit; the shares will be issued when the sale price is collected in full. Subscribed shares = **1,000.**
Outstanding number of shares: The number of shares currently owned by stockholders; that is, the number of shares authorized minus the total number of unissued shares.	Tye Corporation: Authorized shares . . . . 100,000 Unissued shares . . . . 70,000 Outstanding shares **30,000***

* Observe that outstanding shares and issued shares are the same (i.e., 30,000 shares) in this situation. **Treasury stock** (i.e., shares that have been issued then subsequently repurchased by the issuing corporation) will be discussed later. When treasury stock is held, the number of shares issued and the number outstanding will differ by the number of shares of treasury stock held (treasury stock is included in "issued" but not in "outstanding").

Types of Capital Stock

All corporations must issue **common stock,** which may be viewed as the "normal" stock of a corporation because it has voting rights. A corporation may issue preferred stock which grants **preferences** that the common stock does not have. These preferences usually specify, as a minimum, that the preferred stockholders must receive their dividends **before** any dividends can be declared or paid to the common stockholders. Because of the important differences between common and preferred stock, they are identified separately in accounting and reporting (and on the stock exchanges).

Common Stock

When only one class of stock is issued, it must be common. It is often called the **residual equity** because it ranks **after** the preferred stock for dividends and assets distributed upon liquidation of the corporation. Common stock does not have a fixed dividend rate (as does most preferred stock). As a result, common stock may pay higher dividends and have significant increases in market value. Common stock may be either par value or nopar value stock.

Par Value and Nopar Value Stock
Many years ago, all capital stock had to specify a par value. Par value is a **nominal** value per share established in the charter of the corporation. Stock that is sold by the corporation to investors above par value is said to sell at a **premium;** whereas, stock sold below par is said to sell at a **discount.** The initial sale of stock by the corporation to investors cannot be below par value.[3] Originally, the concept of par value was established as protection for creditors by specifying a permanent amount of capital that could not be withdrawn by the owners as long as the corporation existed. This permanent amount of capital is called **legal capital.** The original idea that par value represented protection for creditors was ill conceived. Today, par value, when specified, only identifies the stated or legal capital of the corporation (otherwise, par value has no particular significance). Par value has no relationship to market value.

Many states permit the issuance of **nopar value stock.** Nopar value stock does not have an amount per share specified in the charter. It may be issued at any price without a **discount or premium.** When nopar stock is issued by a corporation, the legal, or stated, capital is as defined by the state law.

The definition of **legal capital** varies among states, but legal capital usually is viewed as the par value of the stock outstanding. In the case of nopar stock, legal

---

[3] Our discussions concerning the sale of capital stock refer to the **initial** sale of the stock by the corporation rather than to later sales between investors as is the common situation in the day-to-day transactions of the stock markets. Because the sale of stock by a corporation at a discount no longer is legal, no further discussion of it is included. The sale of stock among **individuals** is not recorded in the accounts of the corporation.

capital is viewed as either the stated value set by the company or the amount for which the stock was sold originally. Legal capital usually cannot be used as the basis for dividends, and it represents the amount of capital that must remain invested in the corporation until it is liquidated.

Preferred Stock

When stock other than common stock is issued, it is called **preferred stock.** A corporation may issue several types of preferred stock. Preferred stock has some characteristics that make it different from the common stock. The usual characteristics of preferred stock are:

1. Dividend preferences.
2. Conversion privileges.
3. Asset distributions.
4. Nonvoting specifications.

Preferred stock may be nopar value, although typically it has a par value. Most preferred stock has a fixed dividend rate. For example, "6% **preferred stock,** par value $10 per share" would pay an annual dividend of 6% of par, or $0.60 per share. If the preferred stock is nopar value, the preferred dividend would be specified as $0.60 per share.

The dividend preferences of preferred stock take precedence over the common stock, up to a specified limit. Dividend preferences will be discussed in Part B of the chapter. The other features of preferred stock are explained below.

Convertible Preferred Stock

Convertible preferred stock provides preferred stockholders the option to exchange their preferred share for shares of **common** stock of the corporation. The terms of the conversion will specify dates and a conversion ratio. A charter could read: "Each share of preferred stock, at the option of the stockholder, can be converted to two shares of common stock anytime after January 1, 19H."

Asset Distributions

Two **asset distributions** usually are specified on preferred stock. One is provided with preferred stock that is **callable.** At the option of the issuing corporation, holders of callable preferred stock can be required to return the shares to the corporation for a specified amount of cash. The call price usually is higher than the par value. For example, a corporate charter could specify that preferred stock with a $10 par value was callable at $15. At this rate, a holder of the preferred stock would receive $15 per share on "call" by the corporation.

The other asset distribution on the preferred stock occurs if the corporation goes out of business. Preferred stock usually has a specified amount per share that must be paid upon dissolution to the preferred stockholders before any assets can be distributed to the common stockholders.

Nonvoting Specifications

Nonvoting preferred stock is customary, even though the nonvoting feature is undesirable from the perspective of the investors. This feature denies the preferred stockholder the right to vote at stockholder meetings. It is one method for obtaining capital without diluting the control of the common stockholders.

Demand for Preferred Stock

There are a variety of economic reasons why corporations issue preferred stock and why investors buy it. Corporations issue preferred stock because it permits them to raise large amounts of capital without diluting control by giving voting rights to the preferred stockholders. Corporations often provide specific privileges on preferred stock to attract different types of investors who otherwise would not invest in the corporation.

Investors buy preferred stock because they want certain special characteristics. Many investors are willing to give up voting rights to have the additional protection associated with dividend preferences. For example, someone on a retirement income may be more concerned about receiving regular dividends than voting at a stockholders' meeting.

Most investors find common stock more attractive than preferred stock. There is no limit on the amount of dividends that can be paid on common stock, but most preferred stock has a fixed rate. If a corporation is profitable, investors usually can earn a higher return on common stock.

Accounting for Capital Stock

There are two primary sources of stockholders' equity.

1. **Contributed capital**—the amount invested by stockholders through the purchase of shares of stock from the corporation. Contributed capital has two distinct components: (*a*) stated capital—par or stated value derived from the sale of capital stock; and (*b*) additional contributed capital—amounts in excess of par or stated value. This often is called **additional paid-in capital.**
2. **Retained earnings**—the **cumulative** amount of net income earned since the organization of the corporation less the cumulative amount of dividends paid by the corporation since organization.

Sale and Issuance of Par Value Capital Stock

When par value stock is sold for cash, three accounts are affected: (1) Cash is debited for the sale price, (2) the par value amount is credited to an appropriately designated stockholders' equity account, and (3) any difference between the sale price and the par value of the stock is credited to a separate stockholders' equity account called Contributed Capital in Excess of Par. The par value is recorded in a separate account because it represents legal capital.

The sale of par value common and preferred stock by Tye Corporation is shown in Exhibit 12–3. Notice in the first journal entry that the preferred and common stock accounts were credited for the **par value** of the shares sold. The differences between the sale prices and the par values were credited to two capital in excess of par accounts. Tye Corporation recognized **two** different sources of stockholders' equity—preferred and common stock—and each source was subdivided between the par value and the excess received over par.

Capital Stock Sold and Issued for Noncash Assets and/or Services

Often **noncash** considerations, such as buildings, machinery, and services (e.g., attorney fees), are received in payment for capital stock. In these cases, the assets received (or expenses incurred in the case of services) should be recorded at the **market value** of the stock issued at the date of the transaction in accordance with the **cost principle.** If the market value of the stock issued cannot be determined, then the market value of the consideration received should be used. Assume Tye Corporation issued 100 shares of preferred stock for legal services when the stock was selling at $12 per share. The second journal entry given in Exhibit 12–3 records this transaction. Notice that the value of the legal services received is assumed to be the same as the value of the stock that was issued. This assumption is reasonable because two independent parties usually would keep negotiating a deal until the point where the value of what is given up is equal to the value of what is received.

Reporting Stockholders' Equity

The **full-disclosure principle** requires that the major classifications of stockholders' equity be reported separately. Also, the subdivisions of each of these major classifications must be reported. Exhibit 12–3 shows the typical reporting of **contributed capital** and its subdivisions. Notice the separation of each type of stock and of par values and amounts in excess of par. Also, notice that the number of **shares** of each kind of stock authorized, issued, and outstanding are reported.

Sales and Issuance of Nopar Capital Stock

The laws of all states specify how legal capital must be determined if a par value is not stated in the corporate charter. There are two typical specifications, depending on the particular state that issued the charter:

1. In its bylaws, the corporation must specify a **stated** value per share as legal capital. This stated value is a substitute for par value.
2. The corporation must record the **total** proceeds received from each sale and issuance of nopar stock as legal capital.

Recall that **legal capital** is credited to the capital stock account (e.g., common or preferred stock). Any excess of sale price over legal capital is credited to a

Exhibit 12-3 Issuance of par value capital stock

Issuance for cash:

Preferred stock, 1,000 shares @ $12.
Common stock, 30,000 shares @ $5.

Cash (1,000 × $12) + (30,000 × $5)	162,000	
Preferred stock (1,000 × par $10)		10,000
Common stock (30,000 × par $1)		30,000
Contributed capital in excess of par, preferred		
[1,000 × ($12 − $10)]		2,000
Contributed capital in excess of par, common		
[30,000 × ($5 − $1)]		120,000

Issuance for services:

Issued 100 shares of preferred stock for legal services when the stock was selling at $12.

Legal expense	1,200	
Preferred stock (100 × par $10)		1,000
Contributed capital in excess of par, preferred		
[100 × ($12 − $10)]		200

Reporting on the financial statements:

Balance sheet—stockholders' equity:

Contributed capital:
Preferred stock, 6% (par $10; authorized 10,000 shares, issued and outstanding, 1,100 shares)	$ 11,000	
Common stock (par $1; authorized 100,000 shares, issued and outstanding, 30,000 shares)	30,000	
Contributed capital in excess of par:		
Preferred stock	2,200	
Common stock	120,000	
Total contributed capital		$163,200
Retained earnings (illustrated later)		

Income statement:

Legal expense		1,200

Exhibit 12-4 Issuance of nopar capital stock

Case A—The state law requires that the corporation set a **stated** value per share to represent legal capital for nopar stock. The company's charter specified a stated value of $0.50 per share.

Cash (60,000 × $6)	360,000	
Common stock (nopar, with stated value of $0.50; 60,000 × $0.50)		30,000
Contributed capital in excess of stated value [60,000 × ($6.00 − $0.50)]		330,000

Case B—The state law requires that the total proceeds be recorded as legal capital.

Cash	360,000	
Common stock (nopar)		360,000

separate account (e.g., Contributed Capital in Excess of Stated Value, Nopar Common, or Preferred, Stock).

Exhibit 12–4 illustrates the issuance of nopar capital stock.

Treasury Stock

Treasury stock is a corporation's own capital stock that was issued to stockholders, **reacquired** subsequently by the corporation, and is still held by the corporation. Treasury stock often is bought for sound business reasons, such as to obtain shares needed for employee bonus plans; to increase the earnings per share amount; or to have shares on hand for use in the acquisition of other companies. Treasury stock, while held by the issuing corporation, has no voting, dividend, or other stockholder rights.

When a corporation buys its own capital stock, the assets (usually cash) of the corporation and the stockholders' equity are reduced by equal amounts. When treasury stock is sold, the opposite effects occur. Purchases of treasury stock are recorded by debiting its cost to a stockholders' equity account called Treasury Stock (by type of stock) and crediting Cash. Because the Treasury Stock account has a debit balance, it often is called a contra stockholders' equity account. When treasury stock is sold, the Treasury Stock account is credited at cost, and Cash is debited. Usually the purchase and sale prices of treasury stock are different, necessitating recording the difference in an appropriately designated **contributed capital** account.[4]

Accounting for treasury stock is shown in Exhibit 12–5. In the journal entry for January 2, 19B, the **Treasury Stock account** is debited for the **cost** of the treasury stock purchased ($3,600). The journal entry on February 15, 19B, credits the Treasury Stock for the **cost** of the 100 shares of treasury stock sold. A corporation is not permitted by GAAP to report income from investment in its own stock because transactions with the owners are not considered to be normal profit-making activities. In Exhibit 12–5, upon sale of the treasury stock, **contributed capital** was increased by $100, which was the difference between the cost and the sales price of the treasury shares sold [i.e., 100 shares × ($13 − $12)]. This difference was **not** recorded as a gain as would be done for the sale of investments in marketable securities.

The Treasury Stock account never has a credit balance, even though owners' equity accounts normally carry a credit balance. The balance in the Treasury Stock account reflects a **contraction** of stockholders' equity. Therefore, it is a contra equity account. The debit balance in the Treasury Stock account represents the acquisition **cost** of the treasury stock still held at the date of the balance sheet. Observe this deduction on the balance sheet for May Corporation at the bottom of Exhibit 12–5. That balance sheet reports the number of shares as:

---

[4] Two alternative approaches are used to account for treasury stock—the cost method and the par value method. We will limit our discussions to the cost method because it is less complex and used more widely. The par value method is discussed in most accounting texts at the intermediate level.

Exhibit 12–5 Accounting for treasury stock

Situation of May Corporation on January 1, 19B:

MAY CORPORATION
Summarized Balance Sheet
January 1, 19B

Assets		**Stockholders' Equity**	
Cash	$ 30,000	Contributed capital:	
Other assets	70,000	Common stock (par $10, authorized 10,000 shares, issued	
		8,000 shares)	$ 80,000
		Retained earnings	20,000
Total assets	$100,000	Total stockholders' equity	$100,000

Purchase of treasury stock:

On January 2, 19B, May Corporation purchased 300 of its own outstanding shares of common stock at $12 per share.

Treasury stock, common (300 shares @ $12 per share)	3,600	
Cash		3,600

Note: This transaction reduces both assets and stockholders' equity by $3,600.

Sale of treasury stock:

On February 15, 19B, May sold one third of the treasury stock at $13 per share.

Cash (100 shares @ $13)	1,300	
Treasury stock, common (100 shares @ cost, $12)		1,200
Contributed capital, treasury stock transactions		100

Note: This transaction increases both assets and stockholders' equity by $1,300.

Reporting treasury stock:

MAY CORPORATION*
Summarized Balance Sheet
February 15, 19B

Assets		**Stockholders' Equity**	
Cash	$27,700	Contributed capital:	
Other assets	70,000	Common stock (par $10, authorized 10,000 shares, issued 8,000, of which 200 shares are held as treasury stock)	$ 80,000
		Contributed capital, treasury stock transactions	100
		Total contributed capital	80,100
		Retained earnings	20,000
		Total	100,100
		Less cost of treasury stock held	2,400
Total assets	$97,700	Total stockholders' equity	$ 97,700

* Reflects the additional effects of the two transactions given above.

Classification	Shares
Authorized	10,000
Unissued	(2,000)
*Issued	8,000
Treasury shares	(200)
*Outstanding	7,800

* Different by the number of treasury
shares held.

Neither the purchase nor sale of treasury stock affects the number of shares of stock that are issued or unissued. Treasury stock only affects the number of shares of **outstanding** stock. The basic difference between treasury stock and unissued stock is that treasury stock has been sold at least once.

To illustrate the **resale** of treasury stock at a price **less than cost,** assume that an additional 50 shares of the treasury stock were resold by May Corporation on April 1, 19B, at $11 per share; that is, $1 per share below cost. The resulting journal entry is:

April 1, 19B:

```
Cash . . . . . . . . . . . . . . . . . . . . . . . . . . . . . . . . . . . . 550
Contributed capital, treasury stock transactions . . . . . . . . . . . . . . . . . . . .   50
    Treasury stock, common (50 shares) . . . . . . . . . . . . . . . . . . . . .        600
   Sold 50 shares of treasury stock at $11 per share; cost, $12 per share.
```

Notice that the difference between sale price and cost was debited to the same contributed capital account to which the difference in the preceding journal entry (Exhibit 12–5) was credited. Retained Earnings would be debited for some or all of the amount of the difference only if there were an insufficient credit balance in the account Contributed Capital, Treasury Stock Transactions.

PART B—ACCOUNTING FOR DIVIDENDS, RETAINED EARNINGS, AND UNINCORPORATED BUSINESSES

Dividends Defined

Usually a dividend is a distribution of cash to stockholders of a corporation. Dividends must be approved (i.e., declared) by the board of directors before they can be paid. A corporation does not have a legal obligation to pay dividends. Creditors can force a company into bankruptcy if it does not meet required interest payments on debt, but stockholders do not have a similar right if a corporation is unable to pay dividends.

Without a qualifier, the term **dividend** means a cash dividend. Dividends can be paid in assets other than cash. Some corporations issue **stock dividends,** which are dividend distributions of the corporation's own stock.

The most common type of dividend is a cash dividend. While a corporation does not have a legal obligation to pay dividends, a liability is created when the board formally declares a dividend. A typical dividend declaration would be:

> On December 1, 19E, the Board of Directors of Box Corporation hereby declares an annual cash dividend of $2 per share on the common stock and 6% per share on the preferred stock to the stockholders on date of record, December 10, 19E, payable on December 30, 19E.

After the declaration of the dividend, Box Corporation must record a liability, as follows:

December 1, 19E:

Retained earnings (or Dividends declared, which is closed to Retained earnings)	12,400	
Dividends payable (a current liability)		12,400

Declaration of a cash dividend:
Preferred stock (2,000 shares × par $20 × rate 6%) = $ 2,400.
Common stock (5,000 shares × $2)   =   10,000.

The subsequent payment of the liability on December 30, 19E, is recorded as follows:

Dividends payable	12,400	
Cash		12,400

Notice that the declaration and payment of a cash dividend reduces assets (cash) and stockholders' equity (retained earnings) by the same amount. There are two fundamental requirements for the payment of a cash dividend:

1. **Sufficient retained earnings.** The corporation must have accumulated a sufficient amount of retained earnings to cover the amount of the dividend. State incorporation laws usually place restrictions on cash dividends. For example, the state laws often limit cash dividends to the balance in retained earnings. To meet growth objectives, most corporations do not disburse more than 40–60% of the average net income amount as dividends.

2. **Sufficient cash.** The corporation must have access to sufficient cash to pay the dividend and to meet the continuing operating needs of the business. The mere fact that there is a large **credit** in the Retained Earnings account does not mean that the board of directors can declare and pay a cash dividend. The cash generated in the past by earnings represented in the Retained Earnings account may have been expended to acquire inventory, buy operational assets, and/or pay liabilities. Consequently, there is no necessary relationship between the balance of retained earnings and the balance of cash on any particular date (simply, retained earnings is not cash).

Some companies overcome a cash constraint (at least temporarily) by borrowing cash to pay cash dividends. The balance in retained earnings is a more inflexible constraint because retained earnings cannot be borrowed.

Dividends on Preferred Stock

Recall that preferred stock gives certain rights that have precedence over the rights of common stock. The primary distinguishing characteristics of preferred stock are dividend preferences. The **dividend preferences** may be classified as follows:

1. Current dividend preference.
2. Cumulative dividend preference.
3. Participating dividend preference.

The term **dividend preference** does not imply that preferred stockholders have a legal right to receive dividend payments. As was the case with dividends on common stock, preferred stock dividends must be declared by the board of directors. The corporation has no legal obligation to pay preferred dividends until they are declared by the board.

Preferred stock may have one or a combination of dividend preferences. The corporate charter will specify which preferences exist.

Current Dividend Preference on Preferred Stock

Preferred stock always carries a **current dividend preference.** It requires that the current preferred dividend must be declared and paid before any dividends can be declared and paid on the common stock. When the current dividend preference is met (and no other preference is operative), dividends then can be paid to the common stockholders. The current dividend preference on par value preferred stock is a specified percent of the par value of the preferred stock.

Declared dividends must be **allocated** between the preferred and common stock. First, the preferences of the preferred stock must be met, then the remainder of the total dividend can be allocated to the common stock. Exhibit 12–6, Case A, illustrates the allocation of the **current dividend** preference under four different assumptions concerning the **total** amount of dividends to be paid.

Cumulative Dividend Preference on Preferred Stock

Cumulative preferred stock has a preference that states if all or a part of the specified current dividend is not paid in full, the unpaid amount becomes **dividends in arrears.** The amount of any cumulative preferred dividends in arrears must be paid before any common dividends can be paid. Of course, if the preferred stock is **noncumulative,** dividends never can be in arrears. Therefore any dividends passed (i.e., not declared) are lost permanently by the preferred stockholders. Because preferred stockholders are not willing to accept this unfavorable feature, preferred stock is usually cumulative.

The allocation of dividends between **cumulative** preferred stock and common stock is illustrated in Exhibit 12–6, Case B, under four different assumptions concerning the total amount of dividends to be paid. Observe that the dividends

Exhibit 12–6 Dividends on preferred stock

Case A—current dividend preference only:

Preferred stock outstanding, 6%, par $20; 2,000 shares = $40,000 par.
Common stock outstanding, par $10; 5,000 shares = $50,000 par.

Allocation of dividends between preferred and common stock assuming
current dividend preference only:

| | | Amount of dividend paid to stockholders of— | |
| | | --- | --- |
Assumptions	Total dividends paid	6% preferred stock (2,000 shares @ $20 par = $40,000)*	Common stock (5,000 shares @ $10 par = $50,000)
No. 1	$ 1,000	$1,000	–0–
No. 2	2,000	2,000	–0–
No. 3	3,000	2,400	$ 600
No. 4	18,000	2,400	15,600

* Preferred dividend preference, $40,000 × 6% = $2,400; or 2,000 shares × $1.20.

Case B—cumulative dividend preference:

Preferred and common stock outstanding—same as above. Dividends in **arrears** for the
two preceding years.

Allocation of dividends between preferred and common stock assuming **cumulative** preferred stock:

| | | Amount of dividend paid to stockholders of— | |
| | | --- | --- |
Assumptions (dividends in arrears, 2 years)	Total dividends paid	6% preferred stock (2,000 shares @ $20 par = $40,000)*	Common stock (5,000 shares @ $10 par = $50,000)
No. 1	$ 2,400	$2,400	–0–
No. 2	7,200	7,200	–0–
No. 3	8,000	7,200	$ 800
No. 4	30,000	7,200	22,800

* Current dividend preference, $40,000 × 6% = $2,400; dividends in arrears preference, $2,400 × 2
years = $4,800; and current dividend preference plus dividends in arrears = $7,200.

---

in arrears are paid first, next the current dividend preference is paid, and,
finally, the remainder is paid to the common stockholders.

Some preferred stock may provide dividends that are greater than the required minimum amount. Participating preferred stock is discusssed in Chapter
Supplement 12A.

Stock Dividends

The board of directors may vote to declare and issue a stock dividend instead of
a cash dividend. **A stock dividend is a distribution of additional shares of a
corporation's own capital stock on a pro rata basis to its stockholders at no cost.**

Stock dividends usually consist of common stock issued to the holders of common stock. **Pro rata basis** means that each stockholder receives additional shares equal to the percentage of shares already held. A stockholder with 10% of the outstanding shares would receive 10% of any additional shares issued as a stock dividend. Therefore, a stock dividend does not change the proportionate ownership of any stockholder. It does not involve the distribution of any assets of the corporation to the stockholder, and it does not affect the **total** stockholders' equity of the issuing corporation. Assume King Corporation has outstanding 100,000 shares of common stock, par $5, originally sold at $8 per share. The board of directors voted to declare and issue a 10% common stock dividend (i.e., 10,000 shares) when the market value of the common stock was $11 per share. The entry by King Corporation to record the declaration and issuance of this stock dividend would be:

```
Retained earnings (10,000 shares × $11) . . . . . . . . . . . . . . . . . . . . .  110,000
      Common stock [par $5 (10,000 shares × $5)]  . . . . . . . . . . . . . .            50,000
      Contributed capital in excess of par, common stock
         [10,000 shares × ($11 − $5)]  . . . . . . . . . . . . . . . . . . . . . .        60,000
      Common stock dividend of 10% distributed when the market
      value per share was $11.
```

Observe in the above entry that **retained earnings** was **decreased** by $110,000 and that common stock and contributed capital in excess of par were increased by $110,000. The stock dividend did **not** change total stockholders' equity—it only changed some of the balances of the accounts that comprise stockholders' equity. This process of transferring an amount from retained earnings to contributed (i.e., permanent) capital often is called **capitalizing earnings** because it reduces the amount of retained earnings available for future dividends.

After a stock dividend, each **stockholder** has the same **proportionate** ownership of the corporation as before, and no additional assets are received by the stockholders (only more shares to represent the same total value previously held). Because more shares now represent the same "value," the **market** price per share of the stock should drop proportionately.

Notice in the previous journal entry, the amount that was transferred from Retained Earnings to Contributed Capital was the **current market value** of the shares issued as a stock dividend. Market value amount is considered appropriate when the stock dividend is small; that is, when it is less than 25% of the previously outstanding shares. In those cases where a stock dividend is large (i.e., more than 25%), the amount transferred should be the total par value of the shares issued.

Reasons for Stock Dividends

Stock dividends often serve useful purposes for both the corporation and the individual stockholder. The two primary purposes of a stock dividend are:

1. **Maintain dividend consistency.**   Many corporations prefer to declare dividends each year. During a cash shortage, the dividend record may

be maintained by issuing a stock dividend. Stock dividends tend to satisfy the demands of stockholders for continuing dividends and yet avoid the demand on cash. Stockholders view stock dividends as quite different from cash dividends.

2. **Capitalize retained earnings.** A stock dividend is used to transfer retained earnings to permanent capital and thus remove such earnings from cash dividend availability. When a corporation consistently retains a large percent of its earnings for growth, the related funds often are invested permanently in long-term assets such as plant and other property. Therefore, it is realistic to transfer those accumulated earnings to permanent capital. A stock dividend is a convenient approach to capitalize retained earnings.

Stock Splits

Stock splits are **not** dividends. They are similar to a stock dividend but are quite different in terms of their impact on the stockholders' equity accounts. In a stock split, the **total** number of authorized shares is increased by a specified amount, such as a two-for-one split. In this instance, each share held is called in, and two new shares are issued in its place. Typically, a stock split is accomplished by **reducing the par or stated value** per share of all authorized shares so that the **total** par value of all authorized shares is unchanged. For example, assume 1,000 shares of $20 par value stock were outstanding before a two-for-one split. This stock split would involve reducing the par value of each new share to $10 and the issuance of 2,000 shares of $10 par value stock. In contrast to a stock dividend, a stock split does **not** result in a transfer of retained earnings to contributed capital. No transfer is needed because the reduction in the par value per share compensates for the increase in the number of shares. The primary reason for a stock split is to **reduce the market price per share,** which tends to increase the market activity of the stock.

In both a stock dividend and a stock split, the stockholder receives more shares of stock but does not disburse any additional assets to acquire the additional shares. A stock dividend requires a journal entry, while a stock split does not require a journal entry.

The **comparative effects** of a stock dividend versus a stock split may be summarized as follows:

	Stockholders' equity		
	Before	After a 100% stock dividend	After a two-for-one stock split
Contributed capital:			
Number of shares outstanding	30,000	60,000	60,000
Par value per share	$ 10	$ 10	$ 5
Total par value outstanding	300,000	600,000	300,000
Retained earnings	650,000	350,000	650,000
Total stockholders' equity	950,000	950,000	950,000

Dividend Dates

A typical dividend declaration is as follows:

> On November 20, 19B, the Board of Directors of XY Corporation hereby declares a $0.50 per share cash dividend on the 200,000 shares of nopar common stock outstanding. The dividend will be paid to stockholders of record at December 15, 19B, on January 15, 19C.

This declaration specifies **three important dates:**

1. **Declaration date—November 20, 19B.** This is the date on which the board of directors officially approved the dividend. As soon as the declaration is made, a **dividend liability** is created. On the date of declaration, XY Corporation would record the following journal entry:

   November 20, 19B:

   ```
   Retained earnings (or Dividends declared) . . . . . . . . . . . .  100,000
       Dividends payable . . . . . . . . . . . . . . . . . . . . . . . . .         100,000
       Cash dividend declared: 200,000 shares × $0.50 = $100,000.
   ```

   The December 31, 19B, balance sheet would report **Dividends Payable as a current liability.**

2. **Date of record—December 15, 19B.** This date follows the declaration date, usually by about one month, as specified in the declaration. It is the date on which the corporation prepares the list of current stockholders based on the **stockholder records.** The dividend is payable only to those names listed on the record date. Thus, share transfers between investors reported to the corporation before this date result in the dividend being paid to the new owner. Changes reported **after** this date result in the dividend being paid to the old owner; the new owner will receive all subsequent dividends. No journal entry would be made on this date.

3. **Date of payment—January 15, 19C.** This is the date on which the **cash** is disbursed to pay the dividend liability. It follows the date of record as specified in the dividend announcement. The entry to record the cash disbursement by XY Corporation is as follows:

   January 15, 19C:

   ```
   Dividends payable . . . . . . . . . . . . . . . . . . . . . . . . . . . .  100,000
       Cash . . . . . . . . . . . . . . . . . . . . . . . . . . . . . . . . .         100,000
       To pay the liability for a cash dividend declared and
       recorded on November 20, 19B.
   ```

For instructional purposes the time lag between the date of declaration and the date of payment may be ignored because it does not pose any substantive issues. Also, when all of the three dates fall in the same accounting period, a single entry on the date of payment may be made in practice for purely practical reasons.

Reporting Retained Earnings

Many corporations prepare a separate statement of retained earnings (Exhibit 12–7). It is not a required statement because corporations may elect to report the required information in the retained earnings section of the balance sheet or on the income statement. The statement of retained earnings explains how the balance of retained earnings changed during the accounting period. The typical causes of changes are net income for the period, dividends (cash or stock), and prior period adjustments.

Prior Period Adjustments

The income statement reports revenues that were earned during the accounting period and expenses that were matched with the related revenues. Under rare circumstances, an accounting error may occur in one period and be discovered in a subsequent period. Prior period adjustments are corrections of accounting errors that occurred in the financial statements of prior periods.

If an accounting error from a previous period were corrected by making an adjustment to the current income statement, net income for the current period would be improperly measured. To avoid this problem, prior period adjustments are reported as an adjustment of the beginning balance of retained earnings because the incorrect amount of net income from the earlier year was closed to retained earnings in the year the error was made. Prior period adjustments are not reported on the current income statement. Exhibit 12–7 illustrates the reporting of a prior period adjustment.

Exhibit 12–7 Statement of retained earnings

FERRARI CORPORATION
Statement of Retained Earnings
For the Year Ended December 31, 19C

Retained earnings balance, January 1, 19C		$226,000
Prior period adjustment:		
Deduct adjustment for correction of prior		
accounting error (net of income tax)		10,000
Balance as restated		216,000
Net income for 19C		34,000
Total		250,000
Deduct dividends declared in 19C:		
On preferred stock	$ 6,000	
On common stock	12,000	18,000
Retained earnings balance, December 31, 19C		$232,000

Restrictions on Retained Earnings

Often corporations have restrictions on retained earnings. Such a **restriction temporarily removes an amount of retained earnings from availability for dividends.** Restrictions on retained earnings may be voluntary or involuntary. An **involuntary** restriction may be part of a loan agreement when a corporation borrows money from a bank. For additional security, some banks want to limit the amount of dividends that a corporation can pay by placing a restriction on their retained earnings. The management or the board of directors may **voluntarily** establish a restriction on earnings for expansion of the business or for any other purpose. This restriction can be removed by the management or board of directors at any time.

The **full-disclosure principle** requires that restrictions on retained earnings be reported on the financial statements or in a separate note to the financial statements.

A practice used widely in past years, but now used less often, was to set up a separate retained earnings account for special purposes and call the account appropriated retained earnings. Such accounts, somewhat illogically, often were called reserves. A journal entry to establish an appropriation of retained earnings would be:

```
Retained earnings . . . . . . . . . . . . . . . . . . . . . . . . . . . . . .  100,000
    Appropriated retained earnings for future
        plant expansion . . . . . . . . . . . . . . . . . . . . . . . . . . .              100,000
```

When management determines that the appropriation is no longer required, the following entry is made:

```
Appropriated retained earnings for future
    plant expansion . . . . . . . . . . . . . . . . . . . . . . . . . . . . .  100,000
        Retained earnings . . . . . . . . . . . . . . . . . . . . . . . . . .              100,000
```

An appropriation (or restriction) of retained earnings is **not cash.** Observe in the above journal entries that cash was not affected; the **only** effect was to remove a specific amount of retained earnings from dividend availability. To set aside cash for a special purpose, Cash is credited and a **fund** account (e.g., building construction fund) is debited. Such fund accounts are assets similar to a savings account. Thus, there is no necessary relationship between appropriations of retained earnings and cash.

Accounting and Reporting for Unincorporated Businesses

There are three forms of business organizations: **corporations, sole proprietorships** (i.e., one owner), and **partnerships** (i.e., two or more owners). The fundamentals of accounting and reporting for unincorporated businesses are the same as for a corporation except for **owners' equity.** Typical account structures for the three forms of business organizations are outlined in Exhibit 12–8.

Accounting for sole proprietorships and partnerships is discussed in Chapter Supplement 12B.

Exhibit 12–8 Comparative account structures among types of business entities

TYPICAL ACCOUNT STRUCTURE		
Corporation (stockholders' equity)	**Sole Proprietorship** (owner's equity)	**Partnership** (partners' equity)
Capital stock Contributed capital in excess of par	Doe, capital	Able, capital Baker, capital
Retained earnings	Not used	Not used
Dividends paid	Doe, drawings	Able, drawings Baker, drawings
Income summary (closed to Retained Earnings)	Income summary (closed to Doe, Capital)	Income summary (closed to Able, Capital and Baker, Capital)
Revenues, expenses, gains, and losses	Same	Same
Assets and liabilities	Same	Same

DEMONSTRATION CASE

(Try to resolve the requirements before proceeding to the suggested solution that follows.)

This case focuses on the organization and operations for the first year of Shelly Corporation, which was organized on January 1, 19A. The laws of the state specify that the legal capital for nopar stock is the full sale amount. The corporation was organized by 10 local entrepreneurs for the purpose of operating a business to sell various operating supplies to hotels. The charter **authorized** the following capital stock:

Common stock, nopar value, 20,000 shares.

Preferred stock, 5%, $100 par value, 5,000 shares (cumulative, nonparticipating, nonconvertible, and nonvoting; liquidation value, $110).

The following summarized transactions, selected from 19A, were completed on the dates indicated:

1. Jan.   Sold a total of 7,500 shares of nopar common stock to the 10 entrepreneurs for cash at $52 per share. Credit the Nopar Common Stock account for the total sales amount.

2. Feb.   Sold 1,890 shares of preferred stock at $102 per share; cash collected in full.

3. Mar. Purchased land for a store site and made full payment by issuing 100 shares of preferred stock. Early construction of the store is planned. Debit Land (store site). The preferred stock is selling at $102 per share.

4. Apr. Paid $1,980 cash for organization costs. Debit an intangible asset account called Organization Cost.

5. May Issued 10 shares of preferred stock to A. B. Cain in full payment of legal services rendered in connection with organization of the corporation. Assume the preferred stock is selling regularly at $102 per share. Debit Organization Cost.

6. June Sold 500 shares of nopar common stock for cash to C. B. Abel at $54 per share.

7. July Purchased 100 shares of preferred stock that had been sold and issued earlier. The stockholder was moving to another state and "needed the money." Shelly Corporation paid the stockholder $104 per share.

8. Aug. Sold 20 shares of the preferred treasury stock at $105 per share.

9. Dec. 31 Purchased equipment for $600,000; paid cash. No depreciation expense should be recorded in 19A.

10. Dec. 31 Borrowed $20,000 cash from the City Bank on a one-year, interest-bearing note. Interest is payable at a 12% rate at maturity.

11. Dec. 31 Gross revenues for the year amounted to $129,300; expenses, including corporation income tax but excluding amortization of organization costs, amounted to $98,000. Assume that these summarized revenue and expense transactions were paid in cash. Because the equipment and the bank loan transactions were on December 31, no related adjusting entries at the end of 19A are needed.

12. Dec. 31 Shelly Corporation decided that a reasonable amortization period for organization costs, starting as of January 1, 19A, would be 10 years. This intangible asset must be amortized to expense. Give the required adjusting entry for 19A.

Required:

a. Give appropriate journal entries, with a brief explanation for each of the above transactions.

b. Give appropriate closing entries at December 31, 19A.

c. Prepare a balance sheet for Shelly Corporation at December 31, 19A. Emphasize full disclosure of stockholders' equity.

Suggested Solution

Requirement a—Journal entries:

1. January 19A:

Cash 390,000
  Nopar common stock (7,500 shares)   390,000
  Sale of nopar common stock ($52 × 7,500 shares =
  $390,000).

2. February 19A:

Cash 192,780
  Preferred stock, 5% (par $100; 1,890 shares)   189,000
  Contributed capital in excess of par, preferred stock
   [1,890 shares × ($102 − $100)]   3,780
  Sale of preferred stock ($102 × 1,890 shares =
  $192,780).

3. March 19A:

Land (store site) 10,200
  Preferred stock, 5% (par $100; 100 shares)   10,000
  Contributed capital in excess of par, preferred stock   200
  Purchased land for future store site; paid in full by issuance
  of 100 shares of preferred stock. The market value is $102 ×
  100 shares = $10,200.

4. April 19A:

Organization cost 1,980
  Cash   1,980
  Paid organization cost.

5. May 19A:

Organization cost 1,020
  Preferred stock, 5% (par $100; 10 shares)   1,000
  Contributed capital in excess of par, preferred stock   20
  Organization cost (legal services) paid by issuance of 10
  shares of preferred stock. The implied market value is $102
  × 10 shares = $1,020.

6. June 19A:

Cash 27,000
  Nopar common stock (500 shares)   27,000
  Sold 500 shares of the nopar common stock ($54 × 500
  shares = $27,000).

7. **July 19A:**

Treasury stock, preferred (100 shares at $104)	10,400	
Cash		10,400

Purchased 100 shares of preferred treasury stock ($104 × 100 shares = $10,400).

8. **August 19A:**

Cash (20 shares at $105)	2,100	
Treasury stock, preferred (20 shares at $104)		2,080
Contributed capital from treasury stock transactions		20

Sold 20 shares of the preferred treasury stock at $105.

9. **December 31, 19A:**

Equipment	600,000	
Cash		600,000

Purchased equipment.

10. **December 31, 19A:**

Cash	20,000	
Note payable		20,000

Borrowed on one-year, 12% interest-bearing note.

11. **December 31, 19A:**

Cash	129,300	
Revenues		129,300
Expenses	98,000	
Cash		98,000

To record summarized revenues and expenses.

12. **December 31, 19A:**

Expenses	300	
Organization cost		300

Adjusting entry to amortize organization cost for one year [($1,980 + $1,020) ÷ 10 years = $300].

Requirement b—Closing Entries:
13. **December 31, 19A:**

Revenues	129,300	
Income summary		129,300
Income summary	98,300	
Expenses ($98,000 + $300)		98,300
Income summary	31,000	
Retained earnings		31,000

($129,300 − $98,300 = $31,000.)

Requirement c:

SHELLY CORPORATION
Balance Sheet
At December 31, 19A

Assets

Current assets:		
Cash		$ 50,800
Tangible assets:		
Land	$ 10,200	
Equipment (no depreciation assumed in the problem)	600,000	610,200
Intangible asssets:		
Organization cost (cost, $3,000 less amortization, $300)		2,700
Total assets		$663,700

Liabilities

Current liabilities:		
Note payable, 12%		$ 20,000

Stockholders' Equity

Contributed capital:		
Preferred stock, 5% (par value $100; authorized 5,000 shares,		
issued 2,000 shares of which 80 shares are held as		
treasury stock)	$200,000	
Common stock (nopar value; authorized 20,000 shares,		
issued and outstanding 8,000 shares)	417,000	
Contributed capital in excess of par, preferred stock	4,000	
Contributed capital from treasury stock transactions	20	
Total contributed capital	621,020	
Retained earnings	31,000	
Total	652,020	
Less cost of preferred treasury stock held (80 shares)	8,320	
Total stockholders' equity		643,700
Total liabilities and stockholders' equity		$663,700

SUMMARY OF CHAPTER

This chapter discussed accounting for owners' equity for corporations. Sole proprietorships and partnerships are discussed in Chapter Supplement 12B. Except for owners' equity, accounting basically is unaffected by the type of business organization. Each specific source of owners' equity should be accounted for separately. The two basic sources of owners' equity for a corporation are contributed capital and retained earnings. Separate accounts are kept for each type of capital stock.

The earnings of a corporation that are not retained in the business for growth and expansion are distributed to the stockholders by means of dividends. Dividends are paid only when formally declared by the board of directors of the corporation. A cash dividend results in a decrease in assets (cash) and a commensurate decrease in stockholders' equity (retained earnings). In contrast, a stock dividend does not change assets, liabilities, or total stockholders' equity. A stock dividend results in a transfer of retained earnings to the permanent or contributed capital of the corporation by the amount of the stock dividend. Therefore, a stock dividend affects only certain account balances within stockholders' equity. A stock split affects only the par value of the stock and the number of shares outstanding; the individual equity account balances are not changed. Frequently a corporation purchases its own stock in the marketplace. Stock previously issued by the corporation and subsequently reacquired is known as **treasury stock** as long as it is held by the issuing corporation. The purchase of treasury stock is viewed as a contraction of corporate capital, and the subsequent resale of the treasury stock is viewed as an expansion of corporate capital.

CHAPTER SUPPLEMENT 12A

Participating Dividend Preference on Preferred Stock

Preferred stock may be nonparticipating, fully participating, or partially participating. Participation relates to the dividends that can be paid on preferred stock **after** dividends in arrears and **after** the current dividend preference.

Most preferred stock is **nonparticipating.** Preferred stock that is **participating** may be either noncumulative or cumulative.

Fully participating and **noncumulative** preferred stock receives a first priority for the current dividend preference; then a matching proportionate amount is allocated to the common stock; any remaining balance of the total dividend is allocated on a proportionate basis to the preferred and common stock as shown in Exhibit 12–9, Case A.

Fully participating and **cumulative** preferred stock receives a first priority on both dividends in **arrears** and the current dividend preference. After those preferences are satisfied, a proportionate amount is allocated to the common stock; any remaining balance of total dividends to be paid is allocated on a proportionate basis to the preferred and common stock as shown in Exhibit 12–9, Case B.

Partially participating preferred stock essentially is the same as fully participating. However, the participating preference in excess of the current dividend rate is limited to a stated percent of par, such as an additional 2% of par. Fully participating and partially participating preferred stock preferences are rare.

CHAPTER SUPPLEMENT 12B

Accounting for Owners' Equity for Sole Proprietorships and Partnerships

A sole proprietorship is an unincorporated business owned by one person. The only owner's equity accounts needed are (1) a capital account for the proprietor

Exhibit 12-9　Dividends on participating preferred stock

Situation: Box Corporation

Preferred stock, 6%, par $20; shares outstanding, 2,000 = $40,000.
Common stock, par $10; shares outstanding, 5,000 = $50,000.
Dividends in arrears for the two previous years.

Allocation of dividends between preferred and common stock assuming fully participating:

| | Amount of dividends paid | | |
Assumptions (dividends in arrears, two years)	6% preferred stock (total par, $40,000)	Common stock (total par, $50,000)	Total dividends paid
Case A—Preferred stock is fully participating and non-cumulative (two years in arrears). Total dividends paid, $7,200:			
Current dividend ($40,000 × 6%)	$ 2,400		$ 2,400
Equivalent amount to common ($50,000 × 6%)		$3,000	3,000
Subtotal			5,400
Full participation—balance allocated in ratio of par values:			
($40,000/$90,000) × ($7,200 − $5,400)	800		800
($50,000/$90,000) × ($7,200 − $5,400)		1,000	1,000
Totals	$ 3,200	$4,000	$ 7,200
Case B—Preferred stock is fully participating and cumulative (two years in arrears). Total dividends paid, $16,500:			
Arrears ($2,400 × 2 years)	$ 4,800		$ 4,800
Current preference ($40,000 × 6%)	2,400		2,400
Equivalent amount to common ($50,000 × 6%)		$3,000	3,000
Subtotal			10,200
Full participation—balance allocated in ratio of par:			
($40,000/$90,000) × ($16,500 − $10,200)	2,800		2,800
($50,000/$90,000) × ($16,500 − $10,200)		3,500	3,500
Totals	$10,000	$6,500	$16,500

(for example, J. Doe, Capital); and (2) a drawing (or withdrawal) account for the proprietor (for example, J. Doe, Drawings). The **capital account** of a sole proprietorship is used for two purposes: to record investments by the owner and to accumulate the periodic income or loss. Thus, the **Income Summary account** is closed to the capital account at the end of each accounting period. The **drawing account** is used to record withdrawals of cash or other assets by the owner from the business. The drawing account is closed to the capital account at the end of each accounting period. The capital account reflects the cumulative total of all investments by the owner, plus all earnings of the entity, less all withdrawals of resources from the entity by the owner. In most respects, the accounting for a sole proprietorship is the same as for a corporation.

Exhibit 12–10 presents the recording of selected transactions and the owner's equity section of the balance sheet of Doe Retail Store to illustrate the accounting for **owner's equity** for a sole proprietorship.

A sole proprietorship does not pay income taxes. Therefore, the financial statements of a sole proprietorship will not reflect income tax expense or income taxes payable. The net income of a sole proprietorship is taxed when it is included on the **personal** income tax return of the owner. Also, because an employer/employee contractual relationship cannot exist with only one party involved, a "salary" to the owner is not recognized as an expense of a sole proprietorship. The salary of the owner is accounted for as a distribution of profits (i.e., a withdrawal).

Owners' Equity for a Partnership

The Uniform Partnership Act, which has been adopted by most states, defines a partnership as "an association of two or more persons to carry on as co-owners of a business for profit." The partnership form of business is used by small businesses and professionals, such as accountants, doctors, and lawyers. A partnership is formed by two or more persons reaching mutual agreement about the terms of the partnership. The law does not require an application for a charter as in the case of a corporation. The agreement between the partners constitutes a **partnership contract** that should be in writing. The partnership agreement should specify such matters as division of periodic income, management responsibilities, transfer or sale of partnership interests, disposition of assets upon liquidation, and procedures to be followed in case of the death of a partner. If the partnership agreement does not specify on these matters, the laws of the resident state will be binding. The primary advantages of a partnership are (1) ease of formation, (2) complete control by the partners, and (3) no income taxes on the business itself. The primary disadvantage is the unlimited liability of each partner for the liabilities of the partnership.

As with a sole proprietorship, accounting for a partnership follows the same underlying fundamentals of accounting as any other form of business organization, **except for those entries that directly affect owners' equity.** Accounting for partners' equity follows the same pattern as illustrated earlier for a sole proprietorship, except that separate partner capital and drawings accounts must be established for **each** partner. Investments by each partner are credited to the partner's capital account. Withdrawals from the partnership by each partner are debited to the respective drawings account. The net income for a partnership is divided between the partners in the **profit ratio** specified in the partnership agreement. The Income Summary account is closed to the respective partner capital accounts. The respective drawings accounts also are closed to the partner capital accounts. Therefore, after the closing process, the capital account of each

Exhibit 12–10 Accounting for owner's equity for a sole proprietorship

Selected entries during 19A:

January 1, 19A:

    J. Doe started a retail store by investing $150,000 of personal savings. The journal entry for the business would be as follows:

Cash	150,000	
J. Doe, capital		150,000
Investment by owner.		

During 19A:

    Each month during the year, Doe withdrew $1,000 cash from the business for personal living costs. Accordingly, each month the following journal entry was made.

J. Doe, drawings	1,000	
Cash		1,000
Withdrawal of cash by owner for personal use.		

    Note: At December 31, 19A, after the last withdrawal, the drawings account will reflect a debit balance of $12,000.

December 31, 19A:

    Usual journal entries for the year, including adjusting and closing entries for the revenue and expense accounts, resulted in an $18,000 **credit balance** in the Income Summary account (i.e., $18,000 net income). The next closing entry will be:

Income summary	18,000	
J. Doe, capital		18,000
Closing entry to transfer net income for the year to the owner's equity account.		

December 31, 19A:

    The journal entry required on this date to close the drawings account would be:

J. Doe, capital	12,000	
J. Doe, drawings		12,000
Closing entry to transfer drawings for the year to the capital account.		

Balance sheet December 31, 19A (partial):

Owner's Equity

J. Doe, capital, January 1, 19A	$150,000	
Add: Net income for 19A	18,000	
Total	168,000	
Less: Withdrawals for 19A	12,000	
J. Doe, capital December 31, 19A		$156,000

Exhibit 12–11 Accounting for partners' equity

Selected entries during 19A:

January 1, 19A:

AB Partnership was organized by A. Able and B. Baker on this date. Able contributed $60,000 and Baker $40,000 cash in the partnership and agreed to divide net income (and net loss) 60% and 40%, respectively. The journal entry for the business to record the investment would be:

Cash	100,000	
A. Able, capital		60,000
B. Baker, capital		40,000

Investment to initiate a partnership.

During 19A:

It was agreed that in lieu of salaries, Able would withdraw $1,000 and Baker $650 per month in cash. Accordingly, **each month** the following journal entry for the withdrawals was made:

A. Able, drawings	1,000	
B. Baker, drawings	650	
Cash		1,650

Withdrawal of cash by partners for personal use.

December 31, 19A:

Assume the normal closing entries for the revenue and expense accounts resulted in a $30,000 **credit balance** in the Income Summary account (i.e., $30,000 net income). The next closing entry would be:

Income summary	30,000	
A. Able, capital		18,000
B. Baker, capital		12,000

Closing entry to transfer net income to the respective capital accounts. Net income divided as follows:

A. Able, $30,000 × 60% = $18,000
B. Baker, $30,000 × 40% = 12,000

    Total $30,000

December 31, 19A:

The journal entry required to close the drawings account would be:

A. Able, capital	12,000	
B. Baker, capital	7,800	
A. Able, drawings		12,000
B. Baker, drawings		7,800

Closing entry to transfer drawings for the year to the respective capital accounts.

Exhibit 12–11 *(concluded)*

> After the closing entries the partners' accounts would reflect the following balances:
>
> | | |
> |--------------------------|----------|
> | Income summary | –0– |
> | A. Able, drawings | –0– |
> | B. Baker, drawings | –0– |
> | A. Able, capital | $66,000 |
> | B. Baker, capital | 44,200 |
>
> **Reporting partners' distribution of net income and partners' equity:**
>
> **Income statement for the year ended December 31, 19A:**
>
> | | |
> |---|---|
> | Net income | $ 30,000 |
>
> Distribution of net income:
>
> | | | |
> |---|---|---|
> | A. Able (60%) | $18,000 | |
> | B. Baker (40%) | 12,000 | |
> | | $30,000 | |
>
> **Balance sheet December 31, 19A:**
>
> **Partners' Equity**
>
> | | |
> |---|---|
> | A. Able, capital | $66,000 |
> | B. Baker, capital | 44,200 |
> | Total partners' equity | $110,200 |
>
> A separate statement of partners' capital similar to the following customarily is prepared to supplement the balance sheet:
>
> **AB PARTNERSHIP**
> **Statement of Partners' Capital**
> **For the Year Ended December 31, 19A**
>
> | | A. Able | B.Baker | Total |
> |--|----------|----------|-----------|
> | Investment, January 1, 19A | $60,000 | $40,000 | $100,000 |
> | Add: Additional investments during the year | –0– | –0– | –0– |
> | Net income for the year | 18,000 | 12,000 | 30,000 |
> | Totals | 78,000 | 52,000 | 130,000 |
> | Less: Drawings during the year | 12,000 | 7,800 | 19,800 |
> | Partners' equity, December 31, 19A | $66,000 | $44,200 | $110,200 |

partner reflects the cumulative total of all investments of the individual partner, plus the partner's share of all partnership earnings, less all withdrawals by the partner.

Exhibit 12–11 presents selected journal entries and partial financial statements of AB Partnership to illustrate the accounting for the distribution of income and partners' equity.

The financial statements of a partnership follow the same format as a corporation, except (1) the income statement includes an additional section entitled "Distribution of net income," (2) the partners' equity section of the balance sheet is detailed for each partner in conformity with the full-disclosure principle, (3) there is no income tax expense or income taxes payable because partnerships do not pay income tax (each partner must report his or her share of the partnership profits on the individual tax return), and (4) salaries paid to partners are not recorded as expense but are treated as a distribution of earnings (i.e., withdrawals).

IMPORTANT TERMS DEFINED IN THIS CHAPTER

Authorized Shares Maximum number of shares of the corporation that can be issued as specified in the charter. *p. 580*

Charter of a Corporation The legal articles of incorporation by the state that create a corporation; specifies purpose and capital. *p. 578*

Common Stock The basic, normal, voting stock issued by a corporation; not preferred stock; residual equity. *p. 581*

Convertible Preferred Stock Preferred stock that is convertible, at the option of the holder, to common stock. *p. 582*

Cumulative Dividend Preference Preferred stock preference that dividends not declared for a particular year cumulate as a subsequent preference. *p. 590*

Current Dividend Preference The basic dividend preference on preferred stock for a particular year. *p. 590*

Dividend Dates:

Declaration Date dividend declared; entry for cash dividend; dividends payable. *p. 594*

Payment Date on which a cash dividend is paid to the stockholders of record; cash is disbursed. *p. 594*

Record Date on which the stockholders are individually identified to receive a declared dividend. *p. 594*

Dividends in Arrears Dividends on cumulative preferred stock that have not been declared in prior years. *p. 590*

Issued Shares Total shares of stock that have been issued; shares outstanding plus treasury shares held. *p. 580*

Legal or Stated Capital Defined by state law; usually par value; provides a "cushion" for creditors; cannot be used for dividends. *p. 581*

Nopar Value Stock Shares of capital stock that have nopar value specified in the corporate charter. *p. 581*

Outstanding Shares Shares of stock, in total, that are owned by stockholders on any particular date. *p. 580*

Partnership An unincorporated business owned by two or more persons. *p. 604*

Par Value Nominal value per share of capital stock; specified in the charter; basis for legal capital. *p. 581*

Preferred Stock Shares of stock that have specified rights over the common stock. *p. 582*

Prior Period Adjustments Amounts debited or credited directly to retained earnings resulting from correction of accounting errors. *p. 594*

Restrictions on Retained Earnings Temporary removal of some or all of the balance of retained earnings from dividend availability. *p. 596*

Sole Proprietorship An unincorporated business owned by only one person (one owner). *p. 602*

Stock Certificate Evidence of the number of shares of stock held by an investor; ownership interest. *p. 579*

Stock Dividends Distribution of additional shares of stock to current stockholders on a proportional basis at no cost; decreases retained earnings. *p. 591*

Stock Splits The total number of authorized shares is increased by a specified ratio; issued at no cost; does not change proportional ownership of each stockholder; does not decrease retained earnings. *p. 593*

Treasury Stock A corporation's own stock that has been issued, then reacquired and still held by that corporation. *p. 586*

Unissued Shares Shares of a corporation's stock that have never been issued. *p. 580*

QUESTIONS

Part A: Questions 1–10

1. Define a corporation and identify its primary advantages.
2. What is the charter of a corporation?
3. Explain each of the following terms: (*a*) authorized capital stock, (*b*) issued capital stock, (*c*) unissued capital stock, and (*d*) outstanding capital stock.
4. Distinguish between common stock and preferred stock.
5. Explain the distinction between par value stock and nopar value capital stock.
6. What are the usual characteristics of preferred stock?
7. What are the two basic sources of stockholders' equity? Explain each.

8. Owners' equity is accounted for by source. What is meant by source?

9. Define treasury stock. Why do corporations acquire treasury stock?

10. How is treasury stock reported on the balance sheet? How is the "gain or loss" on treasury stock which has been sold reported on the financial statements?

Part B: Questions 11–18

11. What are the two basic requirements to support a cash dividend? What are the effects of a cash dividend on assets and stockholders' equity?

12. Distinguish between cumulative and noncumulative preferred stock.

13. Define a stock dividend. How does it differ from a cash dividend?

14. What are the primary purposes of issuing a stock dividend?

15. Identify and explain the three important dates in respect to dividends.

16. Define retained earnings. What are the primary components of retained earnings at the end of each period?

17. Define prior period adjustments. How are they reported?

18. What is meant by restrictions on retained earnings?

EXERCISES

Part A: Exercises 12–1 to 12–7

E12–1   (Match Definitions with Terms)
Match each definition with its related term by entering the appropriate letter in each space provided.

Terms	Definitions
_____ (1) Unissued shares	A. Specified by the corporate charter, the maximum number of shares of capital stock the corporation can issue.
_____ (2) Stock dividends	
_____ (3) Dividends in arrears	
_____ (4) Authorized shares	B. The class of stock that is issued when only one kind is issued.
_____ (5) Nopar value stock	C. Provides the option of being exchanged for common stock.
_____ (6) Common stock	
_____ (7) Declaration date	D. Requires that if dividends are not paid in full, the unpaid amount of dividends accumulates.
_____ (8) Stock splits	
_____ (9) Cumulative dividend preference	E. The date on which the board of directors officially approves a dividend.
_____ (10) Record date	F. The date on which the corporation prepares a list of those owning outstanding shares.
_____ (11) Issued shares	G. The date cash dividends are disbursed.
_____ (12) Par value	H. The accumulated unpaid preferred stock dividends.
_____ (13) Legal or stated capital	

Terms	Definitions
_____ (14) Payment date	I. Includes treasury stock.
_____ (15) Treasury stock	J. Par value.
_____ (16) Convertible pre-	K. Stock that cannot be sold at a premium or dis-
ferred stock	count.
_____ (17) Preferred stock	L. Nominal value per share established for the
_____ (18) Prior period	stock in the charter of the corporation.
adjustment	M. Stock whose characteristics usually include divi-

M. Stock whose characteristics usually include dividend preferences, conversion privileges, asset preferences, and nonvoting specification.

N. Correction of an error in the financial statements of a prior period that must be reported on the statement of retained earnings.

O. A board of directors may declare and issue this instead of a cash dividend; it decreases retained earnings.

P. Similar to a stock dividend but does not decrease retained earnings.

Q. Capital stock reacquired which reduces cash and stockholders' equity by equal amounts.

R. Authorized shares minus issued shares.

E12–2   (Preparing the Stockholders' Equity Section of the Balance Sheet)

Newman Corporation was organized in 19A to operate an engineering service business. The charter authorized the following capital stock: common stock, par value $11 per share, 10,000 shares. During the first year, the following selected transactions were completed:

1. Sold and issued 5,000 shares of common stock for cash at $25 per share.
2. Issued 500 shares of common stock for a piece of land that will be used for a facilities site; construction began immediately. Assume the stock was selling at $27 per share at the date of issuance. Debit land.
3. Sold and issued, 1,000 shares of common stock for cash at $27 per share.
4. At year-end, the Income Summary account reflected a $12,000 loss. Because a loss was incurred, no income tax expense was recorded.

Required:

a. Give the journal entry required for each of the transactions listed above.

b. Prepare the stockholders' equity section as it should be reported on the year-end balance sheet.

E12–3   (Analysis of Transactions Affecting Stockholders' Equity)

Bently Corporation was organized in January 19A by 12 stockholders to operate an air conditioning sales and service business. The charter issued by the state authorized the following capital stock:

Common stock, $1 par value, 100,000 shares.

Preferred stock, $10 par value, 8%, nonparticipating, noncumulative, 30,000 shares.

During January and February 19A, the following stock transactions were completed:

1. Collected $30,000 cash from each of the 12 organizers and issued 1,000 shares of common stock to each of them.

2. Sold 7,000 shares of preferred stock at $30 per share; collected the cash and immediately issued the stock.

Required:

a. Give the journal entries to record the above stock transactions.

b. Net income for 19A was $35,000; cash dividends declared and paid at year-end were $20,000. Prepare the stockholders' equity section of the balance sheet at December 31, 19A.

E12–4   (Issuing Common and Preferred Stock)
Wells, Incorporated, was issued a charter on January 15, 19A, that authorized the following capital stock:

Common stock, nopar, 80,000 shares.

Preferred stock, 8%, par value $10 per share, 10,000 shares.

The board of directors established a stated value on the nopar common stock of $5 per share.

During 19A, the following selected transactions were completed in the order given:

1. Sold and issued 30,000 shares of the nopar common stock at $30 cash per share.

2. Sold and issued 4,000 shares of preferred stock at $21 cash per share.

3. At the end of 19A, the Income Summary account had a credit balance of $42,000.

Required:

a. Give the journal entry indicated for each of the above transactions.

b. Prepare the stockholders' equity section of the balance sheet at December 31, 19A.

E12–5   (Stockholders' Equity Transactions, Including Noncash Consideration)
Cooke Corporation obtained a charter at the start of 19A that authorized 40,000 shares of nopar common stock and 10,000 shares of preferred stock, par value $10. The corporation was organized by five individuals who "reserved" 51% of the common stock shares for themselves. The remaining shares were to be sold to other individuals at $50 per share on a cash basis. During 19A, the following selected transactions occurred:

1. Collected $20 per share cash from four of the organizers and received two adjoining lots of land from the fifth organizer. Issued 3,000 shares of common stock to each of the five organizers and received title to the land.

2. Sold and issued 5,000 shares of common stock to an "outsider" at $50 cash per share.

3. Sold and issued 6,000 shares of preferred stock at $15 cash per share.

4. At the end of 19A, the Income Summary account, after income taxes, reflected a credit balance of $25,000.

Required:

a. Give the journal entries indicated for each of the transactions listed above.

b. Prepare the stockholders' equity section of the balance sheet at December 31, 19A.

c. Explain the basis that you used to determine the cost of the land.

E12–6 (Finding Missing Amounts from the Stockholders' Equity Section)

The stockholders' equity section on the December 31, 19D, balance sheet of Carbide Corporation was:

Stockholders' Equity

Contributed capital:
Preferred stock (par $30; authorized 8,000 shares, ___?___ issued,
of which 600 shares are held as treasury stock) $165,000
Common stock (nopar; authorized 10,000 shares, issued and
outstanding 7,000 shares) 630,000
Contributed capital in excess of par, preferred 7,150
Contributed capital, treasury stock transactions 2,000
Retained earnings 40,000
Cost of treasury stock, preferred 15,000

Required:
Complete the following statements and show your computations.

a. The number of shares of preferred stock issued was _____.

b. The number of shares of preferred stock outstanding was _____.

c. The average sale price of the preferred stock when issued was $_____ per share.

d. Have the treasury stock transactions (1) increased corporate resources _____; or (2) decreased resources _____? By how much? _____.

e. How much did the treasury stock transactions increase (decrease) stockholders' equity?

f. How much did the treasury stock held cost per share? $_____

g. Total stockholders' equity is $_____.

h. What was the average issue price of the common stock? $_____.

i. Assuming one third of the treasury stock is sold at $40 per share, the remaining balance in the Treasury Stock account would be $_____.

E12–7 (Accounting for Treasury Stock Transactions)

The balance sheet (summarized) of Roman Corporation reflected the information shown below at December 31, 19B:

ROMAN CORPORATION
Balance Sheet
At December 31, 19B

Assets		Liabilities	
Cash	$115,000	Current liabilities	$ 75,000
All other assets	412,000	Long-term liabilities	80,000
			155,000
		Stockholders' Equity	
		Contributed capital:	
		Common stock (par $20;	
		authorized 20,000 shares,	
		outstanding 12,000 shares) . . .	240,000
		Contributed capital in	
		excess of par	72,000
		Retained earnings	60,000
		Total liabilities and	
Total assets	$527,000	stockholders' equity	$527,000

During the next year, 19C, the following selected transactions affecting stockholders' equity occurred:

Feb.   1   Purchased in the open market, 500 shares of the company's own common stock at $40 cash per share.

July 15   Sold 100 of the shares purchased on February 1, 19C, at $41 cash per share.

Sept. 1   Sold 20 more of the shares purchased on February 1, 19C, at $38 cash per share.

Dec. 15   Sold an additional 80 of the treasury shares at $35 per share.

     31   The credit balance in the Income Summary account was $26,500.

Required:

a. Give the indicated journal entries for each of the five transactions.

b. Prepare the stockholders' equity section of the balance sheet at December 31, 19C.

Part B: Exercises 12–8 to 12–13

E12–8   (Comparing Various Types of Preferred Stock)
The records of Golden Company reflected the following balances in the stockholders' equity accounts at December 31, 19H:

Common stock, par $5 per share, 30,000 shares outstanding.

Preferred stock, 7%, par $10 per share, 3,000 shares outstanding.

Retained earnings, $150,000.

On September 1, 19H, the board of directors was considering the distribution of a $42,000 cash dividend. No dividends were paid during 19F and 19G. You have been asked to determine the total and per share amounts that would be paid to the common stockholders and to the preferred stockholders under three independent assumptions (show computations):

a. The preferred stock is noncumulative and nonparticipating.

b. The preferred stock is cumulative and nonparticipating.

c. The preferred stock is cumulative and fully participating (solve this assumption only if Chapter Supplement 12A is assigned for study).

    d. Give the journal entry to record dividends separately for preferred and common stock under each assumption.

    e. Explain why the dividends per share of common stock were less for each assumption than for the preceding assumption.

    f. What factor would cause a more favorable per share result to the common stockholders?

E12–9 (Recording Dividends)

Common Corporation has the following capital stock outstanding at the end of 19B:

Preferred stock, 8%, par $20, outstanding shares, 6,000.

Common stock, par $5, outstanding shares, 20,000.

On October 1, 19B, the board of directors declared dividends as follows:

Preferred stock, the full cash preference amount; payable December 20, 19B.

Common stock, a 10% common stock dividend (i.e., one additional share for each 10 held), issuable December 20, 19B.

On December 20, 19B, the market prices were preferred stock, $50, and common stock, $25.

Required:

    a. Give any required journal entry(s) to record the declaration and subsequent payment of the dividend on the preferred stock.

    b. Give any required journal entry(s) to record the declaration and issuance of the stock dividend on the common stock.

    c. Explain the overall effect of each of the dividends on the assets, liabilities, and stockholders' equity of the company.

E12–10 (Analysis of Stock Dividends)

On December 31, 19E, the stockholders' equity section of the balance sheet of Tech Corporation reflected the following:

Common stock (par $10; authorized 50,000 shares, outstanding 20,000 shares)	$200,000
Contributed capital in excess of par	15,000
Retained earnings	85,000

On February 1, 19F, the board of directors declared a 15% stock dividend to be issued April 30, 19F. The market value of the stock on February 1, 19F, was $16 per share. The market value will be capitalized.

Required:

    a. Give any required journal entry(s) to record the declaration and issuance of the stock dividend.

    b. For comparative purposes, prepare the stockholders' equity section of the balance sheet (1) immediately before the stock dividend and (2) immediately after the stock dividend. (Hint: Use two amount columns for this requirement.)

    c. Explain the effects of this stock dividend on the assets, liabilities, and stockholders' equity.

E12–11   (Preparation of a Statement of Retained Earnings)

The following account balances were selected from the records of Hamilton Corporation at December 31, 19E, after all adjusting entries were completed:

Common stock (par $5; authorized 200,000 shares, issued 120,000 shares, of
 which 500 shares are held as treasury stock) $600,000
Contributed capital in excess of par 280,000
Bond sinking fund 70,000
Dividends declared and paid in 19E 24,000
Retained earnings, January 1, 19E 110,000
Correction of prior period accounting error (a debit, net of income tax) 10,000
Treasury stock at cost (500 shares) 3,000
Income summary for 19E (credit balance) 45,000

Restriction on retained earnings equal to the cost of treasury stock held is required
 by law in this state.

Required:

Based on the above data, prepare (*a*) the statement of retained earnings for 19E and (*b*) the stockholders' equity section of the balance sheet at December 31, 19E.

E12–12   (Preparing the Statement of Retained Earnings)

The data given below were selected from the records of Bing Corporation at December 31, 19B.

Common stock (par $2; authorized 300,000 shares, issued 110,000 shares, of
 which 1,000 are held as treasury stock [purchased at $8 per share]) $220,000
Preferred stock, 6% (par $10; authorized 20,000 shares, issued and
 outstanding 15,000 shares) 150,000
Contributed capital in excess of par:
 Common stock 230,000
 Preferred stock 120,000
Dividends declared and paid during 19B 16,000
Net income for 19B 64,000
Retained earnings balance, January 1, 19B 130,000
Prior period adjustment (gain, net of income tax) 10,000
Extraordinary loss (unusual and infrequent, net of income tax) 45,000

Required:

a. Prepare a statement of retained earnings for the year ended December 31, 19B.

b. Prepare the stockholders' equity section of the balance sheet dated December 31, 19B.

E12–13   (Comparison of Stock Dividends and Splits)

On July 1, 19B, Green Corporation had the following capital structure:

    Common stock (par $2; authorized shares) 100,000
    Common stock (par $2; unissued shares) 80,000
    Contributed capital in excess of par, $60,000.
    Retained earnings, $120,000.
    Treasury stock, none.

Required:

a. The number of issued shares is _____.

b. The number of outstanding shares is _____.

c. Total stockholders' equity is _____.

d. Assume the board of directors declared and issued a 20% stock dividend when the stock was selling at $11 per share. Give any required journal entry(s). If none is required, explain why.

e. Disregard the stock dividend in (d) above. Assume that the board of directors voted a six-to-five stock split (i.e., a 20% increase in the number of shares). The market price prior to the split was $11 per share. Give any required journal entry(s). If none is required, explain why.

f. Complete the following comparative tabulation followed by comments on the comparative effects:

Items	Before Dividend and Split	After Stock Dividend	After Stock Split
Common stock account	$	$	$
Par per share	$2	$	$
Shares outstanding	#	#	#
Contributed capital in excess of par	$ 60,000	$	$
Retained earnings	$120,000	$	$
Total stockholders' equity	$	$	$

PROBLEMS

Part A: Problems 12-1 to 12-5

P12-1 **(Preparation of the Stockholders' Equity Section of the Balance Sheet)**
Wright Corporation received its charter during January 19A. The charter authorized the following capital stock:

Preferred stock, 6%, par $10, authorized 10,000 shares.

Common stock, par $5, authorized 100,000 shares.

During 19A, the following transactions occurred in the order given:

1. Issued a total of 60,000 shares of the common stock to the six organizers at $6 per share. The company collected cash in full from five of the organizers, legal services were received from the other organizer in full payment for the shares. The stock was issued immediately.

2. Sold 3,000 shares of the preferred stock at $22 per share. Collected the cash and issued the stock immediately.

3. Sold 2,000 shares of the common stock at $7 per share and 1,000 shares of the preferred stock at $30. Collected the cash and issued the stock immediately.

4. Total revenues for 19A, $206,000, and total expenses (including income tax), $150,000.

Required:

a. Give all of the journal entries required for the above items including closing entries.

b. Prepare the stockholders' equity section of the balance sheet at December 31, 19A.

c. What was the average issue price of the common stock?

d. Explain the basis you used to value the legal services in the first journal entry.

P12–2   (Analysis of Transactions Affecting Stockholders' Equity)

Ewing Corporation began operations in January 19A. The charter authorized the following capital stock:

Preferred stock, 6%, $10 par, authorized 20,000 shares.

Common stock, nopar, authorized 100,000 shares.

The corporation, in conformance with state laws, established a stated value per share of $4 for the nopar common stock.

During 19A, the following transactions occurred in the order given:

1. Issued 30,000 shares of the nopar common stock to each of the three organizers. Collected $8 cash per share from two of the organizers and received a plot of land, with a small building thereon, in full payment for the shares of the third organizer and issued the stock immediately. Assume that 20% of the noncash payment received applies to the building.

2. Sold 4,000 shares of the preferred stock at $15 per share. Collected the cash and issued the stock immediately.

3. Sold 200 shares of the preferred stock at $16 and 1,000 shares of the nopar common stock at $10 per share. Collected the cash and issued the stock immediately.

4. Operating results at the end of 19A were as follows:

$$
\begin{array}{ll}
\text{Revenue accounts} & \text{\$190,000} \\
\text{Expense accounts, including income taxes} & \text{105,000}
\end{array}
$$

Required:

a. Give the journal entries indicated (including closing entries) for each of the above transactions.

b. Prepare the stockholders' equity section of the balance sheet at December 31, 19A.

c. Explain what you used to determine the cost of the land and the building in the first journal entry.

P12–3   (Comparison of Par and Nopar Stock)

Rand Company was issued a charter in January 19A, which authorized 75,000 shares of common stock. During 19A, the following selected transactions occurred in the order given:

1. Sold 8,000 shares of the stock for cash at $70 per share. Collected the cash and issued the stock immediately.

2. Acquired land to be used as a future plant site; made payment in full by issuing 500 shares of stock. Assume a market value per share of $75.

3. At the end of 19A, the Income Summary account reflected a credit balance of $65,000.

Three independent cases are assumed as follows for comparative study purposes:

Case A—Assume the common stock was $30 par value per share. The state law specifies that par value is legal capital.

Case B—Assume the common stock was nopar and that the total sale price is credited to the Common Stock, Nopar account because the state law specifies this amount as legal capital.

Case C—Assume the common stock is nopar with a stated value, specified by the board of directors, of $10 per share.

Required:

For each independent case:

a. Give the journal entries for each of the three transactions.

b. Prepare the stockholders' equity section of the balance sheet at December 31, 19A.

c. Should total stockholders' equity be the same amount among the three independent cases? Explain.

d. Should the noncash asset (land) be recorded at the same cost under each of the three independent cases? Explain.

P12–4   **(Analysis of Stockholders' Equity Transactions)**

Global Company obtained a charter from the state in January 19A, which authorized 100,000 shares of common stock, $1 par value. The stockholders comprised 20 local citizens. During the first year, the following selected transactions occurred in the order given:

1. Sold 80,000 shares of the common stock to the 20 stockholders at $5 per share. Collected the $400,000 cash and issued the stock.

2. During the year, one of the 20 stockholders needed cash and wanted to sell the stock back to the company. Accordingly, the company purchased the investor's 5,000 shares at $7 cash per share.

3. Two months later, 1,000 of the shares of treasury stock (purchased in 2) were resold to another individual at $8 cash per share.

4. An additional 1,500 shares of the treasury stock were sold at $6.50 cash per share.

5. On December 31, 19A, the end of the first year of business, the Income Summary account reflected a credit balance of $47,200.

Required:

a. Give the indicated journal entry for each of the above items.

b. Prepare the stockholders' equity section of the balance sheet at December 31, 19A.

c. What dollar effect did the treasury stock transactions have on the assets, liabilities, and stockholders' equity of the company? Explain.

P12–5   **(Analysis of Stockholder Transactions Including Noncash Consideration)**

Ansul Company was granted a charter that authorized the following capital stock:

Common stock, nopar, 50,000 shares. Assume the nopar stock is not assigned a stated value per share.

Preferred stock, 6%, par $10, 10,000 shares.

During the first year, 19A, the following selected transactions occurred in the order given:

1. Sold 20,000 shares of the nopar common stock at $30 cash per share and 3,000 shares of the preferred stock at $22 cash per share. Collected cash and issued the stock immediately. For the nopar stock, credit the full selling price to the common stock account.

2. Issued 1,500 shares of preferred stock as full payment for a plot of land to be used as a future plant site. Assume the stock was selling at $22.

3. Purchased 2,000 shares of the nopar common stock sold earlier; paid cash, $26 per share.

4. Sold all of the treasury stock (common) purchased in 3 above. The sale price was $29 per share.

5. Purchased 500 shares of the company's own preferred stock at $24 cash per share.

6. At December 31, 19A, the Income Summary account reflected a credit balance of $24,500.

Required:

a. Give the journal entries indicated for each of the above transactions.

b. Prepare the stockholders' equity section of the balance sheet at December 31, 19A, end of the annual accounting period.

Part B: Problems 12–6 to 12–12

P12–6 **(Comparison of Stock and Cash Dividends)**

Hydro Company had the following stock outstanding and retained earnings at December 31, 19E:

Common stock (par $10; outstanding 20,000 shares)	$200,000
Preferred stock, 6% (par $20; outstanding 5,000 shares) . . .	100,000
Retained earnings	240,000

The board of directors is considering the distribution of a cash dividend to the two groups of stockholders. No dividends were declared during 19C or 19D. Three independent cases are assumed:

Case A—The preferred stock is noncumulative and nonparticipating; the total amount of dividends is $36,000.

Case B—The preferred stock is cumulative and nonparticipating; the total amount of dividends is $18,000.

Case C—Same as Case B, except the amount is $75,000.

Required:

a. Compute the amount of dividends, in total and per share, that would be payable to each class of stockholders for each case. Show computations.

b. Give the journal entry to record the cash dividends declared and paid in 19E for Case C only. Assume that the declaration and payment occurred simultaneously on December 31, 19E.

c. Give the required journal entry assuming, instead of a cash dividend, the declaration and issuance of a 10% common stock dividend on the outstanding common stock. Assume the market value per share of common stock was $25.

d. Complete the following comparative schedule including explanation of the comparative differences.

Item	Amount of Dollar Increase (Decrease)	
	Cash Dividend—Case C	Stock Dividend
Assets	$	$
Liabilities	$	$
Stockholders' equity	$	$

P12–7   **(Recording Dividends)**

Carter Company has outstanding 50,000 shares of $5 par value common stock and 15,000 shares of $15 par value preferred stock (8%). On December 1, 19B, the board of directors voted an 8% cash dividend on the preferred stock and a 15% common stock dividend on the common stock. At the date of declaration, the common stock was selling at $40 and the preferred at $30 per share. The dividends are to be paid, or issued, on February 15, 19C. The annual accounting period ends December 31.

Required:

a. Give any journal entry(s) required to record the declaration and payment of the cash dividend.

b. Give any journal entry(s) required to record the declaration and issuance of the stock dividend.

c. Explain the comparative effects of the two dividends on the assets, liabilities, and stockholders' equity (1) through December 31, 19B; (2) on February 15, 19C; and (3) the overall effects from December 1, 19B, through February 15, 19C. A schedule similar to the following might be helpful:

Item	Comparative Effects Explained	
	Cash Dividend on Preferred	Stock Dividend on Common
1. Through December 31, 19B: Assets		
etc.		

P12–8   (Analysis of Stockholders' Equity Transactions Including Treasury Stock)
The accounts of Stone Corporation reflected the following balances on January 1, 19C:

Preferred stock, 5% (par $50; cumulative, authorized	
10,000 shares, issued and outstanding 2,000 shares)	$100,000
Common stock (par $10; authorized 100,000 shares,	
outstanding 20,000 shares)	200,000
Contributed capital in excess of par, preferred	5,000
Contributed capital in excess of par, common	10,000
Retained earnings	260,000
Total stockholders' equity	$575,000

The transactions during 19C relating to the stockholders' equity are listed below in order:

1. Purchased 200 shares of preferred treasury stock at $150 per share.
2. The board of directors declared and paid a cash dividend to the preferred stockholders only. No dividends were declared during 19A or 19B. The dividend was sufficient to pay the arrears plus the dividend for the current year.
3. The board of directors declared a 10% common stock dividend on the outstanding common stock. Market value of $20 per share is to be capitalized.
4. Net income for the year was $92,000.

Required:
a. Give the journal entry for each of the above transactions, including the closing entries. Show computations.
b. Prepare a statement of retained earnings for 19C and the stockholders' equity section of the balance sheet at December 31, 19C.
c. Explain the comparative effects on assets and stockholders' equity of (1) the cash dividend and (2) the stock dividend.

P12–9   (Preparing the Stockholders' Equity Section of the Balance Sheet)
Cox Company is completing its year-end accounting, including the preparation of the annual financial statements, at December 31, 19E. The stockholders' equity accounts reflected the following balances at the end of the year, 19E:

Common stock (par $10; shares outstanding, 50,000)	$500,000
Contributed capital in excess of par	50,000
Retained earnings, January 1, 19E (credit)	325,000
Cash dividends declared and paid during 19E (debit)	40,000
Income summary account for 19E (credit balance; after tax) . . .	60,000

The following selected transactions occurred near the end of 19E; they are not included in the above amounts:

1. During 19D, the company was sued for $50,000, and it was clear that the suit would be lost. Therefore, in 19D, the company should have debited a loss and credited a liability for this amount. This journal entry was not made, and the accounting error was found in 19E. (Hint: Credit Liability for Damages.) Disregard any income tax effects.

2. The board of directors voted a voluntary restriction on retained earnings of $250,000. It is to be designated as "Earnings appropriated for plant expansion" effective for the 19E financial statements.

Required:

a. Give the appropriate journal entries for the events listed immediately above. If no entry is given, explain.

b. Prepare a statement of retained earnings for 19E and the stockholders' equity section of the balance sheet at December 31, 19E.

P12–10 **(Preparation of the Statement of Retained Earnings)**

Rye Company has completed all of the annual information processing at December 31, 19D, except for preparation of the financial statements. The following account balances were reflected at that date:

RYE COMPANY
Adjusted Trial Balance
December 31, 19D

	Debit	Credit
Cash	$ 74,000	
Accounts receivable (net)	58,000	
Merchandise inventory, December 31, 19D	120,000	
Long-term investment in Company Y	20,000	
Bond sinking fund	40,000	
Land	20,000	
Buildings and equipment (net)	738,000	
Other assets	29,200	
Accounts payable		$ 86,000
Income taxes payable		18,000
Bonds payable (7%; payable December 31)		100,000
Preferred stock (par $10; authorized 50,000 shares)		100,000
Common stock (par $5; authorized 200,000 shares)		660,000
Contributed capital in excess of par, preferred		6,100
Contributed capital in excess of par, common		19,900
Treasury stock, preferred, 10 shares at cost	1,100	
Retained earnings, January 1, 19D		163,300
19D net income		57,000
19D cash dividends on preferred	26,000	
19D common stock dividends distributed (10,000 shares)	70,000	
19D, discovered an accounting error made in 19A in recording a purchase of land (the correction required a net credit to land of $14,000)	14,000	
	$1,210,300	$1,210,300

Note: Retained earnings is restricted in an amount equal to the bond sinking fund per the provisions of the bond indenture.

Required:

Prepare a statement of retained earnings for 19D and a classified balance sheet at December 31, 19D.

P12-11   (Evaluation of an Inaccurately Prepared Statement)

The bookkeeper for Opps Company prepared the following balance sheet:

OPPS COMPANY
Balance Sheet
For the Year 19W

Assets

Current assets	$ 60,000
Fixed assets (net of depreciation reserves, $85,000) . . .	125,000
Other assets	50,000
Total debits	$235,000

Liabilities

Current liabilities	$ 32,000
Other debts	40,000

Capital

Stock (par $10; authorized 10,000 shares)	60,000
Stock premium	30,000
Earned surplus	58,000
Treasury stock (500 shares)	(10,000)
Reserve for treasury stock (required by law)	10,000
Correction of prior year error (a credit, net)	7,000
Cash dividends paid during 19W	(12,000)
Net profit for 19W	20,000
Total credits	$235,000

Required:

a. List all of the deficiencies you can identify in the above statement. Assume the amounts given are correct.

b. Prepare a statement of retained earnings for 19W.

c. Recast the above balance sheet in good form; focus especially on stockholders' equity.

P12-12   (Based on Chapter Supplement 12B—Comparison of Stockholders' Equity Sections for Alternative Forms of Organization)

Assume for each of the three independent cases below that the annual accounting period ends on December 31, 19W, and that the Income Summary account at that date reflected a debit balance of $30,000 (i.e., a loss).

Case A—Assume that the company is a **sole proprietorship** owned by Proprietor A. Prior to the closing entries, the capital account reflected a credit balance of $70,000 and the drawings account a balance of $6,000.

Case B—Assume that the company is a **partnership** owned by Partner A and Partner B. Prior to the closing entries, the owners' equity accounts reflected the following balances: A, Capital, $50,000; B, Capital, $45,000; A, Drawings, $7,000; and B, Drawings, $6,000. Profits and losses are divided equally.

Case C—Assume that the company is a **corporation**. Prior to the closing entries, the stockholders' equity accounts showed the following: Capital Stock, par $20, authorized 20,000 shares, outstanding 4,000 shares; Contributed Capital in Excess of Par, $2,000; and Retained Earnings, $40,000.

Required:

a. Give all of the closing entries indicated at December 31, 19W, for each of the separate cases.

b. Show how the owners' equity section of the balance sheet would appear at December 31, 19W, for each case.

CASES

C12–1 **(Finding Missing Amounts)**

At December 31, 19E, the records of McDermott Corporation provided the following selected and incomplete data:

> Common stock (par $10; no changes during 19E):
>   Shares authorized, 500,000.
>   Shares issued _?_ issue price $12 per share; cash collected in full, $1,800,000.
>   Shares held as treasury stock, 2,000 shares—cost $20 per share.
> Net income for 19E, $176,000.
> Dividends declared and paid during 19E, $74,000.
> Bond sinking fund balance, $20,000.
> Prior period adjustment—correction of 19B accounting error, $18,000 (a credit, net of income tax).
> Retained earnings balance, January 1, 19E, $180,000.
> State law places a restriction on retained earnings equal to the cost of treasury stock held.
> The treasury stock was acquired after the stock dividend was issued.
> Extraordinary gain (net of income tax), $17,000.

Required:

a. Complete the following tabulation:
      Shares authorized _____.
      Shares issued _____.
      Shares outstanding _____.

b. The balance in the Contributed Capital in Excess of Par account appears to be $_____.

c. EPS on net income is $_____.

d. Dividend paid per share of common stock is $_____.

e. The bond sinking fund should be reported on the balance sheet under the classification _____.

f. Net income before extraordinary items was $_____.

g. The prior period adjustment should be reported on the _____ as an addition _____ or a deduction _____.

h. Treasury stock should be reported on the balance sheet under the major caption _____ in the amount of $_____.

i. The amount of retained earnings available for dividends on January 1, 19E, was $_____.

j. Assume the board of directors voted a 100% stock split (the number of shares will double). After the stock split, the par value per share will be $_____ and the number of outstanding shares will be _____.

k. Assuming the stock split given in (*j*) above, give any journal entry that should be made. If none explain why.

l. Disregard the stock split (assumed in [*j*] and [*k*] above). Assume instead that a 10% stock dividend was declared and issued when the market price of the common stock was $15. Give any journal entry that should be made.

C12–2   (Analysis of Stockholders' Equity for an Actual Company)

JCPenney   Refer to the financial statements of J.C. Penney Company, Inc. given in the appendix immediately preceding the index.

1. What is the par value of the company's stock? How many shares are authorized? How many shares were outstanding at the end of the current year?

2. What was the amount of dividends declared during the current year? What amount of dividends were paid in cash? What were the dividends per share for the current year?

3. Prepare the journal entry that was used to record the stock dividend that was declared on May 1, 1988.

THIRTEEN

MEASURING AND REPORTING LONG-TERM INVESTMENTS

PURPOSE

One corporation may invest in the capital stock of another corporation for a variety of reasons. Often the investment is for a short term, designed to earn a return on idle funds; other investments are for the long term. The latter may be designed to provide the investing corporation with significant influence or control over the other corporation. Long-term investments that do not provide the investor with control are discussed in this chapter. Long-term investments that provide control are discussed in Chapter 14. This chapter also discusses investments in the bonds of another corporation.

The balance sheet often reports the total amount of long-term investments with a note providing additional information. The example on the opposite page is fairly typical.

LEARNING OBJECTIVES

1. Explain and use the cost and equity methods.
2. Account for bonds purchased at par; at a discount; at a premium.
3. Record bonds purchased between interest dates.
4. Use the straight-line and effective-interest amortization methods.
5. Expand your accounting vocabulary by learning the "Important Terms Defined in This Chapter."
6. Apply the knowledge learned from this chapter by completing the homework assigned by your instructor.

ORGANIZATION

Part A—long-term investments in equity securities (stocks)
1. Cost method—no significant influence.
2. Equity method—significant influence but no control.

Part B—long-term investments in debt securities (bonds)
1. Bonds purchased at par.
2. Bonds purchased at a discount.
3. Bonds purchased at a premium.
4. Effective-interest amortization on bonds.
5. Bonds purchased between interest dates.

 **CHRYSLER CORPORATION**

Consolidated Balance Sheet

Chrysler Corporation and Consolidated Subsidiaries

Assets	December 31	
(In millions of dollars)	1987	1986
Current Assets:		
Cash and time deposits	$ 355.4	$ 285.1
Marketable securities—at cost which approximates market (Note 14)	2,054.6	2,394.3
Accounts receivable—trade and other (less allowance for doubtful accounts: 1987–$21.6 million; 1986–$19.9 million)	577.6	372.5
Inventories (Note 3)	2,552.1	1,699.6
Prepaid pension expense (Note 12)	54.1	348.9
Prepaid insurance, taxes and other expenses	577.0	263.6
Total Current Assets	6,170.8	5,364.0
Investments and Other Assets:		
Investments in associated companies (Note 4)	371.8	317.7
Investments in and advances to unconsolidated subsidiaries (Notes 4 and 14)	2,349.1	1,926.0
Intangible assets (Note 2)	2,136.7	386.6
Other noncurrent assets	604.3	287.5
Total Investments and Other Assets	5,461.9	2,917.8
Property, Plant and Equipment (Note 5):		
Land, buildings, machinery and equipment	8,938.9	7,081.5
Less accumulated depreciation	3,089.8	2,767.5
	5,849.1	4,314.0
Unamortized special tools	2,462.8	1,803.8
Net Property, Plant and Equipment	8,311.9	6,117.8
Total Assets	$19,944.6	$14,399.6

Investments and Advances

Note 4

Detail of investments and advances in as follows:

(In millions of dollars)	December 31	
	1987	1986
Investments in Associated Companies:		
Mitsubishi Motors Corporation	$ 242.0	$ 223.1
Diamond-Star Motors Corporation	24.0	50.5
Officine Alfieri Maserati SpA	76.4	41.2
Other	29.4	2.9
Total	$ 371.8	$ 317.7

(In millions of dollars)	December 31	
	1987	1986
Investments in and Advances to Unconsolidated Subsidiaries:		
Chrysler Financial Corporation and Subsidiaries	$ 2,192.4	$ 1,907.5
Other	156.7	18.5
Total	$ 2,349.1	$ 1,926.0

In June 1986, Chrysler sold its equity investment in Peugeot S. A. for $244.3 million net of related selling costs. This sale resulted in a gain before taxes of $144.3 million ($131.9 million net of related taxes).

PART A—LONG-TERM INVESTMENTS IN EQUITY SECURITIES (STOCKS)

A company may invest in the equity securities of other corporations for various reasons. Some of the reasons are to: earn a return on excess cash, exercise influence or control over the other company, attain growth through sales of new products and services, and gain access to new markets and new sources of supply. Usually a corporation will acquire capital stock of another corporation by purchasing outstanding shares from other stockholders for cash (or other assets), or by exchanging some of its own capital stock for outstanding capital stock of the other corporation. A transaction between the acquiring corporation and the stockholders of the acquired corporation affects the accounting records of the acquiring corporation. The transaction has no effect on the accounting records of the acquired corporation.

A corporation may acquire **some or all** of the outstanding stock of the other company. If the purpose of the investment is to gain influence or control, the corporation will acquire **common** stock because it has voting rights. The number of shares of stock acquired by an entity usually depends on the objectives of the investor. For measuring and reporting purposes, **three different levels of ownership** are recognized. The three levels are related to the percentage of the outstanding shares of **voting** capital stock owned by the investor.

Measuring Long-Term Investments in Voting Common Stock

Accounting for long-term investments in voting stock involves measuring the amount of the investment and the periodic investment revenue. At the dates of acquisition of the shares, long-term investments in the stock of another company are recorded as the total consideration given to acquire them. This total includes the market price, plus all commissions and other purchasing costs. Subsequent to acquisition, accounting for long-term investments depends on the relationship between the investor and the investee company. The relevant characteristic of the relationship is the extent to which the investing company can exercise **significant influence or control over the operating and financial policies** of the other company. Significant influence and control are related to the number of voting shares owned of the investee company in proportion to the total number of such shares outstanding.

APB Opinion 18 defines the terms **significant influence** and **control** as follows:

1. **Significant influence**—the ability of the investing company to have an important impact on the operating and financing policies of another company in which it owns shares of the voting stock. Significant influence may be indicated by (*a*) membership on the board of directors of the other company, (*b*) participation in the policy-making processes, (*c*) material transactions between the two companies, (*d*) interchange of management personnel, or (*e*) technological dependency. In the absence

of a clear-cut distinction based on these factors, **significant influence is presumed** if the investing company owns at least 20%, but not more than 50%, of the outstanding voting shares of the other company.

2. **Control**—the ability of the investing company to determine the operating and financing policies of another company in which it owns shares of the voting stock. For all practical purposes, **control is presumed** when the investing company owns more than 50% of the outstanding voting stock of the other company.

The three levels of ownership that relate to the measuring and reporting of long-term investments in voting capital stock are:

Level of ownership	Measuring and reporting approach
1. Neither significant influence nor control	Cost method
2. Significant influence but not control	Equity method
3. Control	Consolidated statement method

Each of these approaches is outlined in Exhibit 13–1. The first two are discussed in this chapter; the third is discussed in Chapter 14.

Cost Method

The cost method of accounting must be used when the number of shares of voting capital stock of a corporation does not give the investing corporation the ability to exercise significant influence or control. An investment in voting stock is accounted for under the cost method if less than 20% of the outstanding stock is held. All nonvoting stock is accounted for under the cost method without regard to the level of ownership.

Under the cost method, an investment in stock is recorded at the acquisition date in conformity with the cost principle. To illustrate the cost method, assume Able Corporation purchased the following long-term investments on February 1, 19A:

Penn Corporation common stock: 1,000 shares at $12 per share. This represents 10% of the outstanding shares. Total cost was $12,000.

South Corporation: 5% preferred stock (par $20) 500 shares at $40 per share. This represents 15% of the outstanding shares. Total cost was $20,000.

The acquisition of the long-term investment is recorded as follows:

Long-term investment 32,000
    Cash 32,000

Able Corporation acquired both common stock and preferred stock. Notice that both types of securities can be recorded in a single Long-Term Investment account.

Exhibit 13–1 Measuring and reporting long-term investments in voting stock of another company

Status of ownership	Method	Measurement at date of acquisition	Measurement after date of acquisition	
			Investment	**Revenue**
1. **Investor can exercise no significant influence or control.** Presumed if investor owns less than 20% of the outstanding voting stock of the investee company.	Cost method	Investor records the investment at cost. Cost is the total outlay made to acquire the shares.	Investor reports the investment on the balance sheet at LCM.	Investor recognizes revenue each period when dividends are declared by the investee company. A realized gain or loss is recognized when the investment is sold.
2. **Investor can exercise significant influence, but not control,** over the operating and financing policies of the investee company. Presumed if the investor owns at least 20%, but not more than 50%, of the outstanding voting stock of the investee company.	Equity method	Same as above.	Investor measures and reports the investment at cost **plus** the investor's share of the earnings (or less the losses) and **minus** the dividends received from (i.e., declared by) the other company. (Dividends received are not considered revenue. To recognize dividends as revenue, rather than as a reduction in the investment, would involve double counting.)	Investor recognizes as revenue each period the investor's proportionate share of the earnings (or losses) reported each period by the investee company.
3. **Investor can exercise control** over the operating and financing policies of the investee company. Control is presumed if the investor owns more than 50% of the outstanding voting stock of the investee company.	Consolidated financial statement method	Same as above.	Consolidated financial statements required each period (discussed in Chapter 14).	

On November 30, 19A, the board of directors declared and paid a $1 per share dividend on Penn Corporation stock. The receipt of the dividend is recorded by Able Corporation as follows:

Cash ($1 × 1,000 shares) 1,000
    Revenue from investments 1,000

Lower of Cost or Market

Subsequent to acquisition, *FASB Statement 12* requires that long-term investments in equity securities accounted for under the cost method must be valued at the lower of cost or market (LCM). The LCM rule for long-term investments is similar to the LCM rule discussed in Chapter 8 for marketable securities. However, there is an important difference between the two rules. When the LCM rule is applied, an unrealized loss is recorded. If the LCM rule is applied to marketable securities, the unrealized loss is reported on the income statement; with long-term investments, the unrealized loss is reported as a contra equity account on the balance sheet. An unrealized loss on long-term investments does not affect the income statement.

To apply the LCM rule to long-term investments, the total cost of the portfolio must be compared to the total market value of the portfolio. Assume the following facts for the stock owned by Able Corporation on December 31, 19A:

	Shares	Market Dec. 31, 19A	Total cost	Total market
Penn Corporation	1,000	13	$12,000	$13,000
South Corporation	500	36	20,000	18,000
			$32,000	$31,000

Able Corporation would record an unrealized holding loss as follows:

Unrealized loss on long-term investments 1,000
    Allowance to reduce long-term investments to market 1,000

The unrealized loss does not affect the net income reported by Able Corporation. The loss is reported in the stockholders' equity section of the balance sheet as a contra equity account, as follows:

Balance sheet:
  Investments and funds:
    Investments in equity securities $32,000
    Less: Allowance to reduce long-term
      investments to market 1,000 $31,000

  Stockholders' equity:
    Unrealized loss on long-term investments . . .   (1,000)

When long-term investments are sold, any difference between the sale price and the acquisition cost is reported as a realized loss or gain, without regard to previously recorded unrealized losses. Assume that on March 1, 19B, Able Corporation sold 300 shares of South Corporation stock for $38 per share. The transaction is recorded as follows:

Cash ($38 × 300 shares) 11,400
Realized loss   600
    Long-term investment ($40 × 300 shares)   12,000

The realized loss is reported on the 19B income statement. It may appear that the Allowance to Reduce Long-Term Investments to Market is overstated, but remember that the account is brought up-to-date at the end of each accounting period with an adjusting entry. Assume the following facts for the shares owned by Able Corporation on December 31, 19B:

	Shares	Market Dec. 31, 19B	Total cost	Total market
Penn Corporation	1,000	$14	$12,000	$14,000
South Corporation	200	41	8,000	8,200
			$20,000	$22,200

Before the adjusting entry at the end of 19B, the balance in the Allowance to Reduce Long-Term Investments to Market account is $1,000. Based on the facts shown above, the balance should be zero. Under the LCM rule, a portfolio may be reduced in value if market is below cost, but it cannot be increased in value if market is above cost. Able Corporation would make the following adjusting entry on December 19B:

Allowance to reduce long-term investments to market 1,000
    Unrealized loss on long-term investments   1,000

This adjusting entry affects two balance sheet accounts and has no impact on the income statement.

The LCM rule must be applied to equity securities only. If Able Corporation held bonds, they would not be included in the LCM computations.

Equity Method

The equity method must be used when significant influence (but not control) exists. The equity method recognizes a proportionate share of the reported income of the investee company as revenue for the investor. Dividends from the investee company are not recognized as income for the investor.

The concept underlying the equity method is that the investor has earned income from the investment equivalent to its ownership share. This income is recorded as a debit to the investment account and a credit to investment revenue. Dividends from the investee company are treated as a return of a part of the investment (i.e., a credit to the investment account). If dividends were also recorded as revenue, there would be a double counting of the proportionate share of income and the distribution of that income.

To illustrate the equity method, assume Micro Corporation bought 3,000 shares of Davis Corporation stock at $120 per share on January 15, 19A. This represents 30% of the outstanding stock of Davis. The initial recording of an investment in stock is the same under the cost method and the equity method. Micro Corporation would record the investment under the equity method as follows:

```
Long-term investment . . . . . . . . . . . . . . . . . . . . . . . . . . . . .  360,000
      Cash ($120 × 3,000 shares)  . . . . . . . . . . . . . . . . . . . . .            360,000
```

Subsequent to the initial recording of an investment, there are significant differences between the cost method and the equity method. When dividends are paid on stock that is accounted for under the equity method, the dividend is treated as a return of part of the investment. Therefore, under the equity method, dividends reduce the carrying value of the investment. Assume Davis Corporation declared and paid a $1 per share dividend on June 14, 19A. Micro would record the dividend as follows:

```
Cash ($1 × 3,000 shares) . . . . . . . . . . . . . . . . . . . . . . . . . .  3,000
      Long-term investment  . . . . . . . . . . . . . . . . . . . . . . . . .          3,000
```

Notice that the dividend does not affect the income reported by Micro Corporation (as it would if the cost method were used). Instead Micro reports a proportionate share of the income earned by Davis Corporation. Assume on December 31, 19A, Davis Corporation reported net income of $40,000. Micro Corporation owns 30% of Davis; therefore, its proportionate share of income is $12,000 ($40,000 × 30%). Micro would make the following entry to record its share of the income reported by Davis:[1]

```
Long-term investment . . . . . . . . . . . . . . . . . . . . . . . . . . . .  12,000
      Revenue from investments* . . . . . . . . . . . . . . . . . . . . . . .          12,000
```
* Sometimes called Equity in Earnings of Partially Owned Company.

At the end of the accounting period, the balance of the Long-Term Investment account does not reflect either cost or market. The investment account is increased for the cost of shares that were purchased and the proportionate share of the investee company's income. The account is reduced by the amount of dividends received from the investee company. Because the account balance does not reflect either cost or market, the LCM rule is not applied to investments accounted for under the equity method.

Under the equity method, an investor must report its share of any loss incurred by the investee corporation. The proportionate share of the loss is recorded with a debit to a loss on investment account and a credit to Long-Term Investment.

The equity method is designed to reflect the economic reality of a situation where one company has a significant influence over another. When a company owns more than 20%, but less than 50%, of the voting stock of another, the

---

[1] This example assumes that the investment was purchased at book value. More complex situations are discussed in advanced accounting courses.

investing company is often involved in making operating and financing decisions for the investee company. In effect, the investor has helped the investee company earn its net income. Therefore, it is appropriate to record a proportionate share of income under the equity method.

An additional characteristic of the equity method is that it prevents income manipulation by the investing company. Dividends are not reported as income under the equity method. If they were, the investing company could exert its significant influence to affect the dividend policy of the investee company. In this way, the investing company could manipulate its own reported income.

PART B—LONG-TERM INVESTMENTS IN DEBT SECURITIES (BONDS)

In Chapter 11, we discussed bonds as long-term liabilities of the issuing corporation. This part of the chapter discusses bonds of another company held as a long-term investment. Bonds offer significantly different investment risks and returns than capital stock. Bonds have a stated rate of interest (which determines the amount of cash that will be received on each interest date) and a specified maturity value (which will be received in cash at maturity date). Stockholders receive cash dividends only when they are declared by the board of directors. Dividends tend to vary with the profitability of the corporation. Stock has an indefinite life and does not have a maturity date.

Bonds are bought and sold in the regular security markets. The market price of bonds fluctuates **inversely** with changes in the **market rate** of interest because the **stated rate** of interest remains constant over the life of the bonds (Chapter 11). If the market rate of interest increases, bond prices fall.

Measuring and Reporting Bond Investments

At the date of acquisition, a bond investment is recorded in conformity with the **cost principle.** The purchase cost, including all incidental acquisition costs (such as transfer fees and broker commissions), is debited to an investment account. The amount recorded is the **current cash equivalent amount.** This amount may be the same as the maturity amount (if acquired at par), less than the maturity amount (if acquired at a discount), or more than the maturity amount (if acquired at a premium).[2] Usually the premium or discount on a bond investment is not recorded in a separate account as is done for bonds payable (Chapter 11). The investment account shows the current book or carrying amount. How-

---

[2] Fees, commissions, and other incidental costs decrease the discount, or increase the premium; therefore, they are amortized over the remaining period to maturity. Alternatively, such costs sometimes are recorded separately and amortized on the same basis as the discount or premium.

ever, the bond investment account can be debited at par, and a separate discount or premium account can be used with the same results.

If a bond investment was acquired at par, the book value remains constant over the life of the investment because there is no premium or discount to be amortized. In this situation, revenue earned from the investment each period is measured as the amount of cash interest collected (or accrued).

When a bond investment is purchased at a discount or premium, measurement of the book value of the investment each period necessitates adjustment of the investment account balance from acquisition cost to maturity amount over the life of the investment. This adjustment is the periodic amortization of the discount or premium. The periodic amortization is made as a debit to the investment account if there is a discount, or credit if there is a premium.

When a bond investment is acquired at a discount or premium, the interest revenue each period is recorded as the cash interest collected (or accrued) plus or minus the periodic amortization of discount or premium. As was illustrated in Chapter 11 for bonds payable, bond discount or premium may be amortized by using either the straight-line or effective-interest method. The former is simpler, whereas the latter is conceptually preferable. In the following paragraphs, we will assume straight-line amortization.

In contrast to long-term investments, discount or premium is not amortized on bonds held as a **short-term** investment because the bonds will not be held to maturity.

Accounting for Bonds Illustrated

On July 1, 19F, Roth Company purchased $10,000, 10-year, 8% bonds in the open market. The bonds were issued originally on July 1, 19A, and mature on June 30, 19K. The 8% interest is paid each June 30.[3] Roth Company's annual accounting period ends December 31. The sequence of journal entries made by Roth Company during 19F are illustrated under three different purchase cost assumptions as follows:

Assumptions	Exhibits
1. Bond investment purchased at par (100)	13–2
2. Bond investment purchased at a discount (98)	13–3
3. Bond investment purchased at a premium (102) . . .	13–4

Bonds Purchased at Par

When bond investors accept a rate of interest on a bond investment that is the **same** as the stated rate of interest on the bonds, the bonds will sell at par (i.e., at 100). Bonds that sell at par will not cause a premium or discount. Exhibit 13–2 illustrates the recording of an **investment** in bonds purchased at par.

---

[3] Bonds usually pay interest semiannually. Annual interest is used in this illustration to reduce the number of repetitive entries. The concepts are applied the same way in either case.

Exhibit 13–2 Bonds purchased at par

Situation:

   On July 1, 19F, Roth Company purchased $10,000, 10-year, 8% bonds of Ellsworth Company for cash, $10,000 (i.e., at par). The bonds were issued originally on July 1, 19A, and mature June 30, 19K. Interest is paid each June 30. Roth's accounting period ends December 31.

July 1, 19F, to record purchase of bond investment at par (100):

   Long-term investment, bonds of Ellsworth Company 10,000
      Cash   10,000
   Purchased at par, $10,000 maturity value, 8% bonds of Ellsworth
   Company. (Note: Because the bonds were purchased on an in-
   terest date, there was no accrued interest.)

December 31, 19F, adjusting entry at end of the accounting period (and each year
   through maturity date):

   Bond interest receivable   400
      Revenue from investments*   400
   Adjusting entry to accrue six months' interest revenue on
   Ellsworth Company bonds ($10,000 × 8% × 6/12 = $400).
   * Alternate titles are Interest Revenue and, sometimes, Interest Income.

June 30, 19G, to record annual interest (and each year until maturity):

   Cash ($10,000 × 8%)   800
      Bond interest receivable (from December 31 entry)   400
      Revenue from investments   400
   Receipt of annual interest payment on the Ellsworth
   Company bonds.

June 30, 19K, maturity date of the bonds; to record cash received for face (maturity)
   amount of the bond investment:

   Cash 10,000
      Long-term investment, bonds of Ellsworth Company   10,000
   Retirement of bonds at maturity date (assumes last interest
   receipt already recorded).

Bonds Purchased at a Discount

When bond investors demand a rate of interest that is higher than the **stated rate,** bonds will sell at a **discount.** When a bond is purchased at a discount, the investor receives the periodic interest payments stated in the bond contract plus the maturity value, which is a greater amount than the initial cash invested. A discount increases the interest revenue earned on a bond investment. Assume that on July 1, 19F, Roth Company purchased a $10,000, 8% bond issued by

Baker Company for $9,800 cash. The bond will mature in five years (in 19K). Interest of $10,000 × 8% = $800 will be collected annually.

Although $800 cash is collected each year, the annual revenue **earned** from the investment is $840. The additional $40 is due to amortization of the discount. Analysis of the interest revenue, using straight-line amortization, is as follows:

```
Cash inflows from the investment:
  Annual interest collected, July 1, 19F, through
    June 30, 19K ($10,000 × 8% × 5 years) . . . . . . . . . $ 4,000
  Collection of bond at maturity date, June 30, 19K . . . . . .  10,000    $14,000

Cash outflow for the investment:
  July 1, 19F—purchase of bond . . . . . . . . . . . . . . . .           9,800

  Difference—net increase in cash (the total
    interest earned) . . . . . . . . . . . . . . . . . . . . . . .       $ 4,200

Revenue per year from investment: $4,200 ÷ 5 years = $840
(assuming straight-line amortization).
```

Exhibit 13–3 illustrates the recording of a bond investment purchased at a discount.

When a bond is purchased, it is recorded at cost. Therefore, when a bond is purchased at a discount, the investment account balance at the purchase date will be less than par or maturity value. Through **amortization** of the discount, the balance of the investment account is **increased** each period so that the book value will be the same as the par amount on the maturity date. Amortization of the discount each period increases the amount of interest revenue earned. The amount of discount amortized each period is debited to the investment account and credited to Interest Revenue.

In Exhibit 13–3, each year Roth Company must amortize a part of the discount ($10,000 − $9,800 = $200), so that the total discount is amortized over the remaining life of the bond investment. Using straight-line amortization, the amount of discount amortized each full year will be $200 ÷ 5 years = $40 per year.

The balance of the long-term investment account will increase from cost at date of purchase to par value at maturity date because of the amortization of the bond discount. Notice that the amortization of a discount or premium on a bond investment is conceptually similar to the amortization for bond liabilities that was discussed in Chapter 11. In this chapter, we are looking at the other side of the transaction.

Bonds Purchased at a Premium

When bond investors are willing to invest at a rate of interest that is **less** than the **stated rate** of interest on bonds, the bonds will sell at a **premium.** When bonds are purchased at a premium, the investment account is debited for an amount greater than the par or maturity value of the bonds. Therefore, the premium must be **amortized** over the **remaining life** of the bonds as a **decrease** in the

Exhibit 13–3 Bonds purchased at a discount

Situation:

Exactly the situation given in Exhibit 13–2, except that on July 1, 19F, Roth Company purchased $10,000 of bonds of Baker Company for $9,800 (i.e., at 98), rather than at par.

July 1, 19F, to record purchase of bond investment at a discount (98):

Long-term investment, bonds of Baker Company (at cost)	9,800	
Cash		9,800
Purchased $10,000 maturity value, 8% bonds of the Baker Company at 98.		

Note: This entry records the investment at its cost; that is, net of any discount or premium. Some accountants prefer to record it at **gross** as follows with the same end result:

Long-term investment	10,000	
Discount on long-term investment		200
Cash		9,800

December 31, 19F, end of accounting year; to record adjusting entry for interest revenue and amortization of discount on bond investment (and each year until maturity):

Bond interest receivable ($10,000 × 8% × 6/12)	400	
Long-term investment, bonds of Baker Company (amortization: $40 × 6/12)	20	
Revenue from investments		420
Adjusting entry to (1) accrue interest revenue for six months and (2) amortize discount on the bond investment for six months (July 1 to December 31); $200 ÷ 5 years = $40 amortization per year.		

June 30, 19G, to record cash interest received and to amortize discount on bond investment (and each year until maturity):

Cash ($10,000 × 8%)	800	
Long-term investment, bonds of Baker Company (amortization: $40 × 6/12)	20	
Bond interest receivable (from December 31 entry)		400
Revenue from investments		420
Receipt of annual interest on Baker Company bonds and amortization of discount for six months (January 1 to June 30).		

June 30, 19K, maturity date; to record cash maturity amount received:

Cash	10,000	
Long-term investment, bonds of Baker Company		10,000
Retirement of bonds at maturity (assumes last interest receipt already recorded).		

balance of the investment account so that the investment account balance will be the par value on maturity date. The amortization is similar to the procedure illustrated for a discount, except that each period the investment account is credited and the premium amortization **decreases** interest revenue.

Exhibit 13–4 Bonds purchased at a premium

Situation:

Exactly the same situation given in Exhibit 13–2, except that on July 1, 19F, Roth Company purchased $10,000 of bonds of Garden Company for $10,200 (i.e., at 102), rather than at par.

July 1, 19F, to record purchase of bond investment at a premium (102):

Long-term investment, bonds of Garden Company (at cost)	10,200	
Cash		10,200

Purchased $10,000 maturity value, 8% bonds of Garden Company at 102.

December 31, 19F, end of accounting year; to record adjusting entry for interest revenue and amortization of premium on bond investment (and each year until maturity):

Bond interest receivable ($10,000 × 8% × 6/12)	400	
Long-term investment, bonds of Garden Company (amortization: $40 × 6/12)		20
Revenue from investments		380

Adjusting entry to (1) accrue interest revenue for six months and (2) amortize premium on the investment for six months (July 1 to December 31); $200 ÷ 5 years = $40 amortization per year.

June 30, 19G, to record cash interest received and to amortize premium on bond investment (and each year until maturity):

Cash ($10,000 × 8%)	800	
Bond interest receivable (per December 31 entry)		400
Long-term investment, bonds of Garden Company (amortization: $40 × 6/12)		20
Revenue from investments		380

Receipt of annual interest revenue on Garden Company bonds and amortization of premium for six months (January 1 to June 30).

June 30, 19K, maturity date; to record cash maturity amount received:

Cash	10,000	
Long-term investment, bonds of Garden Company		10,000

Retirement of bonds at maturity (assuming the last interest receipt has been recorded).

Assume Roth Company purchased Garden Company bonds on July 1, 19F, for $10,200 cash. The bonds have an 8% interest rate and mature in five years from that date, on June 30, 19K. Using straight-line amortization, the cash outflow and inflows for this investment may be analyzed to illustrate the effect of the premium on interest revenue as follows:

Cash inflows from the investment:
Annual interest collected, July 1, 19F, through
 June 30, 19K ($10,000 × 8% × 5 years) . . . . $ 4,000
 June 30, 19K, collection of bond at maturity 10,000 $14,000

Cash outflow for the investment:
 July 1, 19F—purchase of bond   10,200

 Difference—net increase in cash (the total
  interest revenue earned) . . . . $ 3,800

Revenue per year from investment: $3,800 ÷ 5 years = $760
(assuming straight-line amortization).

Exhibit 13–4 presents the journal entries for the investor, Roth Company.

Effective-Interest Amortization on Bond Investments

Effective-interest amortization of the discount or premium on a bond investment is similar to the procedures discussed for bonds payable in Chapter 11. This method of amortization is conceptually preferable because (1) interest revenue is measured correctly each period for income statement purposes, and (2) the book value of the investment is measured correctly for balance sheet purposes at the end of each accounting period. Assume that on January 1, 19A, Farmer Company purchased a $10,000, five-year, 8% bond of Research Corporation as a long-term investment. Interest is payable each December 31. The purchase price, based on a 12% effective-interest rate, was $8,558 (a $1,442 discount).[4] The acquisition was recorded by Farmer Company as follows:

Long-term investment, Research Corporation bonds
 (maturity amount $10,000) 8,558
 Cash   8,558
Purchase of long-term investment.

Farmer Company used the effective-interest amortization method to amortize the bond discount. The journal entries for a bond investment are the same regardless of the amortization method used, except for some of the **amounts** in the periodic interest entries.

Computation of effective-interest amortization is shown in Exhibit 13–5. Notice that the effective rate of interest of 12%, rather than the stated rate of 8%, is used to compute the interest revenue amounts.

The first column in Exhibit 13–5 shows the cash inflow each period for interest (based on the stated rate). The second column shows the interest revenue that should be reported on the income statement each period (based on the effective rate). The third column shows the amount of the discount that is amortized (which is the difference between the interest revenue earned and the amount of

---

[4] Given the effective rate of 12%, the price of the bonds can be computed as follows:

$10,000 × $p_{n=5,\ i=12\%}$ = $10,000 × 0.5674 (Table 10–2) $5,674
$800 × $\mathbf{P}_{n=5,\ i=12\%}$ = $800 × 3.6048 (Table 10–4)   2,884
Bond price (*PV* of future cash flows) $8,558

Exhibit 13–5   Schedule of effective-interest amortization

Date	Cash Interest Received Each Interest Date	Interest Revenue (based on beginning balance of investment)	Amortization (increase investment)	Net Investment
1/1/19A (acquisition)				$ 8,558
12/31/19A	$ 800	$8,558 × 12% = $1,027	$ 227	8,785
12/31/19B	800	8,785 × 12% = 1,054	254	9,039
12/31/19C	800	9,039 × 12% = 1,085	285	9,324
12/31/19D	800	9,324 × 12% = 1,119	319	9,643
12/31/19E	800	9,643 × 12% = 1,157	357	10,000
Totals	$4,000	$5,442	$1,442	

cash received). The last column shows the book value of the investment (i.e., the unamortized principal) that should be reported on the balance sheet at the end of each period. The entry for interest revenue each period can be taken directly from the schedule:

	Year 1	Year 2	Etc.
Cash	800	800	
Long-term investment	227	254	
Revenue from investments	1,027	1,054	

Conceptually, the effective-interest method derives the true interest revenue earned during each period and the correct book value of the investment at the end of each period. The straight-line approach gives only approximations of these amounts. When there is a material difference between the two methods, *APB Opinion 21* requires use of the effective-interest method. Straight-line amortization often is used because it is simple to apply, and the different amounts of premium or discount amortized each period are not material.

Bonds Purchased between Interest Dates

Investors usually purchase bonds between the interest dates specified on the bonds. In these situations, the investor must pay the amount of **interest accrued** since the last interest date in addition to the purchase price of the bond. The bond market operates in this manner because the seller of the bond is entitled to interest from the last interest date to the date of the sale transaction; but on the next interest payment date, the new owner will receive interest for the full period between interest dates, regardless of the purchase date. Assume Hays Company purchased a $1,000 bond, 12% interest, payable 6% each March 31 and September 30. The bond was purchased on June 1, 19F, at par plus any accrued interest. The purchase of this bond investment is recorded by Hays Company as follows:

June 1, 19F:

Long-term investment, 12% bond 1,000
Interest receivable ($1,000 × 12% × 2/12)*   20
   Cash [$1,000 + ($1,000 × 12% × 2/12)]   1,020

  Purchase of a $1,000, 12% bond as a long-term investment at 100 plus ac-
  crued interest for two months, March 31, 19F (last interest date), to June 1,
  19F (date of purchase).

  * Alternatively, an account, Bond Interest Revenue, could have been debited on June 1 for $20. When
  the interest is received on September 30, $60 would be credited to Interest Revenue. The net effect on
  the two entries is to report $40 revenue, which is the amount earned for four months.

Hayes Company debited the long-term investment account for the cost of the
investment, which **excludes** the accrued interest. The $20 accrued interest was
paid in cash by Hayes Company. However, it will be returned to Hayes Company at the next interest date, September 30, 19F. At that time, Hayes Company
will receive the full amount of cash interest for six months, although it has
owned the bond for only four months (i.e., June 1 to September 30, 19F).

The journal entry to record the first interest collection after the purchase is:

September 30, 19F:

Cash   60
   Revenue from investments   40
   Interest receivable   20

  Collected interest for six months on bond investment
  ($1,000 × 6% = $60).

Sale of a Bond Investment

A long-term investment in bonds is accounted for with the expectation that the
bonds will be held to maturity. This expectation is the basis for amortizing any
premium or discount over the period from the date of purchase to the maturity
date. However, the bonds may be sold prior to their maturity date. When an
investor sells bonds prior to maturity, the difference between the sale price and
the book value of the bonds is recorded as a "Gain (or Loss) on the Sale of
Investments."

Assume Carson Corporation has two $1,000, 12% bonds of Drake Company
that are being held as a long-term investment. Each bond was purchased at 104.
The long-term investment account was debited for $2,080. Because of amortiza-
tion of bond premium to January 1, 19F, the investment account balance is
$2,040. On that date, one of the bonds was sold for $1,000 cash. The entry by
Carson Company to record the sale is:

Cash 1,000
Loss on sale of investments   20
   Long-term investment, Drake Company bonds   1,020
  Sale of long-term investment.

DEMONSTRATION CASE

(Try to resolve the requirements before proceeding to the suggested solution that follows.)

Howell Equipment Corporation sells and services a major line of farm equipment. Both sales and service operations have been profitable. At the beginning of 19S, the company had excess cash. At that time, the management decided to invest in some securities of two of the manufacturers that supply most of the equipment purchased by Howell for resale. The annual accounting period ends on December 31.

This case focuses on the two long-term investments purchased in 19S. One investment was in equity securities, and the other in debt securities. The transactions were:

19S

a. Jan. 1 Purchased 2,000 shares of common stock of Dear Company at $40 per share. This was 1% of the shares outstanding.

b. Aug. 1 Purchased $100,000, 9% bonds payable of the Massey Company at 102 plus any accrued interest. The bonds pay semiannual interest each May 31 and November 30. The bonds mature on May 31, 19X (i.e., five years from June 1, 19S). Brokerage fees were $900.

c. Nov. 30 Received semiannual interest on Massey Company bonds. Use straight-line amortization.

d. Dec. 28 Received $4,000 cash dividend on the Dear Company stock.

e. Dec. 31 Adjusting entry for accrued interest on the Massey Company bonds.

f. Dec. 31 The current market price of the Dear stock is $39 and $103 for the Massey bonds.

g. Dec. 31 Closed Revenue from Investments to Income Summary.

Required:

a. Give the journal entry for each of the above transactions.

b. Show how the two investments, the accrued interest receivable and the related revenue, should be reported on the balance sheet and income statement at December 31, 19S.

Suggested Solution

Requirement a:

a. January 1, 19S:

Long-term investment, stock of Dear Company (2,000 shares) . . .	80,000	
Cash		80,000
Purchased 2,000 shares Dear Company common stock at $40 per share.		

b. August 1, 19S:

Long-term investment, bonds of Massey Company	102,900	
Interest receivable ($100,000 × 9% × 2/12)	1,500	
Cash		104,400
Purchased $100,000 bonds of Massey Company.		

Computation:
Cost ($100,000 × 1.029) = $102,900
Accrued interest for 2 months
    $100,000 × 9% × 2/12 =   1,500
        Total cash paid . . $104,400

c. November 30, 19S:

Cash	4,500	
Long-term investment, bonds of Massey Company		200
Revenue from investments		2,800
Interest receivable		1,500

Computation:
Semiannual interest: $100,000 × 9% × 6/12 = $4,500
Amortization of premium:
    $2,900 ÷ 58 months = $50*
        per month; $50 × 4 months = $200
Interest revenue: $100,000 × 9% × 4/12 = $3,000
Less amortization of premium . . . .   (200)
                                              $2,800

* August 1, 19S, to May 31, 19X = 58 months.

d. December 28, 19S:

Cash	4,000	
Revenue from investments		4,000
Received dividend on Dear Company stock.		

e. December 31, 19S:

Interest receivable	750	
Long-term investment, bonds of Massey Company		50
Revenue from investments		700
Adjusting entry for accrued interest and premium amortization for one month on Massey Company bonds.		

Computation:
Accrued interest receivable:
    $100,000 × 9% × 1/12   = $750
Amortization of premium:
    $50 × 1 month   =   50
    Revenue from investments $700

f. December 31, 19S:

Unrealized loss on long-term equity investment	2,000	
Allowance to reduce long-term investment to LCM		2,000
To record LCM on Dear stock:		
2,000 shares × ($40 − $39) = $2,000.		

g. December 31, 19S:

Revenue from investments	7,500	
Income summary		7,500

Closing entry: ($2,800 + $4,000 + $700 = $7,500).

Requirement b:

HOWELL EQUIPMENT CORPORATION
Balance Sheet (partial)
At December 31, 19S

Current assets:
Interest receivable . . . . $ 750

Investments and funds:
Stock of Dear Company, at LCM, 2,000 shares (cost, $80,000) . . . . $ 78,000*
Bonds of Massey Company, at amortized cost ($100,000
maturity value; market, $103,000) . . . . 102,650†   180,650

Stockholders' equity:
Unrealized loss on long-term equity investments . . . .   (2,000)

* Cost of equity securities . . . . $ 80,000
Less: Allowance to reduce long-term
equity investment to LCM   2,000
Equity investment at LCM . . . . $ 78,000

† Cost of debt securities $102,900
Less: Amortization of premium
($200 + $50)   250
Debt investment at amortized cost $102,650

HOWELL EQUIPMENT CORPORATION
Income Statement (partial)
For the Year Ending December 31,19S
Revenue from investments $7,500

SUMMARY OF CHAPTER

This chapter discussed two types of long-term investments: capital stock (equity securities) and bonds (debt securities) of another company. A corporation may acquire a part or all of the outstanding capital stock of another corporation by **purchase** of its shares or by **exchange** of its own stock for shares in the other company. The measuring and reporting of long-term investments in the capital stock of another company are determined by the percent of shares owned in relation to the total number of shares outstanding.

If the ownership level of **voting** shares is less than 20%, or if the ownership is of nonvoting stock, the **cost method** must be used. Under this method, the investment amount reported by the investor is based on the lower of cost or market, and investment revenue is recognized on the basis of dividends declared by the investee corporation.

If the ownership is at least 20%, but not more than 50%, the **equity method** must be used. Under this method, the investment is recorded at cost by the investor at date of acquisition. Each period thereafter, the investment amount is increased (or decreased) by the proportionate interest in the income (or loss) reported by the investee corporation and decreased by the proportionate share of the dividends declared by the investee corporation. The LCM basis is not used with the equity method. Each period, the investor recognizes as revenue its proportionate share of the income (or loss) reported by the investee company.

If there is a controlling interest—that is, more than 50% ownership of the outstanding voting stock is held by the investor—the financial statements of the affiliated companies (investor and investee) are **consolidated.** This subject is discussed in Chapter 14.

An investor may purchase the bonds of another entity as a long-term investment. In contrast to capital stock, bonds (1) have a specified maturity date and maturity amount; (2) require the payment of a stated rate of interest at regular specified interest dates, and (3) do not confer voting rights. At the date of purchase, a long-term investment in bonds is recorded at cost, which may be at par, at a discount, or at a premium. When purchased at a premium or a discount, amortization of the premium or discount over the **remaining life** of the bonds is required. The periodic amortization adjusts (1) the balance of the investment amount so that the book value will be the same as the par value on the maturity date and (2) the interest revenue which is reported on the income statement.

IMPORTANT TERMS DEFINED IN THIS CHAPTER

Control The ability of an investor to determine the operating and financing policies of another company (the investee). *p. 631*

Cost Method Method used by investor if less than 20% of the voting stock of the investee company is owned by the investor. *p. 631*

Discount A bond that is purchased for less than par value is purchased at a discount; the difference between cost and par of a bond. *p. 638*

Effective Interest The real or true rate of interest; also called the market rate of interest. *p. 642*

Equity Method Method used by investor if 20% to 50% of the voting stock of the investee company is owned by the investor. *p. 634*

Premium A bond that is purchased for more than par value is purchased at a premium; the difference between cost and par of a bond. *p. 639*

Significant Influence The ability of an investor to have an important impact on the operating and financing policies of another company (the investee). *p. 630*

Stated Interest Rate The annual rate of cash interest specified in the bond contract. *p. 636*

QUESTIONS

Part A: Questions 1-7

1. Explain the difference between a short-term investment and a long-term investment.

2. Match the following:

   Measurement method:
   _____ Cost method.
   _____ Equity method.
   _____ Consolidation.

   Level of ownership of the voting capital stock:
   a. More than 50% ownership.
   b. Less than 20% ownership.
   c. At least 20% but not more than 50%.

3. Explain the application of the cost principle to the purchase of capital stock in another company.

4. Under the cost method, when and how is revenue measured by the investor company?

5. Under the equity method, why is revenue measured on a proportionate basis by the investor company when income is reported by the other company, rather than when dividends are declared?

6. Under the equity method, dividends received from the investee company are not recorded as revenue. To record dividends as revenue would involve double counting. Explain.

7. Match the following items that relate to the long-term investment amount reported on the balance sheet of the investor company:

   Measurement method:
   _____ Cost method.
   _____ Equity method.

   Explanation of balance in the investment account:
   a. LCM.
   b. Original cost plus proportionate part of the income of the investee, less proportionate part of the dividends declared by investee.

Part B: Questions 8-13

8. Explain the difference between an equity security and a debt security.

9. Explain why interest revenue must be accrued on a long-term investment in bonds but not on a long-term investment in capital stock.

10. Under what conditions will a bond sell at (*a*) par, (*b*) a discount, and (*c*) a premium?

11. Distinguish between a long-term investment in bonds and a long-term investment in the capital stock of another company.

12. Why is it necessary to amortize a premium or discount that arises from the purchase of a long-term bond investment above or below par? Over what period should the premium or discount be amortized?

13. When a bond investment is purchased between interest dates, the purchaser must pay accrued interest plus the purchase price of the bond. Explain why the accrued interest must be paid.

EXERCISES

Part A: Exercises 13–1 to 13–6

E13–1 **(Match Definitions with Terms)**
Match each definition with its related term by entering the appropriate letter in the space provided.

Terms	Definitions
_____ (1) Significant influence	A. Assumed when the investing company owns more than 50% of the outstanding voting stock of another company.
_____ (2) Discount	
_____ (3) Control	
_____ (4) Effective interest	B. Accounting treatment prescribed when an investing company does not have significant influence or control over the other company.
_____ (5) Equity method	
_____ (6) Stated interest rate	C. Occurs when the stated interest rate is less than the market rate.
_____ (7) Premium	
_____ (8) Cost method	D. Market rate of interest.
	E. Accounting treatment prescribed when an investing company has significant influence, but not control over the other company.
	F. Occurs when the stated interest rate is more than the market rate.
	G. Presumed if the investing company owns 20% to 50% of the outstanding voting shares of the other company.
	H. When this rate matches a bond investor's required rate of return, the bond will sell at par value.

E13–2 **(Compare Primary Characteristics of Cost and Equity Methods)**
Company P purchased a certain number of the outstanding voting shares of Company S at $15 per share as a long-term investment. Company S had outstanding 10,000 shares of $10 par value stock. On a separate sheet complete the following matrix relating to the measurement and reporting by Company P after acquisition of the shares of Company S stock.

	Method of Measurement	
Questions	Cost Method	Equity Method
a. What is the applicable level of ownership by Company P of Company S to apply the method?	Percent	Percent
For (*b*), (*e*), (*f*), and (*g*) that follow, assume: Number of shares acquired of Company S stock Net income reported by Company S in the first year Dividends declared by Company S in the first year Market price at end of first year, Company S stock, $12.	1,000 $40,000 $10,000	3,000 $40,000 $10,000
b. At acquisition, the investment account on the books of Company P should be debited at what amount?	$	$
c. On what basis should Company P recognize revenue earned on the stock of Company S? Explanation required.		
d. After acquisition date, on what basis should Company P change the balance of the investment account in respect to the stock of Company S owned (other than for disposal of the investment)? Explanation required.		
e. What would be the balance in the investment account on the books of Company P at the end of the first year?	$	$
f. What amount of revenue from the investment in Company S should Company P report at the end of the first year?	$	$
g. What amount of unrealized loss should Company P report at the end of the first year?	$	$

E13–3 **(Identification and Use of Proper Method to Account for a Long-Term Investment in Equity Securities)**

During 19B, Yale Company acquired some of the 60,000 outstanding shares of the common stock, par $10, of Cox Corporation as a long-term investment. The accounting period for both companies ends December 31. The following transactions occurred:

19B
July   2   Purchased 9,000 shares of Cox common stock at $20 per share.
Dec. 31   Received the 19B annual financial statement of Cox Corporation that reported net income of $40,000.
    31   Cox Corporation declared and paid a cash dividend of $1 per share.
    31   Market price of Cox stock was $18 per share.

Required:

a. What accounting method should the company use? Why?

b. Give the journal entries for each of the above transactions. If no entry is required, explain why.

c. Show how the long-term investment and the related revenue should be reported on the 19B financial statements of the company.

E13–4 (Recording and Reporting a Long-Term Investment in an Equity Security)

Jones Company acquired some of the 40,000 shares of outstanding common stock (nopar) of Noe Corporation during 19E as a long-term investment. The annual accounting period for both companies ends December 31. The following transactions occurred during 19E:

19E

Jan. 10   Purchased 12,000 shares of Noe common stock at $30 per share.

Dec. 31   Received the 19E financial statement of Noe Corporation which reported net income of $80,000.

    31   Noe Corporation declared and paid a cash dividend of $1.25 per share.

    31   Market price of Noe stock was $25 per share.

Required:

a. What accounting method should the company use? Why?

b. Give the journal entries for each of the above transactions. If no entry is required, explain why.

c. Show how the long-term investment and the related revenue should be reported on the 19E financial statements of the company.

E13–5 (Identify and Use the Proper Method to Account for a Long-Term Investment in an Equity Security)

During 19H, Ross Company purchased some of the 100,000 shares of common stock, par $5, of Salt Marine, Inc., as a long-term investment. The annual accounting period for each company ends December 31. The following transactions occurred during 19H:

19H

Jan. 7   Purchased 10,000 shares of Salt Marine common stock at $15 per share.

Dec. 31   Received the 19H financial statement of Salt Marine, which reported net income of $70,000.

    31   Salt Marine declared and paid a cash dividend of $2 per share.

    31   Market price of Salt Marine stock was $18 per share.

Required:

a. What accounting method should the company use? Why?

b. Give the journal entries for each of the above transactions. If no entry is required, explain why.

c. Show how the long-term investment and the related revenue should be reported on the 19H financial statements of the company.

E13–6 (Identify and Use the Proper Method to Account for a Long-Term Investment in an Equity Security)

Use the same situation for Ross Company and the data given in Exercise 13–5, **except** for the January 7, 19H, transaction. Assume it was as follows:

19H

Jan. 7   Purchased 40,000 shares of Salt Marine stock at $15 per share.

(The data for December 31 are unchanged.)

Required:

a. What accounting method should the company use? Why?

b. Give the journal entries for each transaction (refer also to transactions given in Exercise 13–5). If no entry is required, explain why.

c. Show how the long-term investment and the related revenue should be reported on the 19H financial statements of the company.

Part B: Exercises 13–7 to 13–15

E13–7   **(Accounting for a Debt Security from Purchase Date to Maturity Date)**
On July 1, 19A, Alpha Company purchased at par a $10,000, 20-year, 10% bond of CD Corporation as a long-term investment. The annual bond interest is payable each year on June 30. The accounting period for the company ends December 31. At the date of purchase, the bond had five years remaining before maturity.

Required:
Give the journal entries on the books of the company for the following transactions:
a. July 1, 19A, acquisition date.
b. December 31, 19A.
c. June 30, 19B.
d. Maturity date of the bond, June 30, 19F.

E13–8   **(Accounting for a Debt Security from Purchase Date to Maturity Date)**
On April 1, 19A, Land Company purchased at par ten $1,000, 10-year, 10% bonds of HI Corporation as a long-term investment. The bond interest is payable semiannually each March 31 and September 30. The accounting period for the company ends on December 31. At the date of purchase, the bonds had six years remaining to maturity.

Required:
Give the journal entry for each of the following dates for the long-term investment: April 1, 19A; September 30, 19A; December 31, 19A; March 31, 19B; and the maturity date.

E13–9   **(Recording an Investment in Bonds)**
On February 1, 19A, Sullivan Company purchased at par a $15,000, 30-year, 8% bond of Lam Corporation as a long-term investment. The bond interest is payable semiannually each January 31 and July 31. The accounting period for the company ends December 31. At the date of purchase, the bonds had four years remaining to maturity.

Required:
Give all journal entries required for the investment for the period February 1, 19A, through January 1, 19B, and on the maturity date.

E13–10   **(Compare Bonds Sold at Par; at a Discount; at a Premium)**
On July 1, 19B, Cody Company purchased three different bonds as long-term investments. Data about the three bonds and the purchase prices are:

Bond designation	Par of bond	Annual interest	Payable semiannually	Remaining years to maturity	Market purchase price*
A	$1,000	10%	Dec. 31 and	7	$1,000
B	1,000	9	June 30	10	920
C	1,000	12	each year	5	1,060

* These amounts do not include any accrued interest.

Required:

a. Give the journal entries to record separately the purchase of each bond.

b. Give the journal entries to record separately collection of interest on the first interest date after purchase. Use straight-line amortization of any discount or premium.

c. Give the journal entries to record separately the maturity of each bond.

E13–11   **(Entries and Reporting for a Debt Security Using Straight-Line Amortization)**
On May 1, 19B, North Company purchased $20,000 maturity value bonds of Opel Corporation at 97.6 (plus any accrued interest) as a long-term investment. The bond interest rate is 10% per annum payable 5% each April 30 and October 31. The bonds mature in four years from May 1, 19B.

Required:

a. Give the journal entries for the company on May 1, 19B; October 31, 19B; and December 31, 19B (adjusting entry for accrued interest). Use straight-line amortization and round all amounts to the nearest dollar.

b. Show how this long-term investment and the related revenue should be shown on the December 31, 19B, annual financial statements of the company.

E13–12   **(Entries and Reporting for a Debt Security Using Straight-Line Amortization)**
On May 1, 19B, Wisteria Company purchased $30,000 of the 8% bonds of Cook Corporation, at 106 (plus any accrued interest) as a long-term investment. The bonds pay interest each April 30 and October 31. The bonds mature in five years on April 30, 19G.

Required:

a. Give the journal entries for the company on May 1, 19B; October 31, 19B; and December 31, 19B (adjusting entry for accrued interest). Use straight-line amortization and round to the nearest dollar.

b. Show how this long-term investment should be shown on the December 31, 19B, annual financial statements of the company.

E13–13   **(Entries and Reporting for a Debt Security Purchased between Interest Dates; Straight-Line Amortization)**
On March 1, 19B, Qwest Company purchased $6,000 of the 10% bonds of TU Corporation as a long-term investment. The bonds pay interest each June 30 and December 31. The bonds mature in 10 years on December 31, 19K. The purchase price was $6,236, plus any accrued interest.

Required:

a. Give the journal entry by the company to record the purchase on March 1, 19B.

b. Give the journal entry to record the interest received on June 30 and December 31, 19B. Use straight-line amortization.

c. What was the amount of interest revenue in 19B? At what amount should the bond investment be reported on the balance sheet at December 31, 19B?

E13–14 **(Analysis of an Effective-Interest Amortization Schedule)**

On January 1, 19A, Cotton Company purchased, as a long-term investment, a $3,000 bond of Devons Company for $2,922 (plus any accrued interest). The bond had a stated interest rate of 7%, payable each January 1. The bond matures in three years on December 31, 19C. Cotton Company uses effective-interest amortization. The amortization table given below was developed.

Date	Cash inflow	Interest revenue	Investment change	Investment balance
January 1, 19A				$2,922
End year 19A	$210	$234	$24	2,946
End year 19B	210	?	?	?
End year 19C	210	?	?	3,000

Required:

a. Complete the amortization table.

b. How much was the discount or premium?

c. What was the total cash outflow and the total cash inflow over the life of this investment? What does the difference represent? Explain.

d. How much interest revenue should be recognized on the income statement each year and in total?

e. What amounts should be reported on the balance sheet each year? For the last year give the amounts just prior to collection of the maturity amount.

f. What was the effective rate of interest per year? Show computations.

g. Show how the price of the bond of $2,922 was computed.

E13–15 **(Prepare an Effective-Interest Amortization Schedule; Entries and Reporting)**

On January 1, 19A, Indian Company purchased, as a long-term investment, a $10,000 par value, 12% bond issued by Jackson Corporation. The bond pays interest each year on December 31 and has five years remaining life to maturity from January 1, 19A. The accounting period for Indian Corporation ends December 31.

The bond was purchased to yield a 10% effective rate of interest.

Required:

a. Compute the price of the bond.

b. Give the journal entry for Indian Company to record the purchase of the bond on January 1, 19A.

c. Prepare a schedule of effective-interest amortization.

d. Give the journal entries for the collection of interest on the bond investment during 19A and 19B.

e. Complete the following schedule (show computations):

	December 31	
	19A	**19B**
Income statement:		
Revenue from bond investment . . . . . . $ _____	$ _____	
Balance sheet:		
Bond-interest receivable	_____	_____
Long-term investment, bond of		
Jackson Corporation	_____	_____

PROBLEMS

Part A: Problems 13–1 to 13–5

P13–1   **(Identify, Record, and Report Using the Proper Method to Account for an Equity Investment)**
During January 19A, Circle Company purchased 15,000 shares of the 100,000 outstanding common shares (nopar value) of Eleven Corporation at $40 per share. This block of stock was purchased as a long-term investment. Assume the accounting period for each company ends December 31.

Subsequent to acquisition, the following data were available:

	19A	**19B**
Income reported by Eleven Corporation		
at December 31	$60,000	$70,000
Cash dividends declared and paid by		
Eleven Corporation during the year	25,000	30,000
Market price per share of Eleven common stock		
on December 31	37	39

Required:

a. What accounting method should be used by the company? Why?

b. Give the journal entries for the company for each year (use parallel columns) for the following (if none, explain why):
   (1) Acquisition of Eleven Corporation stock.
   (2) Net income reported by Eleven Corporation.
   (3) Dividends received from Eleven Corporation.
   (4) Market value effects at year-end.

c. Show how the following amounts should be reported on the financial statements for each year:
   (1) Long-term investment.
   (2) Stockholders' equity—unrealized loss.
   (3) Revenues.

P13–2   **(Identify, Record, and Report Using the Proper Method to Account for Two Different Equity Investments)**
During January 19A, Sterling Company purchased the shares listed below as a long-term investment:

Stock	Number of shares		Cost per share
	Out-standing	Purchase	
M Corporation . . . Common (nopar)	80,000	12,000	$10
N Corporation . . . Preferred, nonvoting (par $10)	10,000	4,000	20

Subsequent to acquisition, the following data were available:

	19A	19B
Net income reported at December 31:		
M Corporation	$20,000	$25,000
N Corporation	30,000	38,000
Dividends declared and paid per share during the year:		
M Corporation common stock	$ 1.00	$ 1.10
N Corporation preferred stock	0.80	0.80
Market value per share at December 31:		
M Corporation common stock	8.00	8.00
N Corporation preferred stock	19.00	20.00

Required:

a. What accounting method should be used for the investment in M common stock? N preferred stock? Why?

b. Give the journal entries for the company for each year in parallel columns (if none, explain why) for each of the following:
   (1) Purchase of the investments.
   (2) Income reported by M and N Corporations.
   (3) Dividends received from M and N Corporations.
   (4) Market value effects at year-end.

c. For each year, show how the following amounts should be reported on the financial statements for 19A:
   (1) Long-term investment.
   (2) Stockholders' equity—unrealized loss.
   (3) Revenues.

P13–3   **(Compare Methods to Account for Various Levels of Ownership of Voting Stock)**
Company S had outstanding 20,000 shares of common stock, par value $15 per share. On January 1, 19B, Company P purchased some of these shares at $20 per share. At the end of 19B, Company S reported the following: income, $40,000; and cash dividends declared and paid during the year, $15,000. The market value of Company S stock at the end of 19B was $17 per share.

Required:

a. For each case given below (in the tabulation), identify the method of accounting that should be used by Company P. Explain why.

b. Give the journal entries for Company P at the dates indicated below for each of the two independent cases. If no entry is required, explain why. Use the following format:

Tabulation of items	Case A—3,000 shares purchased	Case B—8,000 shares purchased
1. Entry to record the acquisition at January 1, 19B.	_____	_____
2. Entry to recognize the income reported by Company S for 19B.	_____	_____
3. Entry to recognize the dividends declared and paid by Company S for 19B.	_____	_____
4. Entry to recognize market value effect at end of 19B.	_____	_____

c. Complete the following schedule to show the separate amounts that should be reported on the 19B financial statements of Company P:

	Dollar amounts	
	Case A	Case B
Balance sheet:		
Investments and funds	_____	_____
Stockholders' equity	_____	_____
Income statement:		
Revenue from investments	_____	_____

d. Explain why assets, stockholders' equity, and revenues are different between the two cases.

P13–4 **(Compare the Cost and Equity Methods)**

Lewis Company purchased, as a long-term investment, some of the 100,000 shares of the outstanding common stock of Towns Corporation. The annual accounting period for each company ends December 31. The following transactions occurred during 19E:

19E

Jan. 10   Purchased shares of common stock of Towns at $10 per share as follows:

Case A—10,000 shares.

Case B—40,000 shares.

Dec. 31   Received the 19E financial statements of Towns Corporation; the reported net income was $80,000.

   31   Received a cash dividend of $0.30 per share from Towns Corporation.

   31   Market price of Towns stock, $7 per share.

Required:

a. For each case, identify the accounting method that should be used by the company. Explain why.

b. Give the journal entries for each case for the above transactions. If no entry is required, explain why. (Hint: Use parallel columns for Case A and Case B.)

c. Give the amounts for each case that should be reported on the 19E financial statements. Use the following format:

	Case A	Case B
Balance sheet (partial):		
Investments and funds:		
Investment in common stock, Towns Corporation . . .	_____	_____
Stockholders' equity:		
Unrealized loss	_____	_____
Income statement (partial):		
Revenue from investments	_____	_____

P13–5   **(Compare the Cost and Equity Methods)**

Sub Corporation had outstanding 200,000 shares of nopar common stock. On January 10, 19B, Golf Company purchased a block of these shares in the open market at $30 per share. At the end of 19B, Sub Corporation reported net income of $210,000 and cash dividends of $0.70 per share. At December 31, 19B, the Sub stock was selling at $27 per share. This problem involves two separate cases:

Case A—30,000 shares of Sub common stock were purchased.

Case B—60,000 shares of Sub common stock were purchased.

Required:

a. For each case, identify the accounting method that should be used by the company. Explain why.

b. For each case, in parallel columns, give the journal entries for each of the following (if no entry is required, explain why):
   (1) Acquisition.
   (2) Revenue recognition.
   (3) Dividends received.
   (4) Market value effects.

c. For each case show how the following should be reported on the 19B financial statements:
   (1) Long-term investments.
   (2) Market effects.
   (3) Revenues.

d. Explain why the amounts reported (in Requirement [c]) are different between the two cases.

Part B: Problems 13–6 to 13–10

P13–6   **(Compare Accounting for Equity Securities with Accounting for Debt Securities)**

On January 1, 19B, Uno Company purchased $60,000, 10% bonds of Bye Company as a long-term investment, at 100 (plus any accrued interest). Interest is payable annually on December 31. The bonds have six years to maturity from December 31, 19A. The company's annual accounting period ends December 31. In addition, on January 2, 19B, the company purchased in the market 5% of the 10,000 shares of outstanding common stock of Bye Company at $40 per share.

Required:

a. Give the journal entry to record the purchase of the bonds on January 1, 19B.

b. Give the journal entry to record the purchase of the common stock on January 2, 19B.

    c. Give the journal entry assuming a cash dividend of $2 per share was declared and received on the Bye stock on December 28, 19B.

    d. Give the journal entry for the receipt of the interest on the Bye bonds on December 31, 19B.

    e. Show how the long-term investments and the related revenues should be reported on the 19B annual financial statements. Market price of Bye stock was $43 at the end of 19B.

P13-7   **(Reporting Bond Investments Using Straight-Line Amortization of the Discount)**
On May 1, 19B, Gray Company purchased $60,000, 8% bonds of Taylor Company as a long-term investment. The interest is payable each April 30 and October 31. The bonds have four years to maturity from May 1, 19B. The bonds were purchased at 96 (plus any accrued interest). In addition, brokerage fees of $480 were paid by the company.

Required:

a. Give the 19B journal entries on the following dates:

    May 1   Purchase.
    Oct. 31   First interest date. Use straight-line amortization.
    Dec. 31   Adjusting entry for accrued interest at the end of the annual accounting period.

b. Show how the investment, interest receivable, and related revenue should be reported on the 19B annual financial statements.

c. Give the journal entry at the maturity date of the bonds.

P13-8   **(Reporting for a Debt Security Using Straight-Line Amortization of a Bond Premium)**
On June 1, 19B, Slade Company purchased $30,000, 10% bonds of Gray Company as a long-term investment. The interest is payable each April 30 and October 31. The bonds have five years to maturity from the issue date, May 1, 19B. The bonds were purchased at 105 (plus any accrued interest). The company's annual accounting period ends December 31.

Required:

a. Give the journal entries on the following dates:

    June 1   Purchase plus any accrued interest.
    Oct. 31   First interest date. Use straight-line amortization.
    Dec. 31   Adjusting entry for accrued interest.

b. Show how the investment, interest receivable, and related revenue should be reported on the 19B annual financial statements.

c. Give the journal entry at the maturity date of the bonds, April 30, 19G.

P13–9 **(Compare Entries and Reporting for Bonds Purchased at Par; at a Discount; at a Premium)**

During 19A, Ronald Company purchased the following bonds of Jackson Corporation as a long-term investment:

	Series A	Series B	Series C	Series D
Maturity amount	$10,000	$10,000	$10,000	$10,000
Date purchased	7/1/19A	7/1/19A	7/1/19A	10/1/19A
Interest per annum	9%	8%	10%	10%
Interest dates, annual	June 30	June 30	June 30	June 30
Maturity date	6/30/19F	6/30/19F	6/30/19F	6/30/19F
Purchase price*	100	95	106	100

* Plus any accrued interest.

Required:

a. Give the journal entries to record separately the purchase of the long-term investments.

b. Give the adjusting entries for December 31, 19A, assuming this is the end of the accounting period. Give a separate journal entry for each series. Use straight-line amortization.

c. Give the journal entry for each separate series that should be made on June 30, 19B, for collection of the first interest payment.

d. Complete the following schedule to show the amounts that should be reported on the 19A financial statements (show each series separately):

> **Income statement (19A):**
> Revenue from investments . . . . $ _____
>
> **Balance sheet (at December 31, 19A):**
> Long-term investment, bonds of Jackson Corporation . . . _____

P13–10 **(Analyze Effective-Interest Amortization; Prepare Schedule and Entries)**

On January 1, 19A, Worth Corporation purchased $50,000, 9% bonds of Boston Company to yield an effective rate of 10%. The bonds pay the interest on June 30 and December 31 and will mature on December 31, 19C.

Required:

a. Record the purchase of the bonds on January 1, 19A.

b. What were the stated and effective rates of interest?

c. What was the amount of the discount or premium? What would be the amount of discount or premium amortization each interest period assuming straight-line amortization?

d. Prepare a schedule of effective-interest amortization.

e. Give the journal entries to record interest (including amortization) on June 30 and December 31, 19A, assuming (1) straight-line and (2) effective-interest amortization.

f. Explain when it is appropriate to use each method of amortization.

CASES

C13–1   **(Analyze the Financial Effects of the Cost and Equity Methods)**

On January 1, 19B, Emerson Company purchased 40% of the outstanding common stock of Reed Corporation at a total cost of $780,000. On the December 31, 19B, balance sheet, the investment in Reed Corporation was $950,000, but no additional Reed stock was purchased. The company received $100,000 in cash dividends from Reed. The dividends were declared and paid during 19B. The company used the equity method to account for its investment in Reed. The market price of Reed stock increased during 19B.

Required:

a. Explain why the investment account balance increased from $780,000 to $950,000 during 19B.

b. What amount of revenue from the investment was reported during 19B?

c. If Emerson used the cost method, what amount of revenue from the investment should have been reported in 19B?

d. If the cost method were used, what amount should be reported as the investment in Reed Corporation on the December 31, 19B, balance sheet?

C13–2   **(Analyzing and Understanding Effective-Interest Amortization)**

On January 1, 19A, Mark Corporation purchased, as a long-term investment, a $10,000 bond of Fable Corporation. The following schedule was prepared based on the investment:

	Cash received	Revenue	Amortization	Investment
January 1, 19A				?
End year 19A	?	?	76	?
End year 19B	?	718	?	?
End year 19C	?	?	87	10,094
End year 19D	?	706	?	?

The bond had a stated rate of interest of 8%, payable at the end of each year.

Required:
Respond to the following:

a. Complete the amortization schedule.

b. What was the maturity amount of the bond?

c. What was the acquisition price of the investment?

d. Give the journal entry that Mark Corporation should make at acquisition date.

e. Was the bond acquired at a premium or discount? How much?

f. What method of amortization apparently will be used? Explain.

g. What was the effective rate of interest?

h. What were the total cash inflow and total cash outflow on the investment? What does the difference represent? Explain.

i. How much interest revenue should be reported each period on the income statement? How does this amount relate to the difference in (h)?

j. What amount will be reported on the balance sheet at the end of each year? (Show the amount for year 19D just prior to collection of the maturity amount.)

k. Why is the method of amortization being used conceptually preferable?

C13–3

JCPenney

(Analysis of the Cost and Equity Methods Using an Actual Financial Statement)
Refer to the financial statements of J.C. Penney Company, Inc. given in the appendix immediately preceding the index.

1. Does J.C. Penney use the cost method or the equity method to account for its short-term investments?

2. Does J.C. Penney use the equity method for any long-term investments?

FOURTEEN

CONSOLIDATED STATEMENTS— MEASURING AND REPORTING

PURPOSE

The previous chapter discussed accounting for long-term investments when one company owns less than 50% of the voting stock of another corporation. This chapter discusses those situations in which one corporation has a controlling influence over another corporation as the result of owning more than 50% of the outstanding voting stock of the other corporation. Often, when one corporation has a controlling influence in another, the financial statements for each are combined into a single set of financial statements by an accounting process called consolidation. Because of the complexity of the consolidation process, most corporations include a note to the financial statements that describes the procedures that were used. Notice that the example on the opposite page includes a change in consolidation procedures.

LEARNING OBJECTIVES

1. Identify necessary criteria for consolidated statements.

2. Specify appropriate use of the pooling and purchase methods.

3. Apply the pooling and purchase methods.

4. Compare the pooling and purchase methods.

5. Expand your accounting vocabulary by learning the "Important Terms Defined in This Chapter."

6. Apply the knowledge learned from this chapter by completing the homework assigned by your instructor.

ORGANIZATION

Part A—acquiring a controlling interest
1. Criteria for consolidated financial statements.

2. Pooling of interests method.

3. Purchase method.

Part B—reporting consolidated operations after one year using a worksheet
1. Impact of pooling of interests and purchase methods after acquisition.

2. Comparison of pooling of interests and purchase methods.

Xerox

Notes to Consolidated Financial Statements

1. Summary of Significant Accounting Policies

Basis of Consolidation. The accounts of all subsidiaries are consolidated, except for the Company's financial services and real estate subsidiaries which are accounted for by the equity method. Investments in corporate joint ventures, and other companies in which the Company has a 20% to 50% ownership, are accounted for by the equity method. The accounts of Latin American subsidiaries are included for their fiscal years which generally end on November 30.

Rank Xerox Limited, Rank Xerox Holding B.V. and their respective subsidiaries and the other subsidiaries jointly-owned by the Company and The Rank Organization Plc are referred to as Rank Xerox Companies. The accounts of the Rank Xerox Companies are included for their fiscal years ended October 31.

Consolidated financial statements of Xerox Financial Services, Inc. (XFSI), the Company's domestic financial services subsidiary, are presented, beginning on page 53, in support of the carrying value of the Company's investment in, and equity in the earnings of, XFSI.

New Accounting Pronouncements. There are several recently issued Statements of the Financial Accounting Standards Board which have not yet been adopted by the Company and its subsidiaries as of December 31, 1987. Of these new Statements the following have particular relevance to the Company:

Statement No. 94 – This Statement will require the Company to consolidate, beginning in 1988, all majority-owned subsidiaries. At the present time the Company does not consolidate XFSI or its real estate and international finance subsidiaries. Statement No. 94 will not affect the Company's net income or shareholders' equity, although the presentation and display of substantially all other financial data will materially change. The industry segment data on page 36 summarize the Company's total revenues, total assets and certain other data on a fully consolidated basis. Short and long-term debt will significantly increase under Statement No. 94 primarily as a result of consolidating Xerox Credit Corporation and the international finance subsidiaries. These subsidiaries are, by nature, highly leveraged relative to the Company and their borrowing capabilities are essentially determined on an independent basis. The Company does not anticipate any changes in its, or its subsidiaries', borrowing capabilities or practices as a result of applying Statement No. 94, Statement No. 94 is required to be retroactively applied.

PART A—ACQUIRING A CONTROLLING INTEREST

Criteria for Consolidated Financial Statements

A **parent** and **subsidiary** relationship exists when a company owns more than 50% of the outstanding voting stock of another corporation. The investing corporation is known as the parent company, and the other corporation is called a subsidiary. Both corporations are **separate legal entities.** Each company has its own accounting system, and each prepares its own financial statements. However, because of their special relationship, the parent and its subsidiary are viewed as a **single economic entity** for financial reporting. Because they are viewed as a single economic entity, the parent company is required to prepare **consolidated financial statements.** The individual financial statements of the parent and each of its subsidiaries are combined by the parent company into one overall or consolidated set of financial statements. The consolidated financial statements report on the single economic entity.

There are a number of operating, economic, and legal advantages to the parent-subsidiary relationship. Therefore, most large corporations, and many medium-size corporations, have a controlling interest in one or more other corporations. For example, Sears has acquired a controlling interest in many of the companies that manufacture the products that it sells. As a result, Sears is assured of getting the quality and quantity of product that it wants at the price that it wants to pay.

Consolidated financial statements are appropriate only if the parent is able to exert control over the subsidiary. Control is presumed to exist when one investor owns more than 50% of the outstanding voting stock of an entity. Nonvoting stock is not included in the determination of control because it does not provide the investor with any ability to influence the policies of the subsidiary. Effective control may not exist even though an investor owns more than 50% of the voting stock. This situation may exist when the subsidiary is located in a foreign country where **governmental restrictions** prevent the parent company from exercising meaningful control.

Consolidated statements are not prepared when an investor lacks meaningful control over the other company, even if it owns more than 50% of the voting stock. In such situations, the investment is reported as a long-term asset on the balance sheet of the parent as "Investment in unconsolidated subsidiary." The investment is accounted for under the **equity method** as discussed in Chapter 13 and is not consolidated.

Consolidated statements affect only the **reporting** by the parent company of the financial results of the parent and its subsidiaries. The accounting for each subsidiary company is not affected. The fact that a parent company owns a controlling interest has no effect on the accounting of a subsidiary. At the end of the accounting period, the subsidiary prepares its own financial statements. Also, the parent company accounts for its own operations in the normal manner and prepares its own financial statements at the end of each period.

When consolidation is appropriate, the financial statements of the parent and the subsidiaries are prepared in the normal manner and then are combined by the parent company on an **item-by-item basis.** Thus, the consolidated statement concept does not affect the recording of transactions by the parent and subsidiaries. It affects only the **reporting phase** of the combined entity represented by the parent company and its subsidiaries.

Methods of Acquiring a Controlling Interest

One corporation may acquire a controlling interest in an existing corporation by acquiring the voting capital stock in either of two ways:

1. **Exchanging shares of parent company voting stock for the outstanding voting capital stock of the subsidiary (owned by the stockholders of the subsidiary).**   If certain additional criteria are met, this type of acquisition is called a **pooling of interests.** In this situation, the stockholders of the subsidiary give up their subsidiary shares and become stockholders of only the parent company.
2. **Purchasing by the parent, using cash, other assets, or debt, of the outstanding voting shares from the stockholders of the subsidiary.**   This type of acquisition is known as a **combination by purchase.** In this situation, the stockholders of the subsidiary sell their shares and are not stockholders of either the parent or the subsidiary.[1]

The pooling of interests and purchase methods have different impacts on the consolidated financial statements. In the next few paragraphs, we will discuss the consolidation process and the effects of the alternative methods of acquiring a controlling interest. Throughout the chapter we will use a continuing example to illustrate the consolidation process. We will use data for Company P (the parent) and Company S (the acquired subsidiary) shown in Exhibit 14–1.

Pooling of Interests Method

When one corporation gains control over another corporation by **exchanging** stock (and certain additional criteria are met), the stockholders of the two corporations have pooled their ownership interests. This transaction is not viewed as a purchase/sale transaction; and as a result, the cost principle is **not** applied to pooling of interests acquisitions. Assume Company P acquired 100% of the voting stock of Company S on January 2, 19A, immediately after the financial statements shown in Exhibit 14–1 were prepared. Company P would record the exchange of stock as follows:

---

[1] A rigid list of criteria must be met to qualify as a pooling of interest; otherwise, the combination must be accounted for as a combination by purchase. Because of the criteria, many stock exchanges must be accounted for under the purchase method.

Exhibit 14–1   Illustrative data for consolidation

COMPANY P AND COMPANY S
Separate Balance Sheets
January 1, 19A, Immediately before Acquisition

	Company P	Company S
Assets		
Cash	$205,000	$ 35,000
Accounts receivable (net)*	15,000	30,000
Receivable from Company S	10,000	
Inventories	170,000	70,000
Plant and equipment (net)*	100,000	45,000
Total assets	$500,000	$180,000
Liabilities and Stockholders' Equity		
Liabilities:		
Accounts payable	$ 60,000	$ 20,000
Payable to Company P		10,000
Stockholders' equity:		
Common stock, Company P (par $6)	300,000	
Common stock, Company S (par $10)		100,000
Retained earnings	140,000	50,000
Total liabilities and stockholders' equity	$500,000	$180,000

* Accounts receivable, less the allowance for doubtful accounts; and plant and equipment, less accumulated depreciation. The net amounts are used to simplify the example. The end results will be the same as they would have been had the separate control accounts been used.

Investment in Company S	150,000	
Common stock		60,000
Contributed capital		90,000

The transaction does not affect the financial statements of Company S because it was an exchange of stock between Company P and the stockholders of Company S. Therefore, Company S does not record the transaction.

Notice that the investment in Company S is recorded at the book value of the stock that was acquired (Common stock, $100,000 + Retained earnings, $50,000) and not the fair market value of the stock. Accountants view a pooling of interests as a joining of ownership interests and not a formal exchange transaction that must be accounted for in conformity with the cost principle (Exhibit 4–5). Consolidated financial statements under the pooling of interests method reflect book values and not market values that existed on the date that the subsidiary was acquired.

To illustrate the consolidation process, we will combine the two separate balance sheets shown in Exhibit 14–2 into a single **consolidated balance sheet.** The result of consolidation is the set of financial statements that would appear if

Exhibit 14–2 Balance sheets immediately after acquisition (pooling of interests method)

COMPANY P AND COMPANY S
Separate Balance Sheets (pooling of interests method)
January 2, 19A, Immediately after Acquisition

	Company P	Company S
Assets		
Cash	$205,000	$ 35,000
Accounts receivable (net)	15,000	30,000
Receivable from Company S	10,000	
Inventories	170,000	70,000
Investment in Company S (100%)	150,000*	
Plant and equipment (net)	100,000	45,000
Total assets	$650,000	$180,000
Liabilities and Stockholders' Equity		
Accounts payable	$ 60,000	$ 20,000
Payable to Company P		10,000
Common stock, Company P (par $6)	360,000*	
Common stock, Company S (par $10)		100,000
Contributed capital	90,000*	
Retained earnings, Company P	140,000	
Retained earnings, Company S		50,000
Total liabilities and stockholders' equity	$650,000	$180,000

* Amounts changed from preacquisition balance sheets given in Exhibit 14–1. Notice the transaction does not affect Company S.

there were a **single entity.** Basically, consolidation involves adding together the individual items reported on each company's financial statements. For example, when the parent company consolidates the balance sheets shown in Exhibit 14–2, the consolidated cash balance will be $240,000 (i.e., $205,000 + $35,000). During consolidation, some accounts are **eliminated** (or adjusted) to avoid including amounts that would not be reported if only a single entity existed. For example, the balance sheet of Company P shows a receivable from Company S of $10,000, and the balance sheet of Company S shows a payable to Company P of $10,000. It is impossible for an entity to owe itself money. Therefore, during consolidation, these accounts must be eliminated (which means that they will not be reported on the consolidated balance sheet). The consolidated balance sheet is prepared as if a single entity existed, and it would not be proper to report an amount that the entity owed to itself.

Two items must be eliminated when the balance sheets shown in Exhibit 14–2 are consolidated under the pooling of interests method:

a. Company P shows a receivable of $10,000 from Company S, and the accounts of Company S show this as a payable to Company P. This amount is called an **intercompany debt.** When the two balance sheets are combined into a single consolidated balance sheet, intercompany debt must be eliminated because there is no external debt or receivable for the combined entity. Thus, the following elimination must be made when the two balance sheets are combined:

	Eliminations	
	Consolidated assets	**Consolidated liabilities**
Receivable from Company S—decrease . . .	−$10,000	
Payable to Company P—decrease		−$10,000

b. The individual assets of Company S will be included on the consolidated balance sheet. The "Investment in Company S" account represents Company P's investment in those assets. Therefore, to prevent double counting, the investment account must be eliminated. Related to this elimination is the reduction of stockholders' equity. The credit balance of $100,000 in the Company S common stock account is owned by Company P. Because it is impossible for a company to invest in itself, the Company S stock held by Company P must be eliminated. Finally, the difference between the balances in the investment account and the common stock account of Company S ($150,000 − $100,000 = $50,000) must be eliminated from Contributed Capital (on Company P's books). This elimination is necessary because it is an intercompany account. The elimination can be summarized as follows:

	Eliminations	
	Consolidated assets	**Consolidated stockholders' equity**
Investment account—decrease	$−150,000	
Common stock, Company S—decrease		$−100,000
Contributed capital—decrease (for the difference) . . .		−50,000

The balance sheets of Company P and Company S are shown separately in Exhibit 14–3. In the last column, these balance sheets are combined on a line-by-line basis, after deducting the "Eliminations," to develop the "Consolidated balance sheet." In an external consolidated financial statement, only the last column would be reported by the parent company.

Review the "Consolidated balance sheet" by the pooling of interests method shown in the last column of Exhibit 14–3. Notice the following measurement procedures: (1) the amounts on each line for the consolidated assets, liabilities, and stockholders' equity are the **combined book values** of the parent and the subsidiary as were shown in the separate balance sheets; (2) the intercompany amounts for investment, subsidiary common stock, a part of contributed capital, and the intercompany debt are eliminated; and (3) the **consolidated** retained

Exhibit 14-3 Preparation of consolidated balance sheet (pooling of interests method)

COMPANY P and Its Subsidiary, COMPANY S (100% owned)
Consolidated Balance Sheet (pooling of interests method)
At January 2, 19A, Immediately after Acquisition

	Separate balance sheets		Eliminations	Consolidated balance sheet
	Company P	Company S		
Assets				
Cash	$205,000	$ 35,000		$240,000
Accounts receivable (net)	15,000	30,000		45,000
Receivable from Company S	10,000		(a) – $ 10,000	–0–
Inventories	170,000	70,000		240,000
Investment in Company S	150,000		(b) – 150,000	–0–
Plant and equipment (net)	100,000	45,000		145,000
Total assets	$650,000	$180,000		$670,000
Liabilities				
Accounts payable	$ 60,000	$ 20,000		$ 80,000
Payable to Company P		10,000	(a) – 10,000	–0–
Stockholders' Equity				
Common stock, Company P	360,000			360,000
Common stock, Company S		100,000	(b) – 100,000	–0–
Contributed capital	90,000		(b) – 50,000	40,000
Retained earnings, Company P	140,000			190,000
Retained earnings, Company S		50,000		
Total liabilities and stockholders' equity . . .	$650,000	$180,000		$670,000

Usually a formal worksheet (with debit-credit columns) is used to prepare consolidated statements.

earnings amount is the sum of the two separate retained earnings amounts ($140,000 + $50,000 = $190,000).[2]

The $100,000 balance shown in the capital stock account of Company S is eliminated because it is an intercompany item (all of the capital stock is owned by Company P). Retained earnings of Company S is not eliminated because it is not an intercompany item. The old stockholders of Company P plus the former Company S stockholders (who are now stockholders of Company P) have dividend claims on the **total** of retained earnings for the combined unit.

All of the elimination entries that are necessary to prepare consolidated statements are made on worksheets. These entries are not made in the journals or posted to the ledgers of either Company P or Company S. Basically, consol-

---

[2] The pooling of interests method also requires that all comparative statements presented for prior years must be restated as if consolidated statements had been prepared.

idation is a process that occurs after the parent and subsidiary have prepared their own financial statements. Consolidation entries are made on worksheets and do not affect the basic accounting records of either the parent or the subsidiary.

Purchase Method

The preceding discussion considered the pooling of interests method (an exchange of stock). In contrast, when a corporation pays cash to acquire the stock of another corporation, a **purchase** transaction takes place. The purchase of assets must be recorded in conformity with the **cost principle.** Thus, on the acquisition date, the investment account for the parent company must be measured at cost, which is the **market value of the acquired shares at date of purchase** (i.e., the cash or cash equivalent paid).

To illustrate a combination by **purchase,** we will use the balance sheets of Companies P and S as given in Exhibit 14–1. Assume that on January 2, 19A, Company P **purchased** from stockholders 100% of the outstanding voting stock of Company S for $165,000 and paid cash. On this date, Company P would make the following journal entry in its accounts:

January 2, 19A:

Investment in stock of Company S (10,000 shares, 100%)	165,000	
Cash		165,000
Acquisition by purchase.		

Note that Company P paid $165,000 cash for 100% of the owners' equity of Company S, although the **total book value** of the stockholders' equity of Company S that was purchased was only $150,000. Thus, Company P paid $15,000 more than "book value."

After the above journal entry is posted to the accounts of Company P, the two separate balance sheets would be changed as shown in the first two columns of Exhibit 14–4. Compare these two columns with Exhibit 14–1, and you will see that for (*a*) Company P cash decreased by $165,000 and the investment increased by the same amount and (*b*) Company S accounts are unchanged because the transaction was between Company P and the stockholders of Company S (not Company S itself).

Observe the consolidated balance sheet under the **purchase method** shown in Exhibit 14–4. The two separate balance sheets for Companies P and S were combined immediately after acquisition to develop the consolidated balance sheet. The consolidation process for a purchase is similar to consolidation for a pooling of interests (as illustrated in Exhibit 14–3). There are two intercompany items that require eliminations like those shown for the pooling of interests method. Notice that the elimination of the investment account is significantly different under the purchase method.

Exhibit 14–4 Preparation of a consolidated balance sheet (purchase method)

COMPANY P and Its Subsidiary, COMPANY S (100% owned)
Consolidated Balance Sheet (purchase method)
At January 2, 19A, Immediately after Acquisition

	Separate balance sheets		Eliminations		Consolidated balance sheet
	Company P	Company S			
Assets					
Cash	$ 40,000	$ 35,000			$ 75,000
Accounts receivable (net)	15,000	30,000			45,000
Receivable from Company S	10,000		(a)	– $ 10,000	–0–
Inventories	170,000	70,000			240,000
Investment in Company S	165,000		(b)	– 165,000	–0–
Plant and equipment (net)	100,000	45,000	(b)	+ 5,000	150,000
Goodwill			(b)	+ 10,000	10,000
Total assets	$500,000	$180,000			$520,000
Liabilities					
Accounts payable	$ 60,000	$ 20,000			$ 80,000
Payable to Company P		10,000	(a)	– 10,000	–0–
Stockholders' Equity					
Common stock, Company P	300,000				300,000
Common stock, Company S		100,000	(b)	– 100,000	–0–
Retained earnings, Company P	140,000				140,000
Retained earnings, Company S		50,000	(b)	– 50,000	–0–
Total liabilities and stockholders' equity . .	$500,000	$180,000			$520,000

a. The intercompany debt must be eliminated for the reasons discussed under the pooling of interests. This elimination is as follows:

	Eliminations	
	Consolidated assets	Consolidated liabilities
Receivable from Company S—decrease . . .	– $10,000	
Payable to Company P—decrease		– $10,000

b. The P Company investment account balance of $165,000 represents **market value** at the date of acquisition. It must be eliminated against the stockholders' equity of the subsidiary, which is at **book value.** Company P paid $15,000 more than book value (i.e., $165,000 – $150,000) to acquire Company S for two reasons: (1) the plant and equipment owned by Company S had a market value of $50,000 at acquisition (compared with the book value of $45,000 reported by

Company S), and (2) Company S had developed a good reputation with its customers which increased the overall value of Company S. The difference between the cost and the book value of the investment may be analyzed as follows:

Purchase price for 100% interest in Company S		$165,000
Net assets purchased, value at market:		
Book value, $180,000 + Market value increment		
of plant and equipment, $5,000 = ...	$185,000	
Less liabilities assumed	30,000	
Total market value purchased		155,000
Goodwill purchased		$ 10,000

Company P paid $165,000 cash for Company S, which had net assets (total assets minus liabilities) with a **market** value of $155,000. Therefore, the goodwill of Company S cost $10,000. **Goodwill** is the amount that an investor paid for the good reputation, customer appeal, and general acceptance of the business that an acquired company had developed over the years. All successful companies have some amount of goodwill. Its "value" is never known except when a business is purchased, as it was in this case. To eliminate the Company P investment account and the owner's equity accounts of Company S, the following five steps must be completed:

1. Increase the plant and equipment of Company S from the book value of $45,000 to market value of $50,000; the increase is $5,000.
2. Recognize the $10,000 goodwill purchased as an asset.
3. Eliminate the investment account balance of $165,000.
4. Eliminate the Company S common stock balance of $100,000.
5. Eliminate the Company S retained earnings balance of $50,000.

These five steps are implemented as follows:

	Eliminations	
	Consolidated assets	Consolidated stockholders' equity
Plant and equipment—increase	+$ 5,000	
Goodwill—increase	+ 10,000	
Investment—decrease	− 165,000	
Common stock Company S—decrease		−$100,000
Retained earnings Company S—decrease . . .		− 50,000

When the purchase method is used, the balance of Retained Earnings of the subsidiary at acquisition is eliminated. In contrast, under the pooling of interests method, retained earnings is not eliminated. This elimination is made with the purchase method because the retained earnings of the subsidiary were in effect paid to the former stockholders of Company S when they were bought out for cash.

The accounts of Company S are not affected by a purchase because the transaction was between the parent company and the former stockholders of the subsidiary.

The two "Separate balance sheets" are shown in Exhibit 14–4. After eliminations, they are combined on a line-by-line basis to develop the "Consolidated balance sheet" of Company P shown in the last column. In an external consolidated financial statement of Company P, only the "Consolidated balance sheet" shown in the last column (and not the "Separate balance sheets") would be reported.

To reemphasize, when the purchase method is used, the **market values** at date of acquisition of the subsidiary's assets are added on an item-by-item basis to the **book values** of the parent.

Comparison of the Effects on the Balance Sheet of Pooling of Interests versus Purchase Methods

To examine the differences in balance sheet amounts that arise when the pooling of interests method is used versus the purchase method, we can compare several of the consolidated amounts shown in Exhibits 14–3 and 14–4 as follows:

	Acquisition method		
	Pooling method	Purchase method	Difference
1. Cash	$240,000	$ 75,000	$(165,000)
2. Plant and equipment (net)	145,000	150,000	5,000
3. Goodwill		10,000	10,000
4. Common stock Company P	360,000	300,000	(60,000)
5. Contributed capital from pooling	40,000		(40,000)
6. Retained earnings Company P	190,000	140,000	(50,000)

The $165,000 difference in cash was the purchase price of the subsidiary (under the pooling of interests method, only stock was exchanged). The $100,000 difference in the amount of common stock is due to the effect of issuing stock under pooling of interests rather than paying cash when the purchase method is chosen. The plant and equipment amount is higher when the purchase method is used because the purchase method requires application of the cost principle. Under the cost principle, the **market value** at date of acquisition rather than book value must be recognized for the assets of the subsidiary. Usually, goodwill arises in purchase but not pooling of interests. These higher amounts for assets under the purchase method mean higher expenses will be reported on the income statements in the future periods. In this case, depreciation expense and amortization expense for goodwill will be higher. Finally, under the pooling of interests method, the reported retained earnings amount is higher because the amount of retained earnings of the subsidiary must be added to that of the parent as shown in Exhibit 14–3.

When the pooling of interests and purchase methods are compared, three items usually stand out on the consolidated balance sheet:

1. Operational assets almost always are valued higher under the purchase method because they are recorded at market rather than at the subsidiary's book values.
2. Goodwill often is recorded under the purchase method but never is recorded under the pooling of interests method.
3. Retained earnings is lower under the purchase method because only the parent company's retained earnings is reflected, while under the pooling of interests method consolidated retained earnings always is the sum of the parent and subsidiary retained earnings.

Part B will discuss other significant effects that are reflected on consolidated income statements.

PART B—REPORTING CONSOLIDATED OPERATIONS AFTER ONE YEAR USING A WORKSHEET

A formal worksheet with debit and credit columns can be used to prepare consolidated financial statements instead of the pluses and minuses that were used in Part A of this chapter. The worksheet is prepared by the parent company, but the debits and credits are not posted to the accounts of either the parent company or the subsidiary. Remember, consolidation is the process of combining the financial statements of the parent and its subsidiary without affecting the basic accounting records of the companies. The worksheet that is used in Part B of this chapter does not involve any new accounting concepts. It is based on the same logic as the pluses and minuses that were used in Part A.

Recall that on January 2, 19A, Company P acquired 100% of the outstanding stock of Company S. Assume that it is now December 31, 19A. After operating for a year, each company prepared its separate income statement and balance sheet as shown in Exhibit 14–5. Two sets of financial statements are shown for Company P; the first is based on the assumption that Company S was acquired through an exchange of stock (pooling of interests), and the second is based on the assumption that Company S stock was acquired with cash (purchase).

At the end of 19A, the following additional data were available to Company P:

a. The Investment in Company S balance was the same as at date of acquisition; the balance of Retained Earnings of Company S at acquisition was $50,000.
b. At date of acquisition, January 2, 19A, the plant and equipment of Company S had an acquisition market value of $5,000 above book value and goodwill purchased amounted to $10,000.
c. Intercompany debt owed by Company S to Company P was $6,000 at the end of 19A.

Exhibit 14–5 Illustrative data for consolidated financial statements subsequent to acquisition (100% ownership)

	COMPANY P AND COMPANY S		
	Separate Financial Statements for 19A (unclassified)		
		At December 31, 19A	
	Company P		
	Exchange of stock	Purchase with cash	Company S
Income statement (for 19A):			
Sales revenue	$400,000	$400,000	$110,000
Cost of goods sold	(220,000)	(220,000)	(59,000)
Expenses (not detailed)	(130,000)	(130,000)	(26,500)
Depreciation expense	(10,000)	(10,000)	(4,500)
Income tax expense	(20,000)	(20,000)	(6,000)
Net income	$ 20,000	$ 20,000	$ 14,000
Balance sheet (at December 31, 19A):			
Cash	$216,000	$ 51,000	$ 55,500
Accounts receivable (net)	18,000	18,000	28,000
Receivable from Company S	6,000	6,000	
Inventories	185,000	185,000	65,000
Investment in Company S			
(by purchase, at cost)	150,000*	165,000*	
Plant and equipment (net)	90,000	90,000	40,500
Totals	$665,000	$515,000	$189,000
Accounts payable	$ 55,000	$ 55,000	$ 19,000
Payable to Company P			6,000
Common stock (par $10)	360,000	300,000	100,000
Contributed capital	90,000		
Beginning retained earnings*	140,000	140,000	50,000
Net income for 19A (per above)	20,000	20,000	14,000
Totals	$665,000	$515,000	$189,000

* Balance at date of acquisition.

> *d.* The plant and equipment owned by Company S had a 10-year remaining life from January 1, 19A, for depreciation purposes. The company uses straight-line depreciation.
>
> *e.* Goodwill is to be amortized from January 1, 19A, over 20 years on a straight-line basis.

A consolidated income statement and balance sheet must be prepared at the end of 19A. A separate consolidation worksheet will be discussed for the pooling of interests and purchase methods.

Pooling of Interests Method—Income Statement and Balance Sheet

The worksheet for the pooling of interests method (Exhibit 14–6) has side captions for each income statement and balance sheet account, and column headings for the parent company, the subsidiary company, intercompany eliminations, and the **consolidated balances.** The amounts entered in the first two columns are taken directly from the separate 19A financial statements prepared by the parent and the subsidiary (as given in Exhibit 14–5).

The worksheet is designed so that the eliminations are entered in debit and credit format. This format provides an excellent check on the accuracy of the work. Remember that the elimination entries are **worksheet entries only;** they are never entered into the accounts of either the parent or the subsidiary.

To complete the worksheet, the elimination entries must be entered. Then, each line is accumulated horizontally to derive the consolidated amount in the last column.

Under the pooling of interests method, there are two elimination entries that must be made on the worksheet:

   a. Eliminate the investment in Company S with offsets to the accounts for (1) Common Stock, Company S; and (2) Contributed Capital. These eliminations are entered on the worksheet and are shown below in journal entry format.

Common stock, Company S	100,000	
Contributed capital	50,000	
Investment in Company S		150,000

   b. Eliminate the intercompany debt of $6,000 owed by Company S to Company P. These two eliminations can be accomplished as follows:

Payable to Company P	6,000	
Receivable from Company S		6,000

Notice that these two eliminations entries are similar to the ones that were discussed in Part A of the chapter. Review that section of the chapter if you do not understand why these entries are made.

The far right column of the worksheet (Consolidated Balances) contains the information that is used to prepare both the consolidated balance sheet and consolidated income statement.

Consolidation under the pooling method is relatively simple because the subsidiary's assets are reported at their book value. Consolidation under the purchase method is somewhat more complex.

Purchase Method—Income Statement and Balance Sheet

Under the purchase method, a few more eliminations are needed because of the use of acquisition market values for the subsidiary. The intercompany eliminations on the worksheet (Exhibit 14–7) under the purchase method are:

Exhibit 14–6 Consolidation worksheet (pooling of interests method; 100% ownership)

COMPANY P and Its Subsidiary, COMPANY S
Consolidation Worksheet (pooling of interests) for the Balance Sheet
and Income Statement December 31, 19A (100% ownership)

Items	Statements Company P	Statements Company S	Intercompany Eliminations Debit	Intercompany Eliminations Credit	Consolidated Balances
Income statement:					
Sales revenue	400,000	110,000			510,000
Cost of goods sold	(220,000)	(59,000)			(279,000)
Expenses (not detailed)	(130,000)	(26,500)			(156,500)
Depreciation expense	(10,000)	(4,500)			(14,500)
Income tax expense	(20,000)	(6,000)			(26,000)
Net income (carried down)	20,000	14,000			34,000
Balance sheet:					
Cash	216,000	55,500			271,500
Accounts receivable (net)	18,000	28,000			46,000
Receivable from Company S	6,000			(b) 6,000	
Inventories	185,000	65,000			250,000
Investment in Company S	150,000			(a) 150,000	
Plant and equipment (net)	90,000	40,500			130,500
Totals	665,000	189,000			698,000
Accounts payable	55,000	19,000			74,000
Payable to Company P		6,000	(b) 6,000		
Common stock, Company P	360,000				360,000
Common stock, Company S		100,000	(a) 100,000		
Contributed capital	90,000		(a) 50,000		40,000
Beginning retained earnings, Company P	140,000				140,000
Beginning retained earnings, Company S		50,000			50,000
Net income, 19A (from above; not added across)	30,000*	14,000*			34,000*
Totals	665,000	189,000	156,000	156,000	698,000

* Carried down from above.

Explanation of eliminations:
(a) To eliminate Investment in Company S against Common Stock of Company S and Contributed Capital.
(b) To eliminate the intercompany debt.

> *a.* Eliminate the investment account against the subsidiary owners' equity accounts. This elimination entry will be the same each year because it is based on the values recognized at the date of acquisition. The $15,000 difference between the purchase price and the book value must be allocated to the subsidiary company's assets (including goodwill). The elimination (illustrated in a journal entry format) is as follows:

Exhibit 14–7 Consolidation worksheet (purchase method; 100% ownership)

COMPANY P and Its Subsidiary, COMPANY S
Consolidation Worksheet (by purchase) for the Balance Sheet
and Income Statement
December 31, 19A (100% ownership)

Items	Statements Company P	Statements Company S	Intercompany Eliminations Debit		Intercompany Eliminations Credit		Consolidated Balances
Income statement:							
Sales revenue	400,000	110,000					510,000
Cost of goods sold	(220,000)	(59,000)					(279,000)
Expenses (not detailed)	(130,000)	(26,500)					(156,500)
Depreciation expense	(10,000)	(4,500)	(c)	500			(15,000)
Amortization expense (goodwill)			(d)	500			(500)
Income tax expense	(20,000)	(6,000)					(26,000)
Net income (carried down)	20,000	14,000					33,000
Balance sheet:							
Cash	51,000	55,500					106,500
Accounts receivable (net)	18,000	28,000					46,000
Receivable from Company S	6,000				(b)	6,000	
Inventories	185,000	65,000					250,000
Investment in Company S (at cost)	165,000				(a)	165,000	
Plant and equipment (net)	90,000	40,500	(a)	5,000	(c)	500	135,000
Goodwill			(a)	10,000	(d)	500	9,500
Totals	515,000	189,000					547,000
Accounts payable	55,000	19,000					74,000
Payable to Company P		6,000	(b)	6,000			
Common stock, Company P	300,000						300,000
Common stock, Company S		100,000	(a)	100,000			
Beginning retained earnings, Company P	140,000						140,000
Beginning retained earnings, Company S		50,000	(a)	50,000			
Net income, 19A (from above; not added across)	30,000*	14,000*					33,000*
Totals	515,000	189,000	172,000		172,000		547,000

* Carried down from above.

Explanation of eliminations:
  (a) To eliminate investment account against the subsidiary stockholders' equity and to allocate the difference between purchase price and book value purchased to the appropriate accounts.
  (b) To eliminate the intercompany debt.
  (c) To record additional depreciation for one year on the asset increase resulting from the acquisition.
  (d) To record amortization for one year on the goodwill recognized.

Common stock, Company S	. . . .	100,000
Retained earnings, Company S	. . . .	50,000
Plant and equipment	. . . .	5,000
Goodwill	. . . .	10,000
Investment in Company S	. . . .	

                                                                            165,000

b. Eliminate the intercompany debt of $6,000 with the following entry on the worksheet:

Payable to Company P	. . . .	6,000
Receivable from Company S	. . . .	6,000

The first two eliminations are similar to the ones that were made when the consolidated balance sheet was prepared on the date of acquisition under the purchase method. You should review the explanation of these entries in Part A of the chapter.

c. Because the plant and equipment amount for Company S was increased by $5,000 to reflect acquisition market value, additional depreciation must be recorded on the $5,000 increment. The depreciation reflected on the statements of Company S is based on original acquisition cost and does not include this $5,000 increase to market value. Therefore, the worksheet entry must be:

Depreciation expense (Company S)	. . . .	500
Plant and equipment (Company S)		
(or accumulated depreciation)	. . . .	500

      $5,000 ÷ 10 years = $500.

d. Goodwill must be amortized over a realistic period not longer than 40 years *(APB Opinion 17).* Company P decided to use a 20-year life. The $10,000 goodwill was recognized in entry *(a)* above. This amount must be amortized. Therefore, the worksheet entry to accomplish this effect is:

Amortization expense (goodwill)	. . . .	500
Goodwill	. . . .	500

      $10,000 ÷ 20 years = $500.

After all of the intercompany eliminations have been entered on the worksheet, the consolidated financial statement amounts are determined by accumulating each line horizontally to derive the balances in the last column. The balances in the last column of the worksheet are classified in the normal manner in preparing the consolidated income statement and balance sheet.

Consolidation Procedures in Perspective

As you can see from this brief introduction, consolidation procedures for large corporations can be complex. While some of the procedures are indeed complex, the basic consolidation concept is fairly easy to understand. Basically, consolidation is the accounting process of bringing together financial statements from separate legal entities to make it appear as if there is a single economic entity. This process involves adding together the individual financial statement items and eliminating or adjusting those items that exist because there are separate entities. Clearly, a company cannot invest in itself, so the Investment in Subsidiary account must be eliminated. Also, a company cannot owe itself money, so intercompany receivables and payables must be eliminated. Your study of consolidation procedures will be much easier if you keep in mind the purpose of the consolidation process. Try to understand why adjustments and eliminations are made and not just how to make them.

Financial Statement Analysis

Nearly all large corporations prepare consolidated financial statements. Analysts must understand the consolidation process because the majority of the statements they work with are prepared on a consolidated basis.

The pooling of interests and purchase methods have significantly different effects on consolidated statements. Analysts must be aware of these differences to properly use consolidated statements. Exhibit 14–8 shows a summary of the differences between the pooling of interests and purchase methods. Item 6 identifies the primary financial statement effects.

Some analysts use the return on investment (ROI) ratio to evaluate the effectiveness of the management of a company. Basically, the ratio is calculated as follows:

$$ROI = \frac{\text{Net income}}{\text{Total assets}}$$

The use of pooling of interests versus purchase can have a dramatic effect on the ROI ratio. Under pooling of interests, net income is normally higher because there is no additional depreciation expense associated with the increased asset values reported under the purchase method. Also under pooling of interests, the amount of total assets reported is normally lower because of the use of book values for the assets of the subsidiary. As a result of the higher numerator for the ratio (net income) and the lower denominator (total assets), ROI for companies that use pooling is often significantly higher than ROI for companies that use the purchase method. Analysts must understand consolidation to be sure they identify real economic differences between companies and not differences created by accounting alternatives.

DEMONSTRATION CASE

On January 1, 19A, Connaught Company purchased 100% of the outstanding voting shares of London Company in the open market for $85,000 cash. On the date of acquisition, the market value of the operational assets of London Company was $79,000.

Exhibit 14–8 Differences between the pooling of interests and purchase methods summarized

Item	Pooling of Interests	Purchase
1. Measuring and recording at date of acquisition by the parent company.	Acquisition is accomplished by exchanging shares of stock. A purchase/sale transaction is not assumed; therefore, the cost principle is **not** applied. The investment account is debited for the **book value** of the subsidiary stock acquired.	Acquisition usually is accomplished by purchasing the shares with cash and/or debt. A purchase/sale transaction is assumed; therefore, the cost principle is applied. On acquisition date, the investment account is debited for the **market value** of the resources acquired.
2. Goodwill.	Goodwill is not recognized by the parent company.	Goodwill is recognized by the parent company to the extent that the purchase price exceeds the sum of acquisition market values of the assets (less the liabilities) of the subsidiary.
3. Method of aggregating or combining by the parent company to derive the consolidated balance sheet.	Assets and liabilities (less any eliminations) of the subsidiary are added, at **book value,** to the book values of the parent.	Assets and liabilities (less any eliminations) of the subsidiary are added, at their acquisition **market values,** to the book values of the assets and liabilities of the parent.
4. Method of aggregating or combining by the parent company to derive the consolidated income statement.	Revenues and expenses as reported by each company, less any eliminations, are aggregated.	Revenues as reported, less any eliminations, are aggregated. Expenses, plus additional depreciation and amortization of goodwill, less any eliminations, are aggregated.
5. Eliminations.	Eliminate all intercompany debts, revenues, and expenses. Eliminate investment account on parent's books and owners' equity of the subsidiary, excluding retained earnings.	Eliminate all intercompany debts, revenues, and expenses. Eliminate the investment account on parent's books and common stock and retained earnings of the subsidiary.
6. Usual comparative effects on the consolidated financial statements.	Expenses—lower Net income—higher EPS—higher Noncash assets—lower Liabilities—same Capital stock—higher Retained earnings—higher	Expenses—higher Net income—lower EPS—lower Noncash assets—higher Liabilities—same Capital stock—lower Retained earnings—lower

Required:

a. Was this a combination by pooling of interests or by purchase? Explain.

b. Give the journal entry that should be made by Connaught Company at date of acquisition. If none is required, explain why.

c. Give the journal entry that should be made by London Company at date of acquisition. If none is required, explain why.

d. Analyze the acquisition to determine the amount of goodwill purchased.

e. Should the assets of London Company be included on the consolidated balance sheet at book value or market value? Explain.

Suggested Solution

a. The purchase method should be used because the stock of the subsidiary was acquired for cash.

b. January 1, 19A:

Investment in subsidiary	85,000	
Cash		85,000

c. London Company would not record a journal entry related to the purchase of stock by Connaught Company. The transaction was between Connaught and the stockholders of London Company. The transaction did not directly involve the London Company.

d.

Purchase price for London Company	$85,000
Market value of net assets purchased	79,000
Goodwill	$ 6,000

e. Under the purchase method, the assets of London Company should be included on the consolidated balance sheet at their market values as of the date of acquisition. The cost principle applies because a purchase/ sale transaction is assumed when the combination is accounted for as a purchase. When the pooling of interests method is used, the assets of the subsidiary are reported on the consolidated balance sheet at their book value.

SUMMARY OF CHAPTER

Consolidated financial statements are required in most situations when one corporation owns more than 50% of the outstanding voting stock of another corporation. The concept of consolidation is based on the view that a parent company and its subsidiaries constitute one economic entity. Therefore, the separate income statements, balance sheets, and statements of cash flows should be combined each period on an item-by-item basis as a single set of consolidated financial statements.

Ownership of a controlling interest of another corporation may be accounted for as either a pooling of interests or combination by purchase. The measurement of amounts reported on the consolidated financial statements is influenced by these two different accounting methods.

The pooling of interests method usually is used when the parent company exchanges shares of its own voting stock for a controlling interest in the voting shares of the subsidiary. In this situation, there is no purchase/sale (exchange) transaction. Rather, there was a joining of interests by exchanging stock and the cost principle is not applied. Therefore, in preparing consolidated statements under the pooling of interests method, the book values of each related company are added together. Acquisition market values are disregarded.

Under the purchase method, the parent company usually pays cash and/or incurs debt to acquire the voting shares of the subsidiary. In these circumstances, a purchase/sale transaction has been completed, and the acquisition is accounted for in conformity with the cost principle. Therefore, the assets of the subsidiary must be measured at their acquisition market values when combined with the statements of the parent company.

The acquisition of a controlling interest **does not** affect the accounting and reporting of the subsidiary companies (the subsidiary companies do not prepare consolidated statements).

CHAPTER SUPPLEMENT 14A

Consolidation Procedures—Less than 100% Ownership

When the parent company owns a controlling interest that is less than 100%, most of the consolidation procedures are the same as the procedures for 100% ownership. Certain eliminations differ because they are based on the **proportionate** ownership level. When the parent company does not own 100% of the subsidiary, there will be a group of stockholders of the subsidiary company called the **minority stockholders.** Their interest in the subsidiary is not affected by the parent's interest. The minority stockholders' interest must be accorded appropriate measurement and reporting on the consolidated financial statements. **Minority interest** includes the minority stockholders' proportionate share of both the earnings and the stockholders' equity of the subsidiary.

To illustrate consolidated statements with a minority interest, we will adapt the data for Company P and Company S given in Exhibit 14–1. Assume that on January 2, 19A, Company P purchased 80% of the 10,000 shares of outstanding capital stock of Company S for $132,000 cash.[3] At acquisition date, Company P recorded the purchase of the 8,000 shares of capital stock as follows:

---

[3] Ownership interests of less than 100% usually are on the purchase basis. *APB Opinion 16* does not permit use of the pooling of interests basis when the ownership interest held by the parent company is less than 90%.

```
Investment, stock of Company S (80% ownership) . . . . . . . . . . . .  132,000
    Cash . . . . . . . . . . . . . . . . . . . . . . . . . . . . . . . . . . . . . .              132,000
  Acquisition of 8,000 shares (80%) of the capital stock of
  Company S at $16.50 per share.
```

On the acquisition date, the owners' equity for Company S showed the following amounts: capital stock, $100,000; and retained earnings, $50,000 (total owners' equity was $150,000). Company P paid $132,000 cash for 80% of the owners' equity of Company S. The book value of the investment was $120,000 ($150,000 × 80%). Thus, Company P paid $12,000 more than the book value of Company S. The market value of the subsidiary company's plant and equipment was $5,000 more than its book value. Therefore, of the $12,000 cost in excess of book value that P Company paid, $4,000 (i.e., $5,000 × 80%) was for the greater market value of the plant and equipment. The remaining amount, $8,000, was for **goodwill.** The analysis of the purchase transaction, at date of acquisition, follows:[4]

```
Purchase price for 80% interest in Company S . . . . . . .  $132,000
Net assets purchased, valued at market:
  Book value, $120,000 + market value increment of
    plant and equipment, $5,000 × 80% =  . . . . . . . .   124,000
Goodwill purchased  . . . . . . . . . . . . . . . . . . . . . . .  $  8,000
```

On December 31, 19A, both companies had completed one year's operations as affiliated companies. Each company has prepared the separate 19A financial statements shown in Exhibit 14–9.

Additional data developed by Company P for the consolidation worksheet:

a. Investment account balance of $132,000 to be eliminated against 80% of stockholders' equity of subsidiary.

b. Plant and equipment of Company S to be increased by $4,000 to market value (i.e., the increment acquired by Company P). Goodwill will be recognized, $8,000 (see analysis of purchase transaction above).

c. Company S owed Company P $6,000 on December 31, 19A.

d. The plant and equipment is being depreciated on a straight-line basis over a remaining life of 10 years by Company S (no residual value).

e. Goodwill will be amortized over 20 years.

f. Company S declared and paid $10,000 cash dividends on December 15, 19A.

---

[4] Some accountants believe that the plant and equipment difference should be 100% (i.e., $5,000) rather than 80% (i.e., $4,000). This difference in opinion has not been resolved; however, it appears that most companies currently use the lower amount.

Exhibit 14-9 Illustrative data for consolidation (less than 100% ownership)

	Company P	Company S
COMPANY P AND COMPANY S		
Separate Financial Statements for 19A		
Income statement (for 19A):		
Sales revenue	$400,000	$110,000
Revenue from investments (dividends from		
Company S)	8,000	
Cost of goods sold	(220,000)	(59,000)
Expenses (not detailed)	(130,000)	(26,500)
Depreciation expense	(10,000)	(4,500)
Income tax expense	(20,000)	(6,000)
Net income	$ 28,000	$ 14,000
Balance sheet (at December 31, 19A):		
Cash	$ 92,000	$ 45,500
Accounts receivable (net)	18,000	28,000
Receivable from Company S	6,000	
Inventories	185,000	65,000
Investment in Company S (80%, at cost)	132,000	
Plant and equipment	90,000	40,500
Totals	$523,000	$179,000
Accounts payable	$ 55,000	$ 19,000
Payable to Company P		6,000
Common stock (par $10)	300,000	100,000
Beginning retained earnings	140,000	50,000
Dividends declared and paid during 19A		(10,000)
Net income for 19A (from above)	28,000	14,000
Totals	$523,000	$179,000

The consolidation worksheet under the purchase method is shown in Exhibit 14–10.

On the worksheet, the minority interest (20%) is designated with an "M." In the income statement portion of the worksheet, 20% of the **subsidiary** net income (i.e., $2,800) is coded "M," and the remainder ($30,400) is identified with the parent. Notice that the minority stockholders do not share in the income of the parent company. On the worksheet, the income amounts are carried down to the retained earnings section of the balance sheet. The 20% of subsidiary stockholders' equity owned by the minority stockholders was not eliminated as an intercompany item. Therefore, it is carried across as minority interest and coded "M." Aside from these adaptions, the Consolidated Balances column is completed as previously explained.

Exhibit 14–10 Consolidation worksheet (purchase method; less than 100% ownership)

	Statements		**Intercompany Eliminations**		**Consolidated Balances**
Items	**Company P**	**Company S**	**Debit**	**Credit**	
Income statement:					
Sales revenue	400,000	110,000			510,000
Revenue from investments	8,000		(e) 8,000		
Cost of goods sold	(220,000)	(59,000)			(279,000)
Expenses (not detailed)	(130,000)	(26,500)			(156,500)
Depreciation expense	(10,000)	(4,500)	(c) 400		(14,900)
Amortization expense (goodwill)			(d) 400		(400)
Income tax expense	(20,000)	(6,000)			(26,000)
Net income	28,000	14,000			33,200
Carried down:					
Minority interest ($14,000 × 20%)					2,800 M*
Parent interest income					30,400
Balance sheet:					
Cash	92,000	45,500			137,500
Accounts receivable (net)	18,000	28,000			46,000
Receivable from Company S	6,000			(b) 6,000	
Inventories	185,000	65,000			250,000

COMPANY P and Its Subsidiary, COMPANY S
Consolidation Worksheet (by purchase) for the Balance Sheet and Income Statement
December 31, 19A (80% ownership)

The consolidated income statement and balance sheet, based on the data in the Consolidated Balances column of the worksheet, are shown in Exhibit 14–11. The **minority interest** share of net income is identified separately on the income statement. Also, the minority interest share of stockholders' equity is identified separately on the balance sheet. Alternatively, the minority interest share of stockholders' equity often is shown as a special caption between liabilities and stockholders' equity rather than as illustrated in Exhibit 14–11.

IMPORTANT TERMS DEFINED IN THIS CHAPTER

Consolidation The accounting process of combining financial statements from related companies into a single set of financial statements. *p. 666*

Exhibit 14–10 *(concluded)*

Items	Statements Company P	Statements Company S	Intercompany Eliminations Debit	Intercompany Eliminations Credit	Consolidated Balances
Investment in Company S (at cost)	132,000			*(a)* 132,000	
Plant and equipment (net)	90,000	40,500	*(a)* 4,000	*(c)* 400	134,100
Goodwill			*(a)* 8,000	*(d)* 400	7,600
Totals	523,000	179,000			575,200
Accounts payable	55,000	19,000			74,000
Payable to Company P		6,000	*(b)* 6,000		
Common stock, Company P	300,000				300,000
Common stock, Company S		100,000	*(a)* 80,000		20,000 M
Beginning retained earnings, Company P	140,000				140,000
Beginning retained earnings, Company S		50,000	*(a)* 40,000		10,000 M
Dividends declared and paid during 19A		(10,000)		*(e)* 8,000	(2,000)M
Net income, 19A (from above; not added across)	28,000	14,000			2,800 M 30,400
Totals	523,000	179,000	146,800	146,800	575,200

M—Minority interest.
* The minority inerest in the earnings of the subsidiary is unaffected by the consolidation procedures of the parent company. Thus, the minority interest in the earnings is $14,000 × 20% = $2,800. This amount is subtracted from consolidated income to derive the amount of consolidated income identifiable with the controlling interest. The two separate amounts then are carried down to the balance sheet section.
Explanation of eliminations:
  (a) To eliminate the investment account against 80% of the owners' equity of the subsidiary and to allocate the difference between purchase price and book value to the appropriate accounts.
  (b) To eliminate the intercompany debt.
  (c) To record depreciation for one year on the asset increase resulting from the acquisition.
  (d) To amortize goodwill recognized (one year).
  (e) To eliminate intercompany revenue arising from dividends declared and paid by the subsidiary.

Control Presumed to exist when more than 50% of the voting stock of an entity is owned by one investor. *p. 666*

Goodwill The amount that was paid for the good reputation and customer appeal of an acquired company. *p. 674*

Minority Interest The proportionate share of both the earnings and the contributed capital of the subsidiary that is not "owned" by the parent. *p. 685*

Parent Company The company that has a significant investment in a subsidiary company. *p. 666*

Pooling of Interests An acquisition that is completed by exchanging parent company stock for subsidiary voting capital stock. *p. 667*

Exhibit 14–11   Consolidated financial statements (with minority interest)

COMPANY P and Its Subsidiary, COMPANY S
Consolidated Income Statement (purchase method)
For the Year Ended December 31, 19A

Sales revenue		$510,000
Cost of goods sold		279,000
Gross margin		231,000
Less:		
Expenses (not detailed)	$156,500	
Depreciation expense	14,900	
Amortization expense (goodwill)	400	
Income tax expense	26,000	197,800
Consolidated net income		33,200
Less: Minority interest in net income		2,800
Controlling interest in net income		$ 30,400

EPS of common stock ($33,200 ÷ 30,000 shares) = $1.107
(some accountants prefer to use $30,400 as the numerator).

COMPANY P and Its Subsidiary, COMPANY S
Consolidated Balance Sheet (purchase method)
At December 31, 19A

Assets

Current assets:		
Cash	$137,500	
Accounts receivable (net)	46,000	
Inventories	250,000	$433,500
Tangible operational assets:		
Plant and equipment (net)		134,100
Intangible operational assets:		
Goodwill (or excess of cost over market value of assets		
of subsidiary)		7,600
Total assets		$575,200

Liabilities

Current liabilities:		
Accounts payable		$ 74,000

Stockholders' Equity

Contributed capital:		
Common stock (par $10; 30,000 shares outstanding)	$300,000	
Retained earnings	170,400	
Total	470,400	
Minority interest	30,800*	
Total stockholders' equity		501,200
Total liabilities and stockholders' equity		$575,200

* $20,000 + $10,000 + $2,800 − $2,000 = $30,800.

Purchase An acquisition that is completed by purchasing subsidiary company voting capital stock for cash. *p. 672*

Subsidiary The company that is owned by a parent company as evidenced by more than 50% of the voting capital stock. *p. 666*

QUESTIONS

Part A: Questions 1–11

1. What is a parent-subsidiary relationship?
2. Explain the basic concept underlying consolidated statements.
3. What is the basic element that must be present before consolidated statements are appropriate?
4. The concept of consolidated statements relates only to reporting as opposed to preparing and posting journal entries in the ledger accounts. Explain.
5. What is pooling of interests?
6. What is a combination by purchase?
7. The investing corporation debits a long-term investment account when it acquires a controlling influence in another corporation. In the case of a pooling of interests, describe how to determine the amount that is debited to the investment account.
8. What are intercompany eliminations?
9. Explain why the investment account must be eliminated against stockholders' equity when consolidated statements are prepared.
10. Explain why the "book values" of the parent and subsidiary are aggregated on consolidated statements when there is a pooling of interests, but acquisition market values of the subsidiary assets are used when the combination is by purchase.
11. Why is goodwill not recognized in a pooling of interests? Why is it recognized in a combination by purchase?

Part B: Questions 12–15

12. Explain why additional depreciation expense usually must be recognized on consolidation when the combination was by purchase.
13. What is goodwill?
14. Explain why management of a company might prefer to account for a consolidation using pooling instead of the purchase method.
15. Explain the basis for each of the following statements:
    a. Pooling of interests, given the same situation, reports a higher net income than combination by purchase.
    b. The cash position, other things being equal, usually is better when the combination is by pooling of interests than when the combination is by purchase.
    c. Pooling of interests, other things being equal, reports a higher amount of retained earnings than does combination by purchase.

EXERCISES

Part A: Exercises 14-1 to 14-5

E14-1   (Match Definitions with Terms)
Match each definition with its related term by entering the appropriate letter in the space provided.

Terms	Definitions
_____ (1) Subsidiary	A. Required because a parent and subsidiary are considered one economic entity.
_____ (2) Purchase	
_____ (3) Minority interest	B. Ownership of voting stock provides more than significant influence.
_____ (4) Control	
_____ (5) Consolidation	C. An amount whose "value" is never known except when a business is purchased.
_____ (6) Pooling of interests	
	D. Only comes into existence when there is less than 100% ownership by the parent company.
_____ (7) Goodwill	E. The company that owns more than 50% of the outstanding voting stock of another corporation.
_____ (8) Parent company	
	F. This transaction often is not viewed as a purchase/sale transaction; therefore, the cost principle is not applied.
	G. In this transaction, the purchase of a controlling interest in another company is recorded under the cost principle.
	H. The company that is owned by another company.

E14-2   (Preparation of a Consolidated Balance Sheet)
On January 2, 19A, Company P acquired all of the outstanding voting stock of Company S by exchanging, on a share-for-share basis, its own unissued stock for the stock of Company S. Immediately after the acquisition of Company S, the separate balance sheets showed the following:

	Balances, January 2, 19A, immediately after acquisition	
	Company P	Company S
Cash	$ 38,000	$12,000
Receivable from Company S	7,000	
Inventory	35,000	18,000
Investment in Company S (100%)	60,000	
Operational assets (net of accumulated depreciation)	80,000	50,000
Total assets	$220,000	$80,000
Liabilities	$ 25,000	$13,000
Payable to Company P		7,000
Common stock (Company P, par $5; Company S, par $5) . . .	140,000	40,000
Contributed capital from pooling of interests	20,000	
Retained earnings	35,000	20,000
Total liabilities and stockholders' equity	$220,000	$80,000

Required:

a. Is this a pooling of interests or a combination by purchase? Explain why.

b. Give the journal entry that was made by Company P to record the acquisition.

c. Prepare a consolidated balance sheet immediately after the acquisition.

d. Were the assets of the subsidiary added to those of the parent, in the consolidated balance sheet, at book value or at market value? Explain why.

e. What were the balances in the accounts of Company P immediately prior to the acquisition for (1) investment and (2) common stock? Were any other account balances for either Company P or Company S changed by the acquisition? Explain.

E14–3   **(Comparison of the Pooling of Interests and the Purchase Methods)**
On January 1, 19A, Company P acquired 100% of the outstanding common stock of Company S. At date of acquisition, the balance sheet of Company S reflected the following book values (summarized):

Total assets (market value, $220,000)* . . .	$180,000	
Total liabilities	30,000	
Stockholders' equity:		
Common stock, par $10	100,000	
Retained earnings	50,000	

* One half subject to depreciation; 10-year remaining life and no residual value.

Two separate and independent cases are given below that indicate how Company P acquired 100% of the outstanding stock of Company S.

Case A—Exchanged two shares of its own common stock (par $1) for each share of Company S stock.

Case B—Paid $20 per share for the stock of Company S.

Required:

For each case, answer the following:

a. Was this a combination by pooling of interests or by purchase? Explain.

b. Give the journal entry that Company P should make to record the acquisition. If none, explain why.

c. Give the journal entry in the accounts of Company S to record the acquisition. If none, explain why.

d. Analyze the transaction to determine the amount of goodwill purchased. If no goodwill was purchased, explain why.

e. In preparing a consolidated balance sheet, should the subsidiary assets be included at book value or market value? Explain.

E14–4   (Identification of the Appropriate Consolidation Method)

On January 1, 19A, Company P purchased 100% of the outstanding voting shares of Company S in the open market for $70,000 cash. On that date (prior to the acquisition), the separate balance sheets (summarized) of the two companies reported the following book values:

	Prior to acquisition	
	Company P	Company S
Cash	$ 80,000	$18,000
Receivable from Company P		2,000
Operational assets (net)	80,000	60,000
Total assets	$160,000	$80,000
Liabilities	$ 28,000	$20,000
Payable to Company S	2,000	
Common stock:		
Company S (nopar)	100,000	
Company P (par $10)		50,000
Retained earnings	30,000	10,000
Total liabilities and		
stockholders' equity	$160,000	$80,000

It was determined on date of acquisition that the market value of the operational assets of Company S was $66,000.

Required:

a. Was this a combination by pooling of interests or by purchase? Explain why.

b. Give the journal entry that should be made by Company P at date of acquisition. If none is required, explain why.

c. Give the journal entry that should be made by Company S at date of acquisition. If none is required, explain why.

d. Analyze the acquisition to determine the amount of goodwill purchased.

e. Should the assets of Company S be included on the consolidated balance sheet at book value or market value? Explain.

f. Prepare a consolidated balance sheet immediately after acquisition.

E14–5 **(Preparation of a Consolidated Balance Sheet after Acquisition)**
On January 4, 19A, Company P acquired all of the outstanding stock of Company S for
$10 cash per share. At the date of acquisition, the balance sheet of Company S reflected
the following:

Common stock (par $5) . . . $50,000
Retained earnings 30,000

Immediately after the acquisition, the balance sheets reflected the following:

	Balances, Jan. 4, 19A, immediately after acquisition	
	Company P	Company S
Cash	$ 13,000	$17,000
Receivable from Company P		3,000
Investment in Company S (100%), at cost . . .	100,000	
Operational assets (net)	122,000	70,000*
Total assets	$235,000	$90,000
Liabilities	$ 22,000	$10,000
Payable to Company S	3,000	
Common stock (par $5)	150,000	50,000
Retained earnings	60,000	30,000
Total liabilities and stockholders' equity	$235,000	$90,000

* Determined by Company P to have a market value of $78,000 at date of acquisition.

Required:

a. Was this a combination by pooling of interests or by purchase? Explain why.

b. Give the journal entry that should be made by Company P to record the acquisition.

c. Analyze the acquisition to determine the amount of goodwill purchased.

d. Should the assets of Company S be included on the consolidated balance sheet at book value or market value? Explain.

e. Prepare a consolidated balance sheet immediately after acquisition.

Part B: Exercises 14–6 to 14–7

E14–6 **(Completion of a Consolidation Worksheet)**
On January 1, 19A, Company P acquired all of the outstanding voting stock of Company
S by exchanging one share of its own stock for each share of Company S stock. At the
date of the exchange, the balance sheet of Company S showed the following:

Common stock (par $10) . . . $40,000
Retained earnings 10,000

One year after acquisition the two companies prepared their separate financial statements as shown on the following worksheet:

| | Separate Statements | | | Consolidated |
Items	Company P	Company S	Eliminations	Statements
COMPANY P and Its Subsidiary, COMPANY S (100% owned)				
Consolidated Balance Sheet and Income Statement				
December 31, 19A				
Income statement (for 19A):				
Sales revenue	100,000	42,000		
Cost of goods sold	(60,000)	(25,000)		
Expenses (not detailed)	(17,000)	(10,000)		
Net income	23,000	7,000		
Balance sheet (at December 31, 19A):				
Cash	21,000	23,000		
Receivable from Company P		2,000		
Investment in Company S (100%)	50,000			
Operational assets (net)	59,000	47,000		
Totals	130,000	72,000		
Liabilities	17,000	15,000		
Payable to Company S	2,000			
Common stock, Company P (par $10)	50,000			
Contributed capital	10,000			
Common stock, Company S (par $10)		40,000		
Beginning retained earnings, Company P	28,000			
Beginning retained earnings, Company S		10,000		
Net income, 19A (from above)	23,000	7,000		
Totals	130,000	72,000		

Required:

a. Give the journal entry that was made by Company P to record the pooling of interests on January 1, 19A.

b. Complete the Eliminations column in the above worksheet, then combine the two sets of statements in the last column to develop the consolidated income statement and balance sheet.

E14–7   (Analysis of a Consolidation Worksheet)

On January 1, 19A, Company P purchased all of the outstanding voting stock of Company S at $2.50 per share. At that date the balance sheet of Company S reflected the following:

Common stock (par $1) . . . $20,000
Retained earnings 10,000

One year after acquisition each company prepared its own separate financial statements and Company P set up the following consolidation worksheet (partially completed):

Items	Separate Statements Company P	Separate Statements Company S	Intercompany Eliminations Debit	Intercompany Eliminations Credit	Consolidated Balances
Income statement (for 19A):					
Sales revenue	105,000	53,000			
Expenses (not detailed)	(71,000)	(40,400)			
Depreciation expense	(9,000)	(3,600)	(c) 1,200		
Amortization expense (goodwill)			(d) 400		
Net income	25,000	9,000			
Balance sheet (at December 31, 19A):					
Cash	16,000	6,000			
Receivable from Co. P		4,000		(b) 4,000	
Investment in Co. S	50,000			(a) 50,000	
Operational assets (net)	90,000	40,000*	(a) 12,000	(c) 1,200	
Goodwill (amortize over 20 years)			(a) 8,000	(d) 400	
Totals	156,000	50,000			
Liabilities	15,000	11,000			
Payable to Co. S	4,000		(b) 4,000		
Common stock, Co. P	80,000				
Common stock, Co. S		20,000	(a) 20,000		
Beginning retained earnings, Co. P	32,000				
Beginning retained earnings, Co. S		10,000	(a) 10,000		
Net income, 19A (per above)	25,000†	9,000†			
Totals	156,000	50,000	55,600	55,600	

* Market value of the operational assets at acquisition was $12,000 above book value and their remaining useful life was 10 years.
† Carried down.

Required:
a. Give the journal entry made by Company P on January 1, 19A, to record the purchase of Company S stock.
b. Show how the $8,000 of goodwill was computed.
c. Complete the last column of the worksheet (note that under "Eliminations" debit/credit instead of +/− were used).
d. Give a brief explanation of eliminations (c) and (d).

PROBLEMS

Part A: Problems 14–1 to 14–6

P14–1

(Analysis of Acquisition and Preparation of a Consolidated Balance Sheet)
During January 19A, Company P acquired all of the outstanding voting shares of Company S by exchanging one share of its own unissued voting common stock for two shares of Company S stock. Immediately prior to the acquisition, the separate balance sheets of the two companies reflected the following:

	Balances immediately prior to acquisition	
	Company P	Company S
Cash	$200,000	$ 32,000
Receivable from Company P		3,000
Inventory	75,000	5,000
Operational assets (net of accumulated depreciation)	75,000	80,000
Total assets	$350,000	$120,000
Liabilities	$ 57,000	$ 30,000
Payable to Company S	3,000	
Common stock, Company P (par $4)	180,000	
Common stock, Company S (par $5)		50,000
Contributed capital from pooling		
Retained earnings	110,000	40,000
Total liabilities and stockholders' equity	$350,000	$120,000

Additional Data:
At the date of acquisition, the market price of Company S stock was $16 per share; there was no established market for Company P stock.

The operational assets of Company S were appraised independently at the date of acquisition at $130,000.

Required:
a. Is this a purchase or a pooling of interests? Explain why.
b. What account balances on each of the above balance sheets would be changed by the exchange of shares? List each account and amount.
c. Give the journal entry that should be made by each company to record the exchange; if no entry is required, explain why.
d. How much goodwill should be recognized? Why?
e. Prepare a consolidated balance sheet immediately after the acquisition.
f. Did you use any market values in solving the above requirements? Explain why.

P14–2

(Analysis of Acquisition and Preparation of a Consolidated Balance Sheet)
Assume the same facts given in Problem 14–1 except that instead of an exchange of shares of stock, Company P purchased from the stockholders 100% of the outstanding voting shares of Company S at a cash price of $160,000.

Required:

a. Is this a purchase or a pooling of interests? Explain why.

b. What account balances on each of the balance sheets would be changed by the purchase of the shares? List each account and amount.

c. Give the journal entry that should be made by each company to record the exchange; if no entry is required, explain why.

d. How much goodwill should be recognized? Why?

e. Prepare a consolidated balance sheet immediately after acquisition.

f. Did you use any market values in solving the above requirements? Explain why.

P14–3 **(Analysis of Entry to Record Acquisition and Preparation of a Consolidated Balance Sheet)**

On January 1, 19A, the separate balance sheets of two corporations showed the following:

	Balances, Jan. 1, 19A	
	Company P	**Company S**
Cash	$ 21,000	$ 9,000
Receivable from Company P		4,000
Operational assets (net)	99,000	32,000
Total assets	$120,000	$45,000
Accounts payable	$ 16,000	$10,000
Payable to Company S	4,000	
Common stock (par $20)	60,000	20,000
Retained earnings	40,000	15,000
Total liabilities and stockholders' equity	$120,000	$45,000

On January 3, 19A, Company P acquired all of the outstanding voting shares of Company S by exchanging one share of its own stock for two shares of Company S stock.

Required:

a. Was this a combination by pooling of interests or by purchase? Explain why.

b. Company P made the following journal entry on its books, at the date of acquisition, to record the investment:

January 3, 19A:

Investment in Co. S	35,000	
Common stock		10,000
Contributed capital from pooling of interests		25,000

Explain the basis for each of the three amounts in this entry.

c. Should any goodwill be recognized on the consolidated balance sheet? Explain why.

d. Prepare a consolidated balance sheet immediately after the acquisition.

P14-4   (Analysis of Consolidation Method and Preparation of a Consolidated Balance Sheet)

On January 2, 19A, Company P acquired all of the outstanding stock of Company S by exchanging its own stock for the stock of Company S. One share of Company P stock was exchanged for two shares of Company S stock. Immediately after the acquisition was recorded by Company P, the balance sheets showed the following:

	Balances, Jan. 2, 19A, immediately	
	Company P	Company S
Cash	$ 38,000	$26,000
Receivable from Company S	6,000	
Inventory	30,000	10,000
Investment in Company S (100%)	70,000	
Operational assets (net)	90,000	50,000
Other assets	6,000	4,000
Total assets	$240,000	$90,000
Liabilities	$ 16,000	$14,000
Payable to Company P		6,000
Common stock (par $5)	125,000	50,000
Contributed capital from pooling of interests	45,000	
Retained earnings	54,000	20,000
Total liabilities and stockholders' equity	$240,000	$90,000

Required:

a. Was this a combination by pooling of interests or by purchase? Explain why.

b. Give the journal entry that was made by Company P to record the acquisition on January 2, 19A. Explain the basis for each amount included in the entry.

c. Should the assets of Company S be included on the consolidated balance sheet at book value or market value? Explain.

d. Will any goodwill be recognized on the consolidated balance sheet? Explain why.

e. Prepare a consolidated balance sheet immediately after acquisition.

P14-5   (Analysis of Goodwill and Preparation of a Consolidated Balance Sheet)

On January 5, 19A, Company P purchased all of the outstanding stock of Company S for $100,000 cash. Immediately after the acquisition the separate balance sheets of the two companies showed the following:

	Jan. 5, 19A, immediately after acquisition	
	Company P	Company S
Cash	$ 22,000	$ 9,000
Accounts receivable (net)	14,000	6,000
Receivable from Company S	4,000	
Inventory	50,000	25,000
Investment in Company S (at cost)	100,000	
Operational assets (net)	153,000	67,000
Other assets	7,000	3,000
Total assets	$350,000	$110,000

	Jan. 5, 19A, immediately after acquisition	
	Company P	Company S
Accounts payable	$ 20,000	$ 16,000
Payable to Company P		4,000
Bonds payable	90,000	
Common stock (par $5)	180,000	60,000
Contributed capital in excess of par . . .	8,000	
Retained earnings	52,000	30,000
Total liabilities and stockholders' equity	$350,000	$110,000

The operational assets of Company S were estimated to have a market value at date of acquisition of $71,000.

Required:

a. Was this a combination by pooling of interests or by purchase? Explain why.

b. Give the journal entry that Company P should make at the date of acquisition.

c. Analyze the acquisition to determine the amount of goodwill purchased.

d. Should the assets of Company S be included on the consolidated balance sheet at book value or market value? Explain.

e. Prepare a consolidated balance sheet immediately after acquisition.

P14–6 **(Analysis of an Acquisition and Completion of a Worksheet to Prepare a Consolidated Balance Sheet)**
On January 4, 19A, Company P purchased 100% of the outstanding common stock of Company S for $240,000 cash. Immediately after the acquisition, the separate balance sheets for the two companies were prepared as shown in the worksheet below.

COMPANY P and Its Subsidiary, COMPANY S
Consolidated Balance Sheet
January 4, 19A, Immediately after Acquisition

	Separate balance sheets			Consolidated balance sheet
	Company P	Company S	Eliminations	
Assets				
Cash	$ 80,000	$ 40,000	_____	_____
Accounts receivable (net)	26,000	19,000	_____	_____
Receivable from Company P		8,000	_____	_____
Inventories	170,000	80,000	_____	_____
Long-term investment, bonds, Z Company	15,000		_____	_____
Long-term investment, Company S .	240,000		_____	_____
Land	12,000	3,000	_____	_____
Plant and equipment (net)	157,000	130,000	_____	_____
Goodwill			_____	_____
Total assets	$700,000	$280,000	_____	_____

	Separate balance sheets			Consolidated balance sheet
	Company P	Company S	Eliminations	
Liabilities				
Accounts payable	$ 22,000	$ 40,000	_____	_____
Payable to Company S	8,000		_____	_____
Bonds payable (5%)	100,000	30,000	_____	_____
Stockholders' Equity				
Common stock, Company P	500,000		_____	_____
Common stock, Company S				
(par $10)		150,000	_____	_____
Retained earnings, Company P . . .	70,000		_____	_____
Retained earnings, Company S . . .		60,000	_____	_____
Total liabilities and stockholders'				
equity	$700,000	$280,000	_____	_____

It was determined at the date of acquisition that on the basis of a comparison of market value and book value, the assets as shown on the books of Company S should be adjusted as follows: (*a*) inventories should be reduced by $3,000, (*b*) plant and equipment should be increased to $148,000, and (*c*) land should be increased by $2,000.

Required:

a. Was this a combination by pooling of interests or by purchase? Explain why.

b. Give the journal entry that was made on the books of Company P to record the acquisition.

c. Analyze the acquisition transaction to determine the amount of goodwill purchased. Use data from the worksheet if needed.

d. At what amount will the assets of Company S be included on the consolidated balance sheet? Explain.

e. Complete the Eliminations column in the worksheet and then extend the amounts for the consolidated balance sheet.

Part B: Problems 14–7 to 14–10

P14–7 **(Analysis of Consolidation Elimination Entries and Completion of a Worksheet)**

On January 1, 19A, Company P acquired 100% of the outstanding stock of Company S for $106,000 cash. At the date of acquisition the balance sheet of Company S showed the following:

Total assets (including operational assets*) . . .	115,000
Total liabilities	25,000
Common stock (par $10)	60,000
Retained earnings	30,000

* Book value, $42,000; market value, $48,000 (20-year remaining life).

One year after acquisition the two companies prepared their December 31, 19A, financial statements. Company P developed the following consolidation worksheet (partially completed):

	COMPANY P AND ITS SUBSIDIARY, COMPANY S				

COMPANY P AND ITS SUBSIDIARY, COMPANY S
Consolidation Worksheet
Income Statement and Balance Sheet, December 31, 19A (100% ownership)

Items	Separate Statements		Eliminations		Consolidated Balances
	Company P	Company S	Debit	Credit	
Income statement:					
Sales revenue	84,000	47,000			
Cost of goods sold	(45,000)	(25,000)			
Expenses (not detailed)	(15,000)	(10,000)			
Depreciation expense	(4,000)	(2,000)	(c) 300		
Amortization of goodwill			(d) 500		
Net income	20,000	10,000			
Balance sheet:					
Cash	15,000	14,000			
Accounts receivable (net)	19,000	9,000			
Receivable from Co. P		1,000		(b) 1,000	
Inventories	70,000	50,000			
Investment in Co. S (100%)	106,000			(a) 106,000	
Plant and equipment (net)	80,000	40,000	(a) 6,000	(c) 300	
Goodwill			(a) 10,000	(d) 500	
Totals	290,000	114,000			
Accounts payable	26,000	14,000			
Payable to Co. S	1,000		(b) 1,000		
Common stock, Co. P	200,000				
Common stock, Co. S		60,000	(a) 60,000		
Beginning retained earnings, Co. P	50,000				
Beginning retained earnings, Co. S		30,000	(a) 30,000		
Dividends declared and paid during 19A, Co. P	(7,000)				
Net income (from above)	20,000	10,000			
Totals	290,000	114,000	107,800	107,800	

Required:

a. Was this a purchase or pooling? Explain.

b. Give the journal entry made by each company to record the acquisition.

c. Complete the last column of the worksheet to develop the consolidated income statement and balance sheet.

d. How much goodwill was recognized? How was it computed?

e. Briefly explain each of the eliminations shown on the worksheet. Note that debit and credit rather than plus and minus were used in the Eliminations column.

P14–8   **(Comparison and Analysis of the Pooling of Interests and the Purchase Methods)**
This problem presents the consolidated income statement and the balance sheet for
Company P and its subsidiary, Company S, one year after acquisition, under two
different assumptions: Case A—pooling of interests, and Case B—purchase.

On January 2, 19A, Company P acquired all of the outstanding common stock of
Company S. At that date, the stockholders' equity of Company S showed the following:
common stock, par $10, $50,000; and retained earnings, $20,000. The journal entry made
by Company P to record the acquisition under each case was as follows:

Case A—pooling of interests method:

Investment in Company S (5,000 shares, 100%)	70,000	
Common stock (par $8)		40,000
Contributed capital		30,000

Case B—purchase method:

Investment in Company S (5,000 shares, 100%)	80,000	
Cash		80,000

On January 2, 19A, the acquisition by purchase (Case B) was analyzed to determine the
goodwill as follows:

Purchase price paid for 100% interest in Company S	$80,000
Net assets purchased, value at market:	
Book value of net assets ($50,000 + $20,000 = $70,000 + increase	
of $2,000 in operational assets to market value)	72,000
Goodwill purchased	$ 8,000

For consolidated statement purposes, the operational assets are being depreciated over 10
years remaining life, and the goodwill will be amortized over 20 years.

One year after acquisition, the two companies prepared separate income statements
and balance sheets (December 31, 19A). These separate statements have been consolidated under each case as shown below.

Required:
a. Prepare a schedule of amounts that shows what items are different between each
statement for Case A, compared with Case B.
b. Explain the reasons why net income is different under pooling of interests versus
purchase. Use amounts from the two statements in your explanation and tell why
they are different.
c. Explain why the cash balance is different between the two cases.
d. What was the balance in the Investment in Company S account in each case prior
to its elimination? Explain.
e. Explain why the operational asset (net) amounts are different between the two
cases.
f. Why is there a difference in goodwill between the two cases? Provide computations.
g. How much was eliminated for intercompany debt? Why was it eliminated?
h. What amount of "Common stock, Company S," was eliminated? Why was it eliminated?

i. Why was only $20,000 of the $30,000 of contributed capital eliminated?

j. Explain why "Beginning retained earnings, Company S, $20,000," is shown under Case A (pooling) but not under Case B (purchase).

COMPANY P and Its Subsidiary, COMPANY S (100% owned)
Consolidated Income Statement and Balance Sheet
December 31, 19A

	Consolidated statements December 31, 19A	
	Pooling method (Case A)	Purchase method (Case B)
Income statement (for the year ended December 31, 19A):		
Sales revenue	$236,000	$236,000
Cost of goods sold	(112,000)	(112,000)
Expenses (not detailed to simplify)	(75,500)	(75,500)
Depreciation expense	(12,500)	(12,700)
Amortization expense (goodwill)		(400)
Net income	$ 36,000	$ 35,400
Balance sheet (at December 31, 19A):		
Assets		
Cash	$128,000	$ 48,000
Accounts receivable (net)	53,000	53,000
Receivable from Company S ($5,000, eliminated)		
Inventory	37,000	37,000
Investment in Company S (eliminated)		
Operational assets (net)	125,000	126,800
Goodwill		7,600
Totals	$343,000	$272,400
Liabilities		
Current liabilities	$ 30,000	$ 30,000
Payable to Company P (eliminated)		
Bonds payable	50,000	50,000
Stockholders' Equity		
Common stock, Company P	140,000	100,000
Common stock, Company S (eliminated)		
Contributed capital ($20,000 eliminated)	20,000	10,000
Beginning retained earnings, Company P	47,000	47,000
Beginning retained earnings, Company S	20,000	
Net income, 19A (from income statement above)	36,000	35,400
Totals	$343,000	$272,400

P14-9 **(Preparation of a Consolidated Balance Sheet and Income Statement Using a Worksheet)**

On January 1, 19A, Company P purchased 100% of the outstanding capital stock of Company S for $98,000 cash. At that date, the stockholders' equity section of the balance sheet of Company S showed the following:

Capital stock, $10 par, 5,000 shares outstanding . . .	$50,000
Retained earnings	30,000
	$80,000

At the date of acquisition, it was determined that the market values of certain assets of Company S, in comparison with the book values of those assets as shown on the balance sheet of Company S, should be shown by (*a*) increasing inventories by $2,000 and (*b*) increasing equipment by $8,000.

It is now one year after acquisition, December 31, 19A, and each company has prepared the following separate financial statements (summarized):

	Company P	Company S
Balance sheet (at December 31, 19A):		
Cash	$ 47,000	$ 35,000
Accounts receivable (net)	31,000	10,000
Receivable from Company P		3,000
Inventories	60,000	70,000
Investment in Company S (at cost)	98,000	
Equipment	80,000	20,000
Other assets	9,000	17,000
Totals	$325,000	$155,000
Accounts payable	$ 42,000	$ 30,000
Payable to Company S	3,000	
Bonds payable (10%)	70,000	30,000
Capital stock ($10 par)	140,000	50,000
Beginning retained earnings	50,000	30,000
Dividends declared and paid during 19A	(10,000)	
Net income, 19A (from income statement) . . .	30,000	15,000
Totals	$325,000	$155,000
Income statement (for 19A):		
Sales revenue	$360,000	$140,000
Cost of goods sold	(220,000)	(80,000)
Expenses (not detailed)	(106,000)	(44,000)
Depreciation expense	(4,000)	(1,000)
Net income	$ 30,000	$ 15,000

Additional Data during 19A:

1. The equipment is being depreciated on the basis of a 20-year remaining life (no residual value).

2. Goodwill is to be amortized over a 40-year period.

Required:

a. Give the journal entry that Company P should make to record the acquisition of the capital stock of Company S on January 1, 19A.

b. Analyze the acquisition of the stock to determine the purchased goodwill.

c. Prepare a consolidation worksheet (purchase method) for the year 19A as a basis for the 19A income statement and balance sheet.

d. Prepare a consolidated income statement and balance sheet based on the data provided by the consolidation worksheet.

P14–10 **(Preparation of a Consolidated Balance Sheet and Income Statement with Minority Interest—Based on Supplement 14A)**

On January 1, 19A, Company P purchased 90% of the outstanding voting stock of Company S for $92,800 cash. At the date of acquisition, the stockholders' equity accounts of Company S reflected the following: Capital Stock (par $10), $60,000; Contributed Capital in Excess of Par, $10,000; and Retained Earnings, $12,000. At that date it was determined that the book value of the operational assets was $10,000 less than their market value.

It is now December 31, 19A, and each company has prepared the following separate financial statements (summarized):

	Company P	Company S
Balance sheet (at December 31, 19A):		
Cash	$ 30,200	$ 11,000
Accounts receivable (net)	57,000	13,000
Receivable from Company P		7,000
Inventories	110,000	24,000
Investment in Company S (at cost; 90% owned) . . .	92,800	
Operational assets (net)	120,000	50,000
Other assets	6,000	5,000
Totals	$416,000	$110,000
Accounts payable	$ 30,000	$ 8,000
Payable to Company S	7,000	
Bonds payable (9%)	80,000	10,000
Capital stock ($10 par)	200,000	60,000
Contributed capital in excess of par	4,000	10,000
Beginning retained earnings	80,000	12,000
Dividends declared and paid, 19A	(15,000)	
Net income (from income statement)	30,000	10,000
Totals	$416,000	$110,000
Income statement (for 19A):		
Sales revenue	$202,200	$ 75,000
Cost of goods sold	(115,000)	(43,000)
Expenses (not detailed)	(52,200)	(19,500)
Depreciation expense	(5,000)	(2,500)
Net income	$ 30,000	$ 10,000

Required:

a. Give the journal entry that Company P should make to record the acquisition of the stock of Company S.

b. Analyze the stock purchase to determine the amount of goodwill purchased.

c. Prepare a consolidation worksheet (purchase method) for a balance sheet and income statement for 19A. Assume the operational assets of Company S have a 10-year remaining life and that any goodwill will be amortized over 20 years.

d. Prepare an income statement and balance sheet for 19A based on the data provided by the consolidation worksheet.

e. What is the minority interest claim to earnings and stockholders' equity at December 31, 19A?

CASES

C14–1   **(Comparison of the Pooling of Interests and the Purchase Methods)**
Some analysts believe that management would prefer to account for an acquisition under the pooling of interests method instead of the purchase method. Accounting rules do not permit management to select the method, but these analysts believe that management will structure the transaction so that it will be accounted for as a pooling. One of the alleged benefits of the pooling of interests method for management is that return on investment (net income/total assets) is usually higher under pooling. Why would you expect return on investment to be higher under pooling?

C14–2   **(Analysis of Consolidation Using an Actual Financial Statement)**
JCPenney   Refer to the financial statements of J.C. Penney Company, Inc. given in the appendix immediately preceding the index.

1. Why did J.C. Penney begin consolidating JCPenney Life Insurance Company for the first time in 1988?

2. What method was used to account for JCPenney Life Insurance Company before 1988?

3. How did the consolidation of JCPenney Life Insurance Company affect consolidated net income (compared to the method previously used)?

FIFTEEN

STATEMENT OF CASH FLOWS

PURPOSE

The basic statements required for external reporting purposes are the income statement, balance sheet, and statement of cash flows (SCF). This chapter discusses the purpose of the SCF and shows how it is prepared. Two alternative methods for preparing the SCF (the direct method and the indirect method) are discussed.

The importance of cash flow is illustrated on the opposite page by an excerpt from an annual report.

LEARNING OBJECTIVES

1. Explain the purpose of the SCF.
2. Identify the format and characteristics of the SCF.
3. Classify cash flows from operating, investing, and financing activities.
4. Give examples of cash equivalents.
5. Compare the direct and indirect methods.
6. Prepare the SCF using the direct method.
7. Prepare the SCF using the indirect method.
8. Expand your accounting vocabulary by learning the "Important Terms Defined in This Chapter."
9. Apply the knowledge learned from this chapter by completing the homework assigned by your instructor.

ORGANIZATION

Part A—overview of the statement of cash flows (SCF).
1. Format of the SCF.
2. Comparison of the direct and indirect methods.
3. Schedule approach.
4. Spreadsheet approach.
5. Additional problems in preparation of the SCF.

Part B—preparation of the SCF, indirect method.
1. Schedule approach.
2. Spreadsheet approach.

QUAKER

Perspective: Value = Cash Flow

What does "maximizing shareholder value" really mean? Essentially it means giving shareholders more cash over time—in the form of dividends and capital appreciation—than they invested in our stock when they bought it. Our goal is to deliver this "value" at a level that meets or even goes beyond the initial expectation of the people who invest in Quaker. Cash flow is crucial to reaching this goal because the more cash we can generate today and in the future, the more cash our owners will get on a current basis and over the longer term—through dividend payout and the increase in our stock price. The stock market places a premium on a company's ability to do two things: generate cash at an above-average rate of return and then make the right strategic decisions to invest this cash in projects that, in turn, also generate returns above the cost of capital. If a company proves that it can do both of these things, then its stock price should be valued at a premium to the market and appreciate over time. So, as managers, we have to weigh the business issues and the financial aspects of projects we invest in so both the current and long-term cash flows meet our shareholders' requirements.

PART A—OVERVIEW OF THE STATEMENT OF CASH FLOWS (SCF)

Many of us experience cash flow problems because we may have to make cash payments before we have received cash that is owed to us. Most businesses have this same problem from time to time. For example, a new business usually starts with a cash flow problem that continues intermittently during the first several years of operations. These cash flow problems arise because the timing of cash inflows often lags the timing of cash needs. During periods of depressed economic activities, or due to ineffective planning, large businesses also may experience similar cash flow problems.

Investors, creditors, and other interested parties need to realistically project the future cash flows of the business in order to project their own cash flows. The statement of cash flows (SCF) is designed to help statement users to project their own prospective net cash flows from investments in, and loans to, a business.

Purposes of the SCF

The SCF is designed to help investors, creditors, and other decision makers in two important ways:

1. To assess the **past performance** of the entity to generate, plan, and control the actual cash inflows and outflows.
2. To assess the entity's **probable future cash inflows, outflows, and net cash flows,** including its ability to meet future obligations and to pay dividends. This assessment should help the investor, or creditor, project a return on resources committed to the entity.

The SCF reports information concerning cash inflows and outflows of an entity classified as cash flows from (1) operating activities, (2) investing activities, and (3) financing activities. Also, the statement reports any related investing and financing transactions that do not directly affect cash.

Classifications on the SCF

FASB Statement 95 specifies the basic format for the SCF. Exhibit 15–1 outlines the required format with illustrative amounts. To assure consistent terminology and comparability, *FASB Statement 95* defines each category included in the required SCF. These definitions (with explanations) are as follows:

A. **Cash flows from operating activities.** This classification reports both the cash inflows and cash outflows that are directly related to income from normal operations reported on the income statement. Under this classification, the usual cash flows are:

Inflows—cash received from:	Outflows—cash paid for:
Customers	Purchase of goods for resale
Interest on receivables	Interest on liabilities
Dividends	Income taxes
Refunds from suppliers	Salaries and wages

Exhibit 15–1 Basic format of a SCF

UTEX COMPANY
Statement of Cash Flows
For the Year Ended December 31, 19B
(in thousands)

A. **Cash flows from operating activities:**
   Cash inflows (detailed) $60
   Cash outflows (detailed) . . . . (40)
      Net cash inflow (outflow) from operating activities $20

B. **Cash flows from investing activities:**
   Cash inflows (detailed) 21
   Cash outflows (detailed) . . . . (30)
      Net cash inflow (outflow) from investing activities . . . .   (9)

C. **Cash flows from financing activities:**
   Cash inflows (detailed) 88
   Cash outflows (detailed) . . . . (65)
      Net cash inflow (outflow) from financing activities   23

D. **Reconciliation of beginning and ending cash balance:**
   Net increase (decrease) in cash during the period   34
   Add: Beginning cash balance   42
   Ending cash balance $76

E. **Noncash investing and financing activities**—must be
   disclosed in a separate schedule.

The difference between the above inflows and outflows is called the
net cash inflow (outflow) from operating activities.

B. **Cash flows from investing activities.** This classification reports cash
   inflows and outflows that are related to the acquisition of productive
   facilities used by the company and other noncash assets. Under this
   classification, the **cash outflows** represent the "investments" of cash by
   the entity to acquire its noncash assets; and the **cash inflows** occur
   only when cash is received from the prior investments. Typical cash
   flows from investing activities are:

Inflows—cash received from:
  Disposal of property, plant, and equip-
    ment
  Disposal of investments in securities
  Collection of a loan (excluding interest,
    which is an operating activity)
  Disposal of other assets used in pro-
    ductive activities (excluding
    inventories)

Outflows—cash paid for:
  Property, plant, and equipment
  Purchase of long-term investments
  Lending to other parties
  Other assets used in productive ac-
    tivities, such as a patent (excluding
    inventories, which are an operating
    activity)

The difference between the above cash inflows and outflows is
called **net cash inflow (outflow) from investing activities.**

C. **Cash flows from financing activities.** This classification represents both cash inflows and outflows that are related to **how cash was obtained** to finance the enterprise (including its operations). Under this classification, the **cash inflows** represent the financing activities used to obtain cash for the entity. The **cash outflows** occur only when cash is paid back to the owners and creditors for their prior cash-providing activities. Usual cash flows from financing activities are:

Inflows—cash received from:	**Outflows—cash paid to:**
Owners—issuing equity securities	Owners for dividends and other dis-
Creditors—borrowing on notes, mort-	tributions
gages, bonds, etc.	Owners for treasury stock purchased
	Payment of principal amounts bor-
	rowed (excluding interest, which is
	an operating activity)

The difference between the above cash inflows and outflows is called **net cash inflow (outflow) from financing activities.**

D. **Reconciliation of beginning and ending cash balance.** *FASB Statement 95* requires reporting of the three related amounts (1) net increase (decrease) in cash, (2) beginning cash balance, and (3) ending cash balance, as shown in Exhibit 15–1.

E. **Noncash investing and financing activities.** These activities are the investing and financing transactions that involve some noncash effects. An example is the purchase of a building where there is no cash down payment and the seller provides the mortgage. In this case, there is an investing activity that did not cause a cash outflow and a financing activity that did not cause a cash inflow. Noncash activities must be reported in a separate schedule or set out separately in the disclosure notes.

Cash and Cash Equivalents

FASB Statement 95 requires that a SCF must explain the change during the period in **cash and cash equivalents.** Cash equivalents are defined as "short-term, highly liquid investments" that are both:

a. Readily convertible to known amounts of cash.

b. So near their maturity that they present insignificant risk of changes in value because of changes in interest rates.

Generally, only investments with original maturities of less than three months qualify as a cash equivalent under this definition.[1] Examples of cash equivalents are Treasury bills, money market funds, and commercial paper.

---

[1] Original maturity means original maturity to the entity holding the investment. For example, both a three-month Treasury bill and a three-year Treasury note purchased three months from maturity qualify as cash equivalents. However, a Treasury note purchased three years ago does not become a cash equivalent when its remaining maturity is three months.

Exhibit 15–2 Direct method, statement of cash flows

UTEX COMPANY
Statement of Cash Flows—Direct Method
For the Year Ended December 31, 19B
(in thousands)

A. **Cash flows from operating activities:**
  Cash inflows:
    From customers $60
  Cash outflows:
    Payments to employees . . . . (18)
    Payments to suppliers . . . . (10)
    Administrative and selling expense . . . . (12)
      Net cash inflow from operating activities $20

B. **Cash flows from investing activities:**
  Cash inflows:
    Cash received from sale of plant assets   21
  Cash outflows:
    Cash paid for acquisition of plant assets . . . . (30)
      Net cash outflow from investing activities . . . . . .   (9)

C. **Cash flows from financing activities:**
  Cash inflows:
    Cash received from sale of common stock   48
    Cash received from long-term debt   40
  Cash outflows:
    Cash paid on long-term debt (principal only) . . . . . . (46)
    Cash paid for treasury stock purchased . . . .   (8)
    Cash paid for dividends . . . . (11)
      Net cash inflow from financing activities   23

D. Net increase (decrease) in cash during 19B   34
  Cash balance, January 1, 19B   42

  Cash balance, December 31, 19B $76

Comparison of the Direct and Indirect Methods

There are two alternative approaches for preparing the SCF:

1. The **direct method** which reports the components of cash flows from operating activities as gross receipts and gross payments (such as total cash receipts from customers and total cash payments to employees). This method starts with cash revenues and cash expenses to compute net cash inflow (outflow) from operating activities. Exhibit 15–2 shows an example of a SCF prepared under the direct method.

Exhibit 15–3 Indirect method, statement of cash flows

UTEX COMPANY
Statement of Cash Flows—Indirect Method
For the Year Ended December 31, 19B
(in thousands)

A. **Cash flows from operating activities:**

Net income (from the income statement)	$22	
Add (deduct) to reconcile net income to		
net cash inflow:		
Accounts receivable increase	(6)	
Inventory increase	(2)	
Depreciation expense	4	
Salaries payable increase	2	
Net cash inflow from operating activities		$20

B. **Cash flows from investing activities:**

Cash inflows:		
Cash received from sale of plant assets	21	
Cash outflows:		
Cash paid for acquisition of plant assets	(30)	
Net cash outflow from investing activities		(9)

C. **Cash flows from financing activities:**

Cash inflows:		
Cash received from sale of common stock	48	
Cash received from long-term debt	40	
Cash outflows:		
Cash paid on long-term debt (principal only)	(46)	
Cash paid for treasury stock purchased	(8)	
Cash paid for dividends	(11)	
Net cash inflow from financing activities		23

D. Net increase (decrease) in cash during 19B   34
Cash balance, January 1, 19B   42

Cash balance, December 31, 19B $76

2. The **indirect method** which adjusts net income to compute net cash inflow (outflow) from operating activities. Exhibit 15–3 shows an example of a SCF prepared under the indirect method.

Either method is acceptable, however *FASB Statement 95* **strongly recommends the direct method.**

Notice that the basic difference between the direct and indirect methods (Exhibits 15–2 and 15–3) is the way that **cash flows from operating activities** are reported (boxed for emphasis). The two methods report the same net cash flow from each of the four classifications (A–D). Only the individual amounts within the cash flows from operating activities sections differ.

The **direct method** reports the gross cash flow amount for each revenue and expense. The direct method converts the accrual basis revenues and expenses amounts reported on the income statement to the cash basis amounts reported on the SCF. For example, an income statement might report revenue of $100,000 which included $75,000 cash collected from customers and $25,000 for credit sales (i.e., accounts receivable). Under the direct method, the SCF would report cash collections from customers of $75,000.

In contrast, the **indirect method** starts with accrual basis net income and converts that amount to a cash basis. Under cash flows from operating activities, the indirect method reports only net income, changes in certain balance sheet accounts, and net cash flow from operating activities.

The direct method is discussed in Part A of this chapter, and the indirect method is discussed in Part B.

Preparation of the SCF, Direct Method

The SCF cannot be prepared by using a trial balance, nor with the worksheet that is often used to prepare the income statement and the balance sheet. We will discuss two approaches to develop the SCF.

 a. **Schedule approach.** This approach involves a series of computations to "build up" a SCF, piece by piece. This approach is used primarily for simple cases.
 b. **Spreadsheet approach.** This approach uses a specifically designed spreadsheet which is widely used in accounting practice.

The data needed to prepare a SCF are:

 1. A complete income statement—used primarily in preparing cash flows from operating activities.
 2. Comparative balance sheets—used in preparing the cash flows from all activities (operating, investing, and financing).
 3. Analyses of selected accounts that reflect several different kinds of transactions and events. Analysis of individual accounts is necessary because the total change amount in an account balance during the year often does not reveal the underlying nature of the cash flows.

Exhibit 15–4 shows case data to illustrate the preparation of the SCF.

Schedule Approach to Develop a SCF, Direct Method

The SCF, direct method, of UTEX Company (Exhibit 15–2) can be developed using the schedule approach. This approach involves the following three steps:

Step 1. Obtain an income statement and the comparative balance sheet as shown in Exhibit 15–4. Notice the net increase in the cash balance ($34). The change in the cash balance is the key check figure.

Exhibit 15–4 UTEX Company, current income statement and comparative balance sheet (in thousands)

A. **Income statement for the year ended December 31, 19B:**

Sales revenue	$ 66
Salaries expense	(20)
Cost of goods sold	(8)
Depreciation expense	(4)
Administrative and selling expense (excluding salaries)	(12)
Net income	$ 22

B. **Comparative balance sheet, December 31, 19B:**

Items	12/31/19A	12/31/19B
Cash (no cash equivalents)	$ 42	$ 76
Accounts receivable	21	27
Inventory	10	12
Plant assets	82	81
Less: Accumulated depreciation	(20)	(14)
Total assets	$135	$182
Salaries payable	$ 3	$ 5
Note payable, long term	46	40
Common stock (par $10)	61	101
Contributed capital in excess of par	9	17
Treasury stock	0	(8)
Retained earnings	16	27
Total liabilities and stockholders' equity	$135	$182

C. **Analysis of individual accounts to identify cash flows (source—accounting records):**

  a. Plant Assets account:

    (1) Purchased plant assets for cash, $30.

    (2) Sold old plant assets for cash, $21; recorded as follows (at book value):

Cash	21	
Accumulated depreciation	10	
Plant assets		31

  b. Long-Term Note Payable account:
    Borrowed cash, $40
    Payments on note principal, $46.

  c. Treasury Stock account—purchased treasury stock for $8 cash.

  d. Statement of retained earnings:

Balance, December 31, 19A	$ 16
Net income for 19B	22
Cash dividend paid in cash at end of 19B	(11)
Balance, December 31, 19B	$ 27

  e. Issued common stock for $48 cash.

Step 2. Prepare three schedules to compute:

A—net cash flow from operating activities.

B—net cash flow from investing activities.

C—net cash flow from financing activities.

Schedule B (investing activities) and Schedule C (financing activities) are prepared by analyzing the change in each asset, liability, and equity account to identify the investing and financing cash inflows and outflows. The results of this analysis of individual accounts are shown in Exhibit 15–4, Panel C.

Step 3. Use three schedules to prepare the formal SCF (Exhibit 15–2).

The three schedules needed for UTEX Company are shown, with explanations, in Exhibit 15–5. In the following sections, we discuss the preparation of each major section of the SCF.

Exhibit 15–5   Schedules to prepare SCF, direct method; UTEX Company (in thousands)

Schedule A, direct method—computation of net cash flow from operating activities (conversion of income statement from accrual to cash basis):

Items from income statement and comparative balance sheet	Accrual basis	Cash basis		Explanation
		Change	Amount	
Sales revenue	$66			Accounts receivable increase, $6; subtracted because sales revenue
Accounts receivable—				
increase (−); decrease (+)		−$6	$60	included this amount of credit sales.
Deduct expenses:				
Salaries expense	20			Salaries payable increase, $2; subtracted because less cash was paid
Salaries payable—				
increase (−); decrease (+) . . .		−2	18	for salaries than was reported as salary expense.
Cost of goods sold	8			Inventory increase, $2 added because more cash was paid to suppliers
Inventory—				
increase (+); decrease (−)		+2	10	than was reported as cost of goods sold.
Administrative and selling				No addition or subtraction because
expense	12			there were no accruals; all of this expense was paid in cash this pe-
Accrued expense payable—				
increase (−); decrease (+)		0	12	riod.
Depreciation	4	−4	0	Depreciation expense, $4; always subtracted because it is always a noncash expense.
Net income:				
Accrual basis	$22			
Cash basis			$20	Reported on the SCF (Exhibit 15–2).

Exhibit 15–5 *(concluded)*

Schedule B, direct method—computation of net cash flow from investing activities (analysis of comparative balance sheet and individual accounts):

Items from account analysis	Cash inflows cash (outflows)	Explanation
Purchase of plant assets	$(30)	Payment in full for noncash asset.
Sale of plant assets	21	Total cash received from sale of noncash asset.
Net cash inflow (outflow) from investing activities	$ (9)	Reported on the SCF (Exhibit 15–2).

Schedule C, direct method—computation of net cash flow from financing activities:

Items from account analysis	Cash inflows cash (outflows)	Explanation
Issuance of common stock	$48	From Common Stock account.
Borrowing on long-term note	40	From Long-Term Note Payable account.
Payments on long-term note	(46)	Same as above.
Purchase of treasury stock	(8)	From Treasury Stock account.
Paid cash dividend	(11)	From statement of retained earnings.
Net cash inflow (outflow) from financing activities	$23	Reported on the SCF (Exhibit 15–2).

Computing Net Cash Flow from Operating Activities

Converting Revenues. Under the direct method, each major income statement category (i.e., revenues, gains, expenses, and losses) must be converted to a cash basis as shown in Exhibit 15–5, Schedule A. Accrual basis revenues and expenses often include **noncash** amounts. These noncash amounts cause changes in the balances of accounts receivable, inventories, accounts payable and other accounts related to revenues and expenses. For example, if less cash is collected from customers than the amount of revenue recognized on the accrual basis, the balance of accounts receivable will increase. Under the direct method, the formula to convert amounts from the accrual basis to the cash basis for **all revenues** is:

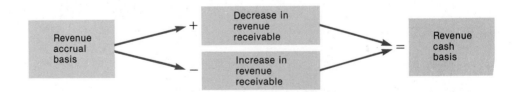

This formula applies to all revenues—service, interest, dividends, royalty, rent, and so on. Notice application of this formula to sales revenue in Exhibit 15–5, Schedule A.

The following cases illustrate use of this formula:

Case	Accounts receivable	Revenue (accrual basis)	Change			Cash basis (inflow)
			A	B	C	
A	No change	$66	—			$66
B	Increase, $6*	66		−$6		60
C	Decrease, $6	66			+$6	72

* The case for UTEX Company.

Converting Expenses. Under accrual accounting, the total amount of an expense category may be different from the cash outflow associated with that activity. For example, the cash payments to employees may be less than the salary expense that is reported. In this case, the unpaid salary expense would cause salaries payable to increase.

Under the direct method, the formula to convert amounts from the accrual basis to the cash basis for **all expenses** is:

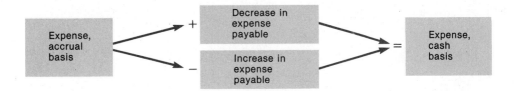

Notice application of this formula to salaries payable in Exhibit 15–5, Schedule A. The following cases illustrate use of this formula:

Cash	Accounts payable	Selling and administrative expense (accrual basis)	Change			Cash basis (outflow)
			A	B	C	
A	No change*	$12	—			$12
B	Increase, $2	12		−$2		10
C	Decrease, $2	12			+$2	14

* The case for UTEX Company.

Noncash expenses, such as bad debt expense and depreciation, are reported on most income statements. Noncash expenses are not reflected on the SCF, direct method because the entry to record these expenses does not involve a credit or debit to cash. The related cash outflow occurred when the asset was purchased or when the debt incurred to buy the asset was paid.

Computing Net Cash Flow from Investing Activities

The analysis of individual accounts is provided in Exhibit 15–4, Item C. The changes in the balances of all of the accounts listed on the balance sheet (Exhibit 15–4, Item B) were analyzed to identify transactions that involved investing activities. In the case of UTEX Comany, the analysis found that the only investing activities involved plant assets. Notice that the purchase of a plant asset and its subsequent sale are both **investing** activities; the former is a cash outflow, and the latter is a cash inflow.

Exhibit 15–6 Spreadsheet to prepare SCF, direct method; UTEX Company, December 31, 19B (in thousands)

Items from Financial Statements	Beginning Balances, 12/31/19A	Analysis of Changes Debit	Analysis of Changes Credit	Ending Balances, 12/31/19B
Phase A—analysis of income statement:				
Revenues:				
Sales			(a) 66	
Expenses:				
Salaries		(b) 20		
Cost of goods sold		(c) 8		
Depreciation		(d) 4		
Administrative and selling (including interest)		(e) 12		
Net income (to retained earnings)		(f) 22		
Phase B—analysis of balance sheet:				
Cash	42	(q) 34		76
Accounts receivable	21	(g) 6		27
Inventory	10	(h) 2		12
Plant assets (analysis needed)	82	(j) 30	(i) 31	81
Less: Accumulated depreciation	(20)	(i) 10	(d) 4	(14)
Total assets	135			182
Salaries payable	3		(k) 2	5
Note payable, long term (analysis needed)	46	(l) 46	(m) 40	40
Common stock (par $10)	61		(n) 40	101
Contributed capital in excess of par	9		(n) 8	17
Treasury stock	0	(o) 8		(8)
Retained earnings	16	(p) 11	(f) 22	27
Total liabilities and stockholders' equity	135			182

Computing Net Cash Flows from Financing Activities

The "financing" type of accounts for UTEX Company include Notes Payable, Common Stock, Contributed Capital in Excess of Par, and Retained Earnings. An analysis of each of these accounts provided the data shown in Exhibit 15–4, Item C. There are two cash inflows (issuance of common stock and borrowing) and three cash outflows (payments on debt, purchase of treasury stock, and cash dividends).

Preparation of the Formal SCF

Step 3 involves preparing the SCF based on the three schedules discussed above. The formal SCF for UTEX Company is shown in Exhibit 15–2. The formal SCF can be prepared using the three completed schedules (A, B, and C, in Exhibit 15–5) and the beginning and ending cash balances reported on the balance sheet.

Exhibit 15–6 (concluded)

Statement of cash flows:	Inflows		Outflows		Subtotals
Cash flows from operating activities:					
From customers—sales	(a)	66			60
Accounts receivable increase			(g)	6	
Paid to employees—salaries			(b)	20	
Salaries payable increase	(k)	2			(40)
Paid to suppliers—cost of goods sold			(c)	8	20
Inventory increase			(h)	2	
Administrative and selling expense			(e)	12	
Cash flows from investing activities:					
Sale of plant assets	(i)	21			
Purchase of plant assets			(j)	30	(9)
Cash flows from financing activities:					
Issuance of common stock	(n)	48			
Borrowing on long-term note	(m)	40			
Payments on long-term note			(l)	46	23
Purchase of treasury stock			(o)	8	
Paid cash dividend			(p)	11	
Net increase (decrease) during the year*			(q)	34	
Totals (to verify)		390		390	34

* Must agree with change in cash reported on the balance sheet.

Spreadsheet Approach to Develop a SCF, Direct Method

Often the use of a spreadsheet to develop the SCF is more efficient than the schedule approach. The primary advantages of the spreadsheet approach are that it (a) brings together all of the needed data, (b) is an organized approach that ties together all of the classifications on the SCF, (c) develops the analysis in the familiar Debts = Credits format, and (d) provides continuing proofs of accuracy. Sometimes the spreadsheet is considered more cumbersome when compared with the schedule approach, but this comparison usually overlooks the advantages of using a spreadsheet when complex problems must be solved.

Exhibit 15–6 shows a completed spreadsheet for UTEX Company (based on the data given in Exhibit 15–4). Notice the following features: (a) it starts with the income statement and balance sheet, (b) it analyzes all changes between the beginning and ending balances by using a series of straightforward debit-credit entries, (c) it provides all of the information for the SCF, and (d) it balances throughout.

How to Prepare a Spreadsheet for the SCF, Direct Method

The SCF spreadsheet is easy to prepare by using the following organized approach:

Step 1. Set up the four money columns with the standard headings shown in Exhibit 15–6.

Step 2. Copy the income statement (amounts in the two middle columns) and the balance sheet (amounts in the first and last money columns) as shown in Exhibit 15–6.

Step 3. Immediately below the income statement and the balance sheet data, write the following side captions (leaving adequate space below each of the captions): Statement of cash flows, Cash flows from operating activities, Cash flows from investing activities, Cash flows from financing activities, Net increase (decrease) during the year, and Totals.

Step 4. Make debit-credit analytical entries under the two Analysis of Changes columns. **The spreadsheet is complete when the changes between the beginning and ending balances on each line are accounted for by the analytical entries.**

Explanation of Spreadsheet Entries.   It is preferable to start with the first item on the income statement and continue in order until all entries are made. The rationale for each entry is given below. For instructional convenience the following abbreviations are used: OA = operating activities, IA = investing activities, and FA = financing activities. Also, entries on the worksheet are coded as (*a*), (*b*), (*c*), etc., for reference purposes.

Enter the income statement amounts as follows:

Entry (*a*)—for revenues:

OA—from customers (a debit to cash flow)*	66	
Sales (to record)		66

* This amount is adjusted in entry (*g*) for the effects of changes in accounts receivable.

Entry (*b*)—for expenses that require cash:

Salaries expense (to record)	20	
OA—paid to employees (a credit to cash outflow)		20

Entry (*c*)—for expenses that require cash:

Cost of goods sold	8	
OA—paid to suppliers (a credit to cash outflow)		8

Entry (*d*)—for noncash expenses; no effect on cash flows:

Depreciation	4	
Accumulated depreciation (on the balance sheet)*		4

* Noncash expenses are not reported on SCF, direct method; no OA, IA, or FA effects.

Entry (*e*)—for expenses that require cash:

Administrative and selling expense (to record)	12	
OA—paid to employees (a credit to cash outflow)*		12

* This amount is all cash because there were no related accruals or deferrals.

Entry (f)—to transfer net income to retained earnings:

Net income (i.e., income summary)   22

Retained earnings*   22

* A noncash transfer, no OA, IA, or FA effects.

After the above entries are made on the spreadsheet, all of the income statement accounts and some of the balance sheet accounts have been reconciled. Those reconciled accounts can be "checked off" because no additional entries will be made to them. Spreadsheet entries "account" for the remaining changes in the account balances reported on the balance sheet. Each entry that follows also classifies cash flows as either OA, IA, or FA. These spreadsheet entries can be made in any order; however, for instructional convenience they follow the worksheet order. Therefore, we start with accounts receivable.

Entry (g)—to record the increase in accounts receivable:

Accounts receivable (check off; this account is now reconciled)   6

OA—from customers*   6

* This adjusts the $66 sales revenue amount to the cash basis, $60. Notice that entry (a) could have been made to include the entry as follows:

OA—from customers ($66–$6)   60
Accounts receivable   6

Sales   66

Entry (h)—to record the increase inventory:

Inventory   2

OA—paid to suppliers   2

Entry (i)—for the sale of old plant assets:

IA—sale of plant assets*   21
Accumulated depreciation (to remove)   10

Plant assets (to remove)   31

* This is the cash inflow; see analysis of plant assets, Exhibit 15–4.

Entry (j)—for the purchase of plant assets:

Plant assets   30

IA—purchase of plant assets*   30

* This is the cash outflow for this transaction; see analysis of plant assets.

Note: After spreadsheet entries (i) and (j) are made, plant assets and accumulated depreciation are fully reconciled.

Entry (k)—for increase in salaries payable:

OA—paid to employees*   2

Salaries payable (increase during year)   2

* This entry is an adjustment of salaries expense entry (b), from the accrual to cash basis. Entry (b) could have included this entry.

Entry (*l*)—for payment of long-term note payable:

Note payable	46	
FA—payment on note*		46

* This is the cash outflow; see analysis of note payable.

Entry (*m*)—for borrowing on note payable:

FA—borrowing on note payable*	40	
Note payable		40

* This is the cash inflow; see analysis of note payable.

Entry (*n*)—for issuance of common stock:

FA—issuance of common stock	48	
Common stock (par $10)		40
Contributed capital in excess of par		8

Entry (*o*)—for purchase of treasury stock:

Treasury stock	8	
FA—purchase of treasury stock		8

Entry (*p*)—for cash dividend paid:

Retained earnings*	11	
FA—payment of dividend		11

* Check off retained earning because it is reconciled (i.e., $16 + $22 − $11 = $27).

Entry (*q*)—to enter, for balancing purposes only, the key check figure which is the change in cash during the period:

Cash	34	
Net increase during the year (to balance)		34

* This fully reconciles the beginning and ending cash balances ($42 + $34 = 76). This is an optional entry on the spreadsheet.

The above entries complete the spreadsheet analysis because all accounts are reconciled. Finally, add the two analysis columns to verify that Debits = Credits. The SCF can now be prepared by using only the bottom part of the spreadsheet (Exhibit 15–2). Notice that the subtotals in the lower right column of the spreadsheet tie in directly with the SCF.

Noncash Investing and Financing Activities

As discussed earlier in this chapter, certain transactions are important investing and financing activities, but they do not have any cash flow effects. For example, the purchase of a $100,000 building with a $100,000 mortgage does not cause either the inflow or the outflow of cash. *FASB Statement 95* requires disclosure of these transactions in either narrative or schedule form. An example of a typical disclosure is shown below.

Alpha Corporation acquired a new factory building for $100,000. The purchase was financed with a 10% mortgage which is held by the seller of the building.

Additional Problems When Preparing the SCF, Direct Method

The previous discussion presented the basic concepts underlying the SCF, direct method. The UTEX Company case was developed to introduce you to the preparation of the SCF. We will now discuss some of the additional issues that are usually encountered in developing a SCF.

Converting Cost of Goods Sold to a Cash Basis

Cost of goods sold represents the cost of merchandise sold during the accounting period. It may be more or less than the amount of cash paid to suppliers during the period. In the case of UTEX Company (Exhibit 15–4), inventory increased during the year. The company bought more merchandise from its suppliers than it sold to its customers. Therefore, UTEX Company paid more cash to its suppliers than the amount of cost of goods sold.

Typically, companies owe their suppliers money (i.e., there will be an accounts payable balance reported on the balance sheet). In these cases, the calculation of cash payments to suppliers is more complex. To convert cost of goods sold, two accounts must be considered—inventory and accounts payable. Cash is required to increase inventory or to decrease accounts payable. Conversely, a decrease in inventory or an increase in accounts payable reduces cash requirements.

Cost of goods sold can be converted to a cash basis in the following manner:

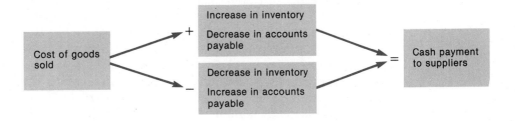

The following cases illustrate this conversion when the schedule approach is used to prepare the SCF, direct method:

Case	Cost of goods sold (accrual basis)	Inventory change increase (decrease)	Accounts payable change increase (decrease)	Cash payments to suppliers
A	$42	$-0-	$-0-	$42
B	42	7	-0-	49
C	42	(7)	-0-	35
D	42	-0-	4	38
E	42	-0-	(4)	46
F	42	7	(4)	53
G	42	(7)	(4)	39

If the spreadsheet approach is used, the entry to record the change in accounts payable is made in the same way as the entry to record the change in inventory (illustrated in Exhibit 15–6).

Gains and Losses

The income statement may include gains and losses from the sale of operational assets. The transactions that cause gains and losses should be classified on the SCF as operating, investing, or financing activities, depending on their dominant characteristics. For example, if the sale of a productive asset (e.g., a delivery truck) produced a gain, it would be classified as an investing activity.

The gain or loss associated with a transaction standing alone does not reflect the complete cash flows caused by the transaction. For example, consider the following entry for Y Corporation to record the disposal of a delivery truck:

Cash	8,000	
Accumulated depreciation	4,000	
Operational assets		10,000
Gain on disposal		2,000

The inflow of cash was $8,000, but the reported gain was only $2,000. This transaction should be reported on the SCF as an investing activity with a cash inflow of $8,000.

To prepare the SCF, the gain of $2,000 must be removed from operating activities (i.e., net income), and the full $8,000 must be shown in the investing activities section of the statement. Under both the schedule and the spreadsheet approach, this is accomplished in the same manner (i.e., a reduction of $2,000 from cash from operating activities and an increase in cash from sale of operational assets). If the $2,000 were not removed from the operating activities section of the SCF, it would be "counted twice" when the $8,000 was reported in the investing activities section. If we avoided the double counting by reporting only $6,000 cash inflow from investing activities, we would misstate the actual effects of the transaction.

When a loss is reported on the income statement, it must also be removed when preparing the SCF. Consider the following entry for Y Corporation to record the sale of a machine:

Cash	25,000	
Accumulated depreciation	15,000	
Loss	5,000	
Machine		45,000

To prepare the SCF, the loss of $5,000 must be removed from operating activities and $25,000 must be shown in the investing activities section of the statement.

Disclosure Requirements under the Direct Method

The SCF, direct method, has the following disclosure requirements:

1. Separately disclose the noncash investing and financing activities.
2. Disclose the policy for determining those items that are treated as cash equivalents.
3. Reconcile net income with net cash inflow (outflow) from operating activities. This reconciliation can be readily prepared using either the schedule or spreadsheet approach. The information contained in the reconciliation is similar to the information reported under the indirect method which is discussed in Part B of this chapter.

PART B—PREPARATION OF THE SCF, INDIRECT METHOD

Part A of this chapter discussed the direct method of preparing the SCF. In this part, we will discuss the indirect method.

The indirect method of reporting cash flows has been used for more than four decades. It continues to be an acceptable alternative to the direct method. Recall from Exhibits 15–2 and 15–3 that it differs from the direct method in an important way. For operating activities, instead of reporting cash inflows from individual revenues and outflows for individual expenses, the indirect method starts with net income and reconciles net income with net cash flows from operating activities.

The direct and indirect methods require the same basic data and the same underlying concepts. Our discussion of the preparation of the SCF under the indirect method is based on the data shown in Exhibit 15–4.

Schedule Approach—SCF, Indirect Method

This approach involves the development of three schedules to compute net cash flow from operating, investing, and financing activities.

The adjustments used to convert accrual income to cash flow from operating activities are varied. Although careful analysis is needed, the following table is useful:

Item	Plus and minus adjustments to net income to reconcile net income with cash flow from operating activities	
	When item increases	When item decreases
Accounts receivable (trade)	−	+
Accounts payable (trade)	+	−
Accrued liability and unearned revenue	+	−
Prepaid asset and accrued revenue	−	+
Inventory	−	+
Depreciation, depletion, and amortization	+	
Amortization of discount on bonds payable	+	
Amortization of premium on bonds payable	−	
Amortization of discount on bond investment . . .	−	
Amortization of premium on bond investment . . .	+	
Gains on the income statement	−	
Losses on the income statement	+	

Exhibit 15–7 shows the three schedules that are used to prepare the SCF with explanations. Notice that Schedules B and C are identical with those prepared using the direct method (Exhibit 15–5).

Spreadsheet Approach—SCF, Indirect Method

When the indirect method is used, the spreadsheet does not include the income statement because the individual revenues and expenses are not analyzed to determine their respective cash flows. Instead, net income is reconciled with cash flow from operating activities. This means that the first analysis on the spreadsheet starts with net income and computes the changes in various balance sheet accounts that reconcile net income and cash flows from operating activities. It follows the pattern shown in the schedule approach (Exhibit 15–7, Schedule A). Exhibit 15–8 shows the spreadsheet for the indirect method. The remaining parts of the analysis—cash flows from investing and financing activities—are the same as when the direct method is used (Exhibit 15–6).

Explanations of spreadsheet entries shown in Exhibit 15–8 using the indirect method are given below.

Entry (a)—for net income:

Net income	22	
Retained earnings		22

This entry is used to start the reconciliation; net income is shown as an inflow to be reconciled by the noncash reconciling entries. The credit to Retained Earnings reflects the effects of the original closing entry. This is the starting point for the reconciliation.

Exhibit 15–7 Schedules to prepare the SCF, indirect method, UTEX Company (in thousands)

Schedule A, indirect method—computation of net cash flow from operating activities (conversion of net income to net cash flow):

Items (Exhibit 15–4)	Amount	Explanation
Net income, accrual basis	$22	From income statement.
Add (subtract) to convert to cash basis:		
Accounts receivable increase	−6	Subtract because cash inflow from sales transactions is less than accrual basis revenues.
Salaries payable increase	+2	Add because cash payments to employees are less than accrual basis salary expense.
Inventory increase	−2	Subtract because cash payments to suppliers are more than accrual basis of cost of goods sold.
Depreciation expense	+4	Add because depreciation expense is a noncash expense.
Net cash inflow from operating activities . .	$20	Reported on the SCF (Exhibit 15–3).

Schedule B, indirect method—computation of net cash flows from investing activities (analysis of comparative balance sheet and individual accounts):

Items from balance sheet and account analysis	Cash inflow cash (outflows)	Explanation
Purchase of plant assets	$(30)	Payment in full for noncash asset.
Sale of plant assets	21	Total cash received from sale of noncash asset.
Net cash inflow (outflow) from investing activities	$ (9)	Reported on the SCF (Exhibit 15–3).

Schedule C, indirect method—computation of net cash flows from financing activities:

Items from balance sheet and account analysis	Cash inflows cash (outflows)	Explanation
Issuance of common stock	$ 48	From Common Stock account.
Borrowing on long-term note	40	From Long-Term Note Payable account.
Payments on long-term note	(46)	Same as above.
Purchase of treasury stock	(8)	From Treasury Stock account.
Paid cash dividend	(11)	From statement of retained earnings.
Net cash inflow (outflow) from financing activities	$ 23	Reported on the SCF (Exhibit 15–3).

Entry (*b*)—for the increase in accounts receivable:

Accounts receivable	6	
Reconciling amount (deduct from net income)		6

This entry reconciles the change in accounts receivable during the period with net income. It is deducted from net income because cash collections from customers were less than sales revenue.

Exhibit 15–8   Spreadsheet to prepare SCF, indirect method, UTEX Company, December 31, 19B (in thousands)

	Beginning Balances, 12/31/19A	Analysis of Changes		Ending Balances, 12/31/19B
		Debit	Credit	
Items from balance sheet:				
Cash	42	(m) 34		76
Accounts receivable	21	(b) 6		27
Inventory	10	(d) 2		12
Plant assets	82	(g) 30	(f) 31	81
Accumulated depreciation	(20)	(f) 10	(e) 4	(14)
Salaries payable	3		(c) 2	5
Note payable, long term	46	(j) 46	(i) 40	40
Common stock (par $10)	61		(h) 40	101
Contributed capital in excess of par	9		(h) 8	17
Treasury stock	0	(k) 8		(8)
Retained earnings	16	(l) 11	(a) 22	27

		Inflows	Outflows	Subtotals
Statement of cash flows:				
Reconciliation of net income to cash flow from operating activities:				
Net income		(a) 22		
Accounts receivable increase			(b) 6	20
Salaries payable increase		(c) 2		
Inventory increase			(d) 2	
Depreciation expense		(e) 4		
Cash flows from investing activities:				
Sale of plant assets		(f) 21		
Purchase of plant assets			(g) 30	(9)
Cash flows from financing activities:				
Issuance of common stock		(h) 48		
Borrowing on long-term note		(i) 40		
Payments on long-term note			(j) 46	
Purchase of treasury stock			(k) 8	23
Paid cash dividend			(l) 11	
Net increase (decrease) during the year			(m) 34	
Totals		284	284	34

Entry (c)—for salaries payable increase:

Reconciling amount (add to net income)   2
    Salaries payable   2

This entry reconciles the change in salaries payable with net income. It is added to net income because payments to employees were less than the accrual basis salary expense.

Entry (d)—for inventory increase:

Inventory	2	
Reconciling amount (deduct from net income)		2

Deduct because cash outflow for inventory was more than accrual basis inventory included in cost of goods sold.

Entry (e)—for depreciation expense:

Reconciling amount (add to net income)	4	
Accumulated depreciation		4

Depreciation expense is a noncash expense. It is added back to net income because this type of expense does not cause a cash outflow when it is recorded.

Entry (f)—for the sale of old plant assets:

Investing activities	21	
Accumulated depreciation (to remove)	10	
Plant assets (to remove)		31

This is a cash inflow; see analysis of plant assets, Exhibit 15–4.

Entry (g)—for the purchase of plant assets:

Plant assets	30	
Investing activities		30

This is the cash outflow for this transaction; see analysis of plant assets.

Entry (h)—for issuance of common stock:

Financing activities	48	
Common stock (par $10)		40
Contributed capital in excess of par		8

This entry recognizes the issuance of common stock which is a financing activity. It is a cash inflow.

Entry (i)—for borrowing on note payable:

Financing activities	40	
Note payable		40

This is a cash inflow; see analysis of note payable (Exhibit 15–4).

Entry (j)—for payment of long-term note payable:

Note payable	46	
Financing activities		46

This is a cash outflow; see analysis of note payable.

Entry (k)—for purchase of treasury stock:

Treasury stock	8	
Financing activities		8

This entry recognizes a cash outflow related to a financing activity. See analysis of retained earnings (Exhibit 15–4).

Entry (*l*)—for payment of cash dividends:

Retained earnings   11
    Financing activities   11

This is a cash outflow that is associated with a financing activity. See analysis of retained earnings.

Entry (*m*)—for balancing purposes:

Cash   34
    Net increase during the year   34

The net increase or decrease reported on the SCF is the same as the change in the cash balance during the year.

The preceding entries complete the spreadsheet analysis because all accounts are reconciled. The accuracy of the analysis can be checked by adding the two analysis columns to verify that Debits = Credits. The formal SCF can be prepared directly from the spreadsheet (Exhibit 15–3).

SUMMARY OF CHAPTER

The SCF is one of the required financial statements. Although it has been used for several decades, *FASB Statement 95* (November 1987) established the requirements for the SCF including a specific format, with detailed guidelines for content.

The primary purpose of the new SCF is to provide cash flow information in a manner that maximizes its usefulness to investors, creditors, and others in projecting future cash flows related to the enterprise.

Two different methods for reporting cash flows are permitted. They are called the direct and indirect methods. These alternative methods differ only in respect to cash flows from operating activities. Investing and financing activities are reported in exactly the same way under both methods. The direct method reports the cash flows from the main classifications of revenues and expenses. In contrast, the indirect method reports operating activities by showing a reconciliation of net income with net cash flow from operating activities. *FASB Statement 95* strongly recommends the direct method because it is more relevant for investors, creditors, and other interested parties.

Two approaches are available for developing the SCF—the schedule approach and the spreadsheet approach. Both approaches are efficient; however, the spreadsheet approach is preferable in complex cases because it is a coordinated and self-checking approach.

CHAPTER SUPPLEMENT 15A

Accounts Receivable and the Allowance for Doubtful Accounts

The first item on the SCF, direct method, is cash inflow from revenues as shown in Exhibit 15–2 for UTEX Company (i.e., $60). The accrual basis revenue amounts reported on the income statement were converted to a cash basis as follows:

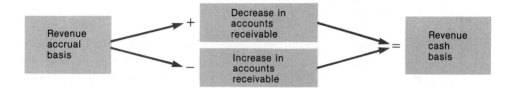

The discussion in the chapter did not consider the case when an **allowance for doubtful accounts** is needed, which is the usual case when some sales are on credit. The accounts receivable and allowance for doubtful accounts involve three different items (entries) as follows: (*a*) the difference between total sales for the period and cash collected for sales, (*b*) recognition of bad debt expense (a noncash entry), and (*c*) the write-off of an uncollectible account (a noncash entry). A cash flow analysis must recognize changes due to each of these three items. Calculation of cash revenue is easiest if you focus on the gross amount of accounts receivable (i.e., before the allowance is subtracted).

To illustrate, assume X Company's financial statements showed the following for 19B (in thousands):

Income statement:

Sales revenue	$60
Bad debt expense	1

Balance sheet:

	Balance		Increase
	12/31/19A	12/31/19B	(decrease)*
Accounts receivable	$10	$12	+$2
Allowance for doubtful accounts . . .	−6	−7	−1
Net	$ 4	$ 5	+$1

* Notice the algebraic implications.

The Allowance for Doubtful Accounts contains only noncash amounts. Therefore, cash flow from sales revenue is computed under the schedule approach as: $60 minus the $2 increase in gross accounts receivable = $58. Notice the existence of the allowance account does not affect the calculation of cash revenue.

If the spreadsheet approach is used, the entries to record sales revenue and accounts receivable would be the same as illustrated for UTEX Company (entries [*a*] and [*g*], Exhibit 15–6). The entry to record bad debt expense is similar to depreciation expense (entry [*d*]) because they are both noncash expenses. The Bad Debt Expense entry on a spreadsheet is:

Bad debt expense   1
    Allowance for doubtful accounts   1

Notice that the entry to record bad debt expense does not include either a debit or credit to Cash. Therefore, bad debt expense does not affect the SCF under the direct method.

Now let's go one step farther—what is the effect of a **bad debt write-off?** A write-off reduces both the allowance account and accounts receivable by the same amount. The write-off of a bad debt **does not affect cash flows.** Nevertheless, the write-off must be considered because it changes the ending balance of accounts receivable. This poses a problem because the change from the beginning to the ending balance of accounts receivable is used to compute cash flows. This problem can be resolved as follows:

Schedule approach—on the schedule, remove (i.e., add back) the write-off from the ending balance of accounts receivable and use the restated balance to compute the cash flow effects of accounts receivable.

Spreadsheet approach—reverse the write-off entry and proceed as if it did not exist.

IMPORTANT TERMS DEFINED IN THIS CHAPTER

Cash Equivalent A short-term, highly liquid investment with original maturity of less than three months. SCF reports changes in cash and cash equivalents. *p. 714*

Cash Flows from Financing Activities Inflows and outflows related to how cash was obtained to finance the enterprise. *p. 714*

Cash Flows from Investing Activities Inflows and outflows related to the acquisition or sale of productive facilities and making or collecting loans. *p. 713*

Cash Flows from Operating Activities Inflows and outflows related to earning net income. *p. 712*

Direct Method Reports components of cash flows from operating activities as gross receipts and gross payments. *p. 715*

Indirect Method Adjusts net income to compute cash flows from operating activities. *p. 716*

Noncash Expense An expense that does not cause an immediate cash outflow; for example, depreciation expense. *p. 721*

Noncash Investing and Financing Activities Transactions that do not have direct cash flow effects; reported on the SCF in narrative or schedule form. *p. 726*

Schedule Approach Used to develop the SCF; efficient method in simple cases. *p. 717*

Spreadsheet Approach Used to develop the SCF; widely used in practice. *p. 717*

Statement of Cash Flows (SCF) A primary financial statement that reports cash inflows and outflows from operating, investing, and financing activities. *p. 712*

QUESTIONS

Part A: Questions 1–11

1. Compare the purposes of the income statement, the balance sheet, and the SCF.
2. What information does the SCF report that is not reported on the other required financial statements? How do investors and creditors use that information?
3. What are the major categories of business activities reported on the SCF? Define each of these activities.
4. What are the typical cash inflows from operating activities? What are the typical cash outflows from operating activities?
5. What are the typical cash inflows from investing activities? What are the typical cash outflows from investing activities?
6. What are the typical cash inflows from financing activities? What are the typical cash outflows from financing activities?
7. What are noncash investing and financing activities? Give two examples. How are they reported on the SCF?
8. What are cash equivalents? How are purchases and sales of cash equivalents reported on the SCF?
9. If a business purchases a Treasury bill that matures in six months, is the Treasury bill considered a cash equivalent? Will that Treasury bill be considered a cash equivalent when it has only three months remaining to maturity?
10. How is the sale of equipment reported on the SCF using the direct method?
11. Should the effects of bad debts expense and the write-off of uncollectible accounts be considered when preparing a SCF? (Based on Supplement 15–A.)

Part B: Questions 12–18

12. Compare the two methods of reporting cash flows from operating activities in the SCF.
13. Under the indirect method, depreciation expense is added to net income to report cash flows from operating activities. Does depreciation cause an inflow of cash?
14. How is depreciation expense handled when preparing a SCF using the direct method? Using the indirect method? What other expenses are handled similar to depreciation?
15. Assume you are preparing a SCF and are trying to determine if there were any investing activities. Where would you find this information?

16. Assume you are preparing a SCF and are trying to determine if there were any financing activities. Where would you find this information?

17. Explain why cash paid during the period for purchases and for salaries is not specifically reported on the SCF, indirect method, as cash outflows.

18. Explain why a $50,000 increase in inventory during the year must be included in developing cash flows for operating activities under both the direct and indirect methods.

EXERCISES

Part A: Exercises 15–1 to 15–12

E15–1   (Classifying Transactions on the SCF)

For each transaction listed below, indicate how the transaction would be reported on a SCF prepared using the direct method. Use the following notations:

Transactions	Notations
___ *a.* Net income	OA = operating activities
___ *b.* Purchase of an operational asset	IA = investing activities
___ *c.* Depreciation expense	FA = financing activities
___ *d.* Collection on a long-term note receivable	S = schedule of noncash investing and financing activities
___ *e.* Issuance of a stock dividend	N = not reported on the SCF
___ *f.* Sale of a long-term investment for cash	
___ *g.* Borrowed cash on a long-term note payable	
___ *h.* Sale of an operational asset at a loss	
___ *i.* Purchase of a long-term investment with cash	
___ *j.* Exchange of common stock for an operational asset	
___ *k.* Exchange of land for equipment	
___ *l.* Sale of treasury stock	
___ *m.* Bad debts expense	
___ *n.* Payment of a cash dividend declared in a previous period	

E15–2   (Reporting Noncash Transactions on the SCF)

An analysis of West Corporation's operational asset accounts provided the following information:

a. West acquired a large machine that cost $22,000. West paid for the machine by giving a $10,000, 15% interest-bearing note due at the end of two years and 200 shares of its common stock, with a par value of $50 per share and a market value of $60 per share.

b. West acquired a small machine that cost $9,500. Full payment was made by transferring a tract of land that had a book value of $9,500.

Required:
Show how this information should be reported on the SCF.

E15–3   **(Calculating Cash Receipts from Customers)**
For each independent case listed in the following schedule, calculate cash receipts from customers.

	Case A	Case B	Case C
Sales revenue	$300,000	$100,000	$150,000
Beginning accounts receivable . . .	12,000	20,000	22,000
Ending accounts receivable	15,000	11,000	22,000
Cash receipts from customers . . .	_____	_____	_____

E15–4   **(Determining Cash Flows from the Sale of an Asset)**
During 19F, Alpha Company sold some excess equipment at a loss. The following information was collected from the company's accounting records:

From the income statement:	
Depreciation expense	$ 800
Loss on sale of equipment	2,000
From the balance sheet:	
Beginning equipment	10,000
Ending equipment	6,000
Beginning accumulated depreciation . . .	2,200
Ending accumulated depreciation	2,500

No new equipment was bought during 19F.

Required:
For the equipment that was sold, determine the original cost, the accumulated depreciation on the equipment, and the cash received from the sale.

E15–5   **(Calculating Cash Flows from Operating Activities, Direct Method)**
The following information pertains to Black Company:

Sales		$100,000
Expenses:		
Cost of goods sold	$60,000	
Depreciation expense	8,000	
Salaries expense	20,000	88,000
Net income		$ 12,000
Accounts receivable increase		$ 3,000
Merchandise inventory decrease		9,000
Salaries payable increase		900

Required:
Prepare the operating activities section of the SCF for Black Company using the direct method.

E15-6   **(Preparing the Operating Activities Section of the SCF, Direct Method)**
The following information pertains to White Company:

Sales		$100,000
Expenses:		
Cost of goods sold	$60,000	
Depreciation expense	8,000	
Salaries expense	20,000	88,000
Net income		$ 12,000
Accounts receivable decrease		$ 3,000
Merchandise inventory increase		9,000
Salaries payable decrease		900

Required:
Prepare the operating activities section of the SCF for White Company using the direct method.

E15-7   **(Calculating Cash Flows from Operating Activities under the Direct Method)**
The Coffey Company completed its income statement and balance sheet for 19D and provided the following information:

Service revenue		$ 60,000
Expenses:		
Salaries	$51,000	
Depreciation	11,000	
Amortization of copyrights	200	
Utilities	4,000	
Other expenses	3,800	70,000
Net loss		$(10,000)
Decrease in accounts receivable		$ 14,000
Bought a small service machine		6,000
Increase in salaries payable		8,000
Decrease in service revenue collected in advance . . .		5,000

Required:
Prepare the operating activities section of the SCF for Coffey Company using the direct method.

E15-8   **(Preparation of the SCF, Direct Method)**
Davis Company completed its income statement and comparative balance sheet at December 31, 19B, and has provided the following data:

Beginning cash balance . . . . $ 85,000
Sales revenue 200,000
Depreciation expense 5,000
Cost of goods sold 120,000
Other expenses 43,000
Sale of long-term investments (sold
   at book value for $6,000 cash) 6,000
Inventory increase during the period 4,000
Declared and paid cash dividends
   during the period 9,000
Borrowed on short-term note 20,000
Payment of long-term note 30,000
Acquired land for future use; issued
   capital stock in payment 25,000
Ending cash balance 105,000

Required:
Prepare a SCF for Davis Company using the direct method.

E15–9 (Preparation of the SCF, Direct Method)

Fisher Corporation completed its income statement and balance sheet on December 31, 19B, and provided the following information:

Beginning cash balance . . . . $ 16,000
Depreciation expense 9,000
Bought treasury stock 4,000
Sold a long-term investment at
   book value 6,000
Service revenue 100,000
Declared and paid cash dividends 7,000
Salaries expense 50,000
Net income 30,000
Salaries recorded but unpaid on
   December 31, 19A* 1,000
Service revenue recorded but un-
   collected on December 31, 19A* 3,000
Issued 200 shares of common stock 1,000
Purchased operational assets for cash . . . 30,000
Other operating expenses 11,000
Ending cash balance 23,000

   * Paid or collected in 19B.

Required:
Prepare the 19B SCF for Fisher Corporation using the direct method.

E15–10 (SCF, Direct Method; Complete Spreadsheet)

Analysis of accounts: (*a*) purchased an operational asset, $30,000, issued capital stock in full payment; (*b*) purchased a long-term investment for cash, $10,000; (*c*) paid cash dividend, $10,000; (*d*) sold operational asset for $5,000 cash (cost, $18,000, accumulated depreciation, $16,000); and (*e*) sold capital stock, 500 shares at $11 per share cash.

	Beginning Balances, 12/31/19A	Analysis of Changes		Ending Balances, 12/31/19B
		Debit	Credit	
Income statement items:				
Sales			120,000	
Cost of goods sold		48,000		
Depreciation		6,000		
Wage expense		22,000		
Income tax expense		10,000		
Interest expense		7,000		
Remaining expenses		2,300		
Gain on sale of operational asset			3,000	
Net income		27,700		
Balance sheet items:				
Cash	19,500			32,200
Accounts receivable	34,000			34,000
Merchandise inventory	78,000			85,000
Investments, long term				10,000
Operational assets	168,500			180,500
Total debits	300,000			341,700
Accumulated depreciation	44,000			34,000
Accounts payable	21,000			19,000
Wages payable	1,500			500
Income taxes payable	2,000			3,500
Bonds payable	104,000			104,000
Common stock, nopar	120,000			155,500
Retained earnings	7,500			25,200
Total credits	300,000			341,700

Statement of cash flows:

	Inflows	**Outflows**
Cash flows from operating activities:		
Cash flows from investing activities:		
Cash flows from financing activities:		
Net increase (decrease) in cash		
Totals		

Required:

Complete the spreadsheet for the SCF, direct method.

E15–11 **(SCF; Cash Flow Analysis of Cost of Goods Sold)**

The records of Jack Company showed cost of goods sold (on the income statement) of $40,000 and a change in the inventory and accounts payable balances. To demonstrate the effect of these changes on cash outflow for cost of goods sold (i.e., payments to suppliers), eight independent cases are used. Complete the following tabulation for each case:

Case	Cost of goods sold	Inventory increase (decrease)	Accounts payable increase (decrease)	Computations	Amount outflow*
A	$40,000	$ –0–	$ –0–	_____	_____
B	40,000	6,000	–0–	_____	_____
C	40,000	(6,000)	–0–	_____	_____
D	40,000	–0–	4,000	_____	_____
E	40,000	–0–	(4,000)	_____	_____
F	40,000	6,000	4,000	_____	_____
G	40,000	(6,000)	(4,000)	_____	_____
H	40,000	(6,000)	(6,000)	_____	_____

* This is the amount of cash paid during the current period for past and current purchases.

E15–12 **(Calculating Cash Payments to Suppliers)**

For each independent case listed in the following schedule, calculate cash payments to suppliers.

	Case A	Case B	Case C	Case D
Cost of goods sold	$20,000	$40,000	$30,000	$30,000
Beginning inventory	15,000	15,000	15,000	20,000
Ending inventory	10,000	15,000	20,000	20,000
Beginning accounts payable . . .	5,000	7,000	6,000	4,000
Ending accounts payable	4,000	8,000	6,000	4,000
Cash payments to suppliers . . .	_____	_____	_____	_____

Part B: Exercises 15–13 to 15–16

E15–13 **(Comparison of the Direct and Indirect Methods)**

To compare SCF reporting under the direct and indirect methods, enter check marks to indicate which items are used with each method.

Cash flows (and related changes)	SCF method	
	Direct	Indirect
1. Revenues from customers	_____	_____
2. Accounts receivable increase or decrease . . .	_____	_____
3. Payments to suppliers	_____	_____
4. Inventory increase or decrease	_____	_____
5. Accounts payable increase or decrease	_____	_____
6. Payments to employees	_____	_____
7. Wages payable, increase or decrease	_____	_____
8. Depreciation expense	_____	_____
9. Net income	_____	_____
10. Cash flows from operating activities	_____	_____
11. Cash flows from investing activities	_____	_____
12. Cash flows from financing activities	_____	_____
13. Net increase or decrease in cash during the period	_____	_____

E15-14   (SCF, Indirect Method; Prepare the Reconciliation for Operating Activities)

The data given below were provided by the accounting records of Ronald Company. Prepare the reconciliation of net income with cash flow from operating activities for inclusion in the SCF, indirect method.

> Net income (accural basis), $60,000.
> Depreciation expense, $7,800.
> Decrease in wages payable, $1,200.
> Decrease in accounts receivable, $1,800.
> Increase in inventory, $2,500.
> Increase in long-term liabilities, $10,000.
> Sale of capital stock for cash, $25,000.
> Accounts payable increase, $4,000.
> Dividend paid, $10,000.

E15-15   (Comparison of Direct and Indirect Methods)

The following information pertains to the Vista Corporation:

Sales		$100,000
Expenses:		
Cost of goods sold	$60,000	
Depreciation expense	8,000	
Salary expense	20,000	88,000
Net income		$ 12,000
Accounts receivable decrease		$ 3,000
Merchandise inventory increase		9,000
Accounts payable increase		500
Salaries payable decrease		900

Required:

a. Prepare the cash flows from operating activities section of the SCF for Vista Corporation using the direct method.

b. Prepare the cash flows from operating activities section of the SCF for Vista Corporation using the indirect method.

E15–16   **(SCF, Indirect Method; Complete Spreadsheet)**

The data used in this exercise are given in Exercise 15–10.

Required:

Complete the SCF, indirect method, spreadsheet given below.

Item	Beginning Balances, 12/31/19A	Analysis of Changes		Ending Balances, 12/31/19B
		Debit	Credit	
Cash plus short-term investments	19,500			32,200
Accounts receivable	34,000			34,000
Merchandise inventory	78,000			85,000
Investments, long term				10,000
Operational assets	168,500			180,500
Totals	300,000			341,700
Accumulated depreciation	44,000			34,000
Accounts payable	21,000			19,000
Wages payable	1,500			500
Income taxes payable	2,000			3,500
Bonds payable	104,000			104,000
Common stock, nopar	120,000			155,500
Retained earnings	7,500			25,200
Totals	300,000			341,700

Statement of cash flows:

Conversion of net income to cash flows from operating activities:

Cash flows from investing activities:

Cash flows from financing activities:

Net increase (decrease) in cash
    Totals

PROBLEMS

Part A: Problems 15–1 to 15–9

P15–1   **(Calculate Cash Flows: Prepare Schedule to Reconcile Net Income with Cash Flows)**

The income statement of Josey Corporation is given below.

JOSEY CORPORATON
Income Statement
For the Year Ended December 31, 19C
Accrual Basis

			Cash flow
Sales revenue (one third on credit; accounts receivable year's end 19A, $11,000; 19B, $15,000)		$300,000	$ _____
Cost of goods sold (one fourth on credit; accounts payable year's end 19A, $9,000; 19B, $8,000; inventory at year's end—19A, $50,000; 19B, $45,000)		180,000	_____
Expenses:			
Salaries and wages (including accrued wages payable at year's end—19A, $500; 19B, $300)	$44,000		_____
Depreciation expense	8,300		_____
Rent expense (no accruals)	6,000		_____
Remaining expenses (no accruals)	11,700		_____
Income tax expense (income taxes payable at year's end— 19A, $2,000; 19B, $3,000)	10,000		_____
Total expenses		80,000	_____
Net income		$ 40,000	
Cash flow from operating activities			$ _____

Required:

a. Provide the cash flow amounts in the blanks given to the right.

b. Prepare a schedule to reconcile net income to net cash provided by operating activities.

P15–2   (Prepare SCF Spreadsheet and SCF Using Direct Method)

Lakeland Company is developing its annual financial statements at December 31, 19B. The income statement and balance sheet are finished, and the SCF is being developed. The income statement and comparative balance sheet are summarized below.

	19A	19B
Balance sheet at December 31:		
Cash	$12,800	$10,800
Accounts receivable	9,000	10,500
Merchandise inventory	6,600	5,000
Operational assets (net)	40,000	43,000
Patent	3,000	2,700
Total assets	$71,400	$72,000
Accounts payable	$11,000	$ 9,000
Income taxes payable	400	500
Note payable, long term	10,000	5,000
Common stock (nopar)	42,000	45,000
Retained earnings	8,000	12,500
Total liabilities and stockholders' equity	$71,400	$72,000
Income statement for 19B:		
Sales revenue		$60,000
Cost of goods sold		35,000
Gross margin		25,000
Expenses (including depreciation, $4,000; patent amortization, $300; income tax expense, $3,000; and other expenses, $10,700)		18,000
Net income		$ 7,000

Additional Data for 19B:

Purchased operational assets for cash, $7,000.
Paid $5,000 on long-term note payable.
Sold and issued common stock for $3,000 cash.
Declared and paid a $2,500 cash dividend on capital stock during 19B.

Required:

a. Prepare a SCF spreadsheet using the direct method to report cash flows from operating activities.

b. Prepare the SCF.

c. Prepare a schedule of noncash investing and financing activities if necessary.

P15-3 **(Prepare SCF Spreadsheet and SCF Using Direct Method)**

Mason Company is developing the annual financial statements at December 31, 19B. The statements are complete except for the SCF. The completed comparative balance sheets and income statement are summarized below:

	19A	19B
Balance sheet at December 31:		
Cash	$ 20,000	$ 31,500
Accounts receivable	26,000	25,000
Merchandise inventory	40,000	38,000
Operational assets (net)	64,000	67,000
	$150,000	$161,500
Accounts payable	$ 24,000	$ 27,000
Wages payable	500	400
Note payable, long term	35,000	30,000
Common stock, nopar	70,000	80,000
Retained earnings	20,500	24,100
	$150,000	$161,500
Income statement for 19B:		
Sales		$ 90,000
Cost of goods sold		(52,000)
Expenses		(32,000)
Net income		$ 6,000

Additional Data:

Bought operational assets for cash, $7,000.
Paid $5,000 on the long-term note payable.
Sold unissued common stock for $10,000 cash.
Declared and paid a $2,400 cash dividend.
Expenses included depreciation, $4,000; wages, $20,000; taxes, $2,000; other, $6,000.

Required:

a. Prepare a SCF spreadsheet using the direct method to report cash flows from operating activities.

b. Prepare the SCF.

c. Prepare a schedule of noncash investing and financing activities if necessary.

P15-4 **(Prepare SCF Spreadsheet and SCF Using Direct Method; Includes Noncash Investing and Financing Activity and the Sale of an Asset at Book Value)**
Hamilton Company is developing the 19B annual report. The following information is provided:

	19A	19B
Cash	$24,000	$32,200
Accounts receivable	26,000	30,000
Inventory	30,000	28,000
Prepaid insurance	1,200	800
Investments, long term	10,800	8,000
Operational assets (net)	30,000	39,000
Patent	3,000	2,700
Accounts payable	21,000	18,000
Wages payable	3,000	2,000
Income taxes payable	1,000	1,200
Note payable, long term	25,000	20,000
Common stock ($10 par)	60,000	70,000
Contributed capital in excess of par	1,000	3,000
Retained earnings	14,000	26,500

Other Information:

Sold long-term investment at book value, $2,800.
Purchased operational assets by issuing 1,000 shares of common stock, market value of common stock, $12 per share.
Revenues, $120,000.
Expenses: depreciation, $3,000; patent amortization, $300; insurance $2,000; wages, $45,000; income taxes, $8,000; and cost of goods sold, $41,700.

Required:

a. Prepare a SCF spreadsheet using the direct method to report cash flows from operating activities.

b. Prepare the SCF.

c. Prepare a schedule of noncash investing and financing activities.

P15-5 **(Prepare SCF Using Direct Method; Includes a Noncash Investing and Financing Activity, and Gain on Disposal of a Machine)**
Texmo Company has prepared its 19B financial statements, which include the following information:

	Comparative	
	19A	**19B**
Balance sheet:		
Cash	$ 40,000	$ 52,000
Inventory	30,000	37,000
Accounts receivable	20,000	17,000
Long-term investment, stock Co. A	10,000	3,000
Machinery and equipment (net)	80,000	75,000
	$180,000	$184,000
Accounts payable	15,000	11,000
Income taxes payable	4,000	6,000
Note payable, long term	20,000	10,000
Bonds payable	30,000	10,000
Common stock (par $10)	100,000	110,000
Contributed capital in excess of par	8,000	11,000
Retained earnings	3,000	26,000
	$180,000	$184,000
Income statement:		
Revenue		$140,000
Cost of goods sold		(65,000)
Depreciation expense		(8,000)
Remaining operating expenses		(29,000)
Income tax expense		(9,000)
Gain on disposal of machine (net of tax) . . .		1,000
Net income		$ 30,000

Additional Data for 19B:

1. Machinery that had a book value of $10,000 was sold for $11,000 cash.

2. Long-term investment (shares of Company A stock) was sold for $7,000 cash; carrying value was $7,000.

3. Equipment was acquired, and payment in full was made by issuing 1,000 shares of capital stock that had a market value of $13 per share.

4. Payments on debt; long-term note, $10,000; bonds payable, $20,000.

5. Declared and paid a cash dividend, $7,000.

Required:

a. Prepare a SCF spreadsheet using the direct method to report cash flows from operating activities.

b. Prepare a SCF.

c. Prepare a schedule of noncash investing and financing activities.

P15–6   **(Prepare SCF Spreadsheet, Using Direct Method; Includes a Noncash Investing and Financing Activity)**

All-Steel Company is preparing the annual financial statements, including a SCF at December 31, 19B. The 19B comparative balance sheet and the income statement and some additional data are summarized below:

	19A	19B
Balance sheet at December 31:		
Cash	$ 15,000	$ 21,500
Accounts receivable	20,000	23,000
Merchandise inventory	22,000	27,000
Prepaid insurance	600	300
Investments, long term (S Corp. stock)		12,000
Operational assets (net)	134,000	220,000
Patent (net)		16,000
Total assets	$191,600	$319,800
Accounts payable	$ 12,000	$ 18,000
Note payable, short term (nontrade)	18,000	10,000
Wages payable	1,000	800
Income taxes payable	600	1,000
Note payable, long term	30,000	10,000
Bonds payable		100,000
Common stock (par $10)	100,000	140,000
Contributed capital in excess of par	5,000	6,000
Retained earnings	25,000	34,000
Total liabilities and stockholders' equity	$191,600	$319,800

Income statement for 19B:	
Sales revenue	$200,000
Cost of goods sold	(126,000)
Expenses (not detailed)	(39,000)
Depreciation expense	(14,000)
Amortization of patent	(1,000)
Income tax expense	(7,000)
Net income	$ 13,000

Additional Data for 19B:

1. Bought patent on January 1, 19B, for $17,000 cash.
2. Bought stock of S Corporation as a long-term investment for $12,000 cash.
3. Paid $20,000 on the long-term note payable.
4. Sold and issued 4,000 shares of common stock for $41,000 cash.
5. Declared and paid a $4,000 cash dividend.
6. Acquired a building (an operational asset) and paid for it by issuing $100,000 bonds payable at par to the former owner—date of transaction was December 30, 19B.

Required:

a. Prepare a SCF spreadsheet using the direct method to report cash flows from operating expenses.
b. Prepare the SCF.
c. Prepare a schedule of noncash investing and financing activities.

P15-7   (Prepare SCF Using Direct Method; Includes Gain on Sale of Equipment)

The income statement, comparative balance sheet, and additional information for Swithin Corporation for 19B appear below.

Income Statement
(in thousands)

Revenues:		
Sales	$1,300	
Gain on sale of equipment	25	$1,325
Expenses:		
Cost of goods sold	600	
Advertising expense	70	
Depreciation expense	90	
Rent expense	60	
Wages expense	127	
Income tax expense	81	
Interest expense on bonds	13	1,041
		$ 284

Comparative Balance Sheet
(in thousands)

	19A	19B
Cash	$ 80	$210
Accounts receivable	28	78
Merchandise inventory	58	258
Prepaid rent	4	14
Equipment	174	244
Accumulated depreciation	(12)	(72)
Totals	$332	$732
Income taxes payable	$ 55	$ 76
Accounts payable	20	120
Wages payable	10	15
Bonds payable	100	100
Common stock	125	125
Retained earnings	22	296
Totals	$332	$732

Other Data:

1. Equipment with an original cost of $50 and accumulated depreciation of $30 was sold for $45.

2. Additional equipment was purchased for cash.

3. No additional bonds were issued or retired during the year.

4. Cash dividends were declared and paid during the year.

Required:

a. Prepare a SCF spreadsheet using the direct method to report cash flows from operating activities.

b. Prepare the SCF.

P15-8 **(Prepare SCF Using Direct Method; Includes a Noncash Investing and Financing Activity, Sale of Equipment at a Loss, and a Net Loss)**

The income statement, comparative balance sheet, and additional information for Wilson Corporation for 19D appear below.

Income Statement
(in thousands)

Revenues:		
Sales		$1,000
Expenses:		
Cost of goods sold	$400	
Depreciation expense	30	
Rent expense	300	
Wage expense	200	
Other operating expenses	100	
Interest expense	9	
Loss of sale of equipment	5	1,044
Net loss		$ (44)

Comparative Balance Sheet
(in thousands)

	19C	19D
Cash	$ 80	$ 16
Accounts receivable	115	95
Merchandise inventory	30	120
Prepaid rent	2	80
Equipment	200	280
Accumulated depreciation	(40)	(62)
Total assets	$387	$529
Accounts payable	$ 10	$ 3
Wages payable	20	8
Notes payable	0	0
Interest payable	0	5
Bonds payable	0	100
Common stock, nopar value	80	180
Retained earnings	277	233
Totals	$387	$529

Other Data:

1. Equipment was purchased during the year by issuing $100 of common stock.
2. Equipment with an original cost of $20 and accumulated depreciation of $8 was sold for $7.
3. Bonds were issued at face value during the year. Interest of $5 was accrued at year-end.
4. $50 was borrowed on a short-term note payable. The note and $4 of interest was repaid.

Required:

a. Prepare a SCF spreadsheet using the direct method to report cash flows from operating activities.
b. Prepare the SCF.
c. Prepare a schedule of noncash investing and financing activities.

P15-9 **(Prepare SCF Using Direct Method; Includes a Noncash Investing and Financing Activity, the Sale of an Asset at a Gain, and a Net Loss)**

The income statement, comparative balance sheet, and additional information for Patrick Corporation appear below.

Income Statement
(in thousands)

Revenues:		
Sales	$800	
Gain on sale of equipment	25	$825
Expenses:		
Cost of goods sold	$600	
Salaries expense	40	
Rent expense	60	
Office supplies expense	30	
Patent amortization expense . . .	10	
Depreciation expense	80	
Interest expense on bonds	97	917
Net loss		$(92)

Comparative Balance Sheet
(in thousands)

	19B	19C
Cash	$ 205	$ 460
Accounts receivable	40	170
Merchandise inventory	400	100
Office supplies	5	7
Long-term investments	50	70
Operational assets	1,800	3,200
Accumulated depreciation	(600)	(660)
Patent	200	190
Totals	$2,100	$3,537
Accounts payable	$ 95	$ 76
Rent payable	5	16
Bonds payable	0	1,037
Common stock ($1 par)	400	500
Contributed capital	900	1,400
Retained earnings	700	608
Treasury stock	-0-	(100)
Totals	$2,100	$3,537

Other Information:

1. Equipment with an original cost of $100 and accumulated depreciation of $20 was sold for $105. Equipment costing $900 was purchased for cash.

2. Land and building valued at $600 were acquired by issuing 100 shares of common stock.

3. Bonds payable were issued during the year.

4. Long-term investments were purchased during the year.

5. Treasury stock was purchased during the year.

Required:

a. Prepare a SCF spreadsheet using the direct method to report cash flows from operating activities.

b. Prepare the SCF.

c. Prepare a schedule of noncash investing and financing activities.

Part B: Problems 15–10 to 15–16

P15–10 **(Prepare SCF, Indirect Method; Use Schedule Approach to Prepare the Statement)**
Jackson Company was organized on January 1, 19A. During the year ended December 31, 19A, the company provided the following data:

Income statement:

Sales revenue	$75,000
Cost of goods sold	(30,000)
Depreciation expense	(2,000)
Remaining expenses	(27,000)
Net income	$16,000

Balance sheet:

Cash	$38,000
Accounts receivable	20,000
Merchandise inventory	10,000
Machinery (net)	23,000
Total assets	$91,000
Accounts payable	$10,000
Accrued expenses payable	17,000
Dividends payable	4,000
Note payable, short term	10,000
Common stock	40,000
Retained earnings	10,000
Total liabilities and stockholders' equity	$91,000

Analysis of Selected Accounts and Transactions:

1. Sold 2,000 shares of common stock, par $10, at $20 per share; collected cash.

2. Borrowed $10,000 on a one-year, 9% interest-bearing note; the note was dated June 1, 19A.

3. During 19A, purchased machinery; paid $25,000.

4. Purchased merchandise for resale at a cost of $40,000 (debited Inventory because the perpetual system is used); paid $30,000 cash, balance credited to Accounts Payable.

5. At December 31, 19A, declared a cash dividend of $6,000; paid $2,000 in December 19A; the balance will be paid March 1, 19B.

Required:
Prepare a SCF, indirect method, using the schedule approach.

P15–11   **(Prepare SCF Spreadsheet, SCF, and Schedules Using Indirect Method; Includes a Noncash Investing and Financing Activity, and a Sale of an Asset at a Loss)**
Riverside Company is preparing its 19B financial statements. The following information is given by the completed 19B comparative balance sheet and income statement:

	19A	19B
Balance sheet:		
Cash	$ 10,000	$ 2,000
Accounts receivable	16,600	21,000
Inventory	17,000	25,000
Prepaid expense	1,400	400
Operational assets (net)	59,000	68,000
Plant site		20,000
Long-term investment	16,000	7,000
Total assets	$120,000	$143,400
Accounts payable	$ 8,000	$ 12,000
Wages payable	1,000	1,500
Short-term note payable (interest,		
December 31)	6,000	3,000
Long-term note payable (interest,		
December 31)	10,000	4,000
Bonds payable (interest,		
December 31)	30,000	50,000
Common stock (par $10)	60,000	60,500
Contributed capital in excess of par	3,000	3,400
Retained earnings	2,000	9,000
Total liabilities and stockholders'		
equity	$120,000	$143,400
Income statement:		
Revenues		$135,000
Depreciation expense		(15,000)
Remaining expenses		(95,000)
Loss of sale of long-term investment . . .		(3,000)
Net income		$ 22,000

Additional Data:

1. Purchased operational asset for cash, $24,000.
2. Sold long-term investment for $6,000 cash; carrying value, $9,000.
3. Sold 50 shares of common stock at $18 cash per share.
4. Declared and paid a cash dividend of $15,000.
5. Payment on short-term note, $3,000.
6. Payment on a long-term note, $6,000.
7. Acquired plant site and issued bonds, $20,000 for full purchase price (the bonds were selling at par).

Required:

a. Prepare a SCF spreadsheet using the indirect method to report cash flows from operating activities.
b. Prepare a SCF.
c. Prepare a schedule of noncash investing and financing activities.

P15–12   **(Comparison of Cash Flows from Operating Activities Using Direct and Indirect Methods)**

The accountants for Alpha Company just completed the income statement and balance sheet for the year and have provided the following information:

Income Statement
(in thousands)

Sales revenue		$15,000
Expenses:		
Cost of goods sold	$8,000	
Depreciation expense	1,000	
Salaries expense	3,000	
Rent expense	1,500	
Insurance expense	500	
Utilities expense	400	
Interest expense on bonds	780	
Loss of sale of investments	100	15,280
Net loss		$ (280)

Selected Balance Sheet Accounts
(in thousands)

	19B	19C
Merchandise inventory	$ 70	$ 95
Accounts receivable	500	400
Accounts payable	260	310
Salaries payable	30	48
Rent payable	5	3
Prepaid rent	10	6
Prepaid insurance	7	12

Other Data:

The company issued $10,000, 8% bonds payable during the year. Investments costing $140,000 were sold for $40,000 during the year.

Required:

a. Prepare the cash flows from operating activities section of the SCF using the direct method.

b. Prepare the cash flows from operating activities section of the SCF using the indirect method.

P15–13   **(Prepare SCF Spreadsheet, SCF, and Schedules Using Indirect Method)**

Required (use the information from Problem 15-3):

a. Prepare a SCF spreadsheet using the indirect method to report cash flows from operating activities.

b. Prepare the SCF.

c. Prepare a schedule of noncash investing and financing activities.

P15–14   **(Prepare SCF Spreadsheet and SCF Using Indirect Method; Includes Noncash Investing and Financing Activity and Sale of an Asset at Book Value)**

Required (use information from Problem 15–4):
a. Prepare a SCF spreadsheet using the indirect method to report cash flows from operating activities.
b. Prepare the SCF.
c. Prepare a schedule of noncash investing and financing activities.

P15–15   **(Prepare SCF Using Indirect Method; Includes a Noncash Investing and Financing Activity, and Gain on Disposal of a Machine)**

Required (use information from Problem 15–5):
a. Prepare a SCF spreadsheet using the indirect method to report cash flows from operating activities.
b. Prepare the SCF.
c. Prepare a schedule of noncash investing and financing activities.

P15–16   **(Prepare SCF Spreadsheet, Using Indirect Method; Includes a Noncash Investing and Financing Activity)**

Required (use information from Problem 15–6):
a. Prepare a SCF spreadsheet using the indirect method to report cash flows from operating activities.
b. Prepare the SCF.
c. Prepare a schedule of noncash investing and financing activities.

CASES

C15–1   **(Critique and Recast a Deficient SCF)**
The following statement was taken from the annual financial statements of Lazy Corporation:

LAZY CORPORATION
Funds Statement
December 31, 19B

Funds generated:

Sales and service revenue	$85,000	
Depreciation	6,000	
Accounts receivable decrease	700	
Merchandise inventory decrease	3,000	
Borrowing (short-term note)	20,000	
Sale of unissued stock	15,000	
Total cash		$129,700

Funds applied:

Cost of sales	$48,000	
Expenses (including depreciation and income tax)	20,000	
Accounts payable decrease	1,000	
Income taxes payable decrease	300	
Payment on long-term mortgage	25,000	
Acquisition of operational asset	9,000	
Dividends (cash) declared and paid during 19B	7,000	
Total		110,300
Increase in funds		$ 19,400

Required:

a. Did Lazy give enough attention to the communication of financial information to stockholders?

b. What was the amount of net income (or loss) reported for 19B?

c. Recast the above statement in good form (and preferred terminology) using the direct method.

d. Did operations generate more or less cash than net income? What caused the difference?

e. Prepare a schedule reconciling net income to net cash provided by operating actvities.

C15–2   (Critique and Recast a Deficient SCF)

The following statement was prepared by Old Corporation:

OLD CORPORATION
Funds Statement
December 31, 19X

Where got:

Revenues	$180,000	
Accounts receivable decrease	15,000	
Expenses (including depreciation and income tax) . . .	(160,000)	
Depreciation	14,000	
Inventory increase	(6,000)	
Accounts payable increase	7,000	
Income taxes payable decrease	(3,000)	
Total		$ 47,000
Sale of permanent assets (at book value)		17,000
Issuance of common stock for land		25,000
Borrowing—short-term note		40,000
Total cash received		$129,000

Where gone:

Dividends	20,000	
Payment on long-term mortgage	80,000	
Machinery	15,000	
Land (5,000 shares of stock)	25,000	
Funds (decrease)	(11,000)	
Total		$129,000

Required:

a. What was the amount of net income for 19X?

b. Did cash increase or decrease? Explain. How can this amount be verified independent of the SCF?

c. Did the company give enough attention to communication of financial information to the stockholders? Explain the basis for your response.

d. Recast the above statement using preferred format and terminology.

e. What was the amount of the difference between net income and cash from operating activities? Why were they different?

f. Do you suspect any potential problems for this company? Explain the basis for your response.

C15–3   (Analysis of an Actual Statement of Cash Flows)

Refer to the financial statements of J.C. Penney Company, Inc. given in the appendix immediately preceding the index.

JCPenney

1. Which of the two basic reporting approaches for the SCF was adopted by the company?

2. Can the accuracy of "Increase (decrease) in cash and short term investments" be useful?

3. Did the company have any noncash financing or investing activities?

4. The SCF shows a $337 million change in cash from customer receivables. Show how this amount was calculated. (Hint: This is a difficult calculation that involves bad debt expense, called "Provision for Doubtful Accounts" in this statement, and "Bad Debts Written Off." (See Chapter Supplement 15–A.)

SIXTEEN

USING AND INTERPRETING FINANCIAL STATEMENTS

PURPOSE

Throughout the preceding chapters, we emphasized the conceptual basis of accounting. An understanding of the rationale underlying accounting is important for both preparers and users of financial statements. In this chapter, we introduce the use and analysis of financial statements. Many widely used analytical techniques are discussed and illustrated. As you study this chapter, you will see that an understanding of accounting rules and concepts is essential for effective analysis of financial statements.

Accounting ratios are used by analysts to evaluate a company's performance. Many financial statements include some key ratios, as shown on the opposite page.

LEARNING OBJECTIVES

1. Identify the major users of financial statements and explain how they use statements.

2. Explain the objectives of ratio analysis.

3. Identify and compute 13 widely used accounting ratios.

4. Interpret accounting ratios.

5. Describe how accounting alternatives affect ratio analysis.

6. Expand your accounting vocabulary by learning the "Important Terms Defined in This Chapter."

7. Apply the knowledge learned from this chapter by completing the homework assigned by your instructor.

ORGANIZATION

1. Financial reports in the decision-making process.

2. Analysis of financial statements.

3. Commonly used ratios.

4. Interpreting ratios.

5. Impact of accounting alternatives on ratio analysis.

QUAKER

Return on Equity from Continuing Operations

Fiscal Years	1983	1984	1985	1986	1987	1988
Asset Turnover	1.71	1.96	1.83	1.78	1.67	1.71
Net Sales						
Average Assets Employed						
Return on Net Sales	×4.35%	×4.03%	×4.37%	×4.76%	×4.20%	×4.80%
Income from Continuing Operations						
Net Sales						
Return on Assets	=7.44%	=7.90%	=8.00%	=8.47%	=7.01%	=8.22%
Income from Continuing Operations						
Average Assets Employed						
Leverage Factor	×2.31	×2.41	×2.42	×2.40	×2.76	×2.66
Average Assets Employed						
Average Common Shareholders' Equity						
Return on Equity	=17.2%	=19.0%	=19.4%	=20.3%	=19.4%	=21.9%
Income from Continuing Operations						
Average Common Shareholders' Equity						

Financial Reports in the Decision-Making Process

The objective of financial statements is to provide information that helps users make better economic decisions. There are two broad groups of decision makers who use financial statements. One group is the management of the business who rely on accounting data to make important management decisions. The second group is "external" decision makers. This group consists primarily of investors (both present and potential owners), investment analysts, creditors, government, labor organizations, and the public. Financial statements serve a diverse group of decision makers with different information needs.

Users of financial statements are interested in three types of information:

1. **Information about past performance.**   Information concerning such items as income, sales volume, cash flows, and return earned on the investment helps assess the success of the business and the effectiveness of the management. Such information also helps the decision maker compare one entity with others.

2. **Information about the present condition of a business.**   This type of information helps answer such questions as: What types of assets are owned? How much debt does the business owe, and when is it due? What is the cash position? What are the EPS, return-on-investment, and debt/equity ratios? What is the inventory position? Answers to these and similar economic questions help the decision maker assess the successes and failures of the past; but, more importantly, they provide useful information in assessing the cash flow and profit potentials of the business.

3. **Information about the future performance of the business.**   Decision makers select from among several alternative courses of action. Each course of action will cause different results. All decisions are future oriented because they do not (and cannot) affect the past. However, in predicting the probable future impact of a decision, reliable measurements of what has happened in the recent past are valuable. For example, the recent sales and earnings trends of a business are good indicators of what might be expected in the future. The primary objective of measuring past performance and the present condition of a business is to aid in predicting the future cash flows of the business.

Some decisions are made intuitively and without much supporting data. Intuitive decision making is used for several reasons. The time and cost of collecting data may prevent a careful analysis. Sometimes the decision maker is unsophisticated and may not understand more systematic approaches to decision making. Unsophisticated decision makers tend to oversimplify the decision-making process, disregard basic information, and often overlook the financial effects of a decision.

In contrast, sophisticated decision makers prepare a systematic analysis of feasible alternatives. Information regarding each alternative is collected and evaluated. For most business decisions, the financial statements provide critical data for effective decision makers.

Financial statement users should understand what was measured and how it was measured. Even if you do not plan to major in accounting, you will use extensively the information that you have studied in this book to evaluate the data presented in the financial reports of a business. One of the objectives of the preceding chapters was to help you understand and evaluate financial statements as a decision maker.

Financial statements are general-purpose statements that are designed primarily to meet the special needs of external decision makers. Because of the varied needs of these users, supplementary financial data may be needed for many decisions.

Investors

The investor group includes current owners, potential owners, and investment analysts (because they advise investors). Investors include individuals, mutual funds, other businesses, and institutions, such as your college or university.

Most investors do not seek a controlling interest when they buy stock. Instead, they invest with the expectation of earning a return on their investment. The return on a stock investment has two components: (1) dividend revenue during the investment period and (2) increases in the market value of the shares owned. When considering a stock investment, the investor must consider the future **income** and **growth** potential of the business. Investors are interested in enterprise income because it is the "source" of future dividends. They are interested in enterprise growth because it tends to cause the market value of the shares to increase. In making these predictions, the investor should consider three factors:

1. **Economy-wide factors.** Often the overall health of the economy will have a direct impact on the performance of an individual business. Investors should consider such data as the gross national product, productivity, unemployment rate, general inflation rate, and changes in interest rates.

2. **Industry factors.** Certain events have a major impact on each company within an industry but have only a minor impact on other companies. For example, a major drought may be devastating for food-related industries but have no effect on the electronics industry.

3. **Individual company factors.** These factors may be either quantifiable or nonquantifiable. Nonquantifiable factors include the introduction of a new product, a lawsuit, and changes in key personnel. Information concerning nonquantifiable factors often is presented in notes to the financial statements. Data pertaining to quantifiable factors are presented in the basic financial statements. The income statement provides direct information, such as revenue from products and services,

Exhibit 16–1   Illustration of comparative financial statements

PACKARD COMPANY
Comparative Income Statements (simplified for illustration)
For the Years Ended December 31, 19B, and 19A

	Year ended Dec. 31		Increase (decrease) 19B over 19A	
	19B	**19A***	**Amount**	**Percent**
Sales revenue	$120,000	$100,000	$20,000	20.0
Cost of goods sold	72,600	60,000	12,600	21.0
Gross margin on sales	47,400	40,000	7,400	18.5
Operating expenses:				
Selling expenses	22,630	15,000	7,630	50.9
Administrative expenses	11,870	13,300	(1,430)	(10.8)
Interest expense	1,500	1,700	(200)	(11.8)
Total expenses	36,000	30,000	6,000	20.0
Pretax income	11,400	10,000	1,400	14.0
Income taxes	2,600	2,000	600	30.0
Net income	$ 8,800	$ 8,000	$ 800	10.0

* Base year for computing percents.

extraordinary items, income tax impacts, net income, and earnings per share. Other relationships, such as gross margin, profit margin, and expense relationships, can be computed. Also, the balance sheet, the statement of cash flows, and the notes to the financial statements provide measurements of past profit performance and current financial position. These data constitute an important base from which predictions of future income and growth can be made. These data are particularly useful when compared with recent past periods as shown in Exhibit 16–1.

Creditors

Suppliers, financial institutions, and individuals provide long-term and short-term credit to businesses. Creditors lend money with the expectation that they will earn a return on their money and that funds will be repaid in accordance with the loan agreement. Creditors are concerned about the following:

1. Profit potential of the business because a profitable entity is more likely to meet its credit obligations.
2. Ability of the business to generate cash from operations because it will be able to pay its debts.

3. Financial position of the business because the assets are security for the debts and the debts indicate the future demand for cash at debt maturity date.

To enhance the credibility of financial reports, creditors often require that the reports be audited by an independent CPA.

Analysis of Financial Statements

Financial statements include a large volume of quantitative data supplemented by disclosure notes. The notes are an integral part of the financial statements and help users interpret the statements. Notes elaborate on accounting policies, major financial effects and events, and certain nonquantifiable events that may contribute to the success or failure of the firm. The notes often include supplemental schedules, such as listings of assets by geographic region or lines of business. The statements also include a letter from the chief executive officer that contains a management discussion and analysis of the operations of the company.

Three techniques are used to help decision makers understand and interpret the external financial statements: (1) comparative financial statements, (2) long-term summaries, and (3) ratio and percentage analyses.

Comparative Financial Statements

Accounting rules require the presentation of **comparative financial statements** covering, as a minimum, the current year and the immediately prior year.

Most financial statements present, side by side, the results for the current and the preceding year (similar to the statements shown in Exhibit 16–1). Analysis of comparative statements is made easier if two additional columns are added for (1) the **amount** of change for each item and (2) the **percent** of change. These data are shown in Exhibit 16–1. Often the percent of change from the prior period is more helpful for interpretive purposes than the absolute dollar amount of change. Notice on each line that the percents are determined by dividing the amount of the change by the amount for the preceding year. For example, in Exhibit 16–1, the percentage on the Sales revenue line was computed as $20,000 \div \$100,000 = 20\%$. The amount from the earlier year is used as the base amount.

Long-Term Summaries

In the interest of full disclosure, annual reports often give 5- to 10-year summaries of certain basic data, such as sales revenue, net income, total assets, total liabilities, total owners' equity, and selected ratios. Data for a series of years are important in interpreting the financial statements for the current period. Misinterpretation is possible when the analyst limits consideration to only the last one or two periods. The vagaries of business transactions, economic events, and accounting techniques are such that the financial reports for a single time period usually do not provide a sound basis for assessing the long-term potential of a business. Sophisticated financial analysts use data for a number of periods so that trends may be identified.

Care should be used in interpreting long-term summaries. Data for a period in the distant past may not be comparable because of changes in the company, industry, and environment. For example, Texaco is a different company now than it was when a gallon of gasoline sold for 25 cents.

In interpreting comparative data, the items showing significant increases and decreases should receive special attention. Analysts should identify significant **turning points** in trends for important items such as net income and cash flow. The turning points often provide indication of significant future trends. Analysts should determine the **underlying causes** for significant favorable or unfavorable changes.

Ratio and Percentage Analyses

Some amounts on financial statements, such as net income, are significant in and of themselves. Other data are more significant when expressed as a relationship to other amounts. Significant relationships can be examined through the use of an analytical tool called **ratio** or **percentage analysis.** A ratio or percent expresses the proportionate relationship between two different amounts. A ratio or percent is computed by dividing one quantity by another quantity. For example, the fact that a company earned net income of $500,000 assumes greater significance when net income is compared with the stockholders' investment in the company. Assuming that stockholders' equity is $5,000,000, the relationship of earnings to stockholder investment is $500,000 ÷ $5,000,000 = 10%. This ratio indicates a different level of performance than would be the case if stockholders' equity was $50,000,000. Ratio analysis helps decision makers to identify significant relationships and to compare companies more realistically than if only single amounts were analyzed.

There are two kinds of ratio analysis: (1) relationships **within one period** and (2) relationships **between periods.** Also, ratios may be computed with amounts within one statement, such as the income statement, or between different statements, such as the income statement and the balance sheet. In Exhibit 16–1, the percents of change represent a percentage analysis between periods within a single statement.

Financial statement analysis is a judgmental process. No single ratio can be identified as appropriate to all situations. Each analytical situation may require the calculation of several ratios. However, there are several ratios that are appropriate to many situations.

Component Percentages

Component percentages are used to express each item on a particular statement as a percentage of a single **base amount** (i.e., the denominator of the ratio). Exhibit 16–2 shows a component analysis for the 19A and 19B income statements and balance sheets for Packard Company. To compute component percentages for the income statement, the base amount is **net sales revenue.** Each expense is expressed as a percent of net sales revenue. On the balance sheet, the base amount is **total assets.** The percents are derived by dividing each balance sheet account by total assets.

Component percentages are useful because they reveal important proportional relationships. For example, on the income statement in Exhibit 16–2, observe that selling expenses were 18.9% of sales revenue in 19B, compared with 15% in 19A. On the balance sheet, notice that merchandise inventory was 36.8% of total assets for 19B, compared with 40% for 19A. These changes in important relationships often suggest the need for further inquiry because they may suggest opportunities for corrective action and increased profitability.

Exhibit 16–2 Illustration of component percentages

PACKARD COMPANY
Income Statements (simplified for illustration)
For the Years Ended December 31, 19B, and 19A

	For the year ended			
	Dec. 31, 19B		Dec. 31, 19A	
	Amount	Percent	Amount	Percent
Sales revenue (net)*	$120,000	100.0	$100,000	100.0
Cost of goods sold	72,600	60.5	60,000	60.0
Gross margin on sales	47,400	39.5	40,000	40.0
Operating expenses:				
Selling expenses	22,630	18.9	15,000	15.0
Administrative expenses	11,870	9.9	13,300	13.3
Interest expense	1,500	1.2	1,700	1.7
Total expenses	36,000	30.0	30,000	30.0
Pretax income	11,400	9.5	10,000	10.0
Income taxes	2,600	2.2	2,000	2.0
Net income	$ 8,800	7.3	$ 8,000	8.0

* Base amount.

Exhibit 16–2 *(concluded)*

PACKARD COMPANY
Balance Sheets (simplified for illustration)
At December 31, 19B, and 19A

	At			
	Dec. 31, 19B		Dec. 31, 19A	
	Amount	Percent	Amount	Percent
Assets				
Current assets:				
Cash	$ 13,000	8.9	$ 9,000	6.0
Accounts receivable (net)	8,400	5.7	7,000	4.6
Merchandise inventory	54,000	36.8	60,000	40.0
Prepaid expenses	2,000	1.4	4,000	2.7
Total current assets	77,400	52.8	80,000	53.3
Investments:				
Real estate	8,000	5.5	8,000	5.3
Operational assets:				
Equipment and furniture	82,500	56.3	75,000	50.0
Less: Accumulated depreciation	(23,250)	(15.9)	(15,000)	(10.0)
Total operational assets	59,250	40.4	60,000	40.0
Other assets	1,900	1.3	2,000	1.4
Total assets*	$146,550	100.0	$150,000	100.0
Liabilities				
Current liabilities:				
Accounts payable	$ 13,200	9.0	$ 12,000	8.0
Notes payable, short term	15,000	10.2	20,000	13.3
Accrued wages payable	7,200	4.9	8,000	5.3
Total current liabilities	35,400	24.1	40,000	26.6
Long-term liabilities:				
Notes payable, long term	7,150	4.9	10,000	6.7
Total liabilities	42,550	29.0	50,000	33.3
Stockholders' Equity				
Common stock (par $10)	85,000	58.0	85,000	56.7
Retained earnings	19,000	13.0	15,000	10.0
Total stockholders' equity	104,000	71.0	100,000	66.7
Total liabilities and stockholders' equity*	$146,550	100.0	$150,000	100.0

* Base amount.

Commonly Used Ratios

Numerous ratios can be computed from a single set of financial statements, but only a selected number may be useful in a given situation. A common approach is to compute certain widely used ratios and then decide which additional ratios are relevant to the particular decision.

Balance sheet amounts relate to one instant in time, and income statement amounts relate to a period of time. Therefore, care should be exercised when calculating ratios that use amounts from both statements. When an income statement amount is compared with a balance sheet amount, a balance sheet **average amount** often is used to reflect changes in the balance sheet amounts. The selected balance sheet amount usually is computed as the average of the amounts shown on the beginning and ending balance sheets. When additional information is available, such as monthly or quarterly data, an average of the additional data often is more representative.

Commonly used financial ratios can be grouped into the five categories shown in Exhibit 16–3.

Tests of Profitability

Profitability is a primary measure of the overall success of a company. Indeed, it is a necessary condition for survival. Investors and creditors would prefer a **single measure** of profitability that would be meaningful in all situations. Unfortunately, no single measure can be devised to meet this comprehensive need. Tests of profitability focus on measuring the adequacy of income by comparing it with one or more primary activities or factors that are measured in the financial statements. Five different tests of profitability are explained below.

1. Return on Owners' Investment (ROI_O)

This ratio is a fundamental test of profitability. It relates income to the investment that was made by the owners to earn the income. This ratio can be used to measure the profitability of any investment, whether for a company or a project. The return on owners' investment ratio is computed as follows:

$$\text{Return on owners' investment} = \frac{\text{Income*}}{\text{Average owners' equity\dag}}$$

$$\text{Packard Company, 19B} = \frac{\$8,800\text{*}}{\$102,000\dag} = 8.6\%$$

Based on Exhibit 16–2.
* Income **before** extraordinary items should be used.
† Average owners' equity is preferable when available, that is ($100,000 + $104,000)
÷ 2 = $102,000.

EXHIBIT 16–3 Widely used accounting ratios

Ratio	Basic computation
Tests of profitability:	
1.* Return on owners' investment (ROI_o).	$\dfrac{\text{Income}}{\text{Average owners' equity}}$
2. Return on total investment (ROI_t).	$\dfrac{\text{Income} + \text{Interest expense (net of tax)}}{\text{Average total assets}}$
3. Financial leverage ($ROI_o - ROI_t$).	$\dfrac{\text{Return on}}{\text{owners' investment}} - \dfrac{\text{Return on}}{\text{total investment}}$
4. Earnings per share.	$\dfrac{\text{Income}}{\text{Average number of shares of common stock outstanding}}$
5. Profit margin.	$\dfrac{\text{Income (before extraordinary items)}}{\text{Net sales revenue}}$
Tests of liquidity:	
6. Current ratio.	$\dfrac{\text{Current assets}}{\text{Current liabilities}}$
7. Quick ratio.	$\dfrac{\text{Quick assets}}{\text{Current liabilities}}$
8. Receivable turnover.	$\dfrac{\text{Net credit sales}}{\text{Average net trade receivables}}$
9. Inventory turnover.	$\dfrac{\text{Cost of goods sold}}{\text{Average inventory}}$
Test of solvency and equity position:	
10. Debt/equity ratio.	$\dfrac{\text{Total liabilities}}{\text{Owners' equity}}$
Market tests:	
11. Price/earnings ratio.	$\dfrac{\text{Current market price per share}}{\text{Earnings per share}}$
12. Dividend yield ratio.	$\dfrac{\text{Dividends per share}}{\text{Market price per share}}$
Miscellaneous ratio:	
13. Book value per share.	$\dfrac{\text{Common stock equity}}{\text{Number of shares of common stock outstanding}}$

* The numbers to the left are used in the following discussions to facilitate reference.

Packard Company earned 8.6%, after income taxes, on the investment provided by the **owners.** Return on owners' investment is a particularly useful measure of profitability from the **viewpoint of the owners.** It relates two fundamental factors—the amount of the owners' investment and the return earned for the owners on that investment.

2. Return on Total Investment (ROI$_t$)

Another view of the return on investment concept relates income to **total assets** (i.e., total investment) used to earn income. Under this broader concept, return on total investment is computed as follows:

$$\text{Return on total investment} = \frac{\text{Income}^* + \text{Interest expense (net of tax)}}{\text{Average total assets}^\dagger}$$

$$\text{Packard Company 19B} = \frac{\$8,800^* + (\$1,500 \times 77\%)}{\$148,275^\dagger} = 6.7\%$$

Based on Exhibit 16–2.
* Income before extraordinary items should be used. This illustration assumes an average income tax of 23%.
† Average total assets should be used; that is ($150,000 + $146,550) ÷ 2 = $148,275.

Packard Company earned 6.7% on the **total resources it used** during the year. Under this concept, **investment** is the amount of resources provided by both owners and creditors. Return is measured as the return to both owners and creditors. To compute return on **total** investment, interest expense (net of income tax) is added back to income because interest is the return on the creditors' investment. It must be added back because it was previously deducted to derive net income. The denominator represents **total** investment; therefore, the numerator (income) must include the total return that was available to the suppliers of funds. Interest expense is measured net of income tax because it represents the net cost to the corporation for the funds provided by creditors.

Return on total investment reflects the combined effect of both the operating and the financing activities of a company as shown in Exhibit 16–4 (remember that total assets always equals total liabilities plus total owners' equity).

Most analysts compute the two return-on-investment ratios shown above. Return on total investment is the preferable measure of **management performance** in using all of the resources available to the company. The return on owners' equity is relevant to the owners because it measures the return that has "accrued" to them.

3. Financial Leverage

Financial leverage is the advantage, or disadvantage, that occurs as the result of earning a return on owners' investment that is different from the return earned

Exhibit 16–4 Components of return on total investment

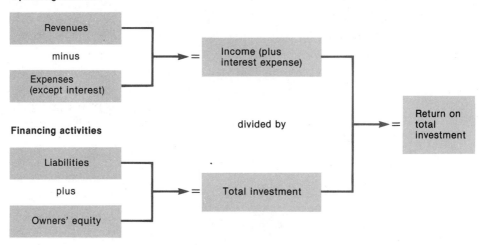

on total investment (i.e., $ROI_o - ROI_t$). Most companies have positive leverage. Positive leverage occurs when the rate of return on a company's investments is higher than the average aftertax interest rate on borrowed funds. Basically, the company borrows at one rate and invests at a higher rate of return.

Financial leverage can be measured by comparing the two return-on-investment ratios as follows:

$$\text{Financial leverage} = \frac{\text{Return on}}{\text{owners' investment}} - \frac{\text{Return on}}{\text{total investment}}$$

Packard Company, 19B = 8.6% − 6.7% = 1.9% (positive leverage)

When a company can borrow funds at an aftertax interest rate and invest those funds to earn a higher aftertax rate of return, the difference "accrues" to the benefit of the owners. This is the primary reason that most companies obtain a significant amount of resources from creditors rather than obtaining resources only from the sale of their capital stock.

4. Earnings per Share (EPS)

This ratio evaluates profitability strictly from the common stockholders' point of view. Instead of being based on the dollar amount of the investment, it is based on the number of shares of common stock outstanding. EPS is computed as follows:

$$\text{Earnings per share} = \frac{\text{Income}}{\substack{\text{Average number of shares of} \\ \text{common stock outstanding}}}$$

$$\text{Packard Company, 19B} = \frac{\$8,800}{8,500} = \$1.04 \text{ per share}$$

EPS usually is computed on three amounts if extraordinary items are reported on the income statement: (1) income before extraordinary items (required), (2) extraordinary items (optional), and (3) net income (required). Of the three EPS amounts, the first one is considered the most relevant because extraordinary items are unusual and do not reoccur.

5. Profit Margin

This percent is based on two income statement amounts. It is computed as follows:

$$\text{Profit margin} = \frac{\text{Income (before extraordinary items)}}{\text{Net sales}}$$

$$\text{Packard Company, 19B} = \frac{\$8,800}{\$120,000} = 7.3\%$$

This profitability test is the percent of each sales dollar, on the average, that is profit. For Packard Company, each dollar of sales generated 7.3 cents of profit. Care must be used in analyzing the profit margin because it does not consider the amount of resources employed (i.e., total investment) to earn income. For example, the income statements of Company A and Company B may show the following:

	Company A	Company B
a. Sales revenue	$100,000	$150,000
b. Income	$ 5,000	$ 7,500
c. Profit margin (*b*) ÷ (*a*)	5%	5%
d. Total investment	$ 50,000	$125,000
e. Return on total investment* (*b*) ÷ (*d*)	10%	6%

* Assuming no interest expense.

In this example, both companies reported the same profit margin (5%). Company A, however, appears to be performing much better because it is earning a 10% return on the total investment versus the 6% earned by Company B. The profit margin percents do not reflect the effect of the $50,000 total investment in Company A compared to the $125,000 total investment in Company B. The effect of the different amounts of investment in each company is reflected in the return on investment (ROI) percents. Thus, the profit margin omits one of the two important factors that should be used in evaluating return on the investment.

Comparing profit margins for companies in different industries is difficult. For example, profit margins in the food industry are low while profit margins in the jewelry business are large. Both types of businesses can be quite profitable because they differ in terms of investment. Grocery stores have small margins but require a relatively small investment. Jewelry stores earn more profit from each sales dollar but require a large investment.

Tests of Liquidity

Liquidity refers to a company's ability to meet its currently maturing debts. Tests of liquidity focus on the relationship between current assets and current liabilities. The ability of a company to pay its current liabilities is an important factor in evaluating short-term financial strength. For example, a company that does not have cash available to pay for purchases on a timely basis will lose its cash discounts and run the risk of discontinued credit by vendors. Two ratios are used to measure liquidity: the current ratio and the quick ratio. Recall that working capital is the difference between total current assets and total current liabilities.

6. Current Ratio

This ratio measures the relationship between total current assets and total current liabilities at a specific date. It is computed as follows:

$$\text{Current ratio} = \frac{\text{Current assets}}{\text{Current liabilities}}$$

$$\text{Packard Company, 19B} = \frac{\$77,400}{\$35,400} = 2.2 \text{ times or 2.2 to 1}$$

At year-end, current assets for Packard Company were 2.2 times current liabilities or, alternatively, for each $1 of current liabilities there were $2.20 of current assets. The current ratio measures the cushion of working capital maintained to allow for the inevitable unevenness in the flow of "funds" through the working capital accounts. Because the current ratio measures the adequacy of working capital, it is sometimes called the working capital ratio.

7. Quick Ratio (or Acid Test Ratio)

This ratio is similar to the current ratio except that it is a more stringent test of short-term liquidity. It is computed as follows:

$$\text{Quick ratio} = \frac{\text{Quick assets}}{\text{Current liabilities}}$$

$$\text{Packard Company, 19B} = \frac{\$21,400}{\$35,400} = 0.60 \text{ times or } 0.60 \text{ to } 1$$

Quick assets are readily convertible into cash at approximately their book values. Quick assets include cash, short-term investments, and accounts receivable (net of the allowance for doubtful accounts). Inventories usually are omitted from quick assets because of the uncertainty of when cash will be received from the sale of inventory in the future. In unusual circumstances, if the inventory will turn to cash very quickly, it should be included. In contrast, prepaid expenses do not "convert" to cash and are excluded from quick assets. Thus, the quick or acid-test ratio is a more severe test of liquidity than is the current ratio.

8. Receivable Turnover

Short-term liquidity often is measured in terms of **turnover** of certain current assets. Two additional ratios that measure nearness to cash are receivable turnover and inventory turnover.

Receivable turnover is computed as follows:

$$\text{Receivable turnover} = \frac{\text{Net credit sales*}}{\text{Average net trade receivables}}$$

$$\begin{array}{l}\text{Packard Company, 19B}\\ \text{(net credit sales assumed}\\ \text{to be } \$77,000 \text{ for 19B)}\end{array} = \frac{\$77,000}{(\$7,000 + \$8,400) \div 2} = 10 \text{ times}$$

* When the amount of credit sales is not known, total sales may be used as a rough approximation.

This ratio is called a turnover because it reflects how many times the trade-receivables were recorded, collected, then recorded again during the period (i.e., "turnover"). Receivable turnover expresses the relationship of the average balance in Accounts Receivable to the transactions (i.e., credit sales) that created those receivables. This ratio measures the effectiveness of the credit-granting and collection activities of the company. A high receivable turnover ratio suggests effective collection activities. Granting credit to poor credit risks and ineffective collection efforts will cause this ratio to be low. A very low ratio is obviously a problem, but a very high ratio can also be a problem. A very high ratio may indicate an overly stringent credit policy that would cause lost sales and profits.

The receivable turnover ratio often is converted to a time basis known as the average age of receivables. The computation is as follows:

$$\text{Average age of trade receivables} = \frac{\text{Days in year}}{\text{Receivable turnover}}$$

$$\text{Packard Company, 19B} = \frac{365}{10} = 36.5 \text{ average days to collect}$$

The effectiveness of credit and collection activities sometimes is judged by the rule of thumb that the **average days to collect** should not exceed 1½ times the credit terms. For example, if the credit terms are 2/10, n/30, the average days to collect should not exceed 45 days (i.e., not more than 15 days past due). Like all rules of thumb, this one has many exceptions. However, an increase or decrease in the average days to collect would suggest changes in the credit policies and/or changes in collection efficiency.

9. Inventory Turnover

Inventory turnover measures the liquidity (i.e., nearness to cash) of the inventory. It reflects the relationship of the inventory to the volume of goods sold during the period. The computation is as follows:

$$\text{Inventory turnover} = \frac{\text{Cost of goods sold}}{\text{Average inventory}}$$

$$\text{Packard Company, 19B} = \frac{\$72,600}{(\$60,000 + \$54,000) \div 2} = 1.3 \text{ times}$$

The inventory for Packard Company "turned over" 1.3 times during the year. Because profit normally is realized each time the inventory is sold (i.e., turned over), an increase in the ratio is usually favorable. However, if the ratio is too high, sales may be lost because of items that are out of stock. The turnover ratio often is converted to a time-basis expression called the **average days' supply in inventory.** The computation is:

$$\text{Average days' supply in inventory} = \frac{\text{Days in year}}{\text{Inventory turnover}}$$

$$\text{Packard Company, 19B} = \frac{365}{1.3}$$

$$= 281 \text{ average day's supply in inventory}$$

Turnover ratios are used extensively because they are easy to understand. Normal (or average) inventory turnover ratios vary significantly by industry classification. Companies in the food industry (grocery stores and restaurants) have high inventory turnover ratios while companies that sell expensive merchandise (automobile dealers and high-fashion clothes) have much lower ratios.

Tests of Solvency and Equity Position

Solvency refers to the ability of a company to meet its **long-term obligations** on a continuing basis. Certain critical relationships can be identified by analyzing how a company has financed its assets and activities. The relative amount of resources provided by creditors and owners is known as a company's **equity position.** The debt/equity ratio is used to reflect the equity position of a company.

10. Debt/Equity Ratio

This ratio expresses the direct proportion between debt and owners' equity.[1] It is computed as follows:

$$\text{Debt/equity ratio} = \frac{\text{Total liabilities (i.e., creditors' equity)}}{\text{Owners' equity}}$$

$$\text{Packard Company, 19B} = \frac{\$42,550}{\$104,000} = 0.41 \text{ (or 41\%)}$$

This ratio means that for each $1 of owners' equity, there was $0.41 of liabilities.

Debt is risky for a company because it imposes important contractual obligations. There are (*a*) specific maturity dates for the principal amounts and (*b*) specific interest payments that must be made. Debt obligations are enforceable by law and do not depend on the earnings of the company. In contrast, dividends for stockholders are always at the discretion of the company and are not legally enforceable until declared by the board of directors. Owner's equity is

---

[1] The relationship between debt and owners' equity alternatively may be calculated with the following two ratios:

$$\text{Owners' equity to total equities} = \frac{\text{Owners' equity}}{\text{Total equities}}$$

$$\text{Packard Company, 19B} = \frac{\$104,000}{\$146,550} = 71\%$$

$$\text{Creditors' equity to total equities} = \frac{\text{Creditors' equity}}{\text{Total equities}}$$

$$\text{Packard Company, 19B} = \frac{\$42,500}{\$146,550} = 29\%$$

"permanent" capital that does not have a maturity date. Thus, equity capital usually is seen as much less risky than debt for a company.

Despite the risk associated with debt, most companies get significant amounts of resources from creditors because of the advantages of financial leverage. Typically, the return on company investments is higher than the aftertax interest rate paid to creditors. By accepting the risk associated with debt, management may earn a higher return for the owners because of positive financial leverage. For example, assume a company is earning a 15% return on total investment while its average interest rate on debt is 7% (net of income tax). The difference between the earnings rate on total resources (15%) and the interest paid to the creditors (7%) "accrues" to the benefit of the stockholders.[2] The stockholders benefit by the 15% earned on the resources provided by them, plus the difference between the 15% return and the 7% interest rate paid on the resources provided by the creditors. A company with a high proportion of debt is **highly levered.** The debt/equity ratio shows the balance that the management has attained between the resources provided by creditors and the resources provided by owners.

Market Tests

Several ratios measure the "market worth" of a share of stock. These market tests relate the current market price of a share of stock to an indicator of the return that might accrue to the investor. The tests focus on the **current market price** of the stock because that is the amount the buyer would invest. Two market test ratios used by analysts and investors are the price/earning ratio and the dividend yield ratio.

11. Price/Earnings (P/E) Ratio

This ratio measures the relationship between the current market price of the stock and its earnings per share. Assuming a current market price of $15.60 per share for Packard Company common stock in 19B and earnings per share of $1.04, the P/E ratio is computed as follows:

$$\text{Price/earnings ratio} = \frac{\text{Current market price per share}}{\text{Earnings per share}}$$

$$\text{Packard Company, 19B} = \frac{\$15.60}{\$1.04} = 15 \text{ (or 15 to 1)}$$

---

[2] Interest expense on debt is a deductible expense on the income tax return; in contrast, dividend payments to stockholders are not deductible. Thus, in addition to the lower stated rate for debt, funds obtained by means of debt tend to be less costly because of the income tax saving. The real cost of debt in the above example depends on the income tax rate.

Packard stock was selling at 15 times the EPS. The P/E ratio often is referred to as the **multiple.** The P/E ratio is used as an indicator of the future performance of the stock. Analysts use the P/E ratio to predict how the stock price may react to a change in the level of the company's earnings.

Sometimes the components of the P/E ratio are inverted, giving the **capitalization rate.** This is the rate at which the stock market apparently is capitalizing the current earnings. Computation of the capitalization rate on current earnings per share for Packard Company would be $\$1.04 \div \$15.60 = 6.67\%$.

12. Dividend Yield Ratio

This ratio measures the relationship between the dividends per share paid and the current market price of the stock. Assuming dividends paid by Packard Company of $0.75 per share for 19B and a current market price per share of $15.60, the ratio is computed as follows:

$$\text{Dividend yield ratio} = \frac{\text{Dividend per share}}{\text{Market price per share}}$$

$$\text{Packard Company, 19B} = \frac{\$0.75}{\$15.60} = 4.81\%$$

This ratio measures the current dividend yield to the investor, based on the dividends per share against the current market price per share. Like the P/E ratio, it is a volatile measure because the price of stock may change materially over short periods of time, and each change in market price or dividend payment changes the ratio.

Miscellaneous Ratio

13. Book Value per Share

The book value per share of stock measures the owners' equity in terms of each share of common stock outstanding. In the case of a simple capital structure, with **only** common stock outstanding, the computation of book value per share is not difficult. To illustrate, assume Day Corporation had total owners' equity of $250,000 and 10,000 shares of common stock outstanding. The computation of book value per share would be as follows:

$$\frac{\text{Book value per}}{\text{common share}} = \frac{\text{Total owners' equity}}{\text{(applicable to common shares)}}{\text{Common shares outstanding}}$$

$$\text{Day Corporation, 19B} = \frac{\$250,000}{10,000 \text{ shares}} = \$25$$

Computation of book value per share is more difficult if both common and preferred shares are outstanding. In this situation, total owners' equity must be allocated between common and preferred stock. This allocation is accomplished by assigning an amount to preferred stock, based on its preferences, and, then, assigning the remaining amount of owners' equity to common stock. Assume Bye Corporation had total owners' equity of $293,000; 1,000 shares outstanding of its 5% preferred stock, par $20, cumulative (no dividends in arrears for past years), and liquidation value of $22 per share; and 10,000 shares of common stock outstanding.

Allocation:
Total owners' equity		$293,000
Less equity allocated to preferred stock:		
Liquidation value (1,000 shares × $22)	$22,000	
Cumulative dividend preference for the current year		
(1,000 shares × $20 × 5%)	1,000	
Amount allocated to preferred stock		23,000
Remainder allocated to common stock		$270,000

Book value per share:
Preferred, $23,000 ÷ 1,000 shares = $23.
Common, $270,000 ÷ 10,000 shares = $27.

Book value per share has limited significance because it has no necessary relationship to market value. Because it is a low conservative amount (historical cost basis), some analysts consider a market value below book value to imply underpriced shares.

Interpreting Ratios

The computation of any particular ratio is not standardized. Neither the accounting profession nor security analysts have prescribed the manner in which a ratio must be computed (except for earnings per share). Thus, users of financial statements should compute the various ratios in accordance with their decision objectives. Before using ratios computed by others, the analyst should determine the computational approach that was used. This section discusses commonly used approaches.

To interpret a ratio, it should be compared with some **standard** that represents an optimal or desirable value. For example, the return-on-investment ratio may be compared with alternative investment opportunities. Some ratios, by their characteristics, are unfavorable if they are **either** too high or too low. For example, analysis may indicate that a current ratio of approximately 2:1 may be considered optimal for a company. In this situation, a ratio of 1:1 may indicate a danger of being unable to meet maturing debts. A ratio of 3:1 may indicate that excess funds are being left idle rather than being employed profitably. Furthermore, an optimal ratio for one company often is not the optimal ratio for another company. Comparisons of ratios for different companies are appropriate only if the companies are indeed comparable. Differences in industry, nature of operations, size, and accounting policies make many comparisons of questionable value.

Most ratios represent **averages.** Therefore, they may obscure underlying factors that are of interest to the analyst. To illustrate, a current ratio of 2:1 may be considered optimal. But even an optimal current ratio may obscure a short-term liquidity problem if the company has a very large amount of inventory and a minimal amount of cash with which to pay debts as they mature. Careful analysis can uncover this liquidity problem. In other cases, careful analysis cannot uncover obscured problems. For example, consolidated statements include financial information about the parent and its subsidiaries. The parent company may have a high current ratio and the subsidiary a low ratio. When the statements are consolidated, the current ratio (in effect, an average of the parent and the subsidiary) may be within an acceptable range. Obscured is the fact that the subsidiary may have a serious liquidity problem.

Despite limitations, ratio analysis is a useful analytical tool. Financial ratios are effective in predicting bankruptcy. Exhibit 16–5 gives the current and debit/equity ratios for Braniff International Corporation for each year before it filed for bankruptcy. Notice the deterioration of these ratios each year. Analysts who studied the financial ratios probably were not surprised by the bankruptcy of Braniff. After selling many of its assets and undergoing a complete financial restructuring, Braniff was able to resume limited flight operations.

Financial analysts often use four types of "standards" against which ratios and percents are compared:

1. **Comparison of the ratios for the current year with the historical ratios for the same company.** Particular attention is given to the **trend** of each ratio over time.

2. **Comparison of the ratios for the current year with ratios of other companies for the same year.** These comparisons include the use of ratios from other similar companies and from industry averages. Industry averages are published by many companies, trade associations, and governmental agencies. For example, a variety of ratios can be found in the publications of Dun & Bradstreet, Inc., Moody's *Manual of Investments*, and Standard & Poor's *Corporation Records*.

Exhibit 16–5   Selected financial ratios for Braniff International

	Years before bankruptcy				
	5	4	3	2	1
Current ratio	1.20	0.91	0.74	0.60	0.49
Debt/equity ratio	2.03	2.45	4.88	15.67	N/A*

* In the year before bankruptcy, Braniff reported negative owners' equity as the result of a large net loss that produced a negative balance in retained earnings. Creditors' equity exceeded total equities.

3. **Experience of the analyst who has a subjective feel for the "right" relationships in a given situation.** These subjective judgments of an experienced and competent observer can be more reliable than purely mechanical comparisons.

4. **Comparison of the ratios for the current year with goals and objectives expressed as ratios.** Many companies prepare comprehensive profit plans (i.e., budgets) that incorporate realistic plans for the future. These plans usually incorporate goals for significant ratios, such as profit margin, return on investment, and EPS. Internal plans seldom are available to external parties because managers are reluctant to share their business plans with competitors. Some companies have begun to experiment with methods to make this information available to users. Days Inn Corporation recently included pro forma (estimated) financial statements for the future as part of their annual report.

Impact of Accounting Alternatives on Ratio Analysis

Financial statements provide information for the average investor. Users who understand basic accounting are able to more effectively analyze the information contained in financial statements. While studying this book, you have developed an understanding of the accounting vocabulary. A knowledge of this vocabulary is necessary to understand financial statements.

Also, familiarity with the underlying accounting concepts is essential for proper analysis of statements. Some unsophisticated users do not understand the cost principle and believe that assets are reported on the balance sheet at their fair market value. We have stressed accounting concepts throughout the book because it is impossible to interpret accounting numbers without an understanding of the concepts that were used to develop the numbers.

When comparing companies, it is rare to find that they use exactly the same accounting policies. If the comparisons are to be useful, the analyst must understand the impact of various accounting alternatives. One company may use conservative accounting alternatives such as accelerated depreciation and LIFO while another may use "income maximizing" alternatives, such as straight-line depreciation and FIFO. Users who do not understand the effects of accounting methods may misinterpret financial results. Perhaps the most important first step in analyzing financial statements is a review of the accounting policies that the company has selected. This information must be disclosed in a note to the statements. An example of this disclosure is shown in the annual report in the appendix preceding the index.

SUMMARY OF CHAPTER

Interpretation of amounts reported on financial statements may be enhanced by expressing certain relationships as ratios or percents. Although many ratios can be calculated, only a few will be useful for a given decision. Having selected the relevant ratios, the analyst has the problem of evaluating the results. This evaluation involves the task of selecting one or more realistic standards with which to compare the results. Four types of standards are used: (1) historical standards, (2) external standards, (3) experience, and (4) planned standards. The interpretation of ratios may suggest strengths and weaknesses in the operations and/or the financial position of the company that should be accorded in-depth investigation and evaluation.

CHAPTER SUPPLEMENT 16A

The Impact of Inflation on Financial Statements

The current rate of inflation in our country is relatively low. However, the United States has experienced periods of rapid inflation. In fact, it now costs more than three dollars to buy the goods and services that one dollar would have bought 20 years ago. Inflation can have a serious impact on the analysis of financial statements because accounting aggregates dollars of different purchasing power. For example, on the income statement, depreciation expense associated with a building acquired 25 years ago (when the dollar had more purchasing power) is matched with revenue earned in the current year (when the dollar has less purchasing power).

Because of the distortion caused by inflation, the FASB experimented with alternatives to historical cost measurements. Beginning in 1979, the FASB required most large companies to disclose inflation-adjusted accounting information as a supplement to their historical cost statements. After several years, the Board concluded that the benefits associated with inflation-adjusted data did not justify the costs of providing the data. As a result, companies are no longer **required** to provide supplementary disclosures concerning the impact of inflation. Nevertheless, an understanding of the alternatives to historical cost measurements is useful because it underscores certain limitations of historical cost financial statements.

Many people incorrectly believe that inflation and changing prices are synonymous terms. They are not. Inflation is the general rise of prices in the economy as the result of an excessive supply of money. Inflation is measured as the change in the general purchasing power of the dollar. Prices of specific goods and services may change more or less rapidly than the general inflation rate. Specific prices may change because of either inflation or changes in the supply and demand for a specific item. Techniques are available to restate historical cost financial statements for either general inflation or specific price changes. We will discuss the impact of general inflation on financial statements (accounting for specific price changes is discussed in advanced courses). Accounting for the impact of general inflation involves the use of price level indexes.

Using Price Level Index Numbers

The federal government publishes several price level indexes, such as the Consumer Price Index which is often reported on the evening news. To construct an index, the price of a group of items in one period is expressed as a relationship to a price at another period. A base year is selected and assigned the base index value of 100. Subsequent changes in prices are expressed in relation to this base. Exhibit 16–6 shows the Consumer Price Index for several recent years.

The use of a price index can be illustrated by considering the effect of general inflation on the cost of renting an apartment. Assume the cost of renting an apartment at Campus Vista changes with the general inflation rate and that in 1967 a three-bedroom apartment cost $200 per month. Using the price indexes in Exhibit 16–6, we can estimate the rental for several years:

Year	CPI	Restatement computation	Restated cost
1967	100		$200.00
1970	116.3	$200 × 116.3/100 =	232.60
1975	161.2	$200 × 161.2/100 =	322.40
1980	246.8	$200 × 246.8/100 =	493.60
1985	322.2	$200 × 322.2/100 =	644.40

This process is called constant dollar (CD) restatement.

Exhibit 16–6   Selected consumer price index values

Year	CPI-U index* Average for the year	At year-end
1967 (base year)	100.0	101.6
1970	116.3	119.1
1971	121.3	123.1
1972	125.3	127.3
1973	133.1	138.5
1974	147.7	155.4
1975	161.2	166.3
1976	170.5	174.3
1977	181.5	186.1
1978	195.4	202.9
1979	217.4	229.9
1980	246.8	258.4
1981	272.4	281.5
1982	289.1	292.4
1983	298.4	303.5
1984	311.1	315.5
1985	322.2	327.4
1986	328.1	331.1
1987	339.6	345.7

* Source: Economic Indicators Joint Economic Committee, U.S. Government Printing Office (monthly).

CD Restatement of Depreciation Expense and Property, Plant, and Equipment

Now consider a company that paid $200,000 for a building in 1967 when the Consumer Price Index (CPI) was 100. Assuming straight-line depreciation, no residual value, and an estimated life of 40 years, the annual depreciation is $5,000 per year. The current year is year 30 (since acquisition) and the current CPI is 300. At the end of year 30, the historical cost (HC) financial statements would show the following amounts:

Balance sheet:
Operational assets:
   Building $200,000
   Accumulated depreciation . . . 150,000
      Carrying value $50,000

Income statement:
Depreciation expense   5,000

All of the amounts shown above represent dollars "valued" 30 years earlier with a purchasing power that is much more than the current period. On the income statement, depreciation expense, expressed in dollars with one purchasing power, is matched with revenue, which is expressed in dollars with a different purchasing power. This mixing of apples and oranges can be corrected with the use of a price index. Historical cost amounts with different purchasing power can be restated to dollars with the same purchasing power by multiplying the historical amount by a price index ratio:

$$\frac{\text{Historical}}{\text{cost amount}} \times \frac{\text{Current period CPI}}{\text{Transaction date CPI}} = \frac{\text{Restated}}{\text{amount}}$$

Example: Depreciation expense.

$$\$5,000 \times 300/100 = \$15,000$$

The restated financial statements are shown below:

	Historical cost	Restatement computation		Restated amount
Balance sheet:				
Operational assets:				
Building	$200,000 ×	300/100	=	$600,000
Accumulated depreciation . . .	150,000 ×	300/100	=	450,000
Carrying value	50,000 ×	300/100	=	150,000
Income statement:				
Depreciation expense	5,000 ×	300/100	=	15,000

CD Restatement of Cost of Goods Sold and Inventory

The CD restatement of cost of goods sold and inventory is accomplished using a price level index ratio that is similar to the one that was used to restate depreciation expense:

$$\frac{\text{Historical}}{\text{cost amount}} \times \frac{\text{Current period CPI}}{\text{Transaction date CPI}} = \frac{\text{Restated}}{\text{amount}}$$

The transaction date CPI is the index that existed on the date that the inventory units were bought. It would be difficult to keep track of the CPI on every date that inventory is purchased. As a result, most accountants assume that inventory is purchased evenly during the year and use the average for the year. If this assumption were not appropriate for a company, it would be necessary to identify the CPI for every date that inventory is purchased.

To illustrate the restatement of cost of goods sold and inventory, assume that Alpha Corporation bought merchandise evenly throughout its first year of operations. The merchandise cost $120,000, and the average CPI for the year was 270. At the end of the year, Alpha reported ending inventory of $30,000 and the CPI was 297. The CD restatement for Alpha is:

Ending inventory:

$$\$30,000 \times 297/270 = \$33,000$$

Cost of goods sold:

$$(\$120,000 - \$30,000) \times 297/270 = \$99,000$$

Purchasing Power Gains and Losses

The value of some balance sheet items does not change during a period of inflation because of their nature or as the result of contract. These items are called monetary items and include cash, payables, and receivables. A complete list of monetary items is shown in Exhibit 16–7. Because inflation does not affect the amount of cash held or the number of dollars to be paid or received for monetary items, these items are not restated on the balance sheet for the effects of inflation.

While monetary items are not restated on the balance sheet, the purchasing power of monetary items is affected by inflation. Consider what would happen if you kept $100 in your wallet during a year in which the inflation rate was 10%. At the end of the year, you could buy less goods and services than you could at the beginning of the year. Your purchasing power loss on this monetary asset is calculated by determining how much cash you would need at the end of the year to have the same $100 purchasing power that you had at the beginning. The purchasing power loss is $10 [($100 × 110/100) − $100] because prices went up $10 during the year but you still have the same amount of cash in your wallet.

Exhibit 16-7 Classification of monetary and nonmonetary items

	Monetary	Nonmonetary
Assets		
Cash	X	
Marketable securities:		
Most common stock		X
Most bonds	X	
Accounts and notes receivable	X	
Allowance for doubtful accounts	X	
Inventories		X
Prepaid expense:		
Claims to future services		X
Prepayments that are deposits or advance payments	X	
Long-term receivables	X	
Property, plant, and equipment		X
Accumulated depreciation		X
Patents and trademarks		X
Goodwill		X
Liabilities		
Accounts and notes payable	X	
Accrued expenses	X	
Cash dividends payable	X	
Bonds payable and other long-term debt	X	
Premium or discount on bonds payable	X	
Deferred income taxes	X	
Owners' Equity		
Preferred stock (nonmonetary if not carried at a fixed redemption price)	X	
Common stock		X
Retained earnings		
This amount usually is restated as a plug or balancing amount		X

Source: Adapted from *FASB Statement 33*, "Financial Reporting and Changing Prices" (Stamford, Conn., September 1979).

If you hold a monetary liability during a period of inflation, you would experience a purchasing power gain because you will be able to pay off the liability with "cheaper" dollars. A dollar owed during a period of inflation is still a dollar owed, but it has less value because it will buy fewer goods at the end of the period.

A company will report a net purchasing power loss during a period of inflation if its losses on monetary assets exceed its gains on monetary liabilities. Conversely, the company will report a net purchasing power gain if its gains on monetary liabilities exceed its losses on monetary assets. The amount of the gain or loss is the difference between the historical cost amount for the monetary items and the restated amount. To illustrate the calculation of a purchasing power gain or loss, assume that during 19A Beta Corporation held a constant balance of cash in the amount $125,000. On July 1, 19A, Beta bought a new factory and signed a note payable for $300,000. The cash and note payable are the only monetary items on the Beta balance sheet. The CPI on January 1, 19A was 200; July 1, 19A, 213; and December 31, 19A, 220. The calculation is:

Historical cost amount	Restatement computation	Restated amount	Purchasing power gain (loss)
$125,000	$125,000 × 220/200 =	$137,500	$(12,500)
300,000	300,000 × 220/213 =	309,860	9,860
	Net purchasing power loss		$ (2,640)

Beta Corporation experienced a net purchasing power loss because the purchasing power loss associated with holding cash exceeded the purchasing power gain on the debt it owed.

Financial Statement Analysis

Historical cost financial statements rest on the unit-of-measure assumption (discussed in Chapter 4) which states that each transaction should be measured in terms of the dollars that existed at the date of each transaction. This assumption implies that the monetary unit is a stable measuring unit without a changing value. Clearly, this assumption is not valid during a period of inflation. The accounting profession experimented with techniques to adjust financial statements to reflect the impact of inflation. Financial analysts argued that inflation adjusted information was useful but the benefits associated with the data were not sufficient to justify the costs of preparation. As a result, inflation adjusted data are no longer required. If we return to the double-digit inflation rates that were experienced in the 1970s and 1980s, there may be renewed interest in inflation-adjusted data.

This discussion of accounting for the impact of inflation identifies an important concern for analysts. Inflation can have a dramatic impact on financial statements, even if the current rate of inflation is low. Buildings and equipment purchased in the 1960s were paid for with dollars that had three times as much purchasing power as current dollars. Financial statements mix dollars with different purchasing power as if they were the same. Analysts must be particularly cautious when comparing companies that are not the same age. One company may report low depreciation expense because it bought its assets before a period of inflation. Another company with the same productive capacity may report higher depreciation because it bought its assets with "cheaper" dollars. The company with lower depreciation expense may report higher net income, but in this case the higher income is more related to inflation than it is related to operating efficiency.

IMPORTANT TERMS DEFINED IN THIS CHAPTER

Common Ratios Selected ratios that are used widely. Exhibit 16–3 presents a list of 13 commonly used accounting ratios. *p. 771*

Comparative Statements Financial statements for several years; amounts are presented side by side for comparative purposes. *p. 767*

Component Percentages A percentage that expresses each item on a particular financial statement as a percent of a single base amount. *p. 769*

Long-Term Summaries Summaries of basic accounting data for many years (typically 10 years). *p. 767*

Market Tests Ratios that tend to measure the "market worth" of a share of stock. *p. 780*

Ratio Analysis An analytical tool designed to identify significant relationships; measures proportional relationship between two financial statement amounts. *p. 768*

Tests of Liquidity Ratios that measure a company's ability to meet its currently maturing obligations. *p. 776*

Tests of Solvency Ratios that measure a company's ability to meet its long-term obligations. *p. 779*

QUESTIONS

1. What are three fundamental uses of external financial statements by decision makers?
2. What are some of the primary items on financial statements about which creditors usually are concerned?
3. Explain why the notes to the financial statements are important to decision makers.
4. What is the primary purpose of comparative financial statements?
5. Why are statement users interested in financial summaries covering several years? What is the primary limitation of long-term summaries?
6. What is ratio analysis? Why is ratio analysis useful?
7. What are component percentages? Why are component percentages useful?
8. Explain the two concepts of return on investment.
9. What is financial leverage? How is financial leverage measured?
10. Is profit margin a useful measure of profitability? Explain.
11. Compare and contrast the current ratio and the quick ratio.
12. What does the debt/equity ratio reflect?
13. What are "market tests?"
14. What are the primary problems when using ratios?

EXERCISES

E16-1   (Match Definition with Terms)

Match each definition with its related term by entering the appropriate letter in the space provided.

Terms	Definitions
_____ (1) Long-term sum-maries	A. Ratios and percentages calculated from financial statements to give greater insight into the profitability, liquidity, solvency, and market status of a company.
_____ (2) Market tests	
_____ (3) Common ratios	
_____ (4) Tests of solvency	
_____ (5) Comparative statements	B. These could be used to compare and contrast a company's financial position from year to year.
_____ (6) Tests of liquidity	C. If you were to compute these percentages for an income statement, the denominator would be net sales revenue.
_____ (7) Component percentages	D. These documents are useful in tracking a company's progress over a long period of time.
_____ (8) Ratio analysis	E. Examples of these are the price/earnings ratio and the dividend yield ratio.
	F. Used to analyze relationships both within one period and between periods.
	G. These tests focus on the relationship between current assets and current liabilities.
	H. An example of this kind of test is the debt/equity ratio.

E16-2   (Analysis of Comparative Financial Statements Using Percentages)

The comparative financial statements prepared at December 31,19B, for Shark Company showed the following summarized data:

	19B	19A
Income statement:		
Sales revenue	$150,000*	$140,000*
Cost of goods sold	90,000	85,000
Gross margin	60,000	55,000
Operating expenses and interest expense	43,000	40,500
Pretax income	17,000	14,500
Income tax	5,000	4,500
Net income	$ 12,000	$ 10,000

	19B	19A
Balance sheet:		
Cash	$ 7,000	$ 8,000
Accounts receivable (net)	12,000	17,000
Inventory	30,000	28,000
Operational assets (net)	50,000	43,000
	$ 99,000	$ 96,000
Current liabilities (no interest)	$ 14,000	$ 17,000
Long-term liabilities (10% interest)	35,000	35,000
Common stock (par $5)	40,000	40,000
Retained earnings†	10,000	4,000
	$ 99,000	$ 96,000

* One third were credit sales.
† During 19B, cash dividends amounting to $8,000 were declared and paid.

Required:

a. Complete the following columns for each item in the above comparative financial statements:

Increase (decrease)
19B over 19A

Amount   **Percent**

b. Answer the following questions:
   (1) Compute the percentage increase in sales revenue, net income, cash, inventory, liabilities, and owners' equity.
   (2) By what amount did working capital change?
   (3) What was the percentage change in the average income tax rate?
   (4) What was the amount of cash inflow from revenues for 19B?
   (5) By what percent did the average markup realized on goods sold change?
   (6) How much did the book value per share change?

E16–3   (Analysis of a Financial Statement Using Component Percentages and Selected Ratios)
Use the data given in Exercise 16–2 for Shark Company.

Required:

a. Present component percentages for 19B only.

b. Answer the following questions for 19B:
   (1) What was the average percentage markup on sales?
   (2) What was the average income tax rate?
   (3) Compute the profit margin. Was it a good or poor indicator of performance? Explain.
   (4) What percent of total resources was invested in operational assets?
   (5) Compute the debt/equity ratio. Does it look good or bad? Explain.
   (6) What was the return on owners' investment?
   (7) What was the return on total investment?
   (8) Compute the financial leverage percent. Was it positive or negative? Explain.
   (9) What was the book value per share of common stock?

E16–4   (Analysis of a Financial Statement Using Each Ratio Discussed in the Chapter)
Use the data given in Exercise 16–2 for Shark Company. Use a separate sheet and complete the following tabulation for 19B only (assume a common stock price of $25 per share); compute the ratios that usually are included under each category:

Name and Computation of the Ratio (show computations)	Brief Explanation of the Ratio
A. Tests of profitability: 1. Return on owners' investment 2. Etc.	
B. Tests of liquidity: 1. Current ratio 2. Etc.	
C. Tests of solvency and equity position: 1. Debt/equity ratio 2. Etc.	
D. Market tests: 1. Price/earnings ratio 2. Etc.	
E. Miscellaneous ratio: 1. Book value per share	

E16–5   (Match Each Ratio with Its Computational Definition)
Match each computation with its related ratio or percent by entering the appropriate letters in the blanks.

Ratios or percents

_____ (1) Profit margin
_____ (2) Inventory turnover ratio
_____ (3) Average collection period
_____ (4) Creditors' equity to total equities
_____ (5) Dividend yield ratio
_____ (6) Return on owners' investment
_____ (7) Current ratio
_____ (8) Debt/equity ratio
_____ (9) Price/earnings ratio
_____ (10) Financial leverage

Computations

A. Income (before extraordinary items) ÷ Net sales.
B. Days in year ÷ Receivable turnover.
C. Income ÷ Average owners' equity.
D. Income ÷ Average number of shares of common stock outstanding.
E. Return on owners' investment − Return on total investment.
F. Quick assets ÷ Current liabilities.
G. Current assets ÷ Current liabilities.
H. Cost of goods sold ÷ Average inventory.
I. Net credit sales ÷ Average net trade receivables.
J. Creditors' equity (debt) ÷ Total equities.
K. Days in year ÷ Inventory turnover.

Ratios or percents	Computations
_____ (11) Receivable turn-over ratio	L. Total liabilities ÷ Owners' equity.
_____ (12) Average days' sup-ply of inventory	M. Dividends per share ÷ Market price per share.
_____ (13) Owners' equity to total equities	N. Owners' equity ÷ Total equities.
_____ (14) Earnings per share	O. Current market price per share ÷ Earnings per share.
_____ (15) Return on total in-vestment	P. Owners' equity ÷ Shares outstanding.
_____ (16) Quick ratio	Q. Income + Interest expense (net of tax) ÷ Total assets.
_____ (17) Book value per share	

E16–6 **(Analysis of the Impact of Selected Transactions on the Current Ratio, Accounts Receivable and Inventory Turnover, and Financial Leverage)**

Case A—Current assets totaled $60,000, and the current ratio was 1.5. Assume the following transactions were completed: (1) purchased merchandise for $3,000 on short-term credit; and (2) purchased a delivery truck for $8,000, paid $2,000 cash, and signed a two-year interest-bearing note for the balance. Compute the cumulative current ratio after each transaction.

Case B—Sales for the year were $600,000 of which one half was on credit. The average gross margin rate was 40% on sales. Account balances were:

	Beginning	Ending
Accounts receivable (net) . . .	$30,000	$20,000
Inventory	20,000	16,000

Compute the turnover for the accounts receivable and inventory, the average age of receivables, and the average days' supply of inventory.

Case C—The financial statements reported the following at year-end:

Total assets	$100,000
Total debt (10% interest)	70,000
Net income (average tax rate 30%) . . .	10,000

Compute the financial leverage. Was it positive or negative?

E16–7 **(Analysis of a Financial Statement Using Ratios and Percentage Changes)**

Brent Company has just prepared the comparative annual financial statements for 19B given below.

BRENT COMPANY
Comparative Income Statement
For the Years Ended December 31, 19B, and 19A

	For the year ended	
	19B	19A
Sales revenue (one half on credit)	$100,000	$ 95,000
Cost of goods sold	48,000	46,000
Gross margin	52,000	49,000
Expenses (including $3,000 interest expense each year)	34,000	33,000
Pretax income	18,000	16,000
Income tax on operations (30%)	5,400	4,800
Income before extraordinary items	12,600	11,200
Extraordinary loss $3,000		
Less income tax saved 900	2,100	
Extraordinary gain	$1,000	
Applicable income tax	300	700
Net income	$ 10,500	$ 11,900

BRENT COMPANY
Comparative Balance Sheet
At December 31, 19B, and 19A

	19B	19A
Assets		
Cash	$ 47,200	$ 20,000
Accounts receivable (net; terms 1/10, n/30)	35,000	30,000
Inventory	30,000	40,000
Operational assets (net)	90,000	100,000
Total assets	$202,200	$190,000
Liabilities		
Accounts payable	$ 60,000	$ 50,000
Income taxes payable	1,500	1,000
Note payable, long term	25,000	25,000
Stockholders' Equity		
Capital stock (par $10)	80,000	80,000
Retained earnings	35,700	34,000
Total liabilities and stockholders' equity	$202,200	$190,000

Required (round percents and ratios to two decimal places):

a. For 19B, compute the tests of (1) profitability, (2) liquidity, (3) solvency, and (4) market. Assume the quoted price of the stock was $25 for 19B. Dividends declared and paid during 19B were $8,000.

b. Respond to the following for 19B:

(1) Compute the percentage changes in sales, income before extraordinary items, net income, cash, inventory, and debt.

(2) What appears to be the pretax interest rate on the note payable?

c. Identify at least two problems facing the company that are suggested by your responses to (a) and (b).

E16–8   **(Based on Chapter Supplement 16A; Use a Price Index to Analyze Price Changes)**
During 1967, a Quality Stereo set sold for $250. Assume that each year this particular set increased in price exactly the same as the changes in the GPL index. However, in 1990 it sold for $795.

Required:

a. What was the selling price in 1970, 1975, and 1978? Use the average CPI-U index values given in the chapter and round to the nearest dollar. Show computations.

b. Analyze the change in price during 1990. Assume that the CPI-U for 1990 was 350.

E16–9   **(Based on Chapter Supplement 16A; CD Restatement of an Operational Asset and the Related Depreciation Expense)**
In 1970, Tower Company purchased a plant site for $23,100. Immediately thereafter, construction of a plant building was started. The building was completed in January 1971 at a cost of $336,000. The building is being depreciated on a straight-line basis assuming an estimated useful life of 30 years and no residual value.

Assume the GPL index in 1970 was 110, in 1971 it was 112, and at the end of 1990 it was 350.

Required:

a. Complete a schedule similar to the following:

	Amount to be reported assuming	
	HC basis	CD restated
Balance sheet at December 31, 1990:		
Operational assets:		
Land		
Building		
Less accumulated depreciation (20 years) . . .		
Income statement for 1990:		
Depreciation expense		

Show your computations.

b. Would the CD restatement affect income tax expense for the company? Explain. Do you think it should? Explain.

PROBLEMS

P16–1   **(Analysis of a Financial Statement Using All of the Ratios Discussed in the Chapter; Emphasis on Assessing Liquidity)**
Winter Corporation has just completed its comparative statements for the year ended December 31, 19B. At this point, certain analytical and interpretive procedures are to be undertaken. The completed statements (summarized) are as follows:

	19B	19A
Income statement:		
Sales revenue	$400,000*	$390,000*
Cost of goods sold	220,000	218,000
Gross margin	180,000	172,000
Operating expenses (including interest on bonds)	147,000	148,000
Pretax income	33,000	24,000
Income tax	9,000	7,000
Net income	$ 24,000	$ 17,000
Balance sheet:		
Cash	$ 5,400	$ 2,700
Accounts receivable (net)	44,000	30,000
Merchandise inventory	30,000	24,000
Prepaid expenses	600	500
Operational assets (net)	150,000	130,000
	$230,000	$187,200
Accounts payable	$ 19,000	$ 20,000
Income taxes payable	1,000	1,200
Bonds payable (10% interest rate)	80,000	50,000
Common stock (par $5)	100,000†	100,000
Retained earnings	30,000‡	16,000
	$230,000	$187,200

* Forty percent were credit sales.
† The market price of the stock at the end of 19B was $20 per share.
‡ During 19B, the company declared and paid a cash dividend of $30,000.

Required:

a. Complete a table similar to the following (show computations; round percents and ratios to two places):

Name and Computation of the 19B Ratio	Brief Explanation of the Ratio
Tests of profitability: 1. Return on owners' investment. 2. Etc. **Tests of liquidity:** 1. Current ratio. 2. Etc. **Tests of solvency and equity position:** 1. Debt/equity ratio. 2. Etc. **Market tests:** 1. Price/earnings ratio. 2. Etc.	

b. Answer the following questions for 19B:
(1) Evaluate the financial leverage. Explain its meaning using the computed amount(s).
(2) Evaluate the profit margin amount and explain how a stockholder might use it.
(3) Explain to a stockholder why the current ratio and the quick ratio are different. Do you observe any liquidity problems? Explain.
(4) Assuming credit terms are 1/10, n/30, do you perceive an unfavorable situation for the company related to credit sales? Explain.

P16–2 **(Use Ratios to Analyze Several Years of Financial Data; Identify Favorable and Unfavorable Factors; Give Recommendations to Improve Operations)**

The following information was contained in the annual financial statements of Oak Company, which started business January 1, 19A (assume account balances only in Cash and Capital Stock on this date; all amounts are in thousands of dollars).

	19A	19B	19C	19D
Accounts receivable (net; terms n/30) . . .	$ 8	$10	$ 16	$ 22
Merchandise inventory	10	12	20	25
Net sales (¾ on credit)	40	60	100	120
Cost of goods sold	26	36	64	80
Net income (loss)	(10)	6	14	10

Required (show computations and round to two decimal places):
a. Complete the tabulation given below.
b. Evaluate the results of the three related ratios 1, 2, and 3, to identify the favorable or unfavorable factors. Give your recommendations to improve the company's operations.
c. Evaluate the results of the last four ratios (4, 5, 6, and 7) and identify any favorable or unfavorable factors. Give your recommendations to improve the company's operations.

Items	19A	19B	19C	19D
1. Profit margin—percent.				
2. Gross margin—ratio.				
3. Expenses as a percent of sales, excluding cost of goods sold.				
4. Inventory turnover.				
5. Days' supply in inventory.				
6. Receivable turnover.				
7. Average days to collect.				

P16-3 **(Compare Alternative Investment Opportunities Using All of the Ratios Discussed in the Chapter; Prepare Investment Recommendations)**

The 19B financial statements for Able and Baker companies are summarized below:

	Able Company	Baker Company
Balance sheet:		
Cash	$ 25,000	$ 11,000
Accounts receivable (net)	30,000	17,000
Inventory	80,000	20,000
Operational assets (net)	125,000	300,000
Other assets	40,000	252,000
Total assets	$300,000	$600,000
Current liabilities	$ 90,000	$ 40,000
Long-term debt (10%)	50,000	60,000
Capital stock (par $10)	120,000	400,000
Contributed capital in excess of par	10,000	60,000
Retained earnings	30,000	40,000
Total liabilities and stockholders' equity	$300,000	$600,000
Income statement:		
Sales revenue (on credit) . . . . ($\frac{1}{3}$)	$600,000 ($\frac{1}{6}$)	$900,000
Cost of goods sold	(350,000)	(450,000)
Expenses (including interest and income tax)	(205,000)	(360,000)
Net income	$ 45,000	$ 90,000
Selected data from the 19A statements:		
Accounts receivable (net)	$ 25,000	$ 19,000
Inventory	70,000	24,000
Long-term debt	50,000	60,000
Other data:		
Per share price at end of 19B (offering price)	$ 20	$ 15
Average income tax rate	30%	30%
Dividends declared and paid in 19B	$ 24,000	$120,000

The companies are in the same line of business and are direct competitors in a large metropolitan area. They have been in business approximately 10 years, and each has had steady growth. The two managements have different viewpoints in many respects; however, Baker is the more conservative, and as the president said, "We avoid what we consider to be undue risks." Neither company is publicly held. Able Company has an annual audit by a CPA but Baker Company does not.

Required:

a. Complete a schedule that reflects a ratio analysis of each company. Compute the ratios discussed in the chapter.

b. A client of yours has the opportunity to buy 10% of the shares in one or the other company at the per share prices given above. Your client has decided to invest in one of the companies. Based on the data given, prepare a comparative evaluation of the ratio analyses (and any other available information) and give your recommended choice with the supporting explanation.

P16–4 **(Comparison of Loan Requests from Two Companies Using All of the Ratios Discussed in the Chapter)**

The 19B financial statements for Doe and Roe companies are summarized below:

	Doe Company	Roe Company
Balance sheet:		
Cash	$ 20,000	$ 40,000
Accounts receivable (net)	60,000	10,000
Inventory	120,000	30,000
Operational assets (net)	500,000	150,000
Other assets	155,000	54,000
Total assets	$855,000	$284,000
Current liabilities	$100,000	20,000
Long-term debt (10%)	200,000	50,000
Capital stock (par $20)	500,000	200,000
Contributed capital in excess of par	25,000	2,000
Retained earnings	30,000	12,000
Total liabilities and stockholders' equity	$855,000	$284,000
Income statement:		
Sales revenue (on credit) . . . . (½)	$900,000	(⅓) $300,000
Cost of goods sold	(522,000)	(180,000)
Expenses (including interest and income tax) . .	(288,000)	(84,000)
Net income	$ 90,000	$ 36,000
Selected data from the 19A statements:		
Accounts receivable, net	$ 50,000	$ 14,000
Long-term debt (12%)	200,000	50,000
Inventory	100,000	45,000
Other data:		
Per share price at end of 19B	$ 15.00	$ 12.00
Average income tax rate	30%	30%
Dividends declared and paid in 19B	$ 20,000	$ 9,000

These two companies are in the same line of business and in the same state but in different cities. Each company has been in operation for about 10 years. Doe Company is audited by one of the national accounting firms, and Roe Company is audited by a local accounting firm. Both companies received an unqualified opinion (i.e., the independent auditors found nothing wrong) on the financial statements. Doe Company wants to borrow $75,000 cash, and Roe Company needs $30,000. The loans will be for a two-year period and are needed for "working capital purposes."

Required:

a. Complete a schedule that reflects a ratio analysis of each company. Compute the ratios discussed in the chapter.

b. Assume you work in the loan department of a local bank. You have been asked to analyze the situation and recommend which loan is preferable. Based on the data given, your analysis prepared in (a), and any other information, give your choice and the supporting explanation.

P16-5   (Assess the Solvency of an Actual Company Using Selected Ratios)
The following information was contained in the actual financial statements of a large manufacturing company that currently is listed on The New York Stock Exchange:

Balance Sheet

	December 31 (millions of dollars)	
	19B	19A
Assets		
Current Assets		
Cash	$ 188.2	$ 123.2
Time deposits	120.8	248.8
Marketable securities	165.3	150.8
Accounts receivable (less allowance for doubtful accounts: 19B—$34.9 million; 19A—$16.7 million)	610.3	848.0
Inventories—at the lower of cost (substantially FIFO) or market	1,873.8	1,980.8
Prepaid insurance, taxes, and other expenses	162.3	210.2
Total Current Assets	3,120.7	3,561.8
Total Investments and Other Assets	1,183.5	1,396.5
Property, Plant, and Equipment		
Land, buildings, machinery, and equipment	3,733.1	3,391.3
Less accumulated depreciation	2,097.1	1,963.9
	1,636.0	1,427.4
Special tools	712.9	595.5
Net Property, Plant, and Equipment	2,348.9	2,022.9
Total Assets	$ 6,653.1	$ 6,981.2
Liabilities and Stockholders' Investment		
Current Liabilities		
Accounts payable	$ 1,530.4	$ 1,725.0
Accrued expenses	807.9	698.0
Short-term debt	600.9	49.2
Payment due within one year on long-term debt	275.6	12.4
Taxes on income	16.8	1.2
Total Current Liabilities	3,231.6	2,485.8
Total Long-term Debt and Other Liabilities	1,559.1	1,564.1
Minority interest in consolidated subsidiaries	38.3	4.8
Preferred stock—nopar value	218.7	217.0
Common stock—par value $6.25 per share	416.9	397.7
Additional paid-in capital	692.2	683.1
Net earnings retained	496.3	1,628.7
Total Liabilities and Stockholders' Investment	$ 6,653.1	$ 6,981.2

Income Statement

	Year Ended December 31 (millions of dollars)	
	---	---
	19B	**19A**
Net sales	$12,004.3	$13,669.8
Cost of goods sold	11,631.5	12,640.1
Depreciation of plant and equipment	180.6	154.0
Amortization of special tools	220.0	198.2
Selling and administrative expenses	598.5	572.1
Pension plans	260.6	262.3
Interest expense	215.4	128.9
	13,106.6	13,955.6
Loss Before Taxes on Income	(1,102.3)	(285.8)
Taxes on income (credit)	(5.0)	(81.2)
Net Loss	$(1,097.3)	$ (204.6)

Required:

a. Calculate the following ratios:
   (1) Return on owners' investment.
   (2) Return on total investment.
       (For purposes of this case, assume that the interest expense reported on the income statement is net of income taxes.)
   (3) Financial leverage.
   (4) Earnings per share.
   (5) Current ratio.
   (6) Quick ratio.
   (7) Inventory turnover.
   (8) Debt/equity ratio.

b. Based on your analysis of the ratios that you calculated in Requirement (a), do you think that this company will be able to continue in existence? Explain. Would you be willing to invest in this company? Explain.

P16-6   (Analysis of the Impact of Alternative Inventory Methods on Selected Ratios)
Aggressive Company uses the FIFO method to cost inventory, and Conservative Company uses the LIFO method. The two companies are exactly alike except for the difference in inventory costing methods. Costs of inventory items for both companies have been rising steadily in recent years, and each company has increased its inventory each year. Each company has paid its tax liability in full for the current year (and all previous years), and each company uses the same accounting methods for both financial reporting and income tax reporting. Identify which company will report the higher amount for each of the following ratios. If it is not possible, explain why.

a. Current ratio.

b. Quick ratio.

c. Debt/equity ratio.

d. Return on owners' investment.

e. Earnings per share.

P16–7   **(Based on Chapter Supplement 16A: CD Restatement of Selected Balance Sheet Accounts and Calculation of the Purchasing Power Gain [Loss] on Monetary Items)**

The HC balance sheet for Fargo Company was prepared on December 31, 19F. Supplemental HC/CD disclosures are to be developed. The following four items were selected from the balance sheet:

Items	HC basis (when acquired)	GPL index (when acquired or incurred)
Receivables	$69,000	115
Investment, common stock	42,000	105
Land, plant site	20,000	100
Payables	99,000	110

The GPL at the end of 19F was 120.

Required:

a. Indicate which items are monetary and which are nonmonetary.

b. Set up a schedule to derive the amount "CD restated basis" that should be shown on the supplementary HC/CD disclosures for each item. Show computations.

c. Compute the purchasing power gain (loss) on monetary items. Show computations.

d. Explain why certain items were omitted from your computation in (c).

P16–8   **(Based on Chapter Supplement 16A; CD Restate Selected Balance Sheet Accounts and Compute Purchasing Power Gain [Loss] on Monetary Items)**

Hill Company has prepared the annual HC basis financial statements at December 31, 19F. The company must prepare supplemental HC/CD disclosures. The following seven items were selected from the balance sheet:

Items	HC basis (when acquired)	GPL index (when acquired or incurred)
1. Cash:		
Beginning balance	$ 20,000	141.5
Debits	38,800	146*
Credits	(44,600)	147*
2. Merchandise inventory (average cost)	58,000	145
3. Accounts receivable (net)	28,800	144*
4. Land (no changes during 19F)	12,000	100
5. Building (net; no changes during 19F)	157,500	105
6. Accounts payable	42,000	140*
7. Bonds payable (no changes during 19F) ...	90,000	110

At the end of 19F the price-level index was 150.
* Average GPL index for these items.

Required:

a. Group the above items into two categories: monetary and nonmonetary.

b. Set up a schedule and compute the amount "CD restated basis" that should be shown on the supplementary HC/CD disclosures for each of the items. Show calculations.

c. Set up a schedule and compute the purchasing power gain or loss on monetary items. Show calculations and round to the nearest $100.

d. Explain why some of the seven items were omitted from your computations in (c).

CASES

C16–1   **(Analysis of the Impact of Alternative Depreciation Methods on Ratio Analysis)**
Fast Company uses the sum-of-years'-digits method to depreciate its property, plant, and equipment, and Slow Company uses the straight-line method. Both companies use 175% declining-balance depreciation for income tax purposes. The two companies are exactly alike except for the difference in depreciation methods.

Required:

a. Identify the financial ratios discussed in Chapter 16 that are **likely** to be affected by the difference in depreciation methods.

b. Which company will report the higher amount for each ratio that you have identified? If you cannot be certain, explain why.

C16–2   **(Analysis of the Impact of Business Transactions on Ratio Analysis)**
Nearly Broke Company requested a sizable loan from Second City National Bank in order to acquire a large tract of land for future expansion. Nearly Broke reported current assets of $1,750,000 ($475,000 in cash) and current liabilities of $975,000. Second City denied the loan request for a number of reasons including the fact that the current ratio was below two to one. When Nearly Broke was informed of the loan denial, the comptroller of the company immediately paid $470,000 that was owed to several trade creditors. The comptroller then asked Second City to reconsider the loan application. Based on these abbreviated facts, would you recommend that Second City approve the loan request? Why?

C16–3   **(Based on Chapter Supplement 16A: Compute and Analyze Purchasing Power Gain on Debt)**
Frank Smith, president of Delta Corporation, has asked that you help him understand inflation accounting. During a meeting, Mr. Smith made the following comments:

I have been told that it is possible to make money by borrowing money during a period of inflation. I plan to recommend that Delta borrow $10 million, at 10% interest, on January 1, 19D, and deposit the money in Delta's checking account (which does not pay interest). One year later, we will repay the money. The average inflation rate during 19D is expected to be 5%, consequently Delta should have a purchasing power gain on the debt. Delta will be able to use the cash from the purchasing power gain to pay a dividend to the stockholders of the company. The only thing I don't understand is why bankers are willing to lend money during a period of inflation. If we can make money by borrowing, don't the bankers lose money by lending money?

Required:

a. Determine the amount of the purchasing power gain that Mr. Smith expects Delta to earn by borrowing $10 million. Will Delta actually earn the purchasing power gain that Mr. Smith expects? Explain why. Would your answer be different if the $10 million were invested in a tract of land during the year? Why?

b. Evaluate Mr. Smith's plan to use cash from a purchasing power gain on monetary items to pay a cash dividend to the stockholders.

c. Prepare a response to Mr. Smith's question concerning why bankers are willing to lend money during a period of inflation.

C16–4 **(Financial Statement Analysis for an Actual Company)**

JCPenney   Refer to the financial statements of J.C. Penney Company, Inc. given in the appendix immediately preceding the index. Compute each of the 13 accounting ratios (for 1988) discussed in the chapter. Assume the tax rate is 34% and that the current market price per share of common stock is $45.

1988 ANNUAL REPORT OF J.C. PENNEY COMPANY, INC.

To Our Stockholders:

The Company's net income in 1988 totaled $807 million, or $6.02 per share. This compared with $608 million, or $4.11 per share, in 1987.

The almost $200 million increase in net income in 1988 reflected primarily an after tax gain of $139 million on the sale of our former headquarters building in New York City. In contrast, two nonrecurring items in the prior year, a provision for the Company's central office relocation to the Dallas, Texas, area and the loss on the sale of the Belgian operation, resulted in an after tax charge of $98 million. An additional supporting factor in 1988 was the decline in our effective income tax rate to 32.3 per cent from 37.9 per cent in 1987.

Net income before the nonrecurring items was $668 million in 1988, about 5 per cent lower than the preceding year's $706 million, with the LIFO impact a significant factor in the decline. Primary earnings per share amounted to $4.96 in 1988, up from $4.77 in 1987. This gain relates to the lesser number of shares outstanding — an average of 17 million fewer — in 1988.

Retail Sales Performance

Retail sales overall, at $14.8 billion, rose 0.4 per cent after excluding sales of the Belgian operation, which was sold in 1987. JCPenney stores' performance lagged, but this was offset by substantial gains by catalog and drug stores.

The decrease in JCPenney stores' sales was accounted for principally by the phaseout during the year of such high volume lines as home electronics, hard sporting goods, and photographic equipment. As we previously reported to you, the elimination of this merchandise, which we continue to offer through catalog, has enabled our stores to devote the much needed space to our major areas of concentration — apparel and soft home furnishings.

Other measurements of store performance are to be commended — in particular the decline in markdowns and the improvement in gross margin in face of steady increases in the costs of goods we purchased. Price inflation, which was greatest in the second half, resulted in a LIFO charge in 1988 of $125 million, as compared with $45 million in 1987.

We made substantial physical adjustments last year to 400 of our largest stores to accommodate broader soft line merchandise assortments. We also continued to open new stores and to close unproductive units. In metropolitan markets, we opened 20 stores, of which the majority were relocations of existing units, and we closed 21. As for geographic stores, 23 were opened and 45 closed.

Record Year for Catalog

Catalog had its third straight record year, with operating profits in excess of the previous year's total despite substantial increases in paper, ink, and postage costs. The success of our catalog in recent years says to us that we know our customers and that they like our merchandise, our quality, our prices, and our service.

Financial Highlights (In millions except per share data)

For the Year	1988	1987	1986
Retail sales	**$14,833**	$15,332	$14,740
Net income	**$ 807**	$ 608	$ 478
Net income per common share			
Primary	**$ 6.02**	$ 4.11	$ 3.19
Fully diluted	**$ 5.92**	$ 4.11	$ 3.17
Dividends per common share	**$ 2.00**	$ 1.48	$ 1.24

Our catalog associates are now doubling their efforts to provide better than expected quality without raising prices. A unique service feature is also on their agenda. Beginning this Summer, consumers throughout the United States will be able to call just one 800 number and whether they're ordering merchandise, checking on its delivery, or questioning an invoice, the person at the other end of the line will have access to their complete file and be able to respond immediately.

Catalog's ties to the JCPenney store remain as strong as ever. A very large part of catalog's business depends on store referrals, and the majority of catalog orders are picked up at stores. A substantial increase in catalog's sales of home electronics last year can be traced to the discontinuance of this line of merchandise in JCPenney stores.

This Spring, we plan to offer a selection of catalog merchandise via JCPenney Television Shopping Channel, utilizing Shop Television Network, Inc. as its exclusive production company for a 24-hour-a-day home shopping network currently available to some 5 million cable subscribers. Merchandise ordered in this way can be picked up at more than 1,400 JCPenney locations and the Penney credit card can be used for purchases.

Thrift Drug's Sales and Profits Up

Strong prescription sales in stores and the mail order operation were major contributors to a successful year for our Thrift Drug operation. Both sales and profits reached record levels. Thirty-four stores were opened in 1988 and at year end, access to our mail order pharmacy was available to some 3.1 million people through some 500 group accounts in all 50 states. Point-of-sale equipment, currently in 140 drug stores, will be installed in an additional 160 units in 1989. The remaining 100 plus stores will be so equipped in 1990. Enhanced efficiency and effectiveness in serving customers' needs are the goals.

Among our specialty retailing businesses, our Units women's specialty stores, which offer poly-cotton free size separates, recorded excellent progress both in terms of sales and profitability in 1988. We were also encouraged by the results turned in by our three Portfolio freestanding furniture stores and plan to open an additional eight units in 1989.

The Company's revenues from other than retail operations totaled $463 million, as compared with $415 million in 1987. The major source of these funds was premiums earned by our insurance operations. Other contributors were the JCPenney National Bank and JCP Realty, Inc. More about these activities can be found in our Financial Review.

The poor results of our casualty insurance activity, coupled with a lack of synergism with JCPenney stores in which it was offered, prompted our decision late last year to exit this business. On February 1, 1989, we disclosed that we were discussing the sale of the field claims, field sales, and home office operations in Westerville, Ohio, with several interested parties. At the time of this writing, we are encouraged by the progress of these talks. We will, of course, continue to operate the JCPenney Life Insurance Company, which offers life, health, and credit insurance through direct response.

Headquarters Plans

As was indicated earlier, we have concluded the sale of our former headquarters building in New York City. The selling price was approximately $350 million. We are now in the early stages of preparing for our eventual central office site in Plano, Texas, just a few miles north of our temporary quarters in the Dallas area. Harwood K. Smith & Partners (HKS) has been selected to design the new offices and prepare a master plan for the 429-acre site. The planning process is expected to take two years, with another two years for actual construction.

Dividend Action

In another development of particular significance to stockholders last year, the Company's Board of Directors increased the regular quarterly dividend by 35 per cent to 50 cents a share. This followed a two-for-one stock split and a 19 per cent dividend increase in 1987. The dividend actions are indicative of the Company's increasingly strong financial condition.

We are, in addition, sufficiently confident of our prospects for profitable future growth that we have continued to buy back our stock. Approximately 28 million shares have been repurchased since Fall 1987 of a total of 35 million authorized by the Board of Directors. Recent purchases have been made in conjunction with the creation of a leveraged employee stock ownership plan (LESOP). The LESOP, which is described in detail in the Financial Review, is intended to enhance cash flow, earnings per share, and return on equity while providing our Penney associates with a more attractive benefit plan.

Personnel Changes

Personnel changes of particular interest in the past year included the retirements of executive vice presidents A. Scott Frahlich and Thomas J. Lyons. Their successors, respectively, are James E. Oesterreicher, who moved from President of the Western Region to Director of JCPenney Stores, and Terry S. Prindiville, who became responsible for real estate and construction services, systems and data processing, company communications, planning and research, and drug stores. Coincident with Mr. Prindiville's appointment, the Southwestern Region that he had headed was consolidated with the southern portion of the Western Region under William J. Ferguson. The northern part of the Western Region became allied with the Central Region, with the ultimate aim of this restructuring a more efficient system for distributing weather-related merchandise to stores. Cost savings will also be realized.

In January 1989, we were saddened by the death of our friend and fellow member of the Board of Directors David B. Meeker. Mr. Meeker had a long career with Hobart Corporation and was that company's president and chief executive officer from 1970 to 1981. He joined our Board in 1983 and in the intervening years served with distinction. We will miss him.

Summing up the year just past, I cannot help but reflect on the changes and the challenges we encountered. Our relocation to the Dallas area; the parting of some long time loyal associates for whom the move was impossible for family or other reasons; the screening and hiring of replacements both from within and outside our own ranks; decisions about homes and schools: all of these situations colored our year both as individuals and as a Company. We have emerged, I believe, reinvigorated; confident of the correctness of our decision to relocate; sure of the soundness of our direction; and eager to continue to expand our businesses step by step and brick by brick.

Warmest regards,

William R. Howell
Chairman of the Board

March 24, 1989

Consolidated Statement of Income (In millions except per share data)

J.C. Penney Company, Inc. and Subsidiaries

For the Year	1988	1987	1986
Revenue			
Retail sales	$14,833	$15,332	$14,740
Other revenue	463	415	411
Total revenue	15,296	15,747	15,151
Costs and expenses			
Cost of goods sold, occupancy, buying, and warehousing costs	9,717	10,152	9,786
Selling, general, and administrative expenses	3,815	3,743	3,668
Costs and expenses of other businesses	487	401	383
Interest expense, net	307	300	350
Nonrecurring items	(222)	172	—
Total costs and expenses	14,104	14,768	14,187
Income before income taxes	1,192	979	964
Income taxes	385	371	434
Income before extraordinary charge	807	608	530
Extraordinary charge on debt restructure, net of income taxes of $49	—	—	52
Net income	$ 807	$ 608	$ 478
Earnings per common share			
Primary			
Income before extraordinary charge	$ 6.02	$ 4.11	$ 3.53
Extraordinary charge, net of income taxes	—	—	.34
Net income	$ 6.02	$ 4.11	$ 3.19
Fully diluted			
Income before extraordinary charge	$ 5.92	$ 4.11	$ 3.51
Extraordinary charge, net of income taxes	—	—	.34
Net income	$ 5.92	$ 4.11	$ 3.17

Consolidated Statement of Reinvested Earnings (In millions)

	1988	1987	1986
Reinvested earnings at beginning of year	$3,213	$3,379	$3,122
Net income	807	608	478
Unrealized change in equity securities and translation adjustment	2	(4)	7
Retirement of common stock	(688)	(514)	(42)
Two-for-one stock split	—	(38)	—
Common stock dividends declared	(260)	(218)	(186)
Preferred stock dividends declared, net	(17)	—	—
Reinvested earnings at end of year	$3,057	$3,213	$3,379

See Summary of Accounting Policies on pages 8 and 9 and 1988 Financial Review on pages 9 through 21.

Consolidated Balance Sheet (In millions)

J.C. Penney Company, Inc. and Subsidiaries

Assets	1988	1987	1986
Current assets			
Cash and short term investments of $653, $84, and $534	$ 670	$ 112	$ 639
Receivables, net	4,233	4,536	4,614
Merchandise inventories	2,201	2,350	2,168
Prepaid expenses	142	132	111
Total current assets	7,246	7,130	7,532
Properties, net of accumulated depreciation and amortization of $1,429, $1,346, and $1,275	3,034	2,910	2,919
Other assets	1,974	1,694	1,395
	$12,254	$11,734	$11,846
Liabilities and Stockholders' Equity			
Current liabilities			
Accounts payable and accrued expenses	$ 1,666	$ 1,595	$ 1,489
Short term debt	756	955	597
Current maturities of long term debt	244	—	484
Deferred taxes, principally installment sales	119	136	142
Total current liabilities	2,785	2,686	2,712
Long term debt	3,064	2,608	2,655
Deferred taxes	1,346	1,375	1,481
Other liabilities	1,102	892	658
Stockholders' equity			
Preferred stock, without par value: Authorized, 25 million shares— issued, 1 million shares of Series B LESOP convertible preferred	706	—	—
Guaranteed LESOP obligation	(668)	—	—
Common stock, par value 50¢: Authorized, 500 million shares— issued, 123, 138, and 150 million shares	862	960	961
Reinvested earnings	3,057	3,213	3,379
Total stockholders' equity	3,957	4,173	4,340
	$12,254	$11,734	$11,846

See Summary of Accounting Policies on pages 8 and 9 and 1988 Financial Review on pages 9 through 21.

Company Statement on Financial Information

The Company is responsible for the information presented in this Annual Report. The consolidated financial statements have been prepared in accordance with generally accepted accounting principles and are considered to present fairly in all material respects the Company's results of operations, financial position, and cash flows. Certain amounts included in the consolidated financial statements are estimated based on currently available information and judgment of the outcome of future conditions and circumstances. Financial information elsewhere in this Annual Report is consistent with that in the consolidated financial statements.

The Company's system of internal accounting controls is supported by written policies and procedures and supplemented by a staff of internal auditors. This system is designed to provide reasonable assurance, at suitable costs, that assets are safeguarded and that transactions are executed in accordance with appropriate authorization and are recorded and reported properly. The system is continually reviewed, evaluated, and, where appropriate, modified to accommodate current conditions. Emphasis is placed on the careful selection, training, and development of professional managers.

An organizational alignment that is premised upon appropriate delegation of authority and division of responsibility is fundamental to this system. Communication programs are aimed at assuring that established policies and procedures are disseminated and understood throughout the Company.

The consolidated financial statements have been audited by independent auditors whose report appears on page 6.

The Audit Committee of the Board of Directors is composed solely of directors who are not officers or employees of the Company. The Audit Committee is responsible for recommending to the Board the engagement of the independent auditors for the purpose of conducting the annual audit of the Company's consolidated financial statements. Company personnel, including internal auditors, and the independent auditors meet periodically with the Audit Committee to review financial statements and discuss auditing and financial reporting matters.

Consolidated Statement of Cash Flows (In millions)

J.C. Penney Company, Inc. and Subsidiaries

For the Year	1988	1987	1986
Operating activities			
Income before extraordinary charge	$ 807	$ 608	$ 530
Gain on sale of headquarters building	(222)	—	—
Deferred taxes	(46)	(112)	273
Depreciation and amortization	258	241	229
Amortization of original issue discount	60	52	46
Nonrecurring items	—	172	—
Change in cash from:			
Customer receivables	337	70	(51)
Inventories, net of trade payables	273	(170)	261
Other assets and liabilities, net	(169)	(56)	(51)
	1,298	805	1,237
Investing activities			
Capital expenditures	(481)	(376)	(348)
Proceeds from sale of headquarters building . .	302	—	—
Other investments	(7)	(55)	(11)
	(186)	(431)	(359)
Financing activities			
Increase (decrease) in short term debt	(199)	427	(143)
Issuance of long term debt	200	202	597
Payments of long term debt	(214)	(728)	(618)
Extraordinary charge on retirement of debt . . .	—	—	(39)
Common stock retired, net	(781)	(589)	(11)
Preferred stock issued	706	—	—
Dividends paid	(266)	(213)	(183)
	(554)	(901)	(397)
Increase (decrease) in cash and short term investments	$ 558	$ (527)	$ 481
Supplemental cash flow information			
Interest paid	$ 278	$ 281	$ 325
Interest received	$ 29	$ 24	$ 27
Income taxes paid	$ 350	$ 407	$ 95

See Summary of Accounting Policies on pages 8 and 9 and 1988 Financial Review on pages 9 through 21.

Independent Auditors' Report

To the Stockholders and Board of Directors of J.C. Penney Company, Inc.:

We have audited the accompanying consolidated balance sheets of J.C. Penney Company, Inc. and Subsidiaries as of January 28, 1989, January 30, 1988, and January 31, 1987, and the related consolidated statements of income, reinvested earnings, and cash flows for the years then ended. These consolidated financial statements are the responsibility of the Company's management. Our responsibility is to express an opinion on these consolidated financial statements based on our audits.

We conducted our audits in accordance with generally accepted auditing standards. Those standards require that we plan and perform the audit to obtain reasonable assurance about whether the consolidated financial statements are free of material misstatement. An audit includes examining, on a test basis, evidence supporting the amounts and disclosures in the financial statements. An audit also includes assessing the accounting principles used and significant estimates made by management, as well as evaluating the overall financial statement presentation. We believe that our audits provide a reasonable basis for our opinion.

In our opinion, the consolidated financial statements referred to above present fairly, in all material respects, the financial position of J.C. Penney Company, Inc. and Subsidiaries at January 28, 1989, January 30, 1988, and January 31, 1987, and the results of their operations and their cash flows for the years then ended, in conformity with generally accepted accounting principles.

1601 Elm, Dallas, Texas 75201
February 16, 1989

Peat Marwick Main & Co.

Management's Discussion and Analysis of Results of Operations and Financial Position

Results of operations	1988	1987	1986
Domestic retail sales, per cent increase	0.4	4.6	6.3
Gross margin, per cent of retail sales	34.5	33.8	33.6
Selling, general, and administrative expenses, per cent of retail sales	25.7	24.4	24.9
Interest expense, net, per cent of retail sales	2.1	2.0	2.3
Income before income taxes and nonrecurring and extraordinary items, per cent of total revenue	6.3	7.3	6.4
Income before nonrecurring and extraordinary items, per cent of total revenue	4.4	4.5	3.5

Income before nonrecurring and extraordinary items decreased 5.4 per cent to $668 million from $706 million in 1987 and compares with $530 million in 1986. The decline in 1988 is primarily attributable to a significant increase in the LIFO reserve and the costs of discontinuing home electronics, hard sporting goods, and photographic equipment. The increase in income in 1987 was attributable to higher sales coupled with slightly higher gross margin and tight expense control. In 1986, income increased due to higher sales and improved gross margin.

Income per share on a primary basis, before nonrecurring and extraordinary items, was $4.96, up from $4.77 in 1987, and $3.53 in 1986. Income per share in 1988 benefited from fewer shares of common stock outstanding, due to the stock buy back programs of 1987 and 1988.

Nonrecurring items in 1988, on a pre-tax basis, included the $222 million gain on the sale of the Company's former corporate headquarters building. On an after-tax basis, this gain increased the Company's earnings by $139 million, or $1.06 per share on a primary basis. In 1987, nonrecurring items included the provision for relocation and the loss on the sale of the Belgian operation, which together reduced net income $98 million, or 66 cents per share.

Net income in 1988 was $807 million, up 32.7 per cent from last year's $608 million. Net income was $478 million in 1986.

Retail sales for 1988 declined 3.3 per cent to $14,833 million from $15,332 million in 1987 due to the sale of the Belgian operation in late 1987. In 1988, the Company continued to sharpen its focus on the lines of merchandise which offer superior profit opportunities: women's, men's, and children's apparel and soft home furnishings. During the year, the Company completed the phase out of home electronics, photography, and hard sporting goods merchandise from retail stores, announced in 1987. If the sales of these discontinued lines and the sales of the Belgian operation were excluded, retail sales increased 3.5 per cent.

Gross margin, as a per cent of retail sales, improved in 1988 due to the greater emphasis on family apparel and the sale of the low margin Belgian operation in 1987. For the year, gross margin exceeded the previous year's by 70 basis points despite the impact of the LIFO method of inventory valuation. As a result of a higher level of inflation in apparel merchandise in 1988 than in the previous two years, the LIFO charge amounted to $125 million, as compared with $45 million in 1987 and $10 million in 1986. Gross margin improved slightly in 1987. Gross margin improved in 1986 primarily as a result of lower markdowns.

Selling, general, and administrative expenses continued to be well controlled in 1988. SG&A expenses increased a modest 1.9 per cent in 1988, 2.0 per cent in 1987, and 6.2 per cent in 1986. As a per cent of retail sales, SG&A expenses increased in 1988 to 25.7 per cent from 24.4 per cent in 1987 as a result of the lower sales volume. In 1987 and 1986, this expense ratio declined slightly. Finance charge revenue, which reduces these expenses, declined in 1988 partially due to the sale of a portion of the Company's credit card receivables.

Costs and expenses of other businesses at $487 million, was $86 million over last year. The increase was attributable to costs associated with the expansion of the banking operation and developmental costs associated with the Company's interactive television program, Telaction, and its video home shopping venture, Shop Television Network (STN). Costs and expenses of other businesses were $383 million in 1986.

Interest expense in 1988 increased slightly because of higher borrowing levels. Interest was favorably affected by the temporary investment of the proceeds from the sale of convertible preferred stock to the leveraged employee stock ownership plan (LESOP) and by reduced borrowings resulting from the sale of a portion of the credit card receivables and the sale of the former headquarters building in New York City. In 1987, interest expense declined as a result of benefits realized from the debt restructure program, lower average borrowing levels, and lower interest rates. Interest expense decreased in 1986 due to lower interest rates and benefits realized from the debt restructure program.

The effective income tax rate for 1988 was 32.3 per cent, as compared with 37.9 and 45.0 per cent for 1987 and 1986, respectively. The reduction was principally due to the change in the statutory rate to 34 per cent in 1988 from 39 per cent in 1987 and 46 per cent in 1986. Additionally, as a result of the Tax Reform Act of 1986, income taxes were reduced $42 million and $17 million in 1988 and 1987 due to the payment of a portion of the taxes on installment sales previously deferred at higher tax rates.

Financial Position. The Company generated sufficient cash in 1988 to meet its operating requirements, capital expenditures, dividend payments, and to support its stock buy back program. Cash generated through operating activities increased $493 million during the year as a result of a lower investment in merchandise inventory and the sale of $250 million of customer receivables. Cash was also generated from the sale of the Company's former headquarters building.

Merchandise inventories decreased to $2.2 billion in 1988, down 6 per cent from 1987. Inventories increased 8 per cent in 1987 and decreased 6 per cent in 1986. In 1988, the Company continued to concentrate its merchandise mix on women's, men's, and children's apparel and soft home furnishings.

Customer accounts receivable were $3.9 billion at the end of 1988, or 8 per cent below the level at the end of 1987. The decline in the 1988 receivables level is principally due to the sale of $250 million of receivables. These receivables were sold through a trust which issued $250 million of asset-backed certificates with an expected maturity of three years. The primary objective of this transaction was to increase the financial flexibility of the Company's capital structure by providing a readily available access to a significant source of funds. Customer accounts receivable were $4.2 billion at the end of 1987, or about 2 per cent below the level at the end of 1986.

Property, plant, and equipment, at $3.0 billion, was $124 million over last year. Capital expenditures in 1988 were $487 million, $111 million above the level of 1987. The increase in capital expenditures was principally related to the cost of converting the space in JCPenney stores from the discontinued home electronics, photography, and hard sporting goods lines to women's apparel. Capital expenditures were $350 million in 1986.

During 1988, the Company continued its debt restructure program by calling a total of $152 million for two issues of high coupon long term debt and by issuing $200 million of 9.45 per cent Notes due 1998. Total debt at year end includes $668 million of borrowings by the LESOP, which is guaranteed by the Company. The source of funds to repay the LESOP debt will be dividends from the Series B preferred stock and cash contributions by the Company, totaling approximately $100 million in each of the next ten years.

Stockholders' equity was $4.0 billion at the end of 1988, a decline of $216 million from last year. Stockholders' equity was reduced in 1988 by $769 million from purchases in the open market of its common stock. In 1988, the Company completed the stock buy back program announced in 1987, totaling 20 million shares, at a total cost of $932 million. The Company is using the proceeds from the issuance of preferred stock to the LESOP to purchase up to an additional 15 million common shares in the open market. By the end of 1988, the Company had purchased 8 million shares of its common stock from this stock buy back program at a cost of $418 million.

The Company anticipates that the major portion of its cash requirements during the next few years to finance its operations and expansion and to repay amounts borrowed will continue to be generated internally from operations. The Company will continue to review all expenditures to maximize financial returns and maintain financial flexibility.

Additional Information. For additional discussion and analysis of 1988, see the 1988 Financial Review on pages 9 through 21.

Summary of Accounting Policies

The dominant portion of JCPenney's business consists of selling merchandise and services to consumers through stores, including catalog operations.

Basis of Consolidation. The consolidated financial statements present the results of J.C. Penney Company, Inc. and its subsidiaries. The accounts of JCPenney Life Insurance Company, JCPenney Casualty Insurance Company, JCPenney National Bank, and JCP Realty, Inc. are, for the first time, included in the Company's consolidated financial statements to reflect the adoption of Financial Accounting Standards Board Statement No. 94, "Consolidation of All Majority-Owned Subsidiaries." This change had no effect on net income; however, the financial statements have been restated to reflect the consolidation of these operations. Prior to 1988, these operations were presented as unconsolidated subsidiaries accounted for under the equity method.

Discussions are under way with several major insurance companies for the sale of the personal lines operations of JCPenney Casualty Insurance Company.

Definition of Fiscal Year. JCPenney's fiscal year ends on the last Saturday in January. Fiscal year 1988 ended January 28, 1989, 1987 ended January 30, 1988, and 1986 ended January 31, 1987. They comprised 52 weeks, 52 weeks, and 53 weeks, respectively. The accounts of JCPenney Life Insurance Company, JCPenney Casualty Insurance Company, and the JCPenney National Bank are on a calendar year basis.

Retail Sales. Retail sales include merchandise and services, net of returns, and exclude sales taxes.

Finance Charge Revenue. Finance charge revenue arising from the JCPenney credit card customer accounts receivable is treated as a reduction of selling, general, and administrative expenses in the consolidated statement of income.

Short Term Investments. Excess cash invested in instruments with maturities of three months or less from time of investment is reflected as short term investments.

Merchandise Inventories. Substantially all merchandise inventories are valued at the lower of cost (last-in, first-out) or market, determined by the retail method.

Depreciation. The cost of buildings and equipment is depreciated on a straight line basis over the estimated useful lives of the assets. The principal annual rates of depreciation are 2 per cent for buildings, 5 per cent for warehouse fixtures and equipment, and 10 per cent for selling fixtures and equipment. Improvements to leased premises are amortized on a straight line basis over the expected term of the lease or their estimated useful lives, whichever is shorter.

Deferred Charges. Expenses associated with the opening of new stores are written off in the year of store opening, except those of stores opened in January, which are written off in the following fiscal year. Catalog preparation and printing costs are written off over the estimated productive lives of the catalogs, not to exceed six months.

1988 Financial Review

Earnings per common share were calculated on the following basis:

Earnings per common share (In millions, except per share data)	1988	1987	1986
Primary			
Net income	$ 807	$ 608	$ 478
Dividend on preferred stock (after-tax)	17	—	—
Adjusted net income	$ 790	$ 608	$ 478
Weighted average number of shares	131	148	150
Net income per share	$6.02	$4.11	$3.19
Fully diluted			
Net income	$ 807	$ 608	$ 478
Weighted average number of shares (primary)	131	148	150
Convertible preferred stock and other	5	—	1
Weighted average number of shares	136	148	151
Net income per share	$5.92	$4.11	$3.17

Nonrecurring items included in the consolidated statement of income in 1988 reflect a pre-tax gain of $222 million on the sale of the Company's former headquarters building in New York City. In 1987, the Company recorded a pre-tax provision of $140 million for the aggregate cost of relocating the corporate headquarters to Dallas, Texas. The move was completed in 1988, and the provision was sufficient to cover all related costs. Also in 1987, the Company's Belgian operation was sold at a pre-tax loss of $32 million. The effect of nonrecurring items increased net income by $139 million, or $1.06 per share, in 1988 and reduced net income by $98 million, or 66 cents per share, in 1987.

Revenue

Retail sales in 1988 were $14,833 million, a decrease of 3.3 per cent from $15,332 million in 1987.

Retail sales (In millions)	1988	Per cent increase (decrease) 1988 vs. 1987 All units	Per cent increase (decrease) 1988 vs. 1987 Comparative units	1987	Per cent increase 1987 vs. 1986 All units	Per cent increase 1987 vs. 1986 Comparative units	1986
JCPenney stores	$13,364	(0.5)	(2.2)	$13,428	4.2	3.9	$12,888
Catalog	2,918	12.9	13.6	2,585	10.9	11.0	2,332
Intracompany elimination	(2,331)	n/a	n/a	(2,033)	n/a	n/a	(1,830)
Total JCPenney stores and catalog	13,951	(0.2)	(1.9)	13,980	4.4	3.9	13,390
Drug stores	882	11.4	9.4	791	8.9	7.2	727
Domestic sales	14,833	0.4	(1.3)	14,771	4.6	4.1	14,117
Belgian operation*	—			561			623
Total	$14,833			$15,332			$14,740

The intracompany elimination represents the duplication of those catalog sales made through JCPenney stores and also included in Catalog. Comparative units are those in operation throughout both the current and prior year. For further analyses of retail sales, see the discussion below and the Five Year Operations Summary on page 23.
*Sold in 1987.

Other revenue includes insurance premiums, income of JCPenney National Bank, and income from real estate development operations.

Other revenue (In millions)	1988	1987	1986
Casualty insurance premiums and investment income	$184	$195	$213
Life insurance premiums and investment income	167	156	150
Bankcard interest and fees	90	41	20
Real estate development operation	22	23	28
Total	$463	$415	$411

Retail Businesses

JCPenney stores' sales (In millions)	1988	Per cent increase (decrease) 1988 vs. 1987		1987	Per cent increase 1987 vs. 1986		1986
		All units	Com-parative units		All units	Com-parative units	
Metropolitan markets	$11,313	(1.3)	(2.2)	$11,463	4.2	6.6	$11,001
Geographic markets	2,051	4.4	2.1	1,965	4.1	4.6	1,887
Total	$13,364	(0.5)	(2.2)	$13,428	4.2	3.9	$12,888

JCPenney stores are organized into two groups of stores, each representing separate and distinct markets.

Metropolitan market stores are located primarily in regional comparison shopping centers.

The Company had 698 stores in metropolitan markets at year end and an aggregate of 95 million gross square feet of space. Sales per square foot were approximately $118 for stores in operation throughout 1988. The Company continues to open new stores as opportunities arise and to close stores that do not meet performance objectives. During 1988, 20 metropolitan market stores were opened and 21 were closed.

Metropolitan market stores' profit was about the same as last year as slightly higher margins were off-set by a decline in sales. Profit increased in 1987 and 1986 due to higher sales, improved gross margin, and expense controls.

Geographic market stores are in nonmetropolitan areas and in satellite towns within metropolitan areas.

At year end, the Company had 657 geographic market stores in operation and an aggregate of 19 million gross square feet of space. Sales per square foot were approximately $113 for stores in operation throughout 1988. During 1988, 23 geographic stores were opened and 45 were closed. The Company continues to expand into new markets and close unproductive stores.

Geographic market stores' profit increased slightly in 1988 due to improved gross margin. Profit increased in 1987 and 1986 due to higher gross margin and expense controls.

Discontinued lines. During 1988, the Company completed the phase out of home electronics, photography, and hard sporting goods merchandise, announced in 1987. These lines will continue to be offered through Catalog. Sales of JCPenney stores, excluding these lines, were as follows:

	1988	1987	1986
Total sales of JCPenney stores	$13,364	$13,428	$12,888
Discontinued lines	131	568	720
Sales of continuing lines	$13,233	$12,860	$12,168
Per cent increase	2.9%	5.7%	6.6%

The more than four million square feet of space made available by discontinued lines was reallocated primarily into the more profitable women's apparel lines. In addition, the concept of segmentation was implemented in the women's department whereby the department is presented in distinct categories that target five different consumer types. These five types are the traditional, updated, conservative, junior, and young junior woman. Each type targets a different lifestyle, a different fashion attitude, and different merchandise needs.

Eight separate departments in women's sportswear and three sub-departments in women's and petites focus on these five distinct consumer types. In effect, each department forms a separate "store" within the larger JCPenney store. This concept works for all JCPenney stores, regardless of size. While smaller stores may not have enough space to separate departments physically, they still organize merchandise by target consumers, using appropriate cues or signals.

As space has been reallocated, JCPenney store's merchandise mix as a per cent of merchandise sales continues to shift more toward women's and men's apparel. The present merchandise mix is approximately 42 per cent women's apparel, 27 per cent men's apparel, 13 per cent children's apparel, and 18 per cent home furnishings.

Several organizational changes occurred within JCPenney stores during the year. The Company's store organization was realigned from five geographical regions to four, and the merchandise and marketing departments were restructured. Both of these changes will enable JCPenney stores to better serve the needs of our targeted middle and middle/upper income families.

Catalog expands the Company's retailing capabilities by offering a wide range of merchandise to complement the stores' assortment. Two general catalogs are published, Fall & Winter and Spring & Summer, and each are circulated to more than 10 million customers. The general catalogs are supplemented by some 50 seasonal, promotional, and specialty catalogs. Merchandise offerings include family fashion and home furnishings, as well as automotive, sporting goods, home electronics, and other hardlines not carried in JCPenney stores.

Virtually all customer orders are called toll free to one of 15 telephone sales centers, where merchandise availability is confirmed or alternate selections offered. Most catalog orders are delivered to their destination within 48 hours from one of six catalog distribution centers. Orders are shipped to catalog departments in all JCPenney stores and selected Drug stores and to freestanding JCPenney catalog sales centers and independent catalog sales merchants. Home delivery orders are shipped directly to customers' homes or offices.

Catalog's profit increased in 1988 due to higher sales and tightly controlled operating expenses. Catalog profit increased dramatically in 1987 and 1986 due to increases in sales combined with improved gross margin and tight controls over advertising and operating expenses.

Catalog sales (In millions)	1988	Per cent increase 1988 vs. 1987 All units	Per cent increase 1988 vs. 1987 Comparative units	1987	Per cent increase 1987 vs. 1986 All units	Per cent increase 1987 vs. 1986 Comparative units	1986
JCPenney stores							
Metropolitan markets	$1,558	13.4	13.5	$1,374	10.7	11.9	$1,242
Geographic markets	597	12.7	14.5	530	8.4	11.5	490
Freestanding operations	176	36.6	12.8	129	31.1	13.2	98
Total	2,331	14.7	13.7	2,033	11.2	11.9	1,830
Drug stores	94	11.6	10.6	84	11.5	8.2	75
Sales merchants	59	33.5	n/a	44	70.7	n/a	26
Other, principally outlet stores	434	2.2	n/a	424	5.4	n/a	401
Total	$2,918	12.9	13.6	$2,585	10.9	11.0	$2,332

Number of catalog units	1988	1987	1986
JCPenney stores, metropolitan markets	698	699	707
JCPenney stores, geographic markets	657	679	696
Freestanding	216	172	144
Drug stores	117	120	118
Sales merchants	176	153	146
Other, principally outlet stores	15	14	14
Total	1,879	1,837	1,825

Drug stores, operating under the name Thrift Drug or The Treasury Drug Center, with an aggregate of 4.4 million square feet of gross selling space, offer typical drug store merchandise, including prescription drugs and health and beauty aid products. Thrift Drug's mail order pharmacy operation services the prescription needs of customers from major organizations by filling prescriptions through the mail. During 1988, 34 drug stores were opened and seven were closed. At year end, the Company operated 434 drug stores.

Drug stores' profits increased in 1988 as a result of higher sales, improved gross margin, and lower operating expenses. Profits declined in 1987 due to a slight decrease in gross margin and the influence of start-up costs associated with the opening of new stores. Profits increased in 1986 as a result of higher sales and improved gross margin.

Other Businesses

Costs and expenses of other businesses were as follows:

Costs and expenses of other businesses (In millions)	1988	1987	1986
Claims costs and expenses of casualty insurance operation	$197	$198	$241
Benefits, claims costs, and expenses of life insurance operation	130	120	110
Interest expense and bad debts of banking operation	75	38	16
Real estate development operation	3	3	2
Other, principally Telaction and Shop Television Network	82	42	14
Total	$487	$401	$383

JCPenney Life Insurance Company markets life, health, and credit insurance through direct response. JCPenney Life Insurance Company's 1988 net income increased from last year as a result of improved underwriting experience.

JCPenney Casualty Insurance Company recorded a net loss of $7 million in 1988 as a result of unfavorable underwriting experience.

Discussions are under way with several major insurance companies for the sale of the personal lines operation of JCPenney Casualty Insurance Company. The Company will not incur any significant gain or loss in exiting the casualty insurance business.

	Year ended December 31		
JCPenney Life Insurance Company (In millions)	**1988**	1987	1986
Premiums earned	**$133**	$121	$112
Investment income	**34**	35	38
Total revenues	**167**	156	150
Benefits, claims, and expenses	**130**	120	110
Income before income taxes	**37**	36	40
Income taxes	**12**	14	13
Net income*	**$ 25**	$ 22	$ 27

*Includes net realized investment gains of $1 million, $4 million, and $9 million in 1988, 1987, and 1986, respectively.

	December 31		
JCPenney Life Insurance Company balance sheet (In millions)	**1988**	1987	1986
Assets			
Investments			
Fixed income, at amortized cost (market: $281, $304, and $248)	**$287**	$307	$239
Short term, at cost which equals market	**2**	14	22
Equity, at market (cost: $17, $18, and $25)	**15**	15	29
Other	**14**	13	12
Total investments	**318**	349	302
Deferred policy acquisition costs	**183**	170	158
Other assets	**50**	58	50
	$551	$577	$510
Liabilities and equity			
Policy and claims reserves	**$219**	$203	$175
Income taxes and other liabilities	**79**	96	81
Equity of JCPenney	**253**	278	254
	$551	$577	$510

	Year ended December 31		
JCPenney Casualty Insurance Company (In millions)	**1988**	1987	1986
Net income (loss)	**$ (7)**	$ 4	$ (13)

	December 31		
JCPenney Casualty Insurance Company (In millions)	**1988**	1987	1986
Net assets of JCPenney Casualty Insurance Company	**$107**	$111	$109

JCPenney National Bank offers Visa and MasterCard credit cards. At the end of the year, about 416 thousand credit cards were issued. Capital contributions and advances to the bank totaled $68 million in 1988, $10 million in 1987, and $28 million in 1986. The bank repaid a $63 million advance by the end of the Company's fiscal year 1988. The bank recorded net income of $5 million in 1988, as compared with breakeven results in 1987 and 1986.

JCPenney National Bank balance sheet (In millions)	December 31		
	1988	1987	1986
Assets			
Cash and short term investments	**$160**	$ 35	$ 15
Receivables, net of allowance for doubtful accounts of			
$17, $9, and $3	**384**	247	128
Other assets	**40**	31	22
	$584	$313	$165
Liabilities and equity			
Deposits	**$474**	$278	$ 85
Other liabilities	**14**	12	4
Due to JCPenney	**63**	—	64
Equity of JCPenney	**33**	23	12
	$584	$313	$165

JCP Realty, Inc. is engaged in the development and operation of real estate through participation in joint ventures.

At year end, JCP Realty had interests in more than 80 projects, primarily regional shopping centers. More than 60 of these were in operation, and the balance were in various stages of development.

JCP Realty recorded profits of $14 million, $13 million, and $18 million in each of the last three years. Included in 1988, 1987, and 1986 results were gains, net of taxes, of $15 million, $9 million, and $14 million, respectively, from sales of its interests in shopping center ventures. JCP Realty has advanced to JCPenney an amount in excess of its equity as follows:

Net investment in JCP Realty, Inc. (In millions)	1988	1987	1986
Amount advanced to JCPenney	**$(144)**	$(127)	$(114)
Equity of JCPenney	**110**	96	83
Net investment of JCPenney	**$ (34)**	$ (31)	$ (31)

Telaction and Shop Television Network. The Company has been involved in testing two television-distributed retail formats, Telaction and Shop Television Network (STN). Expenses, net of revenues, for these businesses were $68 million in 1988, $42 million in 1987, and $14 million in 1986.

Assets

Receivables (In millions)	1988	1987	1986
Customer receivables	**$3,876**	$4,213	$4,291
Less allowance for doubtful accounts	**71**	71	79
Customer receivables, net	**3,805**	4,142	4,212
Other receivables	**428**	394	402
Receivables, net	**$4,233**	$4,536	$4,614

In 1988, the Company transferred $346 million of its customer accounts receivable to a trust which in turn sold $250 million of certificates, representing undivided ownership interests in the trust, in a public offering. The certificates were sold to yield 9.13 per cent with an expected life of three years. As of January 28, 1989, the outstanding balances of the certificates and the receivables were $250 million and $401 million, respectively. The Company owns the remaining undivided interest in the trust not represented by the certificates and will continue to service all receivables for the trust.

Under the terms of the sale, a reserve fund available to the trust was established from the cash flows generated by the receivables to absorb defaulted accounts up to a certain limit. Additionally, the Company has made available to the trust an irrevocable letter of credit that may be drawn upon should the reserve fund be exhausted.

Merchandise inventories (In millions)	1988	1987	1986
Merchandise inventories, at lower of cost (FIFO) or market	**$2,599**	$2,623	$2,396
LIFO reserve	**(398)**	(273)	(228)
Merchandise inventories, at lower of cost (LIFO) or market	**$2,201**	$2,350	$2,168

Properties (In millions)	**1988**	1987	1986
Land	$ 162	$ 164	$ 140
Buildings			
Owned	1,426	1,430	1,458
Capital leases	247	247	247
Fixtures and equipment	2,137	1,983	1,904
Leasehold improvements	491	432	445
	4,463	4,256	4,194
Less accumulated depreciation and amortization	1,429	1,346	1,275
Properties, net	$3,034	$2,910	$2,919

Capital expenditures (In millions)	**1988**	1987	1986
Land	$ 10	$ 56	$ 2
Buildings	81	62	94
Fixtures and equipment	319	218	207
Leasehold improvements	77	40	47
Total capital expenditures	$487	$376	$350

Expenditures for existing stores, primarily modernizations, were $205 million in 1988, as compared with $160 million in 1987 and $172 million in 1986. The increase in capital expenditures for 1988 from 1987 principally represents the cost of converting space in JCPenney stores from the discontinued home electronics, photography, and hard sporting goods lines to primarily women's apparel. The increase in capital expenditures for 1987 from the prior year was related to the relocation of the corporate headquarters.

Other assets (In millions)	**1988**	1987	1986
Life insurance operation, principally investments	$ 551	$ 577	$ 510
Casualty insurance operation, principally investments	308	309	333
Bank operation, principally bankcard receivables	584	313	165
Investment in real estate joint ventures	81	74	58
Other	450	421	329
Total	$1,974	$1,694	$1,395

Liabilities and Stockholders' Equity

Accounts payable and accrued expenses (In millions)	**1988**	1987	1986
Trade payables	$ 646	$ 525	$ 555
Accrued salaries, vacations, profit-sharing, and bonuses	348	401	394
Taxes, including income taxes	300	244	216
Worker's compensation and public liability insurance	95	65	74
Dividend payable	62	51	46
Other	215	309*	204
Total	$1,666	$1,595	$1,489

*Includes provision for relocation of corporate headquarters.

Short term debt (In millions)	**1988**	1987	1986
Commercial paper	$ 663	$ 831	$ 407
Master notes and other	93	124	190
Short term debt	$ 756	$ 955	$ 597
Average borrowings	$1,194	$ 889	$ 955
Peak outstanding	$1,553	$1,922	$1,257
Average interest rates	7.6%	6.7%	6.7%

Current maturities of long term debt (In millions)	**1988**	1987	1986
Bank loan, variable rate, due April, 1989	$ 50	$ —	$ —
Zero coupon note, due 1989, $200 at maturity, yields 14.25%	194	—	—
Sinking fund debentures called for redemption, weighted average rate of 11.5%, with maturities of 2010 to 2015	—	—	274
Other	—	—	210
Total	$244	$ —	$484

Long term debt (In millions)	1988	1987	1986
Original issue discount			
Zero coupon notes and 6% debentures, due 1992 to 1994 and 2006, $700 at maturity, yields 13.5% to 15.1%, effective rates 12.5% to 13.0%	$ 355	$ 488	$ 436
Debentures and notes			
5.375% to 8.875%, due 1991 to 1998	397	414	429
9% to 9.75%, due 1995 to 2016	1,023	831	656
10.2% to 11.875%, due 1990 to 1994	224	239	471
12.125% to 13.75%, due 1991 to 1993	143	295	295
Other	53	128	144
	2,195	2,395	2,431
Present value of commitments under capital leases	201	213	224
Guaranteed LESOP notes, 8.17%, due 1998*	668	—	—
Long term debt	$3,064	$2,608	$2,655
Average interest rates	10.6%	10.9%	11.1%

For further discussion, see LESOP on page 20.

Changes in long term debt (In millions)	1988	1987	1986
Increases			
9% to 11% sinking fund debentures, due 2015 to 2016	$ —	$ —	$ 350
8.375% to 10.875% notes, due 1990 to 1998	200	202	247
Amortization of original issue discount	60	52	46
Guaranteed LESOP notes, 8.17%, due 1998*	700	—	—
	960	254	643
Decreases			
Retirements from debt restructure program			
Open market purchases, weighted average rate of 12% with maturities of 1990 to 2015	—	—	562
Sinking fund debentures called for redemption, weighted average rate of 11.5% with maturities of 2010 to 2015	—	—	274
10.75% and 11.875% notes, due 1990, called in 1987	—	219	—
Other transfers to current maturities of long term debt	244	—	185
13.625% and 13.750% notes, due 1991 and 1999, called in 1988	152	—	—
Other, including LESOP amortization	108	82	66
	504	301	1,087
Net increase (decrease) in long term debt	$456	$ (47)	$ (444)

For further discussion, see LESOP on page 20.

Maturities of long term debt (In millions)	Long term debt	Capital leases
1989	$ 288	$ 24
1990	137	24
1991	192	24
1992	294	24
1993	111	24
1994 to 1998	1,213	94
Thereafter	556	84
Total	$2,791	298
Less future interest and executory expenses		97
Present value		$201

Other liabilities (In millions)	1988	1987	1986
Life insurance operation, principally policy and claims reserves	$ 298	$299	$256
Casualty insurance operation, principally claims reserves	201	198	224
Bank operation, principally customer deposits	488	290	89
Real estate development operation	115	105	89
Total	$1,102	$892	$658

Confirmed lines of credit available to JCPenney amounted to $900 million. None were in use at January 28, 1989.

Stockholders' equity was $3,957 million at year end 1988 compared with $4,173 million at year end 1987 and $4,340 million at year end 1986.

Preferred stock. During 1988, a leveraged employee stock ownership plan (LESOP) was created (see page 20 for further discussion). The LESOP purchased approximately 1.2 million shares of a new issue of Series B convertible preferred stock from the Company. These shares are convertible into approximately 11.8 million shares of the Company's common stock at a conversion rate equivalent to ten shares of common stock for each share of preferred stock. The convertible preferred stock may be redeemed at the option of the Company or the LESOP, under certain limited circumstances. The dividends are cumulative, yield 7.9 per cent, and are payable semi-annually on January 1 and July 1. The first dividend, amounting to $28 million, was declared on January 1, 1989. On an after-tax basis, the dividend amounted to $17 million. The convertible preferred stock issued to the LESOP has been recorded in the equity section and the "Guaranteed LESOP Obligation," representing borrowings by the LESOP, has been recorded as a reduction of stockholders' equity.

Common stock. In 1988, the Company completed the common stock buy back program adopted in 1987 of 20 million shares. Under that program, the Company purchased 7 million shares in 1988 at a cost of $351 million of which $301 million was charged to reinvested earnings and the remainder to common stock. The cost of the entire program was $932 million.

The Company is using the proceeds from the issuance of convertible preferred stock to the LESOP to purchase up to 15 million common shares in the open market. At the end of the year, the Company had purchased 8 million shares at a cost of $418 million, of which $362 million was charged to reinvested earnings and the remainder to common stock. All shares were retired and returned to the status of authorized but unissued shares of common stock.

Effective May 1, 1987, the Board of Directors declared a two-for-one stock split in the form of a 100 per cent stock dividend of the Company's common stock. All references to shares and per share data in the accompanying financial statements were restated to reflect the stock split. In addition, the preferred stock purchase rights which accompany each share of common stock were automatically adjusted in accordance with the rights agreement to entitle the purchase, for each right held, of $\frac{1}{200}$ of a share of Series A junior participating preferred stock at a price of $75 per $\frac{1}{200}$ of a share. Each share of common stock issued as a result of the stock split described above also included one preferred stock purchase right. The rights remain exercisable upon the occurrence of certain events and are redeemable by the Company under certain circumstances, all as described in the rights agreement.

Additionally, in 1988, 1987, and 1986, the Company purchased 568 thousand shares, 420 thousand shares, and 1.2 million shares, respectively, of its common stock from a Company benefit plan at a cost of $28 million, $23 million, and $50 million, of which $25 million, $20 million, and $42 million, respectively, were charged to reinvested earnings. All shares were retired and returned to the status of authorized but unissued shares of common stock.

The quarterly common dividend was 50 cents per share in 1988, 37 cents per share in 1987, and 31 cents per share in 1986, or an annual rate of $2.00 per share in 1988, compared with $1.48 in 1987, and $1.24 in 1986. Common dividends declared were $260 million in 1988, $218 million in 1987, and $186 million in 1986.

Changes in outstanding common stock	Shares (In thousands)			Amounts (In millions)		
	1988	1987	1986	**1988**	1987	1986
Balance at beginning of year	**138,388**	149,640	149,154	**$ 960**	$961	$929
Two-for-one stock split	**—**	—	—	**—**	38	—
Common stock issued	**377**	1,833	1,734	**11**	51	40
Common stock purchased and retired	**(15,935)**	(13,085)	(1,248)	**(109)**	(90)	(8)
Balance at end of year	**122,830**	138,388	149,640	**$ 862**	$960	$961

There were approximately 57 thousand stockholders of record at year end 1988. One of these stockholders was the savings and profit-sharing retirement plan which had 98 thousand participants and held 18.2 million shares of the Company's common stock. Additionally, the LESOP, which had approximately 90 thousand participants, held 1.2 million shares of preferred stock, convertible into 11.8 million shares of common stock. On a combined basis, these plans held approximately 24 per cent of the Company's common shares after giving effect to the conversion of the preferred stock.

1984 Equity Compensation Plan and 1984 Performance Unit Plan. Under the 1984 Equity Compensation Plan, 2.4 million shares of common stock, as well as 3 million shares available under a previous stock option plan, were initially reserved for issuance upon the exercise of options or related stock appreciation rights (SARs) and for payment of stock awards. At year end 1988, 2.4 million shares remained in reserve and were available for grant. Under this plan, ten-year incentive stock options, non-qualified stock options, and SARs and tax benefit rights (TBRs) in tandem with stock options may be granted. Options granted prior to 1987 were exercisable one year from the date of grant. Options granted thereafter generally become exercisable six months from the date of grant.

In 1987 and 1986, the Company granted SARs and TBRs to officers in tandem with certain stock option grants. With respect to SARs and TBRs, about $1 million was paid to participants in each of the last three years. In 1988 and 1987, the Company issued to its officers a total of 370 thousand shares of restricted stock awards which vest over a five year period. The awards have conditions and restrictions which are designed to assure that the officers stay in the Company's service and retain stock ownership for many years. These awards were intended in part to compensate officers for accepting significant limitations placed on an existing program. In conjunction with these awards, a maximum market price for the Company's stock was established upon the exercise of SARs.

Under the 1984 Performance Unit Plan, performance units are earned based on measurements of Company performance determined by the Personnel and Compensation Committee of the Board of Directors. Approximately $9 million was earned in 1988, $8 million in 1987, and $5 million in 1986.

The Board of Directors has approved a new 1989 Equity Compensation Plan, subject to stockholder approval. This plan replaces the 1984 Equity Compensation Plan. Under the 1989 Equity Compensation Plan, 5 million shares of common stock will be reserved for issuance.

	1988		1987		1986	
Stock options	Shares (In thousands)	Weighted average option price	Shares (In thousands)	Weighted average option price	Shares (In thousands)	Weighted average option price
Balance at beginning of year	1,578	$29.15	1,920	$24.55	3,074	$22.12
Granted	1,223	45.65	327	47.12	466	32.53
Exercised	(343)	22.17	(659)	24.60	(1,572)	22.06
Expired and cancelled	(98)	44.14	(10)	31.66	(48)	28.93
Balance at end of year	2,360	$38.10	1,578	$29.15	1,920	$24.55

Additional Financial Data

	1988		1987		1986	
Credit sales	Amounts (In billions)	Per cent of eligible sales	Amounts (In billions)	Per cent of eligible sales	Amounts (In billions)	Per cent of eligible sales
JCPenney credit card	$7.2	49.0	$7.3	49.2	$7.0	50.0
American Express, MasterCard, and Visa	1.5	10.0	1.3	9.2	1.2	8.2
Total	$8.7	59.0	$8.6	58.4	$8.2	58.2

Approximately 90 per cent of sales on the JCPenney credit card were made in accordance with the regular plan and the balance in accordance with the major purchase plan.

At year end, the number of JCPenney credit card accounts with outstanding balances was 16 million under the regular plan and 1.9 million under the major purchase plan. The average balances and maturities are shown in the table below:

	Average account balances			Average maturities (In months)		
	1988	1987	1986	1988	1987	1986
Regular plan	$195	$189	$192	4.0	4.0	4.4
Major purchase plan	$514	$523	$521	9.9	9.9	10.4
All	$229	$230	$233	4.7	4.9	5.2

Includes all customer receivables serviced.

Key JCPenney credit card information (In millions)	1988	1987	1986
Customer receivables			
Regular plan	$3,153	$3,064	$3,110
Major purchase plan	973	1,149	1,181
Total customer receivables serviced	4,126	4,213	4,291
Customer receivables sold	250	—	—
Total customer receivables	$3,876	$4,213	$4,291
Number of accounts with balances	17.9	18.2	18.3
Finance charge revenue	$ 642	$ 676	$ 703
Net bad debts written off	$ 138	$ 167	$ 153
Per cent of customer charges	1.8	2.1	2.0
Provision for doubtful accounts	$ 138	$ 159	$ 160
Accounts 90 days or more past due as a per cent of customer receivables	2.1	2.1	2.5

The Company's policy is to write off accounts when the scheduled minimum payment has not been received for six consecutive months, or if any portion of the balance is more than 12 months past due, or if it is otherwise determined that the customer is unable to pay. Collection efforts continue subsequent to write off, and recoveries are applied as a reduction of bad debt losses.

Advertising expense by the Company for newspapers, television, radio, and other media, excluding catalog preparation and distribution costs, was $424 million in 1988, as compared with $451 million in 1987 and $445 million in 1986.

Interest expense (In millions)	1988	1987	1986
Short term debt	$ 90	$ 59	$ 64
Long term debt	261	258	314
Income on short term investments	(43)	(24)	(27)
Other, net	(1)	7	(1)
Interest expense, net	$307	$300	$350

Rent expense (In millions)	1988	1987	1986
Minimum rent on noncancellable operating leases	$198	$193	$190
Rent based on sales	37	42	42
Minimum rent on cancellable personal property leases	106	115	116
Real estate taxes and common area costs	103	94	95
Total	$444	$444	$443

The Company conducts the major part of its operations from leased premises which include retail stores, distribution centers, warehouses, offices, and other facilities. Almost all leases will expire during the next 20 years; however, most leases will be renewed or replaced by leases on other premises.

Minimum annual rents under noncancellable leases and subleases (In millions)	Gross rents	Net rents*
1989	$ 199	$ 129
1990	189	123
1991	181	117
1992	174	113
1993	179	120
Thereafter	1,398	952
Total	$2,320	$1,554
Present value		$ 850
Weighted average interest rate		10%

Rents are shown net of their estimated executory costs, which are principally real estate taxes, maintenance, and insurance.

Retirement plans (In millions)	1988	1987	1986
Pension			
Service cost	$ 36	$ 39	$ 30
Interest cost	90	80	66
Actual return on assets	(125)	(78)	(137)
Amortization	(6)	(49)	19
Pension credit	(5)	(8)	(22)
Savings and profit-sharing expense	53	50	51
Total	$ 48	$ 42	$ 29

JCPenney's principal pension plan, which is noncontributory, covers substantially all United States employees who have completed 1,000 or more hours of service within a period of 12 consecutive months. In addition, the Company has an unfunded, noncontributory, supplemental retirement program for certain management employees. Benefits under the principal pension plan are 1.5 per cent of final average pay for each year of credited service to normal retirement age up to a maximum of 30 years, less up to 50 per cent of an employee's estimated Social Security benefit, as computed under the plan.

The following table sets forth the funded status of the principal pension plan and the supplemental retirement program:

	December 31		
Pension plans funded status (In millions)	**1988**	1987	1986
Present value of accumulated benefits			
Vested	$ 686	$ 615	$ 564
Non-vested	72	73	60
	$ 758	$ 688	$ 624
Present value of actuarial benefit obligation	$1,001	$ 934	$ 866
Net assets at fair market value	1,164	1,071	1,019
Excess assets	$ 163	$ 137	$ 153
Key assumptions			
Actuarial method	PUC*	PUC*	PUC*
Rate of return on plan assets	9.5%	9.5%	9.5%
Discount rate	9.5%	9.5%	9.0%
Salary progression rate	6.0%	6.0%	6.0%

*Projected unit credit.

The present value of accumulated benefits is based on compensation and service to date. The present value of the actuarial benefit obligation considers estimates of future compensation, but not future service, and is used to determine pension expense (credit) and funding. No contribution was required or made in the past three years.

Certain changes in plan assets and in the actuarial benefit obligation are not recognized as they occur. In addition, at the date of adopting Financial Accounting Standards Board Statement No. 87, the Company had an unrecognized excess of plan assets over the actuarial benefit obligation. These unrecognized changes more than offset the end of year excess of plan assets over the actuarial benefit obligation and are systematically amortized over subsequent periods. The Company's consolidated financial statements reflect a prepaid pension expense. During 1988, that prepaid pension expense was increased by approximately $25 million resulting from a curtailment gain applicable to employee terminations from the Company's relocation to Dallas.

The savings and profit-sharing retirement plan encourages savings by employees through the allocation of 4.5 per cent of the Company's available profits, as defined in the plan, to participants who make deposits under the plan. The eligibility requirement is the same as that of the Company's principal pension plan. After 1988, the Company will not make any contributions to this plan as the plan has been succeeded by the LESOP.

The Company provides post-retirement health care benefits to retired employees and their dependents meeting certain eligibility requirements. The Company recorded expenses for these benefits as incurred in the amounts of $12 million, $11 million, and $9 million in 1988, 1987, and 1986, respectively.

	Savings and profit-sharing			Pension		
	December 31			December 31		
Total assets and equity (In millions)	**1988**	1987	1986	**1988**	1987	1986
JCPenney common stock (18, 20, and 20 million shares at cost: $507, $511, and $442)	$ 919	$ 856	$ 731	$ —	$ —	$ —
Funds with insurance companies	778	681	604	—	—	—
Equity securities (cost: $16, $19, $21, $801, $780, and $643)	39	40	43	889	815	743
Fixed income investments (cost: $2, $7, $6, $172, $161, and $161)	2	7	6	170	156	165
Real estate (cost: $85, $84, and $84)	—	—	—	103	99	103
Other assets, net	38	54	40	2	1	8
Net assets	$1,776	$1,638	$1,424	$1,164	$1,071	$1,019

Changes in fair value of retirement plans' net assets (In millions)	Savings and profit-sharing December 31			Pension December 31		
	1988	1987	1986	**1988**	1987	1986
Net assets at beginning of year	**$1,638**	$1,424	$1,143	**$1,071**	$1,019	$ 903
Company contribution	**47**	50	51	**—**	—	—
Participants' contributions	**117**	112	120	**—**	—	—
Investment income	**132**	142	115	**66**	156	142
Unrealized appreciation (depreciation) of investments	**115**	103	168	**59**	(78)	(5)
Benefits paid	**(273)**	(193)	(173)	**(32)**	(26)	(21)
Net assets at end of year	**$1,776**	$1,638	$1,424	**$1,164**	$1,071	$1,019

LESOP. In 1988, the Company created a leveraged employee stock ownership plan (LESOP). Effective January 1, 1989, the LESOP succeeded the Company's employee savings and profit-sharing retirement plan.

The LESOP borrowed $700 million at an interest rate of 8.17% in a 10-year loan guaranteed by the Company. The LESOP used the proceeds of the loan to purchase a new issue of convertible preferred stock from the Company. The preferred stock is convertible into approximately 11.8 million shares of the Company's common stock at $60 per common share. The dividend yield on the preferred stock is 7.9%; the conversion rate is ten shares of common stock for each share of preferred stock. Each year, one-tenth of the preferred stock held by the LESOP is allocated to participants' accounts.

The Company is using the proceeds from the issuance of preferred stock to the LESOP to purchase up to 15 million common shares in the open market.

The Company has reflected the guaranteed LESOP borrowing as long term debt on its balance sheet. The convertible preferred stock issued to the LESOP for cash was recorded in the equity section. A like amount of "Guaranteed LESOP Obligation" was recorded as a reduction of stockholders' equity. As the Company makes annual contributions to the LESOP, these contributions, plus the dividends paid on the Company's preferred stock held by the LESOP, will be used to repay the loan. As the principal amount of the loan is repaid, the "Guaranteed LESOP Obligation" is reduced accordingly.

The employee eligibility requirement and contribution options of the LESOP are virtually the same as those of the Company's former employee savings and profit-sharing retirement plan.

Income tax expense (In millions)	**1988**	1987	1986
Current			
Federal	**$380**	$411	$127
State and local	**75**	55	15
	455	466	142
Deferred			
Federal	**(66)**	(89)	259
State and local	**(4)**	(6)	33
	(70)	(95)	292
Total income tax expense	**$385**	$371	$434
Effective tax rate	**32.3%**	37.9%	45.0%

Reconciliation of tax rates	Amounts (In millions)			Per cent of pre-tax income		
	1988	1987	1986	**1988**	1987	1986
Federal income tax statutory rate	**$405**	$383	$444	**34.0**	39.0	46.0
Investment tax credits	**—**	—	(7)	**—**	—	(.7)
State and local income taxes, less Federal income tax benefit	**46**	30	26	**3.9**	3.1	2.7
Employee stock ownership plan credits*	**—**	—	(8)	**—**	—	(.8)
Reduction of deferred taxes on installment sales**	**(42)**	(17)	—	**(3.5)**	(1.7)	—
Capital gains benefits and other	**(24)**	(25)	(21)	**(2.1)**	(2.5)	(2.2)
Total income tax expense	**$385**	$371	$434	**32.3**	37.9	45.0

*Expired in 1986.
**Resulting from payment of taxes on installment sales previously deferred at higher tax rates in the financial statements.

Taxes other than income taxes, over half of which were payroll taxes, totaled $374 million in 1988, as compared with $334 million in 1987 and $339 million in 1986.

Deferred taxes consist principally of deferred gross profit on the balances due on installment sales, accelerated depreciation, and accounting for leases.

The Company acquired certain assets under leveraged lease arrangements and purchased tax benefits under the provisions of various federal income tax acts. For income tax purposes, the Company received certain income tax deductions and credits that were used to reduce income taxes otherwise payable. Deferred taxes were provided to reflect the reversal of these tax benefits in future years.

The Tax Reform Act of 1986 eliminated the deferral of income taxes on revolving credit installment sales after fiscal year 1986 and provided that deferred taxes previously established were to be paid over the period 1987 to 1990 in installments of 15, 25, 30, and 30 per cent. At the end of fiscal year 1988, the balance of deferred taxes on installment sales reflected on the balance sheet was $400 million. The amount due within one year is shown in the current portion of deferred taxes at the prevailing statutory rate and is approximately $50 million less than the amount originally provided in the financial statements. Accordingly, income tax expense in fiscal year 1989 will be reduced by that amount.

The Financial Accounting Standards Board issued Statement No. 96 (Accounting for Income Taxes) at the end of 1987. This standard requires an asset and liability approach to accounting for differences between the tax basis of an asset or liability and its reported amount in the financial statements (temporary differences). The standard, as amended in 1988, allows a transition period which provides flexibility for adoption up to 1990. The Company did not adopt this standard in 1988. Under the accounting rules, deferred taxes will be determined by applying the provisions of enacted tax laws, and adjustments will be required for changes in tax laws and rates. If the liability method had been applied in 1988, deferred taxes reflected on the balance sheet would have been reduced by approximately $200 million, and stockholders' equity would have increased by the same amount.

Quarterly Data (Unaudited)

(In millions except per share data)	First			Second			Third			Fourth		
	1988	1987	1986	**1988**	1987	1986	**1988**	1987	1986	**1988**	1987	1986
Retail sales	**$3,174**	3,224	3,045	**3,211**	3,409	3,221	**3,610**	3,756	3,485	**4,838**	4,943	4,989
Per cent increase (decrease)	**(1.6)**	5.9	8.7	**(5.8)**	5.8	6.9	**(3.9)**	7.8	7.4	**(2.1)**	(0.9)	6.5
Total revenue	**$3,279**	3,324	3,146	**3,341**	3,508	3,322	**3,726**	3,863	3,583	**4,950**	5,052	5,100
Per cent increase (decrease)	**(1.4)**	5.7	8.8	**(4.8)**	5.6	6.9	**(3.5)**	7.8	7.6	**(2.0)**	(0.9)	5.9
Gross margin, per cent of retail sales	**36.1**	35.8	34.4	**33.4**	32.9	31.8	**35.8**	34.8	34.4	**33.3**	32.3	33.7
Selling, general, and administrative expenses, per cent of retail sales	**26.9**	26.6	26.4	**27.5**	26.2	26.3	**27.0**	25.1	25.8	**22.8**	21.3	22.4
Income before nonrecurring and extraordinary items	**$ 131**	136	87	**81**	103	57	**160**	171	116	**296**	296	270
Per cent increase (decrease)	**(3.8)**	55.8	73.1	**(21.3)**	81.0	92.9	**(6.7)**	47.6	24.5	**0.1**	9.6	20.5
Net income	**$ 131**	54	63	**81**	103	46	**160**	171	116	**435**	280	253
Net income per common share												
Primary	**$ .96**	.36	.42	**.61**	.68	.30	**1.17**	1.14	.77	**3.28**	1.93	1.70
Fully diluted	**$ .96**	.36	.42	**.61**	.68	.30	**1.16**	1.14	.77	**3.19**	1.93	1.68
Dividends per common share	**$ .50**	.37	.31	**.50**	.37	.31	**.50**	.37	.31	**.50**	.37	.31
Common stock price range												
High	**$ 51**	52	36	**51**	60	43	**55**	65	42	**54**	48	44
Low	**$ 40**	40	29	**44**	46	34	**46**	38	35	**51**	38	36

Five Year Financial Summary

J.C. Penney Company, Inc. and Subsidiaries

Results for year (In millions)	1988	1987	1986	1985	1984
Retail sales	$14,833	15,332	14,740	13,747	13,451
Sales of JCPenney stores and catalog	$13,951	13,980	13,390	12,634	12,372
Per cent increase (decrease)	(0.2)	4.4	6.0	2.1	12.1
Per cent increase in general merchandise inflation	3.2	2.8	1.2	2.0	1.0
Gross margin, per cent of retail sales	34.5	33.8	33.6	32.8	32.9
Selling, general, and administrative expenses, per cent of retail sales	25.7	24.4	24.9	25.1	25.1
Interest, net, per cent of retail sales	2.1	2.0	2.3	2.7	2.6
Depreciation and amortization	$ 258	241	229	212	198
Income before income taxes and nonrecurring items	$ 970	1,151	964	679	711
Per cent of total revenue	6.3	7.3	6.3	4.8	5.2
Income taxes	$ 385	371	434	282	276
Income before nonrecurring and extraordinary items	$ 668	706	530	397	435
Per cent increase (decrease) from prior year	(5.4)	33.2	33.5	(8.7)	(6.8)
Per cent of stockholders' equity	16.0	16.3	13.1	10.4	12.2
Net income	$ 807	608	478	397	435
Earnings per common share					
Primary					
Income before nonrecurring and extraordinary items	$ 4.96	4.77	3.53	2.66	2.90
Net income	$ 6.02	4.11	3.19	2.66	2.90
Fully diluted					
Income before nonrecurring and extraordinary items	$ 4.90	4.77	3.51	2.63	2.89
Net income	$ 5.92	4.11	3.17	2.63	2.89
Per common share					
Dividends	$ 2.00	1.48	1.24	1.18	1.18
Stockholders' equity	$ 32.18	30.15	29.00	27.16	25.63
Financial position (In millions)					
Receivables, net	$ 4,233	4,536	4,614	4,504	4,019
Merchandise inventories	$ 2,201	2,350	2,168	2,298	2,383
Properties, net	$ 3,034	2,910	2,919	2,812	2,608
Capital expenditures	$ 487	376	350	426	505
Total assets	$12,254	11,734	11,846	11,131	10,293
Total debt	$ 4,064	3,563	3,736	3,839	3,774
Stockholders' equity	$ 3,957	4,173	4,340	4,051	3,812
Number of common shares outstanding at year end (In millions)	123	138	150	149	148
Weighted average common shares (In millions)					
Primary	131	148	150	150	150
Fully diluted	136	148	151	151	151
Number of employees at year end (In thousands)	190	181	176	177	180

All per share amounts reflect the 1987 two-for-one stock split.

Five Year Operations Summary

J.C. Penney Company, Inc. and Subsidiaries

	1988	1987	1986	1985	1984
JCPenney metropolitan market stores					
Number of stores	698	699	707	729	749
Gross selling space (In million sq. ft.)	94.7	95.4	96.1	96.7	97.2
Sales (In millions)	$11,313	11,463	11,001	10,382	10,093
Sales per gross square foot	$ 118	119	114	107	105
JCPenney geographic market stores					
Number of stores	657	679	696	753	821
Gross selling space (In million sq. ft.)	18.6	18.2	18.4	18.8	19.2
Sales (In millions)	$ 2,051	1,965	1,887	1,783	1,820
Sales per gross square foot	$ 113	106	101	93	95
Number of JCPenney stores	1,355	1,378	1,403	1,482	1,570
Catalog					
Number of sales facilities	1,879	1,837	1,825	1,733	1,804
Number of distribution centers	6	6	6	6	6
Distribution space (In million sq. ft.)	11.4	11.4	11.4	11.4	11.4
Sales (In millions)	$ 2,918	2,585	2,332	2,000	1,928
Drug stores					
Number of stores	434	407	390	374	369
Gross selling space (In million sq. ft.)	4.4	4.2	4.1	4.0	3.9
Sales (In millions)	$ 976	875	802	702	649
Sales per gross square foot	$ 236	215	204	180	170

Catalog sales made through JCPenney stores and drug stores are included in the sales of those stores as well as in Catalog. Sales per gross square foot include only those sales from stores in operation throughout both the current and prior year.

Public Affairs

The Company made significant progress during 1988 in its commitment to contributing to the health and vitality of the communities in which we do business. Involvement in this commitment occurred at all levels of the organization in such broad areas of concern as charitable contributions, community service programs, and minority affairs.

Charitable contributions in 1988 were $18.4 million compared with $14.5 million in 1987. Approximately 70 per cent of the contributions were made by JCPenney units to community based organizations and 30 per cent to national organizations that impact communities in which the Company operates. JCPenney employees pledged an additional $5.9 million to local United Ways through payroll deductions and one-time gifts.

Community service programs were expanded during 1988 with the introduction of the Golden Rule Network. The Network utilizes the Company's business television network to provide information and materials that address social issues to communities in which we do business. The initial broadcast dealt with teenage substance abuse.

Volunteerism continued to be encouraged through the annual Community Service Awards, which recognize employees for outstanding volunteer activities and providing a contribution to their community organization. The Golden Rule Award program provides similar recognition to volunteers outside the Company. This program was expanded to 55 markets in 1988, and through it the Company contributed $259 thousand to local organizations.

The Company is committed to programs fostering equal opportunity for all and has continued to expand the purchase of merchandise and services from minority-owned companies. During 1988, minority purchases increased to $263.2 million, representing relationships with 1,487 suppliers.

▽